Chartered Institute of Housing

CIH is a registered charity and not-for-profit organisation. This means that the money we make is put back into the organisation and funds the activities we carry out to support the housing sector.

We have a diverse membership of people who work in both the public and private sectors in 20 countries on five continents across the world. We were granted a Royal Charter in 1984, and our work is governed by our Royal Charter and Byelaws, overseen by the Privy Council. We are also a registered charity, with education at the core of our charitable status. That means we must comply with the requirements of the law relating to charities. The Charity Commissioners regulate our activities in England and Wales and the Office of the Scottish Charity Regulator in Scotland.

England charity number 244067/R and Scotland number SCO40324.

Chartered Institute of Housing
Suites 5 and 6
First Floor, Rowan House
Westwood Way
Coventry
CV4 8HS

Telephone: 024 7685 1700

E-mail: *customer.services@cih.org*

Website: *www.cih.org*

Shelter

Shelter exists to defend the right to a safe home and fight the devastating impact the housing emergency has on people and society. We do this with campaigns, advice and support – and we never give up. We believe that home is everything.

88 Old Street
London
EC1V 9HU

Telephone: 0300 330 1234

Website: *shelter.org.uk*

For online housing advice and access to our emergency helpline, visit *shelter.org.uk/housing_advice*

© Shelter, the National Campaign for Homeless People Limited 2023.

Registered charity in England & Wales (263710) and Scotland (SC002327).

Contents

1	Introduction	1
2	Who can get HB	13
3	Occupying your home	29
4	The people in your home	41
5	Liability for rent	55
6	Calculating HB	71
7	Which eligible rent rules	83
8	Service charges	97
9	Social renter rules	111
10	Private renter rules	121
11	The size of your home	137
12	Applicable amounts	149
13	Income	163
14	Earned income	187
15	Capital	217
16	Claims	241
17	Changes	253
18	Payments	267
19	Overpayments	279
20	Decisions and appeals	301
21	Subsidy	317
22	State pension credit	329
23	Other help with housing costs	345
Appendix 1	Legislation	357
Appendix 2	Selected weekly benefit rates from April 2023	361
Appendix 3	Equivalent CTR footnote references	363
	Index	383

Chartered
Institute of
Housing

Help with Housing Costs:

Guide to Housing Benefit

2023-24

Sam Lister, Martin Ward
and Roger Thwaits

SHELTER

Guide to Housing Benefit
Peter McGurk and Nick Raynsford, 1982-88
Martin Ward and John Zebedee, 1988-90

Guide to Housing Benefit and Community Charge Benefit
Martin Ward and John Zebedee, 1990-93

Guide to Housing Benefit and Council Tax Benefit
John Zebedee and Martin Ward, 1993-2003
John Zebedee, Martin Ward and Sam Lister, 2003-12
Sam Lister and Martin Ward, 2012-13

Guide to Housing Benefit and Council Tax Rebates
Sam Lister and Martin Ward, 2013-14

Guide to Housing Benefit
Sam Lister and Martin Ward, 2014-17

Help with Housing Costs: Guide to Housing Benefit
Sam Lister and Martin Ward, 2015-23
Sam Lister, Martin Ward and Roger Thwaits, 2023-24

Sam Lister is policy and practice officer at the Chartered Institute of Housing (email: *sam.lister@cih.org*) and a founding director of Worcester Citizens Advice. He has specialised in housing benefit and social security since 1993.

Martin Ward is an independent consultant and trainer on housing and benefit related matters (e-mail: *mward@knowledgeflow.org.uk*). He has provided consultancy services and training for several national organisations as well as many local authorities and large and small housing providers across the UK since 1982.

Roger Thwaits studies and writes about HB, CTR and UC. He has been involved with these schemes since they began in 1982, 1990 and 2013. At present he is focusing on supported accommodation and how vulnerable people's housing costs are met.

ISBN 978-1-9993510-9-0

Edited and typeset by Davies Communications
(www.daviescomms.com)

Printed by MBA Group Ltd

Preface

This guide explains the rules about housing benefit, focusing on help with housing costs. It gives the rules which apply from 6th April 2023, using information available on that date.

We welcome comments and criticisms on the contents of our guide and make every effort to ensure it is accurate. However, the only statement of the law is found in the relevant Acts, regulations, orders and rules (chapter 1).

We are grateful for the help and encouragement of many people who have been essential to the writing and production of this guide.

In particular, we thank Richard Stanier (Shelter) for his invaluable comments and help throughout each year, John Zebedee for the original material, Linda Davies and Peter Singer (editing and production), and staff from the Department for Work and Pensions and the Rent Service.

Sam Lister, Martin Ward and Roger Thwaits

April 2023

List of tables

Table   **Page**

1.1 HB terminology 1
1.2 Key HB statistics 3
1.3 Summary of HB changes from April 2022 11
2.1 Basic and financial conditions for HB 13
2.2 Pension age or working age HB 14
2.3 Supported or temporary accommodation 17
2.4 Care, support or supervision 20
2.5 Migrants and recent arrivals: eligible groups 24
2.6 Students: eligible groups 26
3.1 Time limits for HB during an absence 31
4.1 Who is a young person 44
4.2 Children and young persons who are not included in your family 45
4.3 People who are not your non-dependants 49
5.1 Payments that count as rent for HB purposes 56
5.2 Payments that aren't rent for HB purposes 57
5.3 Liability for rent 60
5.4 Excluded liabilities 64
5.5 Commerciality 65
5.6 Contrivance 66
6.1 Passport benefits 71
6.2 No non-dependant deductions 74
6.3 Weekly non-dependant deductions: 2023-24 76
6.4 Calculating HB benefit cap reductions 79
6.5 Exceptions to the benefit cap 80
7.1 Eligible rent rules and who they apply to 84
8.1 Rent and service charges summary 98
8.2 Standard weekly fuel deductions 2023-24 105
8.3 Standard weekly meals deductions 2023-24 106
9.1 Exceptions to the bedroom tax 114
9.2 Rent restrictions under the old scheme 115

10.1	LHAs: national maximums	124
10.2	LHAs: one-bedroom categories	126
10.3	Relevant changes in rent referral cases	131
10.4	Eligible rent in rent referral cases	133
11.1	The HB size criteria	141
11.2	What counts as a bedroom: case law	147
12.1	Weekly HB applicable amounts: 2023-24	150
12.2	Premiums after a period in hospital	161
13.1	Disregarded state benefits, pension, etc	165
13.2	Counted state benefits, pensions etc	166
13.3	People on savings credit: adjusting the DWP's figures	168
13.4	War disablement and bereavement pensions	170
13.5	Disregarded council payments	172
13.6	Income from maintenance	174
13.7	Rent from people in your home	175
13.8	Rent from property other than your home	176
13.9	Student maintenance loans	178
13.10	Student grants	179
13.11	Other unearned income disregards	181
14.1	Employed earnings	188
14.2	Self-employed earnings: exclusions	195
14.3	Self-employed expenses	199
14.4	Notional tax and NICs: 2023-24 tax year	203
14.5	The standard earned income disregard	208
14.6	Child care providers	210
14.7	The additional earned income disregard	213
15.1	Capital disregards relating to property	224
15.2	Capital disregards: arrears of benefits	233
15.3	Deprivation of capital: case law	236
16.1	Your date of claim	246
16.2	Good cause: case law	249
17.1	Changes you should notify	254

17.2   When changes of circumstances take effect 255

17.3   When HB changes if you move home 257

17.4   When changes in state benefits take effect 260

18.1   Paying HB to your landlord/agent 271

19.1   Overpayment types 279

19.2   Official error overpayments: case law 281

19.3   Realising there was an overpayment 283

19.4   How overpayments affect your rent: council tenants 290

19.5   How overpayments affect your rent: all other tenants 290

19.6   Maximum deductions from HB (2023-24) 292

19.7   DWP benefits overpaid HB can be recovered from 293

19.8   Notices and effect on recovery: case law 296

20.1   Decision notices about claims 302

20.2   HB reconsiderations and appeals 305

20.3   When reconsidered decisions take effect 309

20.4   Non-appealable HB decisions 311

21.1   Overpayments subsidy categories 320

21.2   Subsidy limits in temporary accommodation 326

22.1   Appropriate minimum guarantee: 2023-24 332

22.2   Savings credit threshold and maximum: 2023-24 335

22.3   Allowable housing costs 338

Abbreviations

The principal abbreviations used in the guide are given below.

AA	Attendance allowance
CTC	Child tax credit
CTR	Council tax rebate
DHP	Discretionary housing payment
DLA	Disability living allowance
DFC	The Department for Communities in Northern Ireland
DLUHC	The Department for Levelling Up, Housing and Communities
DMG	The DWP's *Decision makers' guide: staff guide*
DWP	The Department for Work and Pensions in Great Britain
ESA	Employment and support allowance
ESA(IR)	Income-related employment and support allowance
GLHA	The DWP's *Guidance local housing allowance*
GM	The DWP's *HB/CTB Guidance manual*
GSH	The DWP's *HB Guidance for supported housing claims*
HB	Housing benefit
HMCTS	His Majesty's Courts and Tribunals Service
HMO	House in multiple occupation
HMRC	His Majesty's Revenue and Customs
IS	Income support
JSA	Jobseeker's allowance
JSA(IB)	Income-based jobseeker's allowance
NIHE	The Northern Ireland Housing Executive
OG	The DWP's *HB/CTB Overpayments guide*
PIP	Personal independence payment
SDA	Severe disablement allowance
SMI	Support for mortgage Interest
SPC	State pension credit (guarantee credit and savings credit)
UC	Universal credit
UK	England, Scotland, Wales and Northern Ireland
WTC	Working tax credit

Key to footnotes

Each reference applies to Great Britain only unless otherwise stated.
If prefixed by 'NI' (e.g. NIAA) it applies to Northern Ireland only.

AA	The Social Security Administration Act 1992 [section number]
AC	Appeal Cases, published by The Incorporated Council of Law Reporting for England and Wales, London
All ER	All England Law Reports, published by Butterworths
art	Article number
BC	Borough Council
BMLR	Butterworths Medico-Legal Reports
CA	Court of Appeal for England and Wales
C&P87	The Social Security (Claims and Payments) Regulations 1987, SI No 1968
CBA	The Social Security Contributions and Benefits Act 1992 [section number]
CC	City Council
ChD	High Court (England and Wales) Chancery Division
COD	Crown Office Digest, published by Sweet & Maxwell
CPR	The Housing Benefit and Council Tax Benefit (Consequential Provisions) Regulations 2006, SI No 217 [regulation number]
CPSA	The Child Support, Pensions and Social Security Act 2000 [section number]
CS	Court of Session, Scotland
DAR	The Housing Benefit and Council Tax Benefit (Decisions and Appeals) Regulations 2001, SI No 1002 [regulation number]
DAR99	The Social Security and Child Support (Decisions and Appeals) Regulations 1999, SI No 991 [regulation number]
DC	District Council
DFA	The Discretionary Financial Assistance Regulations 2001, SI No 1167 [regulation number]
EHCR	European Court of Human Rights (neutral citations)
ECJ	European Court of Justice
EWCA Civ	Court of Appeal Civil Division for England & Wales (neutral citation)

EWHC Admin	High Court for England & Wales, Administrative Court (neutral citation)
FTPR	The Tribunal Procedure (First-tier Tribunal) (Social Entitlement Chamber) Rules 2008, SI No 2685 [rule number]
HB	The Housing Benefit Regulations 2006, SI No 213 [regulation number]
HB66+	The Housing Benefit (Persons who have attained the age for state pension credit) Regulations 2006, SI No 214 [regulation number]
HBRB	Housing Benefit Review Board
HLR	Housing Law Reports, published by Sweet & Maxwell
LBC	London Borough Council
MBC	Metropolitan Borough Council
NIAA	The Social Security Administration (Northern Ireland) Act 1992 [section number]
NICBA	The Social Security Contributions and Benefits (Northern Ireland) Act 1992 [section number]
NIC&P87	The Social Security (Claims and Payments) Regulations (Northern Ireland) 1987, NISR No 465
NICPR	The Housing Benefit (Consequential Provisions) Regulations (Northern Ireland) 2006, SR No 407 [regulation number]
NICPSA	The Child Support, Pensions and Social Security Act (Northern Ireland) 2000 [section number]
NIDAR	The Housing Benefit (Decisions and Appeals) Regulations (Northern Ireland) 2001, SR No 213 [regulation number]
NIDAR99	The Social Security and Child Support (Decisions and Appeals) Regulations (Northern Ireland) 1999, SR No 162 [regulation number]
NIDFA	The Discretionary Financial Assistance Regulations (Northern Ireland) 2001, SR No 216 [regulation number]
NIED	The Housing Benefit (Executive Determinations) Regulations (Northern Ireland) 2008, SR No 100 [regulation number]
NIHB	The Housing Benefit Regulations (Northern Ireland) 2006, SR No 405 [regulation number]
NIHB66+	The Housing Benefit (Persons who have attained the age for state pension credit) Regulations (Northern Ireland) 2006, SR No 406 [regulation number]
NIPC	The State Pension Credit Regulations (Northern Ireland) 2003, NISR No 28
NISPCA	The State Pension Credit Act (Northern Ireland) 2002

NISR	Statutory Rules of Northern Ireland (equivalent to Statutory Instruments in GB)
NISSCPR	The Social Security Commissioners (Procedure) Regulations (Northern Ireland) 1999, SR No 225 [regulation number]
NIWRO	The Welfare Reform (Northern Ireland) Order 2015, SI 2015 No 2006
NIUC	The Universal Credit Regulations (Northern Ireland) 2016, NISR No 216
NIUCTP	The Universal Credit (Transitional Provisions) Regulations (Northern Ireland) 2016, NISR No 226
PC	The State Pension Credit Regulations 2002, SI No 1792
QBD	High Court (England and Wales) Queens Bench Division
reg	regulation [regulation number]
ROO	In England and Wales, The Rent Officers (Housing Benefit Functions) Order 1997, SI 1984; in Scotland, The Rent Officers (Housing Benefit Functions) (Scotland) Order 1997, SI 1995 [in both cases followed by article number or schedule and paragraph number]
sch	Schedule
SI	Statutory Instrument [year and reference number]
SLT	Scots Law Times, published by W. Green, Edinburgh
SO	The Income Related Benefits (Subsidy to Authorities) Order 1998, SI No 562
SPCA	The State Pension Credit Act 2002
SSI	Scottish Statutory Instrument
SSWP	Secretary of State for Work and Pensions
TCEA	Tribunals, Courts and Enforcement Act 2007 [section number]
UC	The Universal Credit Regulations 2013, SI No 376
UCTP	Universal Credit (Transitional Provisions) Regulations 2014, SI No 1230 [regulation number]
UKHL	House of Lords, UK case (neutral citation)
UKSC	Supreme Court (neutral citation)
UTPR	The Tribunal Procedure (Upper Tribunal) Rules 2008, SI No 2698 [rule number]
WLR	Weekly Law Reports, published by The Incorporated Council of Law Reporting for England and Wales, London
WRA	The Welfare Reform Act 2012

Help with housing costs: what you can claim

	Working age	Pension age
Renters		
Rent payments	UC	HB
Service charge payments	UC	HB
Renters in supported or temporary accommodation		
Rent payments	HB	HB
Service charge payments	HB	HB
Owners		
Owner occupier payments	SMI	SMI
Service charge payments	UC	SPC
Shared owners		
Owner occupier payments	SMI	SMI
Rent payments	UC	HB
Service charge payments	UC	HB
All		
Living costs	UC	SPC
Council tax (Great Britain)	CTR	CTR
Rates (Northern Ireland)	RR	RR
Other help	DHPs etc	DHPs etc

Volume 1: Guide to Universal Credit and Council Tax Rebates
Universal credit (UC)
Support for mortgage interest (SMI)
Council tax rebate (CTR)
Rate rebate (RR)
Volume 2: Guide to Housing Benefit
Housing benefit (HB)
State pension credit (SPC)
Discretionary housing payments (DHPs)

Chapter 1 **Introduction**

- Summary of HB and how it is changing: see paras 1.2-14.
- Using this guide, the law and guidance: see paras 1.15-21.
- Summary of related benefits: see paras 1.22-38.

1.1 Welcome to this guide, which describes housing benefit (HB) throughout the UK. The guide is used by people claiming HB, advisers, landlords, benefit administrators and appeal tribunals. It gives the rules from April 2023. Table 1.1 summarises the main terminology.

The HB scheme

1.2 HB can help you pay your rent. Chapters 2 and 3 give the details about who is eligible and this depends partly on your age (paras 1.3-4). Nearly 2.6 million people get HB (table 1.2).

Pension age HB

1.3 Pension age HB is mainly for single people over 66 and couples both over 66 (table 2.2). You can make a claim for pension age HB at any time, or if you are already on pension age HB you can continue to get it.

Working age HB

1.4 Working age HB is mainly for single people under 66 and couples if at least one is under 66 (table 2.2). You can make a claim for working age HB if you live in supported or temporary accommodation (table 2.3). In other kinds of accommodation, you can make a claim for universal credit (UC) towards your rent, or if you are already on working age HB you can continue to get it until you transfer to UC (para 1.26).

Table 1.1 **HB terminology**

Tenant/tenancy and landlord/agent

Tenant and tenancy refer to any kind of rent-payer (for example a licensee). Your landlord or agent is the person your rent is due to.

Rent rebate and rent allowance

A rent rebate means HB for a council tenant or NIHE tenant and is paid by reducing your rent. A rent allowance means HB for anyone else and is paid by a cash transfer to your bank account.

Social renter and private renter

If you rent from the council, the NIHE or a housing association you are usually a social renter. If you rent from any other landlord you are usually a private renter.

Eligible rent

Your eligible rent is the amount of rent HB can meet.

Local housing allowance

LHAs are the main way of working out eligible rent for private renters.

Family

Your HB is based on your circumstances and those of the following members of your family:

- your partner if you are in a couple (or partners in a polygamous marriage); and/or
- each child or young person you or your partner are responsible for.

Single person

You are a single person if you do not have a partner. HB law uses 'lone parent' if you have at least one child or young person or 'single claimant' if you don't.

Couple

You are a couple if you are two people who are married or in a civil partnership or living together as a couple. HB law uses 'couple' whether or not you have children or young persons.

Polygamous marriage

You have a polygamous marriage if you (or your husband or wife) are married to more than one person under the law of a country that permits this.

Child and young person

A child is someone under the age of 16. A young person is someone aged 16 to 19 who is in, or has recently left, secondary education or approved training.

Claimant and partner

If you are in a couple or polygamous marriage, only one of you is the claimant. The other one (or each of the others) is your partner.

Benefit week

HB is calculated on a weekly basis. Each weekly period begins on a Monday and ends at midnight on the following Sunday night. This is called a benefit week.

Maximum HB and applicable amount

The calculation of your HB is based on your income and capital, your maximum HB and your applicable amount. Your maximum HB is your eligible rent minus any non-dependant deductions. Your applicable amount is made up of the personal allowances, premiums and components you qualify for.

Non-dependants

A non-dependant is an adult who lives with you but who doesn't count as a member of your family doe HB purposes. If you have one or more non-dependants they may be expected to contribute towards your rent.

Table 1.2 **Key HB statistics**

HB claims in Great Britain on 1st May 2022

Number of cases	2,584,414

Of which:

In receipt of passport benefit	68.3%
Pension age claims	43.2%
Local authority tenants	31.4%
Housing association tenants	46.1%
Private tenant LHA cases	18.3%
Private tenant non-LHA cases	4.2%

■ Source: DWP, Stat-Xplore [www]

The amount of your HB

1.5　　HB helps you pay your rent. How much you get depends on your financial and other circumstances (paras 1.6-7) and your eligible rent (para 1.8). Chapter 6 gives the calculation.

1.6　　You get maximum HB if you are on a passport benefit (para 1.7). If you aren't on a passport benefit, your HB is based on:

(a)　your income and capital: see chapters 13 to 15; and

(b)　your 'applicable amount' – this reflects your basic living needs: see chapters 4 and 12.

In either case, your HB can be reduced if you have one or more non-dependants – these are adults who live with you and are expected to contribute (paras 4.26-32).

The passport benefits

1.7　　The 'passport benefits' are:

(a)　the guarantee credit of state pension credit (SPC) (chapter 22);

(b)　universal credit (UC) in supported or temporary accommodation (para 2.15);

(c)　income-based jobseeker's allowance (JSA(IB));

(d)　income-related employment and support allowance (ESA(IR)); and

(e)　income support (IS).

These help you meet basic living needs other than your rent (such as food and heating).

Your eligible rent

1.8   Your eligible rent is the figure used in calculating your HB:

  (a) in most social sector lettings, your eligible rent equals the rent payable on your home (reduced in certain cases if the home is larger than you need), apart from any charges included in the rent for particular services which HB cannot meet (paras 8.32-51);

  (b) in most private sector lettings, your eligible rent is a fixed 'local housing allowance' figure depending on where you live and the size of accommodation you need.

Chapters 7-11 give the details.

How to get HB

1.9   To get HB you make a claim to the authority that administers HB for your area (para 1.13). We call this 'your council'. If you are a couple, your claim includes both of you. See chapter 16 for how to claim.

1.10   If a council owns properties outside its area, the tenants there claim HB from their landlord council. And if your council contracts out its administration of HB to another council, or group of councils, or a private company, you may have to claim HB from them.

1.11   You can usually claim council tax rebate (in Great Britain) or rate rebates (in Northern Ireland) at the same time as HB.

HB payments and appeals

1.12   HB is a weekly benefit based on 'benefit weeks' which begin each Monday. If you are a council (or NIHE) tenant it is paid as a rebate to your rent account. If you are a private tenant it is usually paid fortnightly or four weekly, or in some cases to your landlord. If you are overpaid you may have to repay it. If you think your HB is wrong (or you have been refused HB), you can ask your council (or NIHE) to reconsider it and appeal to an independent tribunal. See chapters 18-20.

Authorities that administer HB

1.13   HB is administered (along with CTR or rate rebates) by:

  (a) district or borough councils (called housing authorities) in parts of England with two layers of local government;

  (b) London councils or unitary councils in other parts of England;

  (c) Welsh county or county borough councils;

  (d) Scottish local councils;

  (e) the Northern Ireland Housing Executive.

Non-unitary county councils in England don't administer HB but in some cases receive HB claims on behalf of district or borough councils.

Who administers other benefits

1.14   The DWP in Great Britain and DFC in Northern Ireland administer most other state benefits, including UC (para 1.22), SPC (chapter 22) and the passport benefits. But HMRC administers tax credits, child benefit and guardian's allowance.

Using this guide

1.15   The HB rules in this guide apply from April 2023 and recent changes are in table 1.3. The next edition will give the rules from April 2024.

HB and other benefit figures

1.16   The HB figures in this guide apply from:

(a)   Monday 3rd April 2023 if your rent is due weekly or in multiples of weeks; or

(b)   Saturday 1st April 2023 in all other cases.

The figures for most other benefits (appendix 2) apply from week commencing Monday 3rd April, and affect your HB from 1st or 3rd April (para 17.37).

Abbreviations and footnotes

1.17   The tables at the front of this guide give:

(a)   a list of the abbreviations used in the text; and

(b)   a key to the abbreviations used in the footnotes.

The footnotes throughout this guide refer to the law governing HB. All the references are to the law as amended.

HB law

1.18   In Great Britain the main law about HB is in:

(a)   the Social Security Contributions and Benefits Act 1992;

(b)   the Social Security Administration Act 1992;

(c)   the Housing Benefit Regulations 2006 No 213;

(d)   the Housing Benefit (Persons who have attained the qualifying age for state pension credit) Regulations 2006 No 214;

(e)   the Universal Credit (Transitional Provisions) Regulations 2014 No 1230.

Equivalent law applies in Northern Ireland and appendix 1 gives the full details for both GB and NI. See also paras 20.23-25.

1.13   AA 134(1),(1A),(1B),(2),(5), 139(1),(2), 191; NIAA 126(2),(3)

1.16   AA 150(10); NIAA 132(1); HB 79(3); HB66+ 59(3); NIHB 77(5); NIHB66+ 57(5)

DWP guidance

1.19   The DWP publishes guidance on HB for councils in Great Britain including:

  (a)   Housing Benefit and Council Tax Benefit Guidance Manual (GM);

  (b)   Local Housing Allowance Guidance Manual and Good Practice Guide;

  (c)   HB Guidance for Supported Housing Claims (GSH);

  (d)   HB Overpayments Guide (OG) and Recovery Good Practice Guide;

  (e)   Subsidy Guidance Manual;

  (f)   Guidance on Discretionary Housing Payments;

  (g)   Circulars in the 'A' series (about adjudication and operations);

  (h)   Circulars in the 'S' series (about subsidy matters);

  (i)   Circulars in the 'U' series (about urgent matters); and

  (j)   LA Welfare Direct bulletins (on general matters).

In Northern Ireland the DFC provides the Housing Benefit Decision Makers Guide. Its HB Memos provide further guidance.

Case law

1.20   Case law refers to the body of principles established by judges while deciding cases in courts of record such as the Upper Tribunal. These set a precedent and are binding on local authority decision makers and First-tier Tribunals. The cases referred to in this guide are about HB, or other benefit law which is relevant because of its similarities with HB law. Generally speaking, case law from one part of the UK is regarded as binding in other parts of the UK.

Obtaining the law and guidance

1.21   The Acts, regulations, government guidance and case law are available online [www].

Universal credit

1.22   UC can help working age claimants meet basic living needs (such as food and heating), the costs of disability and childcare, and also rent (except in supported or temporary accommodation: para 2.15). By 2025, the DWP expects UC to have fully replaced the legacy benefits (para 1.37). For full details see volume 1.

1.21   GB law: www.legislation.gov.uk
         NI law: www.communities-ni.gov.uk/services/law-relating-social-security-northern-ireland-blue-volumes
         Guidance: www.gov.uk/guidance/housing-benefit-information-guidance-and-good-practice-for-local-authority-staff
         www.gov.uk/government/collections/local-housing-allowance-information-for-local-authorities
         GB case law before January 2016: www.tinyurl.com/29f8bcfw
         GB case law from January 2016: https://www.gov.uk/administrative-appeals-tribunal-decisions
         NI guidance: https://tinyurl.com/HB-NI-Guidance
         NI case law: www.communities-ni.gov.uk/services/northern-ireland-digest-case-law

Who can get UC

1.23 The main conditions for UC are:

(a) you must be working age (under 66);

(b) you must not be an excluded student;

(c) you must not be an excluded migrant, under 18 years old, prisoner, hospital detainee or member of a religious order – but prisoners can continue getting UC for their rent payments during their first six months in prison;

(d) you must in most cases be present in the UK;

(e) your capital (combined if you are a couple) must not be over £16,000;

(f) your income (combined if you are a couple) must be low enough.

1.24 If you are single you must meet all the conditions in para 1.23. If you are a couple, you get UC as a couple if you both meet them all or only one of you meets conditions (a) or (b), but you get UC as a single person if only one of you meets conditions (c) or (d).

UC claims and payments

1.25 You claim UC from the DWP in Great Britain or DFC in Northern Ireland. It is awarded for 'assessment periods' of one month (normally beginning on the same day of each month) and is paid in arrears. Most changes in your circumstances take effect from the beginning of the assessment period they occur in.

Migrating to UC

1.26 Transferring from legacy benefits to UC is called 'migration' (paras 1.27-28). When you transfer, your HB stops (paras 17.19-24), as do any other legacy benefits you are on. You get a two-week run-on of HB and other benefits and you may qualify for transitional protection (paras 1.29-30).

Natural and voluntary migration

1.27 These occur when you transfer to UC without having received a migration notice from the DWP:

(a) 'natural migration' is when your HB or another legacy benefit ends, and you can only replace your lost income by claiming UC;

(b) 'voluntary migration' is when you simply choose to claim UC, usually because you consider you will be better off as a result.

In HB law, both are called 'natural migration'.

1.28 'Managed migration' is when you transfer to UC because you have received a migration notice advising you to claim UC.

1.27   UCTP 7, 8; NIUCTP 5, 6

1.28   UCTP 44-46; NIUCTP 45-47

Examples: Migration to UC

1. Natural migration

Katey is getting HB and IS. She moves to a new council area (her new home is not supported or temporary accommodation).

- ■ She can't claim HB at her new home so she claims UC, and this ends her HB and IS.
- ■ She qualifies for a two-week run-on but not for transitional protection (paras 1.29-30).

2. Voluntary migration

Nicky is getting HB and ESA(IR). He decides to claim UC.

- ■ Claiming UC ends his HB and ESA(IR).
- ■ He qualifies for a two-week run-on but not for transitional protection (paras 1.29-30).

3. Managed migration

Marley is getting HB and JSA(IB). He receives a letter from the DWP saying he needs to claim UC instead.

- ■ Claiming UC ends his HB and ESA(IR).
- ■ He qualifies for a two-week run-on and for transitional protection (paras 1.29-30).

Two-week run-on

1.29   When you transfer to UC, you get a two-week run-on of HB which overlaps with the beginning of your UC (paras 17.20). If you were on JSA(IB), ESA(IR) or IS, you also get a two-week run-on of that benefit. You get these run-ons whether your transfer is due to natural, voluntary or managed migration, but not when you become a couple with someone who is already on UC.

Transitional protection

1.30   If you are worse off on UC than on legacy benefits, you get a transitional element in your UC. This applies to:

(a)   severely disabled people who transfer due to natural or voluntary migration; and

(b)   anyone who transfers due to managed migration.

For (a), you only count as severely disabled if you were getting a severe disability premium in your JSA(IB), ESA(IR) or IS. Getting that premium in your HB is not enough by itself, though in this case you may be able to get discretionary help from your council (paras 23.1-2).

1.29   UCTP 8A, 8B; NIUCTP 6A, 6B

1.30   UCTP 48-55, 63; NIUCTP 49-56, 64

Other related benefits

State pension credit

1.31   SPC can help pension age claimants meet basic living needs (such as food and heating) and the costs of disability and childcare (chapter 22). From 2029 onwards, the DWP plans to transfer claimants on HB to SPC, which will then include a housing element towards rent (table 1.3).

Council tax rebates in Great Britain

1.32   Many people in Great Britain get council tax rebates (CTR) from their council as well as HB. You are likely to qualify for CTR if:

(a) you are on the guarantee credit of SPC; or

(b) you are on UC, JSA(IB), ESA(IR) or IS; or

(c) you have a low income; or

(d) you have a non-dependant who is the second adult in your home and has a low income.

For full details see volume 1 chapters 15-18.

Main CTR

1.33   'Main CTR' is the most common type of CTR. The main rules are:

(a) your weekly main CTR equals your weekly council tax minus:

- amounts for non-dependants and

- 20% of your excess income;

(b) the amounts non-dependants are expected to contribute are much lower than in HB;

(c) in some cases, the council uses the DWP's figures for your earned and unearned income;

(d) applicable amounts are sometimes different from HB (para 1.34);

(e) the rules for working age claims in England are sometimes different (para 1.35).

Chapters 12-15 give footnotes for applicable amounts, capital and income in HB and appendix 3 gives equivalent footnotes for main CTR.

CTR applicable amounts

1.34   The differences from HB are as follows:

(a) the personal allowances (table 12.1) are higher in CTR for children and young persons in Scotland and for working age adults in Wales (volume 1 appendix 2);

(b) the lower rate personal allowance (para 12.8) doesn't apply to CTR;

(c) the two-child limit (para 12.10) doesn't apply to CTR in Scotland and Wales;

(d) the family premium (para 12.24) continues to apply in Wales;

(e) the transitional addition if you transfer onto ESA (para 12.50) no longer applies to CTR in Wales.

1.31   WRA 34, sch 4; NIWRO 40, sch 4

Local CTR for working age claims in England

1.35   In England, local councils can devise their own schemes for working age CTR. These sometimes:

(a)   use different figures for applicable amounts and non-dependant contributions;

(b)   assess income and capital differently;

(c)   deduct up to 35% of excess income; or

(d)   have a completely different method of calculation.

Your local council should tell you how its own local scheme works.

Rate rebates in Northern Ireland

1.36   Many people in Northern Ireland get rate rebate as well as HB. You are likely to qualify for rate rebate if:

(a)   you are on the guarantee credit of SPC; or

(b)   you are on UC, JSA(IB), ESA(IR) or IS; or

(c)   you have a low income; or

(d)   you are a lone pensioner.

For full details see volume 1 chapter 19.

The legacy benefits

1.37   The legacy benefits UC is replacing are:

(a)   HB for working age claimants (except in supported or temporary accommodation);

(b)   income-based JSA (JSA(IB));

(c)   income-related ESA (ESA(IR));

(d)   income support (IS);

(e)   child tax credit (CTC); and

(f)   working tax credit (WTC).

New style JSA/ESA (para 1.38), PIP, DLA, carer's allowance, child benefit and all other state benefits continue alongside UC (appendix 2).

New style JSA and ESA

1.38   'New style' jobseeker's allowance (JSA) and employment and support allowance (ESA) are contributory benefits. New style JSA can help when you are looking for work and new style ESA can help when you unable to work due to illness or disability. Their old names were JSA(C) and ESA(C).

1.37   WRA 33; NIWRO 39

1.38   www.gov.uk/guidance/new-style-jobseekers-allowance
         www.gov.uk/guidance/new-style-employment-and-support-allowance

Table 1.3 **Summary of HB changes from April 2022**

3rd May 2022 SI 2022/449 15th Sep 2022 NISR 2022/202	Nationals from the ECSMA and ESC treaty member states who have limited leave with a 'no public funds' condition are excluded from HB and SPC. Existing awards can continue until entitlement ends.
28th June 2022	Social Security Additional Payments Act 2022 introduces two additional payments amounting to £650 for people on SPC, ESA(IR), IS, JSA(IB), UC, CTC or WTC. These payments are all disregarded for HB (section 8 of the Act).
1st Oct 2022 SI 2022/942 NISR 2022/211	New exceptions to the LHA shared accommodation rate (para 9.20) for victims of domestic abuse and human trafficking.
18th Oct 2022 SI 2022/990 NISR 2022/230	Irish citizens who left Ukraine due to the Russian invasion are exempt from the habitual residence test.
31st Jan 2023 1st/4th Apr 2023 SI 2023/6 NISR 2023/4	LHA rates frozen during 2023-24 at their April 2020 levels.
1st/4th Apr 2022 SI 2023/316 SI 2023/335	Benefits up-rating based on September 2022 consumer prices index of 10.1 per cent. Benefit cap raised by the same amount.

Planned changes

2022 – April 2025	'Managed migration' of claimants on legacy benefits onto UC on an area-by-area basis resumes, with transitional protection against losses. Claimants living in supported or temporary accommodation continue to get HB.
2023-24	Changes to the rules for 'exempt accommodation' (para 10.3) that include minimum standards for support provided and changes to the definition of 'care, support or supervision'.

October 2023	Further new exceptions to the LHA shared accommodation rate covering rough sleepers aged 16-24 and care leavers up to the age of 25 (HM Treasury, Budget Red Book 2020, HC 121, paras 1.190 and 2.20).
April 2026 – March 2028	State pension age is gradually rising from 66 to 67.
April 2028	The transfer of pension age claimants from HB to SPC starts, with a new housing element meeting housing costs in a similar way to UC. Start date revised to align with completion of UC roll-out (HM Treasury, Autumn Budget and Spending Review 2022, CP 751, para 5.14).

T1.3   WRA 34, sch 4; NIWRO 40, sch 4
        Pensions Act 1995, sch 4 para 1(7)-(8)
        Pensions (Northern Ireland) Order 1995, sch para 1(8)-(9)

Chapter 2 **Who can get HB**

- Basic rules for pension age and working age HB: see paras 2.1-7.
- Mixed age couples and polygamous marriages: see paras 2.8-14.
- Supported or temporary accommodation: see paras 2.15-37.
- Migrants and recent arrivals, care leavers, students and trainees: see paras 2.38-50.

Basic rules

2.1 To get HB you must make a valid claim and provide your national insurance number (chapter 16). You must also meet the conditions in table 2.1.

2.2 Once you qualify, your HB continues until you stop meeting those conditions or you have some other change that ends your HB (paras 17.34-35).

2.3 Many of the HB rules depend on:

(a) whether you have a pension age or working age HB claim (table 2.2); and

(b) whether you live in supported or temporary accommodation (STA) or in general accommodation (table 2.3 and para 2.17).

Table 2.1 **Basic and financial conditions for HB**

(a) You must occupy a dwelling as your home (chapter 3).

(b) The payments you make there must count as rent for HB purposes (table 5.1).

(c) You must be liable or treated as liable for the payments (paras 5.6-19).

(d) Your liability must not be excluded (paras 5.20-38)

(e) You must not be an excluded migrant, care leaver or student (paras 2.38-50).

(f) Your capital (apart from disregarded capital) must not be over £16,000 (paras 15.2-4).

(g) Your income and any non-dependant deductions must not be too high for you to qualify (paras 6.2-7).

(h) For working age HB only, you must live in supported or temporary accommodation or have claimed under earlier rules (paras 2.6-7).

2.1   AA 1(1),(1A),(1B),(1C),(4)(b); NIAA 1(1),(1A),(1B),(1C),(4)(b)

2.2   CPSA sch 7 para 4; DAR 7; NICPSA sch 7 para 4; NIDAR 7

T2.1   CBA 130(1),134,137(2)(a),(h)-(j); NICBA 129(1),130,133(2)(a),(h)-(j)

Table 2.2 **Pension age or working age HB**

Single person

   (a) Aged 66 or over   Pension age HB

   (b) Under 66 – all cases   Working age HB

Couple or polygamous marriage

   (c) Both (all) aged 66 or over   Pension age HB

   (d) Both (all) under 66   Working age HB

   (e) Mixed ages   Working age HB

Note: For further details see paras 2.4-14.

Pension age HB

2.4   Pension age HB is for single people aged 66 or over and couples if you are both aged 66 or over (table 2.2). You can make a claim for pension age HB whether you live in general, supported or temporary accommodation.

2.5   Pension age HB is usually more generous than working age HB because:

  (a) you can get pension age HB if you live in any kind of accommodation;

  (b) there is no cap to the total benefits you can get in a week (table 6.5);

  (c) there are no size criteria for social tenants (para 9.11 and table 9.1);

  (d) the HB personal allowances are higher (table 12.1);

  (e) more kinds of income and capital are disregarded (tables 13.6, 14.5 and 15.1);

  (f) you can have more capital before it affects your HB (para 15.5);

  (g) backdating for three months is automatic (16.36).

Working age HB

2.6   Working age HB is for single people under 66 and couples if at least one of you is under 66 (table 2.2). You can only make a claim for working age HB if you live in the kinds of supported or temporary accommodation in table 2.3.

2.7   You can no longer make a claim for working age HB in general accommodation; instead, you can get UC towards your housing costs. People now on working age HB claimed under earlier rules.

T2.2   HB66+ 5; UCTP 6A(4); SI 2019/37 arts 4,7; NIHB66+ 5; NIUCTP 4A(4); NISR 2019/4 arts 4,7

2.4   HB66+ 5; UCTP 6A(4); NIHB66+5; NIUCTP 48(4)

2.6   HB 5; UCTP 6A(1),(2); NIHB 5; NIUCTP 4A(1),(2)

2.7   UCTP 5(1), 6A(1), 8; NIUCTP 3(1), 4A(1), 6

Mixed age couples and polygamous marriages

2.8   You are a 'mixed age' couple if one of you is aged 66 or over and one aged under 66. Or you are a mixed age polygamous marriage if at least one of you is aged 66 or over and at least one aged under 66. This section explains whether you can get pension age or working age HB. For DWP guidance see HB circular A9/2019 [www].

General rule for mixed age couples

2.9   If you are a mixed age couple, you can only make working age claims. In other words:

(a)   you can claim UC; and

(b)   you can claim working age HB in supported or temporary accommodation, but not in general accommodation.

General rule for mixed age polygamous marriages

2.10   If you are a mixed age polygamous marriage, you have to make separate claims:

(a)   the two of you who were married earliest can claim as a couple;

(b)   the other(s) can claim as a single person; and

(c)   each of these claims can be for HB or UC as explained in paras 2.4-7.

When you become a mixed age couple or polygamous marriage

2.11   You become a mixed age couple if:

(a)   you are a single person under 66, and become a couple with someone aged 66 or over; or

(b)   you are a single person aged 66 or over, and become a couple with someone under 66;

(c)   you are a couple both under 66, and the older partner reaches 66.

Becoming a mixed age polygamous marriage is similar. It can arise as a result of marrying or reaching 66.

2.12   When you become a mixed age couple or polygamous marriage (para 2.11), your HB ends. You can then reclaim HB or claim UC as described in paras 2.9-10.

2.8   Pensions Act 1995, sch 4 para 1(6); HB 2(1) – 'qualifying age for state pension credit', 5; HB66+ 2(1), 5; UCTP 6A(4); SI 2019/37 art 2(2),(3); Pensions (Northern Ireland) Order 1995, sch 2 para 1(7); NIHB 2(1), 5; NIHB66+ 2(1), 5; NIUCTP 4A(4); NISR 2019/4 art 2(2),(3) https://tinyurl.com/A9-2019

2.9   HB 5; HB66+ 5; UCTP 5(1),(2)(a), 6A(1),(2); SI 2019/37 art 6; NIHB 5; NIHB66+ 5; NIUCTP 3(1),(2)(a), 4A(1),(2); NISR 2019/4 art 6

2.10   UC 3(4); SI 2019/37 art 7; NIUC 3(3); NISR 2019/4 art 7

2.11   SI 2019/37 art 2(2); NISR 2019/4 art 2(2)

2.12   SI 2019/37 art 6; NISR 2019/4 art 6

Exception if you claimed SPC or pension age HB before 15th May 2019

2.13   You can make a claim for pension age HB as a mixed age couple or polygamous marriage if you (the claimant):

(a) have been a mixed age couple since before 15th May 2019; and

(b) have been on SPC or HB since before that date.

You can also claim SPC if you meet these conditions.

Exception if your partner(s) can't get UC

2.14   You can make a claim for pension age HB as if you were a single person if:

(a) you (the claimant) are in a mixed age couple or polygamous marriage; and

(b) your partner(s) can't get UC because of being an excluded migrant (para 2.39), absent from the UK, a prisoner, hospital detainee, member of a religious order, or under 18 years old (volume 1 chapter 2).

Examples: Mixed age couples

1. Becoming a mixed age couple while on HB

Linda is aged 67 and has been getting pension age HB (but not since before 15th May 2019). Elsa is aged 62 and moves in with her as her partner.

- ■   Linda's HB ends, and Linda and Elsa can make a claim for UC as a couple (para 2.12).

2. On SPC since before 15th May 2019

Haoyu and Beatha are a mixed age couple (one over 66 and one under). They have been on SPC since before 15th May 2019 and are now moving from a relative's home to a rented home.

- ■   They can claim pension age HB as a couple at their new home (para 2.13).

3. On HB since before 15th May 2019

Oleksiy and Kateryna are a mixed age couple. They have been on pension age HB since before 15th May 2019 and are now moving to a rented home in a new council area.

- ■   They can claim pension age HB as a couple at their new home (para 2.13).

4. Claimant with a partner who is an excluded migrant

Aadan and Abidemi are a pension age couple. Abidemi is an excluded migrant (para 2.39).

- ■   Aadan can claim pension age HB as a single person (para 2.14).

2.13   SI 2019/37 art 4; NISR 2019/4 art 4

2.14   UC 3(3); UCTP 6A(1),(5); SI 2019/37 arts 4, 7(1),(3); NIUC 3(2); NIUCTP 4A(1),(5); NISR 2019/37 arts 4, 7(1),(3)

Table 2.3 **Supported or temporary accommodation**

Supported accommodation

(a) Exempt accommodation (with support provided by or on behalf of your landlord)

- You rent from a non-profit landlord (para 2.18); and
- you receive care, support or supervision (table 2.4); and
- the care, support or supervision is provided by your landlord or by someone on your landlord's behalf.

(b) Managed accommodation (with support provided by someone else)

- You rent from a non-profit landlord; and
- you receive care, support or supervision; and
- you were admitted to the accommodation to meet a need for care, support or supervision.

(c) Domestic violence refuges

- You rent from a non-profit landlord or from a local council (para 2.20); and
- the building (or the part you live in) is wholly or mainly used as non-permanent accommodation for people who have left their home as a result of domestic violence (para 2.21); and
- the accommodation is provided to you for that reason.

(d) Local council hostels

- The building (or the part you live in) is owned or managed by a local council; and
- it provides non-self-contained domestic accommodation with meals or food preparation facilities (and is not a care home or independent hospital); and
- you are provided with care, support or supervision by your landlord, or by someone else (this needn't be on your landlord's behalf).

Temporary accommodation

(e) Temporary accommodation for homeless people

- You rent from a local council or a registered housing association; and
- the accommodation is provided to you by your council because you were homeless or to prevent you becoming homeless; and
- it isn't exempt accommodation ((a) above).

Note: For further details see paras 2.15-29.

T2.3(a)-(d)   HB 2(1) definitions: 'hostel', 'housing association', 'voluntary organisation', 75H; NIHB 2(1), 73H
https://tinyurl.com/HB-08-2014

T2.3(e)   UC sch 1 para 3B; NIUC sch 1 para 4A

Supported or temporary accommodation

2.15   'Supported or temporary accommodation' (STA) means any of the kinds of accommodation in table 2.3. Your landlord should normally be able to tell you if your home is STA. Useful advice is given in the DWP's 'Housing benefit guidance for supported housing claims' (GSH) and the DLUHC's 'Supported housing: national statement of expectations' [www].

2.16   If you live in STA, you can't get UC or SPC towards your rent; you get HB instead. The government doesn't plan to change this [www], but plans to work with councils, landlords, care providers and bodies representing residents, to 'improve quality and value for money' (GSH para 11).

Terminology for types of accommodation

2.17   In this guide we use the following terms:

(a) 'supported accommodation' means any accommodation described in table 2.3(a)-(d);

(b) 'exempt accommodation' means accommodation described in table 2.3(a), whether or not it also meets any of descriptions (b)-(d);

(c) 'temporary accommodation' means accommodation described in table 2.3(e);

(d) 'general accommodation' means ordinary houses, flats, etc – in other words, anywhere not in table 2.3.

In the law, supported accommodation (table 2.3(a)-(d)) is called 'specified accommodation'.

Non-profit landlord

2.18   A 'non-profit landlord' (table 2.3) means:

(a) a registered or unregistered housing association (paras 7.15-17);

(b) a charity in England and Wales that is registered with the Charity Commission or exempt from registration, or in Scotland on the Charity Register;

(c) a voluntary organisation (para 2.19); or

(d) a county council in an area of England that has both district councils and a separate county council.

They must be your immediate landlord (CH/3900/2005; [2009] UKUT 12 (AAC)), and not, for example, the superior landlord or a managing agent (para 7.9).

2.15   www.gov.uk/government/publications/housing-benefit-guidance-for-supported-housing-claims
        www.gov.uk/government/publications/supported-housing-national-statement-of-expectations

2.16   UC sch 1 paras 3(h),(i), 3A, 3B; UCTP 6A(2)
        www.gov.uk/government/news/all-supported-housing-funding-to-be-retained-in-welfare-system

2.17   CPR sch 3 para 4(10); UCTP 2(1) – 'specified accommodation', 'temporary accommodation'; NICPR sch 3 para 4(9); NIUCTP 2(1)

2.18   CPR sch 3 para 4(10); NICPR sch 3 para 4(9)

Voluntary organisation

2.19   A 'voluntary organisation' is a 'body, other than a public authority or council, the activities of which are carried on otherwise than for profit' – for example, a community benefit society or co-operative registered with the Financial Conduct Authority. Whether a landlord meets this description can involve looking at all the circumstances (not just the landlord's written constitution), and it is a 'commercial reality' that a voluntary organisation is likely to have contracts with profit-making third parties ([2013] UKUT 291 (AAC)).

Local council

2.20   A 'local council' means:

(a)   a district, borough or city council in England; or

(b)   a council in Scotland, Wales or Northern Ireland.

Domestic violence

2.21   'Domestic violence' includes controlling or coercive behaviour, violence, or psychological, physical, sexual, emotional, financial or other abuse, regardless of the gender or sexuality of the victim. The domestic violence doesn't have to be from a partner or family member, it can be from others, including a neighbour or landlord (GSH para 83).

What is care, support or supervision (CSS)

2.22   'Care, support or supervision' (table 2.4) has its ordinary English meaning. But there have been many appeals about this and the main cases are summarised in table 2.4.

2.23   The DWP recognises that 'the needs of tenants living in supported housing… vary greatly', and gives useful advice about how councils should check what services are provided, that there is a need for them, and that the provision is more than minimal (GSH paras 136-137, 142-155).

Providing CSS

2.24   In exempt accommodation (table 2.3(a)), CSS must either be provided by your landlord, or arranged by your landlord and provided by someone else e.g. a charity, organisation or firm that your landlord uses (GSH paras 138-141) but this need not be the only or main form of CSS provided to you. For example yiu may also be in receipt of a separate care package provided by social services ([2010] AACR 2). In managed accommodation and local council hostels (table 2.3(b), (d)), CSS can be provided or arranged by anyone (GSH paras 76-79).

Paying for CSS

2.25   You can't get HB towards charges for CSS or any other kind of counselling or support (para 8.41). This nearly always means your landlord or someone else has to pay for it – for example social services, another non-profit body and so on.

2.19   HB 2(1) – 'voluntary organisation'; HB 2(1); Co-operative and Community Benefit Societies Act 2014, s2; NIHB 2(1); NIHB66+ 2(1)

2.20   HB 2(1) – 'relevant authority', 75H(4),(5); NIHB 2(1), 73H(4),(5)

2.21   HB 2(1) defs: 'domestic violence', 'coercive behaviour', 'controlling behaviour'; NIHB 2(1)

2.25   HB sch 1 para 1(e)-(f); HB66+ sch 1 para 1(e)-(f); NIHB sch 1 para 1(e)-(f); NIHB66+ sch 1 para 1(e)-(f)

Table 2.4 **Care, support or supervision**

(a) Meaning of care, support or supervision (CSS)

This part of the table applies to supported accommodation generally (table 2.3(a), (b) and (d).

Meaning of CSS: Supported accommodation means 'accommodation in which a measure of care, support or supervision is provided to assist the occupants with the practicalities of day-to-day living' and the phrase 'care, support or supervision' has its ordinary English meaning (R(H) 2/07 confirmed in R(S) v Social Security Commissioners and Others).

Availability of CSS: The CSS must be available in reality to the tenant, and there must be a real prospect that they will find the service of use (R(H) 4/09 and [2009] UKUT 109 (AAC)).

Meaning of 'support': 'Support' might well be characterised as 'the giving of advice and assistance to the claimant in coping with the practicalities of [their] life, and in particular [their] occupation of the property' ([2010] AACR 2). It is more than ordinary housing management ([2010] AACR 2).

Continuity of support: The support provided must be ongoing (R(H) 4/09). Help with gaining exemption from the council tax because the tenant is severely mentally impaired is more like a setting up cost and is not enough ([2010] AACR 2).

Need for and provision of 'support': 'What matters is simply whether support is provided to more than a minimal extent, and it is… implicit that support is not "provided" unless there is in fact some need for it ([2009] UKUT 150 (AAC)).

Dwellings in a group: A dwelling in a group (e.g. sheltered accommodation) doesn't qualify as supported accommodation just because other dwellings in the group do: CSS must be provided to that particular dwelling (CH/1289/2007).

Amount of CSS: CSS must be more than minimal. An average of ten minutes per tenant per week was not enough (in R(H) 7/07), but three hours per tenant per week might be enough (in CH/1289/2007). Just helping with HB claims and reviews, and carrying out safety and security inspections, was not more than minimal; but 'proactively considering what physical improvements or alterations to the properties could be usefully made' in the case for adaptations for disability could be enough ([2010] AACR 2). In the test of what is or is not minimal it is 'unfortunately inherent… that some landlords may just about scrape over the line… while others will not do so' ([2012] UKUT 52 (AAC)).

When there is no relevant history: In a new development it is necessary to look at what is contemplated ([2009] UKUT 109 (AA)).

(b) Provision of CSS in exempt accommodation

This part of the table applies only to exempt accommodation (table 2.3(a)).

CSS provided by the landlord: A landlord can provide CSS by making arrangements for it, or by paying for someone to do it ([2010] AACR 2).

CSS provided on behalf of the landlord: For CSS to be provided 'on behalf of' the landlord, there must be 'a sense of agency between the [CSS provider and the landlord], or… a contract, or something akin to it'. A joint venture is not enough; nor is a contract between the CSS provider and e.g. social services (R(S) v Social Security Commissioner, confirming R(H) 2/07).

CSS provided by landlord as well as care provider: The landlord may provide CSS without being the principal provider of it to that particular tenant ([2010] AACR 2).

Landlord not registered to provide CSS: In Scotland, if CSS is in fact provided but the landlord isn't registered to provide it under the Public Services Reform (Scotland) Act 2010, this leaves the landlord open to legal action, but doesn't stop the claimant's home being exempt accommodation ([2017] UKUT 110 (AAC)).

Availability of CSS from elsewhere: 'The likely nature, extent and frequency of [the CSS], and the extent of support available to the claimant from elsewhere' are to be taken into account in considering whether the CSS provided by a landlord is more than minimal ([2010] AACR 2).

Who pays for the CSS? It is irrelevant that the landlord is (or is not) paid to provide the CSS by someone else ([2010] AACR 2).

Support vs housing management: 'Support' means that the landlord does more than an ordinary landlord would do (R(H) 4/09). It is more than ordinary housing management, e.g. repairs and maintenance. But if the tenancy agreement 'imposes unusually onerous repairing and maintenance obligations on the landlord', this can amount to support; as can the fact that a claimant's disabilities impose a 'materially greater burden on the landlord' ([2010] AACR 2). Intensive (enhanced) housing management activities may be support for exempt accommodation purposes but not an ineligible service. 'The two provisions are capable of operating independently' ([2019] UKUT 304 (AAC)).

Live-in carers: While the presence of a live-in carer may or may not amount to CSS (depending on who provides the carer), the case law on carers can affect whether the size of the accommodation is reasonable (paras 9.23 and 11.10).

Claiming HB in STA

2.26   When you claim HB in STA, the council is likely to ask you and/or your landlord to give lengthy details about your rent and what services and other charges it includes. This is to check your home counts as STA, and also to decide which service charges are eligible for HB (para 8.21).

Claiming HB at the same time as UC

2.27   If you live in STA and are under pension age (or in a couple and at least one of you is under pension age), you need to:

(a) tell the DWP (in your UC claim) that you live in supported or temporary housing; and

(b) claim HB from the council towards your housing costs.

T2.4   R(S) v Social Security Commissioner and Ors [2018] EWHC 3097 Admin and [2009] EWHC 2221 Admin
        [2010] AACR 2, was [2009] UKUT 107 (AAC)

2.27   UC sch 1 paras 3(h),(i), 3A, 3B; UCTP 6A(2); NIUC sch 1 paras 3(e),(ea), 4, 4A; NIUCTP 4A(2)

2.28   If the council then decides your home doesn't meet the definition of STA, you need to go back and ask the DWP to include your housing costs in your UC. The DWP says that your UC housing costs 'will be revised back to the date you originally declared you were living in the accommodation' (GSH paras 64-68).

Claiming HB at the same time as SPC

2.29   If you live in STA and are over pension age (or in a couple and you are both over pension age), you need to claim SPC from the DWP and HB from the council (see also para 16.11 if you are claiming both).

Examples of supported accommodation

2.30   The DWP gives a good description of supported housing [www], and this applies similarly to supported accommodation (table 2.3(a)-(d)). It is 'any housing scheme where housing is provided alongside care, support or supervision to help people live as independently as possible in the community. It covers a range of different housing types, including hostels, refuges, supported living complexes, extra care schemes and sheltered housing... [It] can provide long-term support for years for some vulnerable groups such as older people and disabled people or very short-term immediate emergency help for when people are in times of crisis, such as use of hostels and refuges.'

2.31   Based on the DWP's description, the types of people in supported housing include (among others):

(a)   older people with support needs;

(b)   people at risk of or recovering from homelessness;

(c)   people with learning disabilities;

(d)   people with mental health problems;

(e)   people with physical or sensory disabilities;

(f)   people with drug or alcohol problems;

(g)   people experiencing or at risk of domestic abuse;

(h)   vulnerable young people such as care leavers or teenage parents;

(i)   ex-offenders;

(j)   vulnerable armed forces veterans;

(k)   migrants and refugees with support needs;

(l)   rough sleepers and those without a settled way of life.

2.29   HB66+ 5; UCTP 6A(4); NIHB66+ 5; NIUCTP 4A(4)

2.30-31 Supported Accommodation Review, DWP/DCLG (2016)
        https://tinyurl.com/Supported-Accom-Review-2016
        Funding for Supported Housing Consultation, DCLG/DWP (2016)
        https://tinyurl.com/Funding-Supported-Hsg-2016

Eligible rent in STA

2.32   Eligible rent in supported or temporary accommodation is worked out as follows in both working age and pension age HB:

(a)   for exempt accommodation (table 2.3(a)) the 'old scheme' rules apply (paras 9.17-39);

(b)   in other cases (table 2.3(b)-(e)) the rules for social or private renters apply in the same way and with the same exceptions as for other renters (paras 9.4-16 and chapter 10).

Getting benefit on two homes in STA

2.33   If you claim pension age HB and are liable for housing costs on two homes, you can get HB on both in any of the situations in para 3.40. This is the case whether one or both are supported or temporary accommodation.

2.34   If you claim working age HB and are liable for housing costs on two homes:

(a)   if both are supported or temporary accommodation, you can get HB on both in any of the situations in para 3.40;

(b)   if only one is supported or temporary accommodation, you can get HB on that one and UC towards your housing costs on the other, but only if you are absent due to fear of violence (para 3.16).

The benefit cap in STA

2.35   If you are on UC, HB on supported or temporary accommodation isn't included in the HB benefit cap. If you aren't on UC (for example, you are on a legacy benefit or are working with a low income):

(a)   HB on supported accommodation (table 2.3(a)-(d)) isn't included in the benefit cap;

(b)   HB on temporary accommodation (table 2.3(e)) is included in the benefit cap unless the accommodation also meets the definition of supported accommodation.

Paras 6.27-28 give further details, including the rules that apply when you qualify for benefit on two homes.

Decisions and appeals about STA

2.36   Decisions about whether your home is supported or temporary accommodation are made by your council. If you are working age and claiming UC, the DWP follows the council's decision [www].

2.37   If you disagree with the council's decision, you can ask the council to reconsider and appeal to a tribunal using the HB appeals procedure (chapter 20).

2.34   HB 7(6)(a)-(e); HB66+ 7(6)(a)-(e); UC sch 3 para 6; UCTP 6A(2), 7(5), 8(3);
          NIHB 7(6)(a)-(e); NIHB66+ 7(6)(a)-(e); NIUC sch 3 para 5; NIUCTP 4A(2), 5(5), 6(3)

2.35   HB 75C(2)(a), 75F(1)(g), 75H; UC sch1 paras 3A, 3B; NIHB 73C(2)(a), 73F(1)(g), 73H; NIUC sch 1 paras 4, 4A

2.36   DWP Operational Guidance (2022) supported accommodation (version 6.0) https://tinyurl.com/OG-supported-accom-2022

Table 2.5 **Migrants and recent arrivals: eligible groups**

(a) You are a national of the Common Travel Area (CTA) and you:
- are habitually resident in the CTA; or
- are present in the UK as a result of your deportation, removal or expulsion from another country.

(b) You are a national of any other EEA country and you have EU pre-settled status (or you applied for it on or before 30th June 2021 and are waiting for a decision) and you:
- are a worker, a self-employed person (or are out of work but have retained your worker/self-employed status)
- are the family member of a worker, self-employed person, or a retained worker/self-employed person, or
- have an EEA right to reside other than as a jobseeker and you are habitually resident in the CTA

(c) You are a national of any other country (or an EEA national without pre-settled status) and you:
- claimed asylum and have been granted refugee status, humanitarian protection or discretionary leave
- are the partner of a British citizen or a settled person and you have been granted leave under the destitution domestic violence concession
- are a sponsored migrant and either you have been resident in the UK for five years or your sponsor (or all of them if there was more than one) has died, or
- have leave to be in the UK without a 'no public funds' condition (including EU settled status).

In the case of the last two you must also be habitually resident in the CTA.

Notes
- The CTA means the UK (England, Scotland, Wales and Northern Ireland), the Republic of Ireland, the Channel Islands and the Isle of Man.
- The EEA means (apart from Ireland) Austria, Belgium, Bulgaria, Cyprus, Czech Republic, Denmark, Estonia, Finland, France, Germany, Greece, Hungary, Iceland, Italy, Latvia, Lichtenstein, Lithuania, Luxembourg, Malta, Netherlands, Norway, Poland, Portugal, Romania, Slovakia, Slovenia, Spain, Sweden and Switzerland.

T2.5   Immigration and Asylum Act 1999, s115; HB 10; HB66+ 10; NIHB 10; NIHB66+ 10; SI 2000/636 reg 2(1) sch part 1 paras 2-3; NISR 2000/71 reg 2(1), sch part 1 paras 2-3; SI 2020/1209 regs 4(4),(6), 11; SI 2020/1309 regs 64-65, 68-69, 83, sch 4 paras 1-4

Migrants, care leavers, students and trainees

2.38 This section explains which migrants, recent arrivals, care leavers, students and trainees can get HB.

Migrants and recent arrivals

2.39 If you are a migrant or have recently arrived in the UK, you can only get HB if you are in one of the eligible groups in table 2.5. These apply to both pension age and working age HB. Further details are in volume 1 chapters 20 and 21.

Children in care and care leavers

2.40 You can't get HB if you are:

(a) a child in care ('looked after by a local authority'); or

(b) a care leaver under the age of 18 (paras 2.41-42).

This is because social services are responsible for providing your accommodation.

Who is a care leaver

2.41 You are a 'care leaver' (and can't get HB until you reach the age of 18) if you were in care for one or more periods that:

(a) began after your 14th birthday or (in Scotland) following a children's hearing; and

(b) continued until after your 16th birthday or (except in Scotland) until you went into hospital or detention if you were still there on your 16th birthday; and

(c) totalled at least 13 weeks.

2.42 But you aren't a 'care leaver' (and can get HB) if:

(a) you lived in a family placement for at least six months (either while you were in care or after you left care) and the family placement didn't end by breaking down; or

(b) you were in a pre-planned series of placements each lasting no more than four weeks, and at the end of each placement you returned to your parent(s) or the person with parental responsibility for you.

2.39   CBA 130(1)(4), 137(2)(a) Immigration and Asylum Act 1999 s115; HB 10; HB66+ 10; NIHB 10; NIHB66+ 10;
        SI 2000/636 reg 2(1), sch part 1 paras 2-3; NISR 2000/71 reg 2(1), sch part 1 paras 2-3

2.40(a) Children Act 1989 s22A, 22B, 23B(8)(b); Social Services and Well-being (Wales) Act 2014 s79, 80, 109(1)(b);
        Children (Scotland) Act 1995 s25(1), 26(1); The Children (Northern Ireland) Order 1995 No 755 art 21(1), 27(1)

2.40(b) Children (Leaving Care) Act 2000 s6, 8(6); Children (Leaving Care) Act (Northern Ireland) 2002 s6

2.41-42 Children Act 1989 s23A, sch 2 para 19B; The Children (Leaving Care) (England) Regulations 2001 No 2874 regs 3,4;
        Social Services and Well-being (Wales) Act 2014 s104(2); The Children (Leaving Care) (Wales) Regulations 2001 No 2189 regs 3, 4;
        SI 2002/1855; SI 2004/1732; The Children (Leaving Care) Social Security Benefits (Scotland) Regulations 2004 No 747 reg 2;
        The Children (Northern Ireland) Order 1995 No 755 art 34A, 34B;
        The Children (Leaving Care) Regulations (Northern Ireland) 2005 No 221 regs 2, 3

2.41   SI 2001/2874, regs 3, 4(3) (E); SSI 2004/747, reg 2(2),(4)(a) (S); SI 2001/2189, regs 3(2)(a), 4(2),(2A) (W); NISR 2005/221, reg 2, 3(3)

2.42   SI 2001/2874, reg 4(5)-(7) (E); SSI 2004/747, reg 2(4)(b),(c) (S); SI 2001/2189, regs 3(2)(b), 4(4),(5) (W); NISR 2005/221, reg 3(5)-(7)

Students

2.43   If you are a working age student living in supported or temporary accommodation (table 2.3), you can't get HB unless:

(a) you are a full-time student (para 2.48) and are in any of the eligible groups in table 2.6; or

(b) you are a part-time student (whether or not you are in those eligible groups).

2.44   If you are a working age student and live in any other kind of accommodation:

(a) you can't make a claim for HB (para 2.7); but

(b) if you are already on HB, you can continue to get it for as long as you are in any of the eligible groups (table 2.6) or are a part-time student (or stop being a student).

2.45   If you are a pension age student, you can get HB in the normal way (whether or not you are in any of the eligible groups).

Table 2.6 **Students: eligible groups**

Paras 2.43-44 explain when these apply to full-time and part-time students.

(a) You are on UC in supported or temporary accommodation (table 2.3).

(b) You are on JSA(IB)/ESA(IR)/IS in any accommodation.

(c) You are under 21 and your course is not above A levels, Scottish Highers and equivalent qualifications or you are aged 21 and you are continuing on such a course.

(d) You are responsible for one or more children or young persons (para 4.14).

(e) You are single and have a foster child placed with you.

(f) You qualify for a severe disability premium (para 12.25) or disability premium (para 12.37).

(g) You have been accepted for ESA purposes as having limited capacity for work for at least 28 weeks (ignoring gaps of up to 12 weeks).

(h) You have a UK grant that includes an amount for deafness.

(i) You had an agreed absence from your studies due to sickness or providing care and less than one year has passed since the absence ended, but you haven't yet resumed your studies and can't get a grant or student loan.

(j) You are claiming pension age HB (table 2.2).

(k) Your partner is a student but you aren't.

2.43-45 CBA 130(1)(a), 137(2)(i); HB 2(1) definitions, 7(6)(b), 8(1), 53(1) definitions, 54, 56, 57(4), 58; HB66+ 2(1), 7(6)(b), 8(1); NICBA 129(1)(a), 133(2)(i); NIHB 2(1), 7(6)(b), 8(1), 50(1) definitions, 51, 53, 54(4), 55; NIHB66+ 2(1), 7(6)(b), 8(1)

Student terminology

2.46   You are a student if you are 'attending or undertaking a course of study at an educational establishment'. This could be a university, college, school or any other establishment used for the purpose of training, education or instruction (GM C2 annex A para C2.04).

2.47   You count as a student from when your course begins to when it ends, or you abandon it or are dismissed from it. This includes:

(a)   all term-times and vacations within the course (but not the vacations after it ends, or between two different courses);

(b)   all periods of work experience in a sandwich course; and

(c)   absences while you remain registered with your educational establishment (for example, because you are sick or caring for someone, or for other personal reasons): O'Connor v Chief Adjudication Officer.

2.48   Your educational establishment tells you whether your course is full-time or part-time, and the council normally accepts this. In many cases 'full-time' means more than 16 hours per week. There is further DWP guidance (GM chapter 2 annex A).

2.49   Your period of study means term-times and short vacations, but not your long summer vacation. If you don't have a summer vacation but are expected to study for at least 45 weeks a year (this applies to many postgraduates and student nurses), your period of study is the whole year.

Trainees

2.50   You can't get HB if you are a trainee on a government sponsored or government approved training course unless you claimed under earlier rules (para 2.7).

2.46-49 HB 2(1) definitions, 53(1) definitions; NIHB 2(1), 50(1)
            O'Connor v Chief Adjudication Officer [1999] EWCA Civ 884 1 FLR 1200

2.50   HB 7(18) definition: 'training course'; HB66+ 7(18); NIHB 7(18); NIHB66+ 7(18)

Chapter 3 **Occupying your home**

- Your home: see paras 3.1-4.
- Absences from home: see paras 3.5-13.
- Fear of violence, care homes, students and prisoners: see paras 3.14-28.
- Moving home and two homes: see paras 3.29-43.

Your home

3.1 The general rule is that you can only get HB on accommodation in the UK which you normally occupy as your home (paras 3.2-4). But there are also rules about absences from home, moving home and getting HB on two homes (paras 3.5-43).

Types of accommodation

3.2 Your home (or 'dwelling') can be any residential accommodation whether or not it is self-contained. This includes a house, flat, mobile home, houseboat, or room in someone else's home or in a hostel. It also includes somewhere converted, such as when two flats have been knocked together to form a single home (R(H) 5/09). It doesn't include business premises or somewhere used only for a holiday.

Your normal home

3.3 Whether you normally occupy accommodation as your home is decided in your and your family's particular circumstances (CH/2521/2002). It means more than paying housing costs or having the right to live there: it means being physically present – though exceptions can arise (R(H) 9/05). If you have more than one home (in the UK or abroad), only one can be your normal home. This is decided on the facts, including how much time you and your family spend in each of them.

Short-term accommodation

3.4 Your home can be somewhere short-term, e.g. if you move a lot or are staying in a hostel or refuge. But it must be a 'home' in the ordinary sense, and this doesn't normally include night shelters where you have no right to live during the day ([2013] UKUT 65 (AAC)).

3.1   CBA 130(1)(a); NICBA 129(1)(a)

3.2   CBA 137(1) definition: 'dwelling'; NICBA 133(1)

3.3   HB 7(1),(2); HB66+ 7(1),(2); NIHB 7(1),(2); NIHB66+ 7(1),(2)

Absences from home

3.5   This section explains when you can get HB during an absence from home. If you are in a couple and your partner is absent, see paras 4.23-25.

Temporary absences

3.6   You can get HB on your normal home during an absence if:

(a) you intend to return (para 3.8);

(b) your expected absence is unlikely to exceed, or substantially exceed, the time limit (para 3.10);

(c) your actual absence hasn't yet reached the time limit (para 3.11);

(d) you remain liable for rent on your normal home; and

(e) the part you normally occupy hasn't been rented out (by you or your landlord) to someone else.

Different rules apply if your home is being repaired or you are trying out a care home (paras 3.13, 3.20).

3.7   Your HB ends (CH/1237/2004) if:

(a) you don't meet the conditions in para 3.6 at the outset of your absence; or

(b) stop meeting them while you are away (including when your intentions change).

In either case, it ends at the end of the week (table 17.2).

Intending to return

3.8   Whether and when you intend to return to your normal home is decided by your own intentions rather than what a relative or official intends for you. Your intentions can depend on the outcome of events, for example:

(a) if you are absent due to fear of violence, you need only intend to return when it becomes safe to do so (para 3.15);

(b) if you are trying out a care home, you need only intend to return if the care home doesn't suit you (para 3.20).

But your return must be possible within the time limit. Wanting to return is not enough if your return is in fact impossible (CSHB/405/2005).

Time limits

3.9   Table 3.1 gives the time limits for temporary absences. They apply to:

(a) your expected absence (unless you are trying out a care home: para 3.20); and

(b) your actual absence (in all cases).

3.6   HB 7(11)-(13),(14)-(17),(18) definition: 'main dwelling'; HB66+ 7(11)-(13),(14)-(17);
           NIHB 7(11)-(13),(14)-(17),(18); NIHB66+ 7(11)-(13),(14)-(17),(18)

Table 3.1 **Time limits for HB during an absence**

Reason for your absence	Time limit
(a) You are a patient in hospital or a similar institution.	UK absences 52 weeks
(b) You are receiving medical treatment or medically approved care or convalescence.	Absences abroad 26 weeks
(c) Your partner or child is receiving medical treatment or medically approved convalescence.	
(d) You fear violence (para 3.14).	
(e) You are receiving care in a care home other than during a trial period (para 3.19).	UK absences 52 weeks
(f) You are providing medically approved care to someone.	Absences abroad four weeks
(g) You are caring for a child whose parent/guardian is away from their home to receive medical treatment or medically approved care.	
(h) You are studying or training (para 3.23).	
(i) You are on remand or on bail (para 3.26).	
(j) You are having a trial period in a care home (para 3.20).	UK absences 13 weeks
(k) You are temporarily absent for other reasons (on holiday, working, serving a sentence, etc).	Absences abroad four weeks
(l) You are outside the UK as a mariner, continental shelf worker or member of HM armed forces.	26 weeks
(m) A member of your family (para 4.2) or close relative of your family (para 5.28) has died outside the UK and you can't return within four weeks.	Eight weeks

Note: For these purposes, Great Britain counts as 'abroad' in Northern Ireland, and vice versa.

Examples: Working away from home

1. Mordred gets HB on a privately rented flat. He gets a contract to work for one term as a cleaner at a school. It is too far for him to commute and he stays rent-free with a friend for the whole of the term.

- He can get HB on his flat because his absence is unlikely to be longer than 13 weeks (table 3.1(k)), but his new income is taken into account.

2. Mordred (who still qualifies for HB) gets a year's contract to work at the school. He goes back to his flat for each of the school holidays.

T3.1   HB 7(11)-(18) definition: 'main dwelling'; HB66+ 7(11)-(18); NIHB 7(11)-(18); NIHB66+ 7(11)-(18)

■ He can continue to get HB on his flat because each absence is less than 13 weeks (table 3.1(k)).

3. Mordred then gets a permanent contract at the school. He keeps his flat on but removes most of his possessions from it and stops going back in the holidays.

■ He stops qualifying for HB on his flat because his absence is now likely to be longer than 13 weeks. Even if he returns occasionally to the flat, it is unlikely to count as his normal home so he can't get HB there (para 3.1).

Your expected absence

3.10 Your expected absence must be:

(a) unlikely to exceed the time limit in table 3.1; or

(b) in exceptional circumstances (except in cases (j) to (m) in the table), unlikely to substantially exceed it.

For UK absences with a time limit of 52 weeks, the DWP advises that 15 months is not 'substantially' longer, and that 'exceptional circumstances' can include unanticipated events such as a relapse in hospital (GM A3.532).

Your actual absence

3.11 Your actual absence can never exceed the time limit. If it reaches the time limit, your HB stops. You can't get working age HB again (except on supported or temporary accommodation), but you can get pension age HB (on any accommodation) when you return to your normal home or have a new home.

Counting the time limits

3.12 The time limits apply to absences that are continuous (R v Penwith DC ex parte Burt). The day you go away counts as a day of absence, but the day you return does not ([2019] UKUT 28 (AAC)). And so long as you return for at least 24 hours, going away again starts a new absence with a new time limit (GM A3.460).

Examples: A long stay in hospital

1. Michaela gets HB on her rented home. She has a serious accident and her doctors expect her to be in hospital for between nine and 15 months.

■ She can get HB because her expected absence is unlikely to substantially exceed 52 weeks (para 3.10)

2. Michaela leaves hospital after 13 months and returns home.

■ She can get HB for the first 52 weeks of her absence in hospital (para 3.11).

■ If Michaela was in a couple and her partner was the HB claimant, HB could be awarded throughout Michaela's absence (paras 4.23-25).

3.12   R v Penwith DC HBRB ex p Burt 26/02/90 QBD 22 HLR 292

Repairs to your normal home

3.13   When you move somewhere temporary because of repairs to your normal home, you can get HB on:

(a) your temporary home if:

- you don't pay rent on your normal home (e.g. you live there with relatives or friends or own it), or

- the rent on your normal home has stopped;

(b) your normal home in any other case (if you rent it).

Fear of violence

3.14   For HB purposes, you have a fear of violence if you fear violence towards yourself or a member of your family (para 4.2) either:

(a) in your normal home (whoever it would be from); or

(b) outside your normal home from a person who was a member of your family but no longer is, for example a former partner.

The DWP says you are normally expected to have reported the matter to the police or another reputable body (GM A3.549). But no violence needs actually to have occurred so long as your fear of it is 'reasonably held' (CH/1237/2004).

Moving out temporarily

3.15   If you leave your normal home due to a fear of violence and intend to return to it, you can get HB for up to 52 weeks on:

(a) your normal home (para 3.3); or

(b) the place you are staying (GM A3.630); or

(c) both of these if you are liable for rent on both (para 3.40) and it is reasonable to award HB on both.

Intending to return when it is safe to do so is normally sufficient.

3.16   But if you claim UC because the place you are staying is in a different council's area (table 17.3), you can get:

(a) UC on one or both homes for up to 12 months; or

(b) HB on one home if it is supported or temporary accommodation (table 2.3) and/or UC on the other for up to 12 months.

3.13   HB 7(4); HB66+ 7(4); NIHB 7(4); NIHB66+ 7(4)

3.14   HB 7(6)(a),(16)(c)(x); HB66+ 7(6)(a),(16)(c)(x); NIHB 7(6)(a),(16)(c)(x); NIHB66+ 7(6)(a),(16)(c)(x)

3.15-16 HB 7(6)(a),(16)(c)(x),(17); HB66+ 7(6)(a),(16)(c)(x),(17); NIHB 7(6)(a),(16)(c)(x),(17); NIHB66+ 7(6)(a),(16)(c)(x),(17)

Moving out permanently

3.17 If you leave your home due to a fear of violence and don't intend to return, you can get:

  (a) HB on your old home for up to four weeks (para 3.37); and/or

  (b) HB on your new home in the ordinary way.

Examples: Fear of violence

1. Morgana gets HB on her council flat. Her partner lives with her and he begins to threaten her with violence. She goes to stay in a refuge, but she intends to return to her flat and has got her parents to tell her ex-partner to leave.

    ■ She can get HB for up to 52 weeks on her flat because she intends to return. She can also get HB on the refuge (para 3.15).

2. After four months in the refuge, Morgana goes to stay with her parents. She still intends to return to her flat and her solicitor has written to her ex-partner instructing him to leave.

A month after that she decides she won't return to her flat.

    ■ She can continue to get HB on her flat until she decides not to return to it (paras 3.10-12).

Care homes

3.18 The following rules apply to care homes, and also to independent (non-NHS) hospitals and Abbeyfield Homes.

Moving temporarily to a care home

3.19 If you are being cared for in a care home and intend to return to your normal home, you can get HB on your normal home for up to 52 weeks (table 3.1). For example, you could be staying in the care home for a period of respite care.

Trying out a care home

3.20 If you are trying out a care home to see if it suits you, you can get HB on your normal home:

  (a) for up to 13 weeks while you are still considering whether to stay; and

  (b) for up to four weeks if and when you do decide to stay (R(H) 4/06) (para 3.37).

You can try out more than one care home and the 13 weeks starts again for each one, but only until you have been absent from your normal home for 52 weeks overall.

3.17   HB 7(1),(2),(6)(d),(7),(10); HB66+ 7(1),(2),(6)(d),(7),(10); NIHB 7(1),(2),(6)(d),(7),(10); NIHB66+ 7(1),(2),(6)(d),(7),(10)

3.18   HB 7(18) definition: 'residential accommodation'; HB66+ 7(18); NIHB 7(18); NIHB66+ 7(18)

3.20   HB 2(1) definitions: 'care home', 'independent hospital', 7(11),(12),(18); HB66+ 2(1), 7(11),(12),(18); NIHB 2(1), 7(11),(12),(18); NIHB66+ 2(1), 7(11),(12),(18)

Moving permanently to a care home

3.21   If you move to a care home and don't intend to return to your normal home, you can get HB on your normal home for up to four weeks (para 3.37).

Leaving a care home

3.22   If you are waiting to leave a care home, you can get HB on your normal home for up to four weeks (para 3.36). This can include a new home you have never yet lived in.

Examples: A care home

1. Betella gets HB on a rented house. She goes into a care home for a six-week trial period.

- She can get HB on her normal home throughout the trial period (para 3.20)

2. At the end of the trial period, Betella decides to stay in the care home and gives notice to her old landlord.

- She can get HB on her old home during the notice period for up to four weeks (para 3.20).

Students

3.23   The following rules apply to students who are in an eligible group (table 2.6), and also to trainees on a government sponsored or approved training scheme. You continue to count as a student during any absences while you remain registered on your course (O'Connor v Chief Adjudication Officer). For example, if you are absent because you are sick, caring for someone or for other personal reasons.

Single students

3.24   When you are a single student renting term-time accommodation away from your normal home:

(a)   if you pay rent on your normal home, you can get HB there for up to 52 weeks while you are staying in your term-time accommodation (para 3.6), but you can't get HB on your term-time accommodation;

(b)   if you don't pay rent or a mortgage on your normal home (e.g. it is a relative's home), you can get HB on your term-time accommodation (but during the summer vacation your HB stops during absences of more than a week);

(c)   if you pay a mortgage on your normal home, you can't get HB on either home.

However, (b) only applies to pension age HB, because you can no longer make a claim for working age HB (para 2.6) and UC has no equivalent rule.

3.21   HB 7(7),(8)(c)(iii); HB66+ 7(7),(8)(c)(iii); NIHB 7(7),(8)(c)(iii); NIHB66+ 7(7),(8)(c)(iii)

3.22   HB 7(7),(10); HB66+ 7(7),(10); NIHB 7(7),(10); NIHB66+ 7(7),(10)

3.23   HB 2(1) definitions, 7(18) definition 'training course', 53(1) definitions; HB66+ 7(18); NIHB 2(1), 7(18), 50(1); NIHB66+ 7(18)
        O'Connor v Chief Adjudication Officer [1999] EWCA Civ 884 1 FLR 1200

3.24   HB 7(1),(3),(16)(iv),(viii),(17), 55; HB66+ 7(1),(3),(16)(iv),(viii),(17);
        NIHB 7(1),(3),(16)(iv),(viii),(17), 52; NIHB66+ 7(1),(3),(16)(iv),(viii),(17)

Student couples

3.25   When you are a couple and at least one of you is a student:

(a) you can get HB on two homes (para 3.40) if this is reasonable and occupying both is unavoidable (e.g. because one of you is studying in one area and the other is studying or working in another);

(b) otherwise you can get HB on one home in the same way as described in para 3.24.

Prisoners

Remand and bail

3.26   You can get HB on your normal home for up to 52 weeks (para 3.6) while you are on remand (awaiting trial or sentencing in prison) or on bail (awaiting trial or sentencing at home or elsewhere).

Serving a sentence

3.27   If you are serving a custodial sentence in prison, you can get HB on your normal home:

(a) for up to 13 weeks if your overall absence is unlikely to exceed 13 weeks; or

(b) for up to four weeks from when you left your normal home (para 3.37).

You are likely to meet the time limit in (a) if you have a fixed term sentence of up to six months (which is 13 weeks after remission) or ten months (if you qualify for home detention curfew). But if you are detained in hospital only (b) applies. For DWP guidance see GM A3.485-518.

Parole and temporary release

3.28   If you are released on parole (licence) you can get HB in the ordinary way. But since 1st September 2021, all prisoners on temporary release count as still being in prison, so you can only get HB as described in para 3.27.

Examples: Remand and conviction

1. Gabriel gets HB on a rented flat. He is arrested and sent to prison on remand.

- ■   He can get HB for up to 52 weeks (para 3.26).

2. Gabriel is found guilty and given a prison sentence of one year.

- ■   His total absence from home is now likely to be six months after remission. So his HB ends when he is sentenced (para 3.27).

- ■   If Gabriel was in a couple and his partner was the HB claimant, HB could be awarded throughout Gabriel's absence (paras 4.23-25).

3.25   HB 7(6)(b); HB66+ 7(6)(b); NIHB 7(6)(b); NIHB66+ 7(6)(b)

3.26   HB 7(16)(c)(i),(16A),(17); HB66+ 7(16)(c)(i),(16A),(17); NIHB 7(16)(c)(i),(16A),(17); NIHB66+ 7(16)(c)(i),(16A),(17)

3.27   HB 7(7),(13); HB66+ 7(7),(13); NIHB 7(7),(13); NIHB66+ 7(7),(13)

3.28   HB 7(14),(15); HB66+ 7(14),(15); NIHB 7(14),(15); NIHB66+ 7(14),(15)

Moving home

3.29 When you move home your HB changes on the date of your move to take account of your new housing costs, unless you move to a different council area, in which case you need to claim HB or UC (table 17.3). But in some cases, you can get HB for up to four weeks before moving in or after moving out (paras 3.31-39).

The date of your move

3.30 The date of your move means the day you physically transfer from one home to another, along with any family members who are moving with you, though there can be exceptions if your move is delayed at the last moment (R (H) 9/05). It doesn't mean the date on the letting agreement (if different) or the day you start getting your new home ready (R (H) 9/05; CH/1911/2006). If you have more than one home, it means the date your normal home changes.

Waiting for adaptations for a disability

3.31 You can get HB on a new home for up to four weeks before the date you move into it if:

(a) your liability for rent started before you moved in;

(b) you were waiting for it to be adapted to meet your disability needs (para 3.33) or those of a member of your family (para 4.2);

(c) you have now moved in; and

(d) your delay in moving was necessary and reasonable.

You need to make a new claim promptly (paras 16.31-33).

3.32 You can get HB on both your old and new home for up to four weeks before the date of your move if:

(a) you are liable for rent on both of them; and

(b) you meet the other conditions in para 3.31.

Your HB for your old home should continue during this period (para 16.50) or the decision to end it can be revised (paras 20.35, 20.38). But you need to make a claim for HB for your new home; or if it in the same council area as your old home, you may just need to give the council details of your move (table 17.3).

3.33 The adaptations can include furnishing, carpeting and redecorating as well as changes to your new home's fabric or structure (R (Mahmoudi) v Lewisham LBC).

3.29   HB 79(2A)(a); HB66+ 59(2A)(a); NIHB 77(3)(a); NIHB66+ 57(3)(a)

3.31   HB 7(8)(c)(i); HB66+ 7(8)(c)(i); NIHB 7(8)(c)(i); NIHB66+ 7(8)(c)(i)

3.32   HB 7(6)(e); HB66+ 7(6)(e); NIHB 7(6)(e); NIHB66+ 7(6)(e)

3.33   R (Mahmoudi) v Lewisham [2014] EWCA 284 www.bailii.org/ew/cases/EWCA/Civ/2014/284.html

Waiting for local welfare assistance

3.34 You can get HB on a new home for up to four weeks before the date you move in if:

(a) your liability for rent there started before you moved in;

(b) you were waiting for local welfare assistance (para 23.35) to help with the move or setting up home;

(c) you (or your partner):

- are aged 66 or over, or

- qualify for a disability premium (paras 12.37-39), or

- have limited capability for work or for work-related activity (para 12.48), or

- have a child under 6, or

- have a child or young person who qualifies for a disabled child premium (para 12.22);

(d) you have now moved in; and

(e) your delay in moving was reasonable.

3.35 You can't get HB on your old home at the same time. So, if you are liable for rent on both your old and new homes, you can get HB on whichever counts as your normal home.

Waiting to leave hospital or a care home

3.36 You can get HB on a new home for up to four weeks before the date you move into it if:

(a) your liability for rent there started before you moved in;

(b) you were waiting to leave hospital or a care home (para 3.18);

(c) you have now moved in; and

(d) your delay in moving was reasonable.

Unavoidable liability for rent

3.37 You can get HB on your old home for up to four weeks from the date you move out of it if:

(a) you continue to be liable for rent there;

(b) your liability could not reasonably have been avoided (para 3.39); and

(c) either:

- you have moved into somewhere new – this can include hospital, a care home, or prison, even though you can't get HB on these (GM A3.688 example 3), or

- you left your old home due to fear of violence (para 3.14) and don't yet have a new address or don't want to say where it is.

You don't need to make a new HB claim for this period, because your original HB claim there continues (para 16.50) or the decision to end it can be revised (paras 20.35, 20.38).

3.34   HB 7(8)(c)(ii); HB66+ 7(8)(c)(ii); NIHB 7(8)(c)(ii); NIHB66+ 7(8)(c)(ii)

3.36   HB 7(8)(c)(iii),(18); HB66+ 7(8)(c)(iii),(18); NIHB 7(8)(c)(iii),(18); NIHB66+ 7(8)(c)(iii),(18)

3.37   HB 7(7),(10); HB66+ 7(7),(10); NIHB 7(7),(10); NIHB66+ 7(7),(10)

3.38 You can get HB on your old home as well as your current home for up to four weeks from the date of your move if:

   (a) you are liable for rent on both of them; and

   (b) your liability on both could not reasonably have been avoided (para 3.39).

This is sometimes called the 'overlapping HB rule'. It doesn't apply when you move out for repairs to be done (para 3.13). Your HB for your old home should continue during this period (para 16.50) or the decision to end it can be revised (paras 20.35, 20.38). But you need to make a claim for HB for your new home; or if it is in the same council area as your old home, you may just need to give the council details of your move (table 17.3).

3.39 Whether your liability for rent could reasonably have been avoided is decided on the facts and any alternatives that were open to you (CH/4546/2002), such as whether and when you gave notice to your landlord. Your situation doesn't have to be 'exceptional' (though DWP advice wrongly says it should be: GM A3.682).

Example: Unavoidable liability (overlapping HB)

Barnaby gets HB on a private rented flat. He is offered a housing association house in the same area and has to take up the tenancy there on the following Monday. He gives notice to his old landlord and is liable for rent on both homes for the overlap period.

■ He can get HB on both homes during the overlap for up to four weeks (para 3.38).

Two homes

3.40 You can get HB on two homes when:

   (a) you have a large family (para 3.42); or

   (b) you are absent from your normal home due to fear of violence (para 3.14); or

   (c) are a couple and one or both of you are a student or a trainee (para 3.25); or

   (d) you are waiting for adaptations for a disability (para 3.32); or

   (e) you are unavoidably liable for rent on both homes (para 3.38).

3.41 In any other case you can only get HB on your normal home (paras 3.3-4). If you start or stop qualifying on two homes, your HB changes on the exact day.

Large families

3.42 You can get HB on two homes (with no time limit) if your council or another housing authority has housed you in both, or arranged for you to be housed in both, due to the size of your family (para 4.2). The DWP advises that both homes must be provided but not necessarily owned by the council, and would normally be next to each other or within a few streets of each other (GM A3.660).

3.38   HB 7(6)(d); HB66+ 7(6)(d); NIHB 7(6)(d); NIHB66+ 7(6)(d)

3.40   HB 7(6); HB66+ 7(6); NIHB 7(6); NIHB66+ 7(6)

3.41   HB 79(2A); HB66+ 59(2A); NIHB 77(3); NIHB66+ 57(3)

3.42   HB 7(6)(c); HB66+ 7(6)(c); NIHB 7(6)(c); NIHB66+ 7(6)(c)

Calculating HB on two homes

3.43   When you qualify for HB on two homes:

   (a) the two eligible rents are added together; but

   (b) deductions for excess income and non-dependants are only made once (paras 6.2, 6.6).

This applies even if the two homes are in different council areas ([2011] UKUT 5 (AAC)). For the benefit cap see paras 2.34-35.

3.43   CBA 130(3)(b); HB 71; HB66+ 51; NICBA 129(3)(b); NIHB 69; NIHB66+ 49

Chapter 4 **The people in your home**

- Your family, couples, children and young persons: see paras 4.2-19.
- Household membership: see paras 4.20-25.
- Non-dependants: see paras 4.26-32.
- Carers, lodgers, joint tenants and others: see paras 4.33-50.

4.1 This chapter explains how the people in your home affect your HB. They are divided into:

(a) you and your family; and

(b) other people, including foster children, non-dependants, carers, lodgers and joint tenants.

Your family

4.2 For HB purposes, your 'family' does not always mean the same as in day-to-day life. It means only the following members of your household:

(a) your partner if you are in a couple (or partners in a polygamous marriage); and/or

(b) each child or young person you or your partner are responsible for.

Table 1.1 gives a summary of family and other terminology.

4.3 You and the members of your family are included when the council decides your applicable amount (para 12.2) and the size of accommodation you need (para 11.10). And your partner's income and capital is included with yours (paras 13.2 and 15.2).

> **Examples: Families and other occupiers**
>
> **1.** Laurel and Oliver are a married couple who rent their home. They have two daughters aged 15 and 21 living with them, a foster son aged 14, and a lodger who rents a room from them. Laurel claims HB.
>
> Laurel is the claimant, with Oliver as her partner. Oliver and the younger daughter are the members of Laurel's family (para 4.2). The older daughter is Laurel's non-dependant (para 4.26). Their foster son and lodger are not included in their family and are not non-dependants (table 4.3).
>
> **2.** Stanley and Hardeep are living together as a couple and rent their home. Hardeep's son aged 7 lives with them and so does Hardeep's adult sister. Stanley claims HB.
>
> Stanley is the claimant, with Hardeep as his partner. Hardeep and his son are the members of Stanley's family. Hardeep's sister is Stanley's non-dependant.

4.2   CBA 137(1) definition: 'family'; NICBA 133(1)

Couples

4.4   This section explains who counts as a couple. If you are in a couple your partner is a member of your family (paras 4.2-3). If you are in a polygamous marriage (table 1.1) you don't count as a couple but your partners are included in the same way.

4.5   You are a couple for HB purposes if you are two people who are:

(a)   married or in a civil partnership; or

(b)   living together as though you were married or in a civil partnership (paras 4.8-12).

You must also be members of the same household (paras 4.20-22) – whether you are married/ civil partners (CIS/72/1994) or living together ([2004] UKUT 17 (AAC)). If your partner is temporarily absent see paras 4.23-25.

4.6   If your relationship has ended, you are no longer a couple if you now maintain separate households even in the same dwelling. In deciding this, your shared understanding that your relationship has ended and your actual living arrangements are more important than whether you still share responsibilities and financial arrangements (CIS/72/1994), but by itself a shared understanding may not be enough if you are still married/civil partners (CIS/2900/1998).

4.7   Someone who no longer counts as your partner (paras 4.5 and 4.25) is not included in your applicable amount. Their income and capital is not included with yours, but income you receive from them is counted as maintenance (table 13.6). If they still live in your dwelling they fall within one of the other descriptions in this chapter (for example they might be your joint tenant or a non-dependant) and the effect on your HB follows from that.

Living together as a couple

4.8   The law doesn't give a fixed definition of:

(a)   living together as though you were a married couple, or

(b)   living together as though you were civil partners;

except to say that these are decided in the same way.

4.9   The decision about this is made by looking at:

(a)   your purpose in living together (Crake and Butterworth v the Supplementary Benefits Commission); and

(b)   (if your purpose is unclear) your relationship and living arrangements.

4.10   The following factors are relevant (Crake case; [2013] UKUT 505 (AAC)):

(a)   whether you share the same household;

(b)   the stability of your relationship;

(c)   your financial arrangement;

4.5   CBA 137(1) definition: 'couple'; NICBA 133(1); HB 2(1) definition: 'couple'; HB66+ 2(1); NIHB 2(1); NIHB66+ 2(1)

4.8   CBA 137(1) definition: 'couple', (1A); NICBA 133(1),(1A)

4.9   Crake and Butterworth v SBC 21/07/80 QBD [1982] All ER 498

4.10   [2017] AACR 10, formerly [2016] CSIH 84

(d) whether you have a sexual relationship;

(e) whether you share responsibility for a child;

(f) whether you publicly acknowledge you are a couple;

(g) the emotional element of your relationship;

The decision should be based on the totality of the evidence, and none of the factors is conclusive in itself ([2017] AACR 10) unless you don't share a household (paras 4.20-22).

4.11   There are many reasons why two people might live in the same household or same dwelling. They might be a couple. But they may be landlord/lady and lodger, house sharers, etc. Even living together for reasons of 'care companionship and mutual convenience' does not by itself mean you are a couple (R(SB) 35/85).

4.12   Detailed advice about living together cases is in volume 3 ch 11 of the DWP Decision Maker's Guide [www]. Guidance on the questions councils should ask is in GM C1 annex A paras A1.07-10.

DWP decisions about couples

4.13   If you have claimed a passport benefit (para 1.7) the council is likely to accept the DWP's decision about whether you are a couple. But:

(a) if the DWP decided you are in a couple, the council must make its own decision about this if you say the DWP is wrong (R(H) 9/04);

(b) if the DWP awarded you a passport benefit on the basis that you aren't in a couple, the council should accept this unless it has evidence of fraud which the DWP is unaware of and hasn't considered (CH/4014/2007).

Children and young persons

4.14   This section explains who counts as a child or young person and when they are included in your family.

4.15   A 'child' means someone who is aged under 16.

4.16   A 'young person' means someone who meets all the following conditions:

(a) they are aged 16 or more but under 20;

(b) they meet the conditions for child benefit to be paid for them (table 4.1) – in practice it is almost always enough if child benefit is actually being paid for them;

(c) they are not a care leaver aged 16 or 17 (paras 2.40-42); and

(d) they are not themself on JSA(IB), ESA(IR), IS or UC.

4.12   www.gov.uk/government/publications/decision-makers-guide-vol-3-subjects-common-to-all-benefits-staff-guide

4.15   CBA 137(1) definition: 'child'; NICBA 133(1); HB 2(1) definition: 'child'; HB66+ 2(1); NIHB 2(1); NIHB66+ 2(1)

4.16   HB 19; HB66+ 19; NIHB 17; NIHB66+ 17

4.17   A child or young person is included in your family (paras 4.2-3) if:

(a)   you or your partner are responsible for them – in other words they normally live with you (paras 4.18-19); and

(b)   they do not fall within any of the exceptions in table 4.2.

They must also be a member of your household (paras 4.20-22) – but this is usually the case if they meet the above conditions. If a child or young person is temporarily absent, see paras 4.23-25.

Responsibility for a child or young person

4.18   You are 'responsible' for a child or young person if they are 'normally living' with you. This is usually straightforward. For example they could be your son or daughter, adopted by you, a step-child, a grandchild, or any other child or young person (whether related to you or not); so long as they normally live with you.

4.19   Each child or young person can only be the responsibility of one person (or one couple) at any one time. This is the person they 'normally' live with, whether or not that person gets child benefit for them. But if this is unclear, or they spend equal time in different households (e.g. when parents have separated), they are the responsibility of:

(a)   the person who gets child benefit for them; or

(b)   if no-one gets child benefit, the person who has claimed it for them; or

(c)   if no-one has claimed it (or more than one person has), the person who has 'primary responsibility' for them. Deciding this may mean looking at a wide range of factors and so may not depend on who they spend most time with ([2018] UKUT 44 (AAC)).

See table 4.2(e) for children and young persons who do not normally live with you.

Table 4.1 **Who is a young person**

Someone aged 16 or more but under 20 is a 'young person' (para 4.16) during any or all of the following periods (the periods in which child benefit can be paid for them):

(a)   Until the 31st August following their 16th birthday (in all cases, whether or not they are in education, training or work).

(b)   While they are undertaking a course of education which:

■   is not above GCE A level or equivalent (national standard level 3) [www]; and

■   takes up more than 12 hours per week on average during term-time of tuition, practical work, supervised study or taking examinations; and

■   they began before their 19th birthday.

(c)   While they are between two courses which meet the above conditions. But this only applies if they are enrolled on and actually start the second course.

4.17   CBA 137(1) definition: 'family'; NICBA 133(1)

4.18   HB 20(1); HB66+ 20(1); NIHB 18(1); NIHB66+ 18(1)

4.19   HB 20(2),(3); HB66+ 20(2),(3); NIHB 18(2),(3); NIHB66+ 18(2),(3)

(d) While they are undertaking approved training which is not provided under an employment contract. This includes many kinds of employment preparation course etc [www].

(e) From when they leave the above education or training until the last day of August, November, February or May, whichever comes first. This is called the 'child benefit terminal date'.

(f) If they are aged 16 or 17, from when they leave the above education or training until the end of the 20th whole week after that. This is called the 'child benefit extension period'. But it only applies if:

- they are not in remunerative work; and

- they are registered for work, education or training with the Careers Service or Connexions Service; and

- an application is made, within three months of the end of the education or training, for child benefit to continue during this period.

For exceptions, see para 4.16 and table 4.2.

Table 4.2 **Children and young persons who are not included in your family**

The following are not included in your family (para 4.17), or your applicable amount (para 12.2).

Fostering and adoption

Fostering is also called 'boarding out' or 'kinship care'.

(a) A child or young person who is placed with you or your partner as a foster child or prior to adoption.

- But they can affect the size criteria (paras 11.21-22).

- And they are included in your family, your applicable amount and the size criteria when you actually adopt them – if they normally live with you (paras 4.17-19).

(b) A child or young person who is placed with someone else as a foster child or prior to adoption.

T4.1   HB 19; HB66+ 19; NIHB 17; NIHB66+ 17
         https//www.gov.uk/what-different-qualification-levels-mean
         www.hmrc.gov.uk/manuals/ccmmanual/ccm18035.htm

T4.2(a) HB 21(3),(6); HB66+ 21(3),(6); NIHB 19(3),(6); NIHB66+ 19(3),(6)

T4.2(b) HB 21(4)(b),(c); HB66+ 21(4)(b)(c); NIHB 19(4)(b),(c); NIHB66+ 19(4)(b)(c)

Local authority care

This is also called 'being looked after by a local authority'.

(c) A child or young person who is in local authority care and is not living with you.

- But they are included in your family, your applicable amount and the size criteria in any benefit week in which they live with you for part or all of that week, if it is reasonable to do so – e.g. if they are visiting you under local authority supervision (GM paras C1.120, C1.150).

Living with you but not a young person

(d) Someone aged 16 or more who lives with you but doesn't count (or no longer counts) as a young person (para 4.16 and table 4.1).

- But they usually count as a non-dependant (para 4.26).
- And they are included in the size criteria (para 11.10(b),(e)).

Not normally living with you

(e) A child or young person who doesn't live with you, or doesn't normally live with you (para 4.19), even if they spend some time with you.*

- But they are included in your family, your applicable amount and the size criteria if they are only temporarily absent (para 4.24).
- And if they normally live with another occupier of your dwelling, see paras 4.32, 4.39, 4.46 and 4.48-49.

* Exclusion from applicable amount: [2013] UKUT 642 (AAC), [2014] UKUT 223 (AAC);
from social sector size criteria: [2015] UKUT 34 (AAC);
from private sector size criteria: R v Swale HBRB ex parte Marchant, [2010] UKUT 208 (AAC).

Household membership

4.20 Someone can only be included in your family if you are members of the same 'household' (paras 4.5 and 4.17). Other HB rules also refer to household membership (e.g. about joint tenants: para 4.45).

4.21 Rather than being defined in the law, a household has its ordinary meaning. It means a domestic arrangement involving two or more people who live together as a unit (R(IS) 1/99), even when they have a reasonable level of independence and self-sufficiency (R(SB) 8/85). It requires a settled course of daily living rather than visits from time to time (R(F) 2/81). And a person can't be a member of two or more households at the same time (R(SB) 8/85).

T4.2(c)   HB 21(4)(a),(5),(6); HB66+ 21(4)(a),(5),(6); NIHB 19(4)(a),(5),(6); NIHB66+19(4)(a),(5),(6)

T4.2(d)   HB 19; HB66+ 19; NIHB 17; NIHB66+ 17

T4.2(e)   HB 20; HB66+ 20; NIHB 18; NIHB66+ 18

T4.2(*)   R v Swale HBRB ex p Marchant 9/11/99 CA 32 HLR 856

4.20   CBA 137(1) definition: 'family'; NICBA 133(1)

4.22 You are not members of the same household if you have:

(a) separate homes in different dwellings (R(SB) 4/83); or

(b) separate households within the same dwelling (CIS/072/1994).

So if you keep your eating, cooking, food storage, finances (including paying your housing costs), living space and family life separate, you are unlikely to be members of the same household.

Absences of family members

4.23 Paras 4.24-25 explain the rules about absences of family members. Different rules apply if you (the claimant) are absent from your home (para 3.5) or a non-dependant is (para 4.31).

4.24 A partner, child or young person who is temporarily living away from you continues to be included in your household and in your family. So they are included in your applicable amount, and normally included when the council decides the size of accommodation you need (paras 11.10-11). They could be on holiday, working or looking for work, studying or training (e.g. a child/young person at boarding school or a partner taking a course), in hospital or receiving or providing care, in prison, and so on.

4.25 But they stop being included if:

(a) they don't intend to resume living with you (this is usually looked at in the same way as in para 3.8); or

(b) their absence is likely to be longer than 52 weeks, unless there are exceptional circumstances and it is unlikely to be substantially longer than this.

'Exceptional circumstances' includes being in hospital and other situations where they have no control over the length of their absence. 'Substantially' longer than 52 weeks is likely to mean longer than 15 months (GM para A3.532).

Non-dependants

4.26 A 'non-dependant' is someone who:

(a) normally resides with you (paras 4.29-31); and

(b) does not fall within any of the exceptions in table 4.3.

For example, an adult daughter, son, relative or friend is usually a non-dependant if they live with you on a non-commercial basis. (See also paras 4.41 and 4.47 for special cases.)

4.27 If you have one or more non-dependants you may get less HB – this is called a non-dependant deduction (para 6.9 and tables 6.2 and 6.3). Non-dependants are not included in your applicable amount, but they are included when the council decides the size of accommodation you need (para 11.10).

4.28 Non-dependants can't get HB themselves (para 5.30). But they may be able to get HB if they take over paying your rent because you aren't paying it (paras 5.15-17).

4.24   HB 21(1); HB66+ 21(1); NIHB 19(1); NIHB66+ 19(1)

4.25   HB 21(2); HB66+ 21(2); NIHB 19(2); NIHB66+ 19(2)

4.26   HB 3; HB66+ 3; NIHB 3; NIHB66+ 3

Normally residing with you

4.29   Someone is only a non-dependant if they 'normally reside' with you (or you 'normally reside' with them). Paras 4.30-31 give the two parts to this rule.

4.30   They must actually share some accommodation with you, and it must be more than just a bathroom, toilet or communal area (halls, corridors, stairways, etc: para 8.43). Sharing a living room is enough to count and sharing a kitchen can also be enough (CPC/1446/2008), as can sharing a house but being unable to make use of the shared areas due to disability (CPC/3379/2008). A person can 'reside' in two places but can't 'normally reside' in more than one; so someone who normally resides elsewhere can't normally reside with you ([2018] UKUT 75 (AAC)).

4.31   You must also have the sort of relationship that means you 'normally reside' with each other in the ordinary sense (Khadim v Brent LBC). For example:

(a)   a temporary visitor is not a non-dependant (CH/4004/2004), unless and until residing with you becomes the normal arrangement (CH/3935/2007);

(b)   a longer absence usually means someone stops counting as a non-dependant (e.g. moving to a care home), but a shorter temporary absence does not (e.g. a holiday).

Some absences always mean there is no non-dependant deduction (table 6.2).

If a non-dependant has a family of their own

4.32   If your non-dependant has their own family, each of them counts as your non-dependant (paras 4.27-28) if they normally reside with you. But:

(a)   there is only one deduction for a non-dependant couple instead of two (para 6.18);

(b)   there is no deduction for any non-dependants aged under 18 (or for many others: para 6.11 and table 6.2);

(c)   a non-dependant's child or young person counts as a member of your own family (instead of being a non-dependant) if they meet the conditions for this (paras 4.14-19).

Example: Three generations living together

■   Gloria's daughter aged 15 lives with her, as does the daughter's baby. Gloria gets child benefit for them both. The council decides that Gloria is responsible for them both, and includes both in Gloria's family (and thus in her applicable amount).

■   Later, (after leaving school) the daughter claims income support for herself. The council decides that the daughter and baby now form a separate family, and so excludes them from Gloria's family (and applicable amount).

In both cases, the daughter and baby are included in deciding the size of accommodation Gloria needs. In the second situation the daughter and baby are Gloria's non-dependants (paras 4.26 and 4.32).

4.29   HB 3(1); HB66+ 3(1); NIHB 3(1); NIHB66+ 3(1)

4.30   HB 3(4), sch 1 para 8; HB66+ 3(4), sch 1 para 8; NIHB 3(4), sch 1 para 8; NIHB66+ 3(4), sch 1 para 8

4.31   Khadim v Brent HBRB [2000] EWCA Civ 344 www.bailii.org/ew/cases/EWCA/Civ/2000/344.html

---

Table 4.3 **People who are not your non-dependants**

None of the following count as your non-dependants (para 4.26):

(a) Members of your family (paras 4.2-25).

(b) Children and young persons who are a foster child, placed for adoption, or in local authority care (table 4.2(a)-(c)).

(c) Carers you pay a voluntary or charitable organisation for (para 4.33).

(d) Lodgers of yours (paras 4.36-41).

(e) Joint tenants of yours (paras 4.42-47).

(f) Separate tenants of your landlord (para 4.48).

(g) Your landlord (para 4.49).

(h) People who normally reside with someone in (d) to (g) (see the paras referred to above).

(i) Anyone else who doesn't normally reside with you (paras 4.29-31).

Other people in your home

Carers provided by a charitable or voluntary organisation

4.33   A carer who lives in your home doesn't count as a non-dependant if:

(a) they are living with you to look after you or your partner;

(b) they are employed or engaged by a charitable or voluntary organisation (not a public or local authority); and

(c) the organisation makes a charge to you or your partner for this.

No deduction is made from your HB for them. But if your dwelling is their home, they are included when the council decides the size of accommodation you need (para 11.10(e)).

Other carers

4.34   Any other carer who lives in your home falls within one of the other descriptions in this chapter, and the effect on your HB follows from that. For example they could be your family member, non-dependant, joint tenant, landlord, etc. If you employ them see para 4.50.

T4.3(a)   HB 3(2)(a),(b); HB66+ 3(2)(a),(b); NIHB 3(2)(a),(b); NIHB66+ 3(2)(a),(b)

T4.3(b)   HB 3(2)(c); HB66+ 3(2)(c); NIHB 3(2)(c); NIHB66+ 3(2)(c)

T4.3(c)   HB 3(2)(f); HB66+ 3(2)(f); NIHB 3(2)(f); NIHB66+ 3(2)(f)

T4.3(d)   HB 3(2)(e)(i); HB66+ 3(2)(e)(i); NIHB 3(2)(e)(i); NIHB66+ 3(2)(e)(i)

T4.3(e)   HB 3(2)(d); HB66+ 3(2)(d); NIHB 3(2)(d); NIHB66+ 3(2)(d)

T4.3(f)   HB 3(1),(4); HB66+ 3(1),(4); NIHB 3(1),(4); NIHB66+ 3(1),(4)

T4.3(g)   HB 3(2)(e)(ii); HB66+ 3(2)(e)(ii); NIHB 3(2)(e)(ii); NIHB66+ 3(2)(e)(ii)

T4.3(h)   HB 3(1),(2)(e)(iii); HB66+ 3(1),(2)(e)(iii); NIHB 3(2)(e)(iii); NIHB66+ 3(2)(e)(iii)

T4.3(i)   HB 3(1); HB66+ 3(1); NIHB 3(1); NIHB66+ 3(1)

4.33   HB 3(2)(f); HB66+ 3(2)(f); NIHB 3(2)(f); NIHB66+ 3(2)(f)

4.35   If you or your partner have overnight care from one or more carers who don't live in your home, this can affect the size of accommodation you need (paras 11.25-33). But no deduction is made from your HB for them.

Lodgers

4.36   A lodger is someone who is liable to make payments to you or your partner, on a commercial basis, in order to live in your home. (We use 'lodger' in this guide because HB law doesn't have a straightforward term for this.) The following rules apply separately for each lodger you have.

4.37   The HB rules divide lodgers into two kinds:

(a) lodgers (sometimes called boarders) whose charge includes meals (para 4.38); and

(b) lodgers (sometimes called sub-tenants) whose charge doesn't include meals.

In either case, they might have people who normally reside with them rather than with you (e.g. their family members or non-dependants).

4.38   A lodger's charge counts as including meals if:

(a) 'at least some meals' are provided as part of the agreement between you (e.g. breakfast every day is enough);

(b) they are cooked or prepared by you or someone else, but not by the lodger or a member of their family; and

(c) they are cooked/prepared and consumed in your home or in associated premises.

4.39   Your lodger, and the people who normally reside with them, affect your HB as follows:

(a) part of the payment you receive from them counts as your income, and the way this is done means you are usually better off if you provide meals than if you don't (table 13.7);

(b) they are included when the council decides the size of accommodation you need (para 11.10(c),(e));

(c) they are not included in your applicable amount; and

(d) they are not your non-dependants (table 4.3).

The lodger can make their own claim for HB and – if they do – the people who reside with them are taken into account in their claim.

4.37   HB sch 5 paras 22,42; HB66+ sch 5 paras 9,10; NIHB sch 6 paras 23,44; NIHB66+ sch 6 paras 10,11

4.38   HB sch 5 para 42(2); HB66+ 2(1) definition: 'board and lodging accommodation'; NIHB sch 6 para 44(2); NIHB66+ 2(1)

Example: A claimant whose lodger also claims HB

Fred rents his home from a commercial landlord. It has three bedrooms and he rents (sub-lets) two of these to Barney, one for Barney and one for Barney's son Dino, aged 8. Fred is working and is on HB. Barney is on JSA(IB) and is also on HB.

Fred's HB

Fred is the claimant, Barney is his lodger (para 4.36), and Dino is Barney's child. So Fred is a single claimant. The rent Barney pays is taken into account as Fred's income (table 13.7). The LHA figure for a three-bedroom dwelling is used to calculate Fred's HB, because Barney and Dino live in his dwelling as his home (para 11.10), as well as Fred.

Barney's HB

Barney is the claimant, Dino is his child, and Fred is his landlord. So Barney is a lone parent. The LHA figure for a two-bedroom dwelling is used to calculate Barney's HB (paras 10.16-17), because just he and his son are taken into account.

Distinguishing lodgers from non-dependants

4.40   The difference between lodgers and non-dependants is that:

(a) a lodger has a commercial relationship with you, and is liable to make payments which usually count as 'rent' in the HB sense (table 5.1);

(b) a non-dependant doesn't have a commercial relationship with you, whether or not they contribute towards your housing costs.

Even if a non-dependant has exclusive occupation (e.g. of their bedroom) this doesn't make them a lodger, because there are 'many examples… of family arrangements and acts of friendship or generosity not… giving rise to a tenancy even when exclusive occupation is given' ([2012] UKUT 114 (AAC)).

When a lodger counts as a non-dependant

4.41   A lodger who has a 'contrived' or other letting for which HB can't be paid (paras 5.20-38) counts instead as a non-dependant. For example if you rent out part of your home to a close relative (para 5.28) they count as a non-dependant not a lodger.

Joint tenants

4.42   A joint tenant is someone who is jointly liable to pay the rent on your home. They could be jointly liable with you, your partner, or both of you. The following rules apply separately for each joint tenant you have.

4.41   HB 3(3); HB66+ 3(3); NIHB 3(3); NIHB66+ 3(3)

4.42   HB 3(2)(d); HB66+ 3(2)(d); NIHB 3(2)(d); NIHB66+ 3(2)(d)

4.43   The HB rules divide joint tenants into two kinds:

(a)   joint tenants who are a member of your family, e.g. your partner or a young person; and

(b)   joint tenants who aren't a member of your family, e.g. a relation or friend who jointly rents your home as your house-sharer or flat-sharer.

Joint tenants who are a member of your family

4.44   A joint tenant who is a member of your family is just included in your family, and the effect on your HB follows from that (paras 4.2-3).

Joint tenants who are not a member of your family

4.45   A joint tenant who is not a member of your family might:

(a)   share your household (paras 4.20-22); or

(b)   maintain a separate household from you.

In either case, they might have people who normally reside with them rather than with you (e.g. their family members or non-dependants).

4.46   The joint tenant, and the people who normally reside with them, affect your HB as follows:

(a)   they affect what your share of the eligible rent on your home is (paras 9.7-8 and table 10.4);

(b)   they are included when the council decides the size of accommodation you need (paras 9.16, 9.23, 9.27, 10.17 and 11.30) as follows:

   ■   in social sector, exempt accommodation and rent referral cases, this applies whether they share your household or maintain a separate household, but

   ■   in private sector (LHA) cases, this applies only if they share your household (para 10.7);

(c)   they are not included in your applicable amount;

(d)   they are not your non-dependants (table 4.3) – except in the case of a non-dependant who normally resides with both you and your joint tenant (para 6.19).

The joint tenant can make their own claim for HB and – if they do – the people who reside with them are taken into account in their claim. For examples see chapters 7, 9 and 10.

When a joint tenant counts as a non-dependant

4.47   A joint tenant who has a 'contrived' or other letting for which HB can't be paid (table 5.4) counts instead as a non-dependant. For example if you and a friend are renting from a resident landlord who is the friend's close relative (para 5.28) the friend counts as either your or your landlord's non-dependant, depending on who they normally reside with (paras 4.29-31).

4.47   HB3(3); HB66+ 3(3); NIHB 3(3); NIHB66+ 3(3)

Separate tenants of your landlord

4.48   If you live in a dwelling which is rented out in separate lettings, the other tenants aren't included when the council decides the size of accommodation you need, and don't affect the amount of your HB in any way. The same applies to people who normally reside with them rather than with you (e.g. their family members or non-dependants).

Resident landlords

4.49   If you have a resident landlord, they aren't included when the council decides the size of accommodation you need, and don't affect the amount of your HB in any way. The same applies to people who normally reside with them rather than with you (e.g. their family members, non-dependants or any other member of their household).

Employees

4.50   If you employ someone who lives in your dwelling as their home (e.g. a nanny, an au pair, or a carer who does not fall within para 4.33):

(a)   they are included when the council decides the size of accommodation you need (para 11.10(e));

(b)   they may count as a non-dependant (paras 4.26-32), but in practice they usually don't unless they work for you free of charge (GM para C1.185);

(c)   they don't affect your HB in any other way.

4.48   HB 3(1),(4); HB66+ 3(1),(4); NIHB 3(1),(4); NIHB66+ 3(1),(4)

4.49   HB 3(2)(e)(ii),(iii); HB66+ 3(2)(e)(ii),(iii); NIHB 3(2)(e)(ii),(iii); NIHB66+ 3(2)(e)(ii),(iii)

Chapter 5 **Liability for rent**

- The conditions for getting HB: see paras 5.1-3
- The housing costs HB can meet: see paras 5.4-5.
- Who is liable or treated as liable for rent: see paras 5.6-19.
- Sham, non-commercial, contrived and other excluded liabilities: see paras 5.20-38.

The conditions for getting HB

5.1 To get HB on your home:

(a) your housing costs must count as 'rent' for HB purposes (table 5.1);

(b) you must be liable or treated as liable for them (paras 5.6-19);

(c) your liability must not be a sham (para 5.21);

(d) your liability must be commercial (para 5.22);

(e) your liability must not be contrived (para 5.23);

(f) your liability must not be excluded for other reasons (paras 5.24-38).

5.2 Meeting these conditions is usually shown by your letting agreement or a letter from your landlord, and the questions you answer on the claim form. You must also meet the financial and other conditions in table 2.1.

Decisions and appeals

5.3 If the council refuses you HB, it must send you a decision notice explaining this (para 20.6). The notice:

(a) should give clear findings of fact (para 20.19-20) ([2012] UKUT 333 (AAC));

(b) should only refuse you HB if the findings of fact support this – e.g. you haven't provided evidence of your liability;

(c) should state which reason applies to you – e.g. that although you are liable for rent, your liability is non-commercial;

(d) may give alternative reasons – e.g. that you aren't liable for rent, and even if you are, your liability is contrived;

(e) shouldn't confuse different reasons – e.g. shouldn't mix up non-liability or sham liability with non-commerciality or contrivance (CSHB/718/2002).

Some of the reasons for refusing HB can depend on the same facts (GM A3.231), can be difficult to distinguish, and can overlap. You can appeal about all of them to the council and/or to a tribunal (chapter 20).

5.1   CBA 130(1)(a),(2), 137(2)(i),(j); HB 8, 9, 11(2), 12(1); HB66+ 8, 9, 12(1)
       NICBA 129(2), 133(2)(i),(j); NIHB 8, 9, 11(2), 13(1); NIHB66+ 8, 9, 13(1)

The housing costs HB can meet

5.4   You can only get HB towards certain housing costs. Table 5.1 lists the housing costs that HB can meet, and these all count as 'rent' for HB purposes. Table 5.2 lists the housing costs that HB can't meet.

'Actual rent' and 'eligible rent'

5.5   In this guide we use the following terms:

(a) your 'actual rent' is the total of all the payments in table 5.1 which you are liable to pay on your home;

(b) your 'eligible rent' means the (often lower) amount used in calculating your HB (para 7.4).

Example: Actual rent and eligible rent

Violetta pays her landlord £150 per week for her flat plus £10 per week for service charges.

■   Her 'actual rent' is £160 per week.

The council tells her that the most it could pay her is £140 per week, because of the HB rules (paras 9.5, 10.5).

■   Her 'eligible rent' is £140 per week.

The council also says that this is reduced to £80 per week, because of her income (para 6.6).

■   Her HB is £80 per week.

Table 5.1 **Payments that count as rent for HB purposes**

You can get HB towards any of these payments. For limits on eligible rent and service charges, see chapters 8-11.

(a) Rent payable under a tenancy agreement (para 5.8).

(b) Rent payable under a shared ownership tenancy (para 7.24) but not mortgage payments.

(c) Licence fees (para 5.9) or payments for use and occupation.

(d) Board and lodging payments (paras 7.25, 8.39).

(e) Rent payable to a co-op (co-operative) – so long as you only have a nominal equity share in the co-op (GM A4.170-172).

(f) Payments in a rental purchase scheme – where instalments to buy your home are payable over a fixed period but your landlord remains the owner until you make the final payment (GM A4.140).

5.5   CBA 130A(1),(5); HB 12(1), 12B(2), 12BA(2), 12C(2), 12D(2)(a); HB66+ 12(1), 12B(2), 12C(2), 12D(2)(a);
           NICBA 129A(1),(5); NIHB 13(1), 13A(2), 13AA(2), 13B(2), 13C(2)(a); NIHB66+ 13(1), 13A(2), 13B(2), 13C(2)(a)

T5.1   CBA 130(2)(b), 137(2)(k); HB 2(4)(b)-(d), 12(1)(a)-(j), Old 12(1)(a)-(j); HB66+ HB 2(4)(b)-(d), 12(1)(a)-(j), Old 12(1)(a)-(j);
           NICBA 129(2), 133(2)(k); NIHB 2(4)(b)-(d), 13(1)(a)-(h), Old 13(1)(a)-(h); NIHB66+ 2(4)(b)-(d), 13(1)(a)-(h), Old 13(1)(a)-(h)

(g) In Scotland, payments for a croft and its associated land.

(h) In Great Britain, contributions towards maintenance and essential services in a charitable almshouse provided by a housing association (para 7.15).

(i) If your home is a caravan or mobile home, site charges (owners and renters) and rent (renters only).

(j) If your home is a houseboat, mooring charges and berthing fees (owners and renters) and rent (renters only). A houseboat includes a narrow boat suitable for permanent residence (R(H) 9/08), and mooring charges include a continuous cruiser licence ([2020] UKUT 158 (AAC)).

(k) Eligible service charges payable as a condition of occupying your home (paras 8.25-26).

(l) Mesne profits (in Scotland, violent profits) payable after your tenancy or right to occupy has terminated (para 5.10).

Table 5.2 **Payments that aren't rent for HB purposes**

You can't get HB towards any of these payments. But in some cases the payments can be included within SPC (chapter 22) or SMI (volume 1 chapter 8).

(a) Mortgage and similar payments on a home you and/or your partner own – this means anywhere you have the right to sell or dispose of, even if this would require the consent of other joint owners.

(b) Mortgage and similar payments on a shared ownership tenancy (for rent and services see table 5.1).

(c) Payments on a long lease (in the law, a 'long tenancy') which was for more than 21 years when first granted and meets the legal formalities for a lease (R(H) 3/07).

(d) Payments on care homes and independent (non-NHS) hospitals.

(e) Payments on bail and probation hostels ('approved premises') – for prisoners being released and in a few cases for prisoners on bail.

(f) Payments on HM armed forces accommodation, Crown tenancies and some other UK government tenancies (GM A3.210-216) – but you can get HB if your home is managed by the Crown Estate Commissioners or you rent from the Duchies of Cornwall or Lancaster (GM A3.217-218).

(g) Payments for a tent or its pitch.

(h) Payments on some night shelters (para 3.4).

(i) Payments in a co-ownership scheme – where you are entitled to a payment related to the value of your home when your membership of the scheme ends.

T5.2   CBA 130(2)(b); HB 2(1) – definition 'Crown tenant', 9(1)(k),(4), 11(2) 12(2)(a)-(f); HB66+ 2(1), 9(1)(k),(4), 12(2)(a)-(f);
          PC sch 2 para 5(1),(1A); NICBA 129(2); NIHB 9(1)(k),(4), 11(2) 13(2)(a)-(d); NIHB66+ 9(1)(k),(4), 13(2)(a)-(d); NIPC sch 2 para 5(1),(1A)

> (j)   Payments under a hire purchase or credit sale agreement – e.g. to buy a mobile home or furniture.
>
> (k)   Payments for furniture, furnishings, white goods or other moveable property under a conditional sale agreement.

Liable or treated as liable for rent

5.6   To get HB you must either be:

(a)   liable for rent on your home (para 5.11); or

(b)   treated as liable for it (paras 5.12).

But some liabilities are excluded (tables 5.2 and 5.4).

What liability is

5.7   Liability for rent means having a legally enforceable obligation to pay it. You should normally have a written agreement (which could be a letter from your landlord or agent) granting you a tenancy or licence. Further details are in table 5.3.

Tenancies

5.8   A tenancy is often described as a stake in the land. It is a contract that:

(a)   gives you the right to occupy a dwelling and exclude others from it ('exclusive possession') (Street v Mountford); and

(b)   requires you to pay rent; and

(c)   is for a length of time that can be established (a 'term certain') – in practice this means it is either:

- a 'fixed term tenancy' – this has a fixed period, such as six months or a year, after which it can be renewed, or

- a 'periodic tenancy' – this has a repeating period, such as weekly or monthly (according to how the rent is paid) and in the common law is ended (made certain) by a notice to quit.

In Wales most tenancies are known in the law as an 'occupation contract'.

Licences and permission to occupy

5.9   A licence is an agreement that gives you the right to occupy and requires you to pay rent (a 'fee') but doesn't give you the right to exclude others. Licences are used in hostels and other accommodation where the landlord (licensor) can place others in the dwelling and/or require you to move rooms (AG Securities v Vaughan). Payments for permission to occupy ('use and occupation payments') are usually accepted by social landlords from people who are not a tenant or licensee, for example a relative who remains after the tenant has died or left.

5.6   CBA 130(1)(a), 137(2)(i),(j); NICBA 129(1)(a), 133(2)(i),(j)

5.8   Street v Mountford [1985] UKHL 4

5.9   AG Securities v Vaughan [1988] UKHL 8

Mesne profits

5.10   A tenancy can end when:

(a)   its fixed term ends; or

(b)   the landlord issues a notice to quit; or

(c)   the tenant forfeits it, for example because they no longer live there.

If the tenant remains, they do so without permission and the landlord can obtain a court order evicting them. Accepting rent may mean the landlord creates a new tenancy, so instead the landlord claims compensation for the lost rent – in the law these payments are called 'mesne profits'. Landlords often call them use and occupation payments, charges or fees.

Who is liable for rent

5.11   You are liable for rent on your home (and can get HB towards it) if:

(a)   you are single and are solely liable for the rent; or

(b)   you are in a couple and both of you are liable for the rent; or

(c)   you are in a couple and you are liable for the rent but your partner is not (if the reverse is true, see para 5.12(a)); or

(d)   you are single or in a couple and are jointly liable with one or more others (for example in a house-share).

In case (d) you usually get HB towards a share of the rent (paras 9.7, 9.21, 10.7, 11.16 and table 10.4.

Who is treated as liable

5.12   You are treated as liable for rent on your home (and can get HB towards it) if:

(a)   you are in a couple and your partner is liable but you are not (para 5.13); or

(b)   your former partner is liable but you have to make the payments (para 5.14); or

(c)   someone else is liable but you have to make the payments (para 5.15); or

(d)   your landlord has agreed you can do work on your home instead of paying rent (para 5.18); or

(e)   you have paid the rent in advance (para 5.19); or

(f)   in some cases, you are incapable of managing your affairs (table 5.3).

5.10   HB 12(1)(c), Old 12(1)(c); HB66+ 12(1)(c), Old 12(1)(c); NIHB 13(1)(c), Old 13(1)(c); NIHB66+ 13(1)(c), Old 13(1)(c)

5.11   HB 8(1)(a), Old 12(5), 12B(4), 12C(2), B13(2)(a), 13D(5),(12), HB66+ 8(1)(a), Old 12(5), 12B(4), 12C(2), 13D(5),(12);
          NIHB 8(1)(a), Old 13(5), 13A(4), 13B(2), B14(2)(a), 14D(5),(10); NIHB66+ 8(1)(a), Old 13(5), 13A(4), 13B(2), 14D(5),(10)

5.12   CBA 137(2)(j); HB 8(1)(b),(c),(2); HB66+ 8(1)(b),(c),(2); NICBA 133(2)(j); NIHB 8(1)(b),(c),(2); NIHB66+ 8(1)(b),(c),(2)

Table 5.3 **Liability for rent**

(a) *Liability and letting agreements:* You are liable for rent if your obligation to pay it is legally enforceable – a moral obligation is not enough (R v Rugby HBRB ex parte Harrison). Letting agreements are usually in writing in the form of a contract or a letter that gives the necessary details. But there is no requirement for this (GM A3.50). An agreement by word of mouth is sufficient to create a legally enforceable liability (R v Poole BC ex parte Ross) except in the (rare) case of tenancies with a fixed term of over three years (Law of Property Act 1925, s54).

(b) *Sham liability:* If evidence shows that there is no intention to enforce the terms of your letting agreement, this can indicate the agreement is a sham so you aren't liable and can't get HB (R(H) 3/03).

(c) *Your circumstances:* It isn't possible to grant a tenancy to yourself (Rye v Rye). And if you already have the right to occupy your home (e.g. as joint owner) no-one can grant you a letting on it (e.g. another joint owner) so you can't be liable.

(d) *Your landlord's circumstances:* A landlord normally has a legal interest in the dwelling as an owner or tenant but this is not always the case (CH/2959/2006), Bruton v London and Quadrant HT, Lambeth LBC v Kay.

(e) *If you have an attorney or appointee:* An attorney or appointee (para 16.5) can enter a letting agreement for you thus making you liable for rent – even when your attorney is your landlord ([2013] UKUT 128 (AAC)).

(f) *If you are incapable of understanding your agreement:* If you are legally incapable of understanding your letting agreement (e.g. you are under 18 or have a mental disability), the law can be more complicated. In England and Wales, your letting agreement is likely to be valid so you are liable for rent ([2012] AACR 41). Or if it isn't valid, you are likely to be liable or treated as liable under section 7 of the Mental Capacity Act 2005 or under the common law principle of paying for necessaries ([2012] AACR 41). In Scotland, your liability needs to be decided on a 'transaction by transaction approach' ([2012] AACR 20), and in some cases your letting agreement may not be valid so you aren't liable for rent and can't get HB.

(g) *Non-payment or arrears of rent:* If your landlord is unlikely to evict you if you don't pay, this can be evidence that you are not liable. Most landlords expect to end an agreement if a tenant doesn't pay, and in some cases, arrears may suggest you aren't liable (CH/1849/2007). However, not paying your rent 'even for an extensive period' or paying less than your agreement says (even if your landlord has agreed to this), doesn't without other evidence mean you aren't liable ([2010] UKUT 43 (AAC)).

T5.3   CBA 130(1)(a); NICBA 129(1)(a)

T5.3(a)   R v Rugby HBRB ex parte Harrison [1994] QBD 28 HLR 36; R v Poole BC ex parte Ross 05/05/95 QBD 28 HLR 351

T5.3(c)   Rye v Rye [1962] AC 496

T5.3(d)   Bruton v London and Quadrant HT [1999] UKHL 26; Lambeth LBC v Kay [2006] UKHL 10

T5.3(f)   [2012] AACR 41, was [2012] UKUT 12 (AAC); [2012] AACR 20, was [2011] UKUT 354 (AAC)

(h) *If your landlord breaks their own occupation agreement by renting to you:* A landlord who is a tenant or leaseholder may have a term in their own agreement banning sub-letting. If they rented your home to you in breach of such a ban, your letting agreement is still valid between you and your landlord (Governors of Peabody Donation Fund v Higgins) unless and until the landlord's own tenancy is terminated. Until then, you are liable and can get HB.

(i) *If your landlord breaks the law by renting to you:* A contract (including a tenancy) that is made with knowledge that carrying it out involves a criminal act, is not enforceable (Nayyar v Denton Wilde Sapte). For example, if your home had a prohibition/closing order (Housing Act 2004, s32; Housing (Scotland) Act 1987, s122) on it when your landlord offered you a tenancy. The law is less clear if the order was made after the start of the tenancy and/or in England and Wales the agreement may be varied by a first-tier tribunal (Housing Act 2004, s34). And in some parts of the UK different rules apply if your landlord needs a licence but does not have one – see (j) to (l).

(j) *If your landlord needs a licence for a house in multiple occupation (HMO) in Scotland or Northern Ireland:* It is an offence to let an HMO in Scotland or Northern Ireland without a council licence (Housing (Scotland) Act 2006, s154; Houses in Multiple Occupation (Northern Ireland) Act 2016, s30) so the rule in (i) applies. But in Scotland the council can also make an order to suspend your rent, so your liability is nil (Housing (Scotland) Act 2006, s144(1)).

(k) *If your landlord needs an HMO or other licence in England or Wales or has a banning order:* In England and Wales if your home should be licensed but isn't, the law says your agreement is enforceable (despite the rule in (i)): Housing and Planning Act 2016, s24, Housing Act 2004, s73. But you can apply to a first-tier tribunal for a rent repayment order, or the council can if it was paid by HB (Housing and Planning Act 2016, s43-45, 51; Housing Act 2004, s73). In England, this also applies if your landlord has a banning order (Housing and Planning Act 2016, s40).

(l) *If your landlord/agent doesn't have a licence to manage property in Wales:* Anyone who carries out private rented property management in Wales must have a management licence from Rent Smart Wales [www]. If your landlord/agent doesn't have one the council can apply for a rent repayment order, or a rent stop order (so your liability is nil) (Housing (Wales) Act 2014, s30, 32).

When your partner is liable for rent but you are not

5.13 You are treated as liable for rent if your partner is liable for the rent on your home but you are not (in other words, the tenancy is in your partner's name but not yours). Unlike in para 5.15(c), you don't have to satisfy a test of reasonableness.

T5.3(h) Governors of Peabody Donation Fund v Higgins 20/06/83 CA 10 HLR 82

T5.3(i) Nayyar v Denton Wilde Sapte [2009] EWHC 3218 (QB)
https://caselaw.nationalarchives.gov.uk/ewhc/qb/2009/3218

T5.3(l) https://www.rentsmart.gov.wales

5.13 HB 8(1)(b); HB66+ 8(1)(b); NIHB 8(1)(b); NIHB66+ 8(1)(b)

When your former partner is liable but you are paying

5.14   You are treated as liable for rent if:

(a)   your former partner is liable for the rent on your home but isn't paying it; and

(b)   you have to make the payments in order to continue living there.

Unlike in para 5.15(c), you don't have to satisfy a test of reasonableness.

When someone else is liable but you are paying

5.15   You are treated as liable for rent if:

(a)   the person who is liable for the rent on your home isn't paying it; and

(b)   you have to make the payments in order to continue living there; and

(c)   it is reasonable to treat you as liable (para 5.16).

5.16   This rule lets you get HB when the liable person stops paying and this makes your home precarious ([2021] UKUT 305 (AAC)) – for example, because their absence (in hospital, a care home, working, studying or elsewhere) is too long for them to get HB (table 3.1) or they have gone away permanently. It only applies if your need to make the payments is caused by the liable person's failure to do so rather than by something separate ([2017] UKUT 40 (AAC)). The rule doesn't let you get HB if you move in after the liable person has stopped paying ([2021] UKUT 305 (AAC)), or if they are excluded from HB for the reasons in paras 5.20-38 (CSHB/606/2005). The council must decide whether treating you as liable is reasonable on all the facts and not on a single issue [2017] UKUT 151 (AAC)) and may decide not to award you HB if it considers this will result in the liable person resuming payment ([2016] UKUT 570 (AAC)).

5.17   The rule in para 5.15 is mainly used when:

(a)   the person who isn't paying the rent is an individual – but it can also be used if they are the executor of a deceased tenant, or a company or other body (R(H) 5/05);

(b)   the HB claimant is over 18 – but HB law doesn't set an age limit, so it can also be used in the case of younger HB claimants if the council decides it is reasonable to do so.

When your landlord agrees you can work on your home rather than pay rent

5.18   You are treated as liable for rent if your landlord has agreed not to collect rent from you ('waived the rent') in return for repairs or redecoration work you have actually carried out on your home. The repairs or redecoration (and the amount the landlord has agreed not to collect) must be reasonable, and the rule is limited to eight weeks each time it applies.

When you have already paid your rent or your rent liability has changed

5.19   If you have already paid your rent, you are treated as liable for it over the period the rent covers. Or if your rent liability for a past period has changed, you are treated as liable for the new amount.

5.14   HB 8(1)(c)(i); HB66+ 8(1)(c)(i); NIHB 8(1)(c)(i); NIHB66+ 8(1)(c)(i)

5.15   HB 8(1)(c)(ii); HB66+ 8(1)(c)(ii); NIHB 8(1)(c)(ii); NIHB66+ 8(1)(c)(ii)

5.18   HB 8(1)(d); HB66+ 8(1)(d); NIHB 8(1)(d); NIHB66+ 8(1)(d)

5.19   HB 8(2); HB66+ 8(2); NIHB 8(2); NIHB66+ 8(2)

Examples: Liable or treated as liable to pay rent

1. Darren and Dean are friends who jointly rent a private flat. Dean loses his job and can't afford his half of the rent.

   ■ Dean can get HB because he is liable for the rent – typically towards half of the total amount (para 5.11(d)).

2. Megan lives with her partner Ffion. The tenancy of their home is only in Ffion's name.

   ■ Ffion can get HB for them both because she is liable for the rent (para 5.11(c)); or

   ■ Meghan can get HB for them both because she is treated as liable for it (para 5.13).

3. Ffion leaves and stops paying the rent, so Meghan has to pay the rent in order to continue living there.

   ■ Meghan can get HB because she is treated as liable for the rent (para 5.14).

4. Lesley is a council tenant and her 18-year-old son Logan lives with her. Lesley goes abroad to work and Logan takes over paying the rent.

   ■ Logan can get HB because he is treated as liable for the rent so long as the council agrees this is reasonable (para 5.18).

5. Carrie is working, and her rent is due at the beginning of each month. She claims HB on 4th July. By then she has already paid July's rent.

   ■ Carrie can get HB because she is treated as liable for rent for rent in July (para 5.19).

Excluded liabilities

5.20　You can't get HB if your liability for rent is excluded. Table 5.4 summarises all the types of excluded liability.

If you aren't liable or your liability is a sham

5.21　You can't get HB if:

(a) you aren't liable (or treated as liable) for rent (para 5.6-19 – in other words, you haven't provided evidence that you have to make payments in order to occupy your home; or

(b) you have a sham (pretended) liability – in other words, you have provided evidence but the arrangements between you and your landlord show there was no intention to create a genuine liability.

In (a), the burden of proof (para 20.22) falls on you to provide evidence of your liability (table 2.1), but in (b) the burden is on the council to show your liability is a sham (R(H) 3/03).

5.20　CBA 130(1)(a), 137(2)(i); HB 9; HB66+ 9; NICBA 129(1)(a), 133(2)(i); NIHB 9; NIHB66+ 9

5.21　CBA 130(1)(a); HB 8(1)(a); HB66+ 8(1)(a); NICBA 129(1)(a); NIHB 8(1)(a); NIHB66+ 8(1)(a)

Table 5.4 **Excluded liabilities**

If any of these apply to you, your liability is excluded from HB. Further details and exceptions are in paras 5.21-38.

(a) You aren't in fact liable to make rent payments, or your liability is sham (para 5.21).

(b) Your liability (your letting) isn't on a commercial basis (para 5.22).

(c) Your liability (your letting) was created to take advantage of the HB scheme ('contrived') (para 5.23).

(d) You are renting from your current partner (para 5.24).

(e) You are renting from an ex-partner (para 5.25).

(f) You are renting from your child's parent (para 5.26).

(g) You are renting from a close relative who lives with you (para 5.27).

(h) You are a non-dependant in your home (para 5.30).

(i) You used to be a non-dependant in your home (para 5.31).

(j) You used to own your home within the past five years (para 5.32).

(k) You live in accommodation that is tied to your job (para 5.34).

(l) You are a member of a religious order (para 5.35).

(m) Your landlord is a company and you or a close relative are a director or employee (para 5.36).

(n) Your landlord is a trustee of a trust and you or a close relative are a beneficiary or trustee (para 5.37).

(o) Your landlord is a trustee of a trust for your child (para 5.38).

If your liability isn't on a commercial basis

5.22 You can't get HB towards your rent if – although you are liable for rent – your liability isn't on a commercial basis. In deciding this, the council should look at your individual circumstances, and must take account of the terms of your letting including any which are not legally enforceable. The burden of proof (para 20.22) falls on the council to show that your liability isn't commercial, not on you to show that it is. Table 5.5 gives a summary of court and tribunal decisions about this; further advice is in GM paras 3.258-265.

T5.4   CBA 137(2)(i); HB 9; HB66+ 9; NICBA 133(2)(i); NIHB 9; NIHB66+ 9

5.22   HB 9(1)(a); HB66+ 9(1)(a); NIHB 9(1)(a); NIHB66+ 9(1)(a)

Table 5.5 **Commerciality**

(a) *What makes a letting commercial:* The primary consideration is about what was agreed between you and your landlord rather than what in fact happens. Not only the financial arrangements between you and your landlord but all the terms of your agreement should be taken into account (R v Sutton LBC ex parte Partridge). Each case must be considered on its individual facts and is a matter of judgment (R(H) 1/03). It is necessary to consider whether your letting agreement contains terms that are not enforceable in law (CH/2899/2005). The arrangements between you should be at 'arm's length' (R v Sheffield HBRB ex parte Smith).

(b) *Claiming HB and rent arrears:* Claiming HB towards your housing costs can be evidence that your agreement is commercial ([2020] UKUT 240 (AAC)). If your landlord accepts what you get in HB rather than your contractual rent this doesn't by itself mean your letting is non-commercial (CH/1076/2002), nor does your landlord's failure to chase up arrears or take possession proceedings against you ([2010] UKUT 43 (AAC)).

(c) *Personal and moral considerations:* If your letting is in fact commercial, friendliness and kindness between you and your landlord doesn't make it non-commercial (R v Poole BC ex parte Ross, CH/4854/2003, [2009] UKUT 13 (AAC)). Conversely, if your letting is in fact non-commercial, the fact that it was drawn up in a way that meets your moral or religious beliefs doesn't make it commercial (R(H) 8/04).

(d) *Lettings between family members or friends:* A letting between family members may or may not be commercial. The family arrangement is not decisive by itself. If the letting enables a disabled family member to be cared for more easily, this is not decisive by itself. Each case depends on its individual circumstances (CH/296/2004, CH/1096/2008, CH/2491/2007). For example, a letting of an annexe to a disabled son was commercial ([2011] UKUT 41 (AAC)), as was a letting by a son to his terminally ill mother (2015] UKUT 565 (AAC)), and a letting to a friend in their time of trouble (CH/1097/2004). See also table 5.6(c).

(e) *Low rents:* Having a low rent doesn't by itself make your letting non-commercial (2015] UKUT 565 (AAC)).

(f) *Statutory tenancies:* A statutory tenancy is one created by law, usually at the end of a contractual tenancy. This does not make it non-commercial (CH/4081/2004).

(g) *If the circumstances of your letting change:* If your letting was commercial when it began, it can become non-commercial if there is an identifiable reason for this (CH/3497/2005).

T5.5   HB 9(1)(a); HB66+ 9(1)(a); NIHB 9(1)(a); NIHB66+ 9(1)(a)
         R v Sutton HBRB ex parte Partridge 04/11/94 QBD 28 HLR 315
         R v Sheffield HBRB ex parte Smith 08/12/94 QBD 28 HLR 36
         R v Poole HBRB ex parte Ross 05/05/95 QBD 28 HLR 351

If your liability was created to take advantage of the HB scheme (contrived)

5.23   You can't get HB towards your rent if – although you are liable for rent and aren't excluded for any other reason – your liability was 'created to take advantage of the HB scheme' by you, your landlord or both. This is usually called a 'contrived letting'. The burden of proof (para 20.22) falls on the council to show that your liability was contrived, not on you to show that it wasn't. Table 5.6 gives a summary of court and tribunal decisions about this; further advice is in GM paras A3.310-319.

Table 5.6 **Contrivance**

(a) *What makes a letting contrived:* Your liability for rent must have been created to take advantage of the HB scheme (contrived). This implies abuse of the HB scheme (in the sense of taking improper advantage, not necessarily bad faith) and there must be evidence that this was a primary or dominant purpose of the agreement (R v Solihull HBRB ex parte Simpson, CH/39/2007). The circumstances and intentions of both you and your landlord should be taken into account (R v Barking and Dagenham HBRB ex parte Mackay, R v Sutton HBRB ex parte Keegan).

(b) *Taking advantage of the HB scheme:* Your letting can't 'take advantage of the HB scheme' (can't be contrived) if no advantage is gained by you or your landlord ([2021] UKUT 193 (AAC)).

(c) *Lettings between family members or providing support:* If your landlord is a relation of yours (e.g. your parent) this does not by itself mean your letting is contrived (Solihull case), though other rules may affect you (table 5.5). Lettings to supported tenants can be contrived, depending on the facts of the case ([2009] UKUT 150 (AAC)). See also table 5.5(d).

(d) *High rents and lettings to people on low incomes:* Having a high rent doesn't mean your letting is contrived (R v South Gloucestershire HBRB ex parte Dadds). There is no objection to landlords letting to people on low incomes to make a profit unless their charges and profits show abuse (CH/39/2007, R v Manchester CC ex parte Baragrove Properties). And if you can't afford your rent or know that you will have to claim HB to pay it, this is not evidence that your letting is contrived (Solihull case).

(e) *Companies and trusts:* If you can show that your letting wasn't contrived under the rules about companies and trusts in paras 5.36-37, it can't be contrived under the general rule in para 5.23 ([2014] UKUT 326 (AAC)).

5.23   HB 9(1)(l); HB66+ 9(1)(l); NIHB 9(1)(l); NIHB66+ 9(1)(l)

T5.3   R v Solihull MBC ex parte Simpson 03/12/93 QBD 26 HLR 370
          R v Barking and Dagenham HBRB ex parte MacKay [2001] EWHC Admin 234
          R v Sutton HBRB ex parte Keegan 15/05/92 QBD 27 HLR 92
          R v South Gloucestershire HBRB ex parte Dadds 1997 QBD 29 HLR 700
          R v Manchester CC ex parte Baragrove Properties 15/03/91 QBD 23 HLR 337

Example: Excluded liabilities

Andy and Nick own a house which they live in with Barney, who is the father of one of them and gets SPC. They also own a flat which they rent out. When the tenants end their tenancy, Barney moves there with a similar tenancy agreement and claims HB.

Andy tells the council the arrangement is to give privacy to both and that they need the rental income. For example, if Barney came into money they would expect him to continue paying. If the council refuses HB, they would have to rent out a spare room in their house or find another way of managing. Barney tells the council he would do his best to continue paying if he doesn't get HB.

The council makes the following decisions and awards Barney HB.

- *Liability?* Barney has a letting agreement which shows he is liable for rent.

- *Sham?* There is nothing to suggest that the letting agreement is a sham – many landlords make broad plans for what they would do if the tenants don't pay the rent.

- *Commercial?* The evidence is that the letting is commercial – it is intended to provide Andy and Nick with an income and Barney with a home.

- *Contrived?* The evidence is that the letting isn't contrived – it is designed to maintain that income while giving them privacy, rather than to abuse the HB scheme.

- *Other exclusions?* None of the other exclusions applies. For example, although Barney is a close relative of Andy and Nick, he doesn't live with them.

If you are renting from your current partner

5.24   You can't get HB towards 'rent' you pay your partner, whether you live together or live separately.

If you are renting from an ex-partner

5.25   You can't get HB towards your rent if your landlord:

(a) used to live in your current home with you as a couple; or

(b) used to live in your current home with your partner as a couple.

This rule doesn't breach human rights (R (Painter) v Carmarthenshire County Council; [2012] AACR 16). In deciding whether you were a couple, the council isn't bound by DWP decisions about awarding other benefits (R(H) 9/04).

If you are renting from your child's parent

5.26   You can't get HB towards your rent if:

(a) you are responsible for a child under 16 – in other words, they are included in your family (paras 4.18-19); and

---

5.24   HB 12(2)(f); HB66+ 12(2)(f); NIHB 13(2)(d); NIHB66+ 13(2)(d);
R (Painter) v Carmarthenshire CC [2001] EWHC Admin 308

5.25   HB 9(1)(c); HB66+ 9(1)(c); NIHB 9(1)(c); NIHB66+ 9(1)(c)

5.26   HB 9(1)(d); HB66+ 9(1)(d); NIHB 9(1)(d); NIHB66+ 9(1)(d); R (Tucker) v Secretary of State for Social Security [2001] EWHC Admin 260
[2012] AACR 16, originally [2011] UKUT 301 (AAC)

(b)   your landlord is the child's parent or adoptive parent – or if you have joint landlords, at least one of them is ([2018] UKUT 417 (AAC)).

This rule doesn't breach human rights (R v Secretary of State for Social Security ex parte Tucker).

If you are renting from a close relative who lives with you

5.27   You can't get HB towards your rent if your landlord:

(a)   is your or your partner's close relative (para 5.28); and

(b)   lives with you (para 5.29).

This rule doesn't breach human rights (R(H) 5/06).

5.28   A 'close relative' is:

(a)   a parent, parent-in-law or step-parent; or

(b)   a daughter/son, daughter/son-in-law or step-daughter/son; or

(c)   a sister/brother or half-sister/brother ([2016] UKUT 517 (AAC)); or

(d)   the partner of any of these.

It is the legal not the blood relationship that is used (R(SB) 22/87). An adopted child's parents are his or her adoptive parents, and their other children (natural or by adoption) are his or her brothers and sisters.

5.29   Your landlord lives with you (in the law, 'resides with you') if you share at least some essential living accommodation (CH/542/2006), even if you have exclusive possession of one of the rooms (CH/3656/2004). The description of 'residing with' in paras 4.30-31 is also likely to apply here, so sharing just a kitchen can be enough to count (CPC/1446/2008), as can sharing a house but being unable to make use of the shared areas due to disability (CPC/3379/2008).

If you are a non-dependant in your home

5.30   You can't get HB towards payments of keep you make as a non-dependant (para 4.26) – because these payments aren't on a commercial basis (paras 4.26, 5.20).

If you used to be a non-dependant in your home

5.31   You can't get HB towards your rent if:

(a)   you used to be a non-dependant (para 4.26) of someone who:

■   lived in your home then, and

■   continues to live in your home now; and

(b)   you are now liable for rent as a tenant; and

5.27   HB 9(1)(b); HB66+ 9(1)(b); NIHB 9(1)(b); NIHB66+ 9(1)(b)

5.28   HB 2(1) – definition 'close relative'; HB66+ 2(1); NIHB 2(1); NIHB66+ 2(1)

5.29   HB 3(4); HB66+ 3(4); NIHB 3(4); NIHB66+ 3(4)

5.30   HB 3(2)(d),(e), 9(1)(g); HB66+ 3(2)(d),(e), 9(1)(g); NIHB 3(2)(d),(e), 9(1)(g); NIHB66+ 3(2)(d),(e), 9(1)(g)

5.31   HB 3(3), 9(1)(g); HB66+ 3(3), 9(1)(g); NIHB 3(3), 9(1)(g); NIHB66+ 3(3), 9(1)(g)

(c) you can't show that your rent liability was created for a genuine reason rather than being contrived to take advantage of the HB scheme (para 5.22).

In (c), the burden of proof (para 20.22) falls on you to show your liability wasn't contrived, not on the council to show it was.

If you used to own your home

5.32 You can't get HB towards your rent if you or your partner:

(a) were an owner or long leaseholder of your current home (table 5.2(a)-(c)) at any time in the past five years – even if you have since moved out and then back in (CH/3698/2008); and

(b) can't show that you had to give up ownership in order to continue living there (para 5.33).

5.33 The council can look at:

(a) why you gave up ownership; and

(b) what other options you reasonably had.

It is usually reasonable to give up ownership if your home was about to be repossessed, or you sold it to a housing association under a mortgage rescue scheme, or (in the case of a shared owner) you sold back some or all of the percentage you were buying. These may have been your only option (GM A3.282-288), even if stress made you sell your home more quickly than you needed to (R(H) 6/07, [2018] UK 322 (AAC)). In other situations, it might be reasonable to get work or take in a tenant to avoid having to sell (CH/1586/2004), but not to use a credit card to pay your mortgage ([2008] UKUT 11 (AAC)). Selling your home due to a moral compulsion is not likely to be regarded as reasonable (CH/3853/2001). Good general advice can be found in circular A5/2009.

If you live in tied accommodation

5.34 You can't get HB towards your rent if you or your partner are required to live in your home as a condition of your current employment (your home is 'tied' to your job), for example, if you are a caretaker of a block of flats and are required to live in one of the flats. But this rule only applies during your employment, not once you are retired (GM A3.291).

If you are a member of a religious order

5.35 You can't get HB towards your rent if you are a member of a religious order and are fully maintained by it. This rule applies if you live in an enclosed order and give up your possessions. It doesn't apply if you live in a religious community and are still allowed to work, have possessions, etc (GM A3.255-257).

5.32   HB 9(1)(h),(ha); HB66+ 9(1)(h),(ha); NIHB 9(1)(h); NIHB66+ 9(1)(h)

5.34   HB 9(1)(i); HB66+ 9(1)(i); NIHB 9(1)(i); NIHB66+ 9(1)(i)

5.35   HB 9(1)(j); HB66+ 9(1)(j); NIHB 9(1)(j); NIHB66+ 9(1)(j)

If your landlord is a company that you or your family are part of

5.36   You can't get HB towards your rent if:

(a) your landlord is a company [www]; and

(b) one or more of the following is a director or employee of the company:

   ■   you or your partner, or

   ■   your or your partner's ex-partner, or

   ■   your or your partner's close relative – but in this case only when that close relative lives with you (para 5.28-29); and

(c) you can't show that your rent liability was created for a genuine reason rather than being contrived to take advantage of the HB scheme (para 5.22).

In (c), the burden of proof (para 20.22) falls on you to show your liability wasn't contrived, not on the council to show it was. If you are an employee of the company you rent from, this rule doesn't apply (GM para 3.275).

If your landlord is the trustee of a trust that you or your family are part of

5.37   You can't get HB towards your rent if:

(a) your landlord is one or more of the trustees of a trust (para 15.37); and

(b) one or more of the following is a beneficiary or trustee of the trust:

   ■   you or your partner, or

   ■   your or your partner's ex-partner, or

   ■   your or your partner's close relative – but in this case only when that close relative lives with you (paras 5.28-29); and

(c) you can't show that your rent liability was created for a genuine reason rather than being contrived to take advantage of the HB scheme (para 5.22).

In (c), the burden of proof (para 20.22) falls on you to show your liability wasn't contrived, not on the council to show it was.

If your landlord is the trustee of a trust for your child

5.38   You can't get HB towards your rent if:

(a) your landlord is one or more of the trustees of a trust (para 15.37); and

(b) a child under 16 in your family is a beneficiary of the trust.

This rule doesn't have an exception like the one in para 5.37(c).

5.36   HB 9(1)(e); HB66+ 9(1)(e); NIHB 9(1)(e); NIHB66+ 9(1)(e)

5.37   HB 9(1)(e); HB66+ 9(1)(e); NIHB 9(1)(e); NIHB66+ 9(1)(e)

5.38   HB 9(1)(f); HB66+ 9(1)(f); NIHB 9(1)(f); NIHB66+ 9(1)(f)

Chapter 6 **Calculating HB**

- How HB is calculated: see paras 6.1-8.
- Non-dependant deductions: see paras 6.9-20.
- The HB benefit cap: see paras 6.21-33.
- Converting figures to weekly amounts: see paras 6.34-38.

How to calculate HB

6.1   This chapter explains how much HB you qualify for. To calculate this, work through the steps in paras 6.2-8.

Maximum benefit

6.2   The starting point for all HB calculations is your weekly 'maximum benefit'. This is:

(a)   your weekly eligible rent;

(b)   minus any non-dependant deductions which apply.

See chapter 7-11 for how your eligible rent is worked out. Paras 6.9-20 give the amounts of the non-dependant deductions and explain when they apply.

People on a passport benefit

6.3   If you are on a passport benefit (table 6.1) you qualify for maximum benefit (para 6.2).

Table 6.1 **Passport benefits**

You are 'on a passport benefit' if you are:

(a)   on the guarantee credit of SPC (or have 'underlying entitlement' to between 1p and 9p of guarantee credit);

(b)   on UC in supported or temporary accommodation (para 2.15);

(c)   on UC during the run-on period (para 1.29) in general accommodation (para 2.17);

(d)   on JSA(IB), ESA(IR) or IS;

(e)   entitled to JSA(IB) or ESA(IR) but not receiving it because of a sanction.

6.2   CBA 130(1),(3), 130A; NICBA 129(1),(3), 129A; HB 70; HB66+ 50; NIHB 68; NIHB66+ 48

6.3   CBA 130(3)(a), NICBA 129(3)(a); HB 2(3),(3A),(3B), sch 5 paras 4,5, sch 6 paras 5,6; HB66+ 2(3),(3A), 26; NIHB 2(3),(3A),(3B), sch 6 paras 4,5, sch 7 paras 5,6; NIHB66+ 2(3),(3A), 24

T6.1   CBA 130(1),(3)(a),130A; NICBA 129(1),(3)(a),129A; HB 2(3),(3A),(3B) sch 5 paras 4,5, sch 6 paras 5,6; HB66+ 2(3),(3A), 26; NIHB 2(3),(3A) sch 6 paras 4,5, sch 7 paras 5,6; NIHB66+ 2(3),(3A), 24

People not on a passport benefit

6.4   If you aren't on a passport benefit (table 6.1):

    (a)   your HB is based on your income and applicable amount, as described in paras 6.5-6;

    (b)   but you don't qualify for HB if your capital is over £16,000.

See chapters 12-15 for how applicable amounts, income and capital are assessed.

Income and excess income

6.5   If you have no income, or your income is less than or equal to your applicable amount, you qualify for maximum benefit (para 6.2).

6.6   If your income is more than your applicable amount, the difference between the two is called 'excess income'. You qualify for:

    (a)   maximum benefit (para 6.2); minus

    (b)   a percentage of this excess income.

The percentage – also called a 'taper' – is 65%.

Minimum benefit

6.7   If the amount of HB calculated as above is less than the 'minimum benefit' figure of 50p per week, then it is not awarded.

Other calculation rules

6.8   The amount of HB can be reduced to recover an overpayment (para 19.40) or, in cases of fraud, to reduce your award for a fixed period (para 19.71) and/or recover an administrative penalty (para 19.75). For working age claims, HB is also subject to a benefit cap (para 6.21).

Non-dependant deductions

6.9   This section explains the deductions that are made if you have one or more non-dependants. The deductions are made from your eligible rent in the calculation of your HB (para 6.2). They can be described as the amount your non-dependants are assumed to contribute towards your rent.

6.10   A non-dependant is usually an adult son, daughter, other relative or friend who lives with you on a non-commercial basis: for details see paras 4.26-32.

6.4   CBA 130(3), 134(1); NICBA 129(3), 130(1); HB 43; HB66+ 28; NIHB 40; NIHB66+ 26

6.5   CBA 130(3)(a); NICBA 129(3)(a)

6.6   CBA 130(3)(b); NICBA 129(3)(b); HB 71; HB66+ 51; NIHB 69; NIHB66+ 49

6.7   CBA 134(4); HB 75; HB66+ 56; NICBA 130(3); NIHB 73; NIHB66+ 54

6.10   HB 3; HB66+ 3; NIHB 3; NIHB66+ 3

When a deduction is made

6.11   Unless any of the exceptions in table 6.2 applies:

(a)   one deduction is made for each non-dependant you have;

(b)   but if two non-dependants are a couple, one deduction is made between them (para 6.18).

There are further rules if you are a joint tenant (para 6.19) or pension age (para 6.20).

The amount of the deduction

6.12   The amounts of the deductions are in table 6.3. These vary depending on whether your non-dependant is working at least 16 hours per week and (if they are) on their gross income (paras 6.14-17).

Assuming the amount of the deduction

6.13   If you don't provide evidence of your non-dependant's circumstances, the council could make an assumption about which deduction applies. It mustn't make an assumption that is unlikely to reflect the non-dependant's actual circumstances (CH/48/2006), but otherwise it could make the highest deduction if they are working at least 16 hours per week. If you then provide evidence showing a lower deduction applies, the council must award you arrears of HB (but see paras 17.13-15 if you delay doing this).

Working at least 16 hours per week

6.14   The rules about working at least 16 hours per week (which the law calls 'remunerative work') apply to non-dependants in the same way as they apply to you (the claimant): for the details see paras 14.69-72. For example, a non-dependant on maternity, paternity, adoption or sick leave doesn't count as working at least 16 hours per week (para 14.72).

Gross income

6.15   When a non-dependant's income is taken into account (table 6.3), the following are wholly disregarded:

(a)   PIP or (in Scotland) adult disability payment;

(b)   DLA or (in Scotland) child disability payment;

(c)   attendance allowance, or constant attendance allowance paid with an industrial injury or war disablement pension;

(d)   armed forces independence payment (AFIP); and

(e)   payments from (or originally derived from) the government-sponsored trust funds listed in para 15.42.

6.11   HB 74(1)-(3); HB66+ 55(1)-(3); NIHB 72(1)-(3); NIHB66+ 53(1)-(3)

6.12-13 HB 74(1),(2); HB66+ 55(1),(2); NIHB 72(1),(2); NIHB66+ 53(1),(2)

6.14   HB 2(1) definition: 'remunerative work', 6; HB66+ 2(1),6; NIHB 2(1),6; NIHB66+ 2(1),6

6.15   HB 2(1) definition: 'attendance allowance', 74(9); HB66+ 2(1), 55(10); NIHB 2(1), 72(9); NIHB66+ 2(1), 53(10)

Table 6.2 **No non-dependant deductions**

Your circumstances:

No deductions are made for any non-dependants you have if you or your partner are:

(a) getting the daily living component of PIP or (in Scotland) adult disability payment;

(b) getting the care component of DLA or (in Scotland) child disability payment;

(c) getting attendance allowance, or constant attendance allowance paid with an industrial injury or war disablement pension;

(d) getting an armed forces independence payment; or

(e) severely sight-impaired, blind or have recently regained sight (para 12.54).

But (a)-(c) don't apply if the benefits mentioned cease – e.g. when you/your partner have been in hospital for four weeks.

Your non-dependant's circumstances:

In any other case, there is no deduction for any single non-dependant who is, or any non-dependant couple who are both:

(f) on state pension credit;

(g) aged under 18;

(h) aged under 25 and:

▪   on JSA(IB),

▪   on the assessment phase of ESA(IR),

▪   on IS, or

▪   on UC without any earned income;

(i) a full-time student (para 2.48) – unless you or your partner are are under 66, it is the student's summer vacation, and the student is working at least 16 hours per week;

(j) getting a government training allowance as a youth trainee;

(k) a member of the armed forces (regular or reserve) who is away on operations;

(l) a patient who has been in hospital or similar institution for more than 52 weeks (ignoring breaks of up to four weeks);

(m) a prisoner, whether sentenced, on remand or on bail; or

(n) a temporary resident or visitor or anyone whose normal home is elsewhere.

T6.2   HB 2(1), definition: 'attendance allowance', 74(6)-(8),(10); HB66+ 2(1), 55(6)-(9);
          NIHB 2(1), 3(2), 72(7),(8),(10); NIHB66+ 2(1), 3(2), 53(7)-(9)

Examples: Calculating HB

Claimant on a passport benefit

Olivia is on a passport benefit (table 6.1). She has no non-dependants. Her eligible rent is £105.00 per week.

Claimants on a passport benefit get maximum benefit – which equals their eligible rent.

Olivia's weekly HB equals	£105.00

Claimant not on a passport benefit

Noah and Sophia are not on any of the passport benefits. They have no non-dependants. Their joint weekly income exceeds their applicable amount by £20.00. Their eligible rent is £130.00 per week.

Claimants with excess income get maximum benefit minus a percentage of their excess income.

Eligible rent	£130.00
minus 65% of excess income (65% x £20.00)	£13.00
Noah and Sophia's weekly HB equals	£117.00

Claimant on ESA(IR) with working non-dependant

Nathan is on ESA(IR). His eligible rent is £150.00 per week. His 26-year-old son Leo lives with him. Leo earns £550 per week gross for a 35-hour week.

Claimants on ESA(IR) get maximum benefit, which in this case involves a non-dependant deduction. Leo works at least 16 hours per week and the level of his gross income means the highest deduction applies in HB (table 6.3).

Eligible rent	£150.00
minus non-dependant deduction	£116.75
Nathan's weekly HB equals	£33.25

Claimant on ESA(IR) with non-dependant on new-style JSA

Leo in the previous example loses his job and starts receiving new-style JSA (para 1.38).

The calculation is as above, except that now the lowest deduction applies in HB (table 6.3).

Eligible rent	£150.00
minus non-dependant deduction	£18.10
Nathan's weekly HB equals	£131.90

Table 6.3 **Weekly non-dependant deductions: 2023-24**

HB for rent

If the non-dependant works at least 16 hours per week and has gross weekly income of:

- at least £511   £116.75
- at least £410 but under £511   £106.35
- at least £308 but under £410   £93.40
- at least £236 but under £308   £57.10
- at least £162 but under £236   £41.60
- under £162   £18.10

Any other non-dependant (regardless of income level)   £18.10

Notes:

- See paras 6.14-17 for how to assess income and table 6.2 for exceptions.

- For comparison, the UC deduction (weekly equivalent) is £19.73 in all cases.

6.16   Apart from that, HB law says that the non-dependant's 'normal weekly gross income' is taken into account, without giving a list of what to include. In practice the council is likely to include:

(a) employed earnings (before tax, national insurance, etc have been deducted);

(b) self-employed net profit (after the deduction of reasonable expenses but before tax, national insurance, etc have been deducted);

(c) social security benefits, pensions and credits (except those in para 6.15);

(d) state, occupational and private pensions;

(e) rental income;

(f) maintenance;

(g) charitable and voluntary income; and

(h) interest on savings.

6.17   Because the 'normal' amount of gross weekly income is taken into account, short-term variations are likely to be ignored, but longer-term changes are taken into account. For example, a non-dependant who is a school assistant could count as working at least 16 hours per week throughout the year (see para 14.70(c)) but changes in their income may mean different levels of non-dependant deduction in term-times and holidays.

T6.3   HB 74(1),(2); HB66+ 55(1),(2); NIHB 72(1),(2); NIHB66+ 53(1),(2); SI 2021/162 regs 24(3), 25(3)

6.16   HB 74(1),(2); HB66+ 55(1),(2); NIHB 72(1),(2); NIHB66+ 53(1),(2)

Non-dependant couples

6.18 If you have non-dependants who are a couple (or a polygamous marriage) only one deduction is made for them. This is the higher (or highest) of the amounts that would have applied if they were single. For the gross income limits in table 6.3, each of them is treated as having the gross income of both (or all) of them.

> ### Example: A non-dependant couple
>
> Lily has two non-dependants, Nick and Pat, who are a couple. Nick works for 30 hours per week and has gross earnings of £350 per week. Pat works for 12 hours and has gross earnings of £200 per week.
>
> If they were single, there would be two deductions, £93.40 for Nick and £18.10 for Pat (table 6.3).
>
> Because they are a couple, there is only one deduction. Their combined gross income is £550 per week, so the deduction from Lily's HB is £116.75 (table 6.3 and para 6.18).

Non-dependant of joint tenants

6.19 The following applies if you are a joint tenant of your home (with someone other than your partner), and there is also a non-dependant living there. If the non-dependant normally resides (para 4.29) with:

(a) only you (and your family), the whole non-dependant deduction is made from your HB;

(b) only your joint tenant (or more than one joint tenant), no non-dependant deduction is made from your HB;

(c) both you and your joint tenant (or more than one joint tenant), each of you gets a share of the non-dependant deduction.

The share mentioned in (c) need not be equal: the council should take into account the number of joint tenants concerned and the proportion of rent each of you pays (paras 9.7-8. 10.7-8 and table 10.4).

Delayed non-dependant deductions for pension age claims

6.20 The following rule applies if:

(a) you or your partner are over 66; and

(b) a non-dependant moves in, or there is any change in a non-dependant's circumstances which causes an increase in the amount of the deduction.

In these cases the change relating to the deduction is not implemented until the day 26 weeks after the change actually occurred; or if that is not a Monday, it is implemented from the following Monday. But the non-dependant is taken into account straight away for other purposes such as the size criteria in chapter 11.

6.18   HB 74(3),(4); HB66+ 55(3),(4); NIHB 72(3),(4); NIHB66+ 53(3),(4)

6.19   HB 74(5); HB66+ 55(5); NIHB 72(5); NIHB66+ 53(5)

6.20   HB66+ 59(10)-(13); NIHB66+ 57(12)-(15)

The HB benefit cap

6.21   The 'benefit cap' sets a limit on the amount of HB and other welfare benefits working age claimants can receive. This section explains when and how it applies. If your HB is reduced because of the benefit cap, you may be able to get help from discretionary housing payments (para 23.8) and/or in Northern Ireland from welfare supplementary payments (para 23.24). The Supreme Court has decided that the benefit cap does not discriminate unlawfully: R (SG and others) v SSWP; R (DA and others) v SSWP.

When the benefit cap applies

6.22   The benefit cap only applies to working age claims (table 2.2). But the council/NIHE doesn't have to apply the benefit cap or reduce your HB unless and until it receives notice from the DWP/DFC (para 6.31).

The amount of the benefit cap

6.23   From April 2023, the annual amount of the benefit cap is:

(a)   for single claimants, £16,967 in Greater London and £14,753 elsewhere;

(b)   for lone parents and couples, £25,323 in Greater London and £22,020 elsewhere.

In each case the annual amount is converted to a weekly figure by dividing by 52 and rounding to the nearest penny. If you are in a polygamous marriage (table 1.1), the benefit cap applies to the two of you who were married earliest as though you were a couple. It doesn't apply to the others.

The amount of the HB reduction

6.24   Table 6.4 explains how the reduction in your HB is calculated. As the table shows, the calculation can't reduce your HB to below 50p per week.

Exceptions

6.25   Table 6.5 and paras 6.29-30 give the situations in which the benefit cap does not apply.

The HB and UC benefit caps

6.26   As well as the HB benefit cap described here, there is also a UC benefit cap (volume 1 chapter 9). Only one of these caps can apply to you at any one time. This is the UC benefit cap if you are on UC (even if you are also getting HB), or the HB benefit cap in any other case. For the details see paras 6.27-28.

6.21   WRA 96; HB 75A; NIWRO 101; NIHB 73A;
             R (SG and others) v SSWP UKSC (2015) www.bailii.org/uk/cases/UKSC/2015/16.html
             R (DA and others) v SSWP UKSC (2019) www.bailii.org/uk/cases/UKSC/2019/21.html

6.22   HB 75B; NIHB 73B

6.23   HB 75CA, 75G definition: 'relevant amount', 'couple'; SI 2023/335; NIHB 73CA, 73G; NISR 2023/42

6.26   HB 75F(1)(g); UCTP 9; NIHB 73F(1)(j); NIUCTP 7

Kinds of accommodation

6.27   The following apply when the benefit cap is calculated in HB (tables 6.4 and 6.5) or UC (volume 1 chapter 9):

(a) if you are on UC (in any kind of accommodation):

  ▪ your HB is never included in the HB benefit cap or the UC benefit cap,

  ▪ but your UC can be affected by the UC benefit cap if your other benefits are high;

(b) if you aren't on UC and live in general accommodation:

  ▪ your HB is always included in the HB benefit cap;

(c) if you aren't on UC and live in supported accommodation (table 2.3(a)-(d):

  ▪ your HB is never included in the HB benefit cap;

(d) if you aren't on UC and live in temporary accommodation (table 2.3(e)):

  ▪ your HB is included in the HB benefit cap – unless your home also meets the definition of supported accommodation (table 2.3(a)-(d)).

If you live in supported or temporary accommodation, the HB benefit cap is in practice unlikely to reduce your HB unless your other state benefits are particularly high.

Table 6.4 **Calculating HB benefit cap reductions**

For each benefit week (para 16.49):

(a) Add together your and your partner's entitlement in that week to:

  ▪ HB, except in supported accommodation (para 6.27);

  ▪ JSA, ESA and IS;

  ▪ child benefit, child tax credit and maternity allowance;

  ▪ severe disablement allowance;

  ▪ widowed mother's/parent's allowance; and

  ▪ widow's pension and bereavement allowance.

(b) If the total exceeds the benefit cap (para 6.23), your HB is reduced by the amount of the excess.

(c) But your HB can't be reduced below 50p per week.

Notes:

  ▪ Use the weekly amount of any benefit before any reductions are made for recovering overpayments, administrative penalties, third party deductions or sanctions. In practice, the DWP's/DFC's Benefit Cap Calculation Team provides the council/NIHE with the figures (HB A15/2013 paras 12 onwards).

  ▪ Paras 6.27-28 give the benefit cap rules if you live in supported or temporary accommodation or get HB on two homes.

6.27   WRA 96(10) – 'welfare benefit'; HB 75C(2)(a), 75F(1)(g); UCTP 9; NIWRO 101(7); NIHB 73C(2)(a), 73F(1)(j); NIUCTP 7

T6.4   WRA 96(10) definition: 'welfare benefit'; NIWRO 101(7); HB 75A, 75C, 75D, 75G definition: 'reference period'; NIHB 73A, 73C, 73D, 73G

Table 6.5 **Exceptions to the benefit cap**

The HB benefit cap doesn't apply in any of the following circumstances:

(a) You or your partner are getting:

- pension age HB (table 2.2),
- universal credit in supported or temporary accommodation (para 2.15),
- working age HB during the 39 week 'grace period' after leaving work (para 6.29),
- working age HB during a four-week 'extended payment' after starting work etc (para 17.32),
- main phase ESA with a support component, or
- industrial injuries disablement benefit.

(b) You, your partner or a child or young person in your family are getting the following, or are entitled to them but not receiving them because of being in a hospital or care home:

- PIP or (in Scotland) adult disability payment,
- DLA or (in Scotland) child disability payment,
- attendance allowance or constant attendance allowance paid with an industrial injury pension (you or your partner only), or
- a war disablement or war bereavement pension (para 13.16) (you or your partner only).

(c) You, your partner or a child or young person in your family are getting the following or are entitled to them but not receiving them (e.g. as in para 12.31):

- carer's allowance,
- guardian's allowance, or
- working tax credit (you or your partner only).

Note:

In practice, the DWP's/DFC's Benefit Cap Calculation Team is expected to notify the council/NIHE when these exceptions apply, apart from those relating to war pensions (HB A15/2013 paras 23 and 52).

Example: The HB benefit cap

Amelia and her children are renting their home in London (it isn't supported accommodation). Before the benefit cap is applied, she qualifies for:

HB	£240.00 per week
Other benefits in table 6.4	£259.60 per week

Because the total of £499.60 per week exceeds the benefit cap of £486.98 per week (para 6.23), her HB is reduced by the difference (£12.62 per week) to £227.38 per week.

T6.5   HB 2(1), definition: 'attendance allowance', 75E,75F; NIHB 2(1), 73E,73F

Benefit on two homes

6.28   If you qualify for benefit on two homes (paras 2.33-34) the DWP advises that any benefit cap reduction should be apportioned between them pro rata (A15/2013).

The 39 week grace period after leaving work

6.29   The HB benefit cap does not apply during the 39 weeks beginning with the day after your or your partner's last day of work if the conditions in para 6.30 are met. The DWP calls this time limited exception a 'grace period'. If you are a couple, either you or your partner must meet all the conditions; and if you each meet all the conditions from different dates, both grace periods apply.

6.30   The conditions are that you/your partner:

(a) have ceased work; and

(b) for at least 50 of the 52 weeks before the last day of work, were engaged in work for which payment was made or expected, and were not entitled to JSA, ESA or IS.

For these purposes, being on maternity, paternity or adoption leave, or getting statutory sick pay, counts as being in work.

Applying, changing and ending benefit cap reductions

6.31   In any particular case, the council need not apply the benefit cap or change the amount of any reduction until it receives notification from the DWP's/DFC's Benefit Cap Calculation Team. The council may however do either of these on its own initiative if it has the relevant information and evidence to do so. If the benefit cap stops applying to you, the council might delay removing it until it receives notice from the DWP/DFC, but must then award you arrears of HB (para 6.32).

When benefit cap reductions take effect

6.32   A benefit cap reduction can apply from the beginning of your HB claim. It can also start, change or end during your award of HB, and when it:

(a) starts or increases, HB changes from the date the council makes the decision to do so (this prevents overpayments of HB occurring as a result of a reduction);

(b) reduces or ends, HB changes from the date entitlement to the relevant welfare benefit (table 6.5) changed (so you get your resulting arrears of HB).

6.33   Claims wrongly decided as to a reduction may be corrected at any time. So if the council wrongly applied a benefit cap to you, you are entitled to arrears of HB no matter how far back they go. If you consider the council got the calculation wrong, you can ask for a reconsideration (para 20.38) or appeal (para 20.42).

6.28   WRA 96(10) – 'welfare benefit'; HB 75D(1); NIWRO 101(7); NIHB 73D(1)

6.29   HB 75E(1),(3)-(5); NIHB 73E(1),(3)-(5)

6.30   HB 75E(4); NIHB 73E(4)

6.31   HB 75B; NIHB 73B

6.32-33 DAR 4(7H), 7(2)(r), 8(14F); NIDAR 4(6E), 7(2)(m), 8(14A)

Conversion to weekly amounts

Rent and service charges

6.34   Whenever a weekly figure is needed for rent, the following rules apply. The same rules apply to service charges:

(a)   for rent due in multiples of weeks, divide by the number of weeks it covers;

(b)   for rent due calendar monthly, multiply by 12 then divide by 52 to find the weekly figure;

(c)   for rent due daily, multiply by seven to find the weekly figure.

Rent-free periods

6.35   No HB is awarded during rent-free periods. HB is awarded only for periods in which rent is due (and if a rent-free period begins or ends part way through a benefit week, the eligible rent that week is calculated on a daily basis).

6.36   During the periods in which rent is due, the calculation factors (i.e. applicable amount, income and any non-dependant deductions) are adjusted as follows:

(a)   if rent is expressed on a weekly basis: multiply the calculation factors by 52 or 53, then divide by the number of weeks when rent is due in that year;

(b)   if rent is not expressed on a weekly basis: multiply the calculation factors by 365 or 366, then divide by the number of days when rent is due in that year.

Income

6.37   Whenever a weekly income figure is needed, the following rules apply:

(a)   for an amount relating to a multiple of weeks, divide by the number of weeks it covers;

(b)   for an amount relating to a calendar month, multiply by 12 then divide by 52;

(c)   for an amount relating to a year, there are two rules. For working age claims, divide the annual amount by 365 or 366 then multiply by seven. For pension age claims, simply divide the annual amount by 52;

(d)   for income relating to a self-employed person's assessment period (para 14.30), divide the amount by the number of days in the assessment period, then multiply by seven;

(e)   for an amount relating to any other period longer than a week, divide the amount by the number of days it covers, then multiply by seven;

(f)   for an amount relating to a period less than a week, that is the weekly amount.

Rounding

6.38   The council may 'if appropriate' round any amount involved in the calculation of HB to the nearest penny, halfpennies being rounded upwards.

6.34   HB 80; HB66+ 61; NIHB 78; NIHB66+ 59

6.35   HB 81(1),(2),(3); HB66+ 62(1),(2),(3); NIHB 79(1),(2),(3); NIHB66+ 60(1),(2),(3)

6.37   HB 33; HB66+ 33; NIHB 30; NIHB66+ 31(a)

6.38   AA 5(1)(l); HB 80(8); HB66+ 61(7); NIAA 5(1)(m); NIHB 78(8); NIHB66+ 59(7)

Chapter 7 **Which eligible rent rules**

- The different way of calculating eligible rent: see paras 7.1-4.
- Terminology and types of landlord: see paras 7.5-22.
- Special kinds of accommodation: see paras 7.23-34.
- Old HB claims and old tenancies: see paras 7.35-41.
- Rent restrictions and protected groups: see paras 7.42-56.

The different ways of calculating eligible rent

7.1   This chapter explains which method is used to calculate your eligible rent, when there are rent restrictions that reduce your eligible rent, and when you are protected against the restrictions.

Eligible rent and the amount of your HB

7.2   Your eligible rent is the amount of rent you can get HB for. It is the starting point in all HB calculations (para 6.2), so the higher it is, the more HB you get.

The eligible rent rules and their names

7.3   We use the following names for the methods of calculating eligible rent:
- (a) the 'social renter rules' for most social renters (9.4);
- (b) the 'old scheme rules' for exempt accommodation and a few very old claims (para 9.17);
- (c) the 'LHA rules' (local housing allowance rules) for most private renters (para 10.4);
- (d) the 'rent referral rules' for boarders, hostels, caravans, mobile homes, houseboats and some old claims (para 10.31).

'Private renter rules' means (c) or (d) or both of them.

Which method applies to you

7.4   Table 7.1 summarises which method applies for calculating your eligible rent. Detailed rules are in this chapter and chapters 8-11.

7.2-3   CPR sch 3 para 5; HB 11(1), 12B, 12BA, 12C, 12D; HB66+ 11(1), 12B, 12C, 12D
          NICPR sch 3 para 5; NIHB 11(1), 13A, 13AA, 13B, 13C; NIHB66+ 11(1), 13A, 12B, 12C

Terminology, landlord types and eligible rent

Actual rent and eligible rent

7.5　　We use 'actual rent' to mean the total amount you are liable to pay on your home, and 'eligible rent' to mean the amount you can get HB towards (para 5.5 and table 5.1).

Tenants

7.6　　We use 'tenant' to mean any kind of rent payer:

(a) whether landlord and tenant law regards you as a tenant or licensee;

(b) whether you rent your home or are a shared owner; and

(c) whether you are a sole tenant or joint tenant (para 4.42).

7.7　　If you are a joint tenant your eligible rent may be based on your share of the rent (paras 9.7, 10.7, 11.16 and table 10.4).

Table 7.1 **Eligible rent rules and who they apply to**

Your tenancy and other details	Which rules apply to you
(a) Council and NIHE tenants	
■ Your home is too large and you are on working age HB	Social renter rules with bedroom tax (chapter 9)
■ Other council and NIHE tenants	Social renter rules without bedroom tax (chapter 9)
(b) Registered housing association tenants	
■ You have a market rent tenancy (para 7.18)	LHA rules (chapter 10)
■ Your landlord provides or arranges care, support or supervision so that your home qualifies as exempt accommodation (table 2.3(a))	Old scheme rules (chapter 9)
■ Your rent is too high	Rent referral rules (chapter 10)
■ Your home is too large and you are on pension age HB	Rent referral rules (chapter 10)

7.5-6　HB 2(1) – 'rent', 12(1)(a)-(j), Old 12(1)(a)-(j); HB66+ 2(1), 12(1)(a)-(j), Old 12(1)(a)-(j)
　　　　NIHB 2(1), 13(1)(a)-(h), Old 13(1)(a)-(h); NIHB66+ 2(1), 13(1)(a)-(h), Old 13(1)(a)-(h)

7.7　　CPR sch 3 para 4(1); HB 12B(4), 12C(2), B13(2)(a), 13D(4),(5),(12); HB66+ 12B(4), 12C(2), 13D(4),(5),(12)
　　　　NICPR sch 3 para 4(1); NIHB 13A(4), 13B(2), B14(2)(a), 14D(4),(5),(10); NIHB66+ 13A(4), 13B(2), 14D(4),(5),(10)

T7.1　HB 12B(1), A13(2), 13(1), 13C(2),(5), 13D(10), 14(1),(2)(b); HB66+ 12B(1), 13(1), 13C(2),(5), 13D(10), 14(1),(2)(b)
　　　　NIHB 13A(1), A14(2), 14(1), 14C(2),(5), 15(1),(3)(b); NIHB66+ 13A(1), 14(1), 14C(2),(5), 15(1),(3)(b)

■ Your home is too large and you are on working age HB	Social renter rules with bedroom tax (chapter 9)
■ Otherwise	Social renter rules without bedroom tax (chapter 9)

(c) Tenants of non-profit landlords

(unregistered housing associations, charities, voluntary organisations, county councils in England)

■ Your landlord provides or arranges care, support or supervision so that your home qualifies as exempt accommodation (table 2.3(a))	Old scheme rules (chapter 9)
■ Otherwise	As (d) below

(d) Private tenants

■ Your HB claim began before 1996	Old scheme rules (chapter 9)
■ You have a pre-1989 registered rent or similar tenancy (paras 7.38-41)	Social renter rules without bedroom tax (chapter 9)
■ Your HB claim began before 7th April 2008 (para 7.36)	Rent referral rules (chapter 10)
■ You live in a hostel, caravan, mobile home or houseboat	Rent referral rules (chapter 10)
■ You are a boarder	Rent referral rules (chapter 10)
■ Otherwise	LHA rules (chapter 10)

Note: In each of sections (a)-(d) take the first entry that applies to you.

Landlords

7.8   We use the following descriptions for types of landlord:

(a) the council you claim HB from (in Great Britain) (para 1.13);

(b) the NIHE (in Northern Ireland) (para 1.13);

(c) registered housing association (para 7.12);

(d) non-profit landlord (para 7.19);

(e) private landlord (para 7.21).

7.9   Your 'landlord' means the person you have a legal liability to pay rent to. It doesn't mean your managing agent. And if your landlord rents from a superior landlord, it doesn't mean them (para 7.10).

7.9-10   CBA 130(1)(a); HB 12(1), Old 12(1); HB66+ 2(1), 12(1), Old 12(1); NICBA 129(1)(a); NIHB 2(1), 13(1), Old 13(1); NIHB66+ 2(1), 13(1), Old 13(1)

7.10   For example:

(a) if your legal liability to pay rent is to a housing association, then it is your landlord even it has leased the property from a private landlord;

(b) if your legal liability to pay rent is to a private landlord, it is your landlord even if a housing association manages your tenancy on its behalf;

(c) if your liability to pay rent is to the council, it is your landlord even if the council manages its homes through a separate company (typically an 'arms-length management organisation' or 'tenant management organisation': ALMO/TMO);

(d) if you are a lodger your landlord is the person your rent is due to (e.g. if you are a lodger of a council tenant your landlord is the tenant, not the council).

Council and NIHE tenants

7.11   If your landlord is the council you claim HB from or the NIHE, the social renter rules apply in all cases (para 9.4). If your landlord is an English county council that doesn't administer HB, see para 7.19.

Tenants of housing associations

7.12   If your landlord is a registered housing association (paras 7.15-17):

(a) in England only, the LHA rules apply (para 10.4) when you have a market rent tenancy rather than a social housing tenancy (para 7.18);

(b) the old scheme rules apply (para 9.17) when your landlord provides care, support or supervision so that your home qualifies as 'exempt accommodation' (table 2.3(a));

(c) the rent referral rules apply (para 10.31) when your rent is too high (pension age and working age HB), or your home is too large (pension age HB only) (para 10.33);

(d) the social renter rules apply (para 9.4) in all other cases. These include rules about when your home is too large (working age HB only) (para 9.9).

7.13   If your landlord is an unregistered housing association:

(a) the old scheme rules apply (para 9.17) when your landlord provides or arranges care, support or supervision so that your home qualifies as 'exempt accommodation' (table 2.3(a));

(b) the private renter rules apply in all other cases (para 10.4, 10.31).

7.11   AA 134(1A),(1B); HB 12B(1), 12BA, A13(1),(2); HB66+ 12B(1); NIAA 126(1)(b), NIHB 13A(1), 13AA, A14(1),(2), NIHB66+ 13A(1)

7.12-13   CPR sch 3 para 4(1)(b); HB 12B(1), A13(1),(2); 13C(5)(a)-(c), 14(1),(2)(b), sch 2 para 3; HB66+ 12B(1), 13C(5)(a)-(c), 14(2)(b), sch 2 para 3; NICPR sch 3 para 4(1)(b); NIHB 13A(1), A14(1),(2), 14C(5)(a)-(c), 15(3)(b), sch 3 para 3; NIHB66+ 13A(1), 14C(5)(a)-(c), 15(3)(b), sch 3 para 3

Stock transfer tenants of housing associations

7.14   You are a 'stock transfer tenant' if your tenancy started with the council/NIHE and was transferred to a registered housing association. In these cases:

(a)   the social renter rules apply (para 9.4), but without the bedroom tax,

(b)   however, if and when you have a rent increase that makes your rent unreasonably high, the rules in paras 7.12-13 apply.

What is a housing association

7.15   A 'housing association' means a society, body of trustees or company:

(a)   whose objects or powers include the power to provide, manage, construct or improve housing; and

(b)   which doesn't trade for profit or, if it does, is limited by its constitution not to pay a dividend.

This applies to all housing associations, registered (paras 7.16-17) or unregistered (GSH para 98).

7.16   A 'registered housing association' is a 'housing association' (para 7.15) that is registered with the appropriate national regulator which is:

(a)   in England, with the Regulator of Social Housing;

(b)   in Scotland, with the Scottish Housing Regulator;

(c)   in Wales, with the Welsh Government;

(d)   in Northern Ireland, with the Department for Communities.

In England all registered housing associations are also private registered providers, a wider term which includes private companies whether that body is a housing association or not (para 7.17).

7.17   In Scotland and Wales, registered housing associations are known as 'registered social landlords'. In England, a housing association or other private company that is registered with the Regulator of Social Housing is known as a 'private registered provider of social housing' (often shortened to 'registered providers'). 'Private' here simply means non-council (because councils are also registered providers). A private registered provider (PRP) is registered with the regulator either as non-profit or profit-making. If it is profit-making only its dwellings that are not market rent (para 7.18) count as social housing and fall within the social renter rules.

7.14   HB 12B(1), A13(2)(a), 13C(5)(c), 14(2)(b), sch 2 para 11; HB66+ 12B(1), 13C(5)(c), 14(2)(b), sch 2 para 11
        NIHB 13A(1), A14(2)(b), 14C(5)(c), 15(3)(b), sch 3 para 5; NIHB66+ 13A(1), 14C(5)(c), 15(3)(b), sch 3 para 5

7.15   Housing Associations Act 1985 s1(1); Housing (Northern Ireland) Order 1992 art 3;
        HB 2(1) definition: 'housing association'; HB66+ 2(1); NIHB 2(1); NIHB66+ 2(1)

7.16-17 HB 2(1) definition: 'registered housing association', 13C(5)(a),(6), sch 2 para 3(1),(1A); HB66+ 2(1), 13C(5)(a),(6), sch 2 para 3(1),(1A);
        NIHB 2(1), 14C(5)(a), sch 3 para 3(b); NIHB66+ 2(1), 14C(5)(a), sch 3 para 3(a),(1A)

Types of housing association tenancy

7.18   In England, tenants of a registered housing association have:

(a) a market rent tenancy if:

   ■   your landlord is profit-making, and

   ■   you have a market rent, and

   ■   you aren't a shared owner (para 7.24);

(b) a social housing tenancy in all other cases.

In Scotland and Wales, tenants of a registered housing association have a social housing tenancy in all cases.

Tenants of non-profit landlords

7.19   You have a 'non-profit landlord' if your landlord is:

(a) a registered or unregistered housing association;

(b) a charity that is registered the with the Charity Commission (in Scotland, on the Charity Register) or is exempt from registration;

(c) a voluntary organisation (para 2.19); or

(d) a county council in an area of England that has both district councils and a separate county council.

The rules for (a) are in paras 7.12-14. The rules for (b)-(d) are in para 7.20.

7.20   For tenants of charities, voluntary organisations and English county councils (paras 7.19(b)-(d)):

(a) the old scheme rules apply (para 9.17) when your landlord provides or arranges care, support or supervision so that your home qualifies as 'exempt accommodation' (table 2.3(a));

(b) the private renter rules apply (paras 10.4, 10.31) in all other cases.

Tenants of private landlords

7.21   You have a 'private landlord' if you rent from an individual or from a company, firm or similar. In these cases your eligible rent is worked out using the private renter rules (paras 10.4, 10.31).

Lodgers

7.22   We use 'lodger' to mean a person who rents a room in someone else's house. In this case your eligible rent is worked out using the private renter rules (paras 10.4, 10.31).

7.18   Housing and Regeneration Act 2008, s68-71 and 77; HB 2(1) – 'registered housing association', 13C(5)(a), sch 2 para 3(1)(a),(1A); HB66+ 2(1), 13C(5)(a), sch 2 para 3(1)(a),(1A)

7.19-20 CPR sch 3 para 4(10); HB 13C(5)(b), HB66+13(5)(b); NICPR sch 3 para 4(9); NIHB 14C(5)(b); NIHB66+ 14C(5)(b)

7.21-22 HB 13C(2), 14(1); HB66+13C(2), 14(1); NIHB 14C(2), 15(1); NIHB66+14C(2), 15(1)

Particular types of accommodation

7.23 This section describes some particular types of accommodation and explains how your eligible rent is calculated in each of these. In all these cases your 'landlord' means the person you pay rent to (paras 7.9-10).

Shared ownership tenancies

7.24 You are a 'shared owner' if you are part renting and part buying your home. This is also called having an 'equity sharing agreement':

(a) if your landlord is the council you claim HB from, the NIHE or a registered housing association, your eligible rent is worked out using the social renter rules (para 9.4), but without the bedroom tax;

(b) if you have a private landlord (para 7.21), your eligible rent is worked out using the private renter rules (paras 10.4, 10.31).

Boarders

7.25 You are a 'boarder' if your rent includes a charge for meals. In this case:

(a) if your landlord is the council you claim HB from, the NIHE or a registered housing association, your eligible rent is worked out in the same way as any other tenant who has that kind of landlord (paras 7.11-13);

(b) if you have a private landlord (para 7.21), the rent officer decides whether your eligible rent is worked out using the LHA rules or rent referral rules (para 10.39).

Hostels

7.26 A hostel is a building that:

(a) provides accommodation for residents or a class of residents that is neither separate nor self-contained;

(b) together with either meals or adequate facilities for preparing food; and

(c) which is not a care home, independent hospital or Abbeyfield Home; and

(d) meets at least one of the operating conditions in para 7.27.

7.27 The operating conditions referred to in para 7.26 are that the building is:

(a) managed by a charity or voluntary organisation which provides care, support or supervision to help people be rehabilitated or resettled within the community; or

(b) run on a non-commercial basis, and wholly or partly funded by a government department or agency or local authority; or

(c) managed or owned by a registered housing association (para 7.16).

7.24 Housing and Regeneration Act 2008, s68(1)(b), 70; HB 2(1) – 'shared ownership lease', 12B(1), A13(2)(b), 13C(5)(a), 14(2)(b), sch 2 para 11A; HB66+ 2(1), 12B(1), 13C(5)(a), 14(2)(b), sch 2 para 12

7.25 HB 12D(1), 13C(5)(e), 13D(10), 14(1); HB66+ 12D(1), 13C(5)(e), 13D(10), 14(1); NIHB 13B, 14C(5)(e), 15(1), sch 2 part 1; NIHB66+ 13B, 14C(5)(e), 15(1), sch 2 part 1

7.26-27 HB 2(1) definition: 'hostel'; HB66+ 2(1); NIHB 2(1); NIHB66+ 2(1)

7.28   For people who live in a hostel (paras 7.26-27):

(a) if your landlord is the council you claim HB from, the NIHE or a registered housing association, your eligible rent is worked out using the social renter rules (para 9.4);

(b) if you have a private landlord (para 7.21), your eligible rent is worked out using the rent referral rules (para 10.31).

Caravans, mobile homes and houseboats

7.29   The following applies if you live in a caravan, mobile home or houseboat and pay site fees or mooring charges:

(a) your eligible rent is worked out using the social renter rules (para 9.4), but without the bedroom tax, when:

- you pay your site fees or mooring charges to a council in Great Britain that administers HB (whether or not you also pay rent for your dwelling and whether or not your rent is paid to the same or a different landlord), or

- you live on a gypsy or traveller site (para 7.30) and your landlord is an English county council;

(b) in any other case, your eligible rent is worked out using the rent referral rules (para 10.31).

In both the cases in (a), your HB is paid as a rent allowance rather than a rent rebate (para 18.6).

7.30   A gypsy or traveller site means a site provided for:

(a) people with a cultural tradition of nomadism or living in a caravan; or

(b) other people with a nomadic or cultural tradition of travelling regardless of their race or religion including travellers, show people, and those who no longer travel through reasons of health or age.

Exempt accommodation

7.31   You live in 'exempt accommodation' if you have a non-profit landlord (para 7.19) and your landlord provides or arranges care, support or supervision (table 2.3(a)). In this case, your eligible rent is worked out using the old scheme rules (para 9.17).

Other supported accommodation

7.32   If your home is supported accommodation but doesn't meet the definition of exempt accommodation in table 2.3(a), there are no special rules. Your eligible rent is worked out in the same way as any other tenant who has the same kind of landlord as you (table 7.1).

7.28   AA 134(1A),(1B); HB 12B, 12C, 13C(5)(d)(ii), 14(1); HB66+ 12B, 12C, 13C(5)(d)(ii), 14(1); NIAA 126(1)(b); NIHB 13A(1), 13B, 14C(5)(d)(ii), 15(1); HB66+ 13A(1), 13B, 14C(5)(d)(ii), 15(1)

7.29   AA 134(1A),(1B); HB 12B, 12C, A13(2)(c), 13C(5)(d)(i), 14(1),(2)(b), sch 2 para 3(1)(b); HB66+ 12B, 12C, 13C(5)(d)(i), 14(1)(2)(b), sch 2 para 3(1)(b); NIAA 126(1)(b); NIHB 13A(1), 13B, A14(2)(c), 14C(5)(d)(i), 15(1); HB66+ 13A(1), 13B, 14C(5)(d)(i), 15(1)

7.30   HB sch 2 para 3(4); HB66+ sch 2 para 3(4)

7.31   CPR sch 3 para 4(1)(b); HB 13C(5)(b), 14(2)(b); HB66+ 13C(5)(b), 14(2)(b); NICPR sch 3 para 4(1)(b); NIHB 14C(5)(b), 15(3)(b); NIHB66+ 14C(5)(b), 15(3)(b)

Temporary accommodation

7.33   You live in 'temporary accommodation' if:

(a) your home was made available to you by the council you claim HB from or the NIHE or by a registered housing association (para 7.16) under an arrangement with the council/NIHE, for the purpose of:

■ satisfying a homelessness duty owed to you following your application for assistance (e.g. permanent housing wasn't available), or

■ preventing you from becoming homeless (as defined in the homeless persons legislation); and

(b) the accommodation is:

■ 'board and lodging' (as defined in para 21.35(a)), or

■ held by the authority or registered housing association on a lease and in the case of an authority in England, is held outside the Housing Revenue Account on a lease granted for a term not exceeding ten years (para 21.35(c)), or

■ which the authority or registered housing association has a right to use under an agreement other than a leasehold agreement (e.g. licensed accommodation – para 21.35(b)).

In this case, your eligible rent is worked out using the social renter rules (para 9.4), but without the bedroom tax. (If the council/NIHE housed you in general accommodation, the social renter rules apply with the bedroom tax.)

Sanctuary scheme accommodation

7.34   You live in sanctuary scheme accommodation if:

(a) your landlord is the council you claim HB from, the NIHE or a registered housing association;

(b) your accommodation is part of a scheme that provides additional security for your home;

(c) you – or someone in your home – have been the victim of actual or threatened domestic violence (para 2.21);

(d) this was from your partner or former partner, or your or their son, daughter, stepchild, grandchild, parent, stepparent, grandparent, sister, brother, aunt, uncle, niece, nephew or first cousin;

(e) that person no longer lives with you (except in the case of a young person: para 4.16), and

(f) a professional person provides confirmation of (b) and (c).

In this case, your eligible rent is worked out using the social renter rules (para 9.4), but without the bedroom tax.

7.33   AA 134(1A),(1B); HB 12B(1), A13(2)(e),(3),(4), 13C(5)(a), sch 2 para 3(1)(a);
        NIAA 126(1)(b); NIHB 13A(1), A14(2)(e),(3),(4), 14C(5)(a), sch 3 para 3

7.34   AA 134(1A),(1B); HB 12B(1), A13(2)(f),(5), 13C(5)(a), sch 2 para 3(1)(a);
        NIAA 126(1)(b); NIHB 13A(1), A14(2)(f),(5), 14C(5)(a), sch 3 para 3

Old claims and tenancies

7.35   This section describes the rules that apply if you have an old HB claim or old tenancy. These rules are all rare.

HB claims made in or before 2008

7.36   Your eligible rent is worked out using the rent referral rules (para 10.31) rather than the LHA rules if:

- ■   you are a private tenant (para 7.21); and
- ■   you have been getting HB continuously since 6th April 2008 or earlier.

If you also meet the conditions in paras 7.37-41, the old scheme rules in those paras apply rather than the above, and if both apply the old scheme rules take precedence.

HB claims made in or before 1996

7.37   Your eligible rent is worked out using the old scheme rules (para 9.17) rather than the LHA rules or rent referral rules if:

- (a)   you are a private tenant (para 7.21); and
- (b)   you have been getting HB continuously since 1st January 1996 in Great Britain or 1st April 1996 in Northern Ireland, ignoring breaks of four weeks or less; and
- (c)   you have not moved home since then, or moved only because your home was made uninhabitable by fire, flood or natural disaster.

Registered rent and similar tenancies in Great Britain

7.38   In Great Britain, your eligible rent is worked out using the social renter rules (para 9.4), but without the bedroom tax, if:

- (a)   you are a private tenant (para 7.21) or your landlord is a registered housing association (para 7.16); and
- (b)   your tenancy began before 15th January 1989 in England or Wales, or 2nd January 1989 in Scotland.

7.39   This rule applies whether or not you have a 'registered rent tenancy'. If in fact you do have a registered rent tenancy, you can ask the rent officer to register the rent – in other words, set the maximum your landlord can charge. (This rent officer duty is different from the rent officer's HB duties in paras 10.39-40.)

7.36   HB 13C(2)(a)-(c); HB66+ 13C(2)(a)-(c); NIHB 14C(2)(a)-(c); NIHB66+ 14C(2)(a)-(c);
            SI 2007/2868 reg 1(5),(6); SI 2007/2869 reg 1(5),(6); NISR 2008/103 reg 1(2),(3)

7.37   CPR sch 3 para 4(1)(a),(2); NICPR sch 3 para 4(1)(a),(2)

7.38   HB 12B(1), 13C(5)(c), 14(2)(b), sch 2 paras 4-8; HB66+ 12B(1), 13C(5)(c), 14(2)(b), sch 2 paras 4-8;

Registered rent tenancies in Northern Ireland

7.40   In Northern Ireland, your eligible rent is worked out using the social renter rules (para 9.4), but without the bedroom tax, if you are a private tenant (para 7.21) and:

(a) in certain circumstances, your tenancy began before 1st October 1978; or

(b) your tenancy began on or after 14th June 2006, and your home was built or converted before 6th November 1956 and doesn't meet the fitness standard.

7.41   In these cases, you have a 'registered rent tenancy' and your rent is controlled (using a historic rateable value) or fixed by a rent officer. (This rent officer duty is different from the rent officer's HB duties in paras 10.39-40).

Rent restrictions and temporary protection

7.42   This section explains the restrictions that can mean your eligible rent is reduced and you get less HB. It also gives the protections that can apply against this.

How rent restrictions can apply

7.43   Rent restrictions only apply when your rent is considered to be too high or your home is considered to be too large for your needs. This is done in different ways:

(a) the social renter rules use the bedroom tax, but only for working age HB (para 9.9);

(b) the old scheme rules use comparisons made by the council or NIHE (para 9.22);

(c) the LHA rules use local housing allowances fixed by the rent officer (para 10.5);

(d) the rent referral rules use individual rent determinations given by the rent officer (para 10.40);

(e) there is also a default power to restrict rents (paras 7.44-45).

The default power to restrict the rent

7.44   If your eligible rent appears greater than it is 'reasonable to meet by way of HB', the council can reduce it to 'such lesser sum as seems reasonable'. If this power is used the council must consider your personal circumstances (R (Laali) v Westminster CC).

7.45   The law is uncertain about when and how this default power can be used. It is only likely to affect you if none of the rules in para 7.43(a)-(d) apply to you ([2011] UKUT 156 (AAC)). In the past, it has been used in the case of a council tenant (Burton v Camden LBC). So one example of when it could be used now, at least in theory, is when you are a council tenant but the bedroom tax doesn't apply because you are on pension age HB.

7.43   NIHB 13A(1), 14C(5)(c), 15(3)(b), sch 3 para 4; NIHB66+ 13A(1), 14C(5)(c), 15(3)(b), sch 3 para 4

7.44   HB 12B(6); HB66+ 12B(6); NIHB 13A(7); NIHB66+ 13A(7)
R (Laali) v Westminster CC HBRB 08/12/00 QBD

7.45   HB 12B(1); HB66+ 12B(1); NIHB 13A(1); NIHB66+ 13A(1)
Burton v Camden LBC 17/12/97 CA 30 HLR 991

Protection from rent restrictions

7.46   You are protected against all the rent restrictions in para 7.43-45:

(a)   for up to 13 weeks if you could previously afford your home; or

(b)   for up to 12 months if you have had a death in your home.

The details of these rules are in paras 7.49-56.

7.47   There is an extra protection that doesn't have a fixed time limit when:

(a)   you live in exempt accommodation (table 2.3(a)) or made your HB claim before 1996 (para 7.37); and

(b)   you are considered vulnerable.

The details of this rule are in paras 9.32-35.

7.48   You should tell the council/NIHE if you think any of these protections apply to you. All of them can be appealed (chapter 20).

People who could previously afford their home

7.49   This protection applies if you meet the following conditions when you make a claim for HB:

(a)   you or any combination of the occupiers of your home (para 7.55) could afford the financial commitments there when your liability for rent was entered into (no matter how long ago that was); and

(b)   you have not received HB for any period during the 52 weeks before your award of HB starts, and nor has your partner (if you have one: table 1.1).

7.50   In this case, the protection lasts for the first 13 weeks of your award of HB. This may give you time to move or change your circumstances (e.g. by getting someone else to move in with you or improving your income) without the additional pressure of having insufficient HB. If you stop receiving HB (during or after the 13 weeks) the protection can only apply to a new HB claim if there are at least 52 weeks between the end of your old HB award and the start of the new one.

7.51   While the protection applies to you, your eligible rent is:

(a)   the full actual rent payable on your home;

(b)   minus an amount for service charges which are ineligible for HB (see paras 8.32-52) and in Northern Ireland an amount for rates unless you are billed separately.

7.49   Social renter: HB 12BA(6),(7); NIHB 13AA(6),(7)
        Private renter: HB 12D(5),(6); HB66+ 12D(5),(6); NIHB 13C(5),(6); NIHB66+ 13C(5),(6)
        Old scheme: HB Old 13(7),(8); HB66+ Old 13(7),(8); NIHB Old 14(7),(8); NIHB66+ Old 14(7),(8)
        Rent referral: HB 13(8), 13ZA(3),(4); HB66+ 13(8), 13ZA(3),(4); NIHB 14(8), 14A(3),(4); NIHB66+ 14(8), 14A(3),(4)

7.50   Social renter: HB 12BA(8); NIHB 13AA(8)
        Private renter: HB 12D(7)(b); HB66+ 12D(7)(b); NIHB 13C(7)(b); NIHB66+ 13C(7)(b)
        Old scheme: HB Old 13(7); HB66+ Old 13(7); NIHB Old 14(7); NIHB66+ Old 14(7)
        Rent referral: HB 13ZA(3); HB66+ 13ZA(3); NIHB 14A(3); NIHB66+ 14A(3)

7.51   Social renter: HB 12BA(6); NIHB 13AA(6)
        Private renter: HB 12D(5); HB66+ 12D(5); NIHB 13C(5); NIHB66+ 13C(5)
        Old scheme: HB Old 13(7); HB66+ Old 13(7); NIHB Old 14(7); NIHB66+ Old 14(7)
        Rent referral: HB 13ZA(3); HB66+ 13ZA(3); NIHB 14A(3); NIHB66+ 14A(3)

People who have had a death in their home

7.52   This protection applies if you meet the following conditions when you make a claim for HB or during your award of HB:

(a) any of the occupiers of your home (para 7.55) has died within the past 12 months (including occupiers who were temporarily absent); and

(b) you were living there on the date of their death, or were temporarily absent in the UK or abroad (paras 3.5-12); and

(c) you have not moved since then.

But if you (the claimant) die, your HB ends. So this protection can only apply to someone who claims HB after your death if you counted as an occupier in their home (para 7.55).

7.53   In this case, the protection lasts for the 12 months following the date of the person's death. This may give you time to move or change your circumstances (e.g. by getting someone else to move in with you or improving your income) without the additional pressure of having insufficient HB. If you stop receiving HB and then make a new claim at the same address within the 12 months, the protection resumes until 12 months after the date of the person's death (in other words, it isn't extended). If you move, the protection ends.

7.54   While the protection applies to you:

(a) if you weren't on HB on the date of the person's death, your eligible rent is worked out in the same way as in para 7.51;

(b) if you were on HB on that date, your eligible rent must not be reduced below whatever it was immediately before that date (but it is increased if any rule requires this).

Occupiers related to a protected renter

7.55   In deciding if you qualify as a protected renter, the only 'occupiers' taken into account are:

(a) you (the claimant) (but only for the rule in paras 7.49-51); and

(b) any members of your family (partner, children, young persons: para 4.2); and

(c) any 'relative' of you or your partner (including non-dependants and lodgers) who has no separate right to occupy the dwelling.

In the law, the term 'linked persons' is also used to refer to these occupiers.

7.52-53 Social renter: HB 12BA(3),(4),(5); NIHB 13AA(3),(4),(5)
Private renter: HB 12D(3),(4),(7)(a); HB66+ 12D(3),(4),(7)(a); NIHB 13C(3),(4),(7)(a); NIHB66+ 13C(3),(4),(7)(a)
Old scheme: HB Old 13(5),(6); HB66+ Old 13(5),(6); NIHB Old 14(5),(6); NIHB66+ Old 14(5),(6)
Rent referral: HB 13(8), 13ZA(1),(2); HB66+ 13(8), 13ZA(1),(2); NIHB 14(8), 14A(1),(2); NIHB66+ 14(8), 14A(1),(2)

7.54 Social renter: HB 12BA(3)(a),(b); NIHB 13AA(3)(a),(b)
Private renter: HB 12D(3)(a),(b); HB66+ 12D(3)(a),(b); NIHB 13C(3)(a),(b); NIHB66+ 13C(3)(a),(b)
Old scheme: HB Old 13(5); HB66+ Old 13(5); NIHB Old 14(5); NIHB66+ Old 14(5)
Rent referral: HB 2(1) definition: 'reckonable rent', 13ZA(1); HB66+ 2(1), 13ZA(1); NIHB 2(1), 14A(1); NIHB66+ 2(1), 14A(1)

7.55 HB 2(1) definition: 'linked person', Old 13(10),(11); HB66+ 2(1), Old 13(10),(11); NIHB 2(1), Old 14(10),(11); NIHB66+ 2(1), Old 14(10),(11)

Who is a 'relative'

7.56   A 'relative' means:

(a)   parent, daughter, son, sister or brother;

(b)   parent-in-law, son-in-law, daughter-in-law, step-son, step-daughter, including equivalent relations arising through civil partnership;

(c)   a partner of any of the above (by marriage or civil partnership or by living together as a married couple or as civil partners); or

(d)   grandparent, grandchild, aunt, uncle, niece or nephew.

This definition applies whenever the term 'relative' is used in this guide, except as shown in paras 7.34 and 10.20(e).

Examples: The protected groups

Redundancy

Hudson makes a claim for HB after he is made redundant. His actual rent is high. He moved to this address when he was in a well-paid job and could easily afford the rent and outgoings. He has not been on HB in the last 52 weeks.

Because of the protection for people who could formerly afford their accommodation, Hudson's eligible rent must not be restricted in any way for the first 13 weeks of his award of HB. During those weeks, his eligible rent is his actual rent minus amounts for any ineligible services.

Bereavement before claiming HB

Mirah makes a claim for HB after the death of her husband. She has not moved since her husband's death. Her actual rent is high.

Because of the protection for people who have had a bereavement, Mirah's eligible rent must not be restricted in any way until the first anniversary of her husband's death. Until then, her eligible rent is her actual rent minus amounts for any ineligible services.

Bereavement while on HB

Reuben is on HB and his mother lives with him as his non-dependant. His eligible rent takes account of the fact that he qualifies for two bedrooms (chapter 11) and is £125 per week. Following the death of his mother he only qualifies for one bedroom.

Because he has been bereaved while on HB, he is a protected renter and his eligible rent must not be reduced below £125 per week until the first anniversary of his mother's death.

7.56   HB 2(1) definitions: 'close relative', 'couple', 'relative'; HB66+ 2(1); NIHB 2(1); NIHB66+ 2(1)

Chapter 8 **Service charges**

- ■ General rules about rent and service charges: see paras 8.1-7.
- ■ Charges that count as rent: see paras 8.8-20.
- ■ General rules about service charges: see paras 8.21-31.
- ■ Eligible and ineligible service charges: see paras 8.32-53.

General rules

8.1 This chapter is about service charges and other charges that may be included in your rent. It explains which of these are eligible for HB and which are not and applies to both ordinary housing and supported accommodation (table 2.3). Table 8.1 summarises the rules and the DWP provides helpful guidance in its Housing Benefit Guidance for Supported Housing Claims (GSH).

8.2 The chapter applies when your eligible rent is calculated using:

(a) the social renter rules (para 9.4); or

(b) the old scheme rules (para 9.17); or

(c) the rent referral rules (para 10.31).

It never applies when your eligible rent is calculated using the LHA rules (para 10.4-9).

What you pay your landlord

8.3 When you rent your home, the amounts your pay your landlord are classified into the following categories:

(a) rent including charges that count as part of your rent;

(b) service charges that are eligible for HB, including most communal charges; and

(c) service charges that are not eligible, including most support charges.

Landlords sometimes give separate figures for these, or sometimes give a global figure that includes everything.

8.2	Social rent:	HB 12B(2), B13(2)(a); HB66+ 12B(2); NIHB 13A(2), B14(2)(a); NIHB66+ 13A(2)
	Old scheme:	HB/HB66+ Old 12(3) in CPR sch 3 para 5(1); NIHB/NIHB66+ Old 13(3) in CPR sch 3 para 5(1)
	Rent referral:	ROO sch 1 paras 6(2A), 7(3); HB 13(2),(9); HB66+ 13(2),(9)
	LHA rules:	HB 13D(4),(12); HB66+ 13D(4),(12); NIHB 14D(4),(10); NIHB66+ 14D(4),(10)
8.3-4	Social rent:	HB 12B(2) B13(2)(a), sch 1 para 1(g); HB66+ 12B(2), sch 1 para 1(g)
		NIHB 13A(2), B14(2)(a), sch 1 para 1(g); NIHB66+ 13A(2), sch para 1(g)
	Old scheme:	HB Old 12(3), sch 1 para 1(g); HB66+ Old 12(3), sch 1 para 1(g)
		NIHB Old 13(3), sch 1 para 1(g); NIHB66+ Old 13(3), sch 1 para 1(g)

What HB can pay

8.4   You can only get HB towards categories (a) and (b) in para 8.3. They are added together to give your eligible rent. But your eligible rent can be reduced if your rent is too high (para 7.42) or your service charges are excessive (para 8.30). Different rules apply in LHA cases (paras 10.5-9).

Classifying your payments

8.5   The council/NIHE must classify the payments you make to your landlord into the categories in para 8.3. The rest of this chapter gives the details and uses 'council' to include the NIHE in Northern Ireland.

8.6   The council may decide that the information in your tenancy agreement is sufficient for it to classify your payments. Or it may need to obtain information from you or your landlord or both, particularly in supported accommodation (GSH paras 134, 168). But these are not conclusive: it is the law that determines how to classify a payment: [2009] UKUT 28 (AAC) (paras 8.23-24). If your landlord classifies a payment wrongly, the council must classify it correctly whether that increases or reduces your eligible rent (CH/3528/2006).

8.7   Errors in classifying payments can result in you getting too little HB. Correct classification is particularly important in supported accommodation, where service charges are usually more numerous and varied. And in exempt accommodation (table 2.3(a)) the subsidy rules for old scheme cases mustn't be allowed to undermine this (paras 9.36-38).

Table 8.1 **Rent and service charges summary**

Charges that count as part of your rent	Eligible for HB
Your basic rent	YES
Your landlord's outgoings or overheads	YES
Water charges for communal areas	YES
Water charges for your own accommodation	NO
Council tax in houses in multiple occupation	YES

8.6   HB Old 12(7), 12(8); HB66+ Old 12(7), 12(8); NIHB Old 13(7), 13(8); NIHB66+ Old 13(7), 13(8)

T8.1   Social rent: HB 12B(2) B13(2)(a), sch 1 para 1(a)-(g); HB66+ 12B(2), sch 1 para 1(a)-(g)
                           NIHB 13A(2), B14(2)(a), sch 1 para 1(a)-(g); NIHB66+ 13A(2), sch para 1(a)-(g)
       Old scheme: HB Old 12(3), sch 1 para 1(g); HB66+ Old 12(3), sch 1 para 1(g)
                           NIHB Old 13(3), sch 1 para 1(a)-(g); NIHB66+ Old 13(3), sch 1 para 1(a)-(g)

Service charges

Cleaning and window cleaning of communal areas	YES
Cleaning and window cleaning of your own accommodation	NO
Fuel for communal areas	YES
Fuel for your own accommodation	NO
Meals	NO
Counselling and support	NO
Furniture and household equipment	YES
Other property related and communal services	YES
Other day-to-day living expenses	NO

Charges that count as rent

8.8   This section gives the rules about rent and charges that are part of your rent. These are included in your eligible rent and can't be restricted unless your overall rent is too high (para 7.42).

Rent

8.9   Your rent (sometimes called your 'core rent') is the basic amount your landlord charges you for providing your home. If you are a social renter, it is usually based on a national formula. If you rent from a non-profit landlord, it usually reflects the landlord's costs. Or if you are a private tenant, it is typically based on the market level.

Charges that are part of your rent

8.10   The general rule is that when a charge relates to the property, is made up of your landlord's costs, and isn't attributable to a service, it is part of your rent and is eligible for HB.

Your landlord's outgoings or overheads

8.11   The following landlord costs count as part of your rent and are eligible for HB:

(a) mortgage repayments (or rent if the landlord leases the property from someone else);

(b) insurance and similar payments;

(c) property maintenance including repairs, replacements, redecoration and gas, electricity and fire safety tests;

(d) other items that are properly considered in setting the rent, such as a sinking fund for property maintenance, bad debt provision, and the cost of vacant lettings (voids) (CH/3528/2006; [2010] UKUT 222 (AAC)).

8.9   www.gov.uk/government/publications/rent-standard
www.gov.uk/government/publications/direction-on-the-rent-standard-from-1-april-2020
www.gov.uk/government/publications/guidance-on-rents-for-social-housing

Water charges

8.12   If your landlord includes an amount for water charges (because the landlord gets the water bill not you):

   (a)   an amount for water for communal purposes counts as part of your rent and is eligible for HB;

   (b)   an amount for water used in your own accommodation is not eligible;

   (c)   an amount that combines both must be separated out ([2016] AACR 19).

8.13   The ineligible amount for water used in your own accommodation is:

   (a)   the actual figure billed by the water company, if your home is separately billed; or

   (b)   a proportion of that figure, if your home is part of a dwelling that is separately billed; or

   (c)   in any other case, a figure that can be identified or estimated in some other way.

Council tax or rates

8.14   If your landlord includs an amount for council tax in Great Britain or rates in Northern Ireland (because the landlord gets the bill not you), this counts as part of your rent and is eligible for HB (GM A4.160-161). This applies when:

   (a)   you live in a house in multiple occupation (HMO) such as a house made up of bedsits, or

   (b)   you are a lodger in someone's home.

Communal areas, gardens, garages etc

8.15   When your home includes communal areas, gardens, a garage, mobility scooter shed, outbuildings or land, a charge for these is eligible for HB if:

   (a)   they are used for occupying the dwelling as a home, and either:

   (b)   you acquired them at the same time as the dwelling and had no option but to rent them at the same time; or

   (c)   you have made or are making reasonable efforts to end your liability for them.

Offices and meeting rooms

8.16   Supported accommodation (table 2.3) often includes staff offices and meeting rooms for staff and residents. When the landlord charges for these, this is not a service charge (GSH para 176) but is a charge that counts as part of your rent and is eligible for HB.

Adaptations

8.17   When your landlord charges you for the costs of installing, repairing, and maintaining adaptations to your home (e.g., a stair lift), this is not a service charge (GSH para 175) but is a charge that counts as rent and is eligible for HB ([2011] UKUT 513 (AAC)).

8.12   HB 2(1) – 'water charges', Old 12(3), 12B(2) B13(2)(a), sch 1 para 1(a),(g); HB66+ 2(1), Old 12(3), 12B(2), sch 1 para 1(a),(g)
        NIHB 2(1), Old 13(3), 13A(2), B14(2)(a), sch 1 para 1(a),(g); NIHB66+ 2(1), Old 13(3), 13A(2), sch para 1(a),(g)

8.14   [2016] AACR 19 was [2015] UKUT 532 (AAC)

8.15   HB 2(4)(a); HB66+ 2(4)(a); NIHB 2(4)(a); NIHB66+ 2(4)(a)

Space for a carer

8.18 If you have a live-in carer, their room counts as part of your accommodation even if it is down a corridor from you ([2009] UKUT 28 (AAC) and [2009] UKUT 116 (AAC)). When the landlord charges you for their room, it is included in your rent and is eligible for HB in the normal way. Or if the carer doesn't live in your home or you have a rota of carers, you may qualify for an additional room for them (paras 11.10, 11.25).

Business premises

8.19 Rent on any part of your home which is used for business, commercial or other non-residential purposes is not included as part of your rent and is not eligible for HB. For example, if you rent both a shop and the flat above it, only the part of the rent relating to the flat is eligible for HB. If you are self-employed and work from home, see paras 14.43-44.

Reductions for prompt payment and increases to cover arrears

8.20 If you have a social landlord that reduces your rent under a government-approved scheme (e.g. for prompt payment or for paying online), the total amount (before the reduction) is eligible for HB. If your rent is increased to recover arrears of rent that you owe personally, that part of the rent is not eligible for HB.

Service charges

8.21 The rest of this chapter gives the rules about service charges, including communal charges, and support charges in supported accommodation. It explains which are eligible for HB and which are not. Different rules apply in LHA cases (paras 10.5-9).

What are service charges

8.22 Most charges that benefit you rather than your landlord count as service charges. These are divided into:

(a) service charges that are eligible for HB, such as fuel and maintenance in common areas and

(b) service charges that are not eligible, such as fuel for your own accommodation, meals and counselling and support.

For the details of individual service charges, see paras 8.32-53.

8.23 HB law gives the following definitions:

(a) 'services' means 'services performed' or 'facilities provided' for you, or 'rights made available' to you; and

(b) a 'service charge' means a periodical charge for these (e.g. weekly, monthly, etc).

8.19   HB Old 12(4), 12B(3), B13(2)(a); HB66+ Old 12(4), 12B(3); NIHB Old 13(4), 13A(3), B14(2)(a); NIHB66+ Old 13(4), 13A(3)

8.20   HB 11(3), Old 12(6A),(6B), 12(2A),(2B); HB66+ 11(3), Old 12(6A),(6B), 12(2A),(2B)

8.22   HB sch 1 para 1(a),(f),(g); HB66+ sch 1 para 1(a),(f),(g); NIHB sch 1 para 1(a),(f),(g); NIHB66+ sch 1 para 1(a),(f),(g)

Distinguishing service charges from rent

8.24   In most cases:

   (a) when you (the tenant) derive a benefit or value from a charge (e.g. fuel, cleaning) it counts as a service charge;

   (b) when a charge is made up of your landlord's own costs (e.g. mortgage repayments, property maintenance and in shared accommodation council tax and water charges), it counts as part of your rent.

But a charge that is for a service or facility (para 8.23) is always a service charge and cannot be rent regardless of how the landlord or the tenancy agreement has classified it ([2009] UKUT 28 (AAC)).

Which service charges are eligible for HB

8.25   You can only get HB towards a service charge if:

   (a) you have to pay it as a condition of occupying your home (para 8.26); and

   (b) it is not excessive in relation to the service provided (paras 8.28-30); and

   (c) the charge is eligible for HB (paras 8.32-52).

Helpful advice is in GM A4.700-950 and GSH paras 166-193.

A condition of occupying your home

8.26   A service charge is only eligible for HB if paying it is a condition of occupying your home. This means you must be liable for the charge in the same way as you are liable for rent (para 5.7). You don't need to have been liable from the start of your tenancy; it is sufficient if you have been liable from whenever you agreed to pay it, if the alternative would have been to lose your home.

Services provided free of charge

8.27   Some not-for-profit landlords provide services which are funded by public or other bodies, donations or other activities of the landlord (GSH paras 161-162). This typically applies to counselling and support and other services that aren't eligible for HB, but sometimes also to eligible services. The landlord doesn't charge you for them, and you can't get HB towards them because you don't have to pay for them (GM A4.1950).

8.25   HB 12(1)(e), 12B(2)(b) sch 1 para 4; HB66+ 12(1)(e), 12B(2)(b) sch 1 para 4
      NIHB 13(1)(e), 13A(2)(c) sch 1 para 4; HB66+ 12(1)(e), 12A(2)(c) sch 1 para 4

8.26   HB 12(1)(e); HB66+ 12(1)(e); NIHB 13(1)(e); NIHB66+ 13(1)(e)

8.27   CBA 130(1)(a); HB 12(1); HB66+ 12(1); NICBA 129(1)(a); NIHB 13(1); NIHB66+ 13(1)

Valuing service charges

8.28   There are individual rules for valuing water charges, fuel and meals (paras 8.13, 8.35, 8.39). For any other service charge, the value is found as follows:

(a) if your landlord provides a figure (in your tenancy agreement or separately), the council uses that;

(b) if your landlord doesn't provide a figure, or provides a figure that is unrealistically low, the council decides what amount is 'fairly attributable' to the service.

But in some cases, the council may decide your service charges are excessive (paras 8.29-30).

Unreasonably high eligible service charges

8.29   An eligible service charge is unreasonably high if:

(a) it is excessive taking account of the cost of comparable services; or

(b) it could be more cheaply provided in a satisfactory way ([2010] UKUT 222 (AAC)).

For example, (b) could apply to staff costs in supported accommodation if your landlord employs more staff than the council considers necessary, even if they are paid at the going rate ([2010] UKUT 222 (AAC)).

8.30   When an eligible service charge is unreasonably high, the council:

(a) allows a reasonable amount as eligible for HB; and

(b) disallows the excess.

In the case of counselling and support charges, the DWP advises the council to work with other departments and councils to establish what is reasonable (GSH para 165), and to take account of your landlord's explanation of how the charge was arrived at (GSH para 181).

Unreasonably low ineligible service charges

8.31   When an ineligible service charge is unreasonably low taking account of comparable charges, the council must substitute a higher ineligible amount.

8.28   HB sch 1 para 3; HB66+ sch 1 para 3; NIHB sch 1 para 3; NIHB66+ sch 1 para 3

8.29-30   HB sch 1 para 4; HB66+ sch 1 para 4; NIHB sch 1 para 4; NIHB66+ sch 1 para 4

8.31   HB sch 1 para 3(2); HB66+ sch 1 para 3(2); NIHB sch 1 para 3(2); NIHB66+ sch 1 para 3(2)

Eligible and ineligible service charges

8.32   This section explains which service charges are eligible for HB and which are not. You can only get HB towards eligible service charges. Different rules apply in LHA cases (paras 10.5-9).

Cleaning and window cleaning

8.33   If your landlord charges you for cleaning or window cleaning:

(a) an amount for cleaning and window cleaning of communal areas (para 8.37) is eligible for HB;

(b) an amount for cleaning the outsides of your own windows is eligible for HB if you and your household can't do it (e.g. because you don't live on the ground floor: GSH para 177);

(c) any other cleaning and window cleaning is not eligible.

Fuel for heating, lighting etc

8.34   Fuel means gas, electricity etc, and includes standing charges or other supply costs. If your landlord charges you for fuel:

(a) an amount for fuel used in communal areas (para 8.37) is eligible for HB, but

(b) an amount for fuel used in your own accommodation is not eligible.

8.35   The ineligible amount for fuel used in your own accommodation is:

(a) the figure your landlord provides in your tenancy agreement or separately, or

(b) a figure that can be identified in some other way, or

(c) in any other case, the standard amount in table 8.2 – this is also used when (a) or (b) are unrealistically low or include an amount for communal areas that can't be separated out.

8.36   The standard amounts in table 8.2 are per HB claim (not per person). When they are used, the council must invite you to provide evidence from which the actual or approximate charge can be estimated.

8.33   HB sch 1 para 1(a)(iv); HB66+ sch 1 para 1(a)(iv); NIHB sch 1 para 1(a)(iv), NIHB66+ sch 1 para 1(a)(iv)

8.34   HB sch 1 para 5; HB66+ sch 1 para 5; NIHB sch 1 para 5; NIHB66+ sch 1 para 5

8.35   HB sch 1 para 6; HB66+ sch 1 para 6; NIHB sch 1 para 6; NIHB66+ sch 1 para 6

8.36   HB sch 1 para 6(4), sch 9 para 9(b); HB66+ sch 1 para 6(4), sch 8 para 9(1)(b)
        NIHB sch 1 para 6(4), sch 10 para 10(c); NIHB66+ sch 1 para 6(4), sch 9 para 9(c)

Meaning of communal areas

8.37   In the case of charges for fuel, cleaning and window cleaning (and also in relation to non-dependants: para 4.30), 'communal areas' mean:

(a) . areas of common access in any type of accommodation, e.g. halls, corridors, stairways and other areas that aren't a 'room'; and

(b) common rooms in sheltered accommodation (para 8.38), e.g. lounge, dining room, meeting room, kitchen or laundry room.

In the case of other services, 'communal' is not defined and has its ordinary English meaning.

8.38   For these purposes, 'sheltered accommodation' includes supported housing in general (table 2.3) as well as sheltered, very sheltered and extra care housing ([2012] AACR 38; [2016] AACR 19).

Table 8.2 **Standard weekly fuel deductions 2023-24**

If the claimant and any family occupy more than one room

Fuel for heating	£35.25
Fuel for hot water	£4.10
Fuel for lighting	£2.85
Fuel for cooking	£4.10
Fuel for any other purpose	NIL
Fuel for all the above	£46.30

If the claimant and any family occupy one room only

Fuel for heating and any hot water and/or lighting	£21.10
Fuel for cooking	£4.10
Fuel for any other purpose	NIL
Fuel for all the above	£25.20

Note: Standard weekly deductions for fuel in 2023-24 remain unchanged from the previous year.

8.37   HB sch 1 para 8; HB66+ sch 1 para 8; NIHB sch 1 para 8; NIHB66+ sch 1 para 8

8.38   [2012] AACR 38 is Oxford CC v Basey [2012] EWCA Civ 115; [2016] AACR 19 was [2015] UKUT 532 (AAC)

T8.2   HB sch 1 para 6(2),(3); HB66+ sch 1 para 6(2),(3); NIHB sch 1 para 6(2),(3); NIHB66+ sch 1 para 6(2),(3)

Table 8.3 **Standard weekly meals deductions 2023-24**

A separate amount is assessed and deducted for each person whose meals are provided.

If at least three meals are provided every day

For the claimant, and each other person from the first Monday in September following his or her 16th birthday	£33.15
For each child	£16.80

If breakfast only is provided

For the claimant, and each other person of any age	£4.05

All other cases

For the claimant, and each other person from the first Monday in September following his or her 16th birthday	£22.10
For each child	£11.05

Meals

8.39   Meals include prepared food and the cost of preparation. They also include unprepared food. If your landlord charges you for meals, this is not eligible for HB. The ineligible amount is always the standard amount in table 8.3 (even if your landlord says meals cost more or less than this).

8.40   The standard amounts in table 8.3 are per person and can be different for each person in your accommodation depending on what meals (if any) are provided to them.

Support and related services

8.41   If your landlord charges you for any of the following, they are not eligible for HB:

(a) counselling and support;

(b) medical, nursing and personal care including assistance at meal times;

(c) emergency alarm systems (to summon assistance in the event of a fall, an accident, etc).

T8.3   HB sch 1 para 2(2)-(5); HB66+ sch 1 para 2(2)-(5); NIHB sch 1 para 2(2)-(5); NIHB66+ sch 1 para 2(2)-(5)

8.40   HB sch 1 para 2(6),(7); HB66+ sch 1 para 2(6),(7); NIHB sch 1 para 2(6),(7); NIHB66+ sch 1 para 2(6),(7)

8.41   HB sch 1 para 1(c)-(f); HB66+ sch 1 para 1(c)-(f); NIHB sch 1 para 1(c)-(f); NIHB66+ sch 1 para 1(c)-(f)

How providing support affects your HB

8.42   HB has two linked rules for landlords who provide support, and it is usually the case that the advantage of (a) outweighs the disadvantage of (b):

(a) providing 'care, support or supervision' usually means:

■ your home is exempt accommodation (tables 2.3 and 2.4), and

■ your eligible rent is less likely to be restricted than in ordinary accommodation (para 9.22);

(b) a charge for providing 'counselling and support':

■ isn't eligible for HB; and

■ usually has to be paid for in some other way (para 8.27).

Meaning of support etc

8.43   Support, counselling, care and supervision have their ordinary English meanings (table 2.4). 'Support' typically has the same meaning for both the rules in para 8.42 but this is not automatically the case ([2019] UKUT 304 (AAC)).

Examples of support

8.44   Support can include a wide range of activities for people who are vulnerable and typically includes:

(a) setting up your home and staying safe and secure in it;

(b) dealing with tenancy or related problems;

(c) applying for benefits and using local services;

(d) budgeting;

(e) keeping healthy and well;

(f) activities relating to the reason you are vulnerable.

Distinguishing support from other charges

8.45   In most cases:

(a) when a charge is concerned with the 'provision of adequate accommodation', it is likely to be a service charge that is eligible for HB, or in some cases part of your rent (para 8.8);

(b) when a charge helps you maintain your tenancy, make use of the facilities, or varies in intensity according to your personal needs, it is likely to be a support charge that is not eligible.

8.46   If your landlord labels a support charge as something else, that doesn't change the fact that it is an ineligible service charge (CH/3528/2006). If they label a charge as 'enhanced (or intensive) housing management', the council has to determine what portion (if any) is eligible for HB ([2019] UKUT 304 (AAC) and GSH para 189).

8.42   CPR sch 3 para 4(1)(b),(10); HB sch 1 para 1(f); HB66+ sch 1 para 1(f)
NICPR sch3 para 4(1)(b),(9); NIHB sch 1 para 1(f); NIHB66+ sch 1 para 1(f)

Staff costs

8.47   In supported accommodation, staff often provide a mixture of services. The general rule ([2010] UKUT 222 (AAC)) is that staff costs:

(a) are eligible for HB when they relate to charges that count as part of your rent (para 8.8) or to eligible services, for example maintaining the property and cleaning communal areas;

(b) are ineligible when they relate to ineligible services, for example counselling and support.

It is therefore common for staff costs to be divided into a percentage that is eligible for HB and a percentage that is ineligible. For offices and meeting rooms in supported accommodation see para 8.16.

Examples: Service charges and other charges

1. A tenant of a bedsit

Alex rents a bedsit from a registered housing association. Her rent is made up of the following weekly payments:

- ■   £90 for rent   this is eligible for HB
- ■   £2 for cleaning communal areas   this is a service charge and is eligible for HB

Her actual rent (the total amount she has to pay on her home) is £92 per week.
Her eligible rent (the amount she can get HB towards) is also £92 pw.

2. A tenant in supported accommodation

Pavel rents a room in a hostel that meets the definition of 'exempt accommodation' (table 2.3(a)). His rent is made up of the following weekly payments:

- ■   £200 for rent   this is eligible for HB
- ■   £4 for council tax   this counts as part of his rent and is eligible for HB
- ■   £2 for communal water charges   this counts as part of his rent and is eligible for HB
- ■   £7 for fuel for communal areas   this is a service charge and is eligible for HB
- ■   £3 for water charges for his own room   this counts as part of his rent but is not eligible
- ■   £20 for fuel for his own room   this is a service charge and is not eligible
- ■   £40 for counselling and support   this is a service charge and is not eligible

His actual rent (the total amount he has to pay on his home) is £276 pw. His eligible rent (the amount he can get HB towards) is the total of the four eligible items, which is £213 pw.

Furniture and household equipment

8.48   If your landlord charges you for furniture or household equipment (such as white goods):

  (a) this is eligible for HB; but

  (b) if there is an agreement that you will only pay for a fixed time and then the furniture or household equipment will belong to you, this is not eligible.

Other property-related and communal services

8.49   If your landlord charges you for other services that relate to the 'provision of adequate accommodation', this is eligible for HB. This typically includes communal services.

8.50   No account is taken of your personal needs. It is only the adequacy of the accommodation that counts, not your ability to take advantage of it or any services you may need to do so (R v Swansea HBRB ex p. Littler, R v St Edmundsbury HBRB ex p Sandys).

8.51   For example, charges for the following services are usually eligible for HB (GSH para 177, GM A4.730):

  (a) lifts, communal telephones and entry phones;

  (b) CCTV or other secure building access ([2010] UKUT 222 (AAC));

  (c) communal laundry and kitchen equipment (washing machine, tumble dryer, stove, toaster, etc);

  (d) refuse removal;

  (e) equipment needed to provide TV;

  (f) maintenance of communal areas both indoors and outdoors, including children's play areas and gardens but not your own garden ([2011] UKUT 22 (AAC)), CH/755/2008);

  (g) services relating to the kind of residents the accommodation is for (CIS/1460/1995; [2016] AACR 19) – for example, residents with disabilities or vulnerable young people.

  (h) staff costs relating to eligible services (para 8.47).

For council tax and other overheads see paras 8.11-14.

8.48   HB 12(1)(e),(2)(d),(8), sch 1 para 1(b); HB66+ 12(1)(e),(2)(d),(8), sch 1 para 1(b)
             NIHB 13(1)(e),(2)(b),(8), sch 1 para 1(b); NIHB66+ 13(1)(e),(2)(b),(8), sch 1 para 1(b)

8.49   HB sch 1 para 1(g); HB66+ sch 1 para 1(g); NIHB sch 1 para 1(g); NIHB66+ sch 1 para 1(g)

8.50   R v Swansea HBRB ex p Littler [1998] EWCA Civ 1214, 48 BMLR 24;
             R v St Edmundsbury HBRB ex p Sandys [1997] EWHC Admin 711, 30 HLR 800

Other day-to-day living expenses

8.52   Charges for items that relate to your or your household's general living expenses are not eligible for HB. Several of these are mentioned earlier in this chapter (e.g. cleaning and fuel for your own accommodation). The following are also not eligible:

(a)   individual laundry costs;

(b)   medical expenses and expenses relating to personal hygiene;

(c)   transport;

(d)   TV licence and subscription fees;

(e)   leisure and sports facilities;

(f)   staff costs relating to ineligible services (para 8.47).

For water charges see para 8.12.

Appeals about service charges

8.53   If you fall within the social renter rules (para 9.4) or the old scheme rules (para 9.17), you can appeal to a tribunal about any matter relating to service charges (paras 20.42). But if you fall within the rent referral rules (para 10.31), you may have to ask for a rent officer redetermination instead (para 10.43).

8.52   HB sch 1 para 1(a)(i)-(iv); HB66+ sch 1 para 1(a)(i)-(iv); NIHB sch 1 para 1(a)(i)-(iv); NIHB66+ sch 1 para 1(a)(i)-(iv)

Chapter 9 **Social renter rules**

- How your eligible rent is calculated using the social renter rules: see paras 9.4-8.
- Eligible rent reductions if your home is too large (the bedroom tax): see paras 9.9-16.
- How your eligible rent is calculated using the old scheme rules: see paras 9.17-39.

Summary

9.1 This chapter explains how your eligible rent is calculated using the social renter rules and the old scheme rules.

9.2 The chapter mainly applies to:

  (a) council tenants and NIHE tenants;

  (b) tenants of registered housing associations; and

  (c) tenants of non-profit landlords whose home is 'exempt accommodation' (para 9.18).

Chapter 7 gives full details and exceptions and table 7.1 summarises which rules apply to you.

9.3 Your eligible rent is calculated in the same way for both the social renter rules and the old scheme rules (paras 9.5, 9.21) but rent restrictions apply to them in different ways (paras 9.9, 9.22).

Social renter rules: eligible rent

When the social renter rules apply

9.4 The social renter rules apply if your landlord is:

  (a) the council you claim HB from (in all cases);

  (b) the NIHE (in all cases);

  (c) a registered housing association (in all cases unless you fall within one of the exceptions in table 7.1); or

  (d) a private landlord only when you have a registered rent or similar old tenancy.

Eligible rent

9.5 Your eligible rent is:

  (a) your actual weekly rent (para 9.6);

  (b) minus any reduction required by the bedroom tax (paras 9.9);

  (c) minus an amount for ineligible service and similar charges (table 8.1).

9.6 Your actual rent means the full weekly amount you are liable to pay on your home.

9.4   HB 12B(1), A13(1); 13C(5)(a)-(c), 14(2)(b), sch 2 paras 3-11; HB66+ 12B(1), 13C(5)(a)-(c), 14(2)(b), sch 2 paras 3-11;
      NIHB 13A(1), A14(1), 14C(5)(a)-(c), 15(3)(b), sch 3 paras 3-5; NIHB66+ 13A(1), 14C(5)(a)-(c), 15(3)(b), sch 3 paras 3-5

9.5-6 HB 12B(2), 12BA(2), B13(2)(a); HB66+ 12B(2); NIHB 13A(2), 13AA(2), B14(2)(a); NIHB66+ 13A(2)

Joint tenants

9.7   If you have at least one joint tenant who is not a member of your family (paras 4.42-46):

(a)   first, the eligible rent for your dwelling is worked out as described in para 9.5;

(b)   then it is apportioned (para 9.8) between you and the other joint tenant(s).

9.8   'Apportioning' means deciding how much is fairly attributable to each of you. To do this the authority takes account of:

(a)   the number of joint tenants, including any who are ineligible for HB such as students (Nagshabandi v Camden LBC);

(b)   the proportion of rent paid by each of you;

(c)   the presence or absence of each of you (CH/3376/2002);

(d)   the size and number of rooms each of you occupies;

(e)   whether there is any written or other agreement between you; and

(f)   any other relevant circumstances.

Social renter rules: bedroom tax

9.9   This section explains how your eligible rent can be reduced if you have more bedrooms in your home than you qualify for. This is often called 'under-occupying' your home. In the law the reduced figure is known as the 'maximum rent social sector'.

Compensation in Scotland and Northern Ireland

9.10   In Scotland and Northern Ireland if a reduction applies you are normally fully compensated through other payments (paras 23.9 and 23.29).

When a reduction applies

9.11   Your eligible rent is reduced when:

(a)   the social renter rules apply (para 9.4);

(b)   you – and also your partner(s) if you are in a couple or polygamous marriage – are under the age of 66;

(c)   you have more bedrooms than you qualify for (para 9.12); and

(d)   none of the exceptions in table 9.1 apply to you.

But if a member of your household has died or you could afford the rent before you claimed HB the reduction can be delayed for up to 13 weeks/one year (paras 7.46-56).

9.7   HB 12B(4), B13(2)(c); HB66+ 12B(4); NIHB 13A(4), B14(2)(c); NIHB66+ 13A(4)

9.8   Nagshabandi v Camden LBC HBRB [2002] EWCA Civ 1038 www.bailii.org/ew/cases/EWCA/Civ/2002/1038.html

9.11   HB A13(1),(2)(d); NIHB A14(1),(2)(d)

The amount of the reduction

9.12   The reduction is calculated as follows:

(a) if your home has one bedroom more than you qualify for (table 11.1), your eligible rent is reduced by 14%;

(b) if it has two or more bedrooms more than you qualify for, your eligible rent is reduced by 25%.

No reduction applies if your home has the same number of bedrooms as you qualify for, or fewer bedrooms.

The reduction for joint tenants

9.13   If you have at least one joint tenant who is not a member of your family (paras 4.42-46):

(a) first, the reduction (of 14% or 25%) is made from the eligible rent for your dwelling;

(b) then the resulting figure is apportioned (para 9.8) between you and the other joint tenant(s).

Eligible rent after a reduction

9.14   The reduced eligible rent is used in calculating your HB. Deductions for non-dependants (para 6.2) and/or because you have excess income (para 6.6) are made from the reduced eligible rent.

The number of bedrooms you qualify for

9.15   You qualify for the appropriate number of bedrooms for the occupiers of your home: see table 11.1.

Which occupiers are taken into account

9.16   The social sector size criteria take account of the occupiers of your dwelling. This means:

(a) you (the claimant) and members of your family (partner, children and young persons: para 4.2);

(b) non-dependants (para 4.26);

(c) lodgers (para 4.36);

(d) joint tenants (para 4.42); and

(e) any other person who occupies your dwelling as their home.

For further details, see paras 11.10-11.

9.12   HB B13(2)(b),(3); NIHB B14(2)(b),(3)

9.13   HB B13(2)(c); NIHB B14(2)(c)

9.15   HB B13(5)-(7); NIHB B14(5)-(7)

9.16   HB B13(5); NIHB B14(5)

Table 9.1 **Exceptions to the bedroom tax**

The bedroom tax doesn't apply to you in any of the following cases:

(a)   you or your partner have reached the age of 66

(b)   you have a shared ownership tenancy (para 7.24)

(c)   You live in a caravan, mobile home or houseboat (paras 7.29-30)

(d)   You live in temporary accommodation for homeless people (para 7.33)

(e)   You live in sanctuary scheme accommodation for people threatened with violence (para 7.34)

(f)   your landlord is a housing association and your home is exempt accommodation (para 9.17)

(g)   your landlord is a registered housing association and the rent referral rules apply because the council/NIHE considers your rent is unreasonably high (para 7.12).

Old scheme rules: eligible rent

When the old scheme rules apply

9.17   The old scheme rules only apply to:

(a)   exempt accommodation (para 9.18); and

(b)   pre-1996 HB claims (para 7.37).

Exempt accommodation

9.18   You live in exempt accommodation if:

(a)   you rent from one of the following non-profit landlords:

■   a registered or unregistered housing association,

■   a charity registered the with the Charity Commission (in Scotland, on the Charity Register),

■   a voluntary organisation (para 2.19), or

■   a county council in an area of England that has both district councils and a separate county council;

(b)   and your landlord or someone on their behalf provides you with care, support or supervision (para 2.22).

T9.1   HB A13(2)(b)-(e),(3); CPR sch 3 para 4(1)(b); NIHB A14(2)(b)-(e),(3); NICPR sch 3 para 4(1)(b)

9.17   CPR sch 3 para 4(1); HB 11(1)(d), A13(1)(c), 13C(5)(b); HB66+ 11(1)(d), 13C(5)(b);
          NICPR sch 3 para 4(1); NIHB 11(1)(d), A14(1)(c), 14C(5)(b); NIHB66+ 11(1)(d), 14C(5)(b)

9.18   CPR sch 3 para 4(10); NICPR sch 3 para 4(9)

9.19   Exempt accommodation is one type of supported accommodation (table 2.3). But there are several types of supported accommodation, and they aren't classed as exempt accommodation unless they meet the definition in para 9.18. The name 'exempt accommodation' arose because the accommodation was exempt (and remains exempt) from changes to the law in 1996.

9.20   If you live in exempt accommodation (or any other type of supported accommodation), you can get HB towards your rent whether you have a pension age or working age claim (para 2.16).

Eligible rent

9.21   When the old scheme rules apply to you:

(a) your eligible rent must be calculated using the social renter rules but without the bedroom tax (para 9.9);

(b) your eligible rent can only be reduced using the old scheme rules (paras 9.22-35);

(c) details of your rent may be referred to the rent officer, but this affects how much subsidy the council gets and doesn't bind the council in its assessment of your eligible rent (paras 9.36-38).

Old scheme rules: rent restrictions

9.22   The rest of this chapter explains when your eligible rent can be restricted under the old scheme rules. There have been many court cases about this, and they are summarised in table 9.2. For guidance see GSH paras 203-241.

Table 9.2 **Rent restrictions under the old scheme**

These cases apply to exempt accommodation and pre-1996 HB claims (para 9.17).

Decisions about unreasonably high rents: The authority must decide:

(a) the actual rent you pay (including all eligible and ineligible service charges);

(b) what would be suitable alternative accommodation (paras 9.24-25) including what services are needed to make it suitable and what other factors need to be taken into account;

(c) what the rent is for such accommodation; and

(d) whether (a) is 'unreasonably high' compared with (c).
     (R v Beverley BC ex parte Hare.)

'Unreasonably high for claimant rather than landlord': The authority must decide whether 'the rent is unreasonably high for the claimant to have to pay', rather than unreasonably

---

9.19   HB 75H; UCTP 2(1) – 'specified accommodation'; UC sch 1 paras 1, 3(h), 3A; NIHB 73H; NIUCTP 2(1); NIUC sch 1 para 3(e), 4

9.20   UCTP 2(1) – 'specified accommodation', 5(2)(a), 6A(2); NIUCTP 2(1), 3(2)(a), 4A(2)

9.21   HB/HB66+ Old 12(3), Old 13 in CPR sch 3 para 5; NIHB/NIHB66+ Old 13(3), Old 14 in NICPR sch 3 para 5 high for a particular landlord to charge given the amount of public funding the landlord receives (SS v Birmingham CC).

'Unreasonably high': This means more than just 'higher' (Malcolm v Tweeddale DC HBRB).

Suitability of alternative accommodation: The authority must have 'sufficient information to ensure that like is being compared with like [...] Unless that can be done, no safe assessment can be made of the reasonableness of the rent in question or the proper level of value' (Malcolm v Tweeddale DC HBRB). Your home should be compared with 'more suitable' rather than 'less suitable' accommodation ([2009] UKUT 162 (AAC)).

Decisions about past periods: A decision about a past period should be made as if it was being made then. If evidence about that period is unavailable or unclear, findings of fact must be made about what was likely to have been the case ([2009] UKUT 162 (AAC)).

Decisions about the amount of a reduction: The authority should:

(a)   consider whether any circumstances may make a small reduction appropriate;

(b)   decide the appropriate level of a reduction; and

(c)   be able to say how it arrived at (b).
       (Mehanne v Westminster CC HBRB and R v Beverley BC ex parte Hare).

Limits to reductions: Your eligible rent must not be reduced below the cost of suitable alternative accommodation (R v Brent LBC ex parte Connery).

People considered 'vulnerable': availability of suitable alternative accommodation: Although suitable alternative accommodation must be available if you are considered 'vulnerable' (para 9.33), this doesn't mean the authority is expected to find a home for you. It is 'quite sufficient if an active market is shown to exist in houses in an appropriate place at the appropriate level' (the level your eligible rent is reduced to). So long as the authority has evidence of this, it is sufficient 'to point to a range of properties, or a bloc of property, which is available without specific identification of particular dwelling houses' (R v East Devon DC HBRB ex parte Gibson). If the authority doesn't have this evidence, it shouldn't reduce your eligible rent (CH/4306/2003).

People considered 'vulnerable': reasonableness of being expected to move: If you are considered 'vulnerable', the authority should have evidence that it has taken into account the effect a move would have (para 9.35) on employment and schooling (R v Sefton MBC ex parte Cunningham).

T9.2   R v Beverley DC HBRB ex parte Hare 21/02/95 QBD HLR 637
          SS v Birmingham CC and SSWP [2016] EWCA Civ 1211, [2017] AACR 8
          Malcolm v Tweeddale DC HBRB 06/08/91 CS 1994 SLT 1212
          R v Westminster HBRB ex parte Mehanne [2001] UKHL 11
          R v Brent LBC ex parte Connery 20/10/89 QBD 22 HLR 40
          R v East Devon DC HBRB ex parte Gibson 10/03/93 CA 25 HLR 487
          R v Sefton MBC ex parte Cunningham 22/05/91 QBD 23 HLR 534

When a rent restriction can apply

9.23   Once your eligible rent is calculated, it can only be restricted if:

(a) your rent is unreasonably high; or

(b) your home is unreasonably large; or

(c) you have a rent increase that is unreasonably high; or

(d) you have a rent increase that is within 12 months of the previous rent increase, and this is unreasonable.

In each case this is decided by reference to suitable alternative accommodation (para 9.24).

Suitable alternative accommodation

9.24   The council/NIHE must always decide what is unreasonable by making a comparison with suitable alternative accommodation. It must take into account:

(a) the nature of the alternative accommodation including any exclusive and shared facilities;

(b) the age and state of health of the occupiers of your home (paras 9.26-28);

(c) only alternative accommodation with security of tenure which is reasonably equivalent to what you have;

(d) accommodation that is either occupied or unoccupied, but at least some of it must be unoccupied if the protection in para 9.32 applies to you.

For example, 'if you are disabled or elderly you might have special needs and require expensive or larger accommodation' (GM para A4.1171).

9.25   The council/NIHE normally only looks at alternative accommodation in its own area. If there is nothing comparable there it can look outside, but not at 'other parts of the country where accommodation costs differ widely from those which apply locally' (GM para A4.1172).

Occupiers of your home who are taken into account

9.26   The council/NIHE must consider the occupiers of your home when it is deciding:

(a) what is suitable alternative accommodation (paras 9.24-25); and

(b) which occupiers are vulnerable (para 9.33).

9.27   For these rules (para 9.26) only the following occupiers are taken into account:

(a) you (the claimant);

(b) members of your family (partner, children and young persons: paras 4.4 and 4.14); and

(c) any 'relative' (para 7.56) of you or your partner who has no separate right to occupy your home.

People can fall within (c) whether they are a non-dependant, lodger, tenant or joint tenant.

9.23   HB/HB66+ Old 13(3), Old 13ZA(1) in CPR sch 3 para 5(2),(3)
            NIHB/NIHB66+ Old 14(3), Old 14ZA(1) in NICPR sch 3 para 5(2),(3)

9.24   HB/HB66+ Old 13(3),(9)(a) in CPR sch 3 para 5(2); NIHB/NIHB66+ Old 14(3),(9)(a) in NICPR sch 3 para 5(2)

9.26   HB/HB66+ Old 13(9)(a) in CPR sch 3 para 5(2); NIHB/NIHB66+ Old 14(9)(a) in NICPR sch 3 para 5(2)

9.27-28 HB/HB66+ Old 13(10) in CPR sch 3 para 5(2); NIHB/NIHB66+ Old 14(10) in NICPR sch 3 para 5(2)

9.28   But when the council/NIHE is deciding the size of suitable alternative accommodation, all the occupiers of your home are taken into account – including non-dependants, lodgers, joint tenants, foster children and carers, whether they are related to you or not. (Unlike all the other HB rules about accommodation size, there are no exceptions.)

The amount of the reduction

9.29   When a rent restriction applies (para 9.23), the council/NIHE must first consider whether any of the protections apply to you (para 9.30). If they don't, the council/NIHE can reduce your eligible rent to the level of rent for suitable alternative accommodation (paras 9.24-25) or make a smaller reduction (but can't make no reduction at all).

Protection from rent restrictions

9.30   You are protected against the restrictions relating to high rents and large accommodation (para 9.23(a),(b)):

(a) for up to 13 weeks if you could previously afford your home (para 7.49); or

(b) for up to 12 months if you have had a death in your home (para 7.52); or

(c) without time limit if the protection for vulnerable people applies (paras 9.32-35).

9.31   You are protected against the restrictions relating to rent increases (para 9.23(c),(d)) for up to 12 months if you have had a death in your home (para 7.52).

Protection for vulnerable people

9.32   If you are vulnerable (para 9.33) or another occupier of your home (para 9.26) is vulnerable, the council/NIHE must not reduce your eligible rent unless:

(a) there is cheaper suitable alternative accommodation available (para 9.34); and

(b) it is reasonable to expect you to move (para 9.35).

9.33   For this rule, you or another occupier are only 'vulnerable' if you or they:

(a) have reached the age of 66; or

(b) are responsible for a child or young person in your household (paras 4.4-19); or

(c) have limited capability for work for social security purposes (for guidance see GSH paras 223-225).

The council/NIHE decides (a) and (b), but (c) is decided by the DWP (CH/4424/2004).

Availability of alternative accommodation

9.34   When the protection for vulnerable people applies, suitable alternative accommodation (para 9.24) must be available, and must be available more cheaply. For example, accommodation you have recently left, or an offer of accommodation you have refused, may be available – but only while it actually remains available to you, not after it has

---

9.29   HB/HB66+ Old 13(3) in CPR sch 3 para 5(2); NIHB/NIHB66+ Old 14(3) in NICPR sch 3 para 5(2)

9.30   HB/HB66+ Old 13(5)-(8) in CPR sch 3 para 5(2); NIHB/NIHB66+ Old 14(5)-(8) in NICPR sch 3 para 5(2)

9.31   HB/HB66+ Old 13ZA(2) in CPR sch 3 para 5(3); NIHB/NIHB66+ Old 14ZA(2) in NICPR sch 3 para 5(3)

9.32-34 HB/HB66+ Old 13(4) in CPR sch 3 para 5(2); NIHB/NIHB66+ Old 14(4) in NICPR sch 3 para 5(2)

been let to someone else. The DWP advises that accommodation is 'not available if, in practice, there is little or no possibility of [you] being able to obtain it, for example because it could only be obtained on payment of a large deposit which [you do] not have' (GM para A4.1222).

Reasonableness of having to move

9.35   When suitable alternative accommodation exists, it must be reasonable to expect you to move. In deciding this, the council/NIHE must take into account:

(a)   your prospects of retaining employment; and

(b)   the effect on the education of any children or young persons in para 9.27 who would have to change school.

The impact of subsidy and of rent officer figures

9.36   In Great Britain, the council can get less government subsidy (paras 21.29-33) if you fall within:

(a)   the old scheme rules because your home is exempt accommodation (para 9.18); and also

(b)   the rent referral rules (para 10.31).

For example, this occurs when you live in a hostel (para 7.26-27) and have a non-profit landlord who provides care, support or supervision.

9.37   In these cases, the council can only take subsidy into account as follows (R v Brent LBC ex p Connery):

(a)   it must not take subsidy into account when it decides whether your rent, accommodation size or rent increase is unreasonable, or any matter relating to the protected groups;

(b)   it may take subsidy into account when deciding the amount of a reduction, but shouldn't reduce your eligible rent on financial grounds alone (GM para A4.1173).

9.38   This means that:

(a)   the old scheme rules are used to assess your eligible rent (para 9.22);

(b)   the rent referral rules are used only for subsidy purposes.

The rent officer's figures aren't binding on the council. They are advisory and shouldn't be used as the sole basis to set your eligible rent.

Appeals about rent and service charges

9.39   In old scheme cases, all appeals about your eligible rent and service charges go to an independent tribunal (para 20.42).

9.35   HB/HB66+ Old 13(9)(b) in CPR sch 3 para 5(2); NIHB/NIHB66+ Old 14(9)(b) in NICPR sch 3 para 5(2)

9.36   SO 16(1), sch 4 paras 2, 7, 8, 10

9.37   HB/HB66+ Old 13(3) in CPR sch 3 para 5(2); NIHB/NIHB66+ Old 14(3) in NICPR sch 3 para 5(2)

9.38   CPR sch 3 paras 4(1), 5; HB Old 13(3), 114A(1)(c); HB66+ Old 13(3), 95A(1)(c); NICPR sch 3 paras 4(1), 5; NIHB/NIHB66+ Old 14(3)

Chapter 10 **Private renter rules**

> - How your eligible rent is calculated using the LHA rules: see paras 10.4-9.
> - The LHA figures and how they are set: see paras 10.10-30.
> - How your eligible rent is calculated using the rent referral rules: see paras 10.31-43.

10.1 This chapter explains how your eligible rent is calculated using the LHA rules and the rent referral rules (together called the 'private renter rules').

10.2 The chapter mainly applies to:

(a) tenants of private landlords (paras 7.21-22); and

(b) tenants of non-profit landlords whose home is not exempt accommodation (para 9.18).

Chapter 7 gives full details and exceptions and table 7.1 summarises which rules apply to you.

10.3 Your eligible rent is calculated in different ways for the LHA rules and the rent referral rules (paras 10.5, 10.40) and rent restrictions apply to them in different ways (para 10.5, table 10.4).

LHA rules: eligible rent

When the LHA rules apply

10.4 The LHA rules apply if:

(a) you have:

- a private landlord (paras 7.21-22) , or
- a non-profit landlord (para 9.18(a)) but your home is not exempt accommodation because your landlord (or someone on their behalf) doesn't provide you with care, support or supervision; and

(b) you don't fall within:

- the rent referral rules (para 10.31), or
- any of the other exceptions in table 7.1.

Eligible rent

10.5 Your eligible rent is the lower of:

(a) the LHA figure that applies to you (para 10.10); and

(b) your actual weekly rent (para 10.6).

10.2   AA 134(1A),(1B); HB 13C(2),(5)(b); HB66+ 13C(2),(5)(b); NIAA 126(1)(c); NIHB 14C(2),(5)(b); NIHB66+ 14C(2),(5)(b)

10.4   HB 13C(2),(5)(a)-(e), 14(2)(b); HB66+ 13C(2),(5)(a)-(e), 14(2)(b); NIHB 14C(2),(5)(a)(e), 15(3)(b); NIHB66+ 14C(2),(5)(a)-(e), 15(3)(b)

10.5   HB 12D(1),(2), 13D(4),(5); HB66+ 12D(1),(2), 13D(4),(5); NIHB 13D(1),(2), 14D(4),(5); NIHB66+ 13D(1),(2), 14D(4),(5)

10.6 Your actual weekly rent means the full weekly amount you are liable to pay on your home. This includes all service charges you are liable to pay, whether or not they would be eligible for HB in other types of HB case.

Examples: Eligible rent and LHAs

1. Karen is aged 66 and moves home from rent-free accommodation to a privately rented flat where she pays rent of £160 per week. In her area, the LHA for a one-bedroom dwelling is £138 per week.

- ■ Karen's eligible rent is the lower of these two figures (para 10.5), which is £138.

2. Valentina is aged 66 and retires from a well-paid job that enabled her to afford an expensive privately rented flat. She pays rent there of £233 per week which doesn't include any services. In her area, the LHA for a one-bedroom dwelling is £167 per week.

- ■ Because Valentina could previously afford her home, her eligible rent is £233 per week for the first 13 weeks (para 7.49).
- ■ After that her eligible rent is £167 per week, but the council may agree to award a discretionary housing payment (para 23.8).

3. Julian is a private tenant aged 42 and has been getting HB for several years. He currently pays his landlord £116 per week. The LHA for one-bedroom accommodation in his area is £121 per week.

- ■ Julian's eligible rent is the lower of these two figures (para 10.5), which is £116 per week.

4. Julian's rent goes up to £126 per week on 1st September and the LHA is still £121 per week.

- ■ His eligible rent is the lower of these two figures, which is now £121 per week.

Joint tenants

10.7 If there is at least one joint tenant who is part of your household but not your family (paras 4.42-46):

(a) first, the eligible rent for your dwelling is the lower of:

- ■ the actual rent for your dwelling, and
- ■ the LHA figure that applies to you (this takes account of you, your family and non-dependants, and also the joint tenant(s), their family members and non-dependants: para 10.17);

(b) then the resulting figure is apportioned (para 9.8) between you and the other joint tenant(s).

10.8 But if you have at least one joint tenant who maintains a separate household from you (paras 4.42-46):

(a) first, the actual weekly rent for your dwelling is apportioned (para 9.8) between you and the other joint tenant(s);

10.6   HB 13D(12); HB66+ 13D(12); NIHB 14D(10); NIHB66+ 14D(10)

10.7-8   HB 12D(2)(a), 13D(4),(5),(12); HB66+ 12D(2)(a), 13D(4),(5),(12); NIHB 13C(2)(a), 14D(4),(5),(10); NIHB66+ 13C(2)(a), 14D(4),(5),(10)

(b) then your eligible rent is the lower of:

- your share of the actual rent, and
- the LHA figure that applies to you (this takes account of you, your family and non-dependants, but not the joint tenant(s), their family members or non-dependants: para 10.17).

Changes to your eligible rent

10.9 Your eligible rent is recalculated in the way described in paras 10.5-8 whenever there is a change in your actual rent or your LHA figure (para 10.15) or in the way the figures are apportioned between joint tenants.

Example: LHA rules for joint tenants

Sara and Janet are friends in their 70s. They jointly rent a flat from a private landlord, and Sara's daughter lives with them. Their actual rent is £252 per week. Sara pays two thirds and Janet pays one third which the council accepts is reasonable. In their area, LHAs are £229 per week for three bedrooms, £190 per week for two bedrooms and £150 per week for one-bedroom dwellings.

1. If Sara and Janet have a shared household (para 10.7):

- the eligible rent for their dwelling is the LHA figure of £229 per week;
- Sara's eligible rent is £152.67 per week (two thirds);
- Janet's eligible rent is £76.33 per week (one third).

2. If Sara and Janet have separate households (para 10.8):

- Sara's share of the actual rent is £168.00, which is higher than her LHA figure of £150, so her eligible rent is £150.00 per week;
- Janet's share of the actual rent is £84.00, which is lower than her LHA figure of £126, so her eligible rent is £84.00 per week.

The LHA figures

10.10 This section (paras 10.11-20) explains which LHA figure applies to you and what size of accommodation you qualify for.

10.11 LHA figures are set by the rent officer in Great Britain and the NIHE in Northern Ireland (para 10.21). In each area there is one figure for each size of accommodation in table 10.1. All the figures are available online [www]; they vary from area to area but can never be greater than the maximum amounts in the table.

10.9 HB 13C(2),(3); HB66+ 13C(2),(3); NIHB 14C(2),(3); NIHB66+ 14C(2),(3)

10.11 ROO 4B(2A),(2B),(3A),(3B), sch 3B para 2(2)(a); SI 2023/6 reg 2; NIED 3(2),(2A),(3),(3A), sch para 2(2)(a); NISR 2023/4 reg 2
Great Britain: https://lha-direct.voa.gov.uk/search.aspx
Northern Ireland: www.nihe.gov.uk/Housing-Help/Local-Housing-Allowance/Current-LHA-rent-levels

10.12   Each year's LHA figures apply from the first Monday in April (3rd April 2023) if your rent is due weekly or in multiples of a week; or 1st April in other cases (e.g. if your rent is due monthly or daily).

Table 10.1 **LHAs: national maximums**

Sizes of accommodation	National weekly maximums
(a) One-bedroom shared accommodation	£295.49
(b) One-bedroom self-contained accommodation	£295.49
(c) Two-bedroom dwellings	£365.92
(d) Three-bedroom dwellings	£441.86
(e) Four-bedroom dwellings	£593.75

In practice, actual LHAs are usually lower (para 10.24), and these figures only affect a small number of areas in inner London. For which size of accommodation applies to you, see paras 10.16-20.

Which LHA figure applies to you

10.13   The LHA figure that applies to you is the one for:

(a) the size of accommodation you qualify for (para 10.16); and

(b) the area your home is in (para 10.27).

When you claim HB

10.14   When you make a claim for HB, your LHA figure is the one that applies on your date of claim (table 16.1).

When your LHA figure changes

10.15   Changes in your LHA figure affect your HB as follows:

(a) when you qualify for a different size of accommodation (e.g. if someone moves in or out), your HB changes from the date the change in circumstances takes effect (para 17.11) or up to 12 months later in the case of a death (para 7.52);

(b) when you move home, your HB changes from the same date as the move (para 17.18);

T10.1   ROO sch 3B para 2(2)(b); SI 2020/371 reg 4; NIED sch para 2(2)(b); NISR 2020/53 reg 4

10.12   DAR 7A(2), 8(15);HB 12D(1),(2), 13C(1),(3); HB66+ 12D(1),(2), 13C(1),(3); NIDAR 7A(2), 8(15);
             NIHB 13D(1),(2), 14C(1),(3); NIHB66+ 13D(1),(2), 14C(1),(3)

10.13   HB 13D(1)(a),(b); HB66+ 13D(1)(a),(b); NIHB 14D(1)(a),(b); NIHB66+ 14D(1)(a),(b)

10.14   HB 13D(1)(a); HB66+ 13D(1)(a); NIHB 14D(1)(a); NIHB66+ 14D(1)(a)

10.15   DAR 7A(2), 8(15); HB 12D(2)(b), 13C(2),(3); HB66+ 12D(2)(b), 13C(2),(3); NIDAR 7A(2), 8(15);
             NIHB 13C(2)(b), 14C(2),(3); NIHB66+ 13C(2)(b), 14C(2),(3)

(c)   when the new figures apply in April, your HB changes from the date in para 10.12;

(d)   when the rent officer/NIHE corrects a wrongly calculated LHA figure (in practice this is rare), your HB changes from:

■   the date in para 10.12, if the new figure is higher, or

■   the Monday following the date of the correction, if the new figure is lower.

The size of the accommodation you qualify for

10.16   This is worked out as follows:

(a)   you qualify for accommodation with the appropriate number of bedrooms for the occupiers of your home: see table 11.1;

(b)   but the maximum number of bedrooms is always four;

(c)   and if you are the only occupier of your home, or you and your partner are, see para 10.18.

Which occupiers are taken into account

10.17   The LHA size criteria take account of the occupiers of your home. This means:

(a)   you (the claimant) and members of your family (partner, children and young persons: para 4.2);

(b)   non-dependants (para 4.26);

(c)   lodgers (para 4.36);

(d)   joint tenants who share your household (para 10.7): [2011] UKUT 156 (AAC); and

(e)   any other person who occupies your dwelling as their home (except joint tenants who maintain a separate household: para 10.8).

For further details see chapter 11.

One bedroom LHA figures

10.18   You qualify for one bedroom if:

(a)   you are a single claimant or couple without children;

(b)   there are no other occupiers in your home (para 10.17); and

(c)   you don't qualify for an additional bedroom for any of the reasons in paras 11.18-41.

But there are two LHA figures for one-bedroom accommodation, one for self-contained and one for shared accommodation. See table 10.2 for which of these applies to you.

10.16   HB 13D(2); HB66+ 13D(2); NIHB 14D(2); NIHB66+ 14D(2)

10.17   HB 13D(3),(12) – 'occupiers'; HB66+ 13D(3),(12); NIHB 14D(3),(10); NIHB66+ 14D(3),(10)

10.18   HB 13D(2)(a),(b); HB66+ 13D(2)(a),(b); NIHB 14D(2)(a),(b); NIHB66+ 14D(2)(a),(b)

When your home counts as self-contained

10.19   For the rules in table 10.2, your home counts as self-contained only if you have exclusive use of:

(a)   one room plus a bathroom and toilet (in the bathroom or separately) and a kitchen or cooking facilities; or

(b)   at least two rooms (counting only bedrooms and living rooms, but regardless of whether you share other facilities).

'Exclusive use' means the right to exclude others; and this must be a legal right, not just what happens in practice: [2011] UKUT 156 (AAC) and [2014] UKUT 36 (AAC). This has applied in the case of a couple who separated but remained in their home as joint tenants with a legal agreement that they each had exclusive use of part of it ([2018] UKUT 416 (AAC)). But it seems unlikely to apply to other joint tenants who maintain separate households (para 10.8).

Table 10.2 **LHAs: one-bedroom categories**

Your circumstances	Your LHA category
Single claimants aged 35 or over	
■ If your home counts as self-contained (para 10.19)	One-bedroom self-contained accommodation
■ Otherwise	One-bedroom shared accommodation
Single claimants aged under 35	
■ If you are in excepted groups (a) or (b) in para 10.20	One-bedroom self-contained accommodation
■ If your home counts as self-contained (para 10.19) and you are in excepted groups (c) to (f) in para 10.20	One-bedroom self-contained accommodation
■ Otherwise	One-bedroom shared accommodation
Couples of any age	
■ If your home counts as self-contained (para 10.19)	One-bedroom self-contained accommodation
■ If you or your partner are in excepted groups (a) or (b) in para 10.20	One-bedroom self-contained accommodation
■ Otherwise	One-bedroom shared accommodation

10.19   HB 13D(2)(b); HB66+ 13D(2)(b); NIHB 14D(2)(b); NIHB66+ 14D(2)(b)

T10.2   HB 13D(2)(a),(b); HB66+ 13D(2)(a),(b); NIHB 14D(2)(a),(b); NIHB66+ 14D(2)(a),(b)

> **Notes:**
> - This table applies when you qualify for only one bedroom (para 10.18).
> - Single claimants under 35 who qualify for one-bedroom shared accommodation are called 'young individuals' in HB law.
> - The shared accommodation rule doesn't amount to unlawful discrimination in the case of disabled people ([2020] UKUT 285 (AAC)).

Excepted groups for one-bedroom accommodation

10.20   In LHA cases (table 10.2) and also in rent referral cases (table 10.4(f)), you are in an excepted group if:

(a) you or your partner meet the conditions for a severe disability premium (para 12.25);

(b) you or your partner are aged under 25, and were previously:

- in social services care under a court order at any time after the age of 16, or
- provided with accommodation by social services;

(c) you are aged 25 or over but under 35, and are an ex-offender managed under a level 2 or 3 multi-agency public protection agreement (MAPPA) (HB Circular A12/2011); or

(d) you are aged 16 or over but under 35, and:

- you have occupied (or at any time formerly occupied) one or more hostels for homeless people for one or more periods totalling at least three months, and
- while you were there, you were offered and you accepted support with rehabilitation or resettlement within the community.

(e) you are a victim of, or have been threatened with, domestic violence (para 2.21) that occurred after you reached 16 and was from your partner or former partner, or your or their son, daughter, stepchild, grandchild, parent, stepparent, grandparent, sister, brother, aunt, uncle, niece, nephew or first cousin;

(f) you are a victim of modern slavery and this has been confirmed by a competent authority under the Trafficking Convention of 2005, e.g. the Home Office Competent Authority (HB A6/2002).

Excepted groups (e) and (f) were introduced on 1st October 2022.

How LHAs are set

10.21   This section explains how the rent officer (in Great Britain) or the NIHE (in Northern Ireland) sets the LHA figures and areas.

10.22   Rent officers are independent of the council. They are government employees in the Valuation Office Agency (in England), the Rent Officers Wales or the Rent Service Scotland.

10.20   HB 2(1),(1A),(1B) definition: 'young individual'; NIHB 2(1),(1A),(1B)
       LHA   13D(2)(a), 14D(2)(a)
       Rent referral   HB 13(6); NIHB 14(6)

Current LHA figures

10.23   LHA figures are announced at the end of January each year and apply from the beginning of April (para 10.12). For the years commencing April 2021, April 2022 and April 2023, they have been frozen at April 2020 levels.

April 2020 LHA levels

10.24   In April 2020 the LHA figures equalled:

(a) the rent at the 30th percentile of the rent officer's/NIHE's data for the year to 30th September 2019; or

(b) if lower, the weekly maximum in table 10.1.

10.25   The 'rent at the 30th percentile' meant the highest rent within the bottom 30% of rents in the rent officer's/NIHE's data. In broad terms this meant that people on HB could afford rents in the lowest third of the rental market.

10.26   For the April 2020 LHA figures, the rent officer/NIHE:

(a) used data obtained during the year ending on 30th September 2019;

(b) included rents on assured tenancies that were in a reasonable state of repair;

(c) excluded the value of all ineligible services (paras 8.28-31);

(d) excluded very high or very low rents that a landlord couldn't 'reasonably have been expected to obtain'; and

(e) excluded rents paid by people on HB.

The LHA areas

10.27   LHA areas are called 'broad rental market areas' (BRMAs) and are defined by postcodes. They are drawn up by the rent officer/NIHE so that:

(a) a person 'could reasonably be expected to live [there] having regard to facilities and services for the purposes of health, education, recreation, personal banking and shopping, taking account of the distance of travel, by public and private transport, to and from those facilities and services';

(b) they contain 'residential premises of a variety of types' held as a 'variety of tenancies'; and

(c) they contain 'sufficient privately rented premises' to ensure that the LHA figures 'are representative of the rents that a landlord might reasonably be expected to obtain in that area'.

They can only be changed on 1st April in any year, and only with the DWP's consent.

10.23-24   ROO 4B(2A),(2B), sch 3B para 2(2),(4); NIED 3(2),(2A), sch para 2(2); SI 2020/1519, reg 2; NISR 2021/14, reg 2

10.25   ROO sch 3B para 2(2)(a),(8); NIED sch para 2(2)(a),(8)

10.26   ROO sch 3B para 2(4),(5),(7); NIED sch para 2(4),(5),(7)

10.27   ROO 4B(1A),(3A), sch 3B paras 4, 5; NIED 3(1),(3), sch paras 4, 5

10.28 BRMAs in Great Britain are on average twice the size of council areas (following changes in the law since large areas were criticised in R (Heffernan) v the Rent Service). Their boundaries don't usually match council boundaries, so some councils are completely within one BRMA and others contain parts of more than one BRMA.

Appeals about LHA figures and areas

10.29 You can't appeal to the rent officer or to a tribunal about:

(a) the amount of an LHA;

(b) the area covered by a BRMA; or

(c) any other matter involving the rent officer's professional judgement.

But it may be possible to challenge these by judicial review (para 20.54).

Appeals about other matters

10.30 You can ask for a reconsideration and appeal to a tribunal (chapter 20) about:

(a) whether the LHA rules apply to you (para 10.4); or

(b) whether the authority has correctly decided the size or category of accommodation you qualify for (paras 10.16-20) and therefore has applied the correct LHA figure.

Or you can ask the rent officer to correct technical errors in their determinations (para 20.59) – for example if a wrong rent was identified as the 30th percentile in setting an LHA.

Rent referral rules: eligible rent

When the rent referral rules apply

10.31 The rent referral rules are becoming less common since they were largely replaced by the LHA rules in 2008. Paras 10.32-34 explain when they apply. For DWP guidance see GM A4.1330-2113.

If you have a private or non-profit landlord

10.32 If you have a private landlord (paras 7.21-22) or a non-profit landlord (para 9.18(a)), the rent referral rules apply when:

(a) you are a boarder (para 10.39); or

(b) you live in a hostel, caravan, mobile home or houseboat (paras 7.26-30); or

(c) you have a pre-2008 HB claim (para 7.36).

10.28   R (Heffernan) v the Rent Service [2008] UKHL 58 www.bailii.org/uk/cases/UKHL/2008/58.html

10.29   CPSA sch 7 para 6(2)(c); ROO 7A(4); NICPSA sch 7 para 6(2)(c); NIDAR 16(1) sch para 6

10.30   CPSA sch 7 para 6(1),(3); ROO 7A(4); NICPSA sch 7 para 6(1),(3); NIDAR 10A

10.31   HB 13C(2); HB66+ 13C(2); NIHB 14C(2); NIHB66+ 14C(2)

10.32   HB 13C(2),(5)(d),(e); HB66+ 13C(2),(5)(d),(e); NIHB 14C(2),(5)(d),(e), 15(3)(a),(4); NIHB66+ 14C(2),(5)(d),(e), 15(3)(a),(4)

If your landlord is a registered housing association

10.33   If your landlord is a registered housing association, the rent referral rules apply when the council considers:

(a) your rent is too high (working age or pension age HB); or

(b) your home is too large (pension age HB only).

These cases are very uncommon.

Exceptions

10.34   The rent referral rules don't apply when:

(a) your HB claim began in or before 1996 (para 7.37); or

(b) you have a registered rent or similar old tenancy (para 7.38); or

(c) you have a shared ownership tenancy (para 7.24).

How the rent referral rules work

10.35   In Great Britain:

(a) the rent officer is independent of the council;

(b) the council refers the details of your rent to the rent officer (para 10.38);

(c) the rent officer makes one or more rental valuations – these are called 'rent determinations' (table 10.4);

(d) the council uses these determinations to decide the amount of your eligible rent (table 10.4);

(e) but if your home is exempt accommodation, the determinations are advisory (paras 9.36-38).

In Northern Ireland, the NIHE itself makes the rent determinations and then uses them to decide the amount of your eligible rent. In the rest of this chapter we use both 'rent officer' and 'council' to include the NIHE.

10.33   HB 13C(5)(a), 14(2)(b), sch 2 para 3; HB66+ 13C(5)(a), 14(2)(b), sch 2 para 3;
           NIHB 14C(5)(a), 15(3)(b), sch 3 para 3; HB66+ 14C(5)(a), 15(3)(b), sch 3 para 3

10.34   CPR sch 3 para 4(1)(a); HB 14(2)(b), sch 2 paras 4-11A; HB66+ 14(2)(b), sch 2 paras 4-12
           NICPR sch 3 para 4(1)(a); NIHB 15(3)(b), sch 3 paras 4, 5; NIHB66+ 15(3)(b), sch 3 paras 4, 5

10.35   Housing Act 1996, s122; ROO 3, sch 1; HB 13(2),(3),(5),(7), 114A(1)(a),(6); HB66+ 13(2),(3),(5), 95A(1)(a),(6)
           NICBA 129(4); NIHB 14(2),(3),(5),(7), 15(1), sch 2; NIHB66+ 14(2),(3),(5),(7), 15(1), sch 2

When the council refers your rent to the rent officer

10.36   The council refers details of your rent to the rent officer:

(a)   when you claim HB;

(b)   when you move into a new home;

(c)   when you have a relevant change in your circumstances (table 10.3);

(d)   when 52 weeks have passed since the rent officer last provided figures;

(e)   up to one month before you move into a new home or renew your tenancy agreement, if you and your landlord request this (GM A4.2050-70).

10.37   But:

(a)   if the rent officer has already provided figures for your home (for example, because someone else claimed HB while they were living there), the council uses these, so long as they don't relate to different circumstances (table 10.3) and less than 52 weeks have passed since they were provided; or

(b)   if you live in a hostel (para 7.26), the council makes one referral to the rent officer each year for each type of room (single, double, shared, etc).

Table 10.3 **Relevant changes in rent referral cases**

Rent determinations are required in all these situations (para 10.36):

Changes that could affect the size of accommodation you qualify for

(a)   There is a change in the number of occupiers in your home – but this doesn't apply if you live in a hostel (para 10.37) or to the beginning or end of an armed forces absence (para 11.15).

(b)   A child in your home reaches the age of 10 or 16 – but only if your most recent rent determination included a size-related rent determination (table 10.4(b)).

(c)   There is a change in the household composition of the occupiers of your home (e.g. two people start or stop being a couple) – but only if your most recent rent determination included a size-related rent determination.

(d)   You start or stop qualifying for an additional bedroom for any of the reasons in para 11.19 (foster parents, overnight carers, and disabled people who need their own bedroom).

(e)   You start to meet the conditions for a single room rent determination (which applies to certain single claimants under the age of 35: table 10.2) – e.g. because you are a care-leaver and have reached the age of 22 (para 10.20).

10.36   HB 14(1)(a)-(h),(8) – 'change relating to a rent allowance'; HB66+14(1)(a)-(h),(8); NIDAR 4(5), 7(2)(d); NIHB 15(1), sch 3 para 2; NIHB66+ 15(1), sch 3 para 2

10.37   HB 14(1)(f),(g),(2),(7), sch 2 para 2; HB66+ 14(1)(f),(g),(2),(7), sch 2 para 2; NIDAR 7A(3); NIHB sch 3 para 2; NIHB66+ sch 3 para 2

T10.3   HB 14(1)(c),(8) – 'change relating to a rent allowance', sch 2 para 2; HB66+14(1)(c),(8), sch 2 para 2; NIDAR 4(5), 7(2)(d); NIHB 15(1), sch 3 para 2; NIHB66+ 15(1), sch 3 para 2

Other changes

(f)   There is a substantial change in the terms of your letting agreement or the condition of your home (e.g. your landlord has made improvements) – this applies whether or not your rent changes (but not if the only change is in your rent).

(g)   Your rent increases – but this only applies if:

 ▪   the increase is under a term of your letting agreement (which needn't be in writing but must be a term of your letting, not just a provision of law: CH/3590/2007);

 ▪   that term is the same (or substantially the same) as when your most recent rent determination was made; and

 ▪   in your most recent rent determination, your referred rent was used as your claim related rent (table 10.4(d)).

Note: Other increases in your rent don't count as a 'relevant change'. For moves, see paras 10.36-37.

The information the council gives the rent officer

10.38   The council gives the rent officer details of:

(a)   your tenancy;

(b)   your rent;

(c)   which eligible and ineligible charges are included in your rent; and

(d)   the occupiers of your home.

The rent officer's decision about who is a boarder

10.39   If your rent includes an element for meals, the rent officer makes a 'board and attendance determination'. This decides whether the meals amount to 'substantial board and attendance'. If they do, the rent referral rules apply to you; if they don't the LHA rules apply. To count as 'board and attendance', there must be an element of preparation, service and clearing away ('attendance') on the premises. And as a rule, anything valued at over 15% of the rent is taken to be 'substantial' and anything under 10% is not (Rent Officer Handbook [www]).

How the rent officer's figures are used to calculate your eligible rent

10.40   Table 10.4 shows the figures the rent officer gives the council and how these are used to calculate your eligible rent (except in exempt accommodation: paras 9.36-38). The rent officer either confirms your rent is reasonable, or makes one or more of the determinations in table 10.4 if it is too high or your home is too large (para 11.5). The rent officer's handbook [www] provides guidance about how the rent officer sets the figures.

10.38   HB 114A(6),(8),(9); HB66+ 95A(6),(8),(9)

10.39   HB 13C(5)(e), 13D(10), 114A(3)-(5); HB66+ 13C(5)(e), 13D(10), 95A(3)-(5); NIHB 14C(5)(e), sch 2 para 7(1); NIHB66+ 14C(5)(e), sch 2 para 7(1)
         https://tinyurl.com/RO-handbook see section on HB referrals, boarders

10.40   HB 13(2),(3),(5)(a),(7); HB66+13(2),(3),(5); NIHB 14(2),(3),(5)(a),(7); NIHB66+14(2),(3),(5)

Table 10.4 **Eligible rent in rent referral cases**

Rent officer figures

(a)	Significantly high rent determination	This is provided when your rent is high compared with rents in the area you live in.
(b)	Size-related rent determination	This is provided when your home is larger than you need (chapter 11).
(c)	Exceptionally high rent determination	This is provided when your home is at the top end of the market.
(d)	Claim-related rent	The rent officer always provides this. It equals the lowest of (a)-(c). Or if none of these applies to you, it equals your actual rent minus all ineligible charges.
(e)	Local reference rent	This is the mid-point of rents for your kind of accommodation in the area you live in. The rent officer provides this if it is lower than (d).
(f)	Single room rent	This is the mid-point of rents for one-bedroom shared accommodation in the area you live in. It only applies if you are the sole occupier of your home and don't fall within any of the excepted groups (para 10.20). The rent officer provides this if it is lower than (d).

Eligible rent and ineligible charges

Your eligible rent equals the lowest of (d)-(f). But all the figures have to be adjusted by the council or the rent officer to exclude ineligible service charges (paras 8.32-52).

(g)	Ineligible charges valued by the council	▪ Water charges (para 8.12)
		▪ Cleaning of your own accommodation (para 8.33(c))
		▪ Fuel for your own accommodation (para 8.34(b))
		▪ Meals (using the standard figures) (para 8.39)
		▪ Support and related services (para 8.41)
(h)	Ineligible charges valued by the rent officer	▪ Acquisition of furniture (para 8.48(b))
		▪ Day-to-day living expenses not included in (g) (para 8.52)

T10.4(a)-(f)   ROO sch 1 paras 1-6(1); NIHB 15(1), sch 2 paras 1-6(1); NIHB66+ 15(1), sch 2 paras 1-6(1)

T10.4(g)-(h)   ROO sch 1 paras 6(2A),(3), 7; HB 13(7), 114A(3)(d)-(f),(4),(6),(8)(a); HB66+ 13(7), 95A(3)(d)-(f),(4),(6),(8)(a)
               NIHB 14(7), sch 2 paras 6(2A),(3), 7; NIHB66+ 14(7), sch 2 paras 6(2A),(3), 7

Exceptions

- If you have one or more joint tenants who are not a member of your family (para 4.43), the figures apart from (f) are apportioned between you.
- If you live in a caravan, mobile home or houseboat, determination (b) doesn't apply.
- If you live in a hostel (paras 7.26-28), determinations (e) and (f) don't apply.
- If your landlord is a registered housing association, determination (f) doesn't apply.

When rent officer figures take effect

10.41   When you claim HB, the rent officer figures take effect from the day your HB starts. If your circumstances change, the new rent officer figures take effect when the change itself takes effect (chapter 17). If 52 weeks have passed, the new figures take effect as follows:

(a) If they go up, on the day after the 52 weeks run out, or if that isn't a Monday, on the preceding Monday;

(b) If they go down, on the day the council receives the rent officer's figures.

Appeals about rent and service charges

10.42   If you live in exempt accommodation (para 9.18) all decisions about rent and services are made by the council and appeals go to an independent tribunal (para 20.42).

10.43   In other rent referral cases:

(a) the rent officer makes all the determinations used in setting your eligible rent, so appeals about these (known as redeterminations) go to another rent officer (paras 20.55-59);

(b) the council values most ineligible service and other charges (table 10.4(g)), so appeals about these go to a tribunal (para 20.42);

(c) the rent officer values some less common service charges (table 10.4(h)), so appeals about this go to another rent officer as in (a).

T10.4 exceptions ROO 6(2), 7; HB 2(1) – 'young individual', 12C(2); HB66+ 12C(2)
                  NIHB 2(1), 13B(2), 15(3),(4), sch 2 paras 12, 13; NIHB66+13B(2), 15(3),(4), sch 2 paras 12, 13

10.41   DAR 8(6A); HB 12C, 14(1)(a); HB66+ 12C, 14(1)(a); NIDAR 8(6A); NIHB 13B, 15(1)(a), NIHB66+ 13B, 15(1)(a)

10.42   CPSA sch 7 para 6(1)-(4); DAR sch; HB/HB66+ old 12, 13; NICPSA sch 7 para 6(1)-(4); NIDAR sch; NIHB/NIHB66+ old 13, 14

10.43   ROO sch 1 paras 6(3), 7(3); HB 13(2),(3),(5),(7), 114A(3)(d)-(f),(4),(6),(8)(a); HB66+ 13(2),(3),(5),(7), 95A(3)(d)-(f),(4),(6),(8)(a)
                  NIHB 14(2),(3),(5),(7), sch 2 paras 6(3), 7(3); NIHB66+ 14(7), sch 2 paras 6(3), 7(3)

Example: Eligible rent in a rent referral case

Suzie is aged 52 and has been getting HB on her home since 2007. She lives in a flat and currently pays her private landlord £110 per week which includes some ineligible services (table 8.1).

This is a rent referral case (table 10.32(c)) and the claim related rent is based on a one room dwelling (para 11.5, table 11.1). The council refers the rent because 52 weeks have passed since the last one was made (para 10.36). The rent officer gives the following determinations:

- a claim-related rent of £110 per week (table 10.4(d));
- no local reference rent (table 10.4(e));
- a service charge determination of £5 per week (table 10.4(h)).

The council calculates Suzie's weekly eligible rent as follows (para 10.40) and table 10.4:

claim related rent	£110.00
minus service charge determination	– £5.00
equals eligible rent	£105.00

Chapter 11 **The size of your home**

- The size criteria and eligible rent: see paras 11.1-9.
- Which occupiers are included: see paras 11.10-16.
- How many bedrooms you qualify for: see paras 11.17-20.
- Details of who qualifies for additional bedrooms: see paras 11.21-41.
- What counts as a bedroom: see paras 11.42-44.

The size criteria and eligible rent

11.1　　This chapter explains what size of home you can get HB towards, and how this affects your eligible rent.

11.2　　We call these rules the 'size criteria'. They are also sometimes called the 'bedroom tax' or the 'spare room subsidy'. They are similar to the rules used in UC (volume 1 chapter 7) but not always identical.

If you fall within the social renter rules

11.3　　If your eligible rent is calculated using the social renter rules (para 9.4):

   (a) you qualify for the number of bedrooms in table 11.1 (with no upper limit);

   (b) your eligible rent is normally reduced if you have more bedrooms than this in your home (paras 9.12).

These rules apply if you are on working age HB, unless any of the exceptions in table 9.1 apply. They never apply if you are on pension age HB.

If you fall within the LHA rules

11.4　　If your eligible rent is calculated using the LHA rules (para 10.4):

   (a) you qualify for the number of bedrooms in table 11.1, but only up to a maximum of four bedrooms;

   (b) if you qualify for only one bedroom, there are further rules about what category of accommodation you qualify for (table 10.2);

   (c) your eligible rent is normally limited to the LHA figure for the size (or category) of accommodation you qualify for (para 10.5).

These rules apply whether you are on pension age HB or working age HB.

11.3　　HB B13(2)(b),(3),(5); HB66+ 12B(1),(6); NIHB B14(2)(b),(3),(5); NIHB66+ 13A(1),(7)

11.4　　HB 13D(2)-(3B); HB66+ 13D(2)-(3B); NIHB 14D(2)-(3B); NIHB66+ 14D(2)-(3B)

If you fall within the rent referral rules

11.5   If your eligible rent is calculated using the rent referral rules (para 10.31):

(a) you qualify for the number of bedrooms (with no upper limit) and living rooms in table 11.1;

(b) if you live in one room, or are single and under 35, there are further rules about the category of accommodation you qualify for (table 10.4(f) and para 10.20);

(c) your eligible rent is normally limited to the rent officer's or NIHE's rent determination for the size (or category) of accommodation you qualify for (table 10.4).

These rules apply whether you are on pension age HB or working age HB.

If you fall within the old scheme rules

11.6   If your eligible rent is calculated using the old scheme rules (para 9.17), this chapter doesn't apply. But other rules about the size of your accommodation may affect your HB (paras 9.23).

Discretionary help

11.7   If your eligible rent is reduced because of the size criteria, you may be able to get discretionary housing payments (paras 23.8-10).

The size criteria and unlawful discrimination

11.8   The European Court of Human Rights has decided that the size criteria don't unlawfully discriminate against:

(a) claimants who have a disabled adult child living with them (JD v UK);

(b) separated parents with shared care of a child (R (Cotton and Others) v SSWP);

(c) gypsy travellers ([2019] UKUT 43 (AAC)).

11.9   Other cases resulted in changes to the law so that the size criteria no longer discriminate between adults and children (R (Daly and Others) v SSWP) or against women living in sanctuary schemes (A v UK).

11.5   HB 13(2),(4),(6); HB66+ 13(2),(3); ROO sch 1 para 2(1), sch 2 paras 1-2;
          NIHB 14(2),(5), sch 2 paras 2(1), 10-11; NIHB66+ 14(2),(3), sch 2 paras 2(1), 10-11

11.8   JD and A v UK [2019] ECHR 753, www.bailii.org/eu/cases/ECHR/2019/753.html
          R (Cotton and Others) v SSWP [2014] EWHC Admin 3437, www.bailii.org/ew/cases/EWHC/Admin/2014/3437.html

11.9   R (Daly and Others) v SSWP [2016] UKSC 58, www.bailii.org/uk/cases/UKSC/2016/58.html

Which occupiers are included

11.10   The size criteria take account of the occupiers of your dwelling. This means:

(a) you (the claimant) and the members of your family (partner, children and young persons: paras 4.4 and 4.14);

(b) non-dependants (para 4.26);

(c) lodgers (para 4.36);

(d) joint tenants (para 11.16); and

(e) any other person who occupies your dwelling as their home – for example family members of people in (b)-(d), resident carers (para 4.33) and employees (para 4.50).

See paras 11.11-41 for further details and exceptions.

11.11   The council decides who is an occupier (not, for example, the rent officer: R v Swale BC HBRB ex p Marchant). In doing so it should have regard to the general HB rules about this (chapter 3); and even though some of the law was written to apply to claimants and partners, it should be adapted to apply to non-dependants (for example): [2010] UKUT 129 (AAC). A decision about which occupiers are included is appealable to a tribunal: [2010] UKUT 79 (AAC).

Children and young persons

11.12   The size criteria take into account children and young persons for whom you, your partner or someone else in your household is responsible (para 4.18), including those who are temporarily absent (para 4.24).

11.13   The following are not included:

(a) children and young persons who are foster children or are placed for adoption (table 4.2(a) and (b)) – but in these cases see paras 11.21-24;

(b) children and young persons who don't live with you, or don't normally live with you (table 4.2(c) and (e)).

Students and others gradually leaving home

11.14   When a student starts at a university and lives in a hall of residence, coming home frequently, it is correct to include them as an occupier of the parent's home: [2009] UKUT 67 (AAC), [2010] UKUT 129 (AAC). By perhaps the second year, especially if the student has taken on the rent of a flat or house, this is less likely to be the case. There is no fixed rule, each case depending on its facts.

11.10   Social renter: HB B13(5); NIHB B14(5)
          Private renter (LHA): HB 13D(3),(12); HB66+ 13D(3),(12); NIHB 14D(3),(10); NIHB66+ 14D(3),(10)
          Rent referral: ROO sch 2 para 1; NIHB sch 2 para 10; NIHB66+ sch 2 para 10

11.11   R v Swale BC HBRB ex p Marchant 09/11/99 CA 32 HLR 856
          http://tinyurl.com/Swale-Marchant

11.12-13 All: HB 2(1) definitions: 'child' etc; HB66+ 2(1); NIHB 2(1); NIHB66+ 2(1)
          Social renter: HB B13(5)(ba)-(e); NIHB B14(5)(b)-(f)
          Private renter (LHA): HB 13D(3)(ba)-(e); HB66+ 13D(3)(ba)-(e); NIHB 14D(3)(ba)-(e); NIHB66+ 14D(3)(ba)-(e)
          Rent referral: ROO sch 2 para 1(ba)-(e); NIHB sch 2 para 10(ba)-(e); NIHB66+ sch 2 para 10(ba)-(e)

Armed forces absences

11.15 If your or your partner's son, daughter, step-son or step-daughter is in the armed forces (regular or reserve), he or she continues to count as an occupier of your home during an absence on operations, so long as he or she:

    (a) was a non-dependant (paras 4.26-32) before that absence (regardless of whether a non-dependant deduction then applied); and

    (b) intends to return to reside in your dwelling when that absence ends.

Joint tenants

11.16 For the social renter and rent referral rules (paras 9.4, 10.31), the size criteria take into account all joint tenants (paras 4.42-46). For the LHA rules (para 10.4), they take into account joint tenants who share your household but not those who maintain a separate household.

How many bedrooms you qualify for

General rules

11.17 The general rules about how many bedrooms you qualify for are given in table 11.1. They take account of all the occupiers in your dwelling (paras 11.10-16).

Sharing a bedroom

11.18 The only occupiers who can be counted as sharing a bedroom (table 11.1) are:

    (a) couples (para 4.5) – and for the size criteria this appears to include (only) two members of a polygamous marriage (table 1.1);

    (b) children (para 4.15) – and if children could share bedrooms in different ways, you qualify for the smaller number of bedrooms (example 2 and para 11.36);

but not young persons (para 4.16) or anyone else aged 16 or over. If a couple or a child can't share a bedroom, see paras 11.34-41.

Additional bedrooms: carers and disabled people

11.19 You may qualify for an additional bedroom for someone in your home who:

    (a) is a foster parent, or has a child placed with them for adoption (paras 11.21-24); or

    (b) requires overnight care from a non-resident carer (paras 11.25-33); or

    (c) can't share a bedroom due to their disability (paras 11.34-41).

11.15   All: HB 2(1) definition: 'member of armed forces away on operations'; HB66+ 2(1); NIHB 2(1); NIHB66+ 2(1)
         Social renter: HB B13(8); NIHB B14(8)
         Private renter (LHA): HB 13D(12); HB66+ 13D(12); NIHB 14D(10); NIHB66+ 14D(10)
         Rent referral: ROO sch 2 para 2(4); NIHB sch 3 para 2(4); NIHB66+ sch 3 para 2(4)

11.16   See footnote to para 11.10

11.17-18   All: HB 2(1) definitions: 'child', 'couple'; HB66+ 2(1); NIHB 2(1); NIHB66+ 2(1)
         Social renter: HB B13(5); NIHB B14(5)
         Private renter (LHA): HB 13D(3); HB66+ 13D(3); NIHB 14D(3); NIHB66+ 14D(3)
         Rent referral: ROO sch 2 para 1; NIHB sch 2 para 10; NIHB66+ sch 2 para 10

11.20 You could qualify for one or more additional bedrooms under each of para 11.19(a), (b) and (c). But if you fall within the LHA rules, the maximum number of bedrooms (under the general rules and these rules) is always four.

Table 11.1 **The HB size criteria**

The social renter, LHA and rent referral size criteria (paras 11.3-5) are based on the occupiers of your dwelling (paras 11.10-16).

Bedrooms (all size criteria)

You qualify for one bedroom for each of the following occupiers:

- each couple (para 4.5);
- each other person aged 16 or over;
- two children under 16 of the same sex;
- two children under 10 of the same or opposite sex;
- each other child under 16.

Additional bedrooms (all size criteria)

You may qualify for one or more additional bedrooms for the following occupiers:

- a foster parent or pre-adopter (paras 11.21-24);
- a person who requires an overnight carer (paras 11.25-33);
- a disabled person who can't share a bedroom (paras 11.34-41).

Living rooms (rent referral size criteria only)

When the social renter or LHA rules apply, living rooms are ignored. But when the rent referral rules apply, you qualify for living rooms as follows:

- one if there are one to three occupiers;
- two if there are four to six occupiers;
- three if there are seven or more occupiers.

This applies regardless of the age of the occupiers.

Notes:

- When the LHA rules apply, the maximum number of bedrooms you can qualify for (including additional bedrooms) is four.
- When the LHA or rent referral rules apply, there are further rules about one-bedroom accommodation (para 10.18 and table 10.4(f)).

T11.1   Social renter: HB B13(5)-(9); NIHB B14(5)-(9)
         Private renter (LHA): HB 13D(2)-(3B),(12); HB66+ 13D(2)-(3B),(12); NIHB 14D(2)-(3B),(10); NIHB66+ 14D(2)-(3B),(10)
         Rent referral: ROO sch 2 paras 1, 1A, 1B, 2, 3; NIHB sch 2 paras 10, 10A, 10B, 11, 15; NIHB66+ sch 2 para 10, 10A, 10B, 11, 15

Examples: bedrooms – general rules

1. A lone parent has two children: a boy aged 7 and a girl aged 12.

Three bedrooms are allowed: one for the lone parent, and one each for the children (because they are not counted as sharing a bedroom: table 11.1).

2. A couple have four children: girls aged 8 and 12 and boys aged 5 and 14.

Three bedrooms are allowed: one for the couple, one for the two girls and one for the two boys (because this is fewer than if the two younger children shared a bedroom and the two older children had a bedroom each: para 11.18).

3. A lone parent has two young persons: daughters aged 17 and 19.

Three bedrooms are allowed: one for the claimant, and one each for the young persons (table 11.1).

4. A single claimant has two non-dependants: sons aged 21 and 25.

Three bedrooms are allowed: one for the claimant, and one each for the non-dependants (table 11.1).

5. A couple have a child of their own, a foster child, and two non-dependants who are themselves a couple.

Under the general rules, three bedrooms are allowed: one for the couple, one for their own child, and one for the non-dependent couple. But an additional bedroom is allowed because they are foster parents (para 11.21).

Foster parents and pre-adopters

11.21　　You may qualify for one or more additional bedrooms if an occupier of your home:

(a) is a foster parent (in Scotland a kinship carer) who has a child or young person placed with them; or

(b) has been approved as a foster parent (kinship carer) and is waiting for a placement or between placements – but only for up to 52 weeks in each period without a placement; or

(c) has a child or young person placed with them prior to adoption.

We use 'foster parent or pre-adopter' to mean any of these.

11.22　　This rule can only apply to you, your partner, or (only if you fall within the social renter rules) a joint tenant or the partner of a joint tenant.

11.21-24　　All: HB 2(1) definition: 'qualifying parent or carer'; HB66+ 2(1); NIHB 2(1); NIHB66+ 2(1)

Social renter: HB B13(6)(b),(7),(9); NIHB B14(6)(b),(7),(9)

Private renter (LHA): HB 13D(3A)(b),(3B); HB66+ 13D(3A)(b),(3B); NIHB 14D(3A)(b),(3B); NIHB66+ 14D(3A)(b),(3B)

Rent referral: ROO sch 2 paras 1A(b), 1B, 3; NIHB sch 2 paras 10, 10A(b), 10B, 15; NIHB66+ sch 2 paras 10, 10A(b), 10B, 15

Social renters

11.23 When you fall within the social renter rules, you are allowed:

(a) one additional bedroom if you or your partner are a foster parent or pre-adopter; and/or

(b) one additional bedroom if a joint tenant or their partner is a foster parent or pre-adopter.

So you could qualify for one additional bedroom under (a), or one under (b), or both of these. And in each case only one is allowed even when someone has more than one child or young person placed with them.

Private renters

11.24 When you fall within the LHA or rent referral rules, only para 11.23(a) applies. So you could qualify for one additional bedroom under (a), but not more.

People who need overnight care

11.25 You may qualify for one or more additional bedrooms if an occupier of your home:

(a) requires overnight care (para 11.29); and

(b) has arrangements in place for this (paras 11.30-31); and

(c) has an actual bedroom in your dwelling (para 11.32) that is in addition to those allowed for anyone else.

You may also qualify if the person is waiting to move in or is temporarily absent (para 11.33).

11.26 This rule can apply to any occupier of your dwelling (para 11.10). For example, you, your partner, a child or young person, a non-dependant, a joint tenant, and so on. Unlike the rest of this chapter, this rule can also apply to a child or young person who is placed with you or your partner as a foster child or prior to adoption.

Social renters

11.27 When you fall within the social renter rules, you are allowed:

(a) one additional bedroom if any occupier of your dwelling requires overnight care; or

(b) two additional bedrooms – but only if:

- you have one or more joint tenants (para 4.42), and
- at least one joint tenant or their partner requires overnight care, and
- at least one other occupier (not a joint tenant or their partner) requires overnight care.

So you could qualify for one additional bedroom under (a), or two under (b), but not more.

Private renters

11.28 When you fall within the LHA or rent referral rules, only para 11.27(a) applies. So you could qualify for one additional bedroom under (a), but not more.

11.25-28   All: HB 2(1) definition: 'person who requires overnight care'; HB66+ 2(1); NIHB 2(1); NIHB66+ 2(1)
Social renter: HB B13(6)(a),(ab),(7),(9); HB66+ B13(6)(a),(ab),(7),(9); NIHB B13(6)(a),(ab),(7),(9); NIHB66+ B13(6)(a),(ab),(7),(9)
Private renter (LHA): HB 13D(3A)(a),(3B); HB66+ 13D(3A)(a),(3B); NIHB 14D(3A)(a),(3B); NIHB66+ 14D(3A)(a),(3B)
Rent referral: ROO sch 2 paras 1A(a), 1B, 3; NIHB sch 2 paras 10, 10A(a), 10B, 15; NIHB66+ sch 2 paras 10, 10A(a), 10B, 15

The need for overnight care

11.29   An occupier of your dwelling 'requires overnight care' (para 11.25) if they:

(a) are in receipt of:

- the daily living component of PIP or (in Scotland) adult disability payment,
- the highest or middle rate of the care component of DLA or (in Scotland) child disability payment,
- attendance allowance, or constant attendance allowance paid with an industrial injury pension, or
- an armed forces independence payment; or

(b) don't receive any of the above, but have sufficient evidence to show that they require overnight care.

For example, someone who gets the lower rate of the care component of disability living allowance doesn't meet (a), but could meet (b), and the fact of getting the lower rate can be used as evidence of this ([2014] UKUT 325 (AAC)). Or someone who hasn't claimed any of the benefits in (a) could meet (b).

The arrangements for overnight care

11.30   For an additional bedroom to be allowed (para 11.25), the person requiring overnight care (or someone on their behalf) must reasonably require, and have in fact arranged, that one or more people who don't occupy your dwelling as their home:

(a) are engaged in providing the overnight care;

(b) regularly stay overnight in your dwelling for that purpose (para 11.31); and

(c) are provided with an additional bedroom for that purpose (para 11.32).

11.31   The carer could be the same person on each night a carer is required, or there could be a rota of carers. It is not enough to require a carer only by day. The carer(s) must stay overnight regularly. 'Regularly' does not mean normally, ordinarily or at reasonably even intervals, but is closer to habitually, customarily or commonly; so the question is whether the need for overnight care 'arises steadily and often enough to require a bedroom to be kept for the purpose', and a minority of nights can be enough: [2014] UKUT 325 (AAC).

11.32   There must be an actual bedroom provided for the carer(s), and it must be additional to those used by you, your family and the other occupiers of your dwelling. In this context, the Upper Tribunal has held that a bedroom means a room which has a bed in or is used for sleeping in: [2014] UKUT 48 (AAC). In that case, the claimant rented a two bedroom bungalow. He qualified for one bedroom for himself and his wife (table 11.1), but on medical advice they slept apart – one in each bedroom. Their daughter was an overnight carer, and she slept in a portable bed or sofa in the lounge. This met the condition for an additional bedroom. For further considerations about what is a bedroom, see paras 11.42-44 and table 11.2.

11.29-30   HB 2(1) definitions: 'attendance allowance', 'person who requires overnight care'; HB66+ 2(1); NIHB 2(1); NIHB66+ 2(1)

Examples: People who require overnight care

1. A couple have a child who requires overnight care

The child meets all the conditions (paras 11.29-32) and their home has three bedrooms which include the one where the child's overnight carer stays. Three bedrooms are allowed: one for the couple, one for the child, and one for the carer to use.

2. A joint tenant who requires overnight care

A brother and sister are joint tenants of a social landlord. The brother meets all the conditions (paras 11.29-32) and their home has three bedrooms, which include the one where his overnight carers stay. Three bedrooms are allowed: one each for the brother and sister and one for the carers to use. (This applies in each claim if they both claim, see para 9.7.)

Overnight care: waiting to move in and temporary absence

11.33   An additional bedroom is also allowed if:

(a) the person requiring overnight care (paras 11.26-28) is waiting to move in or temporarily absent; and

(b) there is an additional bedroom now, and the other arrangements in para 11.30 will be in place when they move in or return.

'Waiting to move in' and 'temporarily absent' have the same meanings as in paras 3.5-12 (adapting these as described in para 11.11).

Disabled people who can't share a bedroom

11.34   You may qualify for one or more additional bedrooms if an occupier of your home who would normally be expected to share a bedroom can't do so because of a disability (paras 11.39-41).

11.35   This rule:

(a) can only apply to couples, and to children (aged under 16) – apart from a foster child or a child placed for adoption;

(b) can't apply to single people, or to young persons (aged 16 or over) – because they qualify for their own bedroom under the general rules (table 11.1).

The couple or child can be any of the occupiers of your dwelling (para 11.10). For example, you and your partner, a child of yours, a couple who are non-dependants, a child of a joint tenant and so on.

11.36   If there are two or more children (para 11.18) in your dwelling, first a bedroom is allowed for each child who can't share a bedroom, then a bedroom or bedrooms are allowed under the general rules (table 11.1) for the other child(ren).

11.34-38   All: HB 2(1) definitions: 'child who cannot share a bedroom', 'member of a couple who cannot share a bedroom', (6);
HB66+ 2(1),(6); NIHB 2(1),(6); NIHB66+ 2(1),(6)
Social renter: HB B13(5)(za),(zb),(ba); NIHB B14(5)(za),(zb),(c);
Private renter (LHA): HB 13D(3)(za),(zb),(ba); HB66+ 13D(3)(za),(zb),(ba); NIHB 14D(3)(za),(zb),(ba); NIHB66+ 14D(3)(za),(zb),(ba)
Rent referral: ROO sch 2 paras 1(za),(zb),(ba),3

Social renters

11.37   When you fall within the social renter rules, you are allowed:

(a) one additional bedroom for each couple who can't share a bedroom; and/or

(b) one additional bedroom for each child who can't share a bedroom.

So you could qualify for one or more additional bedrooms under (a) or (b), or both of these.

Private renters

11.38   When you fall within the LHA or rent referral rules, para 11.37 applies. But for each additional bedroom you are allowed, there must be an actual bedroom in your dwelling (paras 11.42-44) that is in addition to those allowed for anyone else.

Examples: Disabled people who can't share a bedroom

1. A couple can't share a bedroom

The couple meets all the conditions (para 11.39) and their home has two bedrooms. Two bedrooms are allowed: one for each of them.

2. A lone parent has three children, one is disabled

Two of the children are twin girls aged 12, one of whom is disabled and meets all the conditions (para 11.40). The other child is a boy aged 14, and their home has four bedrooms. Four bedrooms are allowed: one for the lone parent, one for the disabled child, and two for the other children because they aren't expected to share (para 11.36 and table 11.1).

Couples who can't share a bedroom

11.39   A couple meet the conditions for an additional bedroom if one partner is (or both partners are):

(a) due to their disability, not reasonably able to share a bedroom with their partner; and

(b) in receipt of:

- the daily living component of PIP or (in Scotland) adult disability payment,

- the highest or middle rate of the care component of DLA, or (in Scotland) child disability payment,

- the higher rate of attendance allowance, or

- armed forces independence payment.

11.39-40   HB 2(1) definitions: 'attendance allowance', 'child who cannot share a bedroom', 'member of a couple who cannot share a bedroom';
            HB66+ 2(1); NIHB 2(1); NIHB66+ 2(1)

Children who can't share a bedroom

11.40 A child (under the age of 16) meets the conditions for an additional bedroom if he or she is:

(a) due to disability, not reasonably able to share a bedroom with another child; and

(b) entitled to (para 12.31) the highest or middle rate of the care component of DLA or (in Scotland) child disability payment.

11.41 DWP advice in relation to children is in circular HB A21/2013. This focuses on whether the child requires overnight care and advises authorities to 'keep in mind the policy intention which is to safeguard the wellbeing of children and prevent them being put at risk of physical harm or having their sleep frequently and significantly disrupted by… sharing a bedroom when it is inappropriate to do so because of severe disability' (HB A21/2013 paras 10-11).

What counts as a bedroom

11.42 Whether a particular room in your home is or isn't a bedroom can be important when the council is deciding the following matters, or when you are appealing about them:

(a) if you fall within the social renter rules, whether you have more actual bedrooms than you qualify for in your HB (para 9.12);

(b) in all cases, whether you have enough actual bedrooms to qualify for an additional bedroom in your HB (paras 11.32 and 11.38).

11.43 There is no definition in the HB regulations of what counts as a bedroom, but there have been a number of court and Upper Tribunal decisions about this. These are summarised in table 11.2.

11.44 The council is entitled to use its judgment in deciding whether a room is or is not a bedroom (para 20.24). Initially it is likely to base this decision on how your landlord has categorised the rooms in your home (circular HB/CTB A4/2012), but it is not bound by this and should consider each case on its individual details in the light of the case law.

Table 11.2 **What counts as a bedroom: case law**

Assessing the room. The Court of Session has held that whether a room is a bedroom is determined by 'an objective assessment of the property as vacant which is not related to the residents or what their actual use or needs might be' ([2017] AACR 41). In the same way, the Court of Appeal has held that the assessment should be 'carried out… in respect of a nominally vacant house' and that 'the characteristics of the particular individuals are irrelevant' ([2019] AACR 27).

The term 'bedroom'. The term 'bedroom' has its ordinary or familiar English meaning ([2015] AACR 21). The landlord's designation of the room or its description in the building's plans

---

T11.2   [2017] AACR 41, was [2017] CSH 35;
         [2019] AACR 27, is SSWP v Hockley [2019] EWCA Civ 1080;
         [2015] AACR 21, was [2014] UKUT 525 (AAC)

can be of use in borderline cases rather than being conclusive ([2015] AACR 21; [2018] UKUT 180 (AAC)). And a room can stop counting as a bedroom if exceptional circumstances relating to the physical or mental disability of an occupier mean it is now used as a living room ([2015] UKUT 282 (AAC)).

The description of the room by the landlord or in the building's plans. The council can take account of the description of the room by the original or current landlord (for example in the letting agreement or marketing materials) or in the plans or designs for the building. But this is 'a starting point' and is not conclusive ([2015] AACR 21).

Practical factors. Factors to be considered include '(a) size, configuration and overall dimensions, (b) access, (c) natural and electric lighting, (d) ventilation, and (e) privacy', taking account of the adults and children referred to in the regulations (para 11.10), and the relationship of the room to the other rooms in the house ([2015] AACR 21, [2018] UKUT 180 (AAC)). So long as the room is accessible, it is not a requirement that the door opens all the way ([2020] UKUT 247 (AAC)). It should be possible to get into bed from within the room, and there should be somewhere to put clothes and a glass of water, for example a bedside cabinet with drawers ([2016] UKUT 164 (AAC); [2017] UKUT 443 (AAC)).

Overcrowding and unfitness. The overcrowding rules differ from the size criteria, taking into account living rooms as well as bedrooms, but they can sound 'warning bells' that a room with very small dimensions may not be a bedroom ([2015] AACR 21); [2016] UKUT 164 (AAC); [2017] UKUT 443 (AAC)). A room contaminated with asbestos cannot be counted as a bedroom ([2018] UKUT 287 (AAC)).

Chapter 12 **Applicable amounts**

- What is an applicable amount: see paras 12.1-3.
- Personal allowances for you and your family: see paras 12.4-18.
- Additional amounts for disability and caring: see paras 12.19-50.
- General rules: see paras 12.51-55.

What is an applicable amount

12.1 Your 'applicable amount' represents your basic living expenses. It is compared to your income when your HB is calculated (paras 6.4-6). It is also used to decide other HB matters, such as the earnings disregards (tables 14.5 and 14.7).

How much is your applicable amount?

12.2 Your applicable amount is the total of:

(a) a personal allowance for you, or for you and your partner (paras 12.5-8);

(b) up to two (or sometimes more) personal allowances for children and young persons in your family (paras 12.9-18); and

(c) additional amounts if someone in your family or someone you provide care for is disabled or long-term sick (paras 12.19-50).

12.3 In this chapter a 'single person' means a single claimant or lone parent. For these and other family terms see table 1.1.

Personal allowances

12.4 This section explains which personal allowances are included in your applicable amount. The figures are in table 12.1.

Personal allowances for you/your partner

12.5 You qualify for a personal allowance for yourself, or for you and your partner:

(a) if you are a single person you get the single rate;

(b) if you are a couple you get the couple rate;

(c) if you are a polygamous marriage you get the couple rate plus the polygamous spouse rate for each spouse beyond two.

These are awarded at one of the rates in paras 12.6-8.

12.2   CBA 135; NICBA 131; HB 22(1)(a),(b),(d)-(f), sch 3; HB66+ 22(a),(b),(e), sch 3; NIHB 20(1)(a),(b),(d)-(f), sch 4; NIHB66+ 20(a),(b),(e), sch 4

12.5   HB 22(1)(a), sch 3 para 1; HB66+ 22(1)(a), sch 3 para 1; NIHB 20(1)(a), sch 4 para 1; NIHB66+ 20(1)(a), sch 4 para 1

Table 12.1 **Weekly HB applicable amounts: 2023-24**

Personal allowances

Single person	new pension age rate	£201.05
	old pension age rate	£217.00
	working age rate	£84.80
	lower rate	£67.20
Couple	new pension age rate	£306.85
	old pension age rate	£324.70
	working age rate	£133.30
	lower rate	£101.50
Polygamous spouse	new pension age rate	£105.80
	old pension age rate	£107.70
	working age/lower rate	£48.50
Child or young person	usually up to two amounts	£77.78

Additional amounts: any age

Disabled child premium	each child/young person	£74.69
Enhanced disability premium (child)	each child/young person	£30.17
Family premium	old HB cases	£18.53
Severe disability premium	single rate	£76.40
	double rate	£152.80
Carer premium	Claimant/partner/each	£42.75

Additional amounts: working age only

Disability premium	single person	£39.85
	couple	£56.80
Enhanced disability premium (adult)	single person	£19.55
	couple	£27.90
Support component	single person/couple	£44.70
WRA component	single person/couple	£33.70

Note: Examples are later in this chapter.

T12.1   HB sch 3 paras 1, 2, 20, 25, 26; HB66+ sch 3 paras 1, 2, 12; SI 2023/316;
         NIHB sch 4 paras 1, 2, 20, 25, 26; NIHB66+ sch 4 paras 1, 2, 12

Pension age rate

12.6   There are two pension age rates depending on when you reached age 66:

(a) the new pension age rate applies if you are:

- a single person and reached 66 on or after 1st April 2021, or

- a couple (or polygamous marriage) and at least one of you reached 66 on or after that date;

(b) the old pension age rate applies if you are:

- a single person and reached 66 before 1st April 2021, or

- a couple (or polygamous marriage) and both (or all) of you reached 66 on or before that date.

Working age rate

12.7   The working age rate applies if you are:

(a) a single person and are aged under 66; or

(b) a couple (or polygamous marriage) and both (or all) of you are aged under 66.

Lower rate

12.8   The lower age rate only applies if you are:

(a) a single claimant under 25 or a lone parent under 18, and aren't on the main phase of ESA (para 12.47); or

(b) a couple (or polygamous marriage) and are both (or all) under 18, and you (the claimant) aren't on the main phase of ESA.

Personal allowances: children and young persons

12.9   You qualify for personal allowances for the children and young persons in your family, but in many cases there is a 'two child limit' (paras 12.10-18).

The two child limit

12.10   The two child limit applies to personal allowances for children/young persons, but not to premiums (paras 12.22-23). The Court of Appeal has ruled that it isn't unlawful discrimination (R(SC and Others) v SSWP [2019] EWCA Civ 615) [www].

How the two child limit works

12.11   If you have one child/young person in your family, you get a personal allowance for him or her. Or if you have two, you get personal allowances for each of them.

12.6   HB66+ sch 3 para 1(1)(b),(2)(b),(4); NIHB66+ sch 4 para 1(1)(b),(2)(b),(4)

12.7   HB sch 3 para 1(1)(a),(b),(2)(a),(b),(3)(a),(b); NIHB sch 4 para 1(1)(a),(b),(2)(a),(b),(3)(a),(b)

12.8   HB sch 3 para 1(1)(c),(2)(c),(3)(c); NIHB sch 4 para 1(1)(c),(2)(c),(3)(c)

12.9   HB 22(1)(b), sch 3 para 2(1); HB66+ 22(1)(b), sch 3 para 2(1); NIHB 20(1)(b), sch 4 para 2(1); NIHB66+ 20(1)(b), sch 4 para 2(1)

12.10-11   HB 22(1)(b); HB66+ 22(1)(b); NIHB 20(1)(b); NIHB66+ 20(1)(b) www.bailii.org/ew/cases/EWCA/Civ/2019/615.html

12.12   But if you have three or more, you only get two personal allowances for them unless you qualify for more because:

(a) you have claimed CTC (paras 12.13-16); or

(b) you get transitional protection (paras 12.17-18).

Exception if you have claimed child tax credit

12.13   This exception to the two child limit applies if:

(a) you have claimed CTC; and

(b) your CTC assessment included more than two children/young persons (para 12.15).

You don't have to be getting CTC. It is enough if you were assessed for it but weren't awarded it (e.g. because of the level of your income). The council can ask to see your CTC decision notice as evidence of this.

12.14   When this exception applies to you, you qualify for an HB personal allowance for each child/young person who is included in your CTC assessment.

12.15   Your CTC can include more than two children/young persons if one or more of them:

(a) is adopted or placed with you for adoption;

(b) receives non-parental care from you and:

   ▪   lives with you under formal arrangements made by social services or a court, or confirmed by you getting guardian's allowance for them, or

   ▪   lives with you under informal arrangements made by you and would otherwise be likely to enter local authority care, or

   ▪   was born to a child under 16 who is in your family; or

(c) is one of twins, triplets or a larger multiple birth; or

(d) was conceived because of rape or controlling or coercive behaviour; or

(e) was born before 6th April 2017 in Great Britain or 11th May 2017 in Northern Ireland.

12.16   HMRC decides – when it assesses your CTC – whether a child/young person meets the conditions in para 12.15. So, it can be necessary to claim CTC (even if you won't qualify for it because of your income) to get HB for more than two of them.

Exception if you haven't claimed CTC

12.17   This exception to the two child limit applies if:

(a) you were entitled to HB on 5th April 2017 in Great Britain or 10th May 2017 in Northern Ireland; and:

(b) you have one or more 'protected' children/young persons – this means anyone who:

   ▪   was included in your family then, and

   ▪   is included in your family now (regardless of absences in between); and

---

12.12   HB 22(2)-(4); HB66+ 22(5A)-(5C); SI 2017/376 reg 9; NIHB 20(2)-(4); NIHB66+ 20(3)-(5); NISR 2017/79 reg 8

12.13   HB 22(2),(3); HB66+ 22(5A),(5B); NIHB 20(2),(3); NIHB66+ 20(3),(4)

12.14   HB 22(3),(4); HB66+ 22(5B),(5C); SI 2017/376 reg 9; NIHB 20(2),(3); NIHB66+ 20(3),(4); NISR 2017/79 reg 8

12.15   The Child Tax Credit (Amendment) Regulations 2017 No. 387, reg 5 (includes Northern Ireland)

(c) you haven't made a new claim for HB since then (e.g. following a break in your entitlement or a move to a new local authority area); and

(d) you haven't claimed CTC (para 12.13).

12.18 When this exception applies to you, you qualify for a personal allowance for:

(a) each protected child/young person (para 12.17(b)) no matter how many this is; and

(b) either:

- one other child/young person (if you have just one protected one), or

- no other children/young persons (if you have two or more protected ones).

In some cases, you could be better off if you claim CTC (paras 12.13-16).

Additional amounts: any age

12.19 The additional amounts in this section (called premiums) are for disabled children and young persons, severely disabled adults and their carers, and certain old HB cases. If you meet their conditions they are included in your applicable amount.

12.20 You can get these additions whatever age you are (working age or pension age). If you are a couple (or polygamous marriage) you can get these whatever age you and your partner(s) are.

12.21 The figures are in table 12.1 and the details are in paras 12.22-33. Paras 12.51-55 give general rules about going into hospital, etc. If you are working age you may also qualify for the premiums and components in paras 12.37-50.

Disabled child premium

12.22 You qualify for this premium for each child or young person in your family who:

(a) receives PIP (either component at any rate) or (in Scotland) adult disability payment; or

(b) receives DLA (either component at any rate) or (in Scotland) child disability payment; or

(c) receives armed forces independence payment (young persons only); or

(d) is severely sight impaired (para 12.54).

Enhanced disability premium (child)

12.23 You qualify for this premium for each child or young person who receives:

(a) the enhanced rate of the daily living component of PIP or (in Scotland) adult disability payment; or

(b) the highest rate of care component of DLA or (in Scotland) child disability payment; or

(c) armed forces independence payment (young persons only).

12.17   SI 2017/376, reg 9; NISR 2017/79, reg 8

12.18   SI 2017/376, reg 9(4)-(9); NISR 2017/79, reg 8(4)-(9)

12.19   HB 22(1)(d)-(f); HB66+ 22(1)(e); NIHB 20(1)(d)-(f); NIHB66+ 20(1)(e)

12.22   HB sch 3 paras 16, 20(9)(b); HB66+ sch 3 paras 8, 12(3); NIHB sch 4 paras 16, 20(9)(b); NIHB66+ sch 4 paras 8, 12(3)

12.23   HB sch 3 paras 15(1)(b),(ba),(c)-(d) 20(9)(a); HB66+ sch 3 paras 7(1)(a),(aa),(b)-(c), 12(2);
         NIHB sch 4 paras 15(1)(aa),(b),(ba),(c), 20(9)(a); NIHB66+ sch 4 paras 7(1)(a),(aa),(b), 12(2)

Examples: Applicable amounts

1. Pension age couple, no children

A couple in their 70s claim HB. They do not have any disabilities.

Personal allowance		
■ Couple, old pension age rate		£324.70
Total weekly applicable amount		£324.70

2. Working age single person, one child

A single person aged 30 claims HB on supported accommodation. She has one child aged three. Neither of them has any disabilities. The claimant gets carer's allowance for caring for her mother.

Personal allowances		
■ Single person, working age rate		£84.80
■ One child		£77.78
Additional amount		
■ Carer premium		£42.75
Total weekly applicable amount		£205.33

3. Pension age single person, one disabled child

A single person who has just reached 66 claims HB. Her grandson aged eight lives with her, and he gets the mobility component of PIP.

Personal allowances		
■ Single person, new pension age rate		£201.05
■ One child		£77.78
Additional amount		
■ Disabled child premium		£74.69
Total weekly applicable amount		£353.52

4. Working age couple, two children, one disabled

A couple in their 40s have been on HB for some time (para 2.7). They have two children aged 11 and 13. One child gets the enhanced rate of the daily living component of PIP.

Personal allowances		
■ Couple, working age rate		£133.30
■ Two children		£155.56
Additional amounts		
■ Disabled child premium		£74.69
■ Enhanced disability premium (child)		£30.17
Total weekly applicable amount		£393.72

Family premium

12.24   This premium has been abolished for new HB claims. You only qualify for it if:

(a) you were entitled to HB on 30th April 2016 in Great Britain or 4th September 2016 in Northern Ireland; and

(b) at least one child or young person has been included in your family since then (not necessarily the same one throughout); and

(c) you haven't made a new claim for HB since then (e.g. following a break in your entitlement or a move to a new local authority area).

Severe disability premium

12.25   You qualify for this premium if:

(a) you receive:

- the daily living component of PIP or adult disability payment, or

- the middle or highest rate of the care component of DLA or (in Scotland) child disability payment, or

- attendance allowance, or

- constant attendance allowance paid with an industrial injury or war disablement pension, or

- armed forces independence payment; and

(b) you have no non-dependants living with you (para 4.26) apart from non-dependants who receive any of the benefits in (a) or are severely sight impaired (para 12.54); and

(c) no-one gets carer's allowance or the carer element of UC for caring for you (para 12.28).

12.26   If you are a single person, you qualify for the single rate of this premium if you meet all three conditions (para 12.25).

12.27   If you are a couple you qualify for:

(a) the double rate if you both meet all three conditions (para 12.25);

(b) the single rate if:

- you (the claimant) meet all three conditions, and

- your partner is severely sight impaired (para 12.54); or

(b) the single rate if:

- one of you meets all three conditions, and

- the other meets only the first two conditions (para 12.25(a)-(b)).

12.24   HB 22(1)(c), sch 3 para 3; HB66+ 22(1)(c), sch 3 para 3;
NIHB 20(1)(c), sch 4 para 3; NIHB66+ 20(1)(c), sch 4 para 3; regs 2,4 of SI 2015/1857, regs 2, 4; NISR 2016/310, regs 3, 5

12.25   HB 2(1) definition: 'attendance allowance', sch 3 para 14(2); HB66+ 2(1), sch 3 para 6(2);
NIHB 2(1), sch 4 para 14(2); NIHB66+ 2(1), sch 4 para 6(2)

12.26   HB sch 3 paras 14(2)(a), 20(6)(a); HB66+ sch 3 paras 6(2)(a), 12(1)(a);
NIHB sch 4 paras 14(2)(a), 20(6)(a); NIHB66+ sch 4 paras 6(2)(a), 12(1)(a)

12.27   HB sch 3 paras 14(2)(b),(3),(4), 20(6)(b); HB66+ sch 3 paras 6(2)(b),(3),(6), 12(1)(b);
NIHB sch 4 paras 14(2)(b),(3),(4), 20(6)(b); NIHB66+ sch 4 paras 6(2)(b),(3),(6), 12(1)(b)

If you are in a polygamous marriage, you qualify for the double rate if you all meet all three conditions; or the single rate if you meet all three conditions and all your partners are severely sight impaired; or the single rate if all but one of you meet all three conditions and the other one meets only the first two conditions.

12.28   For the third condition of this premium (para 12.25(c)), your carer:

(a)   counts as getting carer's allowance or the UC carer element even if it stops when you have been in hospital for four weeks;

(b)   counts as getting carer's allowance even if it stops as a penalty for a benefit fraud conviction;

(c)   doesn't count as getting carer's allowance if it isn't paid because it is overlapped by another benefit;

(d)   doesn't count as getting carer's allowance or UC carer element in periods for which it is backdated. This means that your carer's arrears don't cause your HB to be overpaid.

Carer premium

12.29   You qualify for this premium if:

(a)   you receive carer's allowance; or

(b)   you are 'entitled to' (para 12.31) carer's allowance but it isn't paid because it is overlapped by another benefit or you are taking part in a government training scheme; or

(c)   you stopped being 'entitled to' carer's allowance (for any reason) within the past eight weeks.

12.30   If you are a single person, you get one carer premium if you qualify (para 12.29). If you are a couple (or polygamous marriage) you get a carer premium for each one of you who qualifies.

12.31   You are 'entitled to' a benefit (even if it isn't in payment) if you meet all the qualifying conditions (Insurance Officer v McCaffrey [1985]) and have made a claim for it (SSWP v Nelligan [2003]). The qualifying conditions for carer's allowance are:

(a)   you regularly and substantially care for someone for at least 35 hours per week; and

(b)   that person receives one of the benefits in para 12.25(a); and

(c)   you are not in full time employment or full-time education (both are defined differently to HB).

Once you have claimed a benefit you remain 'entitled to' it for as long as you continue to meet all the qualifying conditions. You don't have to make a further claim for carer's allowance to get the carer premium even if you claim HB later (CIS/367/2003).

12.28   HB sch 3 para 14(6),(7); HB66+ sch 3 para 6(8); NIHB sch 4 para 14(6),(7); NIHB66+ sch 4 para 6(8)

12.29   HB sch 3 paras 7(1),(2), 17(1),(2),(4); HB66+ sch 3 paras 5(1),(2), 9(1),(2),(4);
         NIHB sch 4 paras 7(1),(2), 17(1),(2),(4); NIHB66+ sch 4 paras 5(1),(2), 9(1),(2),(4)

12.30   HB sch 3 para 20(8); HB66+ sch 3 para 12(4); NIHB sch 4 para 20(8); NIHB66+ sch 4 para 12(4)

12.31   AA 1(1); NIAA 1(1); Insurance Officer v McCaffrey [1985]) 1 All ER (HL) 5; SSWP v Nelligan [2003] EWCA Civ 555
         www.bailii.org/ew/cases/EWCA/Civ/2003/555.html

Carer premium and severe disability premium

12.32   These premiums both include conditions relating to carer's allowance (paras 12.25 and 12.29). This means that usually either the carer gets the carer premium or the person cared for gets severe disability premium, but not both at the same time.

12.33   However, when carer's allowance is overlapped by another DWP benefit, the carer gets carer premium (para 12.29(b)) and the person cared for can get the severe disability premium at the same time (para 12.28(c)). And if a couple provide care for each other, it is possible for them to qualify for two carer premiums and a severe disability premium (at the single or double rate) at the same time.

Additional amounts: working age only

12.34   The additional amounts in this section are for adults who are disabled or long-term sick. If you meet their conditions they are included in your applicable amount.

12.35   You can only get these additions if you are working age (which means under 66). If you are a couple (or polygamous marriage) you can only get these if you (the claimant) are working age, but your partner(s) can be working age or pension age.

12.36   The figures are in table 12.1 and the details are in paras 12.37-50. Paras 12.51-55 give general rules about going into hospital, etc. You may also qualify for the additions in paras 12.22-33.

Disability premium

12.37   You qualify for the single rate of this premium if you are a single person and:

(a)   you are under 66; and

(b)   you aren't on ESA or ESA credits (paras 12.45-46); and

(c)   you meet the disability condition (para 12.39).

12.38   You qualify for the couple rate if you are a couple (or polygamous marriage) and:

(a)   you (the claimant) are under 66; and

(b)   you (the claimant) aren't on ESA or ESA credits; and

(c)   either:

   ▪   you meet the disability condition, or

   ▪   your partner is also under 66 and they meet the disability condition.

12.33   HB sch 3 para 19; HB66+ sch 3 para 11; NIHB sch 4 para 19; NIHB66+ sch 4 para 11

12.37   HB sch 3 paras 12, 13(9); NIHB sch 4 paras 12, 13(9)

12.38   HB sch 3 para 20(5); NIHB sch 4 para 20(5)

12.39   You meet the disability condition (see paras 12.37-38) if:

(a) you receive:

- PIP or (in Scotland) adult disability payment (either component at any rate),
- DLA or (in Scotland) child disability payment (either component at any rate),
- the disability element or severe disability element of WTC,
- attendance allowance,
- constant attendance allowance paid with an industrial injury pension or war disablement pension,
- armed forces independence payment, or
- war pensioner's mobility supplement; or

(b) you are severely sight impaired (para 12.54); or

(c) you get DWP payments for car running costs or have an invalid vehicle supplied by the NHS.

The same applies to your partner if they are under 66.

Enhanced disability premium (adult)

12.40   You qualify for the single rate of this premium if you are a single person and:

(a) you are under 66; and

(b) you receive:

- the enhanced rate of the daily living component of PIP or (in Scotland) adult disability payment, or
- the highest rate of the care component of DLA or (in Scotland) child disability payment, or
- armed forces independence payment, or
- the support component of ESA or equivalent ESA credits (paras 12.45-49).

12.41   You qualify for the couple rate if you are a couple (or polygamous marriage) and:

(a) you (the claimant) are under 66; and

(b) either:

- you receive one of the benefits in para 12.40(b), or
- your partner is also under 66 and they receive one of the first three benefits in para 12.40(b) (it is not enough if your partner gets the support component of ESA or equivalent ESA credits).

12.39   HB 2(1) definition: 'attendance allowance', sch 3 para 13(1)(a)(i),(iv),(v); NIHB 2(1), sch 4 para 13(1)(a)(i),(iv),(v)

12.40   HB sch 3 paras 15(1)(a)-(d), 20(9)(b); NIHB sch 4 paras 15(1)(a),(aa),(b),(c), 20(9)(b)

12.41   HB sch 3 paras 15(1)(b)-(d), 20(9)(c); NIHB sch 4 paras 15(1)(aa),(b),(c), 20(9)(c)

Support component

12.42   If you are a single person, you qualify for a support component in your HB if:

(a)   you are under 66;

(b)   you are entitled to ESA or get ESA credits; and

(c)   you are entitled to a support component in your ESA (or would be if you get ESA credits instead).

12.43   If you are a couple (or polygamous marriage), you qualify for a support component in your HB if:

(a)   you (the claimant) are under 66; and

(b)   at least one of you is entitled to ESA or gets ESA credits; and

(c)   at least one of you gets a support component in your ESA (or would do if you get ESA credits instead).

WRA component

12.44   The WRA component was abolished for new claims in 2017. In most cases it is no longer possible to get a WRA component in your HB (or in your ESA).

ESA and ESA credits

12.45   You qualify for ESA or ESA credits if you have a disability or health condition that affects how much you can work. You get:

(a)   ESA if you meet the ESA contribution conditions;

(b)   ESA credits if you don't meet the ESA contribution conditions, or if your ESA(C) has ended because you have been getting it for a year.

For HB applicable amounts, ESA credits are treated as though they were ESA.

New style ESA

12.46   ESA is also called 'new-style ESA', and it used to be called ESA(C) (contributory ESA). It can be awarded at the same time as UC or separately. It is different from ESA(IR) (income-related ESA), which has been replaced by UC.

ESA phases

12.47   The ESA 'assessment phase' runs for the first 13 weeks of your ESA claim, and the ESA 'main phase' runs from week 14 of your ESA claim onwards. Your ESA is 'linked' to a previous ESA award if the gap between them is 12 weeks or less.

12.42-43   HB 22(1)(e), sch 3 paras 1A, 21(1), 22, 24, 26; NIHB 20(1)(e), sch 4 paras 1A, 21(1), 22, 24, 26

12.44   SI 2017/204, sch 1 para 6(7), sch 2 paras 1-7; NISR 2017/51, sch 1 para 6(7), sch 2 paras 1-7

12.45   HB sch 3 para 21(2); NIHB sch 4 para 21(2)

12.46   UCTP 2(1) – 'new style ESA', 'old style ESA'; NIUCTP 2(1)

12.47   SI 2008/794, regs 4(1),(4), 5, 145; NISR 2008/280 regs 4(1),(4), 5, 145

12.48   During the ESA assessment phase (para 12.47), you just get your ESA personal allowance(s), and the DWP assesses whether you are in:

(a)   the 'support group' which is for people who have both limited capability for work and limited capability for work-related activity; or

(b)   the 'work-related activity group' (WRA group) which is for people who have limited capability for work but can carry out work-related activity.

12.49   During the ESA main phase:

(a)   you continue to get your ESA personal allowance(s), and:

(b)   if you are in the support group, you get a support component (in your ESA and in your HB).

Transitional addition if you transferred onto ESA

12.50   You qualify for a transitional addition if your disability premium stopped because you started getting a component (paras 12.42-44) when you transferred from long-term IB, SDA or incapacity credits (under the old fitness for work test) onto ESA/ESA credits. Your transitional addition is the difference between your old and new applicable amount at the time you transferred. After that any increase in your HB applicable amount (due to the annual uprating or a change in your circumstances) is deducted from your transitional addition until:

(a)   it reduces to nil; or

(b)   if earlier, when your ESA(C) or HB ends – unless you start back on HB within 12 weeks in which case it is restored.

General rules

Going into hospital

12.51   If you or a member of your family goes into hospital, you continue to qualify for your personal allowances. In most cases you also continue to qualify for your premiums (table 12.2), and your components continue as long as they do in your ESA.

12.52   But your HB ends if you (the claimant) are likely to be in hospital for more than 52 weeks (paras 3.6-12 and table 3.1). Or if a member of your family is likely to be in hospital for more than 52 weeks, that person stops being included in your applicable amount so your HB reduces (para 4.25).

12.48   Welfare Reform Act 2007, s2, 8, 9; SI 2008/794 regs 19, 34
         Welfare Reform Act (Northern Ireland) 2007, s2, 8, 9; NISR 2008/280 regs 19, 34

12.49   Welfare Reform Act 2007, s2; SI 2008/794 reg 67(3), sch 4 para 13; HB 22(1)(e), sch 3 paras 21, 22, 24, 26
         Welfare Reform Act (Northern Ireland) 2007, s2; NISR 2008/280 reg 67(3), sch 4 para 13; NIHB 20(1)(e), sch 4 paras 21, 22, 24, 26

12.50   HB sch 3 paras 27, 28, 30; NIHB sch 4 paras 27, 28, 30

12.52   HB 21(1),(2); HB66+ 21(1),(2); HB 19(1),(2); HB66+ 19(1),(2)

Table 12.2 **Premiums after a period in hospital**

How PIP and DLA affect HB

(a) If you or your partner go into hospital, PIP/DLA/adult or child disability payment stop after four weeks. If this is the only reason they stop:

- disability premium continues;
- enhanced disability premium (adult) continues;
- severe disability premium ends if you are a single person, but continues at the single rate if you are a couple (or polygamous marriage) and were previously getting the couple rate.

(b) If a young person aged 18 or over goes into hospital, PIP/DLA/adult or child disability payment stop after four weeks.
If this is the only reason they stop:

- disabled child premium continues;
- enhanced disability premium (child) continues.

They also continue if a child or young person under 18 goes into hospital, because in their case PIP/DLA don't stop.

How carer's allowance affects HB

(c) If you or your partner go into hospital, carer's allowance stops after 12 weeks. If this is the only reason it stops:

- carer premium continues for a further eight weeks (making 20 weeks in total).

(d) If the person you or your partner care for goes into hospital, PIP/DLA/adult or child disability payment stop after four weeks. If this is the only reason they stop:

- carer premium continues for a further eight weeks (making 12 weeks in total).

Note:

The four weeks in (a) and (d) don't have to be continuous but can be made up of two or more periods which are less than 29 days apart.

T12.2(a) HB sch 3 paras 13(1)(a)(iii),(iiia),(iiib), 14(5), 15(1)(b),(c),(2), 20(6)(b); HB66+ sch 3 para 6(7);
NIHB sch 4 paras 13(1)(a)(iii),(iiia),(iiib), 14(5), 15(1)(b),(c),(2), 20(6)(b); NIHB66+ sch 4 para 6(7)

T12.2(b) HB sch 3 paras 15(1)(b),(c),(ca),16(a),(d),(da); HB66+ sch 3 paras 7(1)(a),(b), 8(a),(d);
NIHB sch 4 paras 15(1)(b),(c),(ca), 16(a),(d),(da); NIHB66+ sch 4 paras 7(1)(a),(b), 8(a),(d)

T12.2(c) HB sch 3 para 17(2)(b),(4)(b); HB66+ sch 3 para 9(2)(b); NIHB sch 4 para 17(2)(b),(4)(b); NIHB66+ sch 4 para 9(2)(b)

A death in your family

12.53   If a child or young person dies who met the conditions for a disabled child premium or enhanced disability premium (child), these continue for eight weeks after their death. Apart from that, if any member of your family dies your applicable amount changes to take account of your new circumstances; or if you (the claimant) die your HB stops (para 17.36).

Severely sight impaired

12.54   For all HB purposes you count as 'severely sight impaired' if:

(a) a consultant ophthalmologist has certified you as 'severely sight impaired' or 'blind'; or

(b) you have regained your sight and (a) stopped applying to you within the past 28 weeks following the date on which you stopped being certified.

DWP concessionary payments

12.55   For the premiums in this chapter, a DWP concessionary payment compensating for non-payment of a DWP benefit counts as if it was that benefit.

12.53   HB sch 3 paras 15(1A), 16(c); HB66+ sch 3 paras 7(2), 8(c); NIHB sch 4 paras 15(1A), 16(c); NIHB66+ sch 4 paras 7(2), 8(c)

12.54   HB sch 3 para 13(1)(a)(v),(2); HB66+ sch 3 para 6(4),(5); NIHB sch 4 para 13(1)(a)(v),(2); NIHB66+ sch 4 para 6(4),(5)

12.55   HB sch 3 para 18; HB66+ sch 3 para 10; NIHB sch 4 para 18; NIHB66+ sch 4 para 10

Chapter 13 **Income**

- General rules about assessing income: see paras 13.1-8.
- State benefits, pensions and payments: see paras 13.9-22.
- Council benefits and payments: see paras 13.23-25.
- Private pensions, maintenance, rent, student income, etc: see paras 13.26-44.
- Additional rules about income disregards: see paras 13.45-49.
- Notional income: see paras 13.50-61.

Assessing income

13.1   This chapter and chapter 14 explain how your income is assessed for HB purposes, including:

(a)   unearned income (paras 13.9-44);

(b)   earned income (chapter 14);

(c)   notional income (paras 13.50-61); and

(d)   assumed income from your capital (para 15.5).

This section gives rules relating to all types of income.

'Your' income

13.2   If you are single, your own income is taken into account. If you are in a couple, the income of your partner is taken into account as well as yours. If you are in a polygamous marriage, the income of all your partners is included. In this chapter and chapter 14, 'your' income always includes the income of your partner (or partners). But if a child or young person in your family has income of their own, this is never included and nor is the income of a non-dependant (but see para 13.61).

How your income affects your HB

13.3   If you are on a passport benefit (see para 13.5), all your income is disregarded (ignored) and you qualify for maximum HB: para 6.2-3.

13.4   If you are not on a passport benefit, some kinds of income are counted and some are wholly or partly disregarded. The details are in this chapter and chapter 14. The more income you have (apart from disregarded income) above your applicable amount, the less HB you qualify for: para 6.4-6.

13.1   HB 27(1)(a),(b),(4); HB66+ 25, 29(1),(2); NIHB 24(1)(a),(b),(4); NIHB66+ 23, 27(1),(2)

13.2   CBA 136(1); HB 25; HB66+ 23; NICBA 132(1); NIHB 22; NIHB66+ 21

13.3   CBA 130(1)(c)(i),(3)(a); HB sch 4 para 12, sch 5 paras 4,5; HB66+ 26; NICBA 129(1)(c)(i),(3)(a); NIHB sch 5 para 12, sch 6 paras 4,5; NIHB66+ 24

13.4   CBA 130(1)(c),(3); HB 36(2), 38(2), 40(2), sch 4, sch 5; HB66+ 33(8),(9), sch 4, sch 5; NICBA 129(1)(c),(3); NIHB 33(2), 35(2), 37(2), sch 5, sch 6; NIHB66+ 31(8),(9), sch 5, sch 6

The passport benefits

13.5   The passport benefits are:

(a) the guarantee credit of SPC;

(b) universal credit in supported or temporary accommodation (table 2.3);

(c) income-based JSA;

(d) income-related ESA; and

(e) income support.

Current income

13.6   Your current income is taken into account for the period it covers (apart from the amounts which are disregarded). In the case of a state benefit this means the period for which it is payable.

Arrears of income

13.7   The rules in para 13.6 also apply to arrears of income. So income paid for a past period counts as income in that past period (apart from the amounts which are disregarded). Para 15.13 explains when arrears of income turn into capital.

Weekly income

13.8   HB is a weekly benefit, so your income is assessed as a weekly figure. The law says this is done by accurately calculating or estimating the likely amount of your average weekly income. In practice this means:

(a) the actual weekly amount if your income is paid weekly; or

(b) the weekly equivalent if your income is paid on a non-weekly basis (see para 6.37).

In working age HB, unearned income must not be averaged over a period longer than 52 weeks. In pension age HB claims, it is not in practice averaged over a period longer than one year. For earned income see paras 14.8-10 and 14.29-31.

Examples: Assessing income

1. A working age HB claim

Geoff and Julia are on HB and have two children at school. Geoff works full time and his net earnings (after disregards) are £321 pw. He also gets WTC of £5 pw. Julia receives child maintenance from the children's father, child benefit, and CTC of £124 pw. They have £3,000 in a savings account.

13.5   HB sch 4 para 12, sch 5 paras 4,5, sch 6 paras 5,6; HB66+ 26; NIHB sch 5 para 12, sch 6 paras 4,5, sch 7 paras 5,6; NIHB66+ 24

13.6   HB 27(1), 31(1),(2); HB66+ 30(1), 33(1),(6); NIHB 24(1), 28(1),(2); NIHB66+ 28(1), 31(1),(6)

13.7   HB 27(1), 31(1),(2); HB66+ 30(1), 33(1),(6); NIHB 24(1), 28(1),(2); NIHB66+ 28(1), 31(1),(6)

13.8   CBA 136(4); HB 27(1), 29-31; HB66+ 30(1), 33(1); NICBA 132(3); NIHB 24(1), 26-28; NIHB66+ 28(1), 31(1)

Their income is assessed as follows:

- the child benefit and the child maintenance are disregarded (tables 13.1 and 13.6)
- the CTC and WTC are counted as income (para 13.12) £129 pw
- the earnings are counted (chapter 14) £321 pw
- they do not have assumed income from their capital (para 15.5)

So their total income for HB purposes is £450 pw

2. A pension age HB claim

Jacqui is on HB and receives a state pension and a private pension totalling £274.00. She also has a war widow's pension. She has £12,000 in a savings account.

Her income is assessed as follows:

- her council runs a local scheme which disregards the whole of the war widow's pension (paras 13.16-18)
- the state pension and the private pension are counted as her income (paras 13.13 and 13.27) £274 pw
- she has assumed income from her capital (para 15.5) of £4 pw

So her total income for HB purposes is £278 pw

State benefits, pensions and payments

13.9 Table 13.1 lists which state benefits, pensions and other payments are disregarded. Table 13.2 lists the ones which are taken into account, and summarises the other rules which apply.

Table 13.1 **Disregarded state benefits, pension, etc**

Income from all the following is wholly disregarded. For the 'passport benefits' (a)-(c) see also para 13.3.

- (a) the guarantee credit of SPC
- (b) universal credit
- (c) JSA(IB), ESA(IR) and IS
- (d) disability living allowance (DLA) or (in Scotland) child disability payment
- (e) personal independence payment (PIP) or (in Scotland) adult disability payment
- (f) attendance allowance and equivalent benefits (para 13.10)

T13.1   HB 40(2), sch 5; HB66+ 29(1), 33(9), sch 5; NIHB 37(2), sch 6; NIHB66+ 27(1), 31(9), sch 6

T13.1(a)-(c)   HB sch 5 para 4; HB66+ 26, 29(1)(j)(zi); NIHB sch 6 para 4; NIHB66+ 24, 27(1)(h)(zi)

T13.1(d)-(e)   HB sch 5 para 6; HB66+ 29(1)(j)(i),(ia); NIHB sch 6 para 7; NIHB66+ 27(1)(h)(i)

T13.1(f)   HB 2(1) definition: 'attendance allowance', sch 5 para 9; HB66+ 2(1), 29(1)(j) (ii)-(v); NIHB 2(1), sch 6 para 10; NIHB66+ 2(1), 27(1)(h) (ii)-(iv)

(g) bereavement support payments other than the initial lump sum (para 15.51)

(h) child tax credit (CTC) in pension age HB (para 13.12)

(i) child benefit

(j) guardian's allowance

(k) Christmas bonus

(l) social fund payments and local welfare assistance

(m) in Northern Ireland, welfare supplementary payments (23.20)

(n) carer's allowance supplement, Scottish child payment, early years assistance, short-term assistance and funeral expense assistance (all paid by Social Security Scotland)

(o) government and related payments to disabled people to help with obtaining or retaining work (for example by buying special equipment)

(p) payments from government work programme training schemes. There are rare exceptions in working age claims (see GM paras BW 2.597-611), but even in these cases expenses for travel etc are always disregarded

(q) payments compensating for non-payment of:
   ■ (a) to (f) in working age HB
   ■ all the above in pension age HB.

Note: Payments (l) to (p) and in most cases (q) are also disregarded as capital. See paras 15.50-52 for details about this and about arrears of benefits.

Table 13.2 **Counted state benefits, pensions etc**

Income from the following is counted in full.

(a) new-style JSA (JSA(C)) (para 13.11)

(b) new-style ESA (ESA(C)) (para 13.11)

(c) working tax credit (WTC) (para 13.12)

(d) child tax credit (CTC) in working age HB (para 13.12)

T13.1(g)   HB sch 5 para 67; HB66+ 29(1)(j)(xiii); NIHB sch 6 para 65; NIHB66+ 27(1)(h)(xi)

T13.1(h)   HB66+ 29(1); NIHB66+ 27(1)

T13.1(i),(j) HB sch 5 paras 50, 65; HB66+ 29(1)(j)(vi),(viii); NIHB sch 6 paras 52, 64; NIHB66+ 27(1)(h)(v),(vi)

T13.1(k)   HB sch 5 para 32; HB66+ 29(1)(j)(x); NIHB sch 6 para 33; NIHB66+ 27(1)(h)(ix)

T13.1(l)   HB sch 5 paras 31,31A; sch 6 paras 20,20A; HB66+ 29(1)(j)(ix); NIHB sch 6 para 32, sch 7 para 21; NIHB66+ 27(1)(h)(viii)

T13.1(m)   NISR 2016/178 reg 12; NISR 2017/35 reg 14

T13.1(n)   HB sch 5 paras 68-72; HB66+ 29(1)(b)(xviib)-(viih); NIHB sch 6 paras 66-68; NIHB66+ 27(1)(h)(xva)-(xvd)

T13.1(o)   HB sch 5 para 49, sch 6 paras 43,44; HB66+ 29(1); NIHB sch 6 para 51, sch 7 para 44; NIHB66+ 27(1)

T13.1(p)   HB 2(1) definitions, sch 5 paras A2-A5,13,58,60,61; HB66+ 29(1); NIHB 2(1), sch 6 paras 13,15,60; NIHB66+ 27(1)

T13.1(q)   HB 2(1) definition: 'concessionary payment', sch 5 para 7; HB66+ 2(1), 29(1)(u); NIHB 2(1), sch 6 para 8; NIHB66+ 2(1), 27(1)(s)

(e) state retirement pension (para 13.13)

(f) the savings credit of SPC (para 13.14)

(g) carer's allowance (but in Scotland see table 13.1(n))

(h) maternity allowance

(i) severe disablement allowance (SDA)

(j) widow's pension

(k) industrial death benefit

The following have individual rules.

(l) widowed mother's allowance and widowed parent's allowance: disregard £15 per week and count the rest as income (for deaths occurring before 6th April 2017)

(m) industrial injuries disablement benefit: disregard any increase for attendance and count the rest as income

(n) war pensions: see paras 13.16-18

(o) increases in benefits for dependants: see para 13.20

(p) reductions in benefits: see para 13.21

(q) statutory sick, maternity, paternity and adoption pay: count as earned income (see table 14.1(c) and paras 14.15-16)

Note: See table 15.2 for arrears of payments (c), (d) and (f).

Benefits equivalent to attendance allowance

13.10 The following benefits are equivalent to attendance allowance:

(a) increases in industrial injuries benefit for constant attendance or exceptionally severe disablement;

(b) increases in a war disablement pension for attendance, constant attendance or exceptionally severe disablement;

(c) an armed forces independence payment;

(d) payments for attendance under the Personal Injuries (Civilians) scheme; or

(e) the daily living component of adult disability payment and the care component of child disability payment in Scotland.

New-style JSA and ESA

13.11 New-style JSA and new-style ESA (previously called JSA(C) and ESA(C)) are counted in full as your income. See para 13.22 if payments are reduced due to sanctions.

T13.2(a)-(k) HB 31(1),(3), 40(1),(2); HB66+ 29(1)(b),(c),(j); NIHB 28(1),(3), 37(1),(2); NIHB66+ 27(1)(b),(c),(h)

T13.2(l) HB sch 5 para 16; HB66+ sch 5 paras 7,8; NIHB sch 6 para 17; NIHB66+ sch 6 paras 8,9

T13.2(m) HB 2(1) definition: 'attendance allowance', sch 5 para 9; HB66+ 2(1), 29(1)(j)(iii),(n); sch 5 para 2; NIHB 2(1), sch 6 para 10; NIHB66+ 2(1), 27(1)(h)(iii),(l), sch 6 para 3

13.11 UCTP 2(1) – 'new-style ESA', 'new-style JSA'; HB 31(1),(2), 40(1); HB66+ 29(1)(j), 33(6); NIUCTP 2(1); NIHB 28(1),(2), 37(1); NIHB66+ 27(1)(h), 31(6)

WTC and CTC

13.12   Working tax credit is counted in full as your income (in working age and pension age HB). Child tax credit is counted in full as your income in working age HB, but is wholly disregarded in pension age HB. In some uncommon cases, part of the earned income disregards can be deducted from your WTC or CTC: see para 14.61(c) and (d).

State retirement pension

13.13   State retirement pension is counted in full as your income. If you defer your state pension:

(a)   it is not included as your income until you begin receiving it. Any increase you receive (because you deferred it) is then included;

(b)   any lump sum you receive (because you deferred your state pension) is disregarded as your capital until your state pension begins.

Savings credit

13.14   The savings credit of state pension credit (SPC) is counted in full as your income. But if you are also on the guarantee credit of SPC, see para 13.3.

Table 13.3 **People on savings credit: adjusting the DWP's figures**

If you are on savings credit, the following adjustments are made whenever the DWP tells the council your income and capital (para 13.15).

Your income

The DWP tells the council:

■   the amount of your savings credit; and

■   your 'assessed income figure' (AIF). This is the DWP's assessment of your income (apart from savings credit).

The council adds these together, and then deducts the following amounts:

If you receive:	The amount is:
(a) maintenance from a current or former husband, wife or civil partner	the full HB disregard (table 13.6)
(b) a war disablement or bereavement pension	any amount disregarded under a local scheme (in other words, any amount over £10: para 13.18)

13.12   HB 31(1), 32, 40(1),(6),46(9),49(2)(f),(g); HB66+ 29(1)(b),(5), 32; NIHB 28(1), 29, 37(1),(4),43(8),46(2)(f),(g); NIHB66+ 27(1)(b),(5), 30

13.13   HB66+ sch 6 para 26A as implied by CPR 2; SI 2005/2677 regs 11,12; NIHB66+ sch 7 para 28

13.14   HB 31(1),(2), 40(1); HB66+ 27(4)(a), 33(6); NIHB 28(1),(2), 37(1); NIHB66+ 25(4)(a), 31(6)

T13.3   HB66+ 27(3)-(8); NIHB66+ 25(3)-(8)

> (c) earned income and you are a lone parent   £5
>
> (d) earned income from 'permitted work'   £167 or £20 (as shown in table 14.5)
>
> (e) earned income and you qualify   the full HB disregard
> for the HB child care disregard   (para 14.63)
>
> (f) earned income and you qualify for   £17.10
> the HB additional earnings disregard   (para 14.68)
>
> If you have a partner who was excluded from your savings credit claim but is included in your HB claim, the council assesses their income and adds it.
>
> **Your capital**
>
> The DWP tells the council the amount of your capital. The council changes this only if your capital increases to more than £16,000, in which case your HB stops.

Other rules if you are on savings credit

13.15   The following rules apply if you are on savings credit (but not guarantee credit):

(a) the DWP assesses your income and capital as part of your savings credit claim;

(b) the DWP tells the council these income and capital figures (when you first claim HB or savings credit, and then whenever your circumstances change);

(c) the council adjusts these figures as shown in table 13.3;

(d) the council uses the adjusted figures to calculate your HB.

War disablement and bereavement pensions

13.16   Table 13.4 gives the rules for assessing income from:

(a) pensions under the Armed Forces Pensions and Compensation schemes (and similar payments) for:

- war disablement;

- war widows;

- war widowers; and

- war bereaved civil partners;

(b) payments compensating for non-payment of the above;

(c) equivalent payments from governments outside the UK; and

(d) pensions paid by any (non-UK) government to the victims of National Socialist persecution.

The payments in (a) include both 'service attributable pensions' for service before 5th April 2005 and 'guaranteed income payments' for service on or after that date.

13.17   War pensions not included in para 13.16 are assessed in the same way as private pensions: see para 13.27.

13.15   HB66+ 27(1)-(3); NIHB66+ 25(1)-(3)

13.16   HB sch 5 para 15; HB66+ 29(1)(e)-(h),(l)-(m), sch 5 para 1; NIHB sch 6 para 15; NIHB66+ 27(1)(e)-(f),(j)-(k), sch 6 para 1

Local schemes for war disablement and bereavement pensions

13.18   Councils in Great Britain can run a 'local scheme' to disregard more than £10 per week of the war disablement and bereavement pensions in para 13.16 (apart from those which are always wholly disregarded: see table 13.4).

13.19   Most councils do this, and some disregard the whole amount. The government pays councils up to 75% of the cost of running a local scheme (see para 21.4), but decisions about local schemes are not appealable to a tribunal (see table 20.4).

Table 13.4 **War disablement and bereavement pensions**

This table applies to the pensions etc in para 13.16.

Assessment in Great Britain

(a) Disregard the whole amount of:

- 'pre-1973' special payments to war widows, war widowers and war bereaved civil partners (currently £111.74 per week: HB circular A2/2023);

- a mobility supplement paid with any war disablement or bereavement pension; and

- an increase for constant attendance paid with any war disablement pension (including war injured civilians) or an Armed Forces independence payment.

(b) Disregard £10 per week from the total of any other war disablement or bereavement pension. But see paras 13.18-19 (local schemes).

Assessment in Northern Ireland

(c) Disregard the whole amount of all war disablement and bereavement pensions.

Increases in benefits for dependants

13.20   The following applies if you receive an increase for a dependant in any of the state benefits which count as income (table 13.2):

(a) if the increase is for your partner, it is included as your income;

(b) if the increase is for a child or young person in your family, it is included as your income in working age HB, but disregarded in pension age HB;

(c) if the increase is for someone not in your family, it is disregarded.

13.18   AA 134(8)-(10); SI 2007 No. 1619

T13.4   HB 2(1) definitions: 'attendance allowance', 'guaranteed income payment', 'war pension' etc, 27(1)(a), 31(1), 40(1), sch 5 paras 8,9,15,53-55;
          HB66+ 2(1), 29(1)(e)-(h),(l),(m), 30(1)(a), sch 5 paras 1-6; NIHB 2(1), 24(1)(a), 28(1), 37(1), sch 6 paras 9,10,15,55-57;
          NIHB66+ 2(1), 27(1)(f),(j),(k), 28(1)(a), sch 6 paras 1-7

13.20   HB 27(1)(a), 40(1), sch 5 para 52; HB66+ 29(1)(j)(viii), 30(1)(a), sch 5 para 13;
          NIHB 24(1)(a), 37(1), sch 6 para 54; NIHB66+ 27(1)(h)(vii), 28(1)(a), sch 6 para 14

Reductions in benefits

13.21   If you receive a reduced amount of any of the state benefits which count as income (see table 13.2) only the reduced amount is counted as your income if the reduction is:

(a) because of the rules about overlapping state benefits;

(b) because your WTC or CTC is reduced to recover an earlier year's overpayment;

(c) because your incapacity benefit is reduced when you have an occupational pension (CH/51/2008); or

(d) in pension age HB, because a state benefit is reduced when you are in hospital.

13.22   But the gross amount (the amount before the reduction is made) is counted as your income in any other circumstances, for example if a state benefit (but not WTC or CTC) is reduced:

(a) to recover an overpayment; or

(b) to pay your rent, fuel, water or other priority debts; or

(c) as a result of a work-related sanction in new-style JSA or ESA.

Council benefits and payments

13.23   This section gives the rules for benefits, allowances and other payments from local councils.

13.24   Table 13.5 lists which council allowances and payments are disregarded.

Social services and similar payments for care and support

13.25   The payments in table 13.5 (a)-(h) are disregarded if they are paid by:

(a) a social services department in Great Britain;

(b) the Health and Social Services Board, a Health and Social Services Trust or a Juvenile Justice Centre in Northern Ireland;

(c) a voluntary organisation on behalf of the above; or

(d) in the case of respite care payments, a Primary Care Trust.

Other unearned income

13.26   This section gives the rules for private pensions, maintenance, charitable and voluntary payments, rent, student income and other unearned income. For assumed income from capital see para 15.5.

13.21   HB 27(1)(a), 40(1),(6); HB66+ 29(3)-(5), 30(1)(a); NIHB 24(1)(a), 37(1),(4); NIHB66+ 27(3)-(5), 28(1)(a)

13.22   HB 40(1),(5),(5A); HB66+ 29(3),(5); NIHB 37(1),(3),(3A); NIHB66+ 27(3),(5)

13.25   HB 2(1), sch 5 paras 25-28A,57; HB66+ 29(1); NIHB 2(1), sch 6 paras 26-29A,59; NIHB66+ 27(1)

Table 13.5 **Disregarded council payments**

Income from the following is wholly disregarded. For payments (a) to (h) see also para 13.25.

(a) foster care payments, also called kinship care payments in Scotland;

(b) adoption allowances;

(c) special guardianship payments;

(d) payments to avoid taking children into care;

(e) payments to care leavers, including payments passed on to you by a care leaver aged 18 or more who lives with you;

(f) boarding out and respite care payments, including contributions you receive from the person you are caring for;

(g) community care payments;

(h) direct care payments;

(i) supporting people payments, for housing-related support to help you maintain your tenancy;

(j) 'local welfare assistance' or equivalent payments in Scotland, Wales and Northern Ireland (para 23.35);

(k) discretionary housing payments (para 23.1) and in Northern Ireland welfare supplementary payments (para 23.20);

(l) council tax rebates, other council tax reductions, and HB itself;

(m) all fuel and cost of living payments paid on behalf of the government.

Note: In some cases these are also disregarded as capital. See para 15.53 for details about this.

Private pensions

13.27   Income from a private pension is counted in full, after any deductions have been made for tax paid on it. This applies to any kind of:

(a) occupational pension;

(b) personal pension; or

(c) pension from the Pension Protection Fund.

But if a court has ordered part of your pension to be paid to someone else (for example your former partner), that part is disregarded (CH/1672/2007). See also paras 13.54-55 and 13.60.

T13.5(a)-(f)   HB 2(1) definition: 'voluntary organisation', sch 5 paras 25-28A; HB66+ 29(1); NIHB 2(1), sch 6 paras 26-29A; NIHB66+ 27(1)

T13.5(g)-(h)   HB sch 5 para 57; HB66+ 29(1); NIHB sch 6 para 59; NIHB66+ 27(1)

T13.5(i)   HB sch 5 para 63; HB66+ 29(1); NIHB sch 6 para 63; NIHB66+ 27(1)

T13.5(j)   HB 2(1) definition – 'local welfare provision', sch 5 para 31A; HB66+ 29(1)

T13.5(k)   HB sch 5 para 62; HB66+ 29(1); NIHB sch 6 para 62; NIHB66+ 27(1)

T13.5(l)   HB sch 5 para 41; HB66+ 29(1); NIHB sch 6 para 43; NIHB66+ 27(1)

13.27   HB 2(1), definition – 'occupational pension' 31(1), 35(2), sch 5 para 1; HB66+ 2(1), 29(1)(c),(d),(t),(x), 30(1)(a), 33(12), 35(2); NIHB 2(1), 28(1), 32(2), sch 6 para 1; NIHB66+ 2(1), 27(1)(c),(d),(r),(v), 28(1)(a), 31(12), 33(2)

Maintenance

13.28 Table 13.6 gives the rules for assessing maintenance you receive from a former partner or anyone else (other than your current partner).

13.29 If you pay maintenance for a child or anyone else, the amount you pay cannot be deducted when your income is assessed. But if it is for a student son or daughter, see para 13.47.

Charitable and voluntary payments

13.30 Payments of income you receive which are charitable and/or voluntary are wholly disregarded. For example, these could be from a charity, family, friends, etc (but for maintenance see table 13.6). For payments of capital see para 15.54. If the only money you have is charitable or voluntary income, you qualify for maximum HB (see paras 6.5 and 16.30).

Rent

13.31 Table 13.7 gives the rules for assessing rent you receive from people living in your home. Table 13.8 gives the rules for rent you receive on other property. But if you are self-employed and you receive rent as part of your business, see para 15.33. In pension age HB the capital value of the right to receive rent is counted in full when considering the capital limit (para 15.4) but disregarded when calculating assumed income (para 15.5). In working age HB it is disregarded for both purposes.

Annuities

13.32 If you have an annuity, you get payments from an insurance or similar company in return for investing an initial capital sum with them. Payments from an annuity are counted in full as unearned income, after any deductions have been made for tax paid on them. In pension age HB the capital value of the right to receive an annuity is counted in full when considering the capital limit (para 15.4) but disregarded when calculating assumed income (para 15.5). In working age HB it is disregarded for both purposes.

Home income plans

13.33 A home income plan is an annuity in which the invested capital sum is a loan secured against your home. The payments you receive are assessed as unearned income (para 13.32). But if you were over pension age when you began the home income plan (or began it before 6th December 2018 and were over 65), the following amounts are disregarded from the payments:

(a) tax paid on them;

(b) mortgage repayments made using them; and

(c) repayments on the loan.

13.29   HB 31(1); HB66+ 30(1); NIHB 28(1); NIHB66+ 28(1)

13.30   HB sch 5 para 14(1)(a),(b),(2); HB66+ 29(1); NIHB sch 6 para 14(1)(a),(b),(2); NIHB66+ 27(1)

13.31   HB sch 6 para 33; HB66+ 33(11), sch 6 paras 27, 28; NIHB sch 7 para 34; NIHB66+ 33(10), sch 7 paras 29, 30

13.32   HB 41(2), sch 5 para 1, sch 6 paras 31, 32; HB66+ 29(1)(d), 33(11),(12), sch 6 para 29;
         NIHB 38(2), sch 6 para 1, sch 7 paras 32, 33; NIHB66+ 27(1)(d), 31(10),(11), sch 7 para 31

13.33   HB 41(2), sch 5 para 1; HB66+ 29(1)(d), 33(12), sch 5 para 11; NIHB 38(2), sch 6 para 1; NIHB66+ 27(1)(d), 31(11), sch 6 para 12

Table 13.6 **Income from maintenance**

Pension age HB	Assessment
(a) Maintenance for child or young person (all cases)	Disregard in full
(b) Maintenance for you or your partner – if you have a child or young person	
■ paid by your or your partner's spouse or former spouse	Disregard £15 per week
■ paid by someone else	Disregard in full
(c) Maintenance for you or your partner – if you don't have a child or young person	
■ paid by your or your partner's spouse or former spouse	Count in full
■ paid by someone else	Disregard in full
(d) Maintenance for a non-dependant (all cases)	Disregard in full

Working age HB	Assessment
(e) Maintenance for a child or young person	
■ paid by your or your partner's former spouse	Disregard in full
■ paid by the child/young person's parent or step-parent	Disregard in full
■ paid by someone whose maintenance payments mean they can reasonably be treated as their father	Disregard in full
■ paid by someone else	Count in full
(f) Maintenance for you or your partner – if you have a child or young person	
■ paid by your or your partner's former partner	Disregard £15 per week
■ paid by someone else	Disregard in full
(g) Maintenance for you or your partner – if you don't have a child or young person	Count in full
(h) Maintenance for a non-dependant (all cases)	Same as (f) or (g)

Note: 'Partner', 'child', 'young person' and 'non-dependant' have the same meaning as in chapter 4. 'Spouse' means husband, wife or civil partner.

T13.6   HB 31(1), sch 5 paras 47,47A; HB66+ 29(1)(o), sch 5 para 20; NIHB 28(1), sch 6 para 49,49A; NIHB66+ 27(1)(m), sch 6 para 21

Table 13.7 **Rent from people in your home**

(a) Household members

Rent (or 'keep') you receive from a child, young person or non-dependant in your home is wholly disregarded.

(b) Lodgers whose rent includes meals (boarders)

If you receive rent from one or more lodgers in your home and their rent includes meals (see para 4.38):

- start with the total amount your lodger(s) pay you each week (for rent, meals and any other services);
- deduct £20 for each lodger you charge for (counting adults and children);
- divide the result by two;
- this gives your weekly income.

(c) Lodgers whose rent does not include meals

If you receive rent from one or more lodgers in your home and their rent does not include meals:

- start with the total amount your lodger(s) pay you each week (for rent and any other services);
- deduct £20 for each separate letting;
- this gives your weekly income.

Examples: Letting out a room

1. A lodger whose rent does not include meals

Henry and Lucy are on HB and have a spare room. They let it out to a lodger for £80 per week inclusive of fuel and water, but not meals.

Their income from this lodger (table 13.7(c)) is £80 minus £20, which is £60 per week.

2. A lodger whose rent includes meals

Henry and Lucy increase the lodger's rent to £90 per week because they now provide meals.

Their income from the lodger (table 13.7(b)) is now £90 minus £20, which is £70, the result being divided by two, which is £35 per week.

T13.7(a) HB sch 5 para 21; HB66+ 29(1); NIHB sch 6 para 22; NIHB66+ 27(1)

T13.7(b) HB sch 5 para 42; HB66+ 2(1) definition: 'board and lodging accommodation', 2(1), 29(1)(p), sch 5 para 9; NIHB sch 6 para 44; NIHB66+ 27(1)(n), sch 6 para 10

T13.7(c) HB sch 5 para 22; HB66+ 29(1)(v), sch 5 para 10; NIHB sch 6 para 23; NIHB66+ 27(1)(t), sch 6 para 11

Table 13.8 **Rent from property other than your home**

(a) When the rent counts as income

The rent you receive counts as unearned income:

- ■　only in working age HB; and
- ■　only if the property's capital value is disregarded for any of the reasons in table 15.1(b) to (g).

In these cases your unearned income equals the rent you receive on the property, minus outgoings you pay on the property (during the period the rent covers) for:

- ■　mortgage payments (both interest and capital);
- ■　council tax (rates in Northern Ireland);
- ■　water charges; and
- ■　tax paid on the resulting income.

No other outgoings can be deducted.

(b) When the rent counts as capital

The rent you receive counts as capital (not income):

- ■　in working age HB other than as described in (a); and
- ■　in all pension age HB.

In these cases, your capital:

- ■　increases when you receive the rent;
- ■　but decreases when you pay for outgoings on the property, for example agent's fees, repairs, cleaning, etc, as well as those listed in (a).

Equity release schemes

13.34　　If you are in an equity release scheme, the payments you receive are a form of loan secured against your home. In pension age HB, payments from an equity release scheme count in full as unearned income. This also seems likely to be the case in working age HB (because of the way loans are treated in HB: see para 15.55).

Mortgage and loan protection policies

13.35　　If you have insurance against being unable to pay your mortgage or another loan (because of unemployment, sickness, etc), payments you receive from that policy are assessed as follows:

T13.8(a) HB sch 5 paras 1, 17(2),(3); NIHB sch 6 paras 1, 18(2),(3)

T13.8(b) HB 46(4), sch 5 paras 1, 17(1); HB66+ 29(1), sch 5 para 22; NIHB 43(4), sch 6 paras 1, 18(1); NIHB66+ 27(1), sch 6 para 23

13.34　　HB66+ 29(1)(w),(8); NIHB66+ 27(1)(u),(8)

13.35　　HB sch 5 para 29; HB66+ 29(1); NIHB sch 6 para 30; NIHB66+ 27(1)

(a) in pension age HB, the payments are wholly disregarded;

(b) in working age HB, payments for the following are disregarded:

- the mortgage or loan repayments;

- the payments due on the policy;

- in the case of a mortgage protection policy, the payments due on another policy you were required to have to insure against loss or damage to your home,

and the rest (if any) counts as your income.

Income from trusts

13.36 Income you receive from a trust is counted as your unearned income, with the following exceptions:

(a) income from some government supported trust funds is wholly disregarded (para 15.42);

(b) income from personal injury trusts is wholly disregarded (paras 15.43-45);

(c) in pension age HB, if you receive discretionary income from a trust:

- £20 per week is disregarded if it is for your rent (other than any part of the rent which is not met by HB because of a non-dependant deduction), mortgage interest or other housing costs that could be met by the guarantee credit of SPC, council tax (in Northern Ireland rates), water charges, household fuel, food, or ordinary clothing or footwear;

- the whole amount is disregarded if it is for anything else.

For further details about trusts see paras 15.37-41.

Student income

13.37 In pension age HB, student income is wholly disregarded. If you are eligible for working age HB (paras 2.43-44) the rules are in paras 13.38-43, but we have not given all the special cases for loans and grants (see GM chapter C2). If you are a student couple, the rules and disregards apply to each of you separately. Details about student grant and loan awards can be found online [www].

Student loans

13.38 Student maintenance loans (loans towards living costs) are counted as your income as described in table 13.9. But the following are wholly disregarded:

(a) special support loans (for students on means tested benefits); and

(b) student fee loans.

13.36(c) HB 31(1), sch 5 para 14(1)(c); HB66+ 29(1)(i), sch 5 para 12; NIHB 28(1), sch 6 para 14(1)(c); NIHB66+ 27(1)(g), sch 6 para 13

13.37 HB 54; HB66+ 29(1); NIHB 51; NIHB66+ 27(1)
England: www.gov.uk/student-finance
www.practitioners.slc.co.uk/policy/
Scotland: www.saas.gov.uk/
Wales: www.studentfinancewales.co.uk
Northern Ireland: www.studentfinanceni.co.uk
NHS and social work: www.nhsbsa.nhs.uk/student-services

13.38 HB 53(1) definitions: 'contribution', 'student loan', 64(1), 64A; NIHB 50(1), 61(1), 62

Student grants

13.39 Student maintenance grants (loans towards living costs) are counted as your income as described in table 13.10. But the following are wholly disregarded:

(a) special support grants (for students on means-tested benefits);

(b) education maintenance allowances (EMAs);

(c) 16-19 bursary fund payments (the English replacement for EMAs);

(d) parent's learning allowances (awarded for dependants); and

(e) higher education bursaries (awards to care leavers).

Table 13.9   **Student maintenance loans**

(a) Start with the annual amount of your loan, including contributions due from your parents or others even if they don't pay them.

(b) Disregard 70% in the case of a postgraduate master's degree loan.

(c) Subtract £693 (an annual allowance towards books, travel and equipment).

(d) Average the result over the period:

■ from the first Monday in September, or the first Monday in your academic year if it falls in August;

■ to the last Sunday in June (or the last Sunday in your course in your final year).

(e) Disregard £10 (a standard weekly amount) (see also para 13.49).

(f) In your first year, disregard the whole amount in the weeks falling before your course begins (CIS/3735/2004).

Note: Most full-time UK students on courses at level 4 or above (HNCs, HNDs, degrees, etc) qualify for a student loan. If you choose not to apply for one, or to take only part of the loan, you are counted at step (a) as having the full amount you qualify for. Religious beliefs aren't likely to be accepted as preventing you from applying (CH/4422/2006).

Using other income to supplement a student loan or grant

13.40 If you have income from a student loan or grant, you may qualify for an extra disregard towards your expenditure. This is calculated as follows:

(a) work out your expenditure for the year on the items in table 13.10(b), but only include expenditure which is necessary for you to attend your course;

(b) add together the following figures:

■ £693,

■ your higher education bursary (if you get one),

■ any amounts you get in your grant for the items in table 13.10(b);

13.39   HB 53(1) definitions: 'contribution', 'grant', 'grant income', 64(1),(4)(a)(ii),(b)(ii), 66, 67; NIHB 50(1), 61(1),(4)(a)(ii),(b)(ii), 64, 65

T13.9   HB 40(7)-(9), 53(1) definitions: 'academic year', 'last day of course', 64, 64B; NIHB 37(3)-(7), 50(1), 61

(c) if the total of (a) is greater than the total of (b), you qualify for a disregard equal to the difference. In practice this is averaged over the year (or a more appropriate period) to give the weekly amount of the disregard.

But this disregard can only be made from income 'intended' for this purpose (CIS/3107/2003), for example if you have to take a part-time job to pay for your travel. It cannot be made from the student loan or grant, or from income you would have anyway.

Table 13.10 **Student grants**

(a) Start with the annual amount of your grant, including contributions due from your parents or others even if they don't pay them.

(b) Disregard all amounts for:

- any disability you have,

- childcare costs,

- travel,

- books and equipment,

- tuition or examination fees,

- maintenance of two homes,

- term-time residential study away from your educational establishment,

- anyone outside the UK who is not included in your application amount.

(c) If you don't qualify for a student loan (table 13.9), subtract £693, even if amounts are deducted for travel and books and equipment at step (b).

(d) Average the result over the period it is payable for. In many (but not all) cases this means that:

- amounts for an adult or child dependant are averaged over the same period as the student loan if you qualify for one (table 13.9), or over the full calendar year if you don't,

- care leaver's grants are averaged over the summer vacation,

- other amounts are averaged over the academic year, but the long summer vacation is excluded (if you get one), and so are periods of work experience in a sandwich course.

13.40   HB 63; NIHB 60

T13.10   HB 40(7)-(9), 53(1) definition: 'grant income', 59; NIHB 37(3)-(7), 50(1), 56

Access funds, learner support funds and financial contingency funds

13.41   Educational establishments can make payments to students from 'access funds' or 'learner support funds', and Welsh Ministers can make payments to students from 'financial contingency funds'. These are sometimes called hardship payments. They are assessed as follows:

(a) payments towards your living costs (see para 13.42) are counted as your income or capital as appropriate. But if they are income (in other words regular payments):

■ the whole amount is disregarded if they are paid before your course begins, or to tide you over until you receive your student loan,

■ £20 per week is disregarded in other situations (see also para 13.49);

(b) payments for anything else (for example course-related expenses) are disregarded as income and as capital for 52 weeks.

13.42   Your living costs mean rent (other than any part of the rent which is not eligible for HB, or not met by HB because of a non-dependant deduction), council tax (in Northern Ireland rates), water charges, household fuel, food or ordinary clothing or footwear.

Sports Council awards

13.43   Sports Council awards are assessed as follows:

(a) payments towards your living costs (see para 13.42) are counted in full as your income or capital as appropriate;

(b) payments for anything else (including vitamins, minerals or performance-enhancing dietary supplements) are disregarded as income, and as capital for 26 weeks.

Other sources of unearned income

13.44   Any other kind of unearned income is:

(a) disregarded in pension age HB;

(b) counted as unearned income in working age HB, except as in table 13.11 and para 13.46.

Additional rules about income disregards

13.45   The rules about disregards for each kind of unearned income are given earlier in this chapter. Those for earned income are in chapter 14. This section gives further rules about disregards which can apply to more than one kind of unearned or earned income.

Income tax

13.46   Income tax paid on any kind of unearned income is always deducted in the assessment of that income. For earned income see paras 14.19-21 and 14.53-55.

13.41   HB 53(1) definition: 'access funds', 65,68(2),(4); NIHB 50(1), 63,66(2),(4)

13.43   HB 2(1) definition: 'sports award', sch 5 para 59, sch 6 para 50; NIHB 2(1), sch 6 para 61, sch 7 para 49

13.44   HB 31(1), sch 5 para 1; HB66+ 29(1); NIHB 28(1), sch 5 para 1; NIHB66+ 27(1)

13.46   HB sch 5 para 1; HB66+ 33(12); NIHB sch 6 para 1; NIHB66+ 31(11)

Parental contributions to a student

13.47   If you make a parental contribution to a son or daughter who is a UK student, the following amount is disregarded from the total of your unearned and earned income:

(a) if you were assessed as having to make a contribution towards their student loan or grant, the whole of that contribution;

(b) if (a) does not apply, and they are under 25, any amount you contribute up to:

- the lower rate of the single person's personal allowance (table 12.1);

- minus the weekly amount of any discretionary grant they receive.

Income outside the UK

13.48   Unearned or earned income you receive outside the UK is assessed in the normal way (as described in this chapter and chapter 14), and any commission for converting it to sterling is then disregarded. But if you are prohibited (by the country you receive the income in) from bringing it to the UK, the whole amount is disregarded.

The over-riding limit on certain disregards

13.49   If you qualify for more than one of the following unearned income disregards, the disregard from all of them is limited to £20 per week:

(a) the £15 disregard from widowed mother's/parent's allowance (table 13.2(l));

(b) in Great Britain, the £10 disregard from war pensions for disablement or bereavement (table 13.4(b)), but your council may also run a local scheme (para 13.18);

(c) in pension age HB, the £20 disregard from discretionary trust income (para 13.36(c));

(d) in working age HB, the £10 disregard from income from student loans (table 13.9(e));

(e) in working age HB, the £20 disregard from income from student access funds (para 13.41).

Apart from that, you get the full amount of any disregard you qualify for.

Table 13.11 **Other unearned income disregards**

The following kinds of income are wholly disregarded (except as shown in (k) to (n)):

(a) expenses you receive as a volunteer or for charitable or voluntary work;

(b) expenses you receive as a member of a service user group (for example when these are run by local councils, social landlords or health authorities);

13.47   HB sch 4 para 11, sch 5 paras 19,20; HB66+ sch 4 para 6, sch 5 paras 18,19; NIHB sch 6 paras 20,21; NIHB66+ sch 5 para 6, sch 6 paras 19,20

13.48   HB sch 4 paras 13,14, sch 5 paras 24,33; HB66+ 29(1)(k), 33(7), sch 4 para 10, sch 5 paras 16,17; NIHB sch 5 paras 13,14, sch 6 paras 25,34; NIHB66+ 27(1)(i), 31(7), sch 5 para 10, sch 6 paras 17,18

13.49   HB sch 5 para 34; HB66+ sch 5 para 12(3)(b),(c); NIHB sch 6 para 35; NIHB66+ sch 6 para 13(3)(b),(c)

T13.11(a) HB sch 5 para 2; HB66+ 29(1); NIHB sch 6 para 2; NIHB66+ 27(1)

T13.11(b) HB 2(1) definition: 'service user group', 35(2)(d), sch 5 para 2A; HB66+ 29(1), 35(2)(f); NIHB 2(1), 32(2)(d), sch 6 para 2A; NIHB66+ 27(1), 33(2)(e)

(c) expenses you receive from your employer (for exceptions see table 14.1(n));

(d) payments you receive as a teacher under the Student Loans Repayment Scheme (but student loan repayments can't be deducted from any other income);

(e) payments for travel for hospital visits;

(f) payments for health service supplies;

(g) payments replacing free milk and vitamins and/or healthy start vouchers;

(h) payments for travel for prison visits;

(i) payments from the National Emergency Trust and the We Love Manchester Emergency Fund, Grenfell Tower payments, Windrush payments and payments for historical child abuse (DWP A1/2022);

(j) payments you receive as a holder of the Victoria Cross or George Cross, and similar payments (para 15.48);

(k) payments in kind (in other words, in goods rather than money or vouchers)

■ but in working age HB, goods bought for you by someone who receives income on your behalf can count as notional income: see para 13.54;

(l) concessionary coal

■ but in working age HB, cash in lieu of it is counted as unearned income (R v Doncaster MBC and another ex parte Bolton);

(m) juror's allowance

■ but in working age HB, compensation for loss of earnings or state benefits is counted as unearned income;

(n) career development loans paid by banks in Great Britain under arrangements in s2 of the Employment and Training Act 1973

■ but in working age HB, loans for living expenses are counted as unearned income until the course you are on ends;

(o) all fuel and cost of living payments paid by or on behalf of the government.

Note: In working age HB, payments (e) to (i) are also disregarded as capital for 52 weeks.

T13.11(c)   HB 35(2)(b), sch 5 para 3; HB66+ 29(1), 35(2)(b); NIHB 32(2)(b), sch 6 para 3; NIHB66+ 27(1), 33(2)(b)

T13.11(d)   HB sch 5 para 12; HB66+ 29(1); NIHB66+ 27(1)

T13.11(e),(f) HB sch 5 para 44; HB66+ 29(1); NIHB sch 6 para 46; NIHB66+ 27(1)

T13.11(g)   HB sch 5 para 45; HB66+ 29(1); NIHB sch 6 para 47; NIHB66+ 27(1)

T13.11(h)   HB sch 5 para 46; HB66+ 29(1); NIHB sch 6 para 48; NIHB66+ 27(1)

T13.11(i)   HB 2(1), sch 5 para 35; HB66+ 29(1); NIHB 2(1), sch 6 para 37; NIHB66+ 27(1)

T13.11(j)   HB sch 5 para 10; HB66+ 29(1); NIHB sch 6 para 11; NIHB66+ 27(1)

T13.11(k)   HB 35(2)(a), sch 5 para 23; HB66+ 29(1); NIHB 32(2)(a), sch 6 para 24; NIHB66+ 27(1)

T13.11(l)   HB66+ 29(1); NIHB66+ 27(1); R v Doncaster MBC & Another ex p Boulton 11/12/92 QBD 25 HLR 195

T13.11(m)   HB sch 5 para 39; HB66+ 29(1); NIHB sch 6 para 41; NIHB66+ 27(1)

T13.11(n)   HB 41(4), sch 5 para 13(1)(c); HB66+ 29(1)

Notional income

13.50 This section explains when you are counted as having unearned or earned income you do not in fact have. This is called 'notional' income.

13.51 For working age HB, this section also includes rules about notional capital when these are similar. The main rules about notional capital are in paras 15.57-60.

Types of notional income

13.52 You can be counted as having notional income when:

(a) there is income available to you (paras 13.54-56);

(b) in working age HB, you are paid income on behalf of someone else (paras 13.57 and 13.59);

(c) someone else is paid income on your behalf (paras 13.58-59);

(d) you have deprived yourself of income (para 13.60);

(e) a non-dependant has more income and capital than you (para 13.61); or

(f) in working age HB, you are paid less than the going rate for a job (para 14.24).

Assessing notional income

13.53 If you are counted as having notional income, it is assessed in the same way as actual income and all the disregards given earlier in this chapter and in chapter 14 apply. This means this section does not apply if you are on a passport benefit.

Money which is available to you

13.54 If income is available to you and you could get it by applying for it, it is counted as your notional income (but only from when you would get it if you did apply). In working age HB, this rule also applies to capital. For further details see paras 13.55-56.

13.55 In pension age HB, the rule in para 13.54 applies only to income from:

(a) a private pension (para 13.27); or

(b) a state pension unless you have deferred it (para 13.13).

For DWP guidance, see GM paras BP2.680-750.

13.56 In working age HB, the rule in para 13.54 applies to any kind of income or capital except for:

(a) income/capital from a private pension (para 13.27) if you (the claimant) are under 66;

(b) income/capital from a personal injury payment (paras 15.43-44);

(c) income/capital from a discretionary trust;

(d) income/capital from WTC or CTC;

13.53   HB 42(11),(12); HB66+ 25; NIHB 39(11),(12); NIHB66+ 23

13.54   HB 42(2), 49(2); HB66+ 41(1),(4); NIHB 39(2), 46(2); NIHB66+ 39(1),(4)

13.55   HB66+ 41(1)-(7); NIHB66+ 39(1)-(7)

13.56   HB 42(2),(12A), 49(2); NIHB 39(2),(12A), 46(2)

(e)   income from expenses or earnings as a service user group member;

(f)   income from a DWP rehabilitation allowance; or

(g)   capital from a loan you could raise against disregarded property or against other disregarded capital.

The DWP says this rule should not be used in the case of any state benefit if there is a doubt about whether you would qualify or how much you would get (see GM para BW2.682). See also paras 13.53 and 15.61.

Payments received by one person on behalf of another

13.57   In working age HB, if you receive payments of income on behalf of someone else, they are counted as your notional income if you keep or use them for yourself or your family. This rule also applies to payments of capital. For exceptions see para 13.59.

13.58   If someone else receives payments of income on your behalf, they are counted as your notional income if they are from:

(a)   a private pension (paras 13.27 and 13.59(a)); or

(b)   some other source, but in this case only if the payment is used for your or your family's:

- rent (other than any part of the rent which is not eligible for HB, or not met by HB because of a non-dependant deduction);

- council tax (rates in Northern Ireland); or

- water charges, household fuel, food or ordinary clothing or footwear (apart from school uniform/sportswear).

In working age HB, this rule also applies to payments of capital. For exceptions see para 13.59.

13.59   The rules in paras 13.57-58 do not apply to

(a)   income/capital from a private pension (para 13.27) if:

- the person whose pension it is, is bankrupt (or sequestered in Scotland) and has no other income; and

- the person it is paid to is their trustee in bankruptcy or someone else acting on behalf of their creditors;

(b)   income/capital from the government-sponsored trusts and funds in paras 15.42(a) to (d);

(c)   income from Grenfell Tower payments, Windrush payments and payments for historical child abuse;

(d)   income/capital from government work programme training schemes;

(e)   income from expenses or earnings as a service user group member; or

(f)   income from cash in lieu of concessionary coal.

See also paras 13.53 and 15.60.

13.57   HB 42(6)(c), 49(3)(c); NIHB 39(6)(c), 46(3)(c)

13.58   HB 2(1) definition: 'ordinary clothing and footwear', 42(6)(a),(b),(13), 49(3)(a),(b),(8), sch 5 para 23(2); HB66+ 42(1); NIHB 2(1), 39(6)(a),(b),(14), 46(3)(a),(b),(8), sch 6 para 24(2); NIHB66+ 40(1)

13.59   HB 42(7),(7A),(12A), 49(4); HB66+ 29(1), 42(2),(3); NIHB 39(7),(7A),(12A), 46(4); NIHB66+ 27(1), 40(2),(3)

Income you have deprived yourself of

13.60   If you have deprived yourself of income, it is counted as your notional income. To 'deprive' yourself of income means:

(a)   you have disposed of it (for example by stopping it being paid); and

(b)   your purpose in doing so was to make yourself entitled to HB or to more HB.

This rule is likely to be interpreted in a similar way to the rule about deprivation of capital (see table 15.3(a) to (e)). In practice it is rare, but could in some cases apply if you sell your right to receive income from a private pension by 'assigning' your pension annuity (HB G8/2016). It does not apply to income from expenses or earnings as a service user group member, or to income from a state pension you have deferred (para 13.13). See also para 13.53.

If your non-dependant has more income and capital than you

13.61   You are counted as having your non-dependant's income and capital (instead of yours) if:

(a)   they have more income and capital than you; and

(b)   you and they arranged to 'take advantage of' (abuse) the HB scheme, for example by deliberately making them your non-dependant rather than making you their non-dependant.

This rule is in practice rare. It does not apply if you are on a passport benefit.

13.60   HB 42(1),(12A); HB66+ 41(8)-(8C),(11),(12); NIHB 39(1),(12A); NIHB66+ 39(8)-(10A),(13),(14)

13.61   HB 26; HB66+ 24, 27(4)(f); NIHB 23; NIHB66+ 22, 25(4)(f)

Chapter 14 **Earned income**

- General rules: see paras 14.1-4.
- Employed earnings and how they are assessed: see paras 14.5-16.
- Calculating net earnings: see paras 14.17-25.
- Self-employed earnings and how they are assessed: see paras 14.26-35.
- Calculating net profit: see paras 14.36-59.
- Earnings disregards: see paras 14.60-73.

Assessing earned income

14.1   This chapter explains how your earned income is assessed for HB purposes.

14.2   In this chapter, 'your' earned income always includes the earned income of your partner. See paras 13.1-8 for details about this and for other general rules.

14.3   The rules in this chapter apply to income from employment or self-employment in the UK (England, Wales, Scotland and Northern Ireland). If you are claiming HB in Northern Ireland they also apply to income from employment or self-employment in the Republic of Ireland. For other countries see para 13.48.

The amount of your earned income

14.4   For HB purposes, the amount of your earned income is:

(a) the weekly amount of your (and your partner's):
- net earnings from employment (para 14.17), and/or
- net profit from self-employment (para 14.36);

(b) minus the earned income disregards which apply to you (para 14.60).

It can also include notional earnings (see 14.24).

> ### Example: Earned income
>
> One partner in a couple is employed and has net earnings of £230 per week. The other is self-employed and has a net profit of £150 per week. They qualify for a standard earned income disregard of £10 per week.
>
> Their combined earned income after the disregard has been made is £370 per week. This figure is used in calculating their HB.

14.4   HB 2(1) definition: 'earnings', 36(1),(2), 38(1),(2); HB66+ 2(1), 33(8)(a), 36(1), 39(1);
NIHB 2(1), 33(1),(2), 35(1),(2); NIHB66+ 2(1), 31(8)(a), 34(1), 37(1)

Employed earnings

14.5   This section explains what employed earnings are and the information used to assess them. This information is needed to calculate your 'net earnings', which is the figure used in HB. (The calculation is in paras 14.17-32.)

What are employed earnings

14.6   Your employed earnings are your earnings from employment 'under a contract of service' (an employment contract) or 'in an office'. An 'office' means the kind of job that may not have an employment contract. People employed in an office include directors of limited companies, local authority councillors and clergy.

14.7   Table 14.1 explains which payments count as employed earnings and which do not. Payments which count as employed earnings are usually shown on your pay slip. For arrears of earnings see para 13.7.

Table 14.1 **Employed earnings**

The following count as employed earnings:

  (a) Employed earnings generally (see para 14.6).

  (b) Employed earnings paid in a lump sum (see also paras 14.58-59).

  (c) Sick, maternity, paternity, shared parental and adoption pay from your employer.

  (d) Statutory sick, maternity, paternity, shared parental and adoption pay.

  (e) Holiday pay.

  (f) Retainers.

  (g) Bonuses and commission.

  (h) Tips.

  (i) Payments in lieu of notice.

  (j) Payments in lieu of earnings (but for redundancy payments see (q) below).

(k) Non-cash vouchers which are earnings for national insurance purposes.

(l) Councillor's allowances, but for expenses see (n) below (R(IS) 6/92). For detailed guidance see GM paras BW2.83-95.

(m) Company director's income (para 14.6).

The following have individual rules:

(n) Expenses paid by your employer:

- these are disregarded if they are 'wholly, exclusively and necessarily incurred' in carrying out your employment. For example, for travel between workplaces (R(IS) 16/93, CIS 507/94), or all travel if you don't have a fixed workplace and can be asked to work anywhere in your area (CH/1330/2008, in which the claimant was a care worker);

- apart from that, they count as your employed earnings. For example, for travel between your home and workplace, or for caring for a member of your family.

(o) Expenses you receive as a participant service user are disregarded (for example where you are being consulted by councils, social landlords or health authorities).

(p) Compensation payments for unfair dismissal or under laws about equal pay etc, whether made by an employment tribunal or in an out of court settlement:

- count as your employed earnings in working age HB claims;

- do not count as your employed earnings in pension age HB (but are likely to be included as your capital).

(q) Redundancy payments count as your capital, not earnings (but for payments in lieu of notice see (j) above).

(r) Payments in kind (in other words, in goods rather than money or vouchers) are disregarded (see also table 13.11(k)). But payments in private currencies count as your employed earnings, for example in local exchange trading schemes (GM paras BW2.99-101) or in internet currencies.

(s) Bounty payments you receive as a part-time firefighter, a part-time lifeboat worker, an auxiliary coastguard or a member of the Territorial Army or similar reserve forces – all these count as your capital, not earnings, if they are paid to you annually or at longer intervals (see also table 14.5(f)).

T14.1(k)   HB 35(1)(k); HB66+ 35(1)(g); NIHB 32(1)(l); NIHB66+ 33(1)(g)

T14.1(l)   HB 35(1); HB66+ 35(1); NIHB 32(1); NIHB66+ 33(1)

T14.1(m)   HB 35(1); HB66+ 35(1); NIHB 32(1); NIHB66+ 33(1)

T14.1(n)   HB 35(1)(f),(2)(b); HB66+ 35(1)(f),(2)(b); NIHB 32(1)(f),(2)(b); NIHB66+ 33(1)(f),(2)(b)

T14.1(o)   HB 2(5) definition: 'participating as a service user' 35(2)(d); HB66+ 2(6), 35(2)(f); NIHB 2(4A), 32(2)(d); NIHB66+ 2(5A), 33(2)(e)

T14.1(p)   HB 35(1)(g),(gg),(h), 41(3); HB66+ 35(2)(e); NIHB 32(1)(g),(gg),(h), 38(3); NIHB66+ 33(2)(d)

T14.1(q)   HB 35(1)(b), 44(1); HB66+ 35(1)(b), 44(1); NIHB 32(1)(b), 41(1); NIHB66+ 33(1)(b), 44(1)

T14.1(r)   HB 35(2)(a),(3); HB66+ 35(2)(a),(3); NIHB 32(2)(a),(3); NIHB66+ 33(2)(a),(3)

T14.1(s)   HB 46(1); NIHB 43(1)

(t)   Advances of earnings and loans from your employer count as your capital, not earnings.

(u)   Tax refunds on your earnings count as your capital, not earnings.

(v)   Occupational pensions count as your unearned income (para 13.27).

(w)   Strike pay counts as your unearned income in working age HB claims, but is disregarded in pension age HB.

(x)   Self-employed earnings are assessed separately (paras 14.26-35, and for royalties and similar payments paras 14.58-59).

Notes

■   The rules in (b), (s), (t) and (u) are given in the law for working age HB. They are also likely to apply for pension age HB.

■   See also paras 14.13-16 if you are absent from work or your job ends.

Assessing employed earnings

14.8   When your employed earnings are assessed, the purpose is to estimate 'the amount which is likely to be' your average weekly net earnings (for net earnings see para 14.17). This is done using information from an assessment period or employer's estimate (paras 14.9-11), but other relevant information should also be taken into account in order to obtain a fair and accurate result. For these purposes, your earnings count as belonging to the period they cover, whether they are paid at the beginning or end of that period or part way through it.

Assessment periods

14.9   In working age HB claims, when you make your claim your assessment period is usually:

(a)   the two months before you claimed if you are paid monthly; or

(b)   the five weeks before you claimed if you are paid weekly; or

(c)   if you have not been working long enough for the above to apply:

■   the period you have been working if what you have been paid is representative;

■   if what you have been paid is not representative, or you haven't yet been paid, an employer's estimate is used (para 14.11);

(d)   but if your earnings vary, whatever period gives a more accurate result.

If your earnings change while you are on HB, your assessment period is whatever period gives an accurate result. But it must not be longer than 52 weeks, and must not include periods before the change occurred ([2015] UKUT 237 (AAC)).

T14.1(t)   HB 46(5); NIHB 43(5)

T14.1(u)   HB 46(2); NIHB 43(2)

T14.1(v)   HB 35(2)(c); HB66+ 35(2)(c); NIHB 32(2)(c); NIHB66+ 33(2)(c)

T14.1(w)   HB 35(1); HB66+ 29(1); NIHB 32(1); NIHB66+ 27(1)

14.8   HB 27(1)(a), 29(1)-(3), 29A; HB66+ 30(1)(a), 33(2),(2A),(3),(3A); NIHB 24(1)(a), 26(1)-(3), 26A; NIHB66+ 28(1)(a), 31(2),(2A),(3),(3A)

14.9   HB 2(1) definition: 'assessment period', 29(1)-(3); NIHB 2(1), 26(1)-(3);

14.10 In pension age HB, when you make your claim your assessment period usually uses the following information:

(a) your most recent two payments if they are one month or more apart; or

(b) your most recent four payments in other cases; or

(c) whatever payments give a more accurate result;

(d) but if your hours vary over a recognisable cycle (for example you work a regular pattern of shifts, or you work in term-times but not school holidays), information about the whole of that cycle.

If your earnings change while you are on HB, the rules in (c) or (d) usually apply.

Employer's estimates

14.11 Your council can ask your employer to provide information about your earnings (see also para 16.22), or can ask you to obtain this information from your employer. Many councils have a 'certificate of earnings' form which can be used for this.

Examples: Assessing employed earnings

1. Ivy's weekly earnings have been the same over the five weeks before she claimed HB.

   ▪ Her weekly net earnings are calculated from this weekly amount.

2. Adam's monthly earnings have varied over the two months before he claimed HB. Evidence about his earlier earnings shows that an average can fairly be taken over the past six months.

   ▪ His weekly net earnings are calculated from the past six months' figures.

3. Fatima has moved to the area for a new job. She claims HB a few days after starting work.

   ▪ She is asked to provide an employer's estimate, and her weekly net earnings are calculated from that.

Starting a job

14.12 When you start a job, your earnings can be estimated to begin with (paras 14.9(c) and 14.11). They are taken into account from the Monday following the first day you are paid for, even if your first pay day is later on. But if you have been out of work for 26 weeks or more, you may qualify for an 'extended payment' of HB (para 17.32).

Leaving a job

14.13 When you leave a job, your earnings are taken into account until the Sunday following the last day you are paid for. But in working age HB, holiday pay counts as your capital, not earnings, if it is payable more than four weeks after you left.

14.10 HB66+ 2(1) definition: 'assessment period', 33(2),(3); NIHB66+ 2(1),31(2),(3)

14.12 HB 29A(b); HB66+ 33 (2A)(b),(3A)(b); NIHB 26A(b); NIHB66+ 31(2A)(b),(3A)(b)

14.13 HB 35(1)(d), 46(3); NIHB 32(1)(d), 43(3)

14.14   And if your job ended before your first day of entitlement to HB:

(a)   in working age HB, all your earnings from that job are disregarded except for compensation (see table 14.1(p)) and retainers;

(b)   in pension age HB, all your earnings from that job are disregarded.

Absences from work

14.15   When you are absent from work, your earnings are reassessed if they change. This applies to all absences, whether they are:

(a)   due to sickness (with or without leave);

(b)   due to maternity, paternity, shared parental or adoption leave;

(c)   'with good cause' (for example you are furloughed or laid off);

(d)   on holiday;

(e)   on strike; or

(f)   for any other reason (including absences 'without good cause').

But in working age HB, holiday pay counts as your capital, not earnings, if it is payable more than four weeks after your absence began.

14.16   And in working age HB, if your absence:

(a)   began before your first day of entitlement to HB; and

(b)   is for one of the reasons in para 14.15(a), (b) or (c),

all your earnings from that job are disregarded except for employer's and statutory sick, maternity, paternity, shared parental or adoption pay, compensation (table 14.1(p)) and retainers.

Calculating net earnings

14.17   It is your 'net earnings' which are used in assessing your HB. They are calculated as follows, using the information described in paras 14.8-16:

(a)   start with your gross earnings: para 14.18;

(b)   deduct amounts for tax and national insurance: paras 14.19-21;

(c)   deduct half of your pension contributions: para 14.22;

(d)   convert the result to a weekly figure: para 6.37;

(e)   this gives your weekly net earnings: para 14.23.

See also paras 14.60-73 for the earned income disregards.

14.14   HB sch 4 paras 1(a),(b), 2(a),(b),(i), 16; HB66+ sch 4 para 8; NIHB sch 5 paras 1(a),(b), 2(a),(b),(i), 16; NIHB66+ sch 4 para 8

14.15   HB 35(1)(d), 46(3); NIHB 32(1)(d), 43(3)

14.16   HB sch 4 paras 1(c), 2(a),(b),(ii), 16; NIHB sch 5 paras 1(c), 2(a),(b),(ii), 16;

14.17   HB 2(1) definition: 'net earnings', 29(4), 36; HB66+ 2(1), 28, 36; NIHB 2(1), 26(4), 33; NIHB66+ 2(1), 26, 34

Example: Calculation of net earnings

Rosa has gross earnings are £1,450 per month. From this, her employer deducts £80.50 each month for tax, £48.24 each month for class 1 national insurance contributions (NICs), and £30.83 each month towards a pension scheme. Rosa's net earnings are calculated as follows.

From her gross earnings	£1,450 pcm
deduct:	
■ tax	£80.50 pcm
■ NICs	£48.24 pcm
■ half her pension contributions	£15.42 pcm
This gives her net earnings	£1,305.84 pcm

They are converted to a weekly figure:

■ £1,305.84 x 12 ÷ 52	£301.34 pw

The earned income disregards which apply to her are then deducted (para 14.60).

Gross earnings

14.18 Your 'gross earnings' are the total of your employed earnings: see paras 14.5-16 and table 14.1.

Deductions for tax and national insurance

14.19 Deductions are made from your gross earnings for:

(a) income tax; and

(b) class 1 national insurance contributions (NICs).

The deductions equal the amounts deducted by your employer for these. The amounts should be shown on your pay slip. The exceptions to this are in paras 14.20-21.

14.20 If your gross earnings were assessed using an employer's estimate (para 14.11) or you have notional earnings (para 14.24), the deductions are calculated by the council. They equal what would be deducted (if they were actual earnings) for:

(a) income tax, using only the specific personal reliefs that you are entitled to (i.e. the personal allowance, the blind person's allowance, the tax deduction for married couples and civil partners where one was born before 6th April 1935 and the transferable tax allowance for married couples and civil partners) [www]; and using the basic rate of tax, or for a Scottish taxpayer, the Scottish basic rate; and

(b) class 1 NICs.

14.18   HB 35; HB66+ 35; NIHB 32; NIHB66+ 33

14.19   HB 36(3),(a),(d); HB66+ 36(2),(a),(d); NIHB 33(3),(a),(d); NIHB66+ 34(2),(a),(d)

14.20   HB 2(1) definitions: 'basic rate', 'Scottish basic rate', 'Scottish taxpayer', 36(6),(a),(b); 42(12)(a),(b);
         HB66+ 2(1),36(5),(a),(b); NIHB 2(1),33(6),(a),(b),39(12)(a),(b); NIHB66+ 2(1),34(5),(a),(b)
         www.gov.uk/income-tax-rates

14.21   If you are claiming HB in Northern Ireland and work in the Republic of Ireland, the deductions are calculated by the NIHE. They equal what would be deducted for tax and class 1 NICs if you worked in Northern Ireland.

Deductions for pension contributions

14.22   If you make contributions towards an occupational or personal pension, one half of the amount you contribute is deducted from your gross earnings. If your gross earnings were assessed using an employer's estimate (para 14.11) or you have notional earnings (para 14.24), the deduction is calculated by the council. It equals one half of what you would contribute (if they were actual earnings).

Net earnings

14.23   The above calculation (paras 14.18-22) gives your net earnings. They are converted to a weekly figure (para 6.37). No other amounts can be deducted from them, even if you have to pay work expenses which are not met by your employer. Your weekly net earnings are used in calculating your HB (but only after the earned income disregards have been made: paras 14.60-73).

Notional earnings

14.24   In working age HB, you are counted as having 'notional' earnings (para 13.52(f)) if:

(a)   you work or provide a service for someone;

(b)   they pay you less than the rate for comparable employment in the area, or do not pay you; and

(c)   none of the exceptions in para 14.25 apply.

Your notional earnings equal the amount (if any) which would be reasonable for the comparable employment. Apart from that, notional earnings are assessed in the same way as actual earnings (but see paras 14.20 and 14.22).

14.25   The rule in para 14.24 does not apply to work you do or a service you provide:

(a)   for someone whose means are insufficient to pay you, or to pay you more; or

(b)   for a charitable or voluntary organisation or as a volunteer, if it is reasonable for you to work without being paid; or

(c)   in a government work programme training scheme or work placement.

14.21   NIHB 33(7); NIHB66+ 34(6)

14.22   HB 36(3)(b),(c),(4),(5),(6)(c), 42(12)(c); HB66+ 36(2)(b),(c),(3),(4),(5)(c);
        NIHB 33(3)(b),(c),(4),(5),(6)(c), 39(12)(c); NIHB66+ 34(2)(b),(c),(3),(4),(5)(c)

14.23   HB 2(1) definition: 'net earnings', 29(4), 36; HB66+ 2(1), 28, 36; NIHB 2(1), 26(4), 33; NIHB66+ 2(1), 26, 34

14.24   HB 27(4), 42(9),(12); NIHB 24(4), 39(9),(12)

14.25   HB 42(9),(10),(10A),(12A); NIHB 39(9),(10),(10A),(12A)

Self-employed earnings

14.26 This section explains what self-employed earnings are, and the information used to assess them. This information is needed to calculate your 'net profit', which is the figure used in HB. (The calculation is in paras 14.36-57.)

What are self-employed earnings

14.27 Your self-employed earnings are your earnings which:

(a) are from 'gainful employment'; but

(b) are not employed earner's earnings (para 14.6).

This applies whether you are a sole trader or in a partnership. Royalties and similar payments also usually count as self-employed earnings (paras 14.58-59).

14.28 Your self-employed earnings only include payments which:

(a) are income (not capital); and

(b) are 'derived from' your self-employment.

Table 14.2 lists payments which (for those reasons) do not count as self-employed earnings. Apart from that, self-employed earnings include payments in money, in kind (in other words, in goods) and in any other form (for example barter).

Table 14.2 **Self-employed earnings: exclusions**

The following do not count as self-employed earnings:

(a) Your business assets. These are capital (not income) and are disregarded (para 15.33).

(b) Grants and loans to your business. These are usually capital and (if so) are disregarded as part of your business assets.

(c) New enterprise allowance. This can help you start up in business if you are on UC, JSA, ESA or IS [www]. It is unearned income and can include a low cost loan. These are disregarded.

(d) Access to work. This can help you start up in business if you have a disability [www]. It is unearned income and is disregarded (table 13.1(o)).

(e) Other government work programme training schemes. Payments from these are usually disregarded (table 13.1(p)).

(f) Sports Council awards. These are usually disregarded (para 13.43).

(g) Foster care and kinship care payments. These are disregarded (table 13.5(a)).

(h) Boarding out and respite care payments. These are disregarded (table 13.5(f)).

14.27 CBA 2(1)(b); NICBA 2(1)(b); HB 2(1) definition: 'self-employed earner', 37(1); HB66+ 2(1), 38(1); NIHB 2(1), 34(1); NIHB66+ 2(1), 36(1)

14.28 HB 37(1); HB66+ 38(1); NIHB 34(1); NIHB66+ 36(1)

T14.2 HB 37(2); HB66+ 38(2); NIHB 34(2); NIHB66+ 36(2); www.gov.uk/new-enterprise-allowance; www.gov.uk/access-to-work

(i)   Rent you receive on your home (table 13.7).

(j)   Rent you receive on other property: R(FC) 2/92 (table 13.8). But if you rent out property as a business this counts as self-employed earnings (para 15.33).

(k)   Employed earnings are assessed separately (paras 14.5-16).

(l)   Income you receive as a director of a limited company counts as employed earnings (not self-employed earnings).

Assessing self-employed earnings

14.29   When your self-employed earnings are assessed, the purpose is to estimate 'the amount which is likely to be' your average weekly net profit (for net profit see para 14.36). This is done using information from an assessment period, but other information should be taken into account to obtain a fair and accurate result.

Assessment periods

14.30   Your assessment period is whatever period is appropriate to enable the most accurate estimation of your weekly net profit (CH/329/2003, [2003] UKUT 104 (AAC)). In working age HB it must not be longer than one year, and in pension age HB it is a year unless this would not be appropriate.

14.31   When you make your claim for HB your assessment period is usually:

(a)   the most recent full year for which you have accounts or other records; or

(b)   the period you have been self-employed if this is less than a year; or

(c)   in either case, a shorter or different period if this would be more representative;

(d)   but if you are just starting self-employment, an estimated future period (see para 14.33).

If your self-employed earnings change while you are on HB (para 14.35), your assessment period should usually be from the date the change occurred to the most recent date you have figures for (CH/329/2003, [2003] UKUT 104 (AAC)). For DWP guidance on assessment periods see GM paras BW2.330, BW2.333.

Providing accounts or other records

14.32   You are expected to provide information about your income and expenses in your assessment period. You can draw up accounts or other records yourself, or get someone else to do this for you. They can be drawn up on:

(a)   a cash basis, counting income when it comes in, and expenses when you pay them; or

(b)   an accrual basis, counting income when you issue a bill and expenses when you get a bill,

so long as you are reasonable, consistent, and fairly reflect your income and expenses.

14.29   HB 27(1)(a), 30(1); HB66+ 30(1)(a), 37; NIHB 24(1)(a), 27(1); NIHB66+ 28(1)(a), 35

14.30   HB 2(1) definition: 'assessment period', 30(1); HB66+ 2(1), 37; NIHB 2(1), 27(1); NIHB66+ 2(1), 35

Example: Self-employed earnings and net profit

Dennie is a self-employed window-cleaner. The records of his most recent year's trading show he had gross income of £10,268, and spent £354 on telephone, postage and stationery, £3,534 on petrol and other costs for his van, £187 on overalls and disposable equipment, £507 on advertising, and £613 to pay someone to cover his round while he was on holiday. His mileage records show that two-thirds of his use of the van is for his business (para 14.41).

The council decides that year is appropriate as his assessment period (see para 14.31), as the figures are likely to represent his current income and expenses. His pre-tax profit (para 14.46) is calculated as follows.

From his gross income	£10,268 pa
Deduct his allowable expenses (see table 14.3):	
telephone, postage and stationery	£354 pa
business use of van (⅔ of £3,534)	£2,356 pa
overalls and disposable equipment	£187 pa
advertising	£507 pa
holiday cover payments	£613 pa
This gives his pre-tax profit	£6,251 pa

This is used to calculate his weekly net profit (para 14.36). The earned income disregards which apply to him are then deducted (para 14.60).

Starting self-employment

14.33 When you start self-employment, your self-employed earnings can be estimated to begin with (para 14.31(d)). The estimate usually covers the first 13 weeks you will be self-employed. Most councils have a form you can use to give your estimated income and expenses for this period, and expect you to provide records of your actual income and expenses after that. If you have been out of work for 26 weeks or more, you may qualify for an 'extended payment' of HB (para 17.32).

Stopping self-employment

14.34 When you stop self-employment, any self-employed earnings are disregarded from the date you stopped, except for royalties etc (para 14.58-59).

14.34   HB sch 4 para 2A; NIHB sch 5 para 2A

Changes in your self-employed earnings

14.35   Your self-employed earnings can change in different ways. Generally speaking:

(a) short-term variations in your cash flow (for example from month to month) are a normal part of being self-employed, and do not mean your HB should be reassessed; but

(b) significant changes in your trading pattern mean your HB should be reassessed. For example, this could be because you change from full-time to part-time or from part-time to full-time, or gain or lose a major customer, or have a break from trading because you are sick or caring for someone or due to coronavirus.

Calculating net profit

14.36   It is your 'net profit' which the council uses to calculate your HB. It is calculated as follows using the information described in paras 14.29-35:

(a) start with your gross income: para 14.37;

(b) deduct your allowable expenses: paras 14.38-45 or 14.52;

(c) this gives your pre-tax profit (or if you are in a partnership your share is your pre-tax profit): paras 14.46-52;

(d) deduct amounts for tax and national insurance: paras 14.53-55;

(e) deduct half your pension contributions: para 14.56;

(f) convert the result to a weekly figure: para 6.37;

(g) this gives your weekly net profit: para 14.57.

See also paras 14.60-73 for the earned income disregards.

Gross income

14.37   Your gross income is the total of your self-employed earnings before any deductions have been made from them: see paras 14.26-35.

Allowable expenses

14.38   Your allowable expenses are deducted from your gross income. There are two main conditions about this:

(a) expenses are only allowable if they are 'wholly and exclusively incurred' for the purposes of the business: paras 14.40-44;

(b) but expenses are not allowable if they are not 'reasonably incurred': para 14.45.

Some types of expenses also have special rules, and these are all included in table 14.3.

14.39   Table 14.3 summarises which expenses are allowable and which are not, and further details are in paras 14.40-45. Different rules apply if you are a childminder: see para 14.52.

14.36   HB 2(1) definition: 'net profit', 30(2), 38; HB66+ 2(1), 28,39; NIHB 2(1), 27(2), 32; NIHB66+ 2(1), 26,37

14.37   HB 37(1); HB66+ 38(1); NIHB 34(1); NIHB66+ 36(1)

14.38   HB 38(3)(a),(4),(7); HB66+ 39(2)(a),(3),(6); NIHB 35(3)(a),(4),(7); NIHB66+ 37(2)(a),(3),(6)

Table 14.3 **Self-employed expenses**

Allowable expenses

(a) Expenditure (from your income) on repairing an existing business asset, apart from costs covered by an insurance policy.

(b) Capital repayments on a loan used for repairing an existing business asset, apart from costs covered by an insurance policy.

(c) Capital repayments on a loan used for replacing business equipment or machinery (this includes a loan for replacing a car: R(H) 5/07).

(d) Interest payments on any business loan.

(e) Any VAT you pay (minus any VAT you receive).

(f) Any other expenditure which meets the conditions in para 14.38. For example:

■ computer, telephone, postage, stationery and delivery costs,

■ transport and vehicle costs and hire and leasing charges,

■ materials, supplies, stock and protective clothing,

■ advertising and subscriptions to trade and professional bodies,

■ bank charges, insurance costs, and accountancy and legal fees,

■ staff costs and payments to subcontractors,

■ premises costs such as rent, rates, cleaning and fuel.

Non-allowable expenses

(g) Capital expenditure, such as buying a vehicle, equipment of a lasting nature, or business premises.

(h) Capital repayments on a loan, unless (b) or (c) above applies.

(i) Depreciation of capital assets.

(j) Expenditure on setting up or expanding your business (but interest on loans for this is allowable: see (d) above).

(k) Losses you have incurred before your assessment period (paras 14.30-31).

(l) Expenditure on business entertainment.

(m) Unpaid bills you have sent out, unless they are proven bad debts.

(n) Expenditure for domestic or private purposes (see also paras 14.41-44).

(o) Any other expenditure which does not meet the conditions in para 14.38.

T14.3(a)-(e)   HB 38(6),(8)(b); HB66+ 39(5),(7)(b); NIHB 35(6),(8)(b); NIHB66+ 37(5),(7)(b)

T14.3(f)   HB 38(3)(a),(4),(7); HB66+ 39(2)(a),(3),(6); NIHB 35(3)(a),(4),(7); NIHB66+ 37(2)(a),(3),(6)

T14.3(g)-(n) HB 38(5),(8)(a); HB66+ 39(4),(7)(a); NIHB 35(5),(8)(a); NIHB66+ 37(4),(7)(a)

'Wholly and exclusively incurred' expenses

14.40   An expense is wholly and exclusively incurred for your business if all of it is for your business and no part of it is for anything else. For example, if you use a van only for your business (and do not use it for domestic, private or other purposes), your vehicle costs for the van are allowable expenses. See also paras 14.41-44.

Expenses for mixed purposes

14.41   If an expense is partly for your business and partly for another purpose, you can separate it out to find the business part. This is also called 'apportioning' expenses. For example, if you use a car for both business and personal purposes, you can keep records of your mileage and then separate the costs on that basis. The business part is then allowable. But the calculation does not have to be that detailed, so long as the method you use is fair and reasonable.

14.42   Even expenses you would incur anyway can be apportioned. For example you would have to pay for insurance and a vehicle licence on a car (and perhaps repay a car loan) even if you did not use it for your business, but you can apportion these expenses in the same way as the petrol you use (R(H) 5/07, which followed R(FC) 1/91).

Expenses if you work from home

14.43   If you work from home, part of your accommodation costs are an allowable expense. For example, this can include part of your fuel for heating and lighting, standing charges, and rent (see also para 14.44). The business part of these should be calculated in a fair and reasonable way, taking into account the size of your working area compared with the size of the rest of your home, and the amount of time you use it for business rather than domestic purposes. In one case a self-employed claimant used the second bedroom in their home only for business purposes. The difference between the total rent on their home and the rent officer's valuation of the rent for a one-bedroom flat was accepted as an appropriate allowable expense (para 12 of R(H) 5/07).

14.44   But when part of your rent is allowed as a business expense, that part cannot be included in your eligible rent: para 8.19.

14.40   HB 38(3)(a),(4); HB66+ 39(2)(a),(3); NIHB 35(3)(a),(4); NIHB66+ 37(2)(a),(3)

'Reasonably incurred' expenses

14.45   Whether an expense is reasonably incurred depends on the circumstances of the individual case (R(P) 2/54), including how much you earn from your business (R(G) 1/56). If an expense is appropriate and necessary, it should always be considered reasonably incurred unless it is excessive (R(G) 7/62). If an expense is excessive only the part which is reasonable is allowable.

Pre-tax profit (chargeable income)

14.46   Deducting your allowable expenses from your gross income gives your pre-tax profit. In the law it is called your 'chargeable income'. Further rules about pre-tax profit are in paras 14.47-52. See also paras 14.53-56 for deductions for tax etc.

Pre-tax profit for business partnerships

14.47   If you are self-employed in a partnership, your pre-tax profit is worked out for your business and then divided between you. The same applies if you are a share fisherman. The division is made in the same way as you actually share the net profit derived from the business. For example if you are one of two business partners and you get one-third of the net profit (perhaps reflecting the different hours you work in the business or the terms of a partnership agreement), then this is the proportion of the pre-tax profit of the business that the council should use in the calculation of your HB.

Pre-tax profit and couples

14.48   If you are a couple and are also business partners, your pre-tax profit is divided between you (see para 14.47). If you are self-employed and employ your partner, the pre-tax profit isn't shared between you. But the wages or salary you pay them are your allowable expenses, and are your partner's employed earnings.

If you make a loss

14.49   If your allowable expenses are greater than (or equal to) your gross income, your pre-tax profit is nil, so your self-employed earnings are nil (R(H) 5/08).

14.50   Your losses cannot be deducted from any other employed or self-employed earnings you have, or your partner or any other family member has (R(H) 5/08).

Pre-tax profit and drawings

14.51   If you take drawings from your business (for example as a kind of wage or salary you pay yourself), this has no effect on the calculation of your pre-tax profit. Drawings are not part of your gross income (R(H) 6/09) and are not an allowable business expense (GM paras BW2.390-396).

14.45   HB 38(7); HB66+ 39(6); NIHB 35(7); NIHB66+ 37(6)

14.46   HB 38(3)(a); HB66+ 39(3)(a); NIHB 35(3)(a); NIHB66+ 37(3)(a)

14.47   HB 38(1)(b); HB66+ 39(1)(b); NIHB 35(1)(b); NIHB66+ 37(1)(b)

14.50   HB 38(10); HB66+ 39(9); NIHB 35(10); NIHB66+ 37(9)

Pre-tax profit if you are a childminder

14.52   If you are a self-employed childminder:

(a)   your expenses are not deducted from your gross income;

(b)   instead, your pre-tax profit always equals one-third of your gross income.

This is intended to make the calculation easier.

Example: A self-employed childminder

Hendl is a self-employed childminder. She gets gross income from her childminding which averages £240 per week. She works from her home and it would be difficult to assess her expenses, but she does not have to do this because her pre-tax profit is calculated as follows.

Her gross income is	£240
Of this only one-third is counted as her pre-tax profit	£80
This is too low for deductions for tax and national insurance.	
So her net profit is also	£80

The earned income disregards which apply to her are then deducted (para 14.60).

Deductions for tax and national insurance

14.53   Deductions are made from your pre-tax profit for:

(a)   income tax; and

(b)   classes 2 and 4 national insurance contributions (NICs).

The deductions are calculated by the council and are called 'notional tax' and 'notional NICs'. They are unlikely to be the same as the amounts you actually pay HMRC, for a number of reasons, e.g. different assessment periods and differences in what expenses are treated as allowable for income tax and for HB.

14.54   Table 14.4 shows how the deductions are calculated. It gives the figures for the tax year from 6th April 2023 to 5th April 2024 (this tax year contains 365 days). The calculation:

(a)   uses annual figures. So if your pre-tax profit is not an annual amount it is converted to an annual figure;

(b)   uses the tax and NICs figures for the tax year which is 'applicable to' your assessment period (paras 14.30-31). If your assessment period spanned two tax years, councils interpret this in different ways. Many use the most straightforward method of using the figures for the tax year containing your date of claim for HB (or the date your HB is reassessed).

When making the calculation, councils can ignore national changes in the tax and NICs rates and allowances for up to 30 weeks.

14.52   HB 39(3)(b); HB66+ 40(3)(b); NIHB 36(3)(b); NIHB66+ 38(3)(b)

14.53   HB 38(1)(b)(i),(3)(b),(9)(a), 39; HB66+ 39(1)(b)(i),(2)(b),(8)(a), 40; NIHB 35(1)(b)(i),(3)(b),(9)(a), 36; NIHB66+ 37(1)(b)(i),(2)(b),(8)(a), 38

14.54   HB 2(1) definitions: 'basic rate', 'tax year', 'Scottish basic rate', 'Scottish taxpayer', 34, 39(1),(2);
         HB66+ 2(1), 34, 40(1),(2); NIHB 2(1), 31, 36(1),(2); NIHB66+ 2(1), 32, 38(1),(2)

14.55 The calculations in table 14.4 apply in Northern Ireland even if your self-employment is based in the Republic of Ireland.

Table 14.4 **Notional tax and NICs: 2023-24 tax year**

This table shows how your notional tax and national insurance contributions (NICs) are calculated if you are self-employed. All three calculations are made (though one or more of them may give a figure of nil).

(a) Income tax

- start with your annual pre-tax profit
- subtract the personal relief(s) which apply to you, e.g. the £12,570 personal allowance
- if there is a remainder, multiply it by the basic rate of tax (20%) or in the case of a Scottish taxpayer, the Scottish basic rate (20%)
- the result is the annual amount of your notional tax.

(b) Class 2 NICs

- if your annual pre-tax profit is £12,570 or more, the annual amount of your notional class 2 NICs is £179.40.

(c) Class 4 NICs

- start with your annual pre-tax profit;
- multiply the first £12,570 by 0%, the rest up to £50,270 by 9%, and any remainder by 2%;
- the result is the annual amount of your notional class 4 NICs.

Notes:

(a) The personal reliefs that may be applicable dependent upon your circumstances are: the personal allowance, the blind person's allowance, the tax deduction for married couples and civil partners where one was born before 6th April 1935 and the transferable tax allowance for married couples and civil partners [www];

(b) £179.40 is 52 times the weekly class 2 NICs of £3.45, there being 52 Sundays in the 2023-24 tax year. If your pre-tax profit is below £12,570, your notional class 2 NICs are nil (even if you have not applied to HMRC for exemption).

14.55   NIHB 35(12); NIHB66+ 37(11)

T14.4   HB 2(1) definitions: 'basic rate', 'tax year', 'Scottish basic rate', 'Scottish taxpayer', 39; HB66+ 2(1), 40;
CBA s15; Health & Social Care Levy Act 2021 s5(2)(c)
HM Treasury Autumn Statement 2022: CP 751 paras 5.17-18 https://tinyurl.com/AutumnStatement2022
NIHB 2(1), 36; NIHB66+ 2(1), 38; SI 2023/236; NICBA s 15; Health & Social Care Levy Act 2021 s 5(4)(c)
www.gov.uk/income-tax-rates

Example: Notional tax and NICs

Florence is a self-employed book-keeper who lives in England. She provides her most recent accounts for a full year. The council decides that year is appropriate as her assessment period (para 14.31). In that year she had gross income of £15,150 and allowable expenses of £1,400, so her pre-tax profit is £13,750. She doesn't contribute to a pension scheme. Her notional tax and national insurance contributions (NICs) are calculated as follows (table 14.4).

(a) Notional tax

- from her pre-tax profit   £13,750.00 pa
- subtract the personal allowance   £12,570.00 pa
                                                                            = £1,180.00 pa

- and multiply this by the basic rate (20%)
  to give her notional tax   £236.00 pa

(b) Notional class 2 NICs

- her pre-tax profit is greater than £12,570
  so her notional class 2 NICs are   £179.40 pa

(c) Notional class 4 NICs

- from her pre-tax profit   £13,750.00 pa
- subtract the lower earnings threshold   £12,570.00 pa
                                                                            = £1,180.00 pa

- and multiply this by 9% to give her notional class 4 NICs   £106.20 pa

(d) Net profit

- from her pre-tax profit deduct: £13,750.00 pa
  - her notional tax   £236.00 pa
  - her notional class 2 NICs   £179.40 pa
  - her notional class 4 NICs   £106.20 pa
- this gives her annual net profit   £13,228.40 pa
- it is converted to a weekly figure:
  - £13,228.40 ÷ 365 x 7   £253.70 pw

The earned income disregards which apply to her are then deducted (para 14.60).

Deductions for pension contributions

14.56   If you make regular contributions towards a qualifying personal pension scheme (i.e. a scheme that qualifies for tax relief) half of the amount you contribute is deducted from your pre-tax profit. If your contributions change (or you start or stop making contributions) your HB is reassessed.

14.56   HB 2(1) definition: 'personal pension scheme', 38(1)(b)(ii),(3)(c),(9)(b),(11),(12); HB66+ 2(1),39(1)(b)(ii),(2)(c),(8)(b),(10),(11);
NIHB 2(1),35(1)(b)(ii),(3)(c),(9)(b),(11),(13); NIHB66+ 2(1),37(1)(b)(ii),(2)(c),(8)(b),(10),(12)

Example: Pension contributions

A couple of months after Florence (in the previous example) claimed HB, she begins making pension contributions of £40 per month. Her HB is reassessed to take account of this as follows. (Her trading pattern has not changed so her income and expenses do not need to be reassessed: para 14.35.)

Her weekly net profit was	£253.70 pw
From this, deduct the weekly equivalent of half of her qualifying pension contributions (para 14.56):	
▪ £20 x 12 ÷ 365 x 7	£4.60 pw
This gives her new weekly net profit	£249.10 pw

The earned income disregards which apply to her are then deducted (para 14.60).

Net profit

14.57   The above calculation (paras 14.37-56) gives your net profit. This is converted to a weekly figure (para 6.37). The council uses your weekly net profit to calculate your HB (but only after the earned income disregards have been made: paras 14.60-73).

Royalties and similar payments

14.58   The following payments count as earned income. In working age HB they are assessed as self-employed earnings (para 14.36), and in practice this is also done in pension age HB:

(a) royalties or other payments you receive for the use of, or right to use, a copyright, design, patent or trademark;

(b) payments you receive as an author under the Public Lending Right scheme or a similar international scheme; and

(c) in pension age HB, any other 'occasional' payment you earn.

The rules in (a) and (b) only apply if you are the first owner of the copyright etc or an original contributor to the book etc. If you have inherited the right to receive royalties etc, this is unearned income (para 13.44).

14.59   Because these payments are often annual, six monthly or irregular, there are special rules saying what period they cover:

(a) in pension age HB, they are averaged over the year beginning with the date of payment. For example, a payment of £364 is gross income of £7 per week over that year (see para 6.37);

14.57   HB 2(1) definition: 'net profit', 30(2), 38; HB66+ 2(1), 28,39; NIHB 2(1), 27(2), 35; NIHB66+ 2(1), 26,37

14.58   HB 37(3); HB66+ 29(1)(q),(r), 33(5),(8)(b),(8A); NIHB 34(3); NIHB66+ 27(1)(o),(p), 31(5),(8)(b),(8A)

14.59   HB 37(4); HB66+ 33(4); NIHB 34(4); NIHB66+ 31(4)

(b) in working age HB, work through the following steps:

- start with the weekly amount of your HB (calculated as though you did not receive the royalties etc);
- add to that all the earned income disregards which apply to you (para 14.60);
- the result is your gross income for each week until payment is used up. For example, if your HB is £90 per week and you qualify for only the £10 per week earned income disregard, a payment of £364 is gross income of £100 per week for three weeks, then £64 in the fourth week.

Earned income disregards

14.60   This section describes the amounts which are disregarded from your earned income. You may qualify for one, two, or all three of the following:

(a) a standard earned income disregard (para 14.62);

(b) a child care disregard (paras 14.63-67);

(c) an additional earned income disregard (para 14.68).

They can be described as the amounts you are allowed to 'keep' before your earned income affects the amount of your HB.

How the disregards work

14.61   The earned income disregards work as follows:

(a) first add together all your (and your partner's):

- weekly net earnings from employment (para 14.17), and
- weekly net profit from self-employment (para 14.36);

(b) then (from that total) deduct the standard earned income disregard;

(c) then deduct the child care disregard if you qualify for it. But if:

- the result of (b) is not enough to deduct the whole of the child care disregard, and
- you are on working tax credit or child tax credit,

the balance of the child care disregard is deducted from your WTC and/or CTC;

(d) then deduct the additional earned income disregard if you qualify for it. But if:

- the result of (c) is not enough to deduct the whole of the additional earned income disregard (£17.10 as shown in para 14.68), and
- you are on working tax credit,

the whole of the additional earned income disregard (not just the balance) is instead deducted from your WTC.

Except as described in (c) and (d), no part of the earned income disregards can be deducted from your unearned income. (See para 13.47 if you make parental contributions to a student.)

14.61   HB 2(1) definition: 'earnings' 27(1)(c),(2), 36(2), 38(2), sch 4 paras 3-10A, sch 5 para 56; SI 2020/371 reg 5;
HB66+ 2(1), 30(1)(c),(2), 33(8), sch 4 paras 1-5A, 7, 9(1),(3), sch 5 para 21;
NIHB 2(1), 24(1)(c),(2), 33(2), 35(2), sch 5 paras 3-10A, sch 6 para 58; NISR 2020/53 reg 5;
NIHB66+ 2(1), 28(1)(c),(2), 31(8), sch 5 paras 1-5A, 7, 9(1),(3), sch 6 para 22

Examples: Earned income disregards

1. A couple without children

Eli and Mia are in their 40s and are both employed for 35 hours a week. Their combined net earnings are £800 per week. They do not have children.

From their weekly net earnings:	£800.00
Deduct:	
■ the standard earned income disregard for a couple (table 14.5 (g))	£10.00
■ the additional earned income disregard (para 14.68 and table 14.7(b))	£17.10
This gives the figure used in calculating Eli and Mia's HB	£772.90

2. A lone parent with child care costs

Arlo is aged 30. He is self-employed for 20 hours a week, and his net earnings are £250 per week. He pays child care charges of £70 per week for his daughter aged 9.

From his weekly earnings:	£250.00
Deduct:	
■ the standard earned income disregard for a lone parent (table 14.5(b))	£25.00
■ the child care disregard (paras 14.63-64)	£70.00
■ the additional earned income disregard (para 14.68 and table 14.7(c))	£17.10
This gives the figure used in calculating Arlo's HB	£137.90

The standard earned income disregard

14.62   Everyone who has earned income qualifies for a standard earned income disregard. The disregard has different amounts, but whether you are a single claimant, a lone parent, or a couple, you qualify for only one amount. Table 14.5 explains the conditions for each amount, and which one you qualify for.

14.62   HB sch 4 paras 3-10A; HB66+ sch 4 paras 1-5A, 7; NIHB sch 5 paras 3-10A; NIHB66+ sch 5 paras 1-5A, 7

Table 14.5 **The standard earned income disregard**

The standard earned income disregard has different amounts (para 14.62), all given in this table. You qualify for the first amount you meet the conditions for.

(a) 'Permitted work' approved by the DWP: £167 per week

The disregard is £167 per week if you are in 'permitted work'. This means work the DWP has agreed you can do while you are receiving:

- ESA(C);
- incapacity benefit;
- severe disablement allowance; or
- national insurance credits instead of those benefits.

If you are a couple and only one of you is in permitted work, it is disregarded from that one's earned income. But if that is less than £167 per week, the balance up to £20 per week is disregarded from the other one's earned income. The disregard is set at 16 times the national living wage, rounded up to the next 50 pence.

(b) Lone parents: £25 per week

Unless (a) applies to you, the disregard is £25 per week if you are a lone parent.

(c) Sickness or disability: £20 per week: working age HB

In working age HB, unless (a) or (b) apply to you, the disregard is £20 per week if you or your partner:

- get main phase ESA (para 12.47) or national insurance credits instead (para 12.45);
- qualify for a disability premium (para 12.37); or
- qualify for a severe disability premium (para 12.25).

(d) Sickness or disability: £20 per week: pension age HB

In pension age HB claims, unless (a) or (b) apply to you, the disregard is £20 per week if you or your partner:

- receive attendance allowance or constant attendance allowance paid with an industrial injury or war disablement pension;
- receive personal independence payment or disability living allowance.
- receive the disability element or severe disability element of working tax credit;
- receive an armed forces independence payment;

T14.5(a)   HB sch 4 para 10A; HB66+ sch 4 para 5A; NIHB sch 5 para 10A; NIHB66+ sch 5 para 5A
            SI 2008/794 reg 45(3),(9A); SI 2013/379 reg 39(1),(4); NISR 2008/280 reg 45(3),(9A); NISR 2016/219 reg 39(1),(4)

T14.5(b)   HB sch 4 para 4; HB66+ sch 4 paras 1(a),2; NIHB sch 5 para 4; NIHB66+ sch 5 paras 1(a),2

T14.5(c)   HB sch 4 para 3; ; NIHB sch 5 para 3;

T14.5(d)   HB66+ 2(1) definition: 'attendance allowance', sch 4 para 5; NIHB66+ 2(1), sch 5 para 5

■ receive war pensioner's mobility supplement;

■ receive main phase ESA (para 12.47), or national insurance credits instead of it (para 12.45);

■ meet the old work fitness test (incapacity benefit). But in the case of national insurance credits the qualifying period is 28 weeks (not one year). And unlike the rules for the disability premium it can be you or your partner who meets this condition; or

■ qualified for the £20 per week disregard (as described in (c) above) at any time in the eight weeks before you reached pension age (para 2.4), and there have been no breaks in either your entitlement to HB or your employment since you reached that age.

(e) Carers: £20 per week

Unless (a) to (d) apply to you, the disregard is £20 per week if your applicable amount includes a carer premium (para 12.29).

If you are a couple and only one of you is a carer, it is disregarded from the carer's earned income. But if that is less than £20 per week, the balance up to £10 per week is disregarded from the other one's earned income.

(f) Special occupations: £20 per week

Unless (a) to (e) apply to you, the disregard is £20 per week if you or your partner are:

■ a part-time fire-fighter;

■ a part-time lifeboat worker;

■ an auxiliary coastguard; or

■ a member of the Territorial Army or similar reserve forces.

(See also table 14.1(s).)

(g) Couples: £10 per week

For all other couples, the disregard is £10 per week.

(h) Single claimants: £5 per week

For all other single claimants, the disregard is £5 per week.

T14.5(e)   HB sch 4 paras 5,6; HB66+ sch 4 paras 1(b),4; NIHB sch 5 paras 5,6; NIHB66+ sch 5 paras 1(b),4

T14.5(f)   HB sch 4 paras 8,9; HB66+ sch 4 paras 1(b),3; NIHB sch 5 paras 8,9; NIHB66+ sch 5 paras 1(b),3

T14.5(g)   HB sch 4 para 7; HB66+ sch 4 para 7(b); NIHB sch 5 para 7; NIHB66+ sch 5 para 7(b)

T14.5(h)   HB sch 4 para 10; HB66+ sch 4 para 7(a); NIHB sch 5 para 10; NIHB66+ sch 5 para 7(a)

The child care disregard

14.63   You qualify for the child care disregard if:

(a) you pay child care charges to one or more of the providers in table 14.6;

(b) you pay them for one or more children who meet the age condition (para 14.66); and

(c) you are:

- a lone parent and you work at least 16 hours per week, or

- a couple and you both work at least 16 hours per week, or

- a couple and one of you works at least 16 hours per week and the other one meets one or more of the conditions in para 14.67.

Paragraphs 14.69-72 explain when you count as working at least 16 hours per week.

14.64   The disregard equals the weekly amount of child care charges you pay (para 14.65), up to:

(a) £175 per week if the charges are for one child;

(b) £300 per week if the charges are for two or more children.

See para 14.61(c) for further information about how the disregard works.

14.65   Table 14.6 explains which child care charges are taken into account. They are included even if the care is not being provided due to the illness of the carer or the child, so long as the care is expected to resume ([2022] UKUT 224 (AAC)). The weekly amount is found by averaging them over whatever period, up to one year, gives an accurate figure. The council can ask the person providing the care for the information about this.

Table 14.6 **Child care providers**

Charges you have paid or will pay to the following are taken into account for the child care disregard (paras 14.63-66):

(a) A registered child minder, nursery or play scheme.

(b) A child minding scheme that does not have to be registered, for example, one run by a school or local authority or in Northern Ireland on Crown property.

(c) Any child care provider if the child care has been approved for working tax credit purposes.

(d) An out-of-school-hours scheme provided by a school on school premises, by a local authority, or in Northern Ireland by an education and library board or HSS trust. But in this case only, the child must be aged 8 or more.

(e) A foster parent or kinship carer (apart from the child's own foster parent or kinship carer) under the Fostering Services Regulations 2002, or equivalent provisions in Wales, or the Looked After Children (Scotland) Regulations 2009.

14.63   HB 28(1) ; HB66+ 31(1); NIHB 25(1) ; NIHB66+ 29(1)

14.64   HB 27(3); HB66+ 30(3); NIHB 24(3); NIHB66+ 28(3)

14.65   HB 28(5),(10); HB66+ 31(5),(10); NIHB 25(5),(10); NIHB66+ 29(5),(10)

> (f) A domiciliary care worker under the Domiciliary Care Agencies Regulations 2002, or equivalent provisions in Wales.
>
> (g) Anyone else who provides care wholly or mainly in the child's home, for example, a friend who comes in to provide care for the child. But this does not apply if they are your partner or a relative of the child. See para 7.56 for who counts as a 'relative'.
>
> But payments you make in respect of compulsory education do not count towards the child care disregard.

14.66 A child meets the age condition for the child care disregard from birth until:

(a) the first Monday in September following their 15th birthday; or

(b) if they meet the conditions for a disabled child premium (para 12.22), the first Monday in September following their 16th birthday.

14.67 The conditions listed in this paragraph are about the child care disregard for couples (para 14.63(c)). If you are a couple and one of you works at least 16 hours per week, the other one does not have to do so if they:

(a) meet the conditions for:

- a work-related activity component (para 12.44),

- a support component (paras 12.42-43), or

- a disability premium (para 12.37); or

(b) are receiving:

- disability living allowance (DLA) or (in Scotland) child disability payment,

- personal independence payment (PIP) or (in Scotland) adult disability payment,

- attendance allowance, or constant attendance allowance paid with an industrial injury or war disablement pension,

or would do so except that they are in hospital (para 12.51 and table 12.2); or

(c) are receiving:

- main phase ESA (para 12.47), or

- severe disablement allowance; or

(d) have been accepted by the DWP as having limited capability for work (para 12.48(b) or (b)) for a continuous period of 28 weeks, ignoring breaks of up to 12 weeks; or

---

T14.6   HB 28(5),(7)-(9); HB66+ 31(5),(7)-(9); NIHB 25(5),(7)-(9); NIHB66+ 29(5),(7)-(9)

14.66   HB 28(6),(9),(13); HB66+ 31(6),(9),(13); NIHB 25(6),(9),(13); NIHB66+ 29(6),(9),(13)

14.67   HB 28(1)(c),(11); HB66+ 31(1)(c),(11) ; NIHB 25(1)(c),(11); NIHB66+ 29(1)(c),(11)

14.67(a)   HB 28(11)(a),(b),(ba); HB66+ 31(11),(b),(ba); NIHB 25(11)(a),(b),(ba); NIHB66+ 29(11),(b),(ba)

14.67(b),(c) HB 28(11)(d)-(f); HB66+ 31(11),(d)-(f); NIHB 25(11)(d)-(f); NIHB66+ 29(11),(d)-(f)

14.67(d)   HB 28(11)(c),(ca),(12),(12A); HB66+ 31(11)(c),(ca),(12),(12A); NIHB 25(11)(c),(ca),(12),(12A); NIHB66+ 29(11)(c),(ca),(12),(12A)

(e)   have an invalid carriage or similar vehicle; or

(f)   are aged 80 or more; or

(g)   are in hospital; or

(h)   are in prison (serving a sentence or on remand).

Condition (d) only applies to the HB claimant but if you want to swap roles with your partner this usually ends your HB (paras 2.7, 16.2).

The additional earned income disregard

14.68   You qualify for the additional earned income disregard if you meet one or more of the conditions in table 14.7. The amount of the disregard is £17.10 per week. See para 14.61(d) for further information about how the disregard works.

Working at least 16 hours per week

14.69   You count as working at least 16 hours per week if:

(a)   you are employed or self-employed in work for which payment is made or expected; and

(b)   you work at least 16 hours per week every week, or on average (para 14.70).

The law calls this 'remunerative work'.

14.70   If your hours vary, they are averaged as follows:

(a)   if there is no recognisable cycle to your work, over five weeks or whatever period would give a more accurate figure;

(b)   if your work has a recognisable cycle (for example you work a regular pattern of shifts), over the whole of that cycle. In this case, the averaging includes periods you don't work;

(c)   but if your work has a recognisable cycle of a year (for example you work in term-times but not school holidays) over the whole year. In this case, the averaging excludes periods you don't work but the result applies throughout the year. (So if you work at least 16 hours every week in term-times, you count as working at least 16 hours per week throughout the year.)

14.67(e)   HB 2(1) definition: 'invalid carriage', 28(11)(g); HB66+ 2(1), 31(11)(g) ; NIHB 2(1), 25(11)(g); NIHB66+ 2(1), 29(11)(g)

14.67(f)   HB66+ 31(11)(a); ; NIHB66+ 29(11)(a)

14.67(g),(h) HB 28(1)(c); HB66+ 31(1)(c); NIHB 25(1)(c); NIHB66+ 29(1)(c)

14.68   HB sch 4 para 17; HB66+ sch 4 para 9; NIHB sch 5 para 17; NIHB66+ sch 5 para 9

14.69   HB 2(1) definition: 'remunerative work'; HB66+ 2(1), 6(1); NIHB 2(1), 6(1); NIHB66+ 2(1), 6(1)

14.70   HB 6(2)-(4); HB66+ 6(2)-(4); NIHB 6(2)-(4); NIHB66+ 6(2)-(4)

Table 14.7 **The additional earned income disregard**

You qualify for the additional earned income disregard (see para 14.68) if you meet one or more of the conditions (a) to (e). Paras 14.69-73 explain when you count as working at least 16 or 30 hours per week. The examples illustrate how the conditions work for couples.

(a) You receive working tax credit and it includes the WTC '30 hour element'.

If you are a couple, at least one of you has to qualify for the WTC 30 hour element. See example 1.

(b) You:

- are aged 25 or more; and

- work at least 30 hours per week.

If you are a couple, at least one of you has to meet both halves of this condition. See example 2.

(c) You:

- are responsible for one or more children or young persons; and

- work at least 16 hours per week.

If you are a couple, only one of you has to work at least 16 hours per week. See example 3.

(d) In working age HB, you:

- qualify for a work-related activity component, a support component, or a disability premium, or are on main phase ESA but can't get a component (see paras 12.37-39 and 12.42-49); and

- work at least 16 hours per week.

If you are a couple, at least one of you has to meet both halves of this condition. See example 4.

(e) In pension age HB, you:

- qualify for the £20 disregard for sickness or disability (see table 14.5(d)); and

- work at least 16 hours per week

If you are a couple, at least one of you has to meet both halves of this condition. See example 5.

Note:

For condition (a) you have to be on WTC (and getting the WTC 30 hour element). For conditions (b) to (e) you don't have to be on WTC (but they are the same as the conditions used in WTC for getting the 30 hour element).

T14.7   HB sch 4 para 17(2); HB66+ sch 4 para 9(2); NIHB sch 5 para 17(2); NIHB66+ sch 5 para 9(2)

Examples: The additional earned income disregard for couples

1. A couple on working tax credit

A couple are on WTC. One of them has been awarded the WTC '30 hour element'.

■ They qualify for the additional earned income disregard: see table 14.7(a).

2. A couple without children

A couple are aged 22 and 27. The 22-year-old works for 35 hours a week. The 27-year-old does not work.

■ They do not qualify for the additional earned income disregard: see table 14.7(b). (They would qualify if the 27-year-old worked at least 30 hours a week.)

3. A couple with a child

A couple with a baby. One of them works for 20 hours a week. The other one does not work.

■ They qualify for the additional earned income disregard: see table 14.7(c).

4. A working age couple, one with a disability

A couple are in their 50s. One of them receives personal independence payment (PIP) and works for 20 hours a week.

■ They qualify for the additional earned income disregard: see table 14.7(d).

5. A pension age couple, one with a disability

A couple are in their 70s. One of them receives attendance allowance and does not work. The other one works for 20 hours a week.

■ They do not qualify for the additional earned income disregard: see table 14.7(e). (They would qualify if the one on attendance allowance worked at least 16 hours a week, or they both did.)

14.71   Once you count as working at least 16 hours per week (paras 14.69-70):

(a) you continue to do so during the following absences from work:

■ while you are on holiday, or

■ while you are absent from work 'without good cause';

(b) for the purposes of the child care disregard (only), you also continue to do so:

■ while you are on maternity, paternity, shared parental or adoption leave. This only applies while you are getting statutory maternity, paternity, shared parental or adoption pay, or maternity allowance, or income support because of paternity leave (these can be paid for up to 39 weeks; and if you are getting the child element of WTC when they stop, it continues to apply until the WTC child element stops), or

■ while you are on sick leave. This is limited to 28 weeks. And it only applies while you are getting statutory sick pay, incapacity benefit at the short-term lower rate, ESA, income support because of incapacity for work, or national insurance credits instead of these.

14.71-72   HB 2(1) definitions: 'adoption leave', 'maternity leave', 'paternity leave', 'shared parental', 'sports award', 6(1),(5)-(8), 28(2)-(4),(14),(15); HB66+ 2(1), 6(1),(5)-(8), 31(2)-(4),(14)-(16); NIHB 2(1), 6(1),(5)-(8), 25(2)-(4),(14),(15); NIHB66+ 2(1), 6(1),(5)-(8), 29(2)-(4),(14)-(16)

14.72 You do not count as working at least 16 hours per week:

(a) while you are absent from work 'with good cause' (for example you are laid off);

(b) while you are doing unpaid work;

(c) while your only income is from a Sports Council award (para 13.43);

(d) in any benefit week in which you are on JSA(IB), ESA(IR) or income support for more than three days;

(e) while you are on maternity, paternity, shared parental or adoption leave, with the right to return to work under your contract or under employment law; or

(f) while you are absent from work due to illness, whether or not you are being paid.

There are exceptions to (e) and (f) in relation to the child care disregard: see para 14.71(b).

Working at least 30 hours per week

14.73 The rules about whether you count as working at least 30 hours per week are the same as in paras 14.69-72, apart from the different number of hours.

14.73   HB sch 4 para 17(4); HB66+ sch 4 para 9(4); NIHB sch 5 para 17(4); NIHB66+ sch 5 para 9(4)

Chapter 15 **Capital**

- General rules about assessing capital: see paras 15.1-13.
- How capital is valued: see paras 15.14-20.
- Savings and investments: see paras 15.21-27.
- Property and possessions: see paras 15.28-35.
- Trust funds, compensation payments and other capital: see paras 15.36-56.
- Notional capital: see paras 15.57-71.

Assessing capital

15.1 This chapter explains how your capital is assessed for HB purposes, including actual capital (paras 15.21-56) and notional capital (paras 15.57-71). This section gives rules relating to all types of capital.

'Your' capital

15.2 If you are single, your own capital is taken into account. If you are in a couple, the capital of your partner is taken into account as well as yours. If you are in a polygamous marriage, the capital of all your partners is included. In this chapter, 'your' capital always includes the capital of your partner (or partners). But if a child or young person has capital of their own, this is never included.

How your capital affects your HB

15.3 If you are on a passport benefit (para 13.5), all your capital is disregarded (ignored) and you qualify for maximum HB: see paras 6.2-3.

15.4 If you are not on a passport benefit, some kinds of capital are counted and some are disregarded. The details are in this chapter. Once the amount of your capital is valued (paras 15.14-20), it is taken into account as follows:

(a) if it is more than £16,000 you are not entitled to HB; otherwise

(b) the first £6,000 is ignored in working age HB claims;

(c) the first £10,000 is ignored in pension age HB claims;

(d) the remainder up to £16,000 is counted as providing you with an assumed amount of income (para 15.5).

(See also para 13.15 if you are on the savings credit of SPC.)

15.1   HB 44(1); HB66+ 44(1); NIHB 41(1); NIHB66+ 42(1)

15.2   CBA 136(1); HB 25, 45; HB66+ 23; NICBA 132(1); NIHB 22, 42; NIHB66+ 21

15.3   HB sch 6 paras 5,6; HB66+ 26; NIHB sch 7 paras 5, 6; NIHB66+ 24

15.4   CBA 134(1); HB 43, 44(2), 52(1), sch 6; HB66+ 28, 29(2), 43, 44(2); NICBA 130(1), NIHB 40, 41(2), 49(1), sch 7; NIHB66+ 26, 27(2), 41, 42(2)

Assumed income from capital (tariff income)

15.5   The assumed income from your capital (apart from disregarded capital) is calculated as follows (in the law it is also called 'tariff income'):

   (a) in working age HB, deduct £6,000 from your capital and divide the remainder by 250;

   (b) in pension age HB , deduct £10,000 from your capital and divide the remainder by 500;

   (c) if the result of (a) or (b) is not an exact multiple of £1, round the result up to the next £1.

This gives the weekly amount of your assumed income from capital. It is added to your other income: see para 13.1. (For interest and other kinds of actual income from capital see para 15.26.)

Examples: Assessing capital and assumed income from capital

1. A working age HB claim

Leroy is in his 40s and has £14,085 in his bank account. Of this, £2,000 is an insurance payment he received three weeks ago to replace his motorbike after an accident. He has no other capital.

Assessment:

   ■ The £2,000 is disregarded (table 15.1(j))

   ■ So his capital for HB purposes is   £12,085

Assumed income from capital (tariff income):

   ■ From the £12,085, £6,000 is deducted leaving   £6,085

   ■ Dividing this by 250 gives   £24.34

   ■ Rounding up to the next whole pound gives   £25

   ■ So he has £25 per week of assumed income from capital

2. A pension age HB claim

Nadia and Idris are in their 80s and have £15,085 in their bank account. Of this, £3,000 is arrears of attendance allowance they received three months ago after winning an appeal. They have no other capital.

Assessment:

   ■ The £3,000 is disregarded (table 15.2)

   ■ So their capital for HB purposes is   £12,085

Assumed income from capital (tariff income):

   ■ From the £12,085, £10,000 is deducted leaving   £2,085

   ■ Dividing this by 500 gives   £4.17

   ■ Rounding up to the next whole pound gives   £5

   ■ So they have £5 per week of assumed income from capital

15.5   CBA 136(2); HB 27(1)(b), 52; HB66+ 30(1)(b), 29(2); NICBA 132(2); NIHB 24(1)(b), 49; NIHB66+ 28(1)(b), 27(2)

Distinguishing capital from income

15.6   HB law does not give a definition of capital or income. Instead the rules 'operate at a stage after the money has been classified' (CH/1561/2005). But the distinction is usually straightforward: see paras 15.7-13.

Capital you hold

15.7   DWP guidance says 'As a general rule, capital includes all categories of holdings which have a clear monetary value' (GM para BW1.70). The rules for savings, investments, property and other items are given later in this chapter, including when they count as your capital and when they are disregarded.

Capital someone else holds for you

15.8   If someone else holds your capital for you, it counts as yours. For example, this includes money held for you by the Court of Protection ([2011] UKUT 157 (AAC)) or by someone who has power of attorney for you.

Capital you hold for someone else

15.9   If you hold someone else's capital for them, it does not count as yours. For example, you might be looking after your child's savings for them, or someone you are caring for may have put your name on a joint bank account so you can deal with their money for them. It is up to you to provide evidence that the money is not yours, but you do not need to be a formally documented trustee for them ([2010] UKUT 437 (AAC)). (If you are a trustee, see para 15.41.)

Payments of income and capital

15.10   A payment you receive can be income (for example earnings or benefits) or capital (for example an inheritance). This is decided by looking at 'the true characteristics of the payment in the hands of the recipient' (in other words, what it is to you), rather than whether the person pays it you periodically or in a lump sum or whether they (or you) call it 'income' or 'capital' (Minter v Hull City Council). DWP guidance says it is more likely to be capital if it is '(i) made without being tied to a period, (ii) made without being tied to any past payment, and (iii) not intended to form part of a series of payments' (GM para BW1.71).

Payments of arrears of income

15.11   A payment of arrears of income is assessed in both the following ways:
   (a) it is income for a past period, except when that kind of income is disregarded. This may mean you have been overpaid HB (chapter 19);
   (b) it is capital from when you receive it until when you spend it. But arrears of some benefits are disregarded as capital for 52 weeks or longer (para 15.50).

The fact that arrears of income can affect your capital does not stop them being income for a past period. For example a large lump sum settlement of an equal pay claim can be income for a past period if it is 'properly characterised as wages' (Minter vs Hull City Council).

15.10-11   Minter v Hull CC 13/10/11 CA [2011] EWCA Civ 1155 www.bailii.org/ew/cases/EWCA/Civ/2011/1155.html

15.11   HB 27(1), 31(1),(2), 44(1); HB66+ 30, 33(1),(6), 44(1); NIHB 24(1), 28(1),(2), 41(1); NIHB66+ 28, 31(1),(6), 42(1)

Payments of capital in instalments

15.12   If capital is payable to you in instalments, outstanding instalments are assessed as follows:

  (a) in pension age HB, they do not count as your capital until you receive them;

  (b) in working age HB, they count as your capital straight away (in other words even before you receive them). But if they would take your capital over £16,000, they count instead as your income.

When payments of income become capital

15.13   Income you do not spend becomes capital. 'A payment of income… remains income for the period in which it is paid. Any surplus at the end of that period metamorphoses into capital' (CH/1561/2005). This applies to counted income (for example earnings) and also to disregarded income (for example fostering allowances: CIS/3101/2007). So if your income is paid monthly, only what is left at the end of the month is capital. Different rules apply to arrears of income (para 15.11).

Valuing capital

15.14   The value of each item of capital you have (apart from disregarded capital) is assessed by working through the following steps:

  (a) start with its current market or surrender value (para 15.15);

  (b) then deduct 10% if selling it would involve costs (para 15.16);

  (c) then deduct any debt or charge secured against it (para 15.17).

Further rules are in paras 15.18-20. See para 13.15 if you are on the savings credit of state pension credit.

Market or surrender value

15.15   Dwellings, non-residential property, and many other items have a market value. It is what they would fetch if you sold them on the open market. Your council can ask the Valuation Office Agency to assist them in valuing these (forms for this are in GM BW1 annexes D and E, and further DWP guidance is in circular A25/2009). Insurance policies and some other investments have a surrender value. It is what you would be paid if you cashed them in now. For cash in a bank account see para 15.22.

Sales costs

15.16   If selling a capital item would mean you had to pay a fee or other costs, 10% is deducted from its value. For example this applies to property and shares. You do not have to work out what the actual sales costs would be. Instead, the 10% deduction always applies.

15.12   HB 41(1), 44(1), sch 6 para 18; HB66+ 44(1); NIHB 38(1), 41(1), sch 7 para 19; NIHB66+ 42(1)

15.14   HB 47; HB66+ 45; NIHB 44; NIHB66+ 43

15.15   HB 47; HB66+ 45; NIHB 44; NIHB66+ 43

15.16   HB 47(a); HB66+ 45(a); NIHB 44(a); NIHB66+ 43(a)

Secured debts or charges

15.17   Any debt or charge secured against a capital item is deducted from its value. For example this includes the outstanding mortgage on a property. Only secured debts and charges can be deducted (the law calls them 'encumbrances'). Other debts (such as rent arrears) cannot be deducted from your capital (CH/3729/2007).

Jointly owned capital

15.18   If you own a capital item jointly with one or more other people (other than just your partner), only your share of its capital value is taken into account. This means:

(a)   your actual share if you own it in known shares (e.g. if you own a one-third share and another person owns a two-thirds share): R(IS) 4/03 – and in appropriate cases this could be your beneficial share (the share that is intended to be of benefit to you): [2018] UKUT 25 (AAC)

(b)   an equal share in other cases (for example one-half if there are two of you).

Your share is valued as described in paras 15.14-16. The reason your share is valued rather than the whole item, is that the value of a half-share (for example) can be less than half the value of the whole item. In some cases the value of a share of capital can be minimal (CH/1953/2003).

Examples: Valuing capital

1. Shares in a company

Wilma owns 1,000 shares. Their sell price is currently £0.78 each.

▪ Their market value is 1,000 x £0.78		£780
▪ Deduct 10% for sales costs		£78
▪ Their value for HB purposes is		£702

2. Jointly owned land

Fred and his two brothers jointly own some land in equal shares. It is worth £35,000, but the value of a one-third share is £10,500. Fred is on HB. He took out a loan using his share of the land as security and £5,400 of the loan remains to be paid.

▪ The market value of his share is		£10,500
▪ Deduct 10% for sales costs		£1,050
▪ Deduct the loan		£5,400
▪ The value of his share for HB purposes is		£4,050

15.17   HB 47(b); HB66+ 45(b); NIHB 44(b); NIHB66+ 43(b)

15.18   HB 51; HB66+ 49; NIHB 48; NIHB66+ 47

Capital outside the UK or not in sterling

15.19   If you own capital in a country outside the UK:

(a)   its market or surrender value in that country is taken into account (see also para 15.20);

(b)   but if you are prohibited (by that country) from bringing the money to the UK, it is valued at what a willing buyer in the UK would give for it;

(c)   in each case, paras 15.16-17 also apply.

If you have capital in a currency other than sterling, any banking charge or commission for converting it to sterling is deducted.

Disregards for the capital limit and assumed income

15.20   The capital disregards explained in this chapter can affect:

(a)   whether your capital is above the £16,000 limit (para 15.4); and

(b)   if it isn't above £16,000, the amount of your assumed income from it (para 15.5).

In pension age HB, some uncommon disregards (paras 13.31-32, 15.31 and 15.39) only apply for (a), and all other disregards apply for both (a) and (b). In working age HB, all the disregards apply for both (a) and (b).

Savings and investments

15.21   This section gives the rules for savings and various kinds of investment. (For property and possessions, see paras 15.28-35.)

Savings and cash

15.22   Your savings are counted in full as your capital whether you keep them as cash or in a bank, and interest is included as capital from when it is due. But if you have more than one bank account, and the bank has the power to use money in one to pay an overdraft on another, it is the net amount (across those accounts) which is counted: [2011] UKUT 63 (AAC). See also para 15.13 if your income is paid into an account.

Savings certificates

15.23   National Savings and Ulster Savings certificates count in full as your capital. You can find out their current value using an online calculator, and the DWP says your council should use this to value them (GM BW1.440-451).

15.19   HB 48, sch 6 para 23; HB66+ 46, sch 6 para 23; NIHB 45, sch 7 para 24; NIHB66+ 44, sch 7 para 23

15.20   HB66+ sch 6 paras 27-30; NIHB66+ sch 7 paras 29-32

15.22   HB 44(1); HB66+ 44(1); NIHB 41(1); NIHB66+ 42(1)

15.23   HB 44(1); HB66+ 44(1); NIHB 41(1); NIHB66+ 42(1)

Shares and similar investments

15.24   Shares, unit trusts, income bonds and similar investments count in full as your capital. Shares and unit trusts are valued at their current 'sell' price. Then 10% is deducted for sales costs in the case of shares (see para 15.16), but not normally for unit trusts because their sell price already allows for this.

Pension schemes, annuities, life insurance and funeral plans

15.25   Capital held in the following is wholly disregarded:

(a)   an occupational or personal pension scheme (para 13.27);

(b)   an annuity (paras 13.32-33);

(c)   a life insurance policy, including a bond or similar investment which has a life insurance element (R(IS) 7/98) and including compensation paid by the UK government (£5,000) to holders of Equitable Life pre-1992 policies (HB G10/2013);

(d)   in pension age HB claims, a funeral plan contract if its sole purpose is to provide a funeral in the UK for you and/or your partner.

Their surrender value is also disregarded (this means what you would get if you cashed them in), but capital you actually receive from them (if you do cash in part or all) is counted in full.

Interest and other actual income from capital

15.26   Interest you receive on a bank account, and other kinds of actual income you receive on capital, are counted as increasing your capital from when they are due. (They are not counted as income, because instead there are rules about assumed income from capital: see para 15.5.) But see tables 13.7 and 13.8 if you receive rent on property you have let out, and para 15.33 for income you receive on business assets.

The value of your right to receive an asset in the future or future income

15.27   Your right to receive an asset in the future can be sold. And the income from some investments can be sold (the purchaser would receive the income in the future instead of you). So, each of these has a capital value. In pension age claims the capital value of any reversionary interest, rent, a life interest/life rent, occupational and personal pensions, annuities, (paras 13.32, 15.31, table 15.1(g)) is counted in full when considering the capital limit (para 15.4) but disregarded when calculating assumed income (para 15.5). In working age claims it is disregarded for both purposes.

15.24   HB 44(1), 47(a); HB66+ 44(1), 45(a); NIHB 41(1), 44(a); NIHB66+ 42(1), 43(a)

15.25   SI 2013/2980 reg 5; HB 2(1) definition: 'policy of life insurance', sch 6 paras 13,17,32; HB66+ 2(1), sch 6 paras 11,12,24,29; NIHB 2(1), sch 7 paras 13,18,31A,33; NIHB66+ 2(1), sch 7 paras 11,12,24,31,31A

15.26   HB 46(4); HB66+ 29(1)(i), sch 5 paras 22,24; NIHB 43(4); NIHB66+ 27(1)(g), sch 6 paras 23,25

15.27   HB sch 6 paras 7, 13, 15, 16, 31, 33; HB66+ 33(11), sch 6 paras 5, 24, 27-29; NIHB sch 7 paras 7, 13, 16, 17, 32, 34; NIHB66+ 31(10), sch 7 paras 5, 24, 29-31

Table 15.1 **Capital disregards relating to property**

Your home and other property

Working age and pension age HB: disregards (a) to (g)

In (a) to (e) only one dwelling can be a person's home at any one time. In (a) to (c) there is no time limit. (if you rent out property as a self-employed business see para 15.33.)

   (a) Your home, and any land or buildings (including croft land in Scotland) which are part of it or are impracticable to sell separately. For example, your home is disregarded if you are a shared owner, or an owner claiming HB for rates in Northern Ireland, or are claiming HB temporarily on other accommodation (see paras 3.13, 3.14).

   (b) The home of a partner or 'relative' (para 7.56) of yours or of anyone in your family, if that partner/relative:

- has reached state pension age (para 2.4); or

- is 'incapacitated'. This word has its ordinary English meaning. For example it is not limited to people on ESA or similar benefits.

   (c) The home of your partner if:

- you have not divorced, dissolved your civil partnership or become estranged (in other words your relationship has not ended: CH/3777/2007); but

- you no longer count as a couple (or polygamous marriage) for HB purposes (para 4.6).

   (d) A home you intend to occupy if:

- you acquired it within the past 26 weeks*; or

- you are taking steps to obtain possession of it, and first sought legal advice about this or began legal proceedings within the past 26 weeks*; or

- you are carrying out essential repairs or alterations to make it fit for occupation or re-occupation, and began doing so within the past 26 weeks*.

   (e) Your former home, and any land or buildings (including croft land in Scotland) which are part of it or are impracticable to sell separately, if:

- you ceased to occupy it because you have divorced, dissolved your civil partnership or become estranged from your partner (in other words your relationship has ended: [2019] UKUT 360 (AAC)); and either

---

T15.1   HB 44(2), sch 6; HB66+ 44(2), sch 6; NIHB 41(2), sch 7; NIHB66+ 42(2), sch 7

T15.1(a) HB sch 6 para 1; HB66+ sch 6 para 26; NIHB sch 7 para 1; NIHB66+ sch 7 para 26

T15.1(b) HB sch 6 para 4(a); HB66+ sch 6 para 4(a); NIHB sch 7 para 4(a); NIHB66+ sch 7 para 4(a)

T15.1(c) HB sch 6 para 4(b); HB66+ sch 6 para 4(b); NIHB sch 7 para 4(b); NIHB66+ sch 7 para 4(b)

T15.1(d) HB sch 6 paras 2, 27, 28; HB66+ sch 6 paras 1-3; NIHB sch 7 paras 2, 28,29; NIHB66+ sch 7 paras 1-3

T15.1(e) HB sch 6 para 25; HB66+ sch 6 para 6; NIHB sch 7 para 26; NIHB66+ sch 7 para 6

- they are now a lone parent and live in it as their home (in this case there is no time limit); or

- you ceased to occupy it within the past 26 weeks (this time limit cannot be extended).

(f) A home and any other premises you are taking reasonable steps to dispose of, and began doing so within the past 26 weeks*.

(g) Any property you will not own until a future event occurs (for example you reach a particular age). This is called a 'reversionary interest'. (But for a life interest/life rent see para 15.31.)

Money relating to property

Working age HB: disregards (h) to (m)

(h) Money which:

- is from the sale of your former home (including compensation for compulsory purchase but not a home loss payment) and which you intend to use to buy a home within 26 weeks* of the date of sale; or

- was deposited with a housing association as a condition of occupying your home and which you intend to use to buy a home within 26 weeks* of the date the deposit was returned (DMG chapter 28 para 295330).

This disregard does not apply if you haven't yet decided what to do with the money (CH/2255/2006).

(i) A local authority grant you received as a council tenant within the past 26 weeks*, for:

- buying a home; or

- carrying out repairs or alterations to make a future home fit for occupation.

(j) Insurance or compensation payments you received within the past 26 weeks* for repairs or replacements following loss or damage to your home or personal possessions.

(k) Any other payments received within the past 26 weeks* solely for essential repairs or improvements to your home.

(l) Money deposited with a housing association as a condition of occupying your home.

(m) Tax refunds for interest on a mortgage, or on a loan for home repairs or improvements.

T15.1(f)   HB sch 6 para 26; HB66+ sch 6 para 7; NIHB sch 7 para 27; NIHB66+ sch 7 para 7

T15.1(g)   HB sch 6 para 7; HB66+ sch 6 para 5; NIHB sch 7 para 7; NIHB66+ sch 7 para 5

T15.1(h)   HB 2(1) definition: 'housing association', sch 6 paras 3, 11(b); NIHB 2(1) definition: 'housing association', sch 7 paras 3, 11(a)

T15.1(i)   HB sch 6 para 38; NIHB sch 7 para 39

T15.1(j)   HB sch 6 para 10(a); NIHB sch 7 para 10(a)

T15.1(k)   HB sch 6 para 10(b);;NIHB sch 7 para 10(b);

T15.1(l)   HB 2(1) definition: 'housing association', sch 6 para 11(a); NIHB 2(1) definition: 'housing association', sch 7 para 11(a)

T15.1(m)   HB sch 6 para 21; NIHB sch 7 para 22

Pension age HB: disregards (n) to (p)

(n) Any money paid to you (or deposited in your name) within the past year for the sole purpose of buying a home. For example this can include money from the sale of your former home, compensation for compulsory purchase, local authority grants, and gifts or loans from relatives or friends.

(o) Insurance or compensation payments you received within the past year for repairs or replacements following loss or damage to your home or personal possessions.

(p) Any other payments you received within the past year solely for essential repairs or improvements to your home or a future home.

Extending the 26-week time limits

*   The time limits marked with an asterisk can be extended if it is reasonable to do so in the circumstances. But the time limit in (h) is not extended if your only reason for needing longer is that you are taking a hard line in negotiations about your share of the money from the sale of your home (CH/2255/2006).

Examples: Property

1. The home of a relative

Daniel owns a house where his mother Maria lives. Maria is aged 87. Daniel claims HB on the flat he is renting.

■   The value of the house is disregarded: table 15.1(b).

2. A couple end their relationship

Lucy and Caleb jointly own a house where they live with their school-age children. They decide to end their relationship. Caleb moves out and rents a flat. He claims HB there. Lucy remains in the home with the children.

■   Caleb's share of the value of the house is disregarded: table 15.1(e).

3. A new partner moves in

Nine months after Caleb moved out, Lucy's new partner moves in with her and the children.

■   Caleb's share of the value of the house is no longer disregarded, because Lucy is no longer a lone parent and because more than 26 weeks have passed since Caleb moved out: table 15.1(e).

4. The house is put up for sale

Lucy and Caleb decide to sell the house. They put it on the market.

■   Caleb's share of the value of the house is disregarded for 26 weeks, or longer if this is reasonable to allow a sale to take place: see table 15.1(f).

T15.1(n)   HB66+ sch 6 paras 18,20(a); NIHB66+ sch 7 paras 18,20(a)

T15.1(o)   HB66+ sch 6 paras 18,19; NIHB66+ sch 7 paras 18,19

T15.1(p)   HB66+ sch 6 paras 18,20(b); NIHB66+ sch 7 paras 18,20(b)

5. Money for buying a home

Ana sells her home and moves to a rented flat in a new area while she looks for a new property to buy. She claims HB on the flat. She has £240,000 from the sale, and a further £50,000 which her brother gave her towards a new home.

- If Ana is aged 66 or over, both these amounts are disregarded for one year, but no longer: table 15.1(n).
- If Ana is under 66, only the money from the sale is disregarded, and only for 26 weeks or longer if reasonable: see table 15.1(h).

6. A property which is rented out

Joshua and Jason own a house which is rented out to a tenant through an agency. The house has a market value of £200,000 and there is an outstanding mortgage on it of £175,000. They claim HB on a flat they are renting.

- The market value of the house is £200,000.
- Deduct 10% for sales costs, leaving £180,000.
- Deduct the outstanding mortgage, leaving £5,000.
- This £5,000 is Joshua and Jason's capital for HB purposes.
- The rent they receive on the house also counts as their capital (not income), after allowing for the mortgage interest, agency fees, and other outgoings they pay on it: table 13.8(b).

Property and possessions

15.28   This section gives the rules for property, money relating to property, personal possessions, and business assets. (For property held in a trust see paras 15.37-40.)

Property

15.29   The rules about property apply to dwellings and non-residential premises. Your home and some other property is disregarded: see the first part of table 15.1. Property which is not disregarded is counted as your capital. Its value is assessed as described in paras 15.14-20. If you have rented it out, this is taken into account in valuing it. For example the presence of a sitting tenant can reduce the value of a dwelling (CH/1953/2003). If ownership of a property is in dispute, it may have no value until the dispute is settled.

Money relating to property

15.30   Money for buying, repairing or improving a home (e.g. including adaptations for people who are elderly or disabled) can be disregarded: see the second part of table 15.1. If you receive rent on a property you have let out, see table 13.8.

15.29   HB 44, sch 6; HB66+ 44(1),(2), sch 6; NIHB 41, sch 7; NIHB66+ 42(1),(2), sch 7

15.30   HB sch 6; HB66+ sch 6; NIHB sch 7; NIHB66+ sch 7

Life interest and life rent

15.31   If you have a life interest (or in Scotland a life rent) in property or any other asset, this means you have the right to use it until you die, or someone else dies. In some cases, the property or other asset is disregarded (see for example table 15.1). Otherwise, in pension age HB the capital value of the life interest or life rent is counted in full when considering the capital limit (para 15.4) but disregarded when calculating assumed income (para 15.5). In working age HB it is disregarded for both purposes.

Personal possessions

15.32   The value of your personal possessions is disregarded. This means any physical assets apart from land, property and business assets (R(H)7/08). Payments for loss or damage to your personal possessions are also disregarded (table 15.1(j) and (o)). But in working age claims, personal possessions you bought with the purpose of gaining HB are counted as your capital (para 15.64).

Self-employed business assets

15.33   If you are self-employed (para 14.27) your business assets are disregarded:

(a) while you are self-employed;

(b) if you are not self-employed because of sickness or disability but intend to return to the self-employment, for 26 weeks, or longer if you reasonably need longer to return;

(c) if you have ceased to be self-employed, for as long as you reasonably need to dispose of the assets.

'Business assets' means assets held in the course of your self-employment (CH/4258/2004). In some circumstances they can include property you rent out, though this is unlikely if you just rent out one property as a single letting ([2016] UKUT 357 (AAC)). Business capital is disregarded (as a business asset) if it is 'part of the fund employed and risked in the business' (R (SB) 4/85), which is unlikely to be the case unless you keep it separate from your personal savings. But rent and other income you receive on your business assets counts as part of your self-employed earnings (para 14.28).

Company ownership

15.34   Companies can take several different forms: public limited company (PLC), private limited company (Ltd) and so on. A company is separate legal entity from its shareholders (who are its members). Normally its assets cannot be attributed to its members (R(SB) 57/83) – it is your shares that are valued. However, particularly in the case of a small private limited company, the council may consider that your relationship to the business is more like that of a sole owner or partner. In these circumstances the council may, and for pension age claims must, adopt a different approach.

15.31   HB 44(1), sch 6 paras 7, 13, 15, 16, 31, 33; HB66+ 33(11), 44(1), sch 6 paras 5, 24, 27-29;
          NIHB 42(1) sch 7 paras 7, 13, 16, 17, 32, 34; NIHB66+ 31(10), sch 7 paras 5, 24, 29-31

15.32   HB sch 6 para 12; HB66+ sch 6 para 8; NIHB sch 7 para 12; NIHB66+ sch 7 para 8

15.33   HB sch 6 para 8(1),(2); HB66+ sch 6 paras 9,10; NIHB sch 7 para 8(1),(2); NIHB66+ sch 7 paras 9,10

15.34-35 HB 49(5),(6);HB66+ 47(3),(4);NIHB 46(5),(6);NIHB66+ 45(3),(4)

15.35 If the council decides that your relationship in the business is like that of a sole owner or partner it should:

(a) disregard the value of your shares in the company; and

(b) decide whether you are engaged in activities in the course of the company's business (R(IS) 13/93).

If the council decides that you aren't so engaged it must treat you as having notional capital (para 15.57-59) equal to the value (or your share of the value) of the capital of the company, i.e. its net worth (R(IS) 13/93). But if the council decides that you are engaged any notional capital it treats you as having is disregarded.

Trusts and compensation

15.36 This section gives the rules for trusts, personal injury payments, and other compensation and gallantry payments. (For compensation relating to property and possessions see table 15.1.)

Trusts

15.37 Assets held in a trust, such as cash, investments or property are legally owned by the trustees (or trustee) of the trust, and beneficially owned by the beneficiary (or beneficiaries) of the trust. The trustees have a duty to use the assets under the terms of the trust for the benefit of the beneficiary, for example by making payments to them. Paras 15.38-41 explain how this is assessed.

If you are a beneficiary of a trust

15.38 Capital held in a trust for you counts in full as your capital, but see para 15.39 for exceptions. If you are not the only beneficiary of the trust, it is your share of the capital which is taken into account (para 15.18).

15.39 Capital held in a trust for you is disregarded:

(a) if you cannot obtain it until a particular event occurs, for example when you reach a certain age (this is called a 'reversionary' trust); or

(b) if it is charitable or government sponsored (para 15.42) or relates to a personal injury (para 15.43); or

(c) in pension age HB if:

- it is property, and

- the trustees make payments to you, or could do so.

In pension age HB, any other capital held in a trust for you is counted in full when considering the capital limit (para 15.4) but disregarded when calculating assumed income (para 15.5). In working age HB it is counted in full for both purposes.

15.38   HB 44(1); HB66+ 44(1); NIHB 41(1); NIHB66+ 42(1)

15.39   HB sch 6 paras 7,14; HB66+ sch 6 para 30; NIHB sch 7 paras 7,14; NIHB66+ sch 7 para 32

15.40   If you receive a payment of capital from a trust (whether the capital in the trust itself is counted or disregarded):

(a)   it is disregarded if any of the disregards in this chapter apply to it (see for example table 15.1(k), (n) and (p));

(b)   otherwise it counts in full as your capital.

For payments of income from a trust see para 13.36.

Example: Money held in a trust

Elizabeth is aged 75 and makes a claim for HB. She is the sole beneficiary of a trust fund with £11,000 in it. The trust is not charitable or for personal injury or from government funds. She also has savings of £4,000 but no other capital.

- Both these amounts (£15,000) are counted when considering the capital limit, but they are not above £16,000.

- The capital in the trust is disregarded when considering tariff income. Only her savings (£4,000) are counted, but they are not enough to mean she has assumed income (para 15.5).

If you are a trustee of a trust

15.41   Capital you hold as a trustee is wholly disregarded. But to count as a trustee it is not enough just to say that you are holding money (or other assets) for someone else, or plan to give it to them. You must have received it on clearly stated terms requiring you to hold it for them, or you must have clearly and consistently expressed that you hold it for them and have given up all intentions of using it for yourself (R(IS)1/90). If you meet these conditions it is not necessary for the trust to be legally documented ([2012] UKUT 115 (AAC)); [2018] UKUT 63(AAC)).

Government sponsored trust funds

15.42   Any payment of capital or income you receive from the following is disregarded:

(a)   the Independent Living Funds (which help severely disabled people live independently);

(b)   government schemes for people infected with HIV or hepatitis C from NHS blood and other products and government Thalidomide trusts;

(c)   the Variant Creutzfeldt-Jacob Disease (vCJD) Trust; and

(d)   the London Bombings Relief Charitable Fund, the London Emergency Trust and the Manchester Emergency Fund (for victims of the attacks and bombings in 2005 and 2017).

The disregards in (a), (b) and (d) have no time limit. The disregard in (c) has no time limit if the payment is to the person with vCJD or their partner or surviving partner, but is limited to two years if it is to a parent or guardian of a child with vCJD. The disregards in (b) to (d) can continue if the payment is passed on to a relative as a gift or inheritance (but the usual HB definition of 'relative' does not always apply here). For further details see GM para BW2.620.

15.40   HB 44; HB66+ 44(1),(2); NIHB 41; NIHB66+ 42(1),(2)

15.42   HB 2(1) definitions: 'Independent Living Fund' etc, sch 5 para 35, sch 6 paras 24, 34, 55,63; HB66+ 2(1), 29(1), sch 6 paras 14,16,30,26I; NIHB 2(1), sch 6 para 37, sch 7 paras 25,35,52; NIHB66+ 2(1), 27(1), sch 7 paras 14,16,32

Personal injury payments

15.43　The following payments of capital are disregarded if they relate to a personal injury you or your partner have had:

(a) damages for personal injury which are:
- held by a court and administered by it, or
- held by someone else and can only be used under a court order or direction;

(b) any payment for personal injury which is held in a trust; and

(c) any other payment for personal injury except for capital paid to you by a trust (but see para 15.40(a)).

The disregards in (a) and (b) have no time limit. The disregard in (c) has no time limit in pension age HB, but in working age HB it is limited to 52 weeks from the day you receive the first or only payment. (It does not start again if you receive a further payment for that injury.) The 52 weeks is called a 'grace period' because it should give you time to form a trust to hold the money (see (b) above) or invest it in an annuity (para 15.25(b)).

15.44　Payments of income you receive for a personal injury to you or your partner are wholly disregarded. For example this includes income paid to you by a trust or from an annuity in which a personal injury payment was invested. In pension age HB, payments of income are also disregarded if they are paid to you by order of a court for a personal injury to your child.

Examples: Personal injury payments

1. Working age HB

Eliana is in her 20s and is awarded £500,000 for a personal injury. It is paid into her bank account.
- This is disregarded for 52 weeks (para 15.43(c)).

Five months later a trust is formed, with her parents and solicitor as the trustees and her as the beneficiary. The whole of the personal injury payment is paid into the trust.
- This is now disregarded without time limit (para 15.43(b)).

The trust pays Eliana an income of £70 per week.
- This is disregarded in the assessment of her income (para 15.44).

The trust later pays her £75,000 to adapt her home for wheelchair use.
- This is disregarded for 26 weeks, or longer if this is reasonable, to allow the work to take place (para 15.40(a) and table 15.1(k)).

2. Pension age HB

Levi is in his 70s and is awarded £500,000 for a personal injury. It is paid into his bank account.
- This is disregarded without time limit (para 15.43(c)).

15.43　HB sch 6 paras 14, 14A, 45, 46; HB66+ sch 6 para 17; NIHB sch 7 paras 14,15,45; NIHB66+ sch 7 para 17

15.44　HB sch 5 para 14(1)(c)-(e); HB66+ sch 5 paras 14,15; NIHB sch 6 para 14(1)(c)-(e); NIHB66+ sch 6 paras 15,16

Payments compensating for death of a parent

15.45   If you are under 18, compensation you receive for the death of a parent is wholly disregarded if it is held by a court and administered by it, or held by someone else and can only be used under a court order or direction.

Second World War payments

15.46   Payments of compensation are wholly disregarded if they were paid because – during the Second World War – you, your partner, or your or your partner's deceased husband, wife or civil partner:

(a) were a slave labourer or forced labourer; or

(b) suffered property loss or personal injury; or

(c) were a parent of a child who died; or

(d) were imprisoned or interned by the Japanese.

There is no time limit. The disregard in (d) is always £10,000 (which is the standard amount paid in these cases), and £10,000 is disregarded from the total of your capital without any time limit (so you do not need to keep track of the money).

The families of the disappeared

15.47   In Northern Ireland, compensation paid to the families of the disappeared is disregarded for 52 weeks from the date of payment.

Gallantry payments

15.48   Payments you receive as a holder of the Victoria Cross or George Cross, and similar payments, are wholly disregarded:

(a) in working age HB in the assessment of both your income and your capital;

(b) in pension age HB in the assessment of your income.

Other capital

15.49   This section gives the rules for arrears and lump sum payments of benefits, charitable and voluntary payments, loans, and other kinds of capital.

Arrears of benefits and compensation relating to benefits

15.50   Table 15.2 explains when the capital value of arrears of benefits is disregarded. The same rules apply to payments compensating for non-payment of the benefits. Arrears of benefits not included in the table are taken into account as described in para 15.11.

15.45   HB sch 6 para 45, 46; NIHB sch 7 para 45

15.46   HB sch 6 paras 54, 56; HB66+ sch 6 paras 13,15; NIHB sch 7 paras 51,53; NIHB66+ sch 7 paras 13,15

15.47   NIHB sch 7 para 58; NIHB66+ sch 7 para 27

15.48   HB sch 5 para 10, sch 6 para 47; HB66+ 29(1); NIHB sch 6 para 11, sch 7 para 46; NIHB66+ 27(1)

Table 15.2 **Capital disregards: arrears of benefits**

(a) Disregarded arrears

Arrears of all the following are disregarded when your capital is assessed:

- state pension credit (both guarantee credit and savings credit)
- universal credit
- JSA(IB), ESA(IR), IS and HB
- WTC and CTC
- disability living allowance or (in Scotland) child disability payment
- personal independence payment or (in Scotland) adult disability payment
- attendance allowance, or equivalent benefits (para 13.10)
- bereavement support payments (other than the initial lump sum: para 15.51)
- maternity allowance
- any Scottish short-term assistance and, in pension age claims, the benefits in para 15.51(d)-(g)
- discretionary housing payments (para 23.1) and in Northern Ireland welfare supplementary payments (para 23.20).

(b) Standard time limit

The disregard lasts for 52 weeks in working age HB, and one year in pension age HB, in each case beginning with the day you received the arrears.

(c) Extended time limit

If the arrears:

- are £5,000 or more;
- are paid while you are on HB; and
- are because you were underpaid due to official error (paras 20.38-40),

the disregard continues for as long as you or your partner remain continuously on HB (including periods one of you remains continuously on HB after the other one's death).

(d) Arrears of war disablement and bereavement pensions

Arrears of the war disablement and bereavement pensions in table 13.4(a) are disregarded:

- for 52 weeks in working age HB claims (the extended time limit does not apply);
- without time limit in pension age HB claims.

Note:

The rules in (a) to (c) above also apply to payments compensating for non-payment of the benefits.

T15.2   CBA 123 definition: 'income related benefit'; HB 46(9), sch 6 para 9; HB66+ 44(3), sch 6 paras 18, 21(1)(a)-(d),(2), 22; NICBA 122; NIHB 43(8), sch 7 para 9; NIHB66+ 42(3), sch 7 paras 18, 21(1)(a)-(d),(2), 22

Benefits paid as a lump sum

15.51   Lump sum payments of the following are disregarded:

(a) social fund payments (winter fuel payments, cold weather payments, Sure Start maternity grant and funeral expenses payment);

(b) in Northern Ireland, welfare supplementary payments;

(c) for 52 weeks, the initial lump sum of bereavement support payment;

(d) winter heating assistance;

(e) carers assistance (young carers grant);

(f) early years assistance;

(g) funeral expense assistance.

The benefits (d)-(g) are paid by Social Security Scotland.

Employment programmes

15.52   The following are wholly disregarded as capital and also as income (table 13.1):

(a) government and related payments to disabled people to help with finding or retaining employment; and

(b) payments from government work programme training schemes.

Local authority support

15.53   The following are wholly disregarded as capital and also as income (table 13.1):

(a) in working age HB claims:

   ▪   adoption payments,

   ▪   special guardianship payments,

   ▪   payments to avoid taking children into care, and

   ▪   payments to care leavers;

(b) community care payments;

(c) direct care payments;

(d) payment(s) for housing-related support to help you live independently in your home;

(e) 'local welfare assistance' or equivalent payments in Scotland, Wales and Northern Ireland (para 23.35); and

(f) all fuel and cost of living paid by or on behalf of the government.

15.51   HB sch 6 paras 20, 62, 65-68; HB66+ sch 6 paras 18, 21(1),(2)(n),(q),(r),(u),(w) 26H, 26J, 26K
              NIHB sch 7 paras 21, 59, 61, 62; NIHB66+ sch 7 paras 18, 21(1),(2)(m),(o),(p), 28D; NISR 2016/178 reg 12; NISR 2017/35, reg 14

15.52(a)   HB sch 6 paras 43, 44; NIHB sch 7 para 44

15.52(b)   HB 46(7),(8), sch 6 paras A2,A3, 8(3),(4), 35,49,52,55; NIHB 43(7),(8), sch 7 paras 8(3),(4), 36,48,52

15.53(a)   HB sch 6 paras 19,19A,59-61; NIHB sch 7 paras 20,20A,56,57

15.53(b),(c) HB sch 6 para 58; HB66+ sch 6 paras 26D,26F; NIHB sch 7 para 55; NIHB66+ sch 7 para 28C

15.53(d)   HB sch 6 para 57; HB66+ sch 6 paras 18,21(1)(e); NIHB sch 7 para 63; NIHB66+ sch 7 paras 18,21(1)(e)

15.53(e)   HB sch 6 para 20A; HB66+ sch 6 paras 18,21(1)(f)

15.53(f)   Social Security (Additional Payments) Act 2022, s8

Charitable and voluntary payments

15.54 Payments of capital you receive which are charitable and/or voluntary are counted as your capital. But in working age HB claims, payments in kind (in other words in goods not money) are disregarded. For payments of income see para 13.30.

Loans

15.55 Money which was loaned to you (and which you still have) is counted as your capital. But in pension age HB claims, loans for buying a home are disregarded (table 15.1(n)). And the following count as income, not capital:

(a) in working age HB, student loans (para 13.38);

(b) in working age HB, career development loans (table 13.11(n));

(c) in pension age HB, payments from an equity release scheme (para 13.34).

Other loans can be counted as income if the council has clear evidence that they should be (R(IS) 6/03, R(H) 8/08). This is likely to mean that (c) above also applies in working age HB.

Other kinds of capital

15.56 If you have any other kind of capital, it is counted in full. But for payments you receive as an earner see chapter 14.

Notional capital

15.57 This section explains when you are counted as having capital you do not in fact have. This is called 'notional capital'.

Types of notional capital

15.58 In working age HB, you can be counted as having notional capital when:

(a) you have deprived yourself of capital (paras 15.61-63);

(b) there is capital available to you (paras 13.54 and 13.56);

(c) you are paid capital on behalf of someone (paras 13.57 and 13.59);

(d) someone else is paid capital on your behalf (paras 13.58-59);

(e) a non-dependant has more income and capital than you (para 13.61); or

(f) you are counted as an owner or partner in relation to a company (para 15.35).

15.59 In pension age HB, you can be counted as having notional capital when:

(a) you have deprived yourself of capital (paras 15.61-63);

(b) a non-dependant has more income and capital than you (para 13.61); or

(c) you are counted as an owner or partner in relation to a company (para 15.35).

15.54   HB 44(1), 46(6), sch 6 para 34; HB66+ 44(1); NIHB 41(1), 43(6), sch 7 para 35; NIHB66+ 42(1)

15.56   HB 44(1); HB66+ 44(1); NIHB 41(1); NIHB66+ 42(1)

Assessing notional capital

15.60   If you are counted as having notional capital, it is assessed in the same way as actual capital. All the rules and disregards given earlier in this chapter apply. This means this section does not apply if you are on a passport benefit (except as described in table 15.3(e)).

Table 15.3 **Deprivation of capital: case law**

This table is about the deprivation of capital rule (see paras 15.61-63).

(a) *The test of purpose:* To count as depriving yourself of capital, 'the test is one of purpose'. Gaining HB must have formed 'a positive part of [your] planning'. [2011] UKUT 500 (AAC).

(b) *Thinking about the consequences:* You can only count as depriving yourself if you knew what you were doing. If you did not think about the consequences, you cannot have acted with the purpose of gaining HB. [2011] UKUT 500 (AAC). And if you had no legitimate choice but to spend capital, this cannot count as deprivation: [2015] UKUT 15 (AAC).

(c) *Your personal circumstances:* Your mental state and capabilities are taken into account. A schizophrenic man without an appointee, who lived in 'an intolerable level of chaos', spent almost all of a big windfall on 'alcohol and high living'. He did not count as depriving himself, because it was not shown that he appreciated what he was doing or what the consequences would be. R(H)1/06.

(d) *Mixed motives:* If you had some other reason for disposing of capital (which is 'almost always' the case), you count as depriving yourself of it if gaining HB was 'a significant operative purpose' of doing so. This includes looking at 'whether, given [your] knowledge, it was reasonable in all the circumstances' to act as you did, bearing in mind your obligations (for example, to support yourself, and to other people). [2009] UKUT 145 (AAC), which cited CJSA/1425/2005.

(e) *Passport benefits and HB:* If you deprived yourself of capital to gain a passport benefit, you also count as depriving yourself to gain HB if you plainly expected that getting the passport benefit would lead to getting HB. [2009] UKUT 145 (AAC).

(f) *Buying an asset whose capital value is disregarded:* Even if what you bought is disregarded, you count as depriving yourself if your purpose was gaining HB (see para 15.64). [2009] UKUT 145 (AAC), which cited R(SB) 40/85 and R(IS) 8/04.

(g) *Buying personal possessions:* In working age HB claims, if you bought a personal possession with the purpose of gaining HB (in this case, a caravan) its value counts as actual (not notional) capital (see para 15.64). [2009] UKUT 145 (AAC).

(h) *Providing receipts:* If you are asked to provide receipts for capital you have spent, this 'is primarily to enable [the council] to be satisfied the money has not been retained' (see para 15.64). But it 'can also form the basis as to the reasonableness of the expenditure'. [2009] UKUT 145 (AAC).

(i) *Seeking to recover the money:* It is irrelevant whether you seek to recover money you deprived yourself of. [2009] UKUT 96 (AAC).

Capital you have deprived yourself of

15.61   If you have deprived yourself of capital, it is counted as your notional capital. To 'deprive' yourself of capital means:

(a) you have disposed of it (for example by spending it or giving or lending it to someone); and

(b) your purpose in doing so was to make yourself entitled to HB, or to more HB (we use 'gain HB' to cover both these).

This is called the 'deprivation of capital rule'.

15.62   Table 15.3 explains how the rule works. See paras 15.63-65 for exceptions and further details. See paras 15.60 and 15.66-71 for how notional capital is assessed and how it reduces.

Exceptions

15.63   In pension age HB, the deprivation of capital rule does not apply to capital you have used to:

(a) buy goods or services which are reasonable in your circumstances; or

(b) repay or reduce a debt you owe.

In working age and pension age HB, the rule does not apply if you are on a passport benefit, except as described in table 15.3(e).

Distinguishing notional capital from actual capital

15.64   In general terms, capital you have is your actual capital, and capital you disposed of to gain HB is your notional capital. The Upper Tribunal has summarised the following possibilities ([2009] UKUT 145 (AAC)):

(a) if you have spent capital on an item which counts as capital (for example shares), the item is your actual capital;

(b) if you have spent capital with the purpose of gaining HB (and (a) does not apply), this is your notional capital;

(c) the exception to (b) is that in working age HB claims, if you bought personal possessions with the purpose of gaining HB, they are counted as your actual capital;

(d) if you spent capital without the purpose of gaining HB (and (a) does not apply), this is neither actual nor notional capital;

(e) if you say you have spent capital but in fact you still have it (for example in an undisclosed bank account), this is your actual capital.

For pension age HB, see also para 15.63.

15.60   HB 49(7); HB66+ 47(5); NIHB 46(7); NIHB66+ 45(5)

15.61   HB 49(1); HB66+ 47(1); NIHB 46(1); NIHB66+ 45(1)

15.63   HB66+ 47(2); NIHB66+ 45(2)

15.64   HB 44, 49(1), sch 6 para 12; HB66+ 44(1),(2), 47(1),(2); NIHB 41, 46(1), sch 7 para 12; NIHB66+ 42(1),(2), 45(1),(2)

15.65   There are also differences in other situations. For example:

(a) if one person holds capital on behalf of another, there are rules about whether it is your actual capital (paras 15.8-9);

(b) the exception is that in working age HB claims, if one person is paid capital on behalf of another, there are rules about whether it is your notional capital (paras 13.57-59).

Example: Diminishing notional capital

Catalina claims HB

Catalina is aged 68. She has actual capital of £15,000, and with just this she would qualify for HB of £50 per week. But she is found to have deprived herself of £5,000 and this counts as her notional capital (paras 15.61-71).

▪ Notional capital	£5,000
▪ Actual capital	£15,000
▪ Total capital	£20,000

She does not qualify for HB. The notional capital means she has lost £50 per week. This is the fixed rate reduction.

Catalina claims HB 20 weeks later

▪ Notional capital (reduced by 20 x £50 = £1,000)	£4,000
▪ Actual capital (has reduced for other reasons to)	£13,000
▪ Total capital	£17,000

She does not qualify for HB. The fixed rate of reduction is not recalculated (less than 26 weeks have passed).

Catalina claims HB 10 further weeks later

▪ Notional capital (further reduced by 10 x £50 = £500)	£3,500
▪ Actual capital (has not changed)	£13,000
▪ Total capital	£16,500

She does not qualify for HB. The fixed rate of reduction is recalculated (at least 26 weeks have passed). But the new figure turns out to be £40 per week, so the existing £50 per week fixed rate continues.

Catalina claims HB 20 further weeks later

▪ Notional capital (further reduced by 20 x £50 = £1,000)	£2,500
▪ Actual capital (has reduced to)	£12,000
▪ Total capital	£14,500

She qualifies for and is awarded HB. Actual rates of reduction are used while she is on HB.

How notional capital reduces

15.66   If you have notional capital because of the deprivation of capital rule (paras 15.61-63), your notional capital reduces each week: paras 15.67-71. This is called the 'diminishing notional capital rule'. It is illustrated in the example.

The amount of the reduction

15.67   The reduction equals the amount of HB and other benefits you have lost as a result of having notional capital: see paras 15.68-71. But the only benefits taken into account are HB, JSA(IB), ESA(IR), IS and SPC. If the figures for these (apart from HB) relate to a part-week, they are converted to a weekly equivalent.

People who still qualify for HB

15.68   In weeks in which you qualify for HB, the reduction equals the amount you have lost in that particular week.

People who don't qualify for HB

15.69   In weeks in which you don't qualify for HB, the reduction is made at a fixed rate (paras 15.70-71), but only in pension age HB, or in working age HB if you live in supported or temporary accommodation (because otherwise you can't reclaim HB: chapter 2).

15.70   The fixed rate of the reduction equals the amount you lost in the most recent of the following weeks:

(a) the week your notional capital was first taken into account; or

(b) the first week you did not qualify for HB; or

(c) any week in which the fixed rate is recalculated (para 15.71).

15.71   The fixed rate is recalculated only if you make a new unsuccessful claim for HB (in other words you claim but do not qualify for HB) at least 26 weeks after the fixed rate was:

(a) first calculated (para 15.70(a) or (b)); or

(b) most recently recalculated (as described in this paragraph).

The new fixed rate is then used if it is higher than (or equal to) the old fixed rate. If it is lower, the old fixed rate continues (but this still counts as a recalculation for (b) above). The fixed rate is not recalculated if you make an unsuccessful claim for HB within the 26 weeks (but the old fixed rate continues). If you make a successful claim for HB (at any time) see para 15.68.

15.66   HB 49(1), 50; HB66+ 47(1), 48; NIHB 46(1), 47; NIHB66+ 45(1), 46

15.67   HB 50(1)-(4),(8); HB66+ 48(1)-(4),(8); NIHB 47(1)-(4),(8); NIHB66+ 46(1)-(4),(8)

15.68   HB 50(1)(a),(2),(3),(8); HB66+ 48(1)(a),(2),(3),(8); NIHB 47(1)(a),(2),(3),(8); NIHB66+ 46(1)(a),(2),(3),(8)

15.70   HB 50(1)(b),(4),(8); HB66+ 48(1)(b),(4),(8); NIHB 47(1)(b),(4),(8); NIHB66+ 46(1)(b),(4),(8)

15.71   HB 50(1)(b),(5)-(8); HB66+ 48(1)(b),(5)-(8); NIHB 47(1)(b),(5)-(8); NIHB66+ 46(1)(b),(5)-(8)

Chapter 16 **Claims**

- Making a claim: see paras 16.1-21.
- Information and evidence: see paras 16.22-30.
- HB start dates and backdating: see paras 16.31-50.

Making a claim

16.1   You have to make a claim to get HB. This chapter explains how to do this. It applies whether you are making your first ever claim or are claiming again following a period when you weren't on HB.

Pension age and working age HB

16.2   Anyone can make a claim for pension age HB, but you can only make a claim for working age HB if you live in supported or temporary accommodation (table 2.3).

16.3   If you are already on HB and you move home or have another kind of change in your circumstances, see chapter 17.

Who makes the claim

16.4   You make your HB claim yourself, and can ask a friend, relative, advice worker or someone else to help you. If you are a couple (or in a polygamous marriage) you have to choose one of you to be the claimant. Or if you can't agree the council chooses for you.

Attorneys and appointees if you are unable to act

16.5   If you are unable to make a claim for HB yourself, an attorney or appointee (paras 16.6-7) can act for you. The law uses the phrase 'unable, for the time being, to act'. This means the person could act for you for a short period (e.g. until you reach 18 or while you are visiting relatives abroad) or a long period (e.g. when you are seriously mentally impaired). However, no-one can make an HB claim after your death (R(IS) 3/04).

16.6   The council:

(a) must accept an HB claim from someone who:

- has ordinary or lasting power of attorney for you ('your attorney'), or
- is appointed by a court to act for you (a deputy appointed by the Court of Protection in England or Wales, a judicial factor or other guardian in Scotland, or a controller appointed by the High Court in Northern Ireland);

16.1   AA 1, 5; NIAA 1, 5

16.2   UCTP 4A, 5(2)(a), 6(1),(8); NIUCTP 2B, 3(2)(a), 4(1),(8)

16.4   CBA 134(2); HB 82(1); HB66+ 63(1); NICBA 130(2); NIHB 80(1); NIHB66+ 61(1)

16.5-7   HB 82(2)-(6); HB66+ 63(2)-(6); NIHB 80(2)-(6); NIHB66+ 61(2)-(6)

(b) may (in any other case) accept an HB claim from someone who is your 'appointee' (para 16.7).

The person then takes over all rights and responsibilities in relation to your HB claim.

16.7   The council may accept a written request from an individual over 18, or from a firm or organisation, to be your 'appointee' – for example, a friend or relative, a social worker or solicitor, or someone appointed by the DWP in relation to one of your benefits. Either the council or appointee can terminate the appointment by giving four weeks' written notice.

Where to claim

16.8   You claim HB from your council. Or if you are claiming SPC, JSA, ESA or IS, you can claim HB from the DWP.

Claiming HB from the council

16.9   Each council has at least one office where you can make your HB claim (called a 'designated office' in the law). This is normally the council's benefit office. Some councils in England also allow claims at a county council office or via a social landlord's address.

16.10   You can make a claim to the council in writing (typically on the council's claim form but it could be in a letter). The council must provide claim forms free of charge. Alternatively, you may make a claim online via a web form or app if the council allows this. But the council can only accept electronic claims if its Chief Executive has made a direction permitting it (HB A18/2006). You can also claim by telephone if the council has published a number for this purpose. Sometimes the council may require a signed confirmation from you of the details given in the call.

Claiming HB via the DWP

16.11   When you claim SPC, JSA, ESA or IS from the DWP, you can usually claim HB at the same time and in the same way (e.g. at an interview, by telephone, etc). You have made a claim for HB if you answered the question (or ticked the box, etc) about whether you pay rent (CP/3444/2003). You can do this at any time before your SPC/JSA/ESA/IS claim is decided. But when you claim other benefits from the DWP, including UC in temporary or supported accommodation, you have to make a separate HB claim to the council.

16.12   If you claim HB via the DWP, the DWP sends details of your claim to the council. Before that, it may ask you to provide information and evidence for the council. If it does, the rules in paras 16.16-17 also apply to the DWP.

16.8   HB 83(4)(a),(b); HB66+ 64(5)(a),(b); NIHB 81(4)(a),(b); NIHB66+ 62(5)(a),(b)

16.9-10   HB 2(1) definition: 'designated office', 83(1),(4A), 83A, sch 11; HB66+ 64(2),(5A), 64A, sch 10; NIHB 2(1), 81(1),(4A), 81A, sch 11; NIHB66+ 2(1), 62(2),(5A), 62A, sch 10

16.11-12   HB 83(5)(d); HB66+ 64(6)(d); NIHB 81(5)(d); NIHB66+ 62(6)(d)

Telling the council or DWP you want to claim

16.13 If you tell the council or DWP that you intend to claim, this can count as your date of claim (table 16.1(b)). You could notify your intention in any way, such as requesting a claim form or asking how to claim.

Completing your claim

16.14 The council doesn't have to decide your claim or award you HB until your claim is complete.

16.15 A 'complete' (or 'valid') HB claim means one that:

(a) meets the council's instructions – for example you need to answer all the questions that apply to you; and

(b) provides the information and evidence the council requires (para 16.22).

Completing an incomplete claim

16.16 If your claim is incomplete ('defective') the council must give you the opportunity to do whatever is needed to complete it. For example, it should:

(a) send you an application form if you asked for one or tell you how to claim;

(b) ask questions that arise from the information you have provided;

(c) ask questions you haven't yet answered;

(d) ask for information and evidence you haven't yet provided.

16.17 The council must allow you a month to respond, and if you claimed by telephone this period starts from when the council/DWP last drew attention to what it required of you. So long as you respond within the month, or longer if reasonable, your date of claim isn't delayed. This is the case even if the council took a long time to ask you in the first place, for example, if it initially failed to recognise your letter as being a claim (para 16.10) (CP/3444/2003).

Deciding your claim

16.18 Once you complete your claim, the council must decide whether you qualify for HB and, if so, from what date (para 16.31).

16.13   HB 83(4D),(4DA),(4E),(6),(7),(8); HB66+ 64(5E),(EA),(5F),(7),(8),(9)
         NIHB 81(4D),(4DA),(4E),(6),(7),(8); NIHB66+ 62(5E),(5EA),(5F),(7),(8),(9)

16.14   HB 83(1),(6); HB66+ 64(2),(7); NIHB 81(1),(6); NIHB66+ 62(2),(7)

16.15   AA 1(1), 5(1)(a),(1A); HB 83(1),(4C),(9), 86(1); HB66+ 64(2),(5D),(10), 67(1)
         NIAA 1(1), 5(1)(a),(1A); NIHB 81(1),(4C),(9), 82(1); NIHB66+ 62(2),(5D),(10), 63(1)

16.16-17 HB 83(4D),(4DA),(4E),(7),(7A),(8),(8A), 86(1); HB66+ 64(5E),(5EA),(5F),(8),(8A),(9),(9A), 67(1)
         NIHB 81(4D),(4DA),(4E),(7),(8), 82(1); NIHB66+ 62(5E),(5EA),(5F),(8),(9), 63(1)

16.18-20 HB 83(4E),(4F),(8), 89, 90; HB66+ 64(5F),(5G),(9), 70, 71; NIHB 81(4E),(4F),(8), 85, 86; NIHB66+ 62(5F),(5G),(9), 66, 67

16.19   The council must also decide your claim if you don't complete it, and in this case it could:

(a)   decide it has enough information to award you HB; or

(b)   decide that your failure to provide information or evidence, or to answer questions, means that you don't meet the conditions of entitlement to HB (para 16.14); or

(c)   make a reasonable assumption that you don't qualify (draw an 'adverse inference'), for example, assume that you still have capital if you refuse to say where it went.

16.20   Even if the council can't get all the information it needs, it must make a decision (para 16.19), send you a notice (para 20.6) and allow you the appeal rights in chapter 20 (R(H) 3/05).

Amending or withdrawing a claim

16.21   You can amend your HB claim at any time before the council makes a decision on it. Or you can withdraw your claim and the council need take no further action on it – in this case you should be sure you don't want HB.

Information and evidence

16.22   The council can ask you for 'certificates, documents, information and evidence' that it reasonably needs to decide your entitlement to HB. This applies when you make your claim, and also while you are getting HB (para 17.8).

Information and evidence normally requested

16.23   The council should tell you what information and evidence it requires to support your claim. You will always be asked for evidence of your and your partner's identity (i.e. name, address) and (in most cases) national insurance number (paras 16.26-27). But apart from that, any other information and evidence requested depends on the council's approach to verifying claims. Many follow the guidance (HB S11/2011) and adopt a risk-based approach whereby the level of checking depends on the probability of fraud or error associated with your category of claim (e.g. pensioner, hostel-dweller). Your risk category may also determine the form of evidence the council accepts (e.g. electronic submission, photocopies or original documents). Changes in the number and type of HB claims due to the roll-out of UC may lead councils to review their approach to information and evidence gathering.

16.24   When you claim on a paper application form you should sign it. If you are a couple (or in a polygamous marriage) your partner(s) should also sign if the form requires this.

Information and evidence that can't be requested

16.25   The council shouldn't ask you for information and evidence about payments from certain government trust funds (para 15.42) or payments in kind (goods not money) from a charity or most other sources.

16.21   HB 87; HB66+ 68; NIHB 83; NIHB66+ 64

16.22   AA 5(1A); HB 83(1), 86(1); HB66+ 64(2), 67(1); NIAA 5(1A); NIHB 81(1), 82(1); NIHB66+ 62(2), 63(1)

16.25   HB 86(2),(4); HB66+ 67(2),(4); NIHB 82(2),(4); NIHB66+ 63(2),(4)

National insurance numbers

16.26   You must give the council your national insurance number (NINO), and your partner's if you are a couple, along with supporting evidence. Or if you don't have a NINO you must apply for one, but you don't have to apply for a NINO to be allocated before you can claim ([2018] UKUT 50 (AAC)].

16.27   However a NINO isn't required:

(a) for you (or your partner) if you live in a hostel (para 7.26); or

(b) for your partner if s/he requires 'leave' to be in the UK but does not have it (table 2.5) – typically if s/he has an outstanding application with the Home Office. In these cases, where your partner's NINO has been refused due to 'immigration status invalid' the council should allocate a dummy NINO so the claim can be processed (GM D1.284-86). The council may inform the Home Office, because getting a personal allowance as a couple rather than as a single person counts as 'public funds', and this may affect your partner's leave (GM C4.218-19).

Using information supplied by the DWP

16.28   Where the DWP has supplied the council with information about any benefits used in connection with your claim (but not UC) the council must normally use that information without verifying its accuracy. Exceptions to this rule include where the information was given to the council more than 12 months after the DWP used it or the council has reasons for thinking it has changed.

16.29   If you have been awarded a passport benefit (table 6.1), you automatically meet the income and capital conditions for getting maximum HB (R v Penwith DC ex parte Menear; R v South Ribble HBRB ex parte Hamilton). If you have been refused a passport benefit, the council must make its own assessment of your income and capital ([2017] UKUT 362 (AAC)).

Nil income claims

16.30   If you have no income, the council mustn't refuse you HB on the grounds that you 'ought' to claim SPC or UC. If you claim HB while waiting for SPC or UC, the council shouldn't delay your HB if you can show that you are living off voluntary support or your savings.

16.26-27   AA 1(1A)-(1C); HB 4; HB66+ 4; NIAA 1(1A)-(1C); NIHB 4; NIHB66+ 4

16.28   AA 7B; SI 2007/2911; NIAA 5B; NISR 2007/467

16.29   R v Penwith DC ex p Menear 11/10/91 QBD 24 HLR 115
                  R v South Ribble HBRB ex p Hamilton [2000] EWCA Civ 518 www.bailii.org/ew/cases/EWCA/Civ/2000/518.html

HB start dates and backdating

Your HB start date

16.31   The general rule is that your HB starts on the Monday following:

(a)   your date of claim (table 16.1); or

(b)   your backdated date of claim (paras 16.36-42).

If your date of claim or backdated date of claim is a Monday, this means the following Monday. Exceptions to the general rule are in paras 16.32-35.

When you move home

16.32   Paras 16.33-34 apply to claims for HB when you move home or become liable for rent for any other reason. But if you were already on HB at your old address, moves within your council's area are taken into account without you having to make a claim (para 16.50 and table 17.3).

Table 16.1 **Your date of claim**

Date of claim	**Conditions you have to meet**
(a) The day the council or DWP received your HB claim (paras 16.8-12).	All cases unless (b)-(e) give an earlier date.
(b) The day you first told the council or DWP you want to claim HB (para 16.13).	You made your HB claim within one month of telling them or of being sent a claim form (even if the form was issued later).
(c) The day your partner died or you separated, if they were getting HB at the time.	The council or DWP received your HB claim within one month of the death or separation.
(d) The day your SPC guarantee credit or UC began.	The council or DWP received your HB claim within one month of the DWP receiving your SPC/UC claim.
(e) The day your liability for rent began, if you were on SPC guarantee credit or UC at the time.	The council or DWP received your HB claim within one month of the liability beginning.

Note: See paras 16.35-42 for advance and backdated claims.

16.31   HB 76(1); HB66+ 57(1); NIHB 74(1); NIHB66+ 55(1)

T16.1   HB 83(5),(12),(12A); HB66+ 64(1),(1A),(5); NIHB 81(5),(12),(12A); NIHB66+ 62(1),(1A),(5)

The new liability rule

16.33 This rule applies when all the following occur in the same benefit week (para 16.49):

(a) your date of claim (table 16.1) or backdated date of claim (paras 16.36-42) is in that benefit week; and

(b) your or your partner's liability for rent begins in that benefit week; and

(c) you move in during or before that benefit week.

In this case, your HB starts on the day your liability begins, or the day you move in if that is later in the week ([2014] UKUT 411 (AAC)). If you don't meet conditions (a) to (c), the general rule applies.

The rule for daily rents

16.34 This rule only applies if you are liable to pay your rent daily to:

(a) a hostel (para 7.26); or

(b) temporary accommodation (para 7.33).

In this case, your HB starts on the day you move in. This applies regardless of when you make your claim (HB A8/2006, A2/2007), but it is a good idea to make your claim as soon as you can so that you still have the information and evidence you need.

Examples: When HB starts

1. Pension age HB: general rule

Sian is aged 70 and is on a low income. Her online claim for HB is received by the council on Friday 8th September 2023.

- ■ Her date of claim is automatically backdated for three months to Thursday 8th June 2023 (para 16.36).

- ■ Her HB starts on Monday 12th June 2023 (para 16.31).

2. Working age HB: a new home

Murdo is aged 30 and moves into supported accommodation on Monday 15th May 2023. His weekly rent starts on the same day, and his HB application form reaches the council on Friday 18th August 2023.

- ■ His date of claim is Friday 18th August 2023 (table 16.1(a)).

- ■ His HB starts on Monday 21st August 2023 (para 16.31).

16.33   HB 76(2); HB66+ 57(2); NIHB 74(2); NIHB66+ 55(2)

16.34   HB 76(3)-(5); HB66+ 57(2)-(4); NIHB 74(3)-(5); NIHB66+ 55(2)-(4)

Advance claims

16.35   Making an advance claim can mean you get HB when you need it, rather than having to wait for HB and possibly building up rent arrears. You can make an advance claim for HB:

(a) up to 17 weeks before you will become entitled to pension age HB (e.g. because you are approaching pension age or planning to retire from work);

(b) up to 13 weeks before you will become entitled to working age HB (e.g. you are planning to move to your first rented home).

In these cases your date of claim is treated as being in the benefit week (para 16.49) before your entitlement begins and your HB starts on the day you become entitled to it. But this rule only applies if you are habitually resident in the UK or the rest of the CTA (table 2.5).

Backdating pension age HB

16.36   When you claim pension age HB your date of claim is automatically backdated for three months (or back to the date you or your partner reached pension age if this is later). You don't have to request this: it applies in all cases. See paras 16.31-34 for the date your HB starts.

If you also claim SPC

16.37   SPC is also automatically backdated for three months (or back to the date you qualify from if this is later: para 22.42).

16.38   If you claim HB within one month of claiming SPC guarantee credit, your HB date of claim is the day your SPC was backdated to (table 16.1(d)).

Backdating working age HB

16.39   When you claim working age HB, your date of claim is backdated if you:

(a) request this – either when you claim or separately later; and

(b) had continuous 'good cause' (para 16.44) for not making your claim/request earlier.

16.40   If you meet these conditions, your date of claim is backdated for one month before the council received your request or (if shorter) for whatever period you had good cause.

If you also claim UC

16.41   UC is also backdated for up to one month, but normally only if you are disabled, or were ill, or the UC online system wasn't working (volume 1 chapter 3). Your UC housing costs can also be backdated if you claim HB because you consider your home is supported accommodation but the council decides it isn't (paraa 2.27-28).

16.42   If you claim HB within one month of claiming UC, your date of claim is the day your UC was backdated to (table 16.1(d)). If your UC was backdated for less than a month, you can request backdated HB for the remainder of the month (paras 16.39-40).

16.35   HB 83(10),(11); NIHB 81(10),(11)

16.36   HB66+ 64(1),(1A); NIHB66+ 62(1),(1A)

16.38   HB66+ 64(1A),(6)(a); NIHB66+ 62(1A),(6)(a)

16.39-40   HB 83(12),(12A); NIHB 81(12),(12A)

16.42   HB 83(5)(aa),(12),(12A); NIHB 81(5)(aa),(12),(12A)

HB during a backdated period

16.43 During a backdated period, your HB is:

(a) calculated using your circumstances and HB rules that applied then; and

(b) only awarded for the parts of the period in which you qualify.

'Good cause' for backdating working age HB

16.44 You are likely to have good cause for backdating working age HB if:

(a) you were so ill (physically or mentally) or otherwise unable to act that you could not claim and could not ask someone to claim for you;

(b) someone you have been able to rely on (such as the council, the DWP, an advice agency and possibly others) advised you that you could not get HB when in fact you could;

(c) there were good reasons for you not believing you could claim, amounting to more than just not thinking or caring;

(d) some external factor prevented you from making a claim (e.g. failure of the postal services, imprisonment); or

(e) there is some other good reason for your failure to claim or request backdating earlier.

Table 16.2 summarises case law about this.

Table 16.2 **Good cause: case law**

■ *Reasonableness:* Good cause includes 'any fact that would probably have caused a reasonable person to act as the claimant did' (CH/4501/2004 approving C.S. 371/49). What is 'reasonable' is objective rather than subjective ([2010] UKUT 64 (AAC)).

■ *Ignorance of rights and attempts to ascertain them:* Claimants are expected to take reasonable steps to ascertain what their rights may be, but 'cannot always be assumed to have an understanding of public administration' (C.S. 371/49). Though ignorance of itself is not good cause, it may be a factor to take into account since the law does not 'require a person to be acquainted with the "rules and regulations"' ([2010] UKUT 64 (AAC)).

■ *A mistaken belief reasonably held:* Good cause can include a firmly held misunderstanding which amounts to a mistaken belief reasonably held, particularly when the claimant has not been careless or attempted to obtain benefit they are not entitled to (CH/4501/2004 approving earlier cases). This could include believing that you don't have to pay housing costs (and so don't have to claim HB) if you are on a passport benefit (CH/4501/2004), or that you can't get HB if you haven't paid national insurance contributions (CH/2198/2008).

■ *Illness:* Good cause is related not to the severity or seriousness of an illness but to the resulting incapability of the claimant to claim (CH/5135/2001).

■ *Mental incapacity:* In deciding good cause, a mentally disabled person is treated as having their mental age, not their chronological age (CH/393/2003).

- *Inability to speak English:* By itself, an inability to speak English is not normally good cause (CH/3579/2003).
- *Not receiving a document from the council:* Good cause can include non-receipt of a document from the council (e.g. requesting information and evidence) if this meant your HB stopped and you have reapplied (CH/3402/2005).
- *Misleading or incorrect advice and other factors:* Case law about other benefits is binding on HB (CH/5221/2001). Misinformation on an official website such as gov.uk can be misadvice and amount to good cause ([2015] UKUT 616(AAC)).
- *Who has to have good cause:* Only you (the claimant) have to show good cause not, for example, your partner (CH/3817/2004).
- *Good cause and qualifying for HB:* If you have good cause your claim is backdated even if you only qualify for HB for part of the backdated period (CH/1237/2004). But the council doesn't have to consider whether you have good cause if you don't qualify for any of the backdated period (CH/996/2004).

16.45　　When you request backdated HB, you don't have to use legal terminology, so long as you ask for HB for a past period and give your reasons (CH/3402/2005). The council can ask you for information and evidence to support your request and must base its decision on your individual circumstances. You can ask the council to reconsider its decision and appeal to a First-tier Tribunal (para 20.42) and then an Upper Tribunal (para 20.53) because 'good cause' is a question of law as well as fact (R(SB) 39/91).

Lost, mislaid or delayed claim forms

16.46　　If you sent the council a claim form or enquiry about claiming (para 16.13) but the council has no record of this, the question of whether and when it reached the council is decided by looking at the evidence and surrounding circumstances (paras 20.20-22). If the council received your form or enquiry but didn't act on it (for the above or other reasons) your HB is awarded based on the date the council received it, without this counting as 'backdating' your HB (CP/3477/2003). If you claimed SPC/JSA/ESA/IS at the DWP and you indicated on the claim form that you pay rent (usually by ticking a box) this is a HB claim even if the council wasn't made aware of it (CP/3477/2003).

Definition of 'month'

16.47　　Many of the rules in this guide refer to allowing you a 'month' to complete your claim or appeal, etc. This means a calendar month, counted as follows (R(IB) 4/02):

(a) if the council requests something on 26th June, you have provided it within one month if you get it to the council by the end of 26th July;

(b) if the council requests something on 31st January, you have provided it within a month if you get it to the council by the end of 28th (or 29th) February.

16.47　　Interpretation Act 1978 s5, sch 1 – 'month'

16.48 Things sent out by the council (such as requests for information or evidence, decision letters) are counted in the law as being sent out on the date of posting. Things received by the council (such as claims, information and evidence) are counted in the law as being received on the date of receipt. In the case of online communications, this means the date recorded by the computer as the date of sending or receipt unless the council reasonably directs otherwise.

Definition of 'benefit week'

16.49 Many of the rules in this guide refer to 'benefit week'. A benefit week always begins on a Monday and ends on the following Sunday.

Duration of your HB award

16.50 There is no fixed limit to an award of HB. Your award may change if your circumstances change (para 17.1) but this does not end your HB (even if the council asks you to complete a new form). Your HB award continues until one or more of the situations in paras 17.34-35 apply to you.

16.48   DAR 2; HB sch 11 para 4; HB66+ sch 10 para 4; NIDAR 2; NIHB sch 11 para 4; NIHB66+ sch 10 para 4

16.49   HB 2(1) definition: 'benefit week'; HB66+ 2(1); NIHB 2(1); NIHB66+ 2(1)

16.50   HB 79(1),(8); HB66+ 59(1),(8); UCTP 8(2A);
         NIHB 77(1),(10); NIHB66+ 57(1),(10); NIUCTP 6(2A)

Chapter 17 **Changes**

- Changes of circumstances: see paras 17.1-10.
- When changes take effect: see paras 17.11-15.
- Rent increases, moving home, transferring to UC, changes in state benefits, starting work etc: see paras 17.16-39.
- Suspending, restoring and terminating HB: see paras 17.40-45.

Changes of circumstances

17.1   This chapter explains how your HB changes when there is a change in your or someone else's circumstances. It applies when:

(a) you or someone else report a change; or

(b) the council becomes aware of a change without it being reported.

The duty to report changes

17.2   You have a duty to tell the council about any 'relevant' change of circumstances. The same duty applies to anyone acting for you (paras 16.5-7), and your landlord/agent if HB is paid to them (para 18.22). This means any change which you (or they) could reasonably be expected to know might affect:

(a) your entitlement to HB; or

(b) the amount of your HB; or

(c) how your HB is paid or who it is paid to.

17.3   This duty begins on the date your claim is made, and continues for as long as you are receiving HB. Table 17.1 summarises the main changes you should tell the council about.

How to notify changes

17.4   You must notify changes to the council.

17.5   Most councils accept notification by telephone or online, though they can require written rather than telephone notifications, or require written or electronic records to be kept by those making online notifications.

17.6   In all other cases, you must notify changes to the council's 'designated office' (para 16.9). However, the council may accept notification by any other method it agrees to in a particular case.

17.2-3   HB 88(1); HB66+ 69(1); NIHB 84(1); NIHB66+ 65(1)

17.4-5   HB 88(1),(6), 88A, sch 11; HB66+ 69(1),(9), 69A, sch 10; NIHB 84(1),(3), 84A, sch 11; NIHB66+ 65(1),(2), 65A, sch 10

Table 17.1 **Changes you should notify**

(a) Changes in your personal details – e.g. becoming a couple or a single person.

(b) Changes in your family details – e.g. a child or young person moving out or stopping being your responsibility.

(c) Changes relating to non-dependants – e.g. moving in or a change in their income.

(d) Changes in your rent (unless you are a council or NIHE tenant) or letting details.

(e) Stopping qualifying for UC, JSA(IB), ESA(IR) or IS (but it is the DWP's duty to notify changes to SPC).

(f) Changes in other DWP benefits.

(g) Changes in your earned or unearned income or capital.

(h) Changes affecting your entitlement to HB – e.g. becoming a student, or absences likely to be over 13 weeks.

(i) If you are a couple, changes (as above) relating to your partner as well as yourself.

(j) Any other changes affecting your entitlement to HB, the amount of your HB, how it is paid or who it is paid to.

Reporting changes promptly

17.7 You should tell the council promptly about changes. If you delay reporting a change that increases your HB, you may end up getting less HB than you could have (table 17.2).

Information and evidence

17.8 The council can ask you for information and evidence it reasonably requires in order to make a decision about a change (para 16.22), and must take this into account if you provide it within one month, or longer if reasonable.

Decisions and notices

17.9 The council makes a decision about the change, and must send you a decision notice telling you:

(a) how the change affects your HB;

(b) if it does, when the change takes effect;

(c) your rights (para 20.1).

17.10 The change to your HB is also called a 'supersession' or (in a few cases) a 'revision' – these terms are explained in para 20.33.

T17.1   HB 88; HB66+ 69; NIHB; NIHB66+ 65

17.8   AA 5(1A); NIAA 5(1A); HB 86(1); HB66+ 67(1); NIHB 82(1); NIHB66+ 63(1); DAR 4(5), 7(5); NIDAR 4(4), 7(5)

17.9   HB 89(1), 90(1)(b), sch 9; HB66+ 70(1), 71(1)(b), sch 8; NIHB 85(1), 86(1)(b), sch 10; NIHB66+ 66(1), 67(1)(b), sch 9

When changes take effect

17.11   When there is a change in your personal, financial or other circumstances, the change takes effect (alters or ends your HB) as in table 17.2.

17.12   But there are different rules for rent increases, moving home, entitlement to UC, SPC and other benefits, reaching pension age, and starting work (paras 17.16-39).

Table 17.2 **When changes of circumstances take effect**

Type of change	When it takes effect
Changes increasing your HB	
(a) Reported to the council, or made by the council, within the time limit (one month or in some cases up to 13 months: para 17.15)	The Monday following the date the change occurred
(b) Reported outside the time limit	The Monday following the date the change was reported, or the council makes the change (if this is earlier)
Changes reducing or ending your HB	
(c) Changes reducing your HB	The Monday following the date the change occurred
(d) Changes ending your HB	The last day of your HB is the Sunday at the end of the benefit week that contains the change, or the exact day of the change if your rent is due on a daily basis

Notes:
- In the law, (a) to (d) are all supersessions.
- For exceptions see paras 17.16-39.

Example: Late notified change increasing HB

Anjali is on HB. Her capital reduced four months ago when she paid off several debts, but she did not inform the council until today. The council asks why she delayed, but she has no special circumstances.

The change is implemented from the Monday following the day her notification of the change was received by the council. She does not get arrears of HB because she has no special circumstances for notifying late.

T17.2   HB 79(1),(8); HB66+ 59(1),(8); DAR 7(2)(a)(i), 8(2)-(5); NIHB 77(1),(8); HB66+ 57(1),(8); NIDAR 7(2)(a)(i), 8(2)-(5)

Time limit for getting your arrears

17.13   When a change increases your HB, you only get all your arrears if you report it within the time limit. Table 17.2 shows how the time limit affects you. It doesn't apply to changes in most state benefits (para 17.26)

17.14   A change is reported within the time limit if:

(a)   you report the change to the council within one month of when it occurred; or

(b)   you report the change within 13 months and the council agrees to extend the time limit (para 17.15); or

(c)   the council (without being notified by you) makes the change within one month of when it occurred.

Extending the time limit

17.15   The time limit for reporting a change is extended if:

(a)   you report the change within 13 months of when it occurred;

(b)   you say you are reporting it late and give the reasons for your delay;

(c)   there are special circumstances why it wasn't practicable for you to report the change earlier; and

(d)   it is reasonable to accept your delay – the longer you delay the more compelling your special circumstances have to be.

Special cases

Rent increases

17.16   If you are a council or NIHE tenant, an increase (or decrease) in your rent or service charges usually affects your eligible rent (para 9.5). When it does, your HB changes on the exact day, and the rule about late reported changes (para 17.13) doesn't apply.

17.17   For all other tenants, an increase (or decrease) in your rent or service charges may or may not affect your eligible rent (paras 9.5, 10.5 or 10.40). When it does, your HB changes on the exact day, but if you are late reporting the change, you don't get all your arrears (table 17.2(b)).

Moving home

17.18   Table 17.3 shows how and when your HB changes if you move home. See also paras 3.29-38 if you qualify for HB before moving in or after moving out.

17.13   DAR 8(2); NIDAR 8(2)

17.14   DAR 7(2)(a),(3), 8(3),(5); NIDAR 7(2)(a), 8(3),(5)

17.15   DAR 9; NIDAR 9

17.16-17   HB 79(2),(8), 80(3)(b),(c),(8); HB66+ 59(2),(8), 61(3)(b),(c),(8)
            NIHB 77(2),(8), 78(3)(b),(c),(8); HB66+ 57(2),(8), 59(3)(b),(c),(8)

Table 17.3 **When HB changes if you move home**

Details of move	HB on old home	HB on new home

General rules
(all pension age moves – and working age moves unless the exceptions apply)

(a) Moves within the same council's area	Last day of HB = day before move	First day of HB = day of move (if you report the move promptly: para 17.13)
(b) Moves to a different council's area	Last day of HB = end of benefit week that contains day of move (or exact day if daily rent)	First day of HB = day of move (if you claim HB on time: table 16.1)
(c) Moves to somewhere HB can't be paid (paras 5.20-38 or table 5.2)	Last day of HB = end of benefit week that contains day of move (or exact day if daily rent)	You can't get HB

Exception for working age HB if you aren't on UC

(d) Moves to general accommodation in a different council's area	Last day of HB = end of transitional HB (this runs for two weeks from date of UC claim: para 17.19)	You can't get HB, but you can claim UC towards your housing costs

Exception for working age HB if you are on UC
(in supported or temporary accommodation)

(e) Moves to general accommodation in the same or a different council's area	Last day of HB = end of benefit week that contains day of move (or exact day if daily rent)	You can't get HB, but you can claim UC towards your housing costs

Notes:

■ 'Supported or temporary accommodation' means any accommodation in table 2.3.

■ 'General accommodation' means any other accommodation.

■ In situation (d), your UC can be backdated for up to one month (volume 1 chapter 3) if you claim UC promptly when you are told by your new council that you can no longer claim HB ([2020] UKUT 309 (AAC)).

T17.3   HB 79(2A)(a),(8), 80(3)(c),(8); HB66+ 59(2A)(a),(8),61(3)(e), (8); UCTP 5(2)(a), 6(8), 8(1),(2A),(3),(5),(8A); NIHB 77(2A)(a),(8), 78(3)(c),(8); NIHB66+ 57(2A)(a),(8),59(3)(c)(9); NIUCTP 3(2)(a), 4(8), 6(1),(2A),(6A)

Examples: Moving home

1. Moving within a council's area

Ginger moves within a council's area on Friday 27th October 2023. She is liable for rent at her old address up to and including Thursday 26th October and at her new address from Friday 27th October.

- ■ Her HB changes on and from Friday 27th October to reflect her new eligible rent.

2. Moving out of rented accommodation

Fred moves out of rented accommodation (to go and live with his parents) on Saturday 14th October 2023. He is liable for rent at his old address (but not on a daily basis) up to and including Friday 13th October.

- ■ His HB ends at the end of the benefit week containing the day of the move, in other words his last day of HB is Sunday 15th October.

Claiming UC – the two-week run on

17.19   If you are on working age HB and you claim UC:

(a) while you are living in general accommodation (para 2.17); or

(b) when you move to general accommodation in a different council's area (table 17.3(d));

you get a two-week run on of HB and (if you are on them) JSA(IB), ESA(IR) or IS (para 1.29).

Transitional HB

17.20   The HB run on is awarded from the first day of your UC and lasts exactly two weeks. It is designed to help you avoid rent arrears while waiting for your UC decision, and isn't repayable even if you turn out not to qualify for UC.

17.21   If you claimed UC as part of 'natural migration' (para 1.27):

(a) you qualify for maximum HB throughout the two-week HB run on; and

(b) this is calculated in the same way as if you were on any passport benefit (paras 6.2-3), using your current rent and non-dependant details.

17.22   If you claimed UC as part of 'managed migration' (para 1.28):

(a) your two-week HB run on continues at whatever amount your HB was on the first day of the two weeks; and

(b) no changes of circumstances are taken into account after that first day.

17.19   UCTP 8(1),(2A),(3),(5); NIUCTP 6(1),(2A),(3),(5)

17.20   reg 5 of SI 2019/1152; reg 4 of NISR 2019/152

17.21   UCTP 8A(a); NIUCTP 6A(a)

17.22   UCTP 8A(c); NIUCTP 6A(c)

17.23   Your two-week HB run on is paid to you if your HB was being paid to you, or to your landlord/agent if it was being paid to them. But if you claimed UC following a move, it is paid by the council whose area you've left, and must be paid to you, not your landlord/agent.

Examples: Transitional HB

1. Managed migration to UC

Rosemary gets HB of £70 per week. She gets a migration notice from the DWP and claims UC on Friday 11th August 2023.

- The first day of her UC is Friday 11th August.
- She gets two weeks transitional HB from Friday 11th August to Thursday 24th August of £70 per week

2. Natural migration to UC

Arthur is on HB and moves to a rented home in a new area. He claims UC on the day he moves, which is Thursday 6th July 2023.

- The first day of his UC is Thursday 6th July.
- He gets two weeks of transitional HB from Thursday 6th July to Wednesday 19th July, which equals maximum HB (his old weekly eligible rent minus deductions for any non-dependants at his old home).

Becoming a couple with someone on UC

17.24   When you become a couple with someone who is already on UC:

(a) if you move out of your home (e.g. because you are moving in with your partner), the last day of your HB is the Sunday at the end of the HB benefit week (para 16.49) containing the day of your move;

(b) if you remain in your home (e.g. because your partner is moving in with you), the last day of your HB is the day before the first day of the UC assessment period in which you become a couple.

In these circumstances you don't qualify for the two-week HB run on.

Example: Becoming a couple with someone on UC

Jack's new partner, Jill, moves in with him on 19th September. She is on UC and her assessment periods begin on the 7th of each month. Jack is added to Jill's UC claim from 7th September (the first day of the assessment period).

- Their UC starts to include housing costs on Jack's home (now their home) on 7th September.
- The last day of Jack's HB is 6th September.

17.23   UCTP 8A(b); NIUCTP 6A(b)

17.24   UCTP 5(2)(b), 7(1)-(3),(5),(6); NIUCTP 4(2)(b), 5(1)-(3),(5),(6)

Changes in SPC, UC and other benefits

17.25   For other benefits received by (or for) you, your partner or a child or a young person in your family:

(a) table 17.2 applies to changes in WTC and CTC; and

(b) table 17.4 applies to SPC, UC and other state benefits.

17.26   It is the DWP's duty to tell the council about changes in SPC, but your duty to tell them about changes in UC and all other benefits. The rule about late reported changes (para 17.13) applies in the case of WTC and CTC, but not in the case of SPC, UC and other benefits.

Examples: Changes in state benefits

1. Award of PIP following a claim

Bruno is aged 45 and is getting HB. He claims PIP and is awarded it from 18th May. This increases his HB (chapter 12).

- His HB is increased from 18th May (table 17.4(m)).

2. Award of attendance allowance following an appeal

Lilian is aged 75 and is getting HB. Following an appeal she is awarded attendance allowance for the past 18 months. This increases her HB (chapter 12).

- Her HB is increased back to the date her attendance allowance is awarded from (table 17.4(m)) so she gets 18 months of arrears of this increase.

Table 17.4 **When changes in state benefits take effect**

What the change is	When it takes effect
Changes in SPC	
(a) Guarantee credit starts	HB increases on the following Monday
(b) Guarantee credit ends (except as in (c) or (d))	HB reduces on the following Monday
(c) Guarantee credit is replaced by savings credit (except as in (d))	HB reduces on the following Monday or, if later, the Monday following the day the DWP tells the council
(d) Guarantee credit is replaced by savings credit and you delayed telling the DWP about the change that led to that	HB reduces on the Monday following the day savings credit begins
(e) Savings credit starts	HB reduces on the following Monday or, if later, the Monday following the day the DWP tells the council
(f) Savings credit ends (except as in (g))	HB increases on the following Monday

---

17.25-26   DAR 4(7B),(7C), 7(2)(i), 8(14); NIDAR 4(6B),(6C),7(2)(h), 8(12)

(g) Savings credit is replaced by guarantee credit	HB increases on the Monday of the benefit week in which guarantee credit begins
(h) Savings credit increases	HB reduces on the following Monday or, if later, the Monday following the day the DWP tells the council
(i) Savings credit reduces	HB increases on the Monday of the benefit week in which it reduces
Changes in other state benefits	
(j) UC starts in temporary or supported accommodation	HB increases on the exact day
(k) UC ends in temporary or supported accommodation	HB reduces on the following Monday
(l) Any other state benefit starts or increases	HB increases or reduces on the exact day
(m) Any other state benefit reduces or ends	HB increases or reduces on the following Monday

Note: In all the above cases, if the change means your HB ends, it ends as described in table 17.2(d).

Reaching pension age

17.27   The pension age HB rules start to apply to you on the day that:

(a)   you reach 66, if you are single; or

(b)   the younger of you reaches 66, if you are a couple.

When differences between working age and pension age rules affect your HB, the change takes place on the exact day of that birthday.

Start of SPC at pension age

17.28   You can get SPC (para 22.6) from the day you reach 66 (or the younger partner in a couple does) if you claim it no more than four months earlier or three months later (paras 22.42-43). The rules in paras 17.29-30 are designed to help you avoid rent arrears when you claim SPC while you wait for your decision, but in the case of a UC run-on (para 17.29) it applies even if you don't claim or don't qualify for SPC.

T17.4   HB 79(1); HB66+ 59(1), 60; DAR 4(7B),(7C), 7(2)(i), 8(14);
               NIHB 77(1); NIHB66+ 57(1), 58; NIDAR 4(6B),(6C), 7(2)(h), 8(12)

17.27   HB 5; HB66+ 5; NIHB 5; NIHB66+ 5

End of UC at pension age

17.29   If you are getting UC, it continues until the end of the UC assessment period containing the date you reach 66 (or the younger partner in a couple does). Your HB is worked out in the normal way (paras 6.5-6) but your UC is disregarded. After that your new circumstances are taken into account in your HB.

End of JSA(IB)/ESA(IR)/IS at pension age

17.30   If you are getting JSA(IB)/ESA(IR)/IS, it ends on the day before you reach 66 (or the younger partner in a couple does). In this case, you get continuing payment of the maximum HB for four weeks plus any odd days to make it end on a Sunday. After that your new circumstances are taken into account in your HB.

Example: End of UC at pension age

Raj is on UC and HB (in supported accommodation) when he reaches 66 on 26th May. His UC assessment periods begin on the 3rd of each month.

- ▪ His UC continues until 2nd June but is disregarded so he gets maximum HB (para 17.29).
- ▪ By then the DWP has decided he qualifies for guarantee credit of SPC, so he continues to get maximum HB.

Starting and stopping work

17.31   When you or your partner start work, your HB changes on the Monday following your first day of employment or self-employment; and when you or your partner stop work, your HB changes on the Monday following the first day you aren't employed or self-employed (paras 14.12, 14.33-34).

Extended payments of HB

17.32   You qualify for an extended payment of four weeks of HB if:

(a) you or your partner start employment or self-employment, or increase your hours or earnings; and

(b) this is expected to last at least five weeks; and

(c) either:
- ▪ you are on JSA(IB), ESA(IR) or IS which stops due to (a), and
- ▪ you have been on those benefits or JSA(C) in any combination for 26 weeks;

(d) or:
- ▪ you are on ESA(C), IB or SDA which stops due to (a), and
- ▪ you have been on those benefits (in any combination) for 26 weeks.

17.29   HB66+ 27(1)(zi); SI 2013/381, sch 1 para 26; UCTP 5(8A); NIHB66+ 21(1)(zi); NISR 2016/221, sch 1 para 26; NIUCTP 4(8A)

17.30   HB66+ 54; NIHB66+ 52

17.31   HB 79(1); HB66+59(1); NIHB 77(1); NIHB66+ 57(1)

17.32-33   HB 72-73E, 115, 116; HB66+ 52-53E, 96, 97; NIHB 70-71D, 110, 111; NIHB66+51-51C, 94, 95

17.33   In each of the four weeks your extended payment equals:

(a) the weekly amount of HB you were getting before the extended payment began, but ignoring the benefit cap (para 6.21); or

(b) if higher, the amount you qualify for in that particular week under the ordinary HB rules.

But you don't get an extended payment in a rent-free week (para 6.35). And after the four weeks of your extended payment, your HB is calculated under the ordinary HB rules.

Changes ending your HB

17.34   Your HB ends if:

(a) you stop meeting any of the basic and financial conditions (table 2.1) – for example, your income increases and you no longer qualify (para 6.6);

(b) you become a mixed age couple or polygamous marriage (para 2.12);

(c) you move to an area where a different council administers HB (para 17.18);

(d) you fail to respond to a request for information or evidence and this causes your HB to be terminated (para 17.44); or

(e) you voluntarily relinquish your HB award by telling the council you want to end it (HB circular G10/2008 and CJSA/3979/1999).

17.35   If you are working age, your HB also ends if:

(a) you make a claim for UC – unless you live in supported or temporary accommodation (STA);

(b) you are on UC and move from STA to general accommodation;

(c) you become the partner of someone who is already on UC.

Death

17.36   Your HB ends at the end of the benefit week that contains your date of death (because you are no longer occupying your home: table 2.1(a)). Your executors can't continue your HB claim, but a bereaved partner can make their own HB claim (table 16.1(c)).

Amendments to regulations and up-ratings

17.37   When the HB regulations are amended, your HB:

(a) changes from the date of the amendment, if you continue to qualify for HB; or

(b) ends at the end of the benefit week (para 16.49) containing the date of the amendment, if you no longer qualify for HB.

But if the April up-rating for social security benefits or tax credits is different from that for HB (para 1.16), they are treated as up-rated on the same day as HB.

17.34   CBA 130(1),(3); HB 79(1); DAR 14; NICBA 129(1),(3); HB66+59(1); NIHB 77(1); NIHB66+ 57(1); NIDAR 14

17.35   UCTP 7(2),(5), 8(2A),(3); NIUCTP 5(2),(5), 6(2A),(3)

17.36   AA 130(1)(a); HB 79(1); HB66+59(1); NIAA 129(i)(a); NIHB 77(1); NIHB66+ 57(1); NIDAR 14

17.37   HB 79(3); HB66+ 60(3); DAR 7(2)(q),(s), 8(10),(14E),(14G)
          NIHB 77(3); NIHB66+ 58(3); NIDAR 8(12)

New case law

17.38   When new case law (in another person's appeal) affects your HB, it takes effect from the date the Upper Tribunal, Northern Ireland Commissioners or court gives its judgment in that case. The main exception is that your HB can be altered from an earlier date if a First-tier Tribunal 'stayed' your own appeal to await that judgment.

More than one change

17.39   If you have more than one change, each is dealt with in turn. But the following rules apply when changes which actually occur in the same benefit week (para 16.49) would have an effect (under the earlier rules in this chapter) in different benefit weeks:

(a)   If one of the changes is in the annual up-rating in cases when this takes effect on the first Monday in April, the other changes take effect when that applies.

(b)   Otherwise, if one of the changes is in your rent (or your address if you move within the council's area), the other changes take effect when that applies.

(c)   In all other cases, all the changes take effect from the Monday of the benefit week in which the changes actually occur.

Suspending, restoring and terminating HB

17.40   This section describes how the council can suspend, restore and terminate HB. To suspend means stopping making payments for the time being, usually in order to avoid an overpayment or to seek information or evidence. To restore means starting payments again – either at the same amount as before or at a different amount, depending on the circumstances. To terminate means ending an award of HB altogether.

Suspending HB

17.41   The council may suspend HB if any of the following circumstances apply:

(a)   the council doubts whether the conditions of entitlement to HB are fulfilled;

(b)   the council is considering whether to change a decision about HB;

(c)   the council considers there may be a recoverable overpayment of HB;

(d)   a First-tier or Upper Tribunal has made a decision (in this or another case) and the council is awaiting the decision or a statement of reasons, or is considering making a further appeal;

(e)   an appeal has been made, or leave to appeal has been sought, against a decision of a First-tier or Upper Tribunal or court in the case to be suspended;

(f)   an appeal has been made, or leave to appeal has been sought, against a decision of an Upper Tribunal (in Northern Ireland, appeal tribunal/Commissioner) or court in a different HB case, and this may affect the case to be suspended;

17.38   CPSA sch 7 paras 4(5),(6),18; DAR 7(2)(b); NICPSA sch 7 paras 4(4),(5); NIDAR 7(2)(b)

17.39   HB 42(8), 79(4),(5); HB66+ 41(9),(10), 59(4),(5); DAR 7(2)(q), 8(14E);
         NIHB 39(8), 77(6),(7); NIHB66+ 39(11),(12), 57(6),(7); NIDAR 7(2)(h), 8(11)

17.41   DAR 11,13(1),(2); NIDAR 11,13(1),(2)

(g) you (or another person affected) have failed to provide information or evidence needed by the council to consider changing a decision about HB.

In such cases, HB is usually suspended in full (though the law permits the council to suspend only part).

Restoring HB

17.42   When payments of HB have been suspended, the council must restore them (to the extent that you are still entitled) within 14 days or as soon as reasonably practicable after that, as follows:

- in cases (a) to (c) (para 17.41), the council is satisfied that HB is properly payable and no outstanding matters remain to be resolved;
- in case (d), the council decides not to make the further appeal (if it decides to make the further appeal case (e) or (f) then applies);
- in cases (e) and (f), the appeal or request for leave has been determined;
- in case (g), the claimant has responded as required (para 17.43).

Information and evidence

17.43   When payments of HB have been suspended for failure to provide information or evidence (para 17.41(g)), the council must notify you of the suspension and of what information and evidence is required. You must then, within one month or such longer period as the council considers necessary:

(a) provide the information or evidence required; or

(b) satisfy the council that the information or evidence does not exist, or is impossible for you to obtain.

Terminating HB

17.44   When payments of HB have been suspended for failure to provide information or evidence (para 17.41(g)) and you have failed to respond as required (para 17.43) your HB entitlement is terminated from the date on which the payments were suspended (i.e. no further payments are made). The rule cannot be used to end HB from an earlier date ([2020] UKUT 71 (AAC)) so if entitlement did end earlier, this is done as an (ordinary) supersession from that earlier date.

17.42   DAR 12,13(5); NIDAR 12,13(5)

17.43   DAR 13(3),(4); NIDAR 13(3),(4)

17.44   DAR 14; NIDAR 14

Decisions and appeals

17.45   The council must notify you if it suspends, restores or terminates your HB, and you can ask it to reconsider any of these matters. You then have a right of appeal to a tribunal about a decision to terminate HB (CH/402/2007), or to restore HB at a different amount or for a different reason; but not about a determination to suspend HB, or to restore HB at the same amount for the same reasons. A decision to suspend HB may, however, be challenged by judicial review if it is irrational: R (Sanneh) v SSWP.

Example: Suspending and restoring HB

Karel is on HB. The council obtains information that he has changed jobs. It suspends his award immediately and writes to him allowing him one month to respond.

After two weeks, he sends in the necessary information and evidence, and he remains entitled to HB.

The council restores his HB from the date payments were suspended, making any change in his entitlement from the Monday after the day he got the new job.

17.45   R (Sanneh) v SSWP [2012] EWHC 1840 (Admin)
          www.bailii.org/ew/cases/EWHC/Admin/2012/1840.html

Chapter 18 **Payments**

- HB payments: rebates, allowances and payments on account: see paras 18.1-16.
- Paying HB to someone on your behalf: see paras 18.17-21.
- Paying HB to your landlord or agent: see paras 18.22-54.

How HB is paid

18.1　This section explains how and when your HB is paid, how soon the first payment should be made, and who your HB is paid to. You can ask the council to reconsider a decision it makes about any of these things (para 20.26), but only some of them can be appealed to a tribunal (para 20.43 and table 20.4).

Rebate or allowance

18.2　Your HB is paid:

　(a)　as a rent rebate if you are a council or NIHE tenant: see paras 18.4-5;

　(b)　as a rent allowance in all other cases: see paras 18.6-54.

18.3　In England, Scotland and Wales there are two exceptions:

　(a)　if you are renting a houseboat, mobile home or caravan (para 7.29) and you pay:

　　■　your mooring charges or site charges to the council, but

　　■　your rent to someone else (for example a private landlord)

　　your HB for each of these is paid as a rent allowance;

　(b)　if you pay your rent to the council because your home is subject to a management order or empty dwelling management order (EDMO), your HB is paid as a rent allowance.

Rent rebates

18.4　If your HB is paid as rent rebate (paras 18.2-3), this means it is paid straight into your rent account. You do not get a payment yourself, but you have less rent to pay (and in some cases no rent to pay).

When rent rebates are paid

18.5　The council should make the first payment into your rent account within 14 days of the date it receives your HB claim or as soon as reasonably practicable after that. It should then usually make payments into your rent account on the days your rent is due.

18.2　AA 134(1A),(1B),(2); NIAA 126(1),(2); NIHB 88,93(5); NIHB66+ 69, 74(5)

18.3　AA 134(1A); HB 91A; HB66+ 72A

18.4　AA 134(1A); NIAA 126(1)(b),(c)

18.5　HB 91(3); HB66+ 72(3); NIHB 87(3); NIHB66+ 68(3)

Rent allowances

18.6   If your HB is paid as a rent allowance (paras 18.2-3), this means it is paid:

(a) to you (the HB claimant);

(b) to someone on your behalf (paras 18.17-21); or

(c) to your landlord or agent (paras 18.22-54).

The council decides how to make payments, and should take into account your (or the payee's) reasonable needs and convenience. Usually the payments are made by credit transfer straight into a bank account or (increasingly rare) by cheque.

18.7   The council should not insist on paying you by credit transfer if:

(a) you do not have a bank account (R (Spiropoulos) v Brighton and Hove CC) (GM para A6.120). But the council may be able to tell you which banks in your area offer basic accounts, and may give you a letter confirming your identity to help you open an account; or

(b) your bank is unlikely to let you take the money out because you have an overdraft. Although the 'right of first appropriation' in common law says you have the right to instruct your bank that the money will be used to pay your rent rather than reduce your overdraft, this right can be difficult to insist upon (for example, sometimes banks insist on a fresh instruction for each payment).

When rent allowances are paid

18.8   The first payment of your rent allowance should be within 14 days of your HB claim, or as soon as reasonably practicable after that. If the council cannot do this, it should make a payment on account: see paras 18.11-16.

18.9   The council decides how often payments are made after that, and should take into account how often and on what dates your rent is due. It can make:

(a) payments to you (or someone on your behalf):

- ▪   every two weeks – you can insist on this if your HB is more than £2 a week,
- ▪   every four weeks,
- ▪   every calendar month, or
- ▪   every week: see para 18.10;

(b) payments to your landlord or agent:

- ▪   every four weeks,
- ▪   every calendar month (but only if your rent is due calendar monthly).

The first payment to a landlord or agent can be for a shorter period if they have other tenants on HB. This is to allow all of the HB payments to them to be made on the same dates.

18.6   AA 134(1A),(1B); HB 91(1), 94; HB66+ 72(1),75; NIAA 126(1); NIHB 87(1), 91; NIHB66+ 68(1), 72

18.7   R (Spiropoulos) v Brighton and Hove CC [2007] EWHC 342 (Admin) www.bailii.org/ew/cases/EWHC/Admin/2007/342.html

18.8   HB 91(3); HB66+ 72(3); NIHB 87(3); NIHB66+ 68(3)

18.9   HB 92; HB66+ 73; NIHB 89; NIHB66+ 70

18.10 The council may pay you weekly if:

(a) paying you over a longer period is likely to lead to an overpayment; or

(b) your rent is due weekly and it is in your interests to be paid weekly.

For example, (b) could apply if you have difficulty budgeting. The council is not expected to check whether this is the case, but should take account of information provided by you or by someone on your behalf, including a social worker or key worker (GM para A6.143).

Payments on account

18.11 A 'payment on account' is an estimated amount of HB. The council must make a payment on account if:

(a) your HB will be paid as a rent allowance (paras 18.2-3);

(b) the council is unable to decide your claim within 14 days of getting it; and

(c) this is not because you have failed to provide information and evidence: paras 18.12-13.

The rules about how and who it is paid to, are the same as for rent allowances (paras 18.6-7).

18.12 The council does not have to make a payment on account if:

(a) it or the DWP has asked you to provide information or evidence reasonably required to decide your HB claim (see paras 16.22-30; and

(b) you have failed without good cause to provide it.

18.13 But the council does have to make a payment on account if:

(a) it has asked someone other than you for the information and evidence (GM para A6.161). For example it has asked:

- your landlord or agent for confirmation of your rent,

- the rent officer for a determination about your rent,

- the DWP for confirmation of your benefit entitlement, or

- the Home Office for confirmation of your conditions of entry or stay; or

(b) you have not provided information or evidence because :

- you have not been asked for it, or

- you have good cause, for example it does not exist or you cannot get it.

18.14 Payments on account are not discretionary. If you meet the conditions (paras 18.11 and 18.13), the council:

(a) must make a payment on account within 14 days of getting your claim, and should not wait to be asked (R v Haringey LBC ex parte Ayub) (GM para A6.158); and

(b) should continue making payments on account until your HB is decided.

You may need to remind the council to make a payment on account, or your landlord or agent can do this if your HB is likely to be paid to them. For delays, see also paras 20.11-16.

18.10   HB 92(6); HB66+ 73(6); NIHB 89(6); NIHB66+ 70(6)

18.11   HB 93(1); HB66+ 74(1); NIHB 90(1); NIHB66+ 71(1)

18.12   HB 93(1); HB66+ 74(1); NIHB 90(1); NIHB66+ 71(1)

18.14   R v Haringey LBC ex p Ayub 13/04/92 QBD 25 HLR 566 http://tinyurl.com/Ayub-Haringey

Payments on account amounts and adjustments

18.15   The amount of your payment on account is whatever the council decides is reasonable, based on the information available to it about your individual circumstances. It must notify you (or the payee) that if this turns out to be greater than your entitlement to HB, the overpayment will be recovered (para 19.9).

18.16   When the council decides your claim, the following rules apply. If your entitlement to HB is:

(a)   greater than your payments on account, the council must pay the balance;

(b)   less than your payments on account, the council must recover the overpayment by making deductions from your future payments of HB (para 19.40).

If you are not entitled to HB, the council recovers the overpayment from the person it was paid to (para 19.26).

Paying HB to someone on your behalf

18.17   This section explains when the council should pay your HB to someone on your behalf. It only applies if your HB is paid as a rent allowance (paras 18.2-3).

Attorneys, appointees, etc

18.18   If you are unable to act for yourself, the council can pay your HB to an attorney, appointee, etc, who claimed HB on your behalf (paras 16.5-7).

Nominees

18.19   If you want your council to pay your HB to someone else, the council can do this (but if you are unable to act, see instead para 18.18). They are usually called your nominee. You have to write to the council requesting this, and your nominee must either be:

(a)   an individual aged 18 or more (for example an adult relative or friend); or

(b)   a corporate body (for example a firm of solicitors).

18.20   The law does not stop your landlord or agent being your nominee. But:

(a)   if you fall within the LHA scheme in England, Scotland or Wales, the council may not agree to this if it would undermine the main rules about paying HB to your landlord/agent (paras 18.24-37);

(b)   in all other rent allowance cases, it may be simpler to request payment to your landlord/agent using the main rule about this (see para 18.38).

18.15   HB 93(1),(2); HB66+ 74(1),(2); NIHB 90(1),(2); NIHB66+ 71(1),(2)

18.16   HB 93(3); HB66+ 74(3); NIHB 90(3); NIHB66+ 71(3)

18.18   HB 94(2); HB66+ 75(2); NIHB 91(2); NIHB66+ 68(2)

18.19   HB 94(3); HB66+ 75(3); NIHB 91(3); NIHB66+ 68(3)

Personal representatives and next of kin

18.21   If HB is due to you when you die, the council must pay it to your personal representative (i.e. the person responsible for settling your affairs, such as an executor), or (if you do not have a personal representative) your next of kin. Your next of kin is the first person in the following list who is aged 16 or more:

(a) your husband, wife or civil partner;

(b) your children or grandchildren;

(c) your parents, brothers or sisters, or their children.

This rule only applies if the executor or next of kin writes to the council requesting payment within one year of your death, or longer if the council agrees. But it does not apply to HB the council has to pay your landlord/agent: see para 18.29.

Paying HB to your landlord or their agent

18.22   This section explains when the council pays your HB to your landlord or their agent. It only applies if your HB is paid as a rent allowance (paras 18.2-3).

(a) The council must pay your HB to your landlord/agent if paras 18.24-29 apply to you.

(b) Otherwise, it may pay your HB to your landlord/agent if paras 18.30-41 apply to you.

(c) Otherwise, it must pay your HB to you, or to someone on your behalf (see paras 18.17-21).

Table 18.1 summarises these rules. There are exceptions if your landlord/agent is not a 'fit and proper person' (paras 18.42-44) or during the two weeks after you claim UC (para 17.23).

Table 18.1 **Paying HB to your landlord/agent**

This table summarises when your HB is paid to your landlord or their agent (see paras 18.22-23).

When the council must pay your landlord/agent

All rent allowance cases

In all rent allowance cases (paras 18.2-3), the council must pay your landlord/agent if:

(a) you have eight weeks or more rent arrears, unless it is in your overriding interests not to pay your landlord/agent: see paras 18.25-27;

(b) part of your DWP benefit is being paid to your landlord/agent: see para 18.28; or

(c) rent remains due to your landlord/agent when you die: see para 18.29.

18.21   AA 5(1)(q); HB 97(1)-(4); HB66+ 78(1)-(4); NIAA 5(1)(r); NIHB 94(1)-(4); NIHB66+ 75(1)-(4)

18.22   AA 5(1)(p),(6); HB 94(1), 95, 96; HB66+ 75(1), 76, 77; NIAA 5(1)(q),(5); NIHB 91(1), 92 ,93; NIHB66+ 68(1), 73, 74

T18.1   AA 5(1)(p),(6); HB 95, 96, 97(5); HB66+ 76, 77, 78(5); NIAA 5(1)(q),(5); NIHB 92, 93, 94(5); NIHB66+ 73, 74, 75(5)

When the council may pay your landlord/agent

LHA cases in England, Scotland or Wales

In LHA cases (para 10.4) in England, Scotland or Wales, the council may pay your landlord/agent if:

(d) your HB has previously been paid to your landlord/agent under the rules in (a) or (b) above: see para 18.33;

(e) paying your landlord/agent would help you secure or retain your tenancy: see para 18.34;

(f) you are likely to have difficulty managing your finances: see para 18.35;

(g) it is improbable that you will pay your rent: see para 18.36; or

(h) the council is considering whether the rules in (f) or (g) apply to you, but in this case only for up to eight weeks: see para 18.37.

See also (k) and (l) below.

Other rent allowance cases

In other rent allowance cases in England, Scotland and Wales which are not LHA cases, and in all rent allowance cases (including LHA cases) in Northern Ireland, the council/NIHE may pay your landlord/agent if:

(i) you have requested this or consented to it: see para 18.38; or

(j) it is in your and your family's interest: see para 18.39.

See also (k) and (l) below.

All rent allowance cases

In all rent allowance cases, the council may pay your landlord/agent if:

(k) you have not paid part or all of your rent, but this only applies to your first payment of HB (or first payment following a change to your HB): see para 18.40; or

(l) you have left your home and rent remains due to your landlord/agent: see para 18.41.

When the council must not pay your landlord/agent

All rent allowance cases

In all rent allowance cases, the council must not pay your landlord/agent if:

(m) your landlord/agent is not a 'fit and proper person', unless paying them is nonetheless in your and your family's best interests: see paras 18.42-44.

Landlord or agent

18.23   When your HB is payable to your landlord or agent, it is payable to:

(a) your landlord if your landlord collects your rent; but

(b) your landlord's agent if the agent collects your rent.

In the following paras, we use 'landlord/agent' to mean whichever of these applies.

18.23   HB 95(1), 96(4); HB66+ 76(1), 77(4); NIHB 92(1), 93(5); NIHB66+ 73(1), 74(5)

When HB must be paid to a landlord/agent

18.24 Paras 18.25-29 explain when the council must pay your HB to your landlord/agent. The rules about this apply in all rent allowance cases (paras 18.2-3). See also paras 18.42-54.

HB must be paid to landlord: eight weeks rent arrears

18.25 In all rent allowance cases, the council must pay your HB to your landlord/agent if you have eight weeks or more rent arrears (para 18.26) unless it is in your overriding interests not to (para 18.27). This continues to apply until your rent arrears reduce below eight weeks (except as described in para 18.33).

18.26 Whether you have rent arrears, and how much they are, are questions of fact (paras 20.19-20). For these purposes, 'rent arrears':

(a) include arrears of eligible and ineligible service charges;

(b) include any amount whose contractual date for payment has passed, 'whether the rent is due in advance or in arrears' ([2019] AACR 20), so if your rent is due two months in advance, you have at least eight weeks of rent arrears at the outset;

(c) should be reduced by the amount of any deposit your landlord/agent holds from you ([2017] UKUT 93 (AAC)).

The council doesn't have to check every HB claim for rent arrears, but must consider any information you or your landlord/agent provide (R v Haringey LBC ex parte Ayub).

18.27 If you consider it is in your 'overriding interests' why your HB shouldn't be paid to your landlord/agent, it is up to you to give specific reasons (CH/3244/2007). If your rent arrears arose because you used the rent to pay for essential repairs, you should have warned the landlord/agent that you planned to do this, and you could be expected to have sent them a solicitor's letter with a schedule of disrepair (CH/3244/2007).

> ### Example: Eight weeks rent arrears
>
> Kim is a private landlord. She lets a calendar-monthly tenancy from 1st July and charges rent in advance on the 1st of each month. Her tenant does not pay any rent.
>
> So by 2nd August, there are two calendar months of rent arrears. This is more than eight weeks of arrears, so Kim is entitled to require the council to pay the tenant's HB to her.

HB must be paid to landlord: deductions from DWP benefits

18.28 In all rent allowance cases, the council must pay your HB to your landlord/agent if, and for as long as, the DWP is paying part of your SPC, JSA, ESA or IS to them towards your rent arrears or hostel charges (para 23.38). The DWP should inform the council when this rule applies to you (GM para A6.188). But this rule doesn't apply when the DWP is paying part of your UC to your landlord/agent in supported or temporary accommodation (table 2.3), though in most of these cases the council can pay HB to your landlord/agent using the rules in paras 18.34-36.

18.25   HB 95(1)(b); HB66+ 76(1)(b); NIHB 92(1)(b); NIHB66+ 73(1)(b)

18.26   R v Haringey ex p Ayub: see footnote to para 18.14

18.28   HB 95(1)(a); HB66+ 76(1)(a); NIHB 92(1)(a); NIHB66+ 73(1)(a)

HB must be paid to landlord: rent due following death

18.29   In all rent allowance cases, the council must pay your HB to your landlord/agent if:

(a)   HB remains due to you when you die, and rent remains due to your landlord/agent; and

(b)   the council has already decided (before your death) to pay your landlord/agent.

But this is limited to the amount of rent remaining due at the date of your death. Any other HB due to you can be paid to your personal representative or next of kin (para 18.21).

When HB may be paid to a landlord/agent

18.30   Paras 18.33-41 explain when your HB may be paid to your landlord/agent.

(a)   The rules in paras 18.33-37 and 18.40-41 apply if you fall within the LHA scheme (para 9.3) in England, Scotland or Wales.

(b)   The rules in paragraphs 18.38-41 apply in:

  ■   all other rent allowance cases in England, Scotland and Wales (for example housing association, exempt accommodation, rent referral and boarder cases), and

  ■   all rent allowance cases in Northern Ireland.

See also paras 18.42-54. In England, Scotland and Wales, the overall effect of the rules is that HB is more likely to be paid to the landlord/agent in non-LHA cases than in LHA cases.

18.31   The rules in paras 18.33-41 are discretionary. If their conditions are met, the council may (but does not have to) pay your landlord/agent. The DWP has given councils extensive guidance about applying these rules in LHA cases (GLHA 4.00-6.102). But as with all discretions (para 20.25), the council must make its own decision. It should not have fixed rules or follow guidance without question: CH/2986/2005.

18.32   Some of the rules require the council to consider quite personal things about you, for example, your ability to manage your finances, the likelihood that you will pay your rent, and what your and your family's interests are (paras 18.35-36 and 18.39). In these cases, the DWP advises (HB/CTB A26/2009) that the council:

(a)   can take account of information it already has, or gets from a home visit; and

(b)   should also take account of information provided by you or by someone on your behalf, for example a relative or friend, a social worker or leaving care worker, or your landlord/agent.

Although this guidance is about LHA cases in England, Scotland and Wales, it is equally reasonable in other rent allowance cases.

HB may be paid to landlord: following a period when it must be

18.33   In LHA cases in England, Scotland and Wales, the council may pay your HB to your landlord/agent if it has previously done so under the rules in paras 18.25-28. It can do this as soon as your rent arrears reduce below eight weeks, or as soon as the DWP stops making direct payments, or (in either case) at a later date.

18.29   HB 97(5); HB66+ 78(5); NIHB 94(5); NIHB66+ 75(5)

18.33   HB 96(3A)(b)(iii); HB66+ 77(3A)(b)(iii)

HB may be paid to landlord: to secure or retain your tenancy

18.34   In LHA cases in England, Scotland and Wales, the council may pay your HB to your landlord/agent if this will assist you to secure or retain your tenancy (or other form of letting). This could encourage your landlord/agent to let to you (or continue to do so) while you are on HB. Some councils use this power to encourage the landlord to let at a lower rent (for example, a rent within the LHA figure).

HB may be paid to landlord: difficulty managing your finances

18.35   In LHA cases in England, Scotland and Wales, the council may pay your HB to your landlord/agent if you are likely to have difficulty managing your finances. For example, the DWP says (GLHA 5.070-074) this could be because you:

(a)   have difficulty budgeting, debt problems, or an undischarged bankruptcy;

(b)   are illiterate or unable to speak English;

(c)   are fleeing domestic violence;

(d)   are leaving care or prison; or

(e)   are getting Supporting People payments, or help from a charity.

See also paras 18.32 and 18.37.

HB may be paid to landlord: improbable you will pay rent

18.36   In LHA cases in England, Scotland and Wales, the council may pay your HB to your landlord/agent if it is improbable that you will pay your rent. This rule is about whether it is improbable you will pay rent in the future (CH/2986/2005). The DWP says this might be the case if you have regularly failed to pay rent (with no good reason) in the past (GLHA 6.063-064), for example if the council helped you get your tenancy for this reason (HB/CTB A26/2009). See also paras 18.32 and 18.37.

HB may be paid to landlord: while considering who to pay

18.37   In LHA cases in England, Scotland and Wales, the council may pay your HB to your landlord/agent while it is considering whether the rules in paragraphs 18.35-36 apply to you. The council can do this for up to eight weeks. Alternatively, it can pay you during this time. See also para 18.46.

HB may be paid to landlord: at your request or with your consent

18.38   In rent allowance cases in England, Scotland and Wales which are not LHA cases, and in all rent allowance cases in Northern Ireland, the council/NIHE may pay your HB to your landlord/agent if you request this or consent to it. The law does not require you to give a reason, but you can if you wish.

18.34   HB 96(3A)(b)(iv),(4); HB66+ 77(3A)(b)(iv),(4)

18.35   HB 96(3A)(b)(i); HB66+ 77(3A)(b)(i)

18.36   HB 96(3A)(b)(ii); HB66+ 77(3A)(b)(ii)

18.37   HB 96(3B); HB66+ 77(3B)

18.38   HB 96(1)(a),(3A)(a); HB66+ 77(1)(a),(3A)(a)

HB may be paid to landlord: your and your family's interests

18.39   In rent allowance cases in England, Scotland and Wales which are not LHA cases, and in all rent allowance cases in Northern Ireland, the council/NIHE may pay your HB to your landlord/agent if doing so would be in your and your family's interests. Although the rules in paras 18.33-37 do not apply in these cases, in practice the council is likely to take similar considerations into account. See also para 18.32.

HB may be paid to landlord: first payment after a claim or change

18.40   In all rent allowance cases, the council may pay your HB to your landlord/agent if you have not yet paid part or all of your rent for the period HB covers. But this is limited to the first payment following your claim for HB, or following a move or other change affecting your HB. And it only applies when paying your landlord/agent is 'in the interests of the efficient administration' of HB.

HB may be paid to your landlord: when you leave your home

18.41   In all rent allowance cases, the council may pay your HB to your landlord/agent if:

(a)   you have left the accommodation the HB is paid for; and

(b)   rent remains due to your landlord/agent there.

If your landlord/agent is not a fit and proper person

18.42   In all rent allowance cases, the council must not pay your HB to your landlord/agent:

(a)   if your landlord/agent is not a 'fit and proper person' (paras 18.43-44);

(b)   unless paying them is nonetheless in your and your family's 'best interests'.

This rule overrides the rules in paras 18.25-29 and 18.33-41. DWP guidance does not say what your and your family's best interests are, but see para 18.32 for information the council could reasonably take into account.

18.43   DWP guidance (GM A6.198) says the council should only consider whether the landlord/agent is or is not a fit and proper person if it is doubtful about [their] honesty in connection with HB. This could be because they are involved in fraudulent acts relating to HB. The DWP also suggests (GM A6.200) it could be because they have regularly failed to report changes they have a duty to report (para 17.2), or to repay overpayments which are recoverable from them (paras 19.23-26).

18.44   The following do not mean a landlord/agent is not a fit and proper person:

(a)   their undesirable activity in non-HB matters, for example not paying parking fines (GM A6.197);

(b)   using their right to request a reconsideration, or to appeal, before repaying an overpayment; or

(c)   making complaints about maladministration, for example to the Ombudsman.

18.39   HB 96(1)(b),(3A)(a); HB66+ 77(1)(b),(3A)(a)

18.40   HB 96(2); HB66+ 77(2); NIHB 93(2); NIHB66+ 74(2)

18.41   HB 96(1)(c); HB66+ 77(1)(c); NIHB 93(1)(c); NIHB66+ 74(1)(c)

18.42   HB 95(3), 96(3),(4); HB66+ 76(3), 77(3),(4); NIHB 92(3), 93(3),(4); NIHB66+ 73(3), 74(3),(4)

Decisions about paying a landlord/agent

18.45 The council can make a decision about paying your HB to your landlord/agent:

(a) when you claim HB; and/or

(b) when there is a change in your or your landlord/agent's circumstances which affects this.

See paras 18.8-9 for when payments to a landlord/agent are made, and paras 18.11 and 18.14-16 about payments on account.

18.46 The council can suspend payments of HB (para 17.41) while it is deciding who to pay (CH/1821/2006). But the DWP has encouraged councils not to delay payments in this way (GLHA 5.111).

Decision notices about paying a landlord/agent

18.47 The council must issue two decision notices, one to your landlord/agent and one to you, when:

(a) it decides to pay your HB to them, or changes the amount of the payment (para 18.48); or

(b) they have asked the council to pay your HB to them, but the council has refused (CH/180/2006).

These must be in writing, and must be issued within 14 days of when the council makes the decision, or as soon as reasonably practicable after that.

18.48 When the council decides to pay your landlord/agent (or change the amount), the decision notice issued to them must contain:

(a) the amount of HB they will get for you, and when the payments start (or change);

(b) their duty to notify changes of circumstances, and examples of what they might be (para 17.2);

(c) an explanation about recovering overpaid HB from a blameless tenant (table 19.5(f)); and

(d) their rights in relation to the decision (para 18.49);

but it must not contain other information about your HB (for example personal or financial information about you or your household). The decision notice to you must contain the information in (a) to (c), and your rights in relation to the decision. In practice, this is sometimes instead included in the main decision notice about your HB (para 20.6).

Reconsiderations and appeals about paying a landlord/agent

18.49 When the council decides to pay, or not pay, your landlord/agent, both you and they are a 'person affected'. So both you and they have the right to obtain a statement of reasons, and to appeal if the right of appeal applies to the decision (para 20.43) (CH/180/2006).

18.45   HB 89(1), 95, 96, 97(5); HB66+ 70(1), 76, 77, 78(5); NIHB 85(1), 92, 93, 94(5); NIHB66+ 66(1), 73, 74 ,75(5)

18.47   HB sch 9 paras 11,12; HB66+ sch 8 paras 11,12; NIHB sch 10 paras 11,12; NIHB66+ sch 9 paras 11,12

18.48   HB sch 9 paras 11,12; HB66+ sch 8 paras 11,12; NIHB sch 10 paras 11,12; NIHB66+ sch 9 paras 11,12

If the council pays the wrong person

18.50   If the council decided it had a duty to pay your landlord/agent (see para 18.22(a)) but paid you instead, the council must pay your landlord/agent ([2008] UKUT 31 (AAC)). If the council fails to do this, your landlord/agent can appeal (para 20.42). What the council paid you is an overpayment which is likely to be recoverable from you (see para 19.23-26).

18.51   If the council decided it had a discretion to pay your landlord/agent (para 18.22(b)) but paid you instead, the council cannot pay your landlord/agent but they can seek compensation from the council (R(H) 2/08, [2010] UKUT 254 (AAC)). If the council fails to do this, your landlord/agent can't appeal (para 19.66(b)) but can ask the Ombudsman to intervene (para 20.12) as in case nos. 17 012 147 and 18 017 737 [www].

18.52   It seems reasonable (following the reasoning in [2008] UKUT 31 (AAC)) that if the council decided it had a duty to pay you (para 18.22(c)) but paid your landlord/agent instead, the council must pay you. If the council fails to do this, you can appeal (para 20.42). What the council paid your landlord/agent is an overpayment which is likely to be recoverable from them (para 19.23-26).

How paying your landlord/agent affects your rent

18.53   When the council pays your HB to your landlord/agent, this discharges your liability to pay that amount of rent unless the council recovers it as an overpayment from your landlord/agent: see table 19.5.

If your landlord/agent refuses to accept your HB

18.54   A landlord/agent has the right to refuse payments of rent from someone who is not a party to the tenancy agreement (Bessa Plus Plc v Lancaster). Although this is uncommon, it could affect you if:

(a)   you are the HB claimant; but

(b)   your partner is the sole tenant of your home; and

(c)   your landlord/agent refuses to accept payment of your HB (because you are not on the tenancy agreement).

If this happens, you should be able to get the council to pay your HB to you (rather than your landlord/agent), or to your partner as your nominee (paras 18.19-20).

18.51   https://tinyurl.com/LGO-17-012-147
         https://tinyurl.com/LGO-18-017-737

18.53   HB 95(2), 96(4); HB66+ 76(2), 77(4); NIHB 92(2), 93(5); NIHB66+ 73(2), 74(5)

18.54   Bessa Plus plc v Lancaster 17/03/97 CA 30 HLR 48

Chapter 19 **Overpayments**

- Overpayment types and which are recoverable: see paras 19.1-11.
- The amount of an overpayment: see paras 19.12-22.
- Who to recover from: see paras 19.23-33.
- Methods of recovery: see paras 19.34-58.
- Decisions, notices and appeals: see paras 19.59-67.
- Fraud and penalties: see paras 19.68-80.

What is an overpayment

19.1 You are overpaid HB if you get more HB than you are entitled to. This is the case whether the HB is:

(a) paid to you or someone on your behalf; or

(b) paid to your landlord or their agent; or

(c) credited to your rent account (if you are a council tenant).

Table 19.1 summarises the types and causes of overpayments.

19.2 HB overpayments affect both claimants and landlords. Errors in overpayment decisions can worsen their debts, and also mean councils get the wrong amount of government subsidy (para 21.13). DWP guidance is in its HB Overpayments Guide 2020 (OG) and its good practice guide on recovering overpayments [www].

Table 19.1 **Overpayment types**

Official error overpayments (paras 19.5-7)

(a) Council (or NIHE) error overpayments – e.g. the council failed to act on information you provided, or delayed on acting on it, or made a duplicate payment (paid the same HB twice).

(b) DWP or HMRC error overpayments – e.g. the DWP wrongly awarded you a passport benefit, making your HB higher than it should have been.

Other overpayments (para 19.8)

(c) Claimant error overpayments – e.g. you gave the council incorrect information or failed to report a relevant change of circumstances.

19.1   AA 75(1), 134(2); HB 99; NIAA 73(1), 126(2); HB66+ 80; NIHB 96; NIHB66+ 77

19.2   https://www.gov.uk/government/publications/housing-benefit-overpayments-guide
        https://www.gov.uk/government/publications/housing-benefit-overpayment-recovery-good-practice

(d) Landlord/agent error overpayments – e.g. your landlord (while receiving HB for you) gave the council incorrect information about a rent increase.

(e) No-one's fault overpayments – e.g. you were awarded backdated income, and this reduced your HB in the past.

Special cases (para 19.9)

(f) Payment on account overpayments – the council made a payment on account (para 18.11) that turned out to be too great.

(g) Future overpayments – you are a council tenant and HB that was credited to your rent account for a future period turned out to be too great.

(h) Migration overpayments – you transferred from HB to UC but the council continued to pay your HB beyond the two-week run on (paras 1.26-29).

Which overpayments are recoverable

19.3   HB overpayments are either:

(a) recoverable – councils can recover these but have discretion not to (para 19.10); or

(b) not recoverable – councils do not have the power to recover these under HB law.

19.4   Unless a decision is changed by revision or supersession (para 20.33):

(a) an overpayment (whether recoverable or not) can't exist (CH/3439/2004); and

(b) the question of whether it is recoverable doesn't arise ([2022] UKUT 86 (AAC)).

The burden of proof falls on the council to show that there is an overpayment and that it is recoverable (CH/4065/2001).

Official error overpayments

19.5   An official error means an error by the council, the DWP or HMRC – or someone acting on their behalf (e.g. a contractor or partner organisation). But it doesn't include an error that you (the claimant) or the payee or someone acting on your or the payee's behalf 'materially contributed to'. Case law about this is in table 19.2.

19.6   For example, an official error can include:

(a) a mistake about what the facts are;

(b) an error or delay in applying the law or case law;

(c) an accidental error; or

(d) a combination of the above (CH/943/2003).

19.7   An official error overpayment is only recoverable if at the time of receiving the payment or a decision notice about the payment:

(a) you (the claimant) or someone on your behalf could reasonably have been expected to realise it was an overpayment; or

---

19.5   HB 100(3); HB66+ 81(3); NIHB 97(3); NIHB66+ 78(3)

19.7   AA 75(1); HB 100(1)-(3); HB66+ 81(1)-(3); NIAA 73(1); NIHB 97(1)-(3); NIHB66+ 78(1)-(3)

(b) the payee or someone on their behalf could reasonably have been expected to realise it was an overpayment.

This rule protects a claimant who received and spent a payment innocently from having to repay money they can't afford (CH/1176/2003). Case law about this is in table 19.3.

Other overpayments

19.8   All other overpayments are recoverable, including claimant error, landlord/agent error and no-one's fault overpayments (table 19.1(c)-(e)). In the law this is because they aren't due to official error.

Special cases

19.9   Payment on account, future and migration overpayments (table 19.1(f)-(h)) are recoverable however they were caused – even if they were due to official error. For migration overpayments see also para 19.46.

Council discretion not to recover

19.10   When an overpayment is recoverable, the council has discretion (para 20.25) about whether or not to recover it. So, the question of whether an overpayment is recoverable is separate from the question of whether to actually recover it.

Table 19.2 **Official error overpayments: case law**

These cases were about whether an HB overpayment 'arose in consequence of an official error' (para 19.5).

(a)   How the council should make the decision

- The council should decide what is the substantial cause of the overpayment viewed in a commonsense way ([2010] UKUT 57 (AAC)), or who really caused the overpayment ([2011] UKUT 266 (AAC)). For this purpose:

- when an overpayment has more than one cause, they must be separated out. If the claimant delayed reporting a change and then the council delayed acting on it, only the second part is official error ([2016] UKUT 396 (AAC));

- when the facts are in dispute they are decided on the balance of probability (para 20.21). If the claimant says they reported a change but the council has no record of this, it can't be assumed that the council's procedures are infallible ([2014] UKUT 23 (AAC));

19.8   AA 75(1); HB 100(1); HB66+ 81(1); NIAA 73(1); NIHB 97(1); NIHB66+ 78(1)

19.9   HB 93(3), 100(1),(4); HB66+ 74(3), 81(1),(4); UCTP 10; NIHB 90(3), 97(1),(4); NIHB66+ 71(3), 78(1),(4); NIUCTP 10

T19.2   R (Sier) v Cambridge CC HBRB [2001] EWCA Civ 1523
             www.bailii.org/ew/cases/EWCA/Civ/2001/1523.html

- for the overpayment not to count as official error, it is only necessary that the claimant contributed to the error, not necessarily the overpayment (CH/215/2008);
- terms like 'error' and 'mistake' are interchangeable (CH/943/2003).

(b)   Overpayment was official error

The following were found to be council error:

- not asking the claimant fundamental questions about eligibility (CH/4228/2006);
- delays in applying to the rent officer (CH/361/2006);
- issuing an out-of-date application form ([2014] UKUT 201 (AAC));
- a mistake by another department that affected HB (CH/3586/2007);
- a failure by another department to pass information on to benefits staff or advise the claimant to do so (CH/2567/2007).

The following were found to be DWP error:

- telling the claimant it would pass on information to the council and not doing so (CH/3761/2005);
- a DWP decision that an appeal tribunal found to be an error of law ([2015] UKUT 197 (AAC)).

(c)   Overpayment wasn't official error

The following were found not to be council error:

- not cross-checking an HB claim form against information the claimant had given in a previous claim (R(H) 1/04);
- not asking follow-up questions that would have been prompted if the claimant had given accurate information ([2018] UKUT 418 (AAC));
- assessing benefit income wrongly, because the claimant hadn't understood which DWP figure to provide (CH/56/2008);
- not anticipating changes in the claimant's benefit income (CH/687/2006, R(H) 2/04), or earnings (CH/3/2008);
- a short delay (of 24 days) in acting on a change the claimant reported (CH/858/2006);
- having poor performance statistics which in any case weren't the cause of the overpayment ([2018] UKUT 433 (AAC)).

The following was found not to be DWP error:

- not notifying the council that a working age passport benefit had ceased – since this is the claimant's duty (table 17.1) not the DWP's (R (Sier) v Cambridge CC).

Table 19.3 **Realising there was an overpayment**

These cases – which were all official error overpayments – were about whether the claimant or payee 'could reasonably have been expected to realise' they were overpaid HB (para 19.7).

(a) How the council should make the decision

The council should decide whether the claimant or payee could have realised there 'was' an overpayment, not 'might be' (CH/858/2006). This includes considering:

- the claimant's knowledge, experience and capacity, generally and in relation to the HB scheme (R v Liverpool CC ex parte Griffiths);

- what the claimant could have realised from the decision notice they received at the time – not the overpayment notice (CH/1176/2003);

- what the claimant could have realised from the payment they received – or in rent rebate cases from the credit to their rent account (CH/1675/2005);

- when payment was to a landlord and the overpayment was due to the claimant moving out, whether the landlord knew they had left ([2013] UKUT 232 (AAC));

- when payment was to a landlord organisation, what the organisation as a whole could have realised (CH/4918/2003);

- when the decision depends on the burden of proof (para 20.22), this falls on the claimant or payee to show they couldn't have realised – not on the council to show they could (CH/4918/2003, CH/3439/2004).

(b) Claimant could have realised

In these cases it was found that the claimant could reasonably have been expected to realise they were overpaid (so the official error overpayment was recoverable):

- the decision notice gave the basis of the HB calculation and this showed reasonably clearly that there was a mistake (CH/2409/2005);

- although the notice omitted the claimant's earnings, it listed their other income (CH/2554/2002);

- although the notice was wrong, the figures it gave were obviously different from the claimant's actual earnings (CH/2943/2007), or rent ([2008] UKUT 6 (AAC);

- although the notice was wrong, the claimant didn't attempt to reconcile it with their knowledge of their own situation (CH/2943/2007).

(c) Claimant couldn't have realised

In these cases it was found that the claimant couldn't reasonably have been expected to realise they were overpaid (so the official error overpayment wasn't recoverable):

- the decision notice contained 'bundles of figures' and was so unclear that the claimant wouldn't have realised it was wrong ([2020] UKUT 270 (AAC));

- the notice was wrong, but was issued so late that the claimant wouldn't have realised it was wrong ([2016] UKUT 396 (AAC));

- the notice didn't explain that (or how) the claimant's earnings had been averaged ([2015] UKUT 237 (AAC));

- although the notice didn't include the claimant's retirement income, the claimant might easily have assumed this was because everyone of his age received it (CH/2554/2002);

- the claimant thought the notice might be wrong so queried it more than once, but the council kept making payments, so the claimant assumed the council knew what it was doing (CH/3240/2007);

- the notice gave the wrong figure for income, but the council requested (and the claimant had given) details for the wrong period, so the claimant assumed it was right (CH/1780/2005);

- the notice gave the wrong figure for income, but the social security system in the claimant's home country had different assessment rules, so the claimant thought it was right (CH/858/2006);

- the claimant was not offered help understanding the notice, even though the council knew he had needed help with the claim form (CH/2935/2005).

19.11 You can ask the council to use this discretion if repaying the overpayment would cause you or your family hardship. The DWP says councils should have 'due regard' to your circumstances (OG 2.145-147). You can ask the council to reconsider the use of this discretion but you can't appeal to a tribunal about it.

The amount of an overpayment

19.12 The amount of an overpayment for a particular period is:

(a) what was actually paid for the period (including credited to your rent account if you are a council tenant);

(b) minus what you were entitled to for that period.

But the rules in this section can reduce this.

Diminishing capital

19.13 The diminishing capital rule applies when:

(a) a recoverable overpayment arose due to capital being wrongly taken into account (for whatever reason); and

(b) the overpayment period was longer than 13 weeks.

T19.3   R v Liverpool CC ex parte Griffiths [1990] QBD
          www.rightsnet.org.uk/pdfs/liverpool_griffiths.pdf

19.12   HB 99; HB66+ 80; NIHB 96; NIHB66+ 77

19.13-15 HB 103; HB66+ 84; NIHB 100; NIHB66+ 81

19.14   In these cases:

(a) at the end of the first 13 weeks of the overpayment period, the council must treat your capital as reduced by the amount that was overpaid during those 13 weeks;

(b) this gives an imaginary capital figure which is used to calculate your overpayment after that;

(c) the council repeats (a) and (b) at the end of each complete 13 weeks until the end of the overpayment period;

(d) but when the council calculates your HB after the end of the overpayment period, it uses your actual capital (not the imaginary amount).

Example: Diminishing capital

James has been getting HB of £100 per week based on having no capital and a low retirement income. The council then finds he has had undeclared capital of £17,000 for the past 20 weeks.

- To begin with he had capital over the capital limit (para 15.4) so didn't qualify for HB. The overpayment for the first 13 weeks is (13 x £100 =) £1,300.

- His capital is then treated as reduced by £1,300 to £15,700.

- This is below the capital limit and gives him an assumed income of £12.00 per week (para 15.5). When this is added to his retirement income it turns out he would have qualified for HB of £92.20 per week. The overpayment for the remaining seven weeks is (7 x £7.80 =) £54.60.

- The total overpayment is £1,354.60.

- However, James's actual capital is still £17,000. So, he can't get HB until it reduces below £16,000 – which it will do if and when he repays the overpayment.

19.15   This rule sometimes (but not always) reduces your overpayment. It reflects the fact that if the council had awarded you less HB due to taking the capital into account, you might have used some of the capital to pay your rent.

Underlying entitlement

19.16   The council must reduce your overpayment by any 'underlying entitlement' you have. This applies in all cases except overpayments (or any parts of an overpayment) caused by you moving home (in these cases the rule in para 19.20 may apply instead).

19.17   Underlying entitlement is HB that would have been awarded if:

(a) you kept the council fully and promptly informed of your true circumstances throughout the overpayment period, including all changes of circumstances no matter how frequent ([2015] UKUT 423 (AAC)); and

(b) in the case of a couple, your partner was the HB claimant rather than you, if this means you would have qualified for more HB ([2015] UKUT 460 (AAC)).

19.16-18   HB 104(1); HB66+ 85(1); NIHB 101(1); NIHB66+ 82(1)

19.18 This rule undoes failures to report advantageous changes ([2019] UKUT 188 (AAC)) and undoes the effect of reporting them late (paras 17.13-15). But this is only for the purpose of calculating the overpayment so:

(a) all the underlying entitlement that falls within the overpayment period is used to reduce your overpayment, but not underlying entitlement falling outside it;

(b) the overpayment can be reduced as far as nil in some cases, but the balance can't be paid to you.

Examples: Underlying entitlement

1. When there has been late notice of a change

Information: Blythe's non-dependant Gwenyth moved out six months ago, but Blythe did not tell her council until three months ago (and had no special circumstances for the late reporting of this change) so her council removed the non-dependant deduction from three months ago. Today the council discovered that Blythe has undeclared earnings from work over the previous nine months.

Assessment: The underlying entitlement rule mean the council must reduce the amount of the overpayment (due to Blythe's undeclared earnings from work) by the amount it could not award in relation to Gwenyth moving out. This results in a lower recoverable overpayment; it may even reduce the overpayment to nil, but in no circumstances can it result in Blythe getting more HB.

2. Calculation rules

Information: In Bill's HB award, there is a recoverable overpayment of £5 per week for weeks 1 to 20 (20 x £5 = £100), and underlying entitlement (because Bill didn't tell the council about a beneficial change on time) in weeks 11 to 20 of £15 per week.

Assessment: The council uses Bill's underlying entitlement in weeks 11 to 20 (10 x £15 = £150) to reduce the overpayment (£100). This is enough to reduce the recoverable overpayment to nil but the council can't award the remainder of the underlying entitlement to Bill.

19.19 The council should invite you to provide any information and evidence showing you have underlying entitlement. The onus is then on you to provide this (R(H) 1/05) and the council should allow you at least one month to do so. You can ask the council to reconsider decisions about underlying entitlement and appeal to a tribunal about it (para 19.65). But once the appeal time limit and any extended time limit has passed (paras 20.46-47) the council can't allow underlying entitlement based on new information or evidence (CH/360/2006).

19.19   HB 86(1); HB66+ 67(1); NIHB 82(1); NIHB66+ 63(1)

Moving home

19.20   When you move home, there is an overpayment if you are paid HB for longer than you were entitled to on your old home (para 3.29).

19.21   The council may reduce this overpayment by treating it as having been correctly paid for your new home, but only if:

(a) the overpayment was paid as a rent allowance (para 18.6);

(b) you qualify for HB on your new home; and

(c) the HB for your new home is:

- administered by the same council, and

- payable to the same person (you on both homes, or the same landlord/agent on both homes).

Example: Calculating an overpayment when you move home

Bob gets rent allowance of £100 a week. He moves to a new home where he gets HB of £110 a week. Bob doesn't tell the council about the move for three weeks after leaving the earlier address. This results in an overpayment of £300 on the old address.

Bob is entitled to £110 a week on the new address for the same period (making £330 in total). The council may reduce the amount of the recoverable overpayment on Bob's old home by £300, reducing it to nil, and paying Bob the remaining £30 in relation to his new home.

Council tenants who paid more rent than required

19.22   If you are a council tenant and during the period of a recoverable overpayment you paid more rent than you were required to, the council may reduce your overpayment by these excess payments.

Example: A council tenant

Betty is a council tenant and is getting HB of £60 per week based on her state and private pensions. Her private pensions increase by £50 per week. She reports this promptly to the council, but the council doesn't reduce her HB for ten weeks.

However, Betty estimates she should pay an extra £35 per week towards her rent and does so for each of the ten weeks. When the council calculates her overpayment, it is £32.50 per week. Using the extra £35 per week she has paid, reduces her overpayment to nil (and leaves her £2.50 per week credit on her rent account).

19.21   HB 104A; HB66+ 85A; NIHB 101A; NIHB66+ 82A

19.22   HB 104(2); HB66+ 85(2); NIHB 101(2); NIHB66+ 82(2)

Who to recover from

Overpayments due to official error

19.23   When an overpayment was due to official error (para 19.5), it is recoverable from:

(a) you – or someone acting on your behalf – if you/they could reasonably have been expected to realise it was an overpayment;

(b) the payee – or someone on their behalf – if they could reasonably have been expected to realise it was an overpayment;

(c) if both (a) and (b) apply – all of the above.

Overpayments due to claimant, appointee or landlord/agent error

19.24   When an overpayment was caused by you, someone acting on your behalf or your landlord/agent (para 19.25), it is recoverable from:

(a) you, or someone acting on your behalf if you or they caused the overpayment;

(b) the payee or agent if they caused the overpayment.

19.25   For these purposes an overpayment is 'caused' by you or someone acting on your behalf or your landlord/agent if you or they misrepresented, or failed to disclose, a material fact when you claimed or when your circumstances changed. Disputes about this are uncommon, because the alternative (para 19.26) has a similar effect.

Other overpayments

19.26   Any other overpayment is recoverable from you or the payee. For example, this applies to an overpayment which is no-one's fault.

Recovery from you/your partner or someone acting on your behalf

19.27   When an overpayment is recoverable from you (paras 19.23-26) it is also recoverable from:

(a) your partner if you are a couple (paras 19.28-29);

(b) your partners in a polygamous marriage;

(c) an attorney or someone acting on your behalf (para 16.5);

(d) your estate if you die.

Couples

19.28   An overpayment recoverable from you is also recoverable from your partner if:

(a) you were a couple at the time of the overpayment; and

(b) you are a couple at the time of the recovery.

19.23   AA 75(3); HB 101(2)(c),(3A); HB66+ 82(2)(c),(3A); NIAA 73(3); NIHB 98(2)(b),(4); NIHB66+ 79(2)(b),(4)

19.24   AA 75(3); HB 101(2)(b); HB66+ 82(2)(b); NIAA 73(3); NIHB 98(2)(b); NIHB66+ 79(2)(b)

19.25   HB 101(2)(b); HB66+ 82(2)(b); NIHB 98(2)(b); NIHB66+ 79(2)(b)

19.26   AA 75(3); HB 101(2)(a); HB66+ 82(2)(a); NIAA 73(3); NIHB 98(2)(a); NIHB66+ 79(2)(a)

19.27   AA 75(3); HB 102(1ZA); HB66+ 83(1ZA); NIAA 73(3); NIHB 99(1A); NIHB66+ 80(1A)

19.28   HB 102(1ZA); HB66+ 83(1ZA); NIHB 99(1A); NIHB66+ 80(1A)

19.29   In these cases, your partner has the same rights as you to be notified about the overpayment and to ask for a reconsideration or appeal (CH/3622/2006). The council can't recover an overpayment from a former partner (if your relationship has ended, or if you die), or a new partner (if you became a couple after the overpayment period).

Recovery from your landlord or agent

19.30   When an overpayment is recoverable from the payee (paras 19.23-26), it is recoverable from:

(a)   your landlord if the HB was paid to them;

(b)   your landlord's agent if the HB was paid to them – this is the case even if the agent has already paid the money to the landlord (R(H) 10/07);

(c)   a third party who was wrongly paid HB if the overpayment was paid to the wrong person.

19.31   In these cases, the landlord, agent or third party has the same rights as you to be notified about the overpayment and to ask for a reconsideration or appeal. These rights are clearly set out in NSP v Stoke on Trent CC ([2020] UKUT 311 (AAC)).

Further rule for landlords and agents

19.32   The council must not recover overpaid HB from your landlord or agent if:

(a)   you (the claimant) failed to disclose a material fact to the council when you claimed or when your circumstances changed;

(b)   this failure could justify legal proceedings (para 19.68);

(c)   the landlord/agent told the council or DWP in writing that they suspected there was an overpayment before the overpayment was identified (CH/2411/2006); and

(d)   the landlord/agent did not collude in it or contribute to its period or amount.

A choice about who to recover from

19.33   When an overpayment is recoverable from two or more people (paras 19.23-26), each has a joint and several liability to repay the overpayment (R(H) 6/06). The council can choose which to recover from, and change the choice, but should not take steps to recover from both at the same time (CH/2583/2007). For appeals see paras 19.65-66.

Methods of recovery

19.34   This section explains the methods of recovery that are available when overpaid HB is recoverable from you or your landlord/agent, and how these affect your rent.

19.35   In this section, 'you' includes your partner and/or someone acting for you (para 19.27), and your 'landlord/agent' means whichever received the HB payment (para 19.30).

19.30   HB 101(2)(b)(c); HB66+ 82(2)(b),(c); NIHB 98(2)(b),(c); NIHB66+ 79(2)(b),(c)

19.31   DAR 3(1)(d); NIDAR 3(1)(d)

19.32   HB 101(1),(3); HB66+ 82(1),(3); NIHB 98(1),(3); NIHB66+ 79(1),(3)

Table 19.4 **How overpayments affect your rent: council tenants**

Overpayments that are deducted from your on-going HB:

(a) Because your HB is lower, you need to pay more towards your rent to avoid arrears.

Overpayments that are deducted from your DWP benefits or earnings, or that you repay from your own money:

(b) These methods of recovery/repayment are mainly for people who are no longer on HB. They don't affect your rent.

Overpayments that are managed using your rent account:

(c) When overpayments are managed using your rent account, they should be recorded separately so that your rent isn't affected. When you are making a payment you need to say whether you are putting it towards the overpayment or your rent, otherwise it is put towards the earliest debt first.

(d) But if your tenancy agreement expressly allows this, the council can add HB overpayments to your rent account (as an extra rent charge), so you need to pay more towards your rent to avoid arrears.

Table 19.5 **How overpayments affect your rent: all other tenants**

Overpayments that are deducted from your on-going HB:

(a) Because your HB is lower, you need to pay more towards your rent to avoid arrears.

(b) But if the overpayment was due to landlord/agent fraud (for which they have been convicted of an offence or agreed to pay a penalty: paras 19.74-77), the landlord/agent must treat you as having paid rent equal to the amount of the deductions so that your rent isn't affected.

Overpayments that are deducted from your DWP benefits or earnings, or that you repay from your own money:

(c) These methods of recovery /repayment are mainly for people who are no longer on HB. They don't affect your rent.

T19.4(a),(b)   Direct consequences of method of recovery

T19.4(c)   R v Haringey LBC ex parte Ayub 13/04/92 QBD 25 HLR 566
                www.rightsnet.org.uk/pdfs/R_V_Haringey_exp_Ayub.pdf

T19.4(d)   Additional rent clauses, typically to offset the landlord's expenses are a common feature in tenancy agreements.

T19.5(a),(c)   Direct consequences of method of recovery

T19.5(b)   AA 75(5)(b),(6); HB 106(3), 107(1),(2); HB66+ 87(3), 88(1),(2); NIAA 73(5)(b),(6); NIHB 103(3), 104(1),(2); NIHB66+ 84(3), 85(1),(2)

> **Overpayments that are deducted from your landlord/agent's HB, DWP benefits or earnings, or that they repay from their own money:**
>
> (d) Your landlord/agent can add these amounts to your rent account (as an extra charge), so you need to pay more towards your rent to avoid arrears.
>
> **Overpayments that are deducted from a blameless tenant's HB:**
>
> (e) Your landlord/agent must treat the blameless tenant as having paid rent equal to the amount of the deduction so that their rent isn't affected.
>
> (f) Your landlord/agent can add the amount of the deduction to your rent account (as an extra charge), so you need to pay more towards your rent to avoid arrears.
>
> (g) The council's overpayment notice to the landlord/agent says who the blameless tenant is, but no notice is sent to the blameless tenant.

Methods of recovery from you

19.36   For both council and private tenants, when an HB overpayment is recoverable from you, it can be:

(a) deducted from your HB (paras 19.40-43);

(b) deducted from your DWP benefits (paras 19.44-46);

(c) deducted from your earnings (paras 19.47-49); or

(c) recovered by some other lawful method (para 19.50).

Methods of recovery from your landlord/agent

19.37   For private tenants, when an overpayment is recoverable from your landlord/agent, it can be:

(a) deducted from your HB, your landlord/agent's HB, or another (blameless) tenant's HB (paras 19.40-43);

(b) deducted from your landlord/agent's DWP benefits or earnings (paras 19.44-49); or

(c) recovered by some other lawful method (para 19.50).

19.38   When an overpayment is recoverable from both you and your landlord/agent (para 19.33), it can be recovered by any of the methods in paras 19.36-37.

Overpayments and your rent

19.39   When overpayments are recovered this sometimes (but not always) means you need to pay more rent to avoid getting into arrears. Tables 19.4 and 19.5 explain this.

Deductions from HB

19.40   The council can recover an HB overpayment by taking deductions from your on-going HB, including transitional HB awarded to people migrating to UC (para 17.19).

T19.5(d),(f)   HB 95(2); HB66+ 76(2); NIHB 92(2); NIHB66+ 73(2)

T19.5(e)   AA 75(5)(c),(6); HB 106(3); HB66+ 87(3); NIAA

Table 19.6 **Maximum deductions from HB (2023-24)**

The maximum weekly deduction is:

- ■ £21.25 if you have been convicted of an offence or agreed to pay a penalty (para 19.68);
- ■ £12.75 in any other case.

Plus, in all cases, not more than half of:

- ■ any £5, £10, £20, £25 earned income and permitted work disregard (table 14.5);
- ■ any disregard of regular charitable or voluntary payments (para 13.30);
- ■ the £10 disregard of war pensions for bereavement or disablement (table 13.4).

19.41   When the overpayment is recoverable from you, the deductions can only be taken from your or your partner's HB.

19.42   But when the overpayment is recoverable from your landlord/agent, the deductions can be taken from:

(a) your or your partner's HB (para 19.43); or

(b) your landlord/agent's own HB; or

(c) a 'blameless' tenant's HB – this means another tenant whose HB is paid to your landlord/agent.

19.43   Whenever deductions are taken from your or your partner's HB (paras 19.41, 19.42(a)), the deductions:

(a) must not reduce HB below 50p a week;

(b) must not exceed the maximum amount in table 19.6 except when they are taken from lump sum arrears of HB;

(c) can be reduced in cases of hardship.

Deductions from DWP benefits

19.44   If you aren't entitled to HB, the council can recover an overpayment by asking the DWP to take deductions from your on-going benefits.

19.45   When the overpayment is recoverable from you, the deductions can only be taken from your or your partner's DWP benefits. And when the overpayment is recoverable from your landlord/agent, the deductions can only be taken from their DWP benefits.

19.46   But this method of recovery can only be used for:

(a) overpayments caused by your or your landlord/agent's misrepresentation or failure to disclose – these can be recovered from the benefits in table 19.7; and

(b) migration overpayments (table 19.1(h)) – these are always recovered from your UC.

T19.6   HB 102(2)-(6); HB66+ 83(2)-(6); NIHB 99(3)-(5); NIHB66+ 80(3)-(5)

19.44-46   AA 75(4),(5); HB 102(1), 105, 106; HB66+ 83(1), 86, 87; NIAA 73(4),(5); NIHB 99(1), 102, 103; NIHB66+ 80(1), 83, 84

Table 19.7 **DWP benefits overpaid HB can be recovered from**

A recoverable overpayment of HB may be deducted from:

- universal credit
- JSA(IB) and ESA(IR)
- personal independence payment
- retirement pension
- maternity allowance
- industrial injuries benefits
- old style bereavement benefits
- 'new style' JSA/ESA

- state pension credit
- income support
- adult disability payment (Scotland)
- incapacity benefit/SDA
- carer's allowance
- disability living allowance
- attendance allowance
- equivalent EU and Swiss benefits

All of these apply to recovery from a claimant or landlord/agent, but only the top three lines apply to recovery from a partner.

Deductions from earnings

19.47 The council can recover an HB overpayment by requiring an employer to take deductions from future earnings. This is called a 'direct earnings attachment' (DEA) and is usually only used when deductions can't be taken from HB or DWP benefits.

19.48 When the overpayment is recoverable from you, the deductions can be taken from your earnings (but not your partner's as the DWP considers this would be inappropriate: LA Welfare Direct Bulletin 9/2019).

19.49 The main rules about deductions from your earnings are as follows (these also apply to deductions from a landlord/agent's earnings):

(a) the council notifies your employer (and you);

(b) the employer has ten days to confirm (or deny) you are an employee, and to claim exemption from making deductions if they are a new business or a micro business;

(c) the employer calculates the deductions on a fixed scale and notifies you of the amount;

(d) the employer pays the deducted amounts to the council and can take a further £1 per deduction for administrative expenses;

(e) you and the employer must notify the council if you stop employment, and you must notify the council if you start new employment;

(f) it is a criminal offence for the employer not to provide the information required or not to make deductions.

Full information is available online [www].

T19.7   HB 105, 106; HB66+ 86, 87; NIHB 102, 103; NIHB66+ 83, 84

19.47-48   AA 75(8)-(10); HB 106A; HB66+ 87A; NIAA 73(8)-(10); NIHB 103A; NIHB66+ 83A

19.49   Part 6 of the Social Security (Overpayments and Recovery) Regulations 2013 No 384 www.gov.uk/make-benefit-debt-deductions
           Part 6 of the Social Security (Overpayments and Recovery) Regulations (Northern Ireland) 2016 No 224

Other methods of recovery

19.50   The council can recover an HB overpayment by any other lawful method, including asking you to repay it from your own money, making payment arrangements with you, and as a last resort taking court action to enforce recovery of the debt (para 19.52).

Bankruptcy etc

19.51   An overpayment can't be recovered if:

(a) the council made the overpayment decision (para 19.59) before you were granted a bankruptcy order; or

(b) the overpayment was included in a debt relief order (DRO) in England and Wales or a sequestration order in Scotland.

But this doesn't apply (and therefore recovery can be made) if the overpayment was caused by fraud. While the order is in force and after it ends, the council can't recover the overpayment by any method (including by making deductions from your UC or other benefits): SSWP v Payne and Cooper; Re Nortel Companies [www].

Court action

19.52   The DWP advises councils that legal proceedings should only be considered after attempts to recover by other means have failed and there is good reason to believe you can afford to make repayments (OG 7.23). Councils are told that before pursuing recovery through the courts they should allow your appeal period to run out, allow any outstanding appeal to be decided, send at least two letters requesting repayment and make sure that procedures are in place to check that you are getting all the HB and other benefits you may be entitled to (OG 7.20-22). But not all councils follow this guidance. Court action may take the form of civil proceedings for debt, but the following procedure (paras 19.53-58) is simpler.

The simplified debt recovery procedure

19.53   In England, Wales and Northern Ireland the council/DWP (NIHE/DFC) has the power to recover HB overpayments by execution in the County Court as if under a court order; and in Scotland (para 19.56) as if it were an extract registered decree arbitral (OG 7.24-38).

19.54   In England, Wales and Northern Ireland, the council/DWP can register an HB overpayment determination directly as an order of the County Court without the need to bring a separate action. The procedure is explained in DWP guidance (OG 7.24-38). The council/DWP applies to the court on form N322A [www], enclosing a copy of the overpayment notice and the relevant fee. The notice must include all the matters in para 19.61 (OG 5.07). An officer of the court then makes an order and a copy is sent to the council

---

19.50   HB 102(1); HB66+ 83(1); NIHB 99(1); NIHB66+ 80(1)

19.51   SSWP v Payne & Cooper 14/12/11 UKSC [2011] UKSC 60 www.bailii.org/uk/cases/UKSC/2011/60.html
         Re Nortel Companies 24/07/13 UKSC [2013] UKSC 52 www.bailii.org/uk/cases/UKSC/2013/52.html

19.53   AA 75(7); NIAA 73(7); NIAA 73(7)(a)

19.54   AA 75(7)(a)
         HB Overpayments Guide, Part 7 https://tinyurl.com/OPGuidePart7
         https://www.gov.uk/government/publications/form-n322a-application-to-enforce-an-award

and to you. Once the order has been made, the council can use all the normal debt enforcement methods – a third party debt order allowing it to receive money owed to you by a third party; a warrant for the court bailiff to seize your goods; or a charging order against property/land you own.

19.55   You can't appeal against the order, but you or your landlord/agent may apply to the court to set it aside if the overpayment notice was defective or the council has ignored your HB appeal rights. For other kinds of disputes, you should ask the council to reconsider or appeal to a tribunal (Ghassemian v Borough of Kensington and Chelsea).

19.56   In Scotland, an HB overpayment determination is immediately enforceable by the council as if it were an extract registered decree arbitral (OG 7.24). The council/DWP doesn't need to register it with the Sheriff Court. The usual methods of enforcement are available.

Time limits for court action

19.57   In England, Wales and Northern Ireland the council/DWP must start any court enforcement action (paras 19.52-55) within six years. This limitation does not apply to any other method of recovery – such as deductions from future HB (OG 7.00-05). In Scotland your council cannot recover overpayments by any method after 20 years (OG 7.05).

19.58   This time limit does not affect how far back an overpayment can go. But the further the overpayment goes back, the more difficult it may be for the council to provide the evidence needed to prove the overpayment to the court (OG 7.00).

Decisions, notices and appeals

Decisions and notices

19.59   When the council decides you were overpaid, it should send you the following within 14 days or as soon as reasonably practicable:

(a) a decision notice about your corrected HB entitlement (paras 20.2-4) unless the overpayment was due to a duplicate payment (table 19.1(a)); and

(b) an overpayment notice (para 19.61).

These are sometimes combined in one notice.

19.60   The council should also send the overpayment notice to each other 'person affected' (para 19.64). This includes every person from whom the overpayment is recoverable (paras 19.23-26) not just the person the council will actually recover it from (R(H) 6/06), [2021] UKUT 256 (AAC)).

19.55   Ghassemian v Kensington and Chelsea LBC [2009] EWCA Civ 743 www.bailii.org/ew/cases/EWCA/Civ/2009/743.html

19.56   AA 75(7)(b)

19.57   s9, 38(1),(11), the Limitation Act 1980; s7, the Prescription and Limitation (Scotland) Act 1973; the Limitation (Northern Ireland) Order 1989 No. 1339 arts 2(1),(11), 6

19.59   HB 90(1); HB66+ 71(1); NIHB 86(1); NIHB66+ 67(1)

Table 19.8 **Notices and effect on recovery: case law**

This table is about the entitlement and overpayment notices the council should issue when there is an HB overpayment (para 19.59).

(a) The content of the notices

- The notices must be clear and unambiguous, with proper use of statutory language and dates relevant to the revisions and supersessions that resulted in the overpayment (R(IS) 2/96; CH/3439/2004; C3/07-08 (IS); C2/10-11 (HB) [www]).

- The overpayment notice must give the reason why there was an overpayment with enough detail to enable the recipient to judge whether to appeal. Just saying it was due to a 'change in circumstances' isn't enough (R v Thanet DC ex parte Warren Court Hotels Ltd).

- The overpayment notice must name all the parties from whom the overpayment is recoverable. If it is recoverable from both claimant and landlord, naming just the landlord isn't enough (CH/3622/2005).

(b) The effect on recovery of the overpayment

- If one or both notices are omitted, the overpayment is not recoverable ([2013] 208 UKUT (AAC)); R (Godwin) v Rossendale BC.

- If one or both notices are incomplete, this can undermine recovery (Warwick DC v Freeman).

- If a notice is incomprehensibly long (here, over 100 sheets with no summary) this can undermine recovery ([2019] UKUT 45 (AAC));

- Trivial defects that cause no harm don't undermine recovery (Haringey LBC v Awaritefe).

- If the council recovers HB from a landlord before issuing a valid notice, the landlord can apply to a court to get the money returned (Waveney DC v Jones).

- If the landlord voluntarily repays HB before the council issues a valid notice, the landlord can't get the money returned (Norwich CC v Stringer).

19.61 The overpayment notice should contain the following information:

(a) the fact that there is a recoverable overpayment;

(b) the reason why there is a recoverable overpayment;

(c) the amount of the recoverable overpayment;

T19.8   C3/ 07-08 (IS) and C2/ 10-11 (HB) are Northern Ireland Commissioners Decisions
https://iaccess.communities-ni.gov.uk/NIDOC/users/internetsearchpage.aspx
R v Thanet DC ex parte Warren Court Hotels Ltd 06/04/00 QBD https://tinyurl.com/Thanet-v-WCH
R (Godwin) v Rossendale BC [2002] EWCA Civ 726 www.bailii.org/ew/cases/EWCA/Civ/2002/726.html
Warwick DC v Freeman 31/10/94 CA www.rightsnet.org.uk/pdfs/warwick_v_Freeman.pdf
Haringey LBC v Awaritefe [1999] EWCA Civ 1491 www.bailii.org/ew/cases/EWCA/Civ/1999/1491.html
Waveney DC v Jones 01/12/99 CA www.rightsnet.org.uk/pdfs/Waveney_v_Jones.pdf
Norwich CC v Stringer 03/05/00 CA 33 HLR 15

(d)   how that amount was calculated;

(e)   the benefit weeks to which the recoverable overpayment relates;

(f)   if overpaid HB is to be deducted from future HB, the amount of the deduction;

(g)   any other relevant matters;

(h)   your rights to request a written statement, ask the council to reconsider, and to appeal to a tribunal, and how and when to do these (chapter 20).

19.62   The council's notice should be clear about which 'revisions' and 'supersessions' the overpayment results from. These terms are explained in paras 20.32-33 but you are not expected to use them unless you wish to. Errors in a notice can affect the council's ability to recover the overpayment. Case law about this is in table 19.8.

Reconsiderations and appeals

19.63   For all HB overpayments, each of the 'persons affected' (para 19.64) has the right:

(a)   to ask the council to reconsider any matter relating to the overpayment; and

(b)   to appeal to a tribunal about certain matters relating to the overpayment (para 19.65).

Chapter 20 explains how to do this.

Persons affected

19.64   When your HB is overpaid you (the claimant) are always a person affected. Your landlord or agent (or someone else) is also a person affected if the HB was paid to them or is recoverable from them (para 20.44).

Appealable and non-appealable matters

19.65   You have the right to appeal about:

(a)   your true HB entitlement during the HB overpayment period;

(b)   whether the council has made the revisions and supersessions (paras 20.32-33) needed to establish that you have been overpaid (R(H) 3/04);

(c)   the amount of the overpayment;

(d)   whether the resulting overpayment is legally recoverable; and

(e)   which person or persons it is recoverable from.

When your landlord/agent makes an appeal, (b) to (e) apply (CH/1129/2004; [2012] AACR 37), but (a) does not (R(H) 7/04).

19.61   HB sch 9 para 15; HB66+ sch 8 para 15; NIHB sch 10 para 15; NIHB66+ sch 9 para 15

19.63   HB sch 9 paras 2-5; HB66+ sch 8 paras 2-5; NIHB sch 10 paras 2-5; NIHB66+ sch 9 paras 2-5

19.64   HB 2(1) – definition: 'person affected'; HB66+ 2(1); DAR 3; NIHB 2(1); NIHB66+ 2(1); NIDAR 3

19.65-66   CPSA sch 7 para 6; NICPSA sch 7 para 6
            [2012] AACR 37 is Wirral MBC v Salisbury Independent Living [2012] EWCA Civ 84
            www.bailii.org/ew/cases/EWCA/Civ/2012/84.html

19.66   The tribunal doesn't have the power to decide:

(a) whether the council should use its discretion not to recover the overpayment ([2011] UKUT 266 (AAC)); and

(b) which person (if there is more than one) it should be recovered from (R(H) 6/06);

(c) what method the council should use to recover it (CH/2298/2007); or

(d) the rate of recovery (R(H) 7/04).

In some of these cases it may be possible to seek judicial review (para 20.54).

Recovery pending appeal

19.67   The DWP has advised councils that recovery of overpayments should in some cases be delayed in order to allow time to appeal, and that recovery action should be suspended from when an appeal is made to when it is decided (OG 4.240-241, 4.250).

Fraud and penalties

19.68   The DWP's Counter Fraud and Compliance Directorate (CFCD) in Great Britain and the DFC's single Fraud Investigation Service in Northern Ireland are responsible for investigating fraud and related offences across all social security benefits, tax credits and HB. Prosecutions are conducted by the Crown Prosecution Service in England and Wales, the Procurator Fiscal in Scotland and the Public Prosecution Service in Northern Ireland. In some cases (usually less serious) you may be offered the chance to pay a penalty rather than face prosecution (paras 19.75-78).

Fraud offences by the claimant

19.69   You (the claimant) can be prosecuted under one of the social security fraud offences if you:

(a) make a false statement; or

(b) produce, provide or supply any document that is false in a material particular,

with the view to receiving HB (or other DWP benefit). You also commit an offence if you fail to promptly report a change of circumstances that you have a duty to notify (para 17.2) with the knowledge that it affects your award.

19.70   If you are convicted in the magistrates' court you are liable for an unlimited fine or up to three months in prison (or both), or up to six months in prison (and/or a fine) if the offence involved dishonesty. If you are convicted in the crown court for dishonestly making a false statement or failing to report a change, the maximum sentence is seven years in prison (and/or a fine). You are dishonest if you knew you were not telling the truth.

19.71   If you are convicted for fraud or agree to pay a penalty (paras 19.75-78) the council/ DWP can reduce your HB (or other benefits) for a fixed period.

19.69   AA 111A, 112; NIAA 105A, 106

19.70   AA 111A(3), 112(2); NIAA 105A(3), 106(2)

19.71   The Social Security (Loss of Benefit) Regulations 2001 No. 4022; The Social Security (Loss of Benefit) Regulations (Northern Ireland) 2002 No.79

Fraud offences by the landlord

19.72   If you are a landlord/agent you can be prosecuted for fraud (paras 19.69-70) if you assist the claimant by providing false information, etc. If you (the landlord/agent) receive HB on behalf of one (or more) of your tenants (paras 18.22-41) you can also be prosecuted if you fail to report a change of circumstances that you could reasonably be expected to know affects their HB. But in this case the only changes you must report to avoid prosecution are those that relate to your tenant's liability for rent (para 5.1) or their occupation of the dwelling.

19.73   If the landlord is a company, the company is liable for any offence (para 19.72) committed as well as any director, manager, secretary or officer of the company who consented to the act or omission from which the offence arose. If a landlord/agent is convicted of an offence or agrees to a pay a penalty (para 19.75) the council may decide that s/he is not a fit and proper person to receive HB payments (paras 18.42-44).

Fraud and how you use your HB

19.74   Although you have a legal obligation to pay your landlord the rent you owe, failure to do so is not a criminal offence (the landlord has civil remedies instead). And although you can be prosecuted for making a false statement or providing false documentation (para 19.69), you don't have a legal obligation to apply your payments of HB for the purpose of paying your rent, so you can't be prosecuted for how you use your payments of HB (DPP v Huskinson).

Administrative penalties

19.75   The DWP (in consultation with the council) [www] may offer you the chance to pay an 'administrative penalty' rather than face prosecution, if:

(a)   the overpayment was caused by an 'act or omission' on your part; and

(b)   there are grounds for bringing a prosecution against you for an offence relating to that overpayment.

You do not have to agree to a penalty. You can opt for the possibility of prosecution instead. The DWP is expected to advise the council of the outcome of an administrative penalty offer [www].

19.76   The offer of a penalty must be in writing, explain that it is a way of avoiding prosecution, and give other information – including the fact that you can change your mind within 14 days (including the date of the agreement), and that the penalty will be repaid if you successfully challenge it by asking for a reconsideration or appeal. The DWP does not normally offer a penalty (but prosecutes instead) if an overpayment is substantial or there are other aggravating factors (such as you being in a position of trust).

19.72   AA 111A(1C),(1F), 112(1C),(1E); NIAA 105A(1C),(1F), 106(1C),(1E)

19.73   AA 115; NIAA 109

19.74   DPP v Huskinson [1988] Crim LR 620, 9.5.88

19.75   AA 115A(1),(1A),(7A)-(7B); NIAA 109A(1),(1A)

         DWP, Fraud Investigations: staff guide, May 2019 https://www.tinyurl.com/Fraud-Investigations

19.76   AA 115A(2),(4),(5); NIAA 109A(2),(4),(5)

19.77	The amount of the penalty is 50% of the recoverable overpayment. This is subject to a minimum of £350 and a maximum of £5,000 where your act or omission causing the overpayment occurred wholly on or after 1st April 2015. The maximum penalty where the relevant act or omission occurred before that date is £2,000. In Northern Ireland the maximum penalty is still set at £2,000.

19.78	The DWP may also make an offer of a penalty where your act or omission could have resulted in an overpayment and it thinks there are grounds for bringing a prosecution for a related offence. In these cases, the penalty is the fixed amount of £350.

Civil penalties

19.79	In Great Britain the council may impose a civil penalty of £50 on you if you:

(a)	negligently make an incorrect statement or representation or negligently give incorrect information or evidence relating to a claim or award and fail to take reasonable steps to correct the error; or

(b)	without reasonable excuse, fail to provide required information or evidence relating to a claim or award or fail to tell the council about a relevant change of circumstance; and

(c)	in any of these circumstances this results in the council making an overpayment; but

(d)	you have not been charged with an offence or cautioned.

19.80	The amount of the civil penalty is added to the amount of the recoverable overpayment. If you have been successfully prosecuted for fraud or offered an administrative penalty or caution, the council cannot issue you with a civil penalty for the same offence. If you want to appeal against a civil penalty you should appeal against the amount of the overpayment.

19.77	AA 115A(3); NIAA 109A(3)

19.78	AA 115A(1A),(3A); NIAA 109A(1A),(3A)

19.79-80	AA 115-115D; The Social Security (Civil Penalties) Regulations 2012 No.1990

Chapter 20 **Decisions and appeals**

- ■ Decision rights: see paras 20.1-4.
- ■ Decisions, notices and reasons: see paras 20.5-25.
- ■ Reconsiderations and when they take effect: see paras 20.26-41.
- ■ Appeals to a tribunal and further appeals: see paras 20.42-54.
- ■ Appeals about rent officer determinations: see paras 20.55-62.

Decision rights

20.1　This chapter explains the rights that go with HB decisions. The main ones are:

(a) getting reasons for the decision;

(b) asking the council to reconsider; and

(c) appealing to a tribunal.

Persons affected by decisions

20.2　These rights belong to:

(a) you (the HB claimant);

(b) someone acting for you if you are unable to act on your own behalf (for example an attorney or appointee: paras 16.5-7);

(c) your landlord or agent if the decision is about whether to pay your HB to them rather than you (paras 18.22-52);

(d) your landlord or agent or anyone else if the decision is about whether an overpayment is recoverable from them (paras 19.23-33).

The law calls these 'persons affected'. They can include individuals (e.g. you, your private landlord) and corporate bodies (e.g. a housing association, a firm of letting agents).

20.3　Others are not persons affected. For example, a landlord providing you with supported accommodation may be very concerned about how the authority decided the amount of your eligible rent, but they aren't a person affected in relation to that decision ([2012] AACR 37).

20.1　CPSA sch 7 para 6(3); HB 90(2); HB66+ 71(2); DAR 4(1),(2); FTPR 23(2)
　　　NICPSA sch 7 para 6(3); NIHB 86(2); NIHB66+ 67(2); NIDAR 4(1),(2), 18(1),(3)

20.2　DAR 3; HB 2(1) – 'person affected'; HB66+ 2(1); NIDAR 3; NIHB 2(1); NIHB66+ 2(1)

20.3　[2012] AACR 37 is Wirral MBC v Salisbury Independent Living Ltd [2012] EWCA Civ 84
　　　www.bailii.org/ew/cases/EWCA/Civ/2012/84.html

Using your rights

20.4   You have to write requesting the rights in para 20.1 and sign your request. Or a solicitor or other representative aged 18 or over can write your request and sign it for you ([2015] UKUT 28 (AAC)). A non-legally qualified representative should have written authority from you to act on your behalf.

Decisions, notices and reasons

Decisions

20.5   The council/NIHE makes decisions about your HB:

    (a)   when you make your claim (para 16.18);

    (b)   when your circumstances change (para 17.11);

    (c)   when your HB is overpaid (para 19.59); and

    (d)   when you ask for a reconsideration (paras 20.31).

Decision notices

20.6   The council/NIHE sends a decision notice to you (or someone acting for you: paras 16.5-7) and to each other person affected (para 20.2):

    (a)   when you make a claim, the notice must contain the information in table 20.1;

    (b)   when your HB changes, the notice must say what the change is (and can include the information in table 20.1);

    (c)   when you are overpaid, the notice must contain the information in para 19.61.

There are also rules for decision notices sent to landlords and agents about paying them HB (paras 18.47-48) or recovering overpayments (para 19.60).

Table 20.1 **Decision notices about claims**

When the council decides your claim for HB, it must issue a decision notice to you containing the following information.

If you are entitled to HB

    (a)   Your first day of entitlement.

    (b)   The normal weekly amount of your HB.

    (c)   If your HB is a rent allowance, when and how often it will be paid (and if it will be paid to your landlord/agent, see paras 18.47-48).

    (d)   Your duty to notify changes of circumstances, and examples of what these might be (para 17.2).

20.4   DAR 20(1); FTPR 23(2),(6); NIDAR 18(1), 20(1)(b), 23(1); NIDAR99 49(8)

20.6   DAR 10; HB 90(1), sch 9 paras 1, 7, 8; HB66+ 71(1), sch 8 paras 1, 7, 8
        NIDAR 10; NIHB 86(1), sch 10 paras 1, 7, 8; NIHB66+ 67(1), sch 9 paras 1, 7, 8

T20.1   HB sch 9 paras 1-10, 13, 14; HB66+ sch 8 paras 1-10, 13, 14
        NIHB sch 10 paras 1-10, 13, 14; NIHB66+ sch 9 paras 1-10, 13, 14

If you are not entitled to HB

(e) The reason why you are not entitled.

(f) If your HB is less than 50p a week, the amount and an explanation that this is below the minimum award (para 6.7).

All cases whether or not you are entitled

(g) Your weekly eligible rent.

(h) If standard deductions were made for fuel, how to change them (paras 8.35-36).

(i) The amount and category of non-dependant deductions.

(j) Your applicable amount and how it was worked out (unless you are on a passport benefit).

(k) Your weekly earned income and weekly unearned income (unless you are on a passport benefit or savings credit).

(l) If you are on savings credit, the DWP's figures for your income and capital, any deductions from them, and the amount of your savings credit (para 13.15).

(m) Your rights in relation to the decision (para 20.7).

(n) Any other information the council considers relevant.

20.7 Every decision notice (whoever it is issued to) must also contain information about the right to:

(a) get a statement of reasons (para 20.10);

(b) ask for a reconsideration (para 20.26);

(c) appeal, if the right to appeal applies to the decision (para 20.42);

and how to do these things.

Time limits for decisions and notices

20.8 When you make a claim for HB, the council/NIHE must:

(a) make a decision about your entitlement within 14 days of getting the information and evidence it requires (para 16.22), or as soon as reasonably practicable;

(b) send you a decision notice on the day it makes the decision, or as soon as reasonably practicable.

When the council/NIHE makes any other HB decision, it must send you a decision notice within 14 days or as soon as reasonably practicable.

'Decisions' and 'determinations'

20.9 The law about HB and other benefits often distinguishes between these terms. The upper tribunal has described them as follows (R(IB) 6/03; [2022] UKUT 9 (AAC)):

(a) 'a decision upon the actual question whether a claimant is entitled to a particular benefit or not'; and

---

20.7   HB sch 9 paras 2-5; HB66+ sch 8 paras 2-5; NIHB sch 10 paras 2-5; NIHB66+ sch 9 paras 2-5

20.8   HB 89(2), 90(1); HB66+ 70(2), 71(1); NIHB 85(2), 86(1); NIHB66+ 66(2), 67(1)

(b) 'a determination of any matter along the way to a decision'.

For example, a HB determination could be that you have a particular amount of income or capital; and a HB decision would then be that you are entitled to a particular amount of HB or not entitled to HB.

Getting a written statement of reasons

20.10   You (or any other person affected) can request a statement of reasons about anything that wasn't explained in your decision. Your request should be in writing, signed (para 20.4), and made within one month of the date of the decision notice. The council/NIHE should provide the statement within 14 days so far as this is practicable. See paras 20.36 and 20.46 for how this affects the reconsideration and appeal time limits

Delays

20.11   If the council/NIHE delays making a decision, issuing a notice or paying your HB, you can complain to the Ombudsman (para 20.12) normally after using the council's complaints procedure or failing to get a response in a reasonable time. In certain circumstances judicial review may provide an alternative remedy (para 20.54). If the council/NIHE has decided you are entitled to HB but delays paying it, you should get a payment on account if you are a private tenant (para 18.11). If that fails you may be able to get the county court or sheriff court to require it to pay: Waveney DC v Jones.

The Ombudsman

20.12   In cases of bad administration by the council/NIHE you can complain to the Ombudsman. Guidance on how to complain, what constitutes maladministration, and recent Ombudsman's reports are available online [www].

20.13   In their report 'Focus on HB' [www], the Ombudsman emphasises that the council/NIHE:

(a) shouldn't overlook requests for a reconsideration or appeal just because claimants don't use the legal language; and

(b) shouldn't recover overpayments while a reconsideration or appeal is ongoing.

Delays and rent arrears

20.14   In England and Wales, the 'Pre-Action Protocol' [www] provides you with some protection against possession action if HB delays have caused your rent arrears. It applies to social renters.

20.10   DAR 10(2); HB 90(2),(4); HB66+ 71(2),(4); NIDAR 10(2); NIHB 86(2),(4); NIHB66+ 67(2),(4)

20.11   Waveney DC v Jones 01/12/99 CA www.rightsnet.org.uk/pdfs/Waveney_v_Jones.pdf

20.12   Local Government Act 1974, s. 24A, 25(1)(a), 26
           Scottish Public Services Ombudsman Act 2002, s. 2, 9, sch 2 para 7
           Public Services Ombudsman Act (Northern Ireland) 2016, s. 5, 12(1), 14, sch 3
           www.lgo.org.uk (England), www.ombudsman-wales.org.uk (Wales)
           www.spso.org.uk (Scotland), https://nipso.org.uk (Northern Ireland)

20.13   Focus on HB (January 2020) https://tinyurl.com/LGO-Focus-HB-Jan-2020

20.14   Pre-Action Protocol for Possession Claims by Social Landlords, para 1.1 http://tinyurl.com/Rent-Protocol

20.15 Your landlord should not begin possession proceedings against you if:

(a) you have provided all the information and evidence needed to decide your claim,

(b) there is a reasonable expectation that you will qualify for HB, and

(c) you have paid any rent which will not be met by HB.

20.16 If possession proceedings are begun, the council can be ordered to explain any delays and to pay costs if it caused them.

If you disagree with a decision

20.17 If you disagree with a decision about your HB, you can ask the council/NIHE to reconsider it (para 20.26); and/or appeal to a tribunal (para 20.42) if it is an appealable decision. See table 20.2 for a summary.

Table 20.2 **HB reconsiderations and appeals**

HB decision and reasons

One month

Asking the authority to reconsider

One month

One month

Appealing to an independent tribunal

One month

Appealing to the Upper Tribunal or NI Commissioners (in both cases on a point of law only)

Notes:

■ One month means a calendar month and may be extended in special circumstances.

■ Appeals relating to rent officer determinations in rent referral cases are dealt with differently (paras 20.55-62).

20.15   Pre-Action Protocol, para 2.6

20.16   Pre-Action Protocol, para 2.14

20.17   DAR 4(1),(2); FTPR 23(2); NIDAR 4(1),(2), 18(1)

T20.2   DAR 4(1); FTPR 23(2); NIDAR 4(1), 18(1)

20.18 Many of the HB rules about reconsiderations and appeals are the same as in UC and CTR (volume 1 chapters 14 and 18). The main differences are:

(a) in HB you can skip a reconsideration and go straight to an appeal, but in UC and CTR you can only appeal after a reconsideration;

(b) in HB you send appeals to the council/NIHE which forwards them to the tribunal but in UC and CTR (with some exceptions in Scotland) you send them straight to the tribunal.

How decisions are made

20.19 When the council/NIHE makes a decision about your HB, it should:

(a) identify the facts (paras 20.20-22); and

(b) apply the law to those facts (paras 20.23-25).

Deciding the facts

20.20 The council/NIHE should only take account of facts that are relevant to your HB. For example, who lives with you is normally relevant, but their personal characteristics are not.

Balance of probability

20.21 When there is a disagreement about the facts or the facts are uncertain, the council/NIHE should decide what they are based on the weight of evidence each way.

Burden of proof

20.22 When there is no evidence about the facts or where the evidence is balanced equally each way, the council/NIHE should decide who has to demonstrate what. For example:

(a) when you make a claim, it is up to you to demonstrate you are entitled;

(b) when you are told an overpayment is recoverable from you, it is up to the council/NIHE to demonstrate this.

Applying the law

20.23 The words of Acts of Parliament, regulations, orders, etc have their ordinary English meaning. But:

(a) some words or phrases are defined in the law – for example 'child' and 'young person' (paras 4.15-16);

(b) some law has been interpreted by Upper Tribunals and courts in case law (para 1.20) – for example deciding whether two people are a couple (para 4.10);

(c) the Supreme Court has decided that the council/NIHE or a tribunal may disapply a regulation, order, etc (but not an Act of Parliament) if it breaches the Human Rights Act 1998 (RR v SSWP).

The footnotes in this guide give the details of (a) and (b).

20.18 CPSA sch 7 para 6(1),(3); SSA 8(3), 12(1),(3A); FTPR 22(1),(2)(d),(9); 23(1),(2)

20.23 RR v SSWP [2019] UKSC 52 www.bailii.org/uk/cases/UKSC/2019/52.html

Judgment

20.24   The law uses terms like 'reasonable', 'appropriate', 'good cause' or 'special circumstances' to show that the council has to make a judgment. Examples include:

(a)   whether it is 'reasonable' to award HB on two homes in the case of a person in fear of violence (para 3.14);

(b)   how much it is 'appropriate' to restrict the rent in exempt accommodation (para 9.29);

(c)   whether a claimant has 'good cause' for a late claim (para 16.44);

(d)   whether a claimant has 'special circumstances' for their delay in notifying an advantageous change in circumstances (paras 17.15, 20.37, 20.47).

Discretion

20.25   A discretion differs from a judgment in the sense that the council/NIHE may choose what to do. The law usually says that it 'may' do something to show this. Examples include:

(a)   whether to award discretionary housing payments (para 23.4);

(b)   whether to recover a recoverable overpayment of HB (para 19.10);

(c)   in some situations, whether to pay HB to a landlord (para 18.30).

Reconsiderations

20.26   You (or any other person affected) can ask the council/NIHE to reconsider any HB decision it has made.

20.27   The council/NIHE can also reconsider a decision without a request, for example because a case is being checked or there are new regulations or case law.

When you can request a reconsideration

20.28   You can request a reconsideration at any time, but if you don't meet the time limit (paras 20.36-37) you could get less HB (table 20.3(a)-(c)).

How to request a reconsideration

20.29   Requests for a reconsideration must be in writing. Some councils have a form you can use, or you can make the request in a letter or email.

Information and evidence

20.30   When you request a reconsideration you should provide any new information and evidence you have. If the council/NIHE needs information and evidence it should request this, and it must take it into account if you provide it within one month.

20.26   CPSA sch 7 para 3(1)(a); DAR 4(1)(a); NICPSA sch 7 para 3(1)(a); NIDAR 4(1)(a)

20.27   CPSA sch 7 para 3(1)(b); DAR 4(1)(b),(2); NICPSA sch 7 para 3(1)(b); NIDAR 4(1)(b),(2)

20.28   CPSA sch 7 paras 3(1),(3), 4(1),(5); DAR 7(2)(b), 8(4)
         NICPSA sch 7 paras 3(1), 4(1),(4); NIDAR 7(2)(b), 8(4)

20.29   DAR 4(8); NIDAR 4(7)

20.30   DAR 4(1),(5); NIDAR DAR 4(1),(4)

Reconsideration decisions and notices

20.31   The council/NIHE makes a decision about your request, and sends you a decision notice telling you:

(a)   whether it has altered your HB;

(b)   if it has, what it has altered and when from; and

(c)   your rights (para 20.1).

Revisions and supersessions

20.32   In the law, a changed decision is called a revision or supersession, but you don't have to use these terms when you request a reconsideration.

20.33   The terms have the following meanings:

(a)   a 'revision' alters your HB from the same date (in most cases) as the decision it is altering: you get arrears of HB back to then (or have been overpaid since then);

(b)   a 'supersession' alters your HB from a date later than the decision it is altering: you get arrears back to that later date (or have been overpaid since then);

(c)   a 'closed period supersession' is used when a change took place in the past and has already come to an end (CIS/2595/2003): you get arrears for that past fixed period (or have been overpaid during it).

When reconsidered decisions take effect

20.34   When the council/NIHE changes a decision it has reconsidered, the change takes effect (alters your HB) from the date in table 20.3.

Time limit for getting your arrears

20.35   Except for an official error (para 20.38), if you request a reconsideration that increases or reinstates your HB you only get all your arrears if you made your request (or your HB is altered) within the time limit. Table 20.3 shows how your request affects your arrears. A separate (but similar) rule applies instead if your circumstances have changed (paras 17.13-14).

20.36   Your request is within the time limit if it is received within one month of the council's decision notice (para 20.8). But:

(a)   any time is ignored from the date a statement of reasons was requested (para 20.10) to the date it was provided (both dates included);

(b)   if an accidental error is corrected, any time before you were notified is ignored (para 20.41);

(c)   if you have special circumstances the time limit can be extended (para 20.37).

20.31   HB 90(1), sch 9 paras 2-5; HB66+ 71(1), sch 8 paras 2-5
         NIHB 86(1), sch 10 paras 2-5; NIHB66+ 67(1), sch 9 paras 2-5

20.32   DAR 4(9), 7(6); NIDAR 4(8), 7(6)

20.33   CPSA sch 7 paras 3(3), 4(5); NICPSA sch 7 paras 3(3), 4(4)

20.35   CPSA sch 7 paras 3(1),(3), 4(1),(5); DAR 4(1), 7(2), 8(4)
         NICPSA sch 7 paras 3(1),(3), 4(1),(4); NIDAR 4(1), 7(2), 8(4)

20.36   DAR 4(1),(4), 5(1),(4), 10A(3); NIDAR 4(1),(3), 5(1),(4), 10A(3)

Table 20.3 **When reconsidered decisions take effect**

Type of reconsideration	When it takes effect
Decisions increasing or reinstating your HB	
(a) Reconsiderations requested or made within the time limit (one month or in some cases up to 13 months: para 20.37)	The date the original decision took effect (or should have)
(b) Requests made to correct an official error (at any time: para 20.38)	The date the original decision took effect (or should have)
(c) Other cases	The Monday of the benefit week in which the change is requested, or the council/NIHE first takes action to make it (if this is earlier)
Decisions reducing or ending your HB	
(d) All cases	The date the original decision took effect (or should have)

Notes:

- This table doesn't apply to decisions that are wrong due to change of circumstance where there is an equivalent rule (table 17.2).
- In the law, (a), (b) and (d) are revisions and (c) is a supersession (para 20.33).

Extending the time limit

20.37 The time limit for requesting a reconsideration is extended if:

(a) the council/NIHE receives your request within 13 months of the date of its decision notice;

(b) you say you are asking for it to be accepted late and give the reasons for the delay;

(c) your request 'has merit';

(d) there are special circumstances why it wasn't practicable for you to make the request earlier; and

(e) it is reasonable to accept your delay – the longer you delay the more compelling your special circumstances have to be.

When deciding this, the council/NIHE can't take account of ignorance or misunderstanding of the law or the time limits; or of an Upper Tribunal, the NI Commissioners or a court interpreting the law in a new way.

T20.3   CPSA sch 7 paras 3(1),(3), 4(1),(5); DAR 4(1),(2), 6, 7(2), 8(4),(5)
         NICPSA sch 7 paras 3(1),(3), 4(1),(4); NIDAR 4(1),(2), 6, 7(2), 8(4),(5)

20.37   DAR 5(1)-(6); NIDAR 5(1)-(6)

Official errors

20.38   In the case of official errors (paras 20.39-40), there is no time limit for changes. So your reconsideration request can be made at any time, and (if you are successful) you get arrears of HB back to the date the original decision took effect (or should have taken effect)

20.39   An 'official error' means an error by the council, the DWP or HMRC – or someone acting on their behalf (e.g. a contractor or a partner organisation). But it doesn't include an error that you (the claimant) or the payee or someone acting on your or the payee's behalf 'materially contributed to'.

20.40   For example, an official error can include:

  (a)   a mistake about what the facts are (e.g. because the council/NIHE failed to take account of information and evidence it had when the original decision was made);

  (b)   an error in applying the law or case law;

  (c)   an accidental error; or

  (d)   a combination of the above (CH/943/2003).

Accidental errors

20.41   There is an accidental error when the council fails to record, or to put into action its true intentions (e.g. by mis-entering data on a computer). The council/NIHE can correct an accidental error at any time. Any resulting change in your HB takes effect from the date the original decision took effect (or should have).

Appeals to a tribunal

20.42   You (or any other person affected) can appeal about an HB decision to:

  (a)   a First-tier Tribunal in Great Britain; or

  (b)   an Appeal Tribunal in Northern Ireland.

These tribunals are independent of the council/NIHE. You can appeal to them either instead of or after asking the council/NIHE to reconsider its decision.

Which decisions can be appealed

20.43   Any HB decision can be appealed to a tribunal except those in table 20.4. If a decision is non-appealable, you can ask the council to reconsider it (para 20.26) or you may be able to apply for judicial review (para 20.54).

20.38   DAR 4(2); NIDAR 4(2)

20.39   DAR 1(2) –'official error'; NIDAR 1(2)

20.41   CPSA sch 7 para 19(1)(a); DAR 10A(1),(2); NICPSA sch 7 para 19(1)(a); NIDAR 10A(1),(2)

20.42   CPSA sch 7 para 6(1),(3); NICPSA sch 7 para 6(1),(3)

20.43   CPSA sch 7 para 6(2),(4); DAR 16(1), sch; NICPSA sch 7 para 6(2),(4); NIDAR 16(1), sch

Table 20.4 **Non-appealable HB decisions**

(a) Whether or when you should be included in 'managed migration' to UC (para 1.28)

(b) LHA figures and areas (paras 10.21-28)

(c) The DWP's assessed income figure (table 13.3) – but deductions from it are appealable (table 13.3(a)-(f))

(d) Whether the council should run a local scheme for war disablement and bereavement pensions (paras 13.18)

(e) Which partner in a couple is to be the claimant (para 16.4)

(f) Who may claim on behalf of someone who is unable to act (para 16.5)

(g) Suspending or restoring HB (paras 17.41-42) – but terminating HB is appealable (para 17.44)

(h) When and how HB is paid (paras 18.2-8)

(i) The frequency of payment of a rent allowance (paras 18.9-10)

(j) Making a payment on account (paras 18.11-15)

(k) Paying outstanding HB after a death (para 18.21)

(l) Certain matters relating to overpayments (para 19.66)

(m) Rent determinations made by the rent officer/NIHE (para 20.55)

(n) Figures that are specified in the law (e.g. the capital limit, applicable amounts, or the benefit cap)

(o) Appeals in which the reconsideration was refused because it was outside the time limit and was not about official error (R(H) 8/05; [2018] UKUT 404 (AAC))

Appeals about overpayments

20.44 In relation to an overpayment appeal, the persons affected are:

(a) you (the claimant) in all cases -- whoever the overpayment was paid to or is recoverable from;

(b) anyone else that the overpayment was paid to ([2021] UKUT 256 (AAC)) – e.g. your attorney or nominee (para 18.17) or your landlord or their agent (para 18.22); and

(c) anyone else that the overpayment is recoverable from – e.g. the person the overpayment was paid to, your partner or your estate (paras 19.23-33).

This means there are often two (or three) persons affected in the case of an overpayment appeal.

T20.4   CPSA sch 7 para 6(2),(4); DAR 16(1), sch; NICPSA sch 7 para 6(2),(4); NIDAR 16(1), sch

20.44   CPSA sch 7 para 6(6); DAR 3(1)(a),(d),(e); NICPSA sch 7 para 6(6); NIDAR 3(1)(a),(d),(e)

How to appeal

20.45   Your appeal has to meet the tribunal requirements. It should:

(a)   be in writing, signed (para 20.4) and sent to the council/NIHE;

(b)   say what decision you are appealing about and why you consider it is wrong;

(c)   give your name and address, and those of your representative if you have one;

(d)   say which address you want documents about your appeal to be sent to; and

(e)   be within the time limit (paras 20.46-47).

The council/NIHE can't insist on you using an official form so long as you meet these requirements. If you don't meet them, see para 20.48.

Time limit for appealing

20.46   Your appeal is within the time limit if the council/NIHE receives it within one month of its decision notice (paras 20.8-9) or, if you requested a reconsideration, within one month of its decision notice about that (para 20.31). But:

(a)   if you requested a statement of reasons (para 20.10) within that month, the time limit is 14 days after the end of that month, or 14 days after the date the council provides the statement, whichever is later;

(b)   if the time limit runs out on a non-working day it is extended to the next working day;

(c)   if it is in the interests of justice the time limit can be extended (para 20.47).

Disputes about whether your appeal is within the time limit must be referred to the tribunal. And if the council's/NIHE's decision notice is invalid because it didn't meet the necessary requirements, the time limit doesn't start until the council/NIHE issues a valid notice (CH/1129/2004).

Extending the time limit

20.47   The time limit for appealing is extended if:

(a)   the council/NIHE receives your appeal within 12 months of the end of the time limit described in para 20.46; and

(b)   you say why you are asking for it to be accepted late and give reasons for your delay; and

(c)   there are special circumstances meaning it wasn't practicable to make your appeal earlier – because you, your partner or a dependant have suffered a serious illness or died, or you aren't resident in the UK, or postal services were disrupted, or there were other 'wholly exceptional' special circumstances – and the longer your delay the more compelling your special circumstances have to be; and

(d)   it is in the interests of justice to accept your delay – but no account can be taken of ignorance or misunderstanding of the law or the time limits, or of an Upper Tribunal, the NI Commissioners or a court interpreting the law in a new way.

20.45   CPSA sch 7 para 6(8); DAR 20(1); FTPR 23(6); NICPSA sch 7 para 6(8); NIDAR 20(1)

20.46   DAR 19(5),(5A); FTPR 12, 23(2)(a),(7), sch 1; NIDAR 18(1),(2),(4),(5), 19(3),(5)

20.47   DAR 19(5A),(6)-(9); FTPR 23(3)-(5),(8); NIDAR 19(2)-(8)

If the council/NIHE doesn't consider your appeal meets these conditions, it must refer your request for an extension of time to the tribunal. The tribunal has wider powers. For example, it can accept your appeal if you meet condition (a) above and neither the council/NIHE nor any other party objects. Or it can accept your appeal later than the time limit in (a) if the circumstances are truly exceptional and you have done all you can to obtain a hearing ([2022] UKUT 292 (AAC).

Appeals that don't meet the requirements

20.48   If your appeal doesn't meet the requirements in para 20.45, the council/NIHE should write to you asking you to provide what is missing. For example, it might ask you to clarify which decision you are appealing or why you think the decision is wrong. The council/NIHE should allow you at least 14 days to do this and can allow longer. If you provide the information, it is treated as being part of your appeal. If you don't, the council/NIHE must send your appeal to the tribunal to decide whether it meets the requirements. The tribunal notifies you and the council/NIHE about this.

The council's/NIHE's appeal duties

20.49   When the council/NIHE receives your appeal, it must consider:

(a)   whether it agrees with part or all of your appeal;

(b)   whether the outcome is beneficial to you – 'beneficial' means you are awarded HB, or more HB, or HB for a longer period.

The council must do this in all cases unless the tribunal has decided your appeal doesn't meet the requirements (para 20.48), or you withdraw your appeal in writing.

20.50   The council/NIHE must then do one of the following:

(a)   if it agrees with your appeal (either wholly or partly) and the outcome is beneficial, the council must alter its decision, send you a decision notice about its new decision, and award any arrears of HB. Your appeal 'lapses' (it isn't sent to the tribunal);

(b)   if it agrees with your appeal (either wholly or partly) but the outcome is not beneficial, the council must alter its decision and send you a decision notice about its new decision. It must also send your appeal to the tribunal;

(c)   if it disagrees with your appeal, the council must send your appeal to the tribunal.

In cases (a) and (b), you have one month in which you can make further representations about the council's altered decision and about your appeal.

20.48   DAR 20(2),(5)-(8); NIDAR 20(2),(5)-(8)

20.49   DAR 17(1)-(3), 20(7)-(9); FTPR 24(1A); NIDAR 17(1),(3), 18(4), 19(3), 20(7)-(9)

20.50   DAR 17(1),(4),(5); NIDAR 17(1),(4),(5)

Sending your appeal to the tribunal

20.51   As soon as practicable, the council/NIHE sends your appeal to the tribunal – along with its own submission and any relevant documents – and sends a copy to you and any other person affected. The Ombudsman recommends the council should do this within four weeks and can award compensation if the council takes longer [www]. If there is a delay, you can write to the tribunal asking it to issue a direction to the council/NIHE to provide its submission, or asking the tribunal to set a hearing date without waiting for the submission (R(H) 1/07). Or if you have difficulty obtaining evidence, you can write to the tribunal asking it to direct the holder of the evidence to relase it ([2022] UKUT 77 (AAC)).

Appeals and further appeals

20.52   The tribunal writes to you asking (among other things) whether you want there to be a hearing or if you want the appeal to be decided without one. The tribunal will keep you informed about what happens next. Once the tribunal has decided your appeal, it notifies its decision to you, the council/NIHE and any other person affected.

20.53   You can then make a further appeal, but only if you consider the tribunal has made a mistake about the law (and not about the facts), and only if you first ask the tribunal for a statement of its reasons within one month of receiving its decision. The council/NIHE can also do this. The further appeal goes to:

(a)   an Upper Tribunal in Great Britain; or

(b)   the NI Commissioners in Northern Ireland.

For more information about appeals and further appeals, see volume 1 chapter 14. You can also get details of tribunal procedures and rules online [www].

Judicial review

20.54   When using judgment or discretion, councils are bound by the principles of administrative law evolved by the courts. If they ignore these and the decision isn't appealable they can be challenged (as a last resort) by applying to the High Court (or in Scotland the Court of Session) for 'judicial review'. Examples of when a challenge may be successful are if the council:

20.51   FTPR 6, 24(1A),(2)(e),(4),(5); see also footnote para 20.12
         https://tinyurl.com/LGO-Focus-HB-Jan-2020
         https://tinyurl.com/LGO-19-015-569

20.52   FTPR 27(1), 29, 33; NIDAR 23(1); NIDAR99 39, 49(2), 53(1)-(3)

20.53   FTPR 34(2)-(5), 38(3), 39; UTPR 21
         NIDAR 23(1),(3)(f); NIDAR99 53(4), 54(1), 58(1); NISR 1999/225 reg 9
         www.gov.uk/administrative-appeals-tribunal
         www.gov.uk/government/publications/social-entitlement-chamber-tribunal-procedure-rules
         www.justice-ni.gov.uk/articles/appeals-service
         www.nihe.gov.uk/Housing-Help/Housing-Benefit/Appeals

20.54   R v South Hams DC ex p Ash [1999] 32 HLR 405, QBD

(a) fails to consider each case on its merits, instead applying predetermined rules;

(b) takes into account matters which it ought not to consider;

(c) does not consider matters which it ought to take into account; or

(d) reaches a conclusion that no reasonable council could have come to (what is reasonable here means rational rather than what is the best decision).

A judicial review judgment can impose its own decision on the council/NIHE, or can tell the council what factors it should take into account in remaking its own decision (R v South Hams DC ex p Ash, which was about the discretion not to recover an overpayment).

Appeals about rent officer/NIHE rent determinations

20.55   This section explains how to appeal against rent determinations made by the rent officer in Great Britain or NIHE in Northern Ireland, and how errors in them are corrected. It applies to board and attendance determinations and all other rent determinations (para 10.39 and table 10.4). See paras 20.56-61 in Great Britain and para 20.62 in Northern Ireland.

Rent officer re-determinations

20.56   In Great Britain, appeals against rent determinations are dealt with by the council making an application to the rent officer for a 're-determination'. The council:

(a) must make an application within seven days of receiving a valid request from you (para 20.57) – and must include a copy of your request and any information and evidence you provide;

(b) may choose to make an application at any time (with or without a request from you);

(c) can only make a maximum of two applications in the order (a) then (b), or three applications in the order (b) then (a) then (b).

The rules apply each time the rent officer makes a determination (para 10.36).

20.57   Your request is valid if:

(a) it is sent to the council in writing and signed (para 20.4);

(b) it says you disagree with a rent determination, or raises matters which affect a rent determination; and

(c) you make it within one month of the date of a decision notice about your HB (para 20.8).

20.58   The re-determination is made by the rent officer (known as a re-determination officer) with advice from one or two other rent officers. It covers all rent determinations that apply to you (table 10.4), or if appropriate just the board and attendance determination (para 10.39). The rent officer should send the redetermination to the council within 20 days of receiving the application for it or any further information they have requested from the council. They normally include their reasons and send a copy to you [www].

20.56   HB 15, 16; HB66+ 15, 16

20.57   HB 16(1); HB66+ 16(1)

20.58   ROO 2 – definition – 'relevant period', 4, 4D, sch 3
          Rent Officer Handbook: Redeterminations; https://tinyurl.com/RO-handbook

Correcting errors

20.59   In Great Britain, the rent officer provides a substitute determination (or substitute re-determination) if:

(a) the council made an error in the information it gave them (e.g. about the occupiers of your home); or

(b) the rent officer discovers they made an error (e.g. in the data they used).

The council has to request this each time (a) applies, but not normally when (b) applies (DWP circular G5/2005).

Changes to your eligible rent

20.60   If the rent officer's new determination changes the amount of your eligible rent, the council must send you a decision notice about this. Your HB changes as follows:

(a) an increase in your eligible rent takes effect (as a revision: para 20.33) from the date the council's original decision took effect (or should have) – so you are awarded arrears of HB back to then; but

(b) a reduction in your eligible rent takes effect (as a supersession) from the Monday following the date of the rent officer's new determination – so you haven't been overpaid HB before then.

Tribunal appeals

20.61   In Great Britain, you can't appeal to a tribunal about the rent officer's determinations or re-determinations, but you may be able to apply for judicial review (para 20.54). You can appeal to a tribunal (para 20.42) about whether you fall within the rent referral rules (table 10.2) and about the information the council provides to the rent officer ([2010] UKUT 79 (AAC); [2010] AACR 40).

Reconsiderations and appeals in Northern Ireland

20.62   In Northern Ireland, you can ask the NIHE to reconsider any rent determinations it has made. If your HB changes as a result:

(a) an increase in your eligible rent takes effect as described in table 20.3; but

(b) a reduction in your eligible rent normally takes effect from the Monday following the date of the NIHE's new rent determination.

Restrictions on appeals to a tribunal are the same as in Great Britain (para 20.60).

20.59   HB 17, 18, 18A; HB66+ 17, 18, 18A; ROO 4A, 4E, 7A(1),(2)

20.60   HB 90(1), sch 9 paras 9(a), 10(a); HB66+ 71(1), sch 8 paras 9(a), 10(a);
         DAR 4(3), 7(2)(c), 8(4)

20.61   CPSA sch 7 para 6(2)(c)

20.62   NICPSA sch 7 para 6(2)(c); NIHB 15(1); NIHB66+ 15(1);
         NIDAR 4(1),(2), 7(2)(b), 8(4), 16(1), sch para 6

Chapter 21 **Subsidy**

- General rules about subsidy for HB expenditure, local schemes, and administration: see paras 21.1-9.
- The effect of HB overpayments on subsidy: see paras 21.10-26.
- The effect of high rents etc on subsidy: see paras 21.27-40.

General rules

21.1   The councils in Great Britain that have a legal duty to administer and pay housing benefit are part reimbursed for this by the DWP. This reimbursement takes the form of subsidy payments which each council must claim. (For the separate rules about grants towards discretionary housing payments, see paras 23.18-19.)

21.2   The DWP pays councils subsidy for each financial year (1st April to 31st March) towards the:

(a) actual HB paid (paras 21.3-4); and

(b) HB administration costs (para 21.5).

The balance of the council's costs is met from the council's general fund in England and Scotland, or its council fund in Wales.

Subsidy for HB expenditure

21.3   The DWP pays each council subsidy towards the HB it pays in the financial year:

(a) this equals 100% of all HB lawfully paid;

(b) except that a lower amount (or no subsidy) is paid for:

- additional HB paid under a local scheme (para 21.4),
- some overpayments of HB (paras 21.10-26), and
- some payments of HB relating to high rents etc (paras 21.27-40).

Lawfully paid HB includes rebates, allowances, payments on account (chapter 18) and extended payments. It also includes payments made in the financial year for an earlier financial year. But each amount of HB can only get subsidy once.

Subsidy towards local schemes

21.4   If the council runs a local scheme for war disablement and bereavement pensions (paras 13.18-19):

(a) first the council's annual subsidy is calculated (para 21.3), but including only the HB that would be awarded if it did not run a local scheme;

(b) then this is increased to take account of the local scheme. The increase equals the lower of:

- ■   0.2% of the council's annual subsidy,

- ■   75% of the additional HB awarded in the year as a result of the local scheme.

Subsidy for HB administration

21.5   The DWP also pays each council subsidy towards part of its HB administration costs in the financial year (for example staffing, accommodation, training and computers). The amounts for 2023-24 are in circular S2/2023. The DWP calls this a 'cash-limited specific grant'. It is separate from the grant for council tax rebate (CTR) administration, which is paid to councils by the MHCLG in England, or by the Scottish or Welsh Government.

New burdens funding

21.6   The government's 'new burdens doctrine' [www] says that the responsible central government department must assess and properly pay for all new burdens it places on councils. New burdens often arise in the administration of HB. Subsidy details are in the 'S' list of circulars (para 21.8). Recent examples include carrying out improvements to recording HB statistics for claims made in supported and temporary accommodation (S3/2022), carrying out DWP welfare reforms (S4/2022), Verify Earnings and Pensions (VEP) alerts (S6/2021, S8/2022), and the HB Award Accuracy Initiative (S8/2020, S11/2021, S7/2022).

Subsidy claims, payments and overpayments

21.7   To get subsidy, councils have to claim it from the DWP. They may not get their full amount of subsidy if they do not:

(a) claim it on time using the correct procedures;

(b) provide the information and evidence required by the DWP; and

(c) get their final subsidy claim assured/certified by their auditor by 30th November.

Subsidy is paid to the council in instalments throughout the year and a final (balancing) payment is made after the year for which subsidy is being claimed. The DWP has the power to recover subsidy which was overpaid, or was claimed in breach of the subsidy rules: R (Isle of Anglesey County Council) v SSWP, R (Lambeth LBC) v SSWP.

21.4   AA 134(8), SO 12(1)(d),(4)

21.5   AA 140B(4)(a),(4A), SO 12(1)(b), sch 1

21.6   New burdens doctrine: guidance for government departments: https://tinyurl.com/NewBurdens

21.7   SO part II
         R v Anglesey CC v SSWP EWHC 2518 Admin www.bailii.org/ew/cases/EWHC/Admin/2003/2518.html
         R (Lambeth LBC) v SSWP EWHC 637 Admin www.bailii.org/ew/cases/EWHC/Admin/2005/637.html

Subsidy law and guidance

21.8   The law about HB subsidy is in:

(a)   sections 140A-140G of the Social Security Administration Act 1992 (which gives the legal framework); and

(b)   the Income-related Benefits (Subsidy to Authorities) Order 1998, SI 1998 No.562 (which gives the detailed rules).

When the subsidy rules change for each financial year, the Order is usually amended at the end of that year, but advance warning is usually given in the *Subsidy Guidance Manual* and the 'S' series of circulars [www]. The DWP's *HB subsidy claims – local authority best practice guide* (June 2015) provides examples of how to complete subsidy claims [www]. In England the arrangements for the assurance of subsidy claims are set out in DWP circulars S1/2017, S7/2018 and S12/2018. The HB assurance process (HBAP) instructions for English councils and reporting accountants are available on gov.uk [www].

Subsidy and HB decision-making

21.9   When councils make decisions about awarding HB, or recovering overpaid HB, they have a duty to apply HB law fairly, objectively and impartially. If a decision means the council has to use its judgment (para 20.24), it must not allow the subsidy rules to affect this. But if a decision allows the council to use its discretion (para 20.25), it may take its own financial position (including the effect of the subsidy rules) into account as one factor: R v Brent LBC HBRB ex parte Connery. For examples see paras 9.37, 19.10-11 and 21.13.

Overpayments of HB

21.10   This section describes how much subsidy the DWP pays councils towards overpayments of HB.

Subsidy categories

21.11   For subsidy purposes, HB overpayments fall into the categories shown in table 21.1. The table also summarises the amounts of subsidy paid. The details for each category are in paras 21.14-26.

21.12   The rules about which HB overpayments are recoverable do not always correspond to the subsidy categories, but in broad terms:

(a)   departmental error and authority error/administrative delay overpayments may or may not be recoverable: see the rules about official error overpayments in paras 19.5-7;

(b)   other overpayments are usually recoverable: paras 19.8-9.

21.8   DWP Housing Benefit Subsidy Guidance Manual 2020 to 2021 https://tinyurl.com/Subsidy-Guidance
        DWP Housing-Benefit-Subsidy Circulars https://tinyurl.com/SubsidyCirculars
        DWP's HB subsidy claims – local authority best practice guide (June 2015) https://tinyurl.com/DWPBestPractice
        HB Assurance Process documents https://tinyurl.com/HBAssurance

21.9   R v Brent LBC ex p Connery 20/10/89 QBD 22 HLR 40

Table 21.1 **Overpayments subsidy categories**

Subsidy category	Amount of subsidy
(a) Departmental error overpayments	100%
(b) Payment on account overpayments	100%
(c) Duplicate payment overpayments	25%
(d) Technical overpayments	Nil
(e) Authority error/administrative delay overpayments	100%, 40% or nil depending on certain thresholds
(f) Claimant error, fraudulent and other overpayments	40%

Notes

In broad terms:

- subsidy in (a) to (c) is paid only on unrecovered overpayments;
- subsidy in (e) and (f) is paid whether the overpayments are recovered or not.

Detailed rules about the subsidy categories, amounts, etc are in paras 21.14-26. Subsidy categories don't exactly match those in table 19.1.

Deciding subsidy categories

21.13 The council decides which subsidy category each HB overpayment falls into, but this is contentious because there is a strong financial incentive to misclassify: for example, to code a technical error (para 21.20) as a claimant error or not to code an error at all for administrative delay (para 21.21). This problem was recognised in old regulatory guidance for external auditors who were advised to test the classifications to provide assurance that they are correct and 'fairly stated'.

Departmental error overpayments

21.14 For subsidy purposes, a 'departmental error overpayment' means one caused by a mistake of fact or law (whether in the form of an act or omission):

(a) by the DWP or HMRC or someone providing services to them; or

(b) in a decision of a First-tier or Upper Tribunal.

This does not include an overpayment to which the claimant, or someone acting on the claimant's behalf, or the payee, materially contributed (para 21.25(c)). And it does not include an overpayment caused because a court interprets the law differently from how the DWP or HMRC or a tribunal interpreted it (para 21.25(d)).

T21.1   SO 11(2), 13, 18, 19(1)(e)-(i)

21.13   SO 18(4) Audit Commission, Certification Instruction BEN01 (06-07) para 35

21.14   SO 18(4)

21.15   Subsidy on these overpayments is 100% of:

(a) the total departmental error overpayments in the year;

(b) minus the total departmental error overpayments recovered in the year (whether they were overpaid in the year or in a previous year).

This means the council does not qualify for subsidy towards the amount it recovers.

Payment on account overpayments

21.16   A 'payment on account overpayment' means one caused when a payment on account is greater than the amount of HB a claimant qualifies for (paras 18.11-16).

21.17   Subsidy on these overpayments is 100% of:

(a) the total payment on account overpayments in the year;

(b) minus the total payment on account overpayments recovered in the year (whether they were overpaid in the year or in a previous year).

Duplicate payment overpayments

21.18   A 'duplicate payment overpayment' means one caused when:

(a) a duplicate payment of HB is issued because the first one was (or was alleged to have been) lost, stolen or not received; but

(b) the first one is in fact cashed.

21.19   Subsidy on these overpayments is 25% of:

(a) the total duplicate payment overpayments in the year;

(b) minus the total duplicate payments recovered in the year (whether they were issued in the year or in a previous year).

Technical overpayments

21.20   A 'technical overpayment' means one caused because:

(a) a council tenant's liability for rent ends (for example their tenancy ends) or reduces; but

(b) HB has already been credited to their rent account for a period after it ended or reduced.

No subsidy is paid on these overpayments.

21.15   SO 18(1)(b)(i),(2),(3), 19(1)(e)

21.16   SO 18(7B)

21.17   SO 18(1)(f)

21.18-19   SO 18(1)(a)

21.20   SO 18(7),(7A)

Authority error/administrative delay overpayments

21.21   For subsidy purposes:

(a) an 'authority error overpayment' means one caused by a mistake of fact or law (whether in the form of an act or omission) by the council;

(b) an 'administrative delay overpayment' means one caused by a delay (rather than a mistake), but only when the council:

■ is notified of a change of circumstances, and

■ has the information and evidence it needs to make a decision on it, but

■ fails to make the decision before the next HB payment date.

21.22   These do not include an overpayment to which the claimant, or someone acting on the claimant's behalf, or the payee, materially contributed (see para 21.25(c)). And they do not include an overpayment caused because a court interprets the law differently from how the council interpreted it (para 21.25(d)).

21.23   These overpayments are combined for subsidy purposes. The amount of subsidy (para 21.24) depends on:

(a) the total authority error and administrative delay overpayments in the year;

(b) as a percentage of the total HB paid in the year. (This means HB which qualifies for 100% subsidy: para 21.3.)

21.24   If the above percentage is:

(a) not more than 0.48% (the lower threshold), 100% subsidy is paid on all authority error and administrative delay overpayments in the year;

(b) more than 0.48% but not more than 0.54% (the higher threshold), 40% subsidy is paid on all these overpayments;

(c) more than 0.54%, no subsidy is paid on any of these overpayments.

In cases (a) and (b), the council qualifies for this subsidy even if it recovers some or all of these overpayments.

Example: Subsidy for authority error and administrative delay overpayments

A council's annual expenditure on correctly paid HB is £10,000,000.

So its lower threshold is £48,000 and its higher threshold is £54,000 for that year (see para 21.24).

If the total authority error and administrative delay overpayments in that year are:

■ £45,000, the council gets subsidy of 100% of this, which is £45,000;

■ £50,000, the council gets subsidy of 40% of this, which is £20,000;

■ £55,000, the council gets no subsidy for this.

21.21-22   SO 18(6),(6ZA)

21.23   SO 18(6A)

21.24   SO 18(1)(e)

Claimant error, fraudulent and other overpayments

21.25   Any other overpayment qualifies for 40% subsidy, whether it is:

(a) a 'claimant error overpayment'. This means one caused by the claimant, or someone acting on the claimant's behalf, failing to provide required information or evidence;

(b) a 'fraudulent overpayment'. This means one where the claimant has been found guilty of an offence, made an admission under caution, or agreed to pay a penalty as an alternative to prosecution (para 19.75);

(c) an overpayment that would count as departmental error (para 21.14) or authority error/administrative delay, except that the claimant, someone acting on the claimant's behalf, or the payee, materially contributed to it (para 21.22);

(d) an overpayment caused because a court interprets the law differently from how the DWP, HMRC, a tribunal or the council interpreted it (paras 21.14 and 21.22);

(e) an overpayment caused by a third party, for example a landlord, whether or not they are the payee; or

(f) any other overpayment not included in paras 21.14-24.

21.26   Subsidy is 40% of the total of these overpayments in the year. The council qualifies for this subsidy even if it recovers some or all of these overpayments.

High rents etc

21.27   This section describes the subsidy limitations which apply when HB is paid for:

(a) exempt accommodation (paras 21.29-33);

(b) temporary accommodation for homeless people (paras 21.34-38);

(c) council tenants in certain circumstances (para 21.39); and

(d) rent referral cases which the council fails to refer to the rent officer (para 21.40).

21.28   The DWP pays councils 100% subsidy on all other payments of HB (para 21.3) regardless of how high the eligible rent is, so long as it is correctly assessed. In practice most payments of HB fall outside para 21.27 because a private tenant's HB can't exceed the LHA rate or the lowest of the rent officer's determinations (chapter 10) and a social tenant's rent can't exceed the limits set by the national regulator (para 7.16).

21.25(a)   SO 18(4A)

21.25(b)   SO 18(5),(5A)

21.25(c),(d) SO 18(4),(6)

21.25(e),(f) SO 18(2)

21.26   SO 18(1)(b)(iii),(c),(d),(2), 19(1)(ea),(f)

21.28   SO 13(1)(a)

Exempt accommodation

21.29   Exempt accommodation is defined in para 9.18. The subsidy limitations in exempt accommodation only apply if:

(a) the council has to make a referral to the rent officer (para 21.30); and

(b) the claimant's eligible rent exceeds the subsidy limit (paras 21.32-33).

21.30   All exempt accommodation cases have to be referred to the rent officer unless:

(a) the landlord is a registered housing association in most cases (para 10.33), or

(b) the letting is a registered rent or similar old tenancy (para 7.38).

21.31   If the council is not required to make a referral, subsidy is 100% of the claimant's HB. But if the council fails to make a referral when one is required, the DWP pays no subsidy (para 21.40).

The subsidy limit

21.32   The DWP pays the council the following amounts of subsidy:

(a) 100% of weekly HB attributable to eligible rent up to the subsidy limit (para 21.33);

(b) 60% of weekly HB attributable to eligible rent above the subsidy limit when:

- the claimant could formerly afford their accommodation (para 7.49), or

- the claimant has had a death in their household (para 7.52), or

- the claimant or someone in their household is considered vulnerable and there is no suitable cheaper alternative accommodation the claimant can reasonably be expected to move to (para 9.32);

(c) nil for weekly HB attributable to eligible rent above the subsidy limit in other cases.

The weekly HB is attributed first to (b) or (c), then to (a): see the example.

Examples: Subsidy for exempt accommodation

A claimant is renting exempt accommodation where the rent is £230 per week. The rent officer has provided a significantly high rent determination of £200 per week (with no other determinations) so this is the subsidy limit. But the council decides her eligible rent is £230 per week, because she falls into a vulnerable group and there is no suitable cheaper alternative accommodation available. So, her eligible rent exceeds the subsidy limit, the excess being £30 per week.

21.29   SO 13(1)(b)(i),(iii), 16(1),(2), sch 4 paras 2, 3, 6, 7

21.30   SO 16(2); HB 14(1),(2)(b), sch 2 paras 3-8, 11; HB66+14(1),(2)(b), sch 2 paras 3-8, 11

21.31   SO 13(1)(a), 16(1), sch 4 paras 3, 6

21.32   SO 16(1), sch 4 paras 2, 7, 8(2),(3), 10

1. **Claimant gets full HB of £230 per week**

- First, subsidy is calculated on HB attributable to the excess:
  this is 60% of £30 — £18 pw

- Then, subsidy is calculated on HB not attributable to the excess:
  this is 100% of £200 — £200 pw

- Total subsidy — £218 pw

2. **Claimant gets partial HB of £170 per week**

- First, subsidy is calculated on HB attributable to the excess:
  this is 60% of £30 — £18 pw

- Then, subsidy is calculated on HB not attributable to the excess:
  this is 100% of £140 — £140 pw

- Total subsidy — £158 pw

3. **Claimant gets partial HB of £20 per week**

- Subsidy is calculated on HB attributable to the excess:
  this is 60% of £20 — £12 pw

- Total subsidy — £12 pw

21.33 The subsidy limit equals:

(a) the rent officer's size-related rent determination if there is one; or otherwise

(b) the rent officer's exceptionally high rent determination if there is one; or otherwise

(c) the rent officer's significantly high rent determination.

These determinations are described in table 10.4.

Temporary accommodation for homeless people

21.34 'Temporary accommodation' means accommodation which you rent from a local council or a registered housing association (the landlord), and which is provided to you by your council because you were homeless or to prevent you becoming homeless (table 2.3(e)).

21.35 The accommodation can be any of the following types:

(a) 'board and lodging' – this means accommodation in a hotel, guest house, lodging house or similar establishment where the rent includes a charge for at least some meals which are cooked or prepared, and also consumed, in the accommodation or in associated premises (but not a hostel as in para 7.26 or a care home as in table 5.2);

(b) 'licensed' – this means accommodation the landlord holds on a licence;

(c) 'leased' – this means accommodation the landlord holds on a lease, but in the case of

---

21.33   SO sch 4 para 8(1)(a),(b)

21.34   SO 17(1)(a)-(c), 17A(1)(a)-(c), 17B(1)(a)-(c), 17C(1)(a)-(c),

21.35   SO 11(1) – 'board and lodging accommodation', 17(1)(b),(4), 17A(1)(b), 17B(1)(b), 17C(1)(b)

English councils, the lease must be for no longer than ten years and the accommodation must be held outside the council's Housing Revenue Account;

(d) 'owned' – this means accommodation a registered housing association (not the council) owns.

21.36   The subsidy limitations for temporary accommodation are given in table 21.2. But for temporary accommodation that also meets the definition of exempt accommodation, the rules in paras 21.29-33 apply instead. For DWP guidance, see circulars S1/2011, S5/2011 and G10/2012 [www].

Table 21.2 **Subsidy limits in temporary accommodation**

In each HB case, government subsidy is limited to the lowest of:

- the amount of HB awarded;
- the maximum amount in (a) to (e);
- the cap figure in (f) or (g).

Accommodation type	Maximum amount
(a) Board and lodging	The January 2011 LHA figure for
(b) Licensed (non-self-contained)	one-bedroomed self-contained
(c) Licensed (self-contained)	90% of the January 2011 LHA
(d) Leased	figure for accommodation of
(e) Owned by a registered housing association (para 21-35(d))	the appropriate size (para 21.38)

Area (BRMA)	Cap figure
(f) Central London, Inner East London, Inner North London, Inner South East London, Inner South West London, Inner West London and Outer South West London	£500
(g) Elsewhere	£375

Notes

- Accommodation types are explained in para 21.35; and appropriate size in para 21.38.
- The January 2011 LHA rates for England are available on the National Archives [www].

21.36   SO 17B(1)(d), 17C(1)(d)
          https://tinyurl.com/HB-S5-2011
          https://tinyurl.com/HB-S1-2011
          https://tinyurl.com/Bulletin-G10-2012

T21.2   SO 13(1), 17(2),(3), 17A(2),(3), 17B(2),(3), 17C(2),(3), sch 8
          https://tinyurl.com/LHA-England-Jan-2011

Example: subsidy for leased temporary accommodation

A London council houses a homeless family in a house outside London which it holds on a three year lease. The claimant's rent is payable to the London council and the claimant is entitled to HB of £260 per week. The house has three bedrooms and one living room, making four rooms in all. So the January 2011 LHA figure for a three-bedroom dwelling is used to calculate subsidy (table 21.2). In the area the house is in, this figure is £180 per week.

Subsidy is therefore 90% of the January LHA figure, i.e. £162 per week.

21.37   Authorities also get grant funding towards the management costs of temporary accommodation in England through the Homelessness Prevention Grant [www] and in Scotland and Wales through block grants. The Homelessness Prevention Grant replaced the flexible homelessness support grant and homelessness reduction grant from April 2021.

21.38   The appropriate size of dwelling in table 21.2(c)-(e) depends on the number of rooms, counting both bedrooms and living rooms, in the claimant's accommodation (not the size of their household). If their accommodation contains:

(a)   one or two rooms, the appropriate size is one-bedroom self-contained accommodation

(b)   three rooms, the appropriate size is a two-bedroom dwelling

(c)   four rooms, the appropriate size is a three-bedroom dwelling

(d)   five or six rooms, the appropriate size is a four-bedroom dwelling

(e)   seven or more rooms, the appropriate size is a five-bedroom dwelling (in January 2011 there were LHA figures for five-bedroom dwellings).

The law says this because other rooms in the claimant's accommodation must be regarded as living rooms (even if they are in fact bedrooms).

Council tenants

21.39   The following subsidy limitations can apply to council tenants (para 7.11), but in practice they are rare. The DWP's *Subsidy Guidance Manual* [www] gives further details and exceptions:

(a)   The 'rent rebate subsidy limitation scheme' applies in Wales only (section 9 of the manual). If a council increases its tenants' rents by more than its guideline rent increase, no subsidy is payable on the HB attributable to the excess (DWP circulars S8/2018 and S3/2019). The 'specified amounts' and 'guideline weekly rent increases' for each new financial year are set out in a subsidy circular.

21.37   www.gov.uk/government/publications/homelessness-prevention-grant-2023-to-2025

21.38   SO 17(3), 17A(3),(4), 17B(3), 17C(3),(4)

21.39   SO 11(2), 13(1)(a), 15, 15A, 19(1)(a),(c),(2),(3), 20A, sch 4A
          DWP Housing Benefit Subsidy Guidance Manual 2020 to 2021 https://tinyurl.com/Subsidy-Guidance

(b) The 'disproportionate rent increase rule' applies in Wales and Scotland only (see section 5 of the manual). If a council increases rents to its tenants on HB more than it increases its other rents, subsidy on the difference is restricted.

(c) Limitations on 'modular improvement schemes' apply throughout Great Britain (see section 8 of the manual). If a council offers its tenants the right to select optional services or facilities for an increase in rent, no subsidy is payable on the amount of HB attributable to these.

(d) Limitations on 'rent payment incentive schemes' apply throughout Great Britain (see section 8 of the manual). If a council makes payments (in cash or kind) to reward tenants for paying their rent on time, the total value of such payments is deducted from the amount of subsidy paid to the council

Failure to make a rent referral

21.40   'Rent referral cases' are described in paras 10.31-43. If the council:

(a) is required to refer an HB case to the rent officer during the year;

(b) but fails to do so before the date its final subsidy claim has to be submitted for that year,

no subsidy is paid for any of the HB awarded in the year for that case. In the past some councils have lost a significant amount of subsidy for this reason: R (Isle of Anglesey County Council) v SSWP, R (Lambeth LBC) v SSWP.

21.40   SO 13, 16(4)(c), sch 4 para 15; R (Anglesey) v SSWP and R (Lambeth) v SSWP see footnote 21.7

Chapter 22 **State pension credit**

- ■ Overview, basic conditions and how to claim state pension credit (SPC): see paras 22.1-9.
- ■ Calculating SPC: see paras 22.10-21.
- ■ Help with housing costs: basic conditions: see paras 22.22-25.
- ■ Which housing costs are allowable: see paras 22.26-34.
- ■ Calculating your housing costs: see paras 22.35-39.
- ■ Other matters (payment and appeals): see paras 22.40-45.

Overview

22.1   This chapter describes who can get state pension credit (SPC) and which housing costs you can get help with in SPC.

22.2   SPC is for people on a low income who are aged at least 66 (pension age). It is administered in Great Britain by the DWP, and in Northern Ireland by the DFC. About 1.44 million households in the UK were getting SPC in August 2022 [www].

Guarantee credit and savings credit

22.3   There are two kinds of SPC:

(a) guarantee credit; and

(b) savings credit.

22.4   You can be awarded either kind or both, but savings credit is being phased out (para 22.8). Guarantee credit tops up your pension (and other) income to a minimum level (including if you have nil income). Savings credit provides an additional income if you have a modest pension and/or savings income above the amount of the basic state pension (as a 'reward' for saving).

Housing costs if you are on SPC

22.5   While you are on guarantee credit you can get:

(a) HB towards your rent and service charges (but see para 22.45 for future changes);

(b) SMI towards your mortgage interest (volume 1 chapter 8);

(c) SPC towards housing costs that aren't met by HB/SMI (table 22.3).

While you are on savings credit only (a) and (b) apply.

22.2   www.gov.uk/government/collections/dwp-statistical-summaries
www.communities-ni.gov.uk/topics/benefits-statistics

22.3-4   SPCA 1(3), 4(1),(1A),(2); NISPCA 1(3), 4(1),(1A),(2); SI 2019/37; NISR 2019/4

22.5   PC 6(6)(c); NIPC 6(6)(c)

Who can get SPC

22.6   You qualify for SPC if:

(a) you have made a claim for it (para 22.9);

(b) you and your partner (if you have one) are pension age or over;

(c) your partner (if you have one) doesn't get SPC;

(d) you aren't subject to 'immigration control' (or you meet one of the exceptions to this rule, e.g. if you are a refugee or have been granted humanitarian protection by the Home Office);

(e) you are present in Great Britain/Northern Ireland; and

■   you are 'habitually resident' in the Common Travel Area, and

■   you have a 'right to reside' in the UK;

(f)   you meet the low-income condition (para 22.7) or the additional conditions for savings credit (para 22.21) (or both); and

(g) in the case of savings credit you meet the additional condition in para 22.8.

Pension age (for both men and women) is 66. For further details about what is meant by 'immigration control' (including exceptions), 'habitual residence' and 'right to reside', see volume 1 chapter 20.

The low income conditions

22.7   The low-income condition (para 22.6) for guarantee credit is:

(a) you have nil income; or

(b) your income is below the 'appropriate minimum guarantee'.

Your income includes any 'tariff income' from your savings and any income (and tariff income) of your partner. For savings credit you must have a 'qualifying income' that exceeds the savings credit threshold but is not so high that it results in a nil award (paras 22.19-21).

Savings credit: phasing out and restriction on new claims

22.8   Savings credit is being phased out, so you can now only get it if:

(a) you are single and reached pension age before 6th April 2016; or

(b) you are a couple and:

■   both of you reached pension age before 6th April 2016, or

■   at least one of you qualified for savings credit before that date and has been continuously entitled to it since then.

22.6   SPCA 1(2),(3),(6), 2(1), 3(1),(2), 4; AA 1; Pensions Act 1995 sch 4 para 1; PC 2;
             NISPCA 1(2),(3),(6), 2(1), 3(1),(2), 4; NIAA 1; SI 1995/3213 sch 2; NIPC 2

22.7   SPCA 2(1)(a),(b); NISPCA 2(1),(a),(b)

22.8   SPCA 3(2)-(4), 3ZA; PC 7A; NISPCA 3(2)-(4), 3ZA; NIPC 7A

How to claim SPC

22.9   You claim SPC online [www] or by telephone by calling 0800 991234 and your claim is complete if you provide your national insurance number and other information required during the call. You may also be asked to complete a written statement of your circumstances. Alternatively, you can make a claim in writing, but it is advisable to get someone to telephone for a form (such as an advisor or friend). If you complete and return the form within one month, the date of your claim is the date of the phone call. In Northern Ireland, you claim pension credit by calling 0808 1006165 or you can claim in writing by downloading the claim form [www]. For the time limit, backdating and making a claim in advance of your retirement, see paras 22.42-43.

Calculating SPC

How guarantee credit is calculated

22.10   The weekly amount of your guarantee credit equals:

(a)   your 'appropriate minimum guarantee' (para 22.11);

(b)   minus your weekly income (para 22.18).

If the result is between 1p and 9p, it isn't paid unless you get another benefit to pay it with (e.g. state pension). But if you don't, you count as having 'underlying entitlement' so you get 'passport' rights to other benefits (e.g. CTR, cold weather payments).

22.11   Your 'appropriate minimum guarantee' is made up of:

(a)   your 'standard minimum guarantee' (table 22.1); plus

(b)   in certain circumstances, additional amounts for:

- each child or young person you or your partner is responsible for,
- each child or young person (as above) who is disabled,
- severe disability (of you/your partner),
- a carer (for you/your partner), plus

(c)   your weekly eligible housing costs (para 22.37).

The weekly amounts for (a) and (b) are in table 22.1.

Standard minimum guarantee

22.12   Everyone qualifies for a standard minimum guarantee. You qualify for the appropriate rate depending on whether you are single or a couple (table 22.1).

22.9   C&P87 4D(3),(6A),(6B); NIC&P87 4C(3),(6A),(6B)
https://www.gov.uk/pension-credit/how-to-claim
https://www.nidirect.gov.uk/publications/pension-credit-application-form

22.10   SPCA 2(2); PC 13; NISPCA 2(2); NIPC 13

22.11   PC 6(1),(4),(5),(6)(a)-(d),(8), Sch 2A paras 9(1), 10; NIPC 6(1),(4),(5),(6)(a)-(d),(8), sch 2A paras 9(1), 10

22.12   PC 6(1); NIPC 6(1)

Table 22.1 **Appropriate minimum guarantee: 2023-24**

Standard minimum guarantee

Single person	£201.05
Couple	£306.85
Each additional spouse in polygamous marriage	£105.80
First child or young person born before 6th April 2017	£72.31
Child or young person (each child/young person)	£61.88

Additional amounts

Disabled child (each child/young person)	lower rate	£33.67
	higher rate	£104.86
Severe disability	single rate	£76.40
	double rate	£152.80
Carer	claimant/partner/each	£42.75
Housing costs	Your weekly eligible housing costs (para 22.37)	

Additional amounts: children and young persons

22.13   You get an additional amount for each child and young person if:

(a)   you or your partner do not get CTC for them; and

(b)   you claimed SPC or your award is revised on or after 1st February 2019; and

(c)   you or your partner are responsible for that child or young person.

The rules about whether you are responsible for a child/young person are the same as for HB (paras 4.14-19), including the rules about temporary absence (paras 4.24-25).

22.14   The amount is:

(a)   if at least one child/young person was born before 6th April 2017, you get

■   the higher rate for one child/young person, and

■   the lower rate for each of the others;

(b)   otherwise you get the lower rate for each child/young person.

But unlike HB or UC there is no two-child limit.

T22.1   PC 6(1),(5),(8), sch 2A paras 9(1), 10; SI 2023/316; NIPC 6(1),(5),(8), sch 2A paras 9(1), 10

22.13   PC 6(6)(d), sch 2A paras 1-7; NIPC 6(6)(d), sch 2A paras 1-7

22.14   PC sch 2A paras 9(1), 10; NIPC sch 2A paras 9(1), 10

Additional amount(s): disabled child or young person

22.15   You qualify for a further additional amount for each child or young person you are responsible for who meets one of the following conditions:

(a)   you get the higher rate for each child/young person who is:

■   entitled to the highest rate of the care component of DLA or child disability payment, or

■   entitled to the enhanced rate of the daily living component of PIP, or adult disability payment, or

■   certified as blind or severely sight-impaired by a consultant ophthalmologist;

(b)   you get the lower rate for each child/young person who is entitled to disability living allowance or personal independence payment but does not meet the conditions in (a).

Additional amounts: severe disability and carer

22.16   You qualify for these additional amounts if you or you and your partner are severely disabled or a carer: the rules are the same as for HB (paras 12.25-33).

Additional amount: housing costs

22.17   Your weekly eligible housing costs (paras 22.22-39) are added to your standard minimum guarantee and any other additional amounts you qualify for (22.12-16). The total is your appropriate minimum guarantee (para 22.11).

Assessing income and capital for guarantee credit

22.18   Your and your partner's income and capital, including your pension income and most social security benefits, is treated in the same way as for pension age HB, except that:

(a)   there are some differences in the treatment of income; the main ones are:

■   there are no childcare or additional earnings disregards (paras 14.63-68),

■   the standard disregard for lone parents is £20 (table 14.5),

■   you can't qualify for a £20 disregard through having limited capability for work,

■   there is no carry-over of any unused earnings disregard to WTC (para 14.61), and

■   only £10 is disregarded from widowed parent's allowance (table 13.2);

(b)   you can get guarantee credit even if your capital is over £16,000 and if it is your tariff income (para 15.5) is calculated on all your assessed capital (not just the first £16,000);

(c)   your income is generally treated as being paid to you on the first day of your benefit week (para 22.41) in which it is due – or on the day it was due if this was before you made your claim; and

(d)   unlike HB, annual income is always converted into a weekly figure by dividing by 52 (there are no exceptions).

22.15   PC Sch 2A para 9(1)(b),(2),(3); NIPC Sch 2A para 9(1)(b),(2),(3)

22.16   PC 6(5),(6)(a), sch 1 paras 1-4; NIPC 6(5),(6)(a), sch 1 paras 1-4

22.17   PC 6(6)(c), sch 1 paras 1-15; NIPC 6(6)(c), sch 2 paras 1-15

22.18   SPCA 15, 16, 17(1) definition: 'social security benefits'; PC 14-16, sch 4, sch 5; NISPCA 15, 16, 17(1); NIPC 14-16, sch 4, sch 5

Examples: Eligible housing costs on guarantee credit

(a) A single pensioner with no income or capital, living in a leasehold flat

His eligible housing costs (towards service charges) are £30 per week.

His guarantee credit is calculated as follows:

- Appropriate minimum guarantee:

standard minimum guarantee	£201.05
eligible housing costs	£30.00

- He has no income to deduct
- Weekly amount of guarantee credit   £231.05

His guarantee credit meets the whole of his eligible housing costs. He also qualifies for maximum CTR.

(b) A non-dependant moves in with him

The adult daughter of the above leaseholder moves in and a non-dependant deduction of £116.75 applies for her. This reduces his eligible housing costs from £30 to nil (but is not used to reduce any other part of his applicable amount). His guarantee credit is now calculated as follows:

- Appropriate minimum guarantee:

standard minimum guarantee	£201.05
eligible housing costs	£0.00

- He has no income to deduct
- Weekly amount of guarantee credit   £201.05

His guarantee credit no longer meets any of his eligible housing costs. He still qualifies for maximum CTR but with a non-dependant deduction.

(c) A pensioner couple living in a leasehold flat

They have state and private pensions totalling £307.80 per week and have capital of £4,000. Their eligible housing costs (towards service charges) are £27.40 per week. Their guarantee credit is calculated as follows:

- Appropriate minimum guarantee:

standard minimum guarantee	£306.85
eligible housing costs	£27.40

- Minus their weekly income   – £307.80
- Weekly amount of guarantee credit   £26.45

Their guarantee credit meets only part of their eligible housing costs. But they still qualify for maximum CTR.

Calculating savings credit

22.19 The weekly amount of your savings credit depends on:

(a) the 'savings credit threshold' (table 22.2);

(b) the 'maximum savings credit' (table 22.2).

(c) your 'qualifying income' (para 22.20).

Table 22.2 Savings credit threshold and maximum: 2023-24

Threshold	
Single	£174.49
Couple	£277.12

Maximum	
Single	£15.94
Couple	£17.84

22.20 Your total income is the same as calculated for guarantee credit (para 22.18). Your 'qualifying income' is the same as your total income but excluding: new-style ESA and JSA, WTC, SDA, maternity allowance and maintenance payments for you or your partner from a former spouse.

22.21 Your savings credit is worked out as follows:

(a) if your qualifying income is less than or equal to the threshold you don't get savings credit;

(b) if your qualifying income is greater than the threshold:

- your savings credit is 60% of the difference up to the maximum, but

- if your total income exceeds your 'appropriate minimum guarantee' (para 22.11) your savings credit is reduced by 40% of the excess (until it is reduced to nil).

22.19   SPCA 3(2)-(4),(6),(7); PC 7; NISPCA 3(2)-(4),(6),(7); NIPC 7

T22.2   SPCA 3(7); PC 7(2); SI 2023/316; NISPCA 3(7); NIPC 7(2)

22.20   SPCA 3(6); PC 9; NISPCA 3(6); NIPC 9

22.21   SPCA 3(2)-(4),(6),(7); PC 7; NISPCA 3(2)-(4),(6),(7); NIPC 7

Help with housing costs: basic conditions

22.22   Your housing costs are included as an additional amount in your appropriate minimum guarantee (para 22.17) only if:

(a) your housing costs are the kind that are allowable (para 22.26); and

(b) you or your partner:

  ■   is liable for those costs (para 22.23), and

  ■   occupy the home for which those costs are paid (para 22.24); and

(c) the weekly amount of those costs is greater than any non-dependant deductions that apply in your case (para 22.37).

Liability for housing costs

22.23   You are liable for housing costs if you have a legal obligation or duty to pay them. You are treated as liable (whether you have actual liability or not) if:

(a) your partner is liable for them; or

(b) the liable person is not paying them; and

  ■   you (the claimant) must pay them to continue living there, and

  ■   it is reasonable in all the circumstances to treat you as liable for them; or

(c) you share those costs with other members of the household none of whom is a close relative (para 5.28) of you or your partner, and

  ■   one or more of those members is liable to meet those costs, and

  ■   it is reasonable in the circumstances to treat you as sharing responsibility.

See example where (b) might apply.

Example: Claimant treated as liable because the liable person is not paying

Karl gets guarantee credit; it does not include an amount for housing costs because he lives with his sister in her flat. His sister is buying the lease with a mortgage; she also makes service charge payments to the landlord on which her right to occupy depends. His sister dies, and her estate becomes liable to meet the mortgage and service charge payments. But she did not leave a will and her estate is not making any payments. The building society cannot transfer the mortgage to Karl until his sister's estate is settled, but it agrees that if he pays the mortgage he can continue living there. The landlord also agrees to accept service charge payments from Karl.

It is reasonable to treat Karl as liable for mortgage interest payments, and because he gets SPC he can apply for a DWP loan to pay these (volume 1, chapter 8). His SPC is also revised to include an additional amount for his service charge payments.

  ■   Adapted from DMG Volume 13 para 78215.

22.22   PC 6(6)(c), sch 2 para 1(1)(a),(b); NIPC 6(6)(c), sch 2 para 1(1)(a),(b)

22.23   PC sch 2 paras 1(1)(a),(b), 3; NIPC sch 2 paras 1(1)(a),(b), 3

Occupying the home

22.24   To get housing costs as an additional amount in your SPC you (the claimant) must be occupying the home for which those payments are made. You are treated as occupying the home if it is where you and your family normally live and this is decided in the same way as for HB (paras 3.2-4).

Moving home, two homes and temporary absence

22.25   As with HB, there are rules about when you can claim housing costs for two homes, during a temporary absence or if you move home. You are treated as occupying the home and can get a housing costs additional amount:

(a) if you are living in temporary accommodation while essential repairs are carried out, but only in respect of the dwelling you must make payments for, not both (para 3.13);

(b) during a period of temporary absence for up to 13 or, in some cases, 52 weeks (paras 3.5-12);

(c) on your new home for up to four weeks before you move if the delay is because you are:

- waiting for a disability adaptation (para 3.31), or

- waiting for local welfare assistance (para 3.33), or

- leaving care (para 3.36);

(d) on your previous home and your new home for up to four weeks if your liability for both is unavoidable (para 3.37);

(e) on your normal and your temporary home if your temporary absence:

- is due to fear of violence (para 3.14),

- because you are a student or trainee living at your term time address (para 2.45).

And in each case rules work in the same way as they do for HB but read as if 'housing costs' is substituted for rent (and the law is in the footnote for that para).

Allowable housing costs

22.26   Your housing costs are allowable if:

(a) they are one or more of the type of costs in table 22.3; and

(b) the charge (or part of it) isn't an excluded cost (para 22.29).

If you are a homeowner (including a long leaseholder or a shared owner) and make interest payments on a mortgage or loan secured on your home these costs aren't allowable, but you may be able to get a DWP loan towards these if you still qualify for guarantee credit: see volume 1, chapter 8.

22.24   PC sch 2 paras 1(1)(a),(b), 4(1),(2); NIPC sch 2 paras 1(1)(a),(b), 4(1),(2)

22.25   PC sch 2 para 4(3)-(13); NIPC sch 2 para 4(3)-(13)

22.26   PC sch 2 paras 1(1)(b), 5(1), 10, 13(1),(2); NIPC sch 2 paras 1(1)(b), 5(1), 10, 13(1),(2)

Table 22.3 **Allowable housing costs**

The following kinds of housing cost are allowable, to the extent that they aren't excluded (para 22.29). They are included as an additional amount in your 'appropriate minimum guarantee' (para 22.11):

(a) Rent or ground rent on a long tenancy

- A long tenancy is one where the lease is made by deed registered with the land registry and granted for a specified number of years, exceeding 21, or for a fixed term with a promise in the agreement for perpetual renewal (unless it is sub-let, and the original lease was for less than 21 years). It includes a lease granted for life because the law treats these as a 90-year agreement.

(b) Service charges if you are a homeowner or long leaseholder

- A service charge is eligible if it isn't excluded (para 22.29) and your right to occupy is conditional on you paying it (see also para 22.29 if you are a shared owner).

(c) Payments under a co-ownership scheme

- You are a co-owner if your home is let by a housing association (para 7.15) and under the terms of the agreement you are entitled to a payment based on the value of your home when you cease to be a member of the scheme. (See notes for the co-owner/shared owner distinction).

(d) Payments relating to a Crown tenancy or licence

- You are a Crown tenant/licensee if your landlord is the Crown or a government department, except if your home is managed by the Crown Estates Commission or the landlord is the Duchy of Cornwall or Lancaster (in which case you are eligible for HB: table 5.2).

(e) Rentcharges

- A rentcharge (or chief rent) is an annual fee paid by a freehold homeowner to a third party who has no other interest in the property. They are part of an historic system whereby the former land owner is entitled to a fee as a condition of them agreeing to release the land for development. No new rentcharges can be created after 21st July 1977.

(f) Payments for a tent and site fee

- If the dwelling you occupy as your home is a tent, housing costs are allowed for the tent and the pitch on which it stands.

Notes:

- A shared owner means someone who owns a fixed share in their home (typically 25, 50 or 75 per cent) and who rents the remaining share from their landlord (usually a housing association). A shared owner (unlike a co-owner) gets help with their service charges in HB instead of SPC (para 22.29).
- If you are a homeowner, long leaseholder or shared owner with a mortgage or loan secured on your home see para 22.5.

T22.3   PC sch 2 para 13(1)(a)-(f),(6)(a)-(d); NIPC sch 2 para 13(1)(a)-(f),(6)(a)-(d)

Service charges, estimated bills and final adjustments

22.27   Most service charges for long-leases/owner occupied dwellings are based on the landlord/managing agent's actual costs so the charge for each period is variable rather than a fixed amount. The usual practice is for the landlord/managing agent to send a bill based on the estimated costs with final adjustments being made some time after the end of the accounting period.

Length of award and how charges are attributed

22.28   Your housing costs are attributed to a fixed 52-week period from the date your liability first arose. At any one time your award may therefore be made up of housing costs arising from different liabilities notified at different times (para 22.27 and see example).

Examples: Service charge awards

Sora pays service charges on her home and these are eligible for SPC. Her landlord calculates them each financial year (1st April to 31st March) and sends Sora bills:

- in March for estimated charges for the following financial year; and
- in September for the finalised balance for the preceding financial year.

1. On 1st April 2021, Sora claims SPC. She sends the DWP the estimated bill for 2021-22. This is £432.00 for the year, equivalent to £8.31 pw over 52 weeks (paras 22.36, 22.38).

- The DWP awards Sora £8.31 pw for the 52 weeks in the period 1/4/21 to 30/3/22.

2. In March 2022, Sora sends the DWP the estimated bill for 2022-23. This is £565.00 for the year, equivalent to £10.87 pw over 52 weeks.

- The DWP awards Sora £10.87 pw for the 52 weeks in the period 31/3/22 to 29/3/23.

3. On 8th September 2022, Sora sends the DWP the finalised balance for 2021-22. This is £243.85, equivalent to £4.69 pw over 52 weeks.

- The DWP continues to award Sora £10.87 pw (from example 2) until 29/3/23.
- It additionally awards Sora £4.69 pw for the 52 weeks in the period 8/9/22 to 6/9/23.

4. In March 2023, Sora sends the DWP the estimated bill for 2023-24. This is £602.00 for the year, equivalent to £11.58 pw over 52 weeks.

- The DWP continues to award Sora £4.69 pw (from example 3) until 6/9/23.
- It additionally awards Sora £11.58 pw for the 52 weeks in the period 30/3/23 to 28/3/24.

Example adapted from DMG volume 13 para 78487.

22.28   PC sch 2 para 13(3); NIPC sch 2 para 13(3)

Excluded housing costs

22.29   Even if your housing costs are of the kind in table 22.3 they are nevertheless excluded from help if:

(a) they relate to a service charge that is eligible for HB (table 5.1). So, you can't get help with your service charges in your SPC if you are a shared owner (unless you are a co-owner), but you get help in your HB instead (para 7.24);

(b) any part of a charge that relates to business use (para 22.30) if the dwelling is part of a building that is partly residential and partly business;

(c) any charge for 'repairs and improvements' (para 22.31);

(d) any charge or part of a charge that relates to an ineligible service (para 22.32);

(e) any housing cost to the extent that it is considered excessive (paras 22.33-34).

Apportionment for business use

22.30   If your home forms part of a building that is liable for both business rates and council tax, your housing costs are in proportion to the residential part of the building only. That fraction is the current market value of the residential part of the building divided by the combined market values of the business and residential parts. If the building was built or converted before 1st April 1990 the rateable values (as at 31st March 1990) are used instead.

Repairs and improvements

22.31   Any charge that relates to 'repairs or improvements' is excluded from SPC. This includes a wide range of measures undertaken to maintain the fitness of the building for human habitation such as:

(a) provision of washing or sanitary facilities (bath, shower, lavatory) and drainage facilities;

(b) repairs to the heating system;

(c) provision of damp proof measures or insulation;

(d) provision of ventilation or natural lighting;

(e) provision of lighting or power sockets;

(f) repairs of unsafe structural defects;

(g) adapting the dwelling for the needs of a disabled person, or to provide additional bedrooms so that children or young persons of the opposite sex can sleep separately.

But if you are a homeowner or long leaseholder and have taken out a mortgage or secured loan for these you might be able to get DWP loan payments: see volume 1, chapter 8.

22.29   PC sch 2 paras 5(1), 10, 13(2)(a)-(c); NIPC sch 2 paras 5(1), 10, 13(2)(a)-(c)

22.30   PC sch 2 para 6(1)-(3); NIPC sch 2 para 6(1)-(3)

22.31   PC sch 2 paras 12(2), 13(2)(c); NIPC sch 2 paras 12(2), 13(2)(c)

Ineligible service charges

22.32 Any part of your housing costs for services that wouldn't be eligible for HB (paras 8.25 and 8.32) – including any service charge that isn't related to the provision of adequate accommodation: para 8.49 – is deducted from your weekly housing costs.

22.33 The deduction is decided as follows:

(a) if you are a Crown tenant and your rent includes a charge for water, that amount is deducted if it is known, or in any other case the likely amount;

(b) if the charge includes an amount for fuel that isn't separately identified:

- the standard amount as for HB (table 8.2) is deducted, unless

- you provide evidence of the actual or approximate amount that allows the charge to be estimated, in which case the deduction is that estimated amount;

(c) in any other case:

- if the charge is separately identified, that amount is deducted, otherwise

- the part of that payment that is 'fairly attributable' to the cost of providing that service having regard to the costs of comparable services.

Excessive housing costs

22.34 In the past if your allowable housing costs were considered excessive, the DWP could disallow the excess. This no longer applies except for some people who have been getting SPC since before April 2018.

Calculating your housing costs

22.35 Your housing costs are part of your minimum income guarantee (para 22.11). Because SPC is a weekly benefit your housing costs are converted to a weekly figure, even if you pay them over a different cycle (four-weekly, monthly, quarterly, etc).

Conversion to weekly figures

22.36 Where your housing costs are paid other than weekly, the weekly figure is calculated by dividing the yearly amount by 52. It is always 52 weeks, even in a year that has 53 weeks, or if there are period(s) in the year where no payment is due ('rent-free').

22.32-33   PC sch 2 para 13(2)(a),(b),(5); NIPC sch 2 para 13(2)(a),(b),(5)

22.34   LMI sch 5 para 4(c); NILMI sch 5 para 4(c)

22.35   PC sch 2 para 13(1); NIPC sch 2 para 13(1)

22.36   PC sch 2 para 13(3); NIPC sch 2 para 13(3)

Calculating your weekly housing costs

22.37   To calculate your weekly housing costs work through the following steps:

(a) start with the gross weekly figure and deduct the amount amount of ineligible charges;

(b) if part of building is used for business calculate the proportion of those costs that is attributable to residential use;

(c) if you are jointly responsible for payments, your eligible housing costs is the proportion (of (a) or (b)) that you are responsible for (but if a person you share liability with isn't paying you are treated as responsible for their share: para 22.23);

(d) deduct the appropriate weekly amount that applies for each non-dependant (para 22.39).

If the result from (d) is nil (or negative), then your appropriate minimum guarantee (para 22.11) doesn't include an amount for housing costs.

22.38   Where any part of the calculation (para 22.37) results in a fraction of a penny, that figure is rounded up to next whole penny, unless it involves the apportionment of a non-dependant charge (para 6.19(c)) in which case it is rounded (up or down) to the nearest penny.

Non-dependant deductions

22.39   All the rules about non-dependants that apply to pension age HB also apply to SPC. This includes the rules about: who 'resides with you' (paras 4.29-31), the situations when a deduction doesn't apply and the amount of the weekly deduction (tables 6.2 and 6.3). The only differences to HB are:

(a) if you are a shared owner and a deduction has been made from your HB no deduction is made from your SPC housing costs in respect of the same non-dependant;

(b) the following aren't counted as non-dependants:

▪ anyone aged under 20 and who you are responsible for,

▪ anyone who isn't a close relative (para 5.28) of you/your partner and who makes payments to you/your partner on a commercial basis (such as rent),

▪ anyone jointly liable for housing costs or a co-owner with you/your partner.

In the case of (b), in most situations the outcome is the same as for HB but there are very slight differences.

22.37   PC sch 2 paras 5(1), 6(2),(3),(5), 14; NIPC sch 2 paras 5(1), 6(2),(3),(5), 14

22.38   PC sch 2 paras 13(5), 15; NIPC sch 2 paras 13(5), 15

22.39   PC sch 2 para 14; NIPC sch 2 para 14

Other matters

When your SPC is paid

22.40 SPC is usually paid fortnightly or four weekly in arrears on the same day as your state pension, according to the last two digits of your national insurance number as follows:

(a) 00 to 19 – Monday

(b) 20 to 39 – Tuesday

(c) 40 to 59 – Wednesday

(d) 60 to 79 – Thursday

(e) 80 to 99 – Friday

But there are some exceptions to this, the main one being that if your SPC award started before 6th April 2010, it is usually paid weekly in advance on a Monday.

Your benefit week

22.41 Your benefit week is the seven days ending on your pay day if it is paid in arrears or starting on your pay day if it is paid in advance.

Time limit for claiming and backdating

22.42 The time limit for claiming SPC is three months from the date you first became entitled to it. If you claim within the time limit you get all the arrears: there are no further conditions, so you do not need to show 'good cause'. If you claim after the time limit you only get three months arrears. The time limit cannot be extended for any reason.

Advance claims: reaching pension age

22.43 You can make an advance claim for SPC up to four months before the date you reach pension age (and also for state pension). If you are on UC you can get an overlapping payment of your UC and SPC during the UC assessment period in which you become 66 (volume 1, chapter 11).

Appeals about SPC

22.44 Most decisions about your pension credit – including any additional amount for your housing costs – can be reconsidered and then appealed to a tribunal. The rules are similar to UC: the time limit is one month, and you must go through a mandatory reconsideration before you can appeal to a tribunal: see volume 1, chapter 14.

22.40   C&P87 22C, 22CA, 26B, 26BA; NIC&P87 22C, 22CA, 26B, 26BA

22.41   PC 1(1) – definition 'benefit week'; NIPC 1(1)

22.42   C&P87 19(2),(3)(i); NIC&P87 19(2),(3)(i)

22.43   C&P87 4E(2); PC 15(1)(za); NIC&P87 4D(2); NIPC 15(1)(za)

22.44   SI 1999/991 reg 3ZA; FTPR 22(2)-(4); NISR 1999/162 regs 3ZA, 31, 33

Planned changes

22.45   The government plans that payments that are eligible for pension age HB (typically rent: table 5.1) will become part of your eligible housing costs (table 22.3) when pension age HB is abolished; although this isn't expected to happen until April 2028 after all existing working age HB claims have been transferred to UC (table 1.3, planned changes).

Chapter 23 **Other help with housing costs**

- Discretionary housing payments (DHPs) towards your rent or service charges: see paras 23.1-19.
- Welfare supplementary payments in Northern Ireland: see paras 23.20-34.
- Local welfare assistance schemes: see paras 23.35-37.
- Direct payments to your landlord from your SPC or legacy benefits for rent arrears or hostel charges: see paras 23.38-56.

Discretionary housing payments

23.1   This section describes how the council/NIHE can award you a discretionary housing payment (DHP) if you are entitled to HB or a UC housing costs element and need further help towards your rent or related housing costs.

23.2   DHPs are legally separate from HB, but are administered by the same council/NIHE as HB.

The law and guidance on DHPs

23.3   The Acts of Parliament governing DHPs are the Child Support, Pensions and Social Security Act 2000 and its Northern Ireland equivalent. The details of the DHP scheme are in the Discretionary Financial Assistance Regulations 2001 and its Northern Ireland equivalent (see appendix 1). DWP guidance for councils is in its Discretionary Housing Payments Guidance manual (DHPGM) [www]. In Scotland, the Scottish Government is responsible for DHPs.

Who can get DHPs

23.4   To get a DHP you must meet the conditions in paras 23.5-6. DHPs are discretionary: the council doesn't have to award you a DHP even if you meet the conditions so you shouldn't rely on getting one. (But see para 23.9 in Scotland.)

Basic conditions

23.5   The basic conditions for getting a DHP are:

(a) you are entitled to HB or a UC housing costs element; and

(b) you 'appear… to require further financial assistance… in order to meet housing costs'.

There are also some restrictions on what a DHP can be used for (paras 23.10-11).

23.3   CPSA 69,70; Scotland Act 2016 s25 SI 2016/759 reg 3; NICPSA 60,61; SI 2001/1167; NISR 2001/216
        www.gov.uk/government/publications/discretionary-housing-payments-guidance-manual

23.5   DFA 2(1); NIDFA 2(1)

Requiring financial assistance

23.6   DHP law doesn't define what requiring 'some further financial assistance' means. The DWP says you usually need to demonstrate you 'are unable to meet housing costs from [your] available income' or 'have a shortfall as a result of the welfare reforms' (DHPGM 1.18-19). But your (and your family's) circumstances don't have to be 'exceptional' or causing you 'hardship'. And the council/NIHE shouldn't take account of any DLA mobility component you or your partner receive, or have a fixed rule or policy that it always takes account of any DLA care component or equivalent PIP component (Hardy v Sandwell MBC).

Housing costs

23.7   DHP law doesn't list which 'housing costs' you can get help with. They clearly include rent and any eligible service charges you pay (para 8.32). The DWP says (DHPGM 1.16, 4.1-18) they can also include rent in advance; deposits; and other lump sum costs associated with a housing need such as removal costs. But see para 23.11 for items that are excluded.

Uses for DHPs: Great Britain

23.8   In Great Britain DHPs can be used to help with:

(a)   reductions in your HB due to the following:

- the benefit cap (para 6.21),
- the social renter bedroom tax (para 9.4, 9.9) (and this is nearly always the case in Scotland: para 23.9),
- the LHA rules (para 10.4),
- the rent referral rules (para 10.31),
- the income taper (para 6.6),
- non-dependant deductions (para 6.9);

(b)   similar reductions in your UC (DWP circular G8/2016);

(c)   a shortfall in your rent to prevent your household becoming homeless while the housing authority explores other options;

(d)   a rent deposit or rent in advance if you are getting HB/UC on your present home and are waiting to move into a new home;

(e)   the gap between the end of your UC for housing costs and the start of your HB when you move into supported or temporary accommodation (table 17.3).

These are examples, and DHPs can be used in other situations. Examples (a) to (d) are based on DWP guidance (DHPGM 3.2) and for (e) see para 23.15.

23.7   R (Hardy) v Sandwell MBC [2015] EWHC 890 (Admin); www.bailii.org/ew/cases/EWHC/Admin/2015/890.html

Bedroom tax in Scotland

23.9   In Scotland you get a DHP regardless of your circumstances to cover the full reduction due to the social renter bedroom tax (para 9.9). The only exception is if you don't meet the basic conditions because your HB is reduced to nil after the reduction is applied. Apart from that, all the possibilities in para 23.8 apply.

Uses for DHPs: Northern Ireland

23.10   In Northern Ireland you can only get a DHP to help with:

(a) a shortfall between your eligible rent and your actual rent due to the LHA or rent referral rules (paras 10.4, 10.31);

(b) the loss of the family premium (para 12.24); or

(c) a reduction due to the benefit cap (to the extent that the reduction is not met by a WSP: para 23.23-28).

Exceptions

23.11   You can't get a DHP to help with any of the following:

(a) service charges that are ineligible for HB (para 8.32) or (if you aren't on HB) for UC;

(b) any charges for water, sewerage or allied environmental services;

(c) any liability for council tax, or in Northern Ireland rates;

(d) increases to cover rent arrears which are not eligible for HB (para 8.20);

(e) reductions in any benefit due to the recovery of an overpayment of HB/UC, or to sanctions relating to jobseekers, child support or benefit offences.

DHP claims

23.12   You can make your DHP claim in any way the council/NIHE agrees to (e.g. in writing or by telephone) or someone can claim on your behalf if this is reasonable. Some councils have a special DHP form you can use. You should provide information and evidence you are asked for when you claim. And if your circumstance change in a way that could affect your DHPs, you (and the person they are paid to if this is different) should tell the council/NIHE about this. In Scotland you can use the Scottish Government website to apply online [www].

DHP awards

23.13   DHPs can be awarded for a fixed period, an open-ended period or as a lump sum, but see paras 23.14-15 for limits. The council/NIHE can start or stop your award when it thinks fit. This means you may have to reclaim, possibly several times, if you need DHPs for more than a short period.

23.9   www.gov.scot/policies/social-security/support-with-housing-costs/

23.10   NIDFA 2(1)(a)-(d)

23.11   DFA 3(a),(aa),(b),(c),(f)-(p); NIDFA 3(a).(aa),(ab),(b)-(m)

23.12   DFA 5, 6; NIDFA 5, 6
         https://www.mygov.scot/discretionary-housing-payment/

23.13   DFA 5; NIDFA 5

DHP amounts and limits

23.14   When DHPs are awarded for a period, the following limits apply:

(a) if you are on HB, the weekly total of your DHP must not be greater than:

- your actual rent,

- minus any service/support charges that are ineligible for HB (para 8.32);

(b) if you are on UC, the monthly amount of your DHP must not be greater than your UC housing costs element. In other words, not greater than the monthly amount of:

- your actual rent,

- minus any service/support charges that are ineligible for UC (volume 1, chapter 6).

If you are on HB in supported or temporary accommodation (table 2.3) the limit (a) applies, but the law is not completely clear about this if you are also on UC.

23.15   The above limits don't apply when DHPs are awarded:

(a) as a lump sum (e.g. towards a deposit or rent in advance); or

(b) 'for past housing costs (arrears of rent) on the ground that [you are] currently receiving full housing benefit' (Gargett v Lambeth LBC) (and see DHPGM 4.1-4, 4.20).

Payments and overpayments

23.16   The council/NHE can pay your DHP to you, or to someone else if appropriate (e.g. someone acting on your behalf or your landlord). It also has a discretion to recover overpayments of DHPs that are due to you (or someone else) not giving correct information, or due to an error it has made.

Decisions, notifications and appeals

23.17   When you claim a DHP the council/NIHE must decide whether or not to award you one. It must give you written notice of its decision, including reasons, as soon as reasonably practicable. You can ask the council/NIHE to review its decision if you disagree with it, but the detailed rules about reconsiderations don't apply. You can't appeal to a tribunal, but in limited circumstances you may be able to apply for judicial review (para 20.54).

DHP expenditure: government grants and limits

23.18   In England and Wales the DWP makes grants to councils towards their expenditure on DHPs. This is separate from HB subsidy. The details are in the Discretionary Housing Payments (Grants) Order SI 2001/2340. In 2023-24 and 2024-25 the amounts for each English and Welsh council are in circular S1/2023 and the total is £100 million each year. The council has to claim this grant by 30th April in the following financial year, but doesn't have to submit audited accounts. In Scotland, grants to Scottish authorities are allocated by the Scottish Government. The total allocation for 2023-24 is £85.9 million (Scottish Budget 2023-24, table 5.16 [www]).

23.14   DFA 4(1),(2); NIDFA 4(1),(2)

23.15   R (Gargett) v Lambeth LBC [2008] EWCA Civ 1450; www.bailii.org/ew/cases/EWCA/Civ/2008/1450.htm

23.16   DFA 8; NIDFA 8

23.18-19 CPSA 70; SI 2001/2340; SI 2014/2918; SSI 2014/298; www.gov.scot/publications/scottish-budget-2023-24/pages/6/

23.19 The council doesn't have to spend the exact amount of its grant on DHPs; it can spend less or more. In England and Wales the maximum it can spend in any year is two and a half times the amount of its grant for that year. This limit doesn't apply in Scotland, and the Scottish Government provides funding to councils for the additional expenditure on the social renter size criteria (para 23.9).

Welfare supplementary payments in Northern Ireland

23.20 In Northern Ireland, welfare supplementary payments (WSPs) can help people affected by recent changes in HB and other social security benefits. This section describes how WSPs can help with your rent if your HB is reduced as a result of the benefit cap or the social renter size criteria ('bedroom tax'). WSPs are not part of the HB scheme and are administered by the DFC in conjunction with the NIHE.

The law and guidance on WSPs

23.21 The primary legislation governing WSPs is the Welfare Reform (Northern Ireland) Order SI 2015/2006.

23.22 Details about WSPs for the benefit cap are in the Welfare Supplementary Payments Regulations (Northern Ireland) 2016 NISR 2016/178 and the Welfare Supplementary Payment (Amendment) Regulations (Northern Ireland) 2017 NISR 2017/28. WSPs for the benefit cap end on 31st March 2025, but WSPs for the bedroom tax continue beyond that date.

23.23 Details about WSPs for the bedroom tax are in the Housing Benefit (Welfare Supplementary Payment) Regulations (Northern Ireland) 2017 NISR 2017/35.

WSPs for the benefit cap

23.24 The benefit cap is explained in paras 6.21-33. You qualify for benefit cap WSPs if:

(a) you are a lone parent or couple with at least one child or young person in your family (para 4.14);

(b) your HB is reduced as a result of the benefit cap;

(c) you have been entitled to 'welfare benefits' since 31st May 2016 or 7th November 2016 (para 23.25); and

(d) your home is in Northern Ireland (para 23.26).

23.25 'Welfare benefits' means any of the benefits in table 6.4(a). If you were a couple who separated on or after 31st May 2016 and met condition (a) or (b) when you separated, you continue to meet condition (a) and/or (b) whenever your former partner does.

23.21   SI 2015/2006 arts 137, 137A; NISR 2016/178 (as amended by NISR 2016/389); NISR 2017/28 part 2; NISR 2017/35

23.22   NISR 2016/178 reg 4(6)

23.24-28   NISR 2016/178 regs 1-4A, 13-16

23.26   You can only get benefit cap WSPs if you are present and normally resident in Northern Ireland. But during a temporary absence from Northern Ireland you can get them for:

(a)   up to 13 weeks if your absence is to receive medical treatment; or

(b)   up to four weeks if your absence is for any other reasons;

so long as your absence is unlikely to exceed 52 weeks. And you can only get them for the first four weeks you are in prison (in Northern Ireland or elsewhere).

23.27   WSPs for the benefit cap are awarded from the first day your HB is reduced as a result of it. To begin with, they equal the amount of your benefit cap reduction (table 6.4), so you don't lose any money. After that, they go down if your benefit cap reduction goes down, but can never go up.

23.28   WSPs for the benefit cap end when your HB ends or (if earlier) if your benefit cap reduction ends or (in all cases) on 31st March 2025, and can never start again.

WSPs for the bedroom tax

23.29   The bedroom tax (para 9.9) was introduced on 20th February 2017. WSPs can be awarded whenever your HB is affected by size criteria (paras 23.30-32).

23.30   You qualify for bedroom tax WSPs if:

(a)   you rent from the NIHE or a registered housing association;

(b)   your HB is reduced because your home has more bedrooms than the bedroom tax allows (table 11.1); and

(c)   your home is in Northern Ireland (the rules about temporary absence are the same as for HB: para 3.5).

You can't get bedroom tax WSPs if you rent from any other landlord.

23.31   Bedroom tax WSPs are awarded from the first day your HB is reduced as a result of the bedroom tax. They equal the amount of the reduction in your HB (paras 8.12-13), so you don't lose any money. Whenever the reduction in your HB goes up or down, your bedroom tax WSPs go up or down by the same amount. They continue for as long as you qualify for them, and start again whenever you qualify for them again.

WSP awards and appeals

23.32   You are awarded WSPs without having to make a claim. The DFC uses information provided by the NIHE, and by your landlord if you rent from a registered housing association. You can ask the DFC to review your award if you think it is wrong. You can't appeal to a tribunal but may be able to apply for judicial review (para 20.54).

23.29-31   NISR 2017/28 regs 1-7, 14

23.32   NISR 2016/178 reg 2; NISR 2017/28 regs 2(1),(5), 7, 15

WSP payments and overpayments

23.33 WSPs are paid four weekly in arrears. They are paid to you (or someone on your behalf) or to your landlord or agent if your HB is paid to them (but not a private landlord/agent unless they are registered with the Landlord Registration Scheme).

23.34 Overpayments of WSPs are nearly always recoverable – from you and/or the person they were paid to. The methods include making deductions from future payments of WSPs, HB, some other social security benefits, or earnings.

Local welfare assistance/discretionary support

23.35 You may be able to get help from:

(a) a local welfare assistance scheme in England;

(b) the Welsh Discretionary Assistance Fund;

(c) the Scottish Welfare Fund; or

(d) discretionary support in Northern Ireland.

These are not part of the HB scheme. In England they are administered by local councils under their general power to promote well-being. In Scotland, local councils administer the funds according to national rules and guidance. In Wales and Northern Ireland the funds are administered by the national government or their agents.

23.36 To get help you normally have to be 'in need' and without the money to meet the need. But the schemes and funds are discretionary, so you have no right to help. Payments can be a grant or a loan but many councils provide help only (or mainly) on a non-cash basis. In general terms you may be able to get help to:

(a) avoid becoming homeless;

(b) avoid entering institutional care (e.g. residential care, hospital or prison);

(c) set up home after leaving institutional care; or

(d) meet a crisis and avoid harm.

23.37 In Scotland you can't get a grant or loan for rent or mortgage payments, rent in advance, repair costs or any housing costs that could be covered by a DHP. Similar exclusions apply in Northern Ireland but you may get a loan for rent in advance to secure a tenancy [www]. In England local councils set their own rules but in practice similar exclusions are likely to apply.

23.33-34   NISR 2016/178 regs 4(7)-(9), 11; NISR 2017/28 regs 4-13, schs 1, 2; NISR 2017/35 regs 4-13, schs 1, 2

23.35   England: Localism Act 2011, s1;   Scotland: The Welfare Funds (Scotland) Act 2015; SSI 2016/107
Wales: Government of Wales Act 2006, s70;   Northern Ireland: NIWRO 135; NISR 2016/270

23.36-37   Scotland: https://www.mygov.scot/scottish-welfare-fund/
Wales: https://gov.wales/discretionary-assistance-fund-daf
Northern Ireland: https://www.nidirect.gov.uk/articles/extra-financial-support

Direct payments from DWP benefits

23.38   This section describes how the DWP can make deductions from your SPC/JSA/ESA/IS and pay them direct to your landlord to cover your rent arrears and/or any hostel charges not covered by your HB. It gives the rules for Great Britain. Similar rules apply in Northern Ireland but some of the details differ.

23.39   Direct payments are not part of the HB scheme, but are administered by the DWP, and in Northern Ireland by the DFC. The DWP/DFC call them 'third party payments'.

The law and guidance on direct payments

23.40   The law about direct payments is in schedule 9 of the Social Security (Claims and Payments) Regulations SI 1987/1968 and schedule 8A of its Northern Ireland equivalent (see appendix 1). DWP guidance for landlords and mortgage lenders is in *How to Apply for Third Party Payments* and the *Third Party Payments Creditor/Supplier Handbook* [www]. Guidance for councils is in GM D1.570-689.

What direct payments can be used for

23.41   The DWP can make direct payments:

(a) to your landlord towards arrears of rent including service charges;

(b) to your landlord, if you live in a hostel, towards essential services that are not eligible for HB;

(c) to your utility supplier to cover fuel and/or water charges and certain other debts.

They are designed to encourage your landlord to let you stay in your home rather than evict you because of arrears. They cannot be used to repay rent arrears on your former home. This guide does not give the rules about direct payments for utility bills and other debts, except to the extent that these charges are included in your rent, but these are listed in para 23.56).

When direct payments can be made

23.42   The basic conditions for making direct payments are in para 23.43 and further details are in the rest of this section. But direct payments are discretionary. This means the DWP doesn't have to make them even if all the conditions are met, though in practice it usually does.

Basic conditions

23.43   The DWP can only make direct payments if:

(a) you or your partner get a qualifying benefit (para 23.44);

(b) you or your partner also get HB (or you live in a hostel and have made a claim for HB); and

(c) the direct payments are for the dwelling you occupy as your home.

There are also further conditions for each kind of direct payment: see paras 23.46-49.

23.40   C&P87 35(1) and sch 9; NIC&P87 34A(1) and sch 8A
             https://tinyurl.com/creditordeductions

23.43   C&P87 sch 9; NIC&P87 sch 8A

Qualifying benefits

23.44 Direct payments can only be made if you or your partner are:

(a) on state pension credit (SPC) – whether this is guarantee credit or savings credit or both;

(b) on income support (IS);

(c) on income-based JSA;

(d) on income-related ESA;

(e) on new-style JSA and are also entitled to JSA(IB) at the same rate; or

(f) on new-style ESA and are also entitled to ESA(IR) at the same rate.

The last two apply because in these circumstances you are paid new-style JSA/ESA rather than JSA(IB)/ESA(IR).

Direct payments if you get universal credit

23.45 The rules in this section (paras 23.38-56) don't apply if you are on UC, including if you are on UC and HB because you live in supported or temporary accommodation (table 2.3); the UC direct payment rules apply instead (volume 1, chapter 12).

Benefits from which deductions can be made

23.46 When the DWP makes a direct payment, it deducts the same amount from your qualifying benefit (para 23.44). But if the amount of your SPC, IS or JSA(IB) is insufficient to make the deduction, the DWP can make it from any retirement pension, JSA(C), incapacity benefit or severe disablement allowance you or your partner get (whether this is paid separately or together with your SPC/IS/JSA(IB)).

Direct payments for rent arrears

23.47 The DWP can make direct payments to your landlord for rent arrears if:

(a) you meet the basic conditions (para 23.43);

(b) you have rent arrears (para 23.48) of:

- at least four times your weekly rent, or

- if you live in a hostel (para 7.26) at least £100; and

(c) either:

- the arrears have accrued or persisted over at least eight weeks and your landlord has requested direct payments, or

- they have accrued or persisted over less than eight weeks and the DWP considers it is in your and your family's overriding interests to make direct payments, or

- you live in a hostel and are eligible for direct payments of service charges (para 23.49).

When this applies to you, your HB must also be paid to your landlord (para 18.28).

23.43-44 C&P87 sch 9 para 1(1) definition: 'specified benefit', (2),(3); NIC&P87 para 1(1)-(3)

23.45 C&P87 1(3); NIC&P87 1(3)

23.46 C&P87 sch 9 para 5(1),(1A),(2); NIC&P87 para 5(1)(1A),(2)

23.47 C&P87 sch 9 paras 1(1) definition: 'rent', 5(7); NIC&P87 para 5(7)

23.48   For the above purposes (para 23.47), both 'rent' (also called 'gross rent') and 'rent arrears':

(a) include all the following (whether or not they are eligible for HB):

- your rent (or licence fee, etc: table 5.1),
- any service or other charges included in your rent, and
- any separate charge made by your landlord for water or services;

(b) but do not include:

- any fuel charge that is not eligible for HB and varies more than twice a year,
- any unpaid non-dependant charge, or
- any unpaid amount relating to a former home.

The amounts in (b) are also ignored when calculating the period over which your rent arrears have accrued or persisted.

Direct payments for hostel charges

23.49   The DWP can make direct payments to your landlord for hostel charges if:

(a) you meet the basic conditions (para 23.43) – but see para 23.45 if you live in supported or temporary accommodation;

(b) you live in a hostel (para 7.26); and

(c) your hostel charges include an amount for fuel, meals, laundry and/or cleaning (other than communal areas).

This can apply whether or not you have arrears of rent or other charges. When it does apply, your HB must also be paid to your landlord (para 18.28).

Amounts deducted from your benefits

23.50   Paras 23.51-53 explain how much is deducted from your social security benefit and paid to your landlord as a direct payment. Paras 23.54-56 give the limits that can affect this.

23.51   All the amounts in the rest of this section are given as weekly figures. The standard amount of £4.25 (para 23.52) is 5% of the personal allowance for a single person aged 25-plus (table 12.1) rounded up to the next multiple of 5p. It only changes when the personal allowance changes.

Amount for rent arrears

23.52   The amount deducted as a direct payment for rent or mortgage arrears is:

(a) the standard amount of £4.25; plus

(b) (in rent arrears cases) the amount of any fuel and/or water charges that are included in your rent and that aren't eligible for HB.

Once all your rent arrears are cleared, the amount in (b) can continue to be deducted as a direct payment if this is in the 'interests of [your] family'.

23.48   C&P87 sch 9 para 5(1),(1A),(2); NIC&P87 sch 8A para 5(1),(1A),(2)

23.49   C&P87 SI 1987/1968 sch 9 para 4A; NIC&P87 sch 8A para 4A

23.51   C&P87 sch 9 paras 1(1) definition: '5%', 3(2),5(6); NIC&P87 sch 8A paras 1(1),3(2),5(6)

23.52   C&P87 sch 9 paras 2,5(6),(7); NIC&P87 sch 8A paras 2,5(6),(7)

Amount for hostel charges

23.53   The amount deducted as a direct payment for hostel charges equals the amount of your charges for fuel, meals, laundry and/or cleaning (other than communal areas). This is calculated as described in para 8.28 and table 10.4(g) or, if your HB hasn't yet been awarded, the DWP should estimate it.

Limits to amounts for rent arrears

23.54   Once the amount for rent arrears has been calculated (para 23.52):

(a) it is reduced whenever necessary to leave you receiving 10p a week of your qualifying benefit (para 23.44);

(b) if it is higher than 25% of:

- your qualifying benefit's applicable amount,

- plus (if you are on CTC) your CTC and child benefit,

it is reduced to that 25% unless you consent to a higher amount.

Limits when there is more than one direct payment

23.55   Amounts can be deducted from your DWP benefits to make direct payments for other purposes, and in many cases they equal or include a standard amount of £4.25. If more than one direct payment applies to you:

(a) the maximum deduction for standard amounts is £12.75 (3 x £4.25);

(b) the total deduction is reduced whenever necessary to leave you receiving 10p a week of your qualifying benefit (para 23.44).

23.56   If the above limits mean that only some direct payments can be made, they are made in the following order of priority:

(a) rent or mortgage arrears;

(b) fuel;

(c) water;

(d) council tax;

(e) unpaid fines;

(f) child support;

(g) repayments of refugee integration loan;

(h) loan repayments to certain affordable credit lenders (credit unions);

(i) tax credit overpayment debts and self assessment debts.

23.53   C&P87 sch 9 para 4A(3); NIC&P87 sch 8A para 4A(3)

23.54   C&P87 sch 9 para 2(2); NIC&P87 sch 8A para 2(2)

23.55-56   C&P87 sch 9 paras 8,9; NIC&P87 sch 8A paras 8,9

Appendix 1 **Legislation**

England, Wales and Scotland

Main primary legislation (Acts)

The Social Security Contributions and Benefits Act 1992

The Social Security Administration Act 1992

The Child Support, Pensions and Social Security Act 2000

The Welfare Reform Act 2007

The Welfare Reform Act 2012

The Welfare Reform and Work Act 2016

Main secondary legislation (Regulations and Orders)

SI 2006/213	The Housing Benefit Regulations 2006
SI 2006/214	The Housing Benefit (Persons who have attained the qualifying age for state pension credit) Regulations 2006
SI 2006/217	The Housing Benefit and Council Tax Benefit (Consequential Provisions) Regulations 2006
SI 1997/1984	The Rent Officers (Housing Benefit Functions) Order
SI 1997/1995	The Rent Officers (Housing Benefit Functions) (Scotland) Order
SI 1998/562	The Income-related Benefits (Subsidy to Authorities) Order 1998
SI 2001/1002	The Housing Benefit and Council Tax Benefit (Decisions and Appeals) Regulations
SI 2001/1167	The Discretionary Financial Assistance Regulations
SI 2014/1230	The Universal Credit (Transitional Provisions) Regulations 2014

Recent secondary legislation: housing benefit

The following is a list of amendments etc (or otherwise relevant) to the main regulations from 4th April 2022. This list is up to date as at 10th April 2023.

SI 2022/449   The Social Security and Council Tax Reduction Schemes (Amendment) Regulations 2022

SI 2022/530   The Social Security (Disability Assistance for Working Age People) (Consequential Amendments) (No 2)) Order 2022

SI 2022/907   The Renting Homes (Wales) Act 2016 (Consequential Amendments to Secondary Legislation) Regulations 2022

SI 2022/942   The Housing Benefit and Universal Credit (Victims of Domestic Abuse and Victims of Modern Slavery) (Amendment) Regulations 2022

SI 2022/990   The Social Security (Habitual Residence and Past Presence) (Amendment) (No 2) Regulations 2022

SI 2023/6   The Rent Officers (Housing Benefit and Universal Credit Functions) (Modification) Order 2023

SI 2023/134   The Bereavement Benefits (Remedial) Order 2023

SI 2023/316   The Social Security Benefits Up-rating Order 2023

SI 2023/335   The Benefit Cap (Annual Limit) (Amendment) Regulations 2023

Other secondary legislation

SI 2022/752   The Universal Credit (Transitional Provisions) (Amendment) Regulations 2022

Northern Ireland

Main primary legislation (Acts and Acts of Northern Ireland Assembly)

The Social Security Contributions and Benefits (Northern Ireland) Act 1992

The Social Security Administration (Northern Ireland) Act 1992

The Child Support, Pensions and Social Security Act (Northern Ireland) 2000

The Welfare Reform Act (Northern Ireland) 2007

The Welfare Reform Act (Northern Ireland) 2015

The Welfare Reform (Northern Ireland) Order SI 2015/2006

The Welfare Reform and Work (Northern Ireland) Order 2016 SI 2016/999

Main secondary legislation (Statutory Rules and Orders)

NISR 2006/405   The Housing Benefit Regulations (Northern Ireland) 2006

NISR 2006/406   The Housing Benefit (Persons who have attained the qualifying age for state pension credit) Regulations (Northern Ireland) 2006

NISR 2006/407   The Housing Benefit (Consequential Provisions) Regulations (Northern Ireland) 2006

NISR 2008/100   The Housing Benefit (Executive Determinations) Regulations (Northern Ireland) 2008

NISR 2001/213   The Housing Benefit (Decisions and Appeals) Regulations (Northern Ireland) 2001

NISR 2001/216   The Discretionary Financial Assistance Regulations (Northern Ireland) 2001

NISR 2016/226   The Universal Credit (Transitional Provisions) Regulations (Northern Ireland) 2016

Recent secondary legislation: housing benefit

The following is a list of amendments etc (or otherwise relevant) to the main regulations from 4th April 2022. This list is up to date as at 10th April 2023.

NISR 2022/172   The Income-Related Benefits (Local Welfare Provision Disregard) (Amendment) Regulations (Northern Ireland) 2022

NISR 2022/202   The Social Security (Amendment) Regulations (Northern Ireland) 2022

NISR 2022/211   The Housing Benefit and Universal Credit (Victims of Domestic Abuse and Victims of Modern Slavery) (Amendment) Regulations (Northern Ireland) 2022

NISR 2022/230   The Social Security (Habitual Residence and Past Presence) (Amendment No 2) Regulations (Northern Ireland) 2022

NISR 2022/236   The Parental Bereavement Leave and Pay (Consequential Amendments to Subordinate Legislation) (No 2) Regulations (Northern Ireland) 2022

NISR 2023/4   The Housing Benefit and Universal Credit Housing Costs (Executive Determinations) (Modification) Regulations (Northern Ireland) 2023

SI 2023/134   The Bereavement Benefits (Remedial) Order 2023

NISR 2023/42   The Benefit Cap (Annual Limit) (Amendment) Regulations (Northern Ireland) 2023

NISR 2023   The Social Security Benefits Up-rating Order (Northern Ireland) 2023

Other secondary legislation

NISR 2022/194   The Universal Credit (Transitional Provisions) (Amendment) Regulations (Northern Ireland) 2022

Appendix 2 **Selected weekly benefit rates from April 2023**

	£
Attendance allowance	
Higher rate	101.75
Lower rate	68.10
Bereavement support payment	
(higher rate)	80.77
(standard rate)	23.08
Child benefit	
Only or older/oldest child	24.00
Each other child	15.90
Carer's allowance	
Claimant	76.75
Disability living allowance	
Care component	
Highest rate	101.75
Middle rate	68.10
Lowest rate	26.90
Mobility component	
Higher rate	71.00
Lower rate	26.90
Employment and support allowance (new style)	
Personal allowances	
Aged under 25	67.20
Aged 25 or over	84.80
Components	
Work-related activity	33.70
Support	44.70
Guardian's allowance	20.40

£

Industrial injuries disablement benefit

20% disabled	41.52
For each further 10% disability up to 100%	20.76
100% disabled	207.60

Jobseeker's allowance (new style)

Aged under 25	67.20
Aged 25 or over	84.80

Maternity and paternity pay and allowance

Statutory maternity, paternity and adoption pay	172.48
Maternity allowance	172.48

Personal independence payment

Daily living component

Enhanced rate	101.75
Standard rate	68.10

Mobility component

Enhanced rate	71.00
Standard rate	26.90

Retirement pension

New state pension (flat rate)	203.85
Old state pension (basic pension)	156.20
Old state pension spouse or civil partner's insurance (basic pension)	93.60

Severe disablement allowance

Basic rate	92.20

Age-related addition

Higher rate	13.80
Middle and lower rate	7.65

Statutory sick pay

Standard rate	109.40

Widow's/widower's benefits (for deaths before 6th April 2017)

Widowed parent's allowance (standard rate)	139.10
Widow's pension (standard rate)	139.10

For details of other benefit rates from April 2023 (including means-tested benefits, tax credits and war pensions) see Circulars A1/2023 and A2/2023.

Appendix 3 **Equivalent CTR footnote references**

Table A: England

This table shows the equivalent footnote references for the law on council tax rebates in England for chapters 12-15 of this guide

	Prescribed Requirements (SI 2012 No. 2885)	**Default Scheme (SI 2012 No. 2886)**
12.5	sch 1 para 6(1)(a), sch 2 para 1	25(1)(a), 26(1)(a), sch 2 para 1, sch 3 para 1
T12.1	sch 2 paras 1-3, 20; SI 2023/16 reg 7	sch 2 paras 1-3, 12, sch 3 paras 1-4, 17, 23, 24
12.6	sch 2 para 1; SI 2021/29 reg 7	—
12.7	—	26(1)(a), sch 3 para 1(1)(a),(b),(2),(3)
12.8	—	26(1)(a), sch 3 para 1(1)(c)
12.9	sch 1 para 6(1)(b), sch 2 para 2(1)	25(1)(b), 26(1)(b), sch 2 para 2(1), sch 3 para 3(1)
12.10-11	sch 1 para 6(1)(b); SI 2017/1305 reg 7	25(1)(b), 26(1)(b)
12.12	sch 1 para 6(1C); SI 2017/1305 reg 17	—
12.13	sch 1 para 6(1A)-(1C)	—
12.14	sch 1 para 6(1B),(1C)	—
12.17	SI 2017/1305 reg 17	—
12.18	SI 2017/1305 reg 17(4)-(9)	—
12.19	sch 1 para 6(1)(c),(d), sch 2 paras 3, 6-9	25(1)(c),(d), 26(1)(c),(d), sch 2 paras 3, 6-9, sch 3 paras 4, 11-14
12.22	sch 2 paras 8, 12(3)	sch 2 paras 8, 12(3), sch 3 para 13, 17(3)
12.23	sch 2 paras 7, 12(2)	sch 2 paras 7, 12,(2), sch 3 para 12, 17(5)
12.24	sch 1 para 6(1)(c), sch 2 para 3; SI 2015/2041 regs 2(4)(b), 3	25(1)(c), 26(1)(c), sch 2 para 3, sch 3 para 4
12.25	sch 2 para 6	sch 2 para 6, sch 3 para 11
12.26	sch 2 para 12(1)(a)	sch 2 para 12(1)(a), sch 3 para 17(2)(a)
12.27	sch 2 para 12(1)(b)	sch 2 para 12(1)(b), sch 3 para 17(2)(b)
12.28	sch 2 para 6(7)(d),(8)	sch 2 para 6(7)(d),(8), sch 3 para 11(5)(b),(6),(7)
12.29-31	sch 2 para 9(1),(2)	sch 2 para 9(1),(2), sch 3 para 14(1),(2)
12.30	sch 2 para 12(4)	sch 2 para 12(4), sch 3 para 17(4)
12.32	sch 2 para 11	sch 2 para 11, sch 3 para 16
12.33	sch 2 para 11	sch 2 para 11, sch 3 para 16
12.37	—	sch 3 paras 9, 10(8)
12.38	—	sch 3 para 17(1)
12.39	—	sch 3 para 10(1)(a)
12.40	—	sch 3 para 12(1)(a)-(c)
12.41	—	sch 3 para 12(1)(b)-(c)

12.42	—	sch 3 paras 18, 21, 22
12.43	—	sch 3 paras 18, 19
12.44	—	sch 3 paras 20(2), 23, 24
12.46	—	sch 3 paras 2, 18, 19
12.50	—	sch 3 paras 25, 26, 28
12.52	8(1)	8(1)
T12.2(a)	sch 2 paras 6(7)(a)-(c), 12(1)(b)(i)	sch 2 paras 6(7)(a)-(c), 12(1)(b)(i), sch 3 paras 10(1)(a)(iii)-(v), 11(5)(a), 12(1)(b),(c),(3), 17(2)(b)
T12.2(b)	sch 2 paras 7(1)(a),(b), 8(a)	sch 2 paras 7(1)(a),(b), 8(a), sch 7 paras 12(1)(b),(c), 13(a)
T12.2(c)	sch 2 para 9(2)(b)	sch 2 para 9(2)(b), sch 7 para 14(2)(b),(4)(b)
12.53	sch 2 paras 7(2), 8(c)	sch 2 paras 7(2), 8(c), sch 3 paras 12(2), 13(c)
12.54	sch 2 para 6(4),(5)	sch 2 para 6(4),(5), sch 3 para 10(1)(a)(vii),(2)
12.55	sch 2 para 10	sch 2 para 10, sch 3 para 15
13.1	sch 1 paras 16(1),(2), 24(1)(a),(b)	39(1),(2), 57(1)(a),(b)
13.2	sch 1 para 11	33, sch 8 para 25
13.3	sch 1 para 13	38, sch 7 para 14, sch 8 paras 8, 9
13.4	sch 1 para 17(9)-(11), sch 4, sch 5	40(9)-(11), 52(2), 54(2), 61(2), sch 5, sch 6, sch 7, sch 8
13.5	sch 1 para 13	35, sch 7 para 14, sch 8 paras 8, 9
13.6	sch 1 paras 17(1),(7), 24(1)	40(1),(7), 49(1),(2), 57(1)
13.7	sch 1 paras 17(1),(7), 24(1)	40(1),(7), 49(1),(2), 57(1)
13.8	sch 1 paras 17(1), 24(1)	40(1), 47-49, 57(1)
T13.1	sch 1 paras 16(1), 17(11), sch 5	39(1), 40(11), 54(2), sch 6, sch 8
T13.1(a)-(c)	sch 1 paras 13,16(1)(j)(zi)	35, 37, sch 8 paras 8, 9
T13.1(d)-(f)	sch 1 para 16(1)(j)(i)-(v)	39(1)(j)(i)-(v), sch 8 paras 11,14
T13.1(g)	sch 1 para 16(1)(j)(xiii)	39(1)(j)(xiii)
T13.1(h)	sch 1 para 16(1)	39(1)
T13.1(i)	sch 1 para 16(1)(j)(vi)	39(1)(j)(vi), sch 8 para 66
T13.1(j)	sch 1 para 16(j)(vii)	39(1)(j)(vii), sch 8 para 52
T13.1(k)	sch 1 para 16(1)(j)(x)	39(1)(j)(x), sch 8 para 38
T13.1(l)	sch 1 para 16(j)(ix)	39(1)(j)(ix), sch 8 para 37(a), sch 10 para 25(a)
T13.1(n)	sch 1 para 16(1)(j)(xx)-(xxvii)	No equivalent
T13.1(o)	sch 1 para 16(1)	39(1), sch 8 para 51, sch 10 paras 47, 48
T13.1(p)	sch 1 para 16(1)	2(1), 39(1), sch 8 paras 2, 3, 18, 52, 63
T13.1(q)	sch 1 para 16(1)(u)	2(1), 39(1)(u), sch 8 para 12
T13.2(a)-(m)	sch 1 para 16(1)(b),(c),(j)	39(1)(b),(c),(j), 49(1),(3), 54(1)
T13.2(n)	sch 5 paras 7, 8	sch 6 paras 7, 8, sch 8 para 21
T13.2(o)	sch 1 para16(1)(j)(v),(n), sch 5 para 2	2(1), 39(1)(j)(v),(n), sch 6 para 2, sch 8 para 14

13.11	sch 1 paras 16(1)(j), 17(7)	39(1)(j), 40(7), 49(1),(2), 54(1)
13.12	sch 1 paras 16(1)(b), 24	39(1)(b),(3), 49(1), 54(1),(5), 59, 64(10), 67(4)(g),(h)
13.13	sch 6 para 28	sch 9 para 28
13.14	sch 1 paras 14(2)(a), 17(7)	36(2)(a), 40(7)
T13.3	sch 1 para 14(2)-(5)	36(2)-(5)
13.15	sch 1 para 14(1)	36(1)
13.16	sch 1 para 16(1)(e)-(h),(l)-(m), sch 5 para 1	39(1)(e)-(h),(l)-(m), sch 6 para 1, sch 8 para 20
13.18	See Volume 1 para 16.9	See Volume 1 para 16.9
T13.4	2(1), sch 1 paras 16(1)(e)-(h),(l)-(m), 24(1)(a), sch 5 paras 1-6	2(1), 39(1)(e)-(h),(l)-(m), 49(1), 54(1), 57(1)(a), sch 6 paras 1-6, sch 8 paras 13, 14, 20, 54-56
13.20	sch 1 paras 16(1)(j)(viii), 24(1)(a), sch 5 para 13	39(1)(j)(viii), 54(1), 57(1)(a), sch 6 para 13, sch 8 para 53
13.21	sch 1 paras 16(2)-(4), 24(1)(a)	39(2)-(4), 54(1),(4),(5), 57(1)(a)
13.22	sch 1 para 16(3)	39(2), 54(1),(4),(5)
13.25	sch 1 para 16(1)	2(1), 39(1), sch 8 paras 30-34, 59
T13.5(a)-(f)	sch 1 para 16(1)	2(1), 39(1), sch 8 paras 30-34, 59
T13.5(g)-(h)	sch 1 para 16(1)	39(1), sch 8 para 59
T13.5(i)	sch 1 para 16(1)	39(1), sch 8 para 65
T13.5(j)	sch 1 para 16(1)	2(1) definition 'occasional assistance', 39(1)(j)(ix), sch 8 para 37(b)
T13.5(k)	sch 1 para 16(1)	39(1), sch 8 para 64
T13.5(l)	sch 1 para 16(1)	39(1), sch 8 para 45
13.27	2(1), sch 1 paras 16(1)(c),(d),(t),(x), 17(13), 18(2), 24(1)(a)	2(1), 39(1)(c),(d),(t),(x), 40(13), 41(2), 49(1), 51(2), 57(1)(a), sch 8 para 4
13.29	sch 1 para 24(1)	49(1), 57(1)
13.30	sch 1 para 16(1)	39(1), sch 8 para 19(1)(a),(b),(2)
13.32	sch 1 paras 16(1)(d), 17(13)	39(1)(d), 40(13), 55(2), sch 8 para 4
13.33	sch 1 paras 16(1)(d), 17(13), sch 5 para 11,	39(1)(d), 40(13), 55(2), sch 6 para 11, sch 8 para 4
T13.6	sch 1 para 16(1)(o), sch 5 para 20	39(1)(o), 49(1), sch 6 para 20, sch 8 paras 49, 50
T13.7(a)	sch 1 para 16(1)	39(1), sch 8 para 25
T13.7(b)	2(1), sch 1 para 16(1)(p), sch 5 para 9	2(1), 39(1)(p), sch 6 para 9, sch 8 para 27
T13.7(c)	sch 1 para 16(1)(v), sch 5 para 10	39(1)(v), sch 6 para 10, sch 8 para 26
T13.8(a)	—	sch 8 paras 4, 22(2),(3)
T13.8(b)	sch 1 para 16(1), sch 5 para 23	39(1), 64(5), sch 6 para 23, sch 8 paras 4, 22(1)
13.34	sch 1 para 16(1)(w),(5)	39(1)(w),(5)
13.35	sch 1 para 16(1)	39(1), sch 8 para 35
13.36(c)	sch 1 para 16(1)(i), sch 5 para 12	39(1)(i), 49(1), sch 6 para 12, sch 8 para 19(1)(c)
13.37	sch 1 para 16(1)	39(1), 74
13.38	—	20, 24, 73(1), 75(1),(4),(6), 81(1),(6)

13.39	—	73(1), 81(1)(a)(ii),(b)(ii), 83, 84
T13.9	—	54(6)-(9), 73(1), 81
13.40	—	80
T13.10	—	54(6)-(9), 73(1), 76
13.41	—	73(1), 82, 85(2)
13.43	—	2(1), sch 8 para 61, sch 10 para 54
13.44	sch 1 para 16(1)	39(1), 49(1), sch 8 para 4
13.46	sch 1 para 17(13)	40(13), sch 8 para 4
13.47	sch 4 para 7, sch 6 paras 18, 19	sch 5 para 7, sch 6 paras 18, 19, sch 7 para 13, sch 8 paras 23, 24
13.48	sch 1 para 16(1)(k), 40(8), sch 4 para 11, sch 5 paras 16, 17	39(1)(k), 40(8), sch 5 para 11, sch 6 paras 16, 17, sch 7 paras 15, 16, sch 8 paras 29, 39
13.49	sch 5 para 12(3)(b),(c)	sch 6 para 12(3)(b),(c), sch 8 para 40
T13.11(a)	sch 1 para 16(1)	39(1), sch 8 para 5
T13.11(b)	sch 1 paras 16(1), 18(2)(f)	2(1), 41(2)(f), 51(2)(d), sch 8 para 6
T13.11(c)	sch 1 paras 16(1), 18(2)(b)	39(1), 41(2)(b), 51(2)(b), sch 8 para 7
T13.11(d)	sch 1 para 16(1)	39(1), sch 8 para 17
T13.11(e),(f)	sch 1 para 16(1)	39(1), sch 8 para 46
T13.11(g),(h)	sch 1 para 16(1)	39(1), sch 8 para 47
T13.11(i)	sch 1 para 16(1)	39(1), sch 8 para 48
T13.11(j)	sch 1 para 16(1)	39(1), sch 8 para 15
T13.11(k)	sch 1 para 16(1)	39(1), 51(2)(a), sch 8 para 28
T13.11(l)	sch 1 para 16(1)	39(1)
T13.11(m)	sch 1 para 16(1)	39(1), sch 8 para 44
T13.11(n)	sch 1 para 16(1)	39(1), 55(4), sch 8 para 18(1)(c)
13.53	sch 1 para 11(1)	33(1), 56(9),(10)
13.54	sch 1 para 22(1),(4)	45(1),(4), 56(2), 67(4)
13.55	sch 1 para 22(1)-(8)	45(1)-(8)
13.56	—	56(2),(11), 67(4)
13.57	—	56(3)(c), 67(5)(c)
13.58	sch 1 para 23(1)	46(1), 56(3)(a),(b), 67(5)(a),(b), sch 8 para 28(2)
13.59	sch 1 paras 16(1), 23(2),(3)	39(1), 46(2),(3), 56(4),(11), 67(6)
13.60	sch 1 para 22(9)-(12),(15),(16)	45(9)-(12),(15),(16), 56(1),(13)
13.61	sch 1 paras 12, 14(2)(f)	34, 36(2)(f)
14.4	2(1), sch 1 para 17(9)(a), 19(1), 29(1)	40(9)(a), 42(1), 52(1),(2), 61(1),(2)
14.6	2(1), sch 1 para 16(1)(a)	2(1), 39(1)(a)
14.7	sch 1 para 18	41, 51
T14.1(a)	sch 1 para 18(1)	41(1), 51(1)
T14.1(b)	sch 1 para 17(5)	40(5), 55(3)
T14.1(c)	sch 1 para 18(1)(m)	41(1)(m), 51(1)(k)

T14.1(d)	sch 1 para 18(1)(h)-(l)	41(1)(h)-(l), 51(1)(j)
T14.1(e)	sch 1 para 18(1)(d)	41(1)(d), 51(1)(d)
T14.1(f)	sch 1 para 18(1)(e)	41(1)(e), 51(1)(e)
T14.1(g)	sch 1 para 18(1)(a)	41(1)(a), 51(1)(a)
T14.1(h)	sch 1 para 18(1)	41(1), 51(1)
T14.1(i)	sch 1 para 18(1)(c)	41(1)(c), 51(1)(c)
T14.1(j)	sch 1 para 18(1)(b)	41(1)(b), 51(1)(b)
T14.1(k)	sch 1 para 18(1)(g)	41(1)(g), 51(1)(l)
T14.1(l)	sch 1 para 18(1)	41(1), 51(1)
T14.1(m)	sch 1 para 18(1)	41(1), 51(1)
T14.1(n)	sch 1 para 18(1)(f),(2)(b)	41(1)(f),(2)(b), 51(1)(f),(2)(b)
T14.1(o)	2(8), sch 1 para 18(2)(f)	41(2)(f), 51(2)(d)
T14.1(p)	sch 1 para 18(2)(e)	41(2)(e), 51(1)(g)-(i)
T14.1(q)	sch 1 paras 18(1)(b), 31(1)	41(1)(b), 51, 63(1)
T14.1(r)	sch 1 para 18(2)(a),(3)	41(2)(a),(3)
T14.1(s)	—	64(2)
T14.1(t)	—	64(6)
T14.1(u)	—	64(3)
T14.1(v)	sch 1 para 18(2)(c)	41(2)(c), 51(1)(c)
T14.1(w)	sch 1 para 16(1)	39(1), 51(1)
14.8	sch 1 paras 17(2),(3A),(4),(4A) 24(1)(a)	40(2),(4), 47(1)-(3), 57(1)(a)
14.9	—	2(1), 47(1)-(3)
14.10	2(1), sch 1 para 17(2)-(4)	2(1), 40(2)-(4)
14.12	sch 1 para 17(3A),(4A)	No equivalent
14.13	—	51(1)(d), 64(4)
14.14	sch 4 para 9	sch 5 para 9, sch 7 paras 1(a),(b), 2(a),(b),(i), 19
14.15	—	51(1)(d), 64(4)
14.16	—	sch 7 paras 1(c), 2(a),(b),(ii), 19
14.17	2(1), sch 1 paras 15, 19	2(1), 38, 42, 47(4), 52
14.18	sch 1 para 18	41, 51
14.19	sch 1 para 19(2)(a),(d)	42(2)(a),(d), 52(3)(a),(d)
14.20	2(1), sch 1 para 19(5),(a),(b)	2(1), 42(5)(a),(b), 52(6),(a),(b), 56(10)(a),(b)
14.22	sch 1 para 19(2)(b),(c),(3),(4),(5)(c)	42(3)(b),(c),(4),(5),(6)(c), 52(2)(b),(c),(3),(4),(5)(c), 56(10)(c)
14.23	2(1), sch 1 paras 15, 19	2(1), 38, 42, 47(4), 52
14.24	—	56(6),(10)
14.25	—	56(6),(7),(8),(11)
14.27	2(1), sch 1 para 21(1)	2(1), 44(1), 53(1)
14.28	sch 1 para 21(1)	44(1), 53(1)
T14.2	sch 1 para 21(2)	44(2), 53(2)

14.29	sch 1 paras 20, 24(1)(a)	43, 48(1), 57(1)(a)
14.30	2(1), sch 1 para 20	2(1), 43, 48(1)
14.34	—	sch 7 para 3
14.36	2(1), sch 1 paras 15, 29	2(1), 38, 48(2), 61
14.37	sch 1 para 21(1)	44(1), 53(1)
14.38	sch 1 para 29(2)(a),(3),(6)	61(3)(a),(4),(7)
T14.3(a)-(e)	sch 1 para 29(5),(7)(b)	61(6),(8)(b)
T14.3(f)	sch 1 para 29(2)(a),(3),(6)	61(3)(a),(4),(7)
T14.3(g)-(n)	sch 1 para 29(4),(7)(a)	61(5),(8)(a)
14.40	sch 1 para 29(2)(a),(3)	61(3)(a),(4)
14.45	sch 1 para 29(6)	61(7)
14.46	sch 1 para 29(3)(a)	61(3)(a)
14.47	sch 1 para 29(1)(b)	61(1)(b)
14.50	sch 1 para 29(9)	61(10)
14.52	sch 1 para 30(4)(b)	62(4)(b)
14.53	sch 1 para 29(1)(b)(i),(2)(b),(8)(a)	61(1)(b)(i),(2)(b),(9)(a), 62
14.54	sch 1 para 28, 30(1)-(3)	2(1), 60, 62(1)-(3)
14.55	NI Only	NI Only
T14.4	2(1), sch 1 para 30	2(1), 62
14.56	2(1), sch 1 para 29(1)(b)(ii),(2)(c),(8)(b),(10),(11)	2(1), 61(1)(b)(ii),(3)(c),(9)(b),(11),(12)
14.57	2(1), sch 1 paras 15, 29	2(1), 38, 48(2), 61
14.58	sch 1 paras 16(1)(q),(r), 17(9)(b),(10)	39(1)(q),(r), 40(6),(9)(b),(10), 53(3)
14.59	sch 1 para 17(5)	40(5), 53(4)
14.61	2(1), sch 1 paras 17(9), 24(1)(c),(2), sch 4 paras 1-6, 8, 10(1),(3), sch 5 para 21	2(1), 40(9), 52(2), 57(1)(c),(2), 61(2), sch 5 paras 1-6, 8, 10(1),(3), sch 6 para 21, sch 7 paras 4-12, sch 8 para 58
14.62	sch 4 paras 1-6, 8	sch 5 paras 1-6, 8, sch 7 paras 4-12
T14.5(a)	sch 4 para 6	sch 5 para 6, sch 7 para 12
T14.5(b)	sch 4 paras 1(a), 2	sch 5 paras 1(a), 2, sch 7 para 5
T14.5(c)	—	sch 7 para 4
T14.5(d)	2(1) sch 4 para 5	sch 5 para 5
T14.5(e)	sch 4 paras 1(b), 4	sch 5 paras 1(b), 4, sch 7 paras 6, 7
T14.5(f)	sch 4 paras 1(b), 3	sch 5 paras 1(b), 4, sch 7 paras 9, 10
T14.5(g)	sch 4 para 8(b)	sch 5 para 8(b), sch 7 para 8
T14.5(h)	sch 4 para 8(a)	sch 5 para 8(a), sch 7 para 11
14.63	sch 1 para 25(1)	58(1)
14.64	sch 1 para 24(3)	57(3)
14.65	sch 1 para 25(5),(9)	58(5),(10)
T14.6	sch 1 para 25(5),(7)-(8),(17)	58(5),(7)-(9)

14.66	sch 1 para 25(6),(13),(17)	58(6),(9),(14)
14.67	sch 1 para 25(1)(c),(10)	58(1)(c),(11)
14.67(a)	sch 1 para 25(11)(b),(c)	58(11)(b)-(e)
14.67(b),(c)	sch 1 para 25(10)(f),(g),(k)	58(11)(h),(i),(m)
14.67(d)	sch 1 para 25(11)(d),(e),(11),(12)	58(11)(f),(g),(12),(13)
14.67(e)	2(1), sch 1 para 25(11)(g)	58(11)(n)
14.67(f)	sch 1 para 25(10)(l)	58(11)(a)
14.67(g),(h)	sch 1 para 25(1)(c)	58(1)(c)
14.68	sch 4 para 10	sch 5 para 10, sch 7 para 18
14.69	2(1), 10(1)	2(1), 10(1)
14.70	10(2)-(4)	10(2)-(4)
T14.7	sch 4 para 10(2)	sch 5 para 10(2), sch 7 para 18(2)
14.71-72	2(1), 10(1),(5)-(8), sch 1 para 25(2)-(4),(14)-(16)	2(1), 10(1),(5)-(8), 58(2)-(4),(15)-(17)
14.73	sch 4 para 10(4)	sch 5 para 10(4), sch 7 para 18(4)
15.1	sch 1 para 31(1)	63(1)
15.2	sch 1 para 11	33, 63(4)
15.3	sch 1 para 13	35, sch 10 paras 8, 9
15.4	11(2), sch 1 paras 15, 24(1)(b), 31, 37, sch 6	23, 38, 57(1)(b), 63(2), 71, 72, sch 9, sch 10
15.5	sch 1 paras 24(1)(b), 37	57(1)(b), 71, 72
15.10-11	See text	See text
15.11	sch 1 paras 17(1),(7),(12), 24(1), 31(1)	40(1),(7),(12), 49(1),(2), 57(1), 63(1)
15.12	sch 1 para 31(1)	63(1)
15.14	sch 1 para 32	65
15.15	sch 1 para 32	65
15.16	sch 1 para 32(a)	65(a)
15.17	sch 1 para 32(b)	65(b)
15.18	sch 1 para 36	70
15.19	sch 1 para 33	66
15.20	sch 6 para 23	sch 9 para 23, sch 10 para 28
15.22	sch 1 para 31(1)	63(1)
15.23	sch 1 para 31(1)	63(1)
15.24	sch 1 paras 31(1), 32(a)	63(1), 65(a)
15.25	2(1), sch 6 paras 11, 12, 24, 28, 29A, 32	2(1), sch 9 paras 11, 12, 24, 32, sch 10 paras 16, 21, 35, 36
15.26	sch 1 para 16(1)(i), sch 5 paras 22, 23	39(1)(i), 64(5), sch 6 paras 22, 23, sch 8 para 36
15.27	sch 6 paras 5, 31	sch 9 paras 5, 31, sch 10 paras 10, 37
T15.1	sch 1 para 31(2), sch 6	63(1),(2), sch 9, sch 10
T15.1(a)	sch 6 para 26	sch 9 para 26, sch 10 para 4
T15.1(b)	sch 6 para 4(a)	sch 9 para 4(a), sch 10 para 7(a)

T15.1(c)	sch 6 para 4(b)	sch 9 para 4(b), sch 10 para 7(b)
T15.1(d)	sch 6 paras 1-3	sch 9 paras 1-3, sch 10 paras 5, 32, 33
T15.1(e)	sch 6 para 6	sch 9 para 6, sch 10 para 30
T15.1(f)	sch 6 para 7	sch 9 para 7, sch 10 para 31
T15.1(g)	sch 6 para 5	sch 9 para 5, sch 10 para 10
T15.1(h)	—	2(1), sch 10 paras 6, 14(b)
T15.1(i)	—	sch 10 para 41
T15.1(j)	—	sch 10 para 13(a)
T15.1(k)	—	sch 10 para 13(b)
T15.1(l)	—	2(1), sch 10 para 14(a)
T15.1(m)	—	sch 10 para 26
T15.1(n)	sch 6 paras 18, 20(a)	sch 9 paras 18, 20(a)
T15.1(o)	sch 6 paras 18, 19	sch 9 paras 18, 19
T15.1(p)	sch 6 paras 18, 20(b)	sch 9 paras 18, 20(a)
15.29	sch 1 para 31(1),(2), sch 6	63(1),(2), sch 9, sch 10
15.30	sch 6	sch 9, sch 10
15.31	sch 1 para 31(1)	63(1)
15.32	sch 6 para 8	sch 9 para 8, sch 10 para 15
15.33	sch 6 paras 9, 10	sch 9 paras 9, 10, sch 10 para 11
15.34-35	sch 1 para 34(3),(4)	67(7),(8)
15.38	sch 1 para 31(1)	63(1)
15.39	sch 6 para 33	sch 9 para 33, sch 10 paras 10, 17
15.40	sch 1 para 31(1),(2)	63(1),(2)
15.42	2(1), sch 1 para 16(1), sch 6 paras 14, 16, 16A	2(1), 39(1), sch 8 para 41, sch 9 paras 14, 16, sch 10 paras 29, 38, 59
15.43	sch 6 para 17	sch 9 para 17, sch 10 para 50
15.44	sch 5 paras 14, 15	sch 6 paras 14, 15, sch 8 para 19(1)(c)-(e)
15.45	—	sch 10 paras 50, 51
15.46	sch 6 paras 13, 15	sch 9 paras 13, 15, sch 10 paras 58, 60
15.48	sch 1 para 16(1)	39(1), sch 8 para 15, sch 10 para 52
T15.2	sch 1 para 31(3), sch 6 paras 18, 21(a)-(d),(2), 22	63(3), 64(10), sch 9 paras 18, 21(a)-(d),(2), 22, sch 10 para 12
15.51	sch 1 paras 16(1)(j)(xiii); 31(1),	39(1)(j)(xiii), 63(3), sch 10 para 25
15.52(a)	—	sch 10 paras 47, 48
15.52(b)	—	64(8),(9), sch 10 paras 2, 3, 11(3),(4), 39, 53, 56
15.53(a)	—	sch 10 paras 23, 24, 63, 64
15.53(b),(c)	sch 6 paras 29, 29B	sch 9 para 29, sch 10 para 62
15.53(d)	sch 6 paras 18, 21(1)(e)	sch 9 paras 18, 21(1)(e), sch 10 para 61
15.53(e)	sch 6 paras 18, 21(1)(f)	sch 10 para 25(b)
15.54	sch 1 para 31(1)	63(1), 64(7), sch 10 para 38

15.56	sch 1 para 31(1)	63(1)
15.60	sch 1 para 34(5)	67(9)
15.61	sch 1 para 34(1)	67(1)
15.63	sch 1 para 34(2)	67(2)
15.64	sch 1 paras 31(1),(2), 34(1),(2)	63(1),(2), 67(1),(2), sch 10 para 15
15.66	sch 1 paras 34(1), 35	67(1), 68, 69
15.67	sch 1 para 35(1)-(4),(5),(10)	68(1)-(5),(10), 69(1)-(5),(10)
15.68	sch 1 para 35(1)(a),(2),(3),(10)	68(1)(a),(2),(3),(10), 69(1)(a),(2),(3),(10)
15.70	sch 1 para 35(1)(b),(4),(5),(10)	68(1)(b),(4),(5),(10), 69(1)(b),(4),(5),(10)
15.71	sch 1 para 35(1)(b),(7)-(10)	68(1)(b),(7)-(10), 69(1)(b),(7)-(10)

Table B: Scotland and Wales

This table shows the equivalent footnote references for the law on council tax rebates in Scotland and Wales for chapters 12-15 of this guide

	CTR Regulations Scotland		CTR Regulations Wales	
	Working age SSI 2021 No. 249	**Pension age** SSI 2012 No. 319	**Prescribed Requirements** SI 2013 No.3029	**Default Scheme** SI 2013 No. 3035
12.5	35(a), sch 1 para 1(1)	20(1)(a), sch 1 para 2	sch 1 para 1(1)(a), sch 2 para 1, sch 6 para 1(1)(a), sch 7 para 1	23(1)(a), 24(1)(a), sch 2 para 1, sch 3 para 1
T12.1	sch 1 paras 1-5, 17; SI 2023/38 reg 20	sch 1 paras 2, 3, 13; SI 2023/38 regs 25, 27	sch 2 paras 1-3, 12, sch 7 paras 1, 3, 4, 17, 23, 24; SI 2023/47 regs 7, 9	sch 2 paras 1-3, 12, sch 3 paras 1, 3, 4, 17; SI 2023/47 regs 15, 16
12.6	—	sch 1 para 2	sch 2 para 1	sch 2 para 1
12.7	sch 1 para 1(1)	—	sch 7 para 1(a),(b),(2),(3)	sch 3 para 1(a),(b),(2),(3)
12.8	sch 1 para 1(1)	—	sch 7 para 1(1)(c)	sch 3 para 1(1)(c)
12.9	sch 1 para 2	sch 1 para 3	sch 2 para 2, sch 7 para 3	sch 2 para 2, sch 3 para 3
12.10-11	35(b), sch1 para 2	20(1)(b)	sch 1 para 1(1)(b), sch 6 para 1(1)(b)	23(1)(b), 24(1)(b)
12.12-18	Not Scotland	Not Scotland	Not Wales	Not Wales
12.19	35(c)-(d), 98, sch 1 paras 3-5, 13, 14	20(1)(c),(d), sch 1 paras 4, 7-10	sch 1 para 1(1)(c),(d), sch 2 paras 3, 6-9, sch 6 para 1(1)(c),(d), sch 7 paras 4, 11-14	23(1)(c),(d), 24(1)(c),(d), sch 2 paras 3, 6-9, sch 3 paras 4, 11-14
12.22	sch 1 para 3(a)	sch 1 paras 9, 13(3)	sch 2 paras 8, 12(3), sch 7 paras 13, 17(3)	sch 2 paras 8, 12(3), sch 3 paras 13, 17(3)
12.23	sch 1 para 3(b)	sch 1 paras 8, 13(2)	sch 2 paras 7, 12(2), sch 7 paras 12(1)(b),(c), 17(5)(a)	sch 2 paras 7,12(2), sch 3 paras 12(1)(b),(c), 17(5)(a)
12.24	98	20(1)(c), sch 1 para 4; SSI 2016/81, reg 18	sch 1 para 1(1)(c), sch 2 para 3, sch 6 para 1(1)(c), sch 7 para 4	23(1)(c), 24(1)(c), sch 2 para 3, sch 3 para 4
12.25	4(1), sch 1 para 13(2),(3),(4)	2(1), sch 1 para 7(2)	2(1), sch 2 para 6(2), sch 7 para 11(2)	2(1), sch 2 para 6(2), sch 3 para 11(2)
12.26	sch 1 para 17	sch 1 para 13(1)(a)	sch 2 para 12(1)(a), sch 7 para 17(2)(a)	sch 2 para 12(1)(a), sch 3 para 17(2)(a)
12.27	sch 1 para 17	sch 1 para 13(1)(b)	sch 2 para 12(1)(b), sch 7 para 17(2)(b)	sch 2 para 12(1)(b), sch 3 para 17(2)(b)
12.28	sch 1 para 13(5)(b),(6),(7)	sch 1 para 7(7)(b),(8)	sch 2 para 6(7)(d),(8), sch 7 para 11(5)(b),(6),(7)	sch 2 para 6(7)(d),(8), sch 3 para 11(5)(b),(6),(7)
12.29	sch 1 paras 5, 6	sch 1 para 10	sch 2 para 9, sch 7 para 14	sch 2 para 9, sch 3 para 14
12.30	—	sch 1 para 13(4)	sch 2 para 12(4), sch 7 para 17(4)	sch 2 para 12(4), sch 3 para 17(4)
12.33	sch 1 paras 6(1), 16	sch 1 para 12	sch 2 para 11, sch 7 para 16	sch 2 para 11, sch 3 para 16
12.37	sch 1 paras 7,11,12(8)	—	sch 7 paras 9, 10(8)	sch 3 paras 9, 10(8)
12.38	sch 1 para 17	—	sch 7 para 17(1)	sch 3 para 17(1)
12.39	4(1), sch 1 para 12(1)(a),(2)	—	2(1), sch 7 para 10(1)(a)	2(1), sch 3 para 10(1)(a)
12.40	sch 1 para 14(1)	—	sch 7 para 12(1)(a)-(d)	sch 3 para 12(1)(a)-(d)

12.41	sch 1 para 17	—	sch 7 para 12(1)(b)-(d)	sch 3 para 12(1)(b)-(d)
12.42	sch 1 paras 18, 21, 22	—	sch 7 paras 18, 21, 22	sch 3 paras 18, 21, 22
12.43	sch 1 paras 18, 19	—	sch 7 paras 18, 19	sch 3 paras 18, 19
12.44	sch 1 paras 20(2), 23, 24	—	sch 7 paras 20(2), 23, 24	sch 3 paras 20(2), 23, 24
12.46	sch 1 paras 1(2), 18, 19	—	sch 7 paras 2, 18, 19	sch 3 paras 2, 18, 19
12.50	100	—	sch 7 paras 25, 26, 28	sch 3 paras 25, 26, 28
12.52	12, 15	11(1)	8(1)	8(1)
T12.2(a)	sch 1 paras 12(1)(a)(iii), 13(5)(a), 14(1)(b),(c),(3), 17	sch 1 paras 7(7)(a), 13(1)(b)(i)	sch 2 paras 6(7), 12(1)(b)(i), sch 7 paras 10(1)(a)(iii)-(v), 11(5)(a), 12(1)(b)-(d),(3), 17(6)(b	sch 2 paras 6(7), 12(1)(b)(i), sch 3 paras 10(1)(a)(iii)-(v), 11(5), 12(1)(b)-(d),(3), 17(2)(b)
T12.2(b)	sch 1 para 3(a)(i),(b)(ii),(iii)	sch 1 paras 8(1)(a),(b), 9(a)	sch 2 paras 7(1)(a),(b), 8(a), sch 7 paras 12(1)(b),(c), 13(a)	sch 2 paras 7(1)(a),(b), 8(a), sch 3 paras 12(1)(b),(c), 13(a)
T12.2(c)	sch 1 paras 5(5),(6)(b), 6(4)	sch 1 para 10(2)(b)	sch 2 para 9(2)(b), sch 7 para 14(2)(b),(4)(b)	sch 2 para 9(2)(b), sch 3 para 14(2)(b),(4)(b)
12.53	sch 1 para 3	sch 1 paras 8(2), 9(c)	sch 2 paras 7(2), 8(c), sch 7 paras 12(2), 13(c)	sch 2 paras 7(2), 8(c), sch 3 paras 12(2), 13(c)
12.54	4(1), sch 1 para 12(2)	sch 1 paras 7(4),(5)	sch 2 paras 6(4),(5), sch 7 para 10(1)(a)(vii),(2)	sch 2 paras 6(4),(5), sch 3 para 10(1)(a)(vii),(2)
12.55	sch 1 para 15	sch 1 para 11	sch 2 para 10, sch 7 para 15	sch 2 para 10, sch 3 para 15
13.1	38(2)(a),(b), 42(2)(a),(b)	27(1),(2), 28(1),(a),(b)	sch 1 paras 5(1), 8(1),(2), 18(1)(a),(b), sch 6 para 20(1)(a),(b)	30(1), 33(1),(2), 54(1)(a),(b)
13.2	36	2	sch 1 para 5(1), sch 6 para 7, sch 9 para 25	30, sch 7 para 25
13.3	13(11)	26	sch 1 para 9, sch 8 para 14, sch 9 paras 8, 9	35, sch 6 para 14, sch 7 paras 8, 9
13.4	49(6)(d), 50(3)(i), 51(2), 57(1), sch 3	31(8)-(10), sch 2, sch 3	sch 1 para 11(9)-(11), sch 3, sch 4, sch 6 paras 15(2), 17(2), 24(2), sch 8, sch 9	37(9)-(11), 49(2), 51(2), 58(2), sch 4, sch 5, sch 6, sch 7
13.5	4(1), 13(11), 42(2), 57(1)(p),(2)(d)	24	sch 1 para 7, sch 8 para 14, sch 9 paras 8, 9	32, sch 6 para 14, sch 7 paras 8, 9
13.6	38(2), 41(1),(2)	28(1), 31(1),(6)	sch 1 paras 11(1),(7), 18(1), sch 6 paras 12(1),(2), 20(1)	37(1),(7), 46(1),(2), 54(1)
13.7	38(2), 41(1),(2)	28(1), 31(1),(6)	sch 1 paras 11(1),(7), 18(1), sch 6 paras 12(1),(2), 20(1)	37(1),(7), 46(1),(2), 54(1)
13.8	38(2), 39-41	28(1), 31(1)	sch 1 paras 11(1), 18(1), sch 6 paras 10-12, 20(1)	37(1), 44-46, 54(1)
T13.1	57(1)	27(1), 31(10), sch 3	sch 1 paras 10(1), 11(11), sch 4, sch 6 para 17(2), sch 9	36(1), 37(11), 51(2), sch 5, sch 7
T13.1 (a)-(c)	13(11), 42(2)	24, 27(1)(j)(xxvi)	sch 1 para 7, sch 6 para 9, sch 9 paras 8, 9	32, 34, sch 7 paras 8, 9
T13.1 (d)-(e)	57(1)(b)	27(1)(j)(ii),(iii)	sch 1 para 10(1)(j)(i),(ii), sch 9 para 11	36(1)(j)(i),(ii), sch 7 para 11
T13.1(f)	4(1), 57(1)(b)	2(1), 27(1)(j)(iv)-(vi)	2(1), sch 1 para 10(1)(j)(iii)-(v), sch 9 para 14	2(1), 36(1)(j)(iii)-(v), sch 7 para 14
T13.1(g)	57(1)(b)	27(1)(j)(xva)	sch 1 para 10(1)(j)(xiii)	36(1)(j)(xiii)
T13.1(h)	57(1)(r)	27(1)	sch 1 para 10(1)	36(1)
T13.1(i)	57(1)(b)	27(1)(j)(vii)	sch 1 para 10(1)(j)(vi), sch 9 para 66	36(1)(j)(vi), sch 7 para 66
T13.1(j)	57(1)(b)	27(1)(j)(viii)	sch 1 para 10(1)(j)(vii), sch 9 para 52	36(1)(j)(vii), sch 7 para 52

	Working age SSI 2021 No. 249	Pension age SSI 2012 No. 319	Prescribed Requirements SI 2013 No.3029	Default Scheme SI 2013 No. 3035
T13.1(k)	57(1)(b)	27(1)(j)(xii)	sch 1 para 10(1)(j)(x), sch 9 para 38	36(1)(j)(x), sch 7 para 38
T13.1(l)	57(1)	27(1)(j)(x)	sch 1 para 10(1)(j)(ix), sch 9 para 31, sch 10 para 25	36(1)(j)(ix), sch 7 para 31, sch 9 para 25
T13.1(n)	57(1)(b)(iv)	27(1)(j)(xxii)	No equivalent	
T13.1(o)	57(1)	27(1)	sch 1 para 10(1), sch 9 para 51, sch 10 paras 46, 47	36(1), sch 7 para 51, sch 9 paras 46, 47
T13.1(p)	57(1)	2(1), 27(1),	2(1), sch 1 para 10(1), sch 9 paras 2, 3, 18, 52, 63	2(1), 36(1), sch 7 paras 2, 3, 18, 52, 63
T13.1(q)	57(1)	2(1), 27(1)(u)	2(1), sch 1 para 10(1)(u), sch 9 para 12	2(1), 36(1)(u), sch 7 para 12
T13.2 (a)-(k)	57(1)(b)	27(1)(b),(c),(j)	sch 1 para 10(1)(b),(c),(j), sch 6 paras 12(1),(3), 17(1)	36(1)(b),(c),(j), 46(1),(3), 51(1)
T13.2(l)	57(4)	sch 3 paras 6,7	sch 4 paras 7,8 sch 9 para 21	sch 5 paras 7,8, sch 7 21
T13.2(m)	57(1)(b)(ix)	27(1)(j)(v),(vi)	sch 1 para 10(1)(j)(v), sch 9 para 14	36(1)(j)(v), sch 7 para 14
T13.2(n)	57(1)	—	sch 4 paras 7, 8, sch 9 para 21	sch 5 paras 7, 8, sch 7 para 21
T13.2(o)	57(1)(b)	2(1), 27(1)(j)(v),(n)	2(1), sch 1 para 10(1)(j)(v),(n), sch 4 para 2, sch 9 para 14	2(1), 36(1)(j)(v),(n), sch 5 para 2, sch 7 para 14
13.10	4(1)	2(1)	2(1)	2(1)
13.11	57(1)(b)(ii),(iii)	27(1)(j), 31(6)	sch 1 paras 10(1)(j), 11(7), sch 6 paras 12(1),(2), 17(1)	36(1)(j), 37(7), 46(1),(2), 51(1)
13.12	57(1)(q),(r),(5)	27(1)(b),(4)	sch 1 paras 10(1)(b),(3) 21, sch 6 paras 12(1), 17(1),(5), 27(10)	36(1)(b),(3), 46(1), 51(1),(5), 56, 61(10)
13.13	57(1)(a)	sch 4 para 30A	sch 5 para 27	sch 8 para 27
13.14	—	25(2)(a), 31(6)	sch 1 paras 8(2)(a), 11(7)	33(2)(a), 37(7)
T13.3	—	25(2)-(6)	sch 1 para 8(2)-(5)	33(2)-(5)
13.15	—	25(1)	sch 1 para 8(1)	33(1)
13.16	57(1)	27(1)(e)-(h),(l)-(m), sch 3 para 1	sch 1 para 10(1)(e)-(h),(l)-(m), sch 4 para 1, sch 9 para 20	36(1)(e)-(h),(l)-(m), sch 6 para 1, sch 7 para 20
13.18	57(1)	See volume 1 para 16.6	See volume 1 para 16.7	See volume 1 para 16.7
T13.4	57(1)	2(1), 27(1)(e)-(h), (l)-(m), 28(1)(a), sch 6 paras 1-5	2(1), sch 1 paras 10(1)(e)-(h), (l)-(m),18(1)(a), sch 4 paras 1-6, sch 6 paras 12(1), 17(1), 20(1)(a), sch 9 paras 13, 14, 20, 54-56	2(1), 36(1)(e)-(h),(l)-(m), 46(1), 51(1), 54(1)(a), sch 5 paras 1-6, sch 7 paras 13, 14, 20, 54-56
13.20	41(1), 57(1)(b)	27(1)(j)(ix), 28(1)(a), sch 3 para 12	sch 1 paras 10(1)(j)(viii), 18(1)(a), sch 4 para 13, sch 6 paras 17(1), 20(1)(a), sch 9 para 53	36(1)(j)(viii), 51(1), 54(1)(a), sch 5 para 13, sch 7 para 53
13.21	41(1), 57(1)(a),(b)	27(3)-(5), 28(1)(a)	sch 1 paras 10(2)-(4), 18(1)(a), sch 6 paras 17(1),(4),(5), 20(1)(a)	36(2)-(4), 51(1),(4),(5), 54(1)(a)
13.22	41(1)	27(3)	sch 1 paras 10(2), sch 6 para 17(1),(4),(5)	36(2), 51(1),(4),(5)
13.25	57(1)	2(1), 27(1)	2(1), sch para 10(1), sch 9 paras 30-34, 59	2(1), 36(1), sch 7 paras 30-34, 59
T13.5 (a)-(f)	57(1)	2(1), 27(1)	2(1), sch para 10(1), sch 9 paras 30-34, 59	2(1), 36(1), sch 7 paras 30-34, 59

T13.5 (g)-(h)	57(1)	27(1)	sch para 10(1), sch 9 para 59	36(1), sch 7 para 59
T13.5(i)	57(1)	27(1)	sch para 10(1), sch 9 para 65	36(1), sch 7 para 65
T13.5(j)	57(1)	27(1)(j)(xi)	2(1) definition 'occasional assistance', sch 1 para 10(1), sch 9 para 37(b)	2(1), 36(1), sch 7 para 37(b)
T13.5(k)	57(1)	27(1)	sch para 10(1), sch 9 para 64	36(1), sch 7 para 64
T13.5(l)	57(1)	27(1)	sch para 10(1), sch 9 para 45	36(1), sch 7 para 45
13.27	57(1) (a),(e),(n), 58	2(1), 27(1)(c),(d),(t),(x), 28(1)(a), 31(12), 32(2)	2(1), sch 1 paras 10(1)(c),(d),(t),(x), 11(13), 12(2), 18(1)(a), sch 6 paras 2(1), 36(1)(c),(d),(t),(x), 37(13), 12(1), 14(2), 20(1)(a), sch 9 para 4	38(2), 46(1), 48(2), 54(1)(a), sch 7 para 4
13.29	38(2), 41(1)	28(1)	sch 6 paras 12(1), 20(1)	46(1), 54(1)
13.30	57(1)	27(1)	sch 1 para 10(1), sch 9 para 19(1)(a),(b),(2)	36(1), sch 7 para 19(1)(a),(b),(2)
13.32	57(1)(j)	27(1)(d), 31(12),	sch 1 paras 10(1)(d), 11(13), sch 6 para 18(2), sch 9 para 4	36(1)(d), 37(13), 52(2), sch 7 para 4
13.33	57(1)	27(1)(d), 31(12), sch 3 para 10	sch 1 paras 10(1)(d), 11(13), sch 4 para 11, sch 6 para 18(2), sch 9 para 4	36(1)(d), 37(13), 52(2), sch 5 para 11, sch 7 para 4
T13.6	57(1)(d)	27(1)(o), sch 3 para 19	sch 1 para 10(1)(o), sch 4 para 20, sch 6 para 12(1), sch 9 paras 49, 50	36(1)(o), 46(1), sch 5 para 20, sch 7 paras 49, 50
T13.7(a)	57(1)	27(1)	sch 1 para 10(1), sch 9 para 25	36(1), sch 7 para 25
T13.7(b)	57(1)	2(1), 27(1)(p), 8 sch 3 para	2(1), sch 1 para 10(1)(p), sch 4 para 9, sch 9 para 27	2(1), 36(1)(p), sch 5 para 9, sch 7 para 27
T13.7(c)	57(1)	27(1)(v), sch 3 para 9	sch 1 para 10(1)(v), sch 4 para 10, sch 9 para 26	36(1)(v), sch 5 para 10, sch 7 para 26
T13.8(a)	57(1)	—	sch 9 paras 4, 22(2),(3)	sch 7 paras 4, 22(2),(3)
T13.8(b)	57(1)	—	sch 1 para 10(1), sch 4 para 23, sch 6 para 27(5), sch 9 paras 4, 22(1)	36(1), 61(5), sch 5 para 23, sch 7 paras 4, 22(1)
13.34	—	27(1)(w),(6)	sch 1 para 10(1)(w),(5)	36(1)(w),(5)
13.35	57(1)(i)	27(1)	sch 1 para 10(1), sch 9 para 35	36(1), sch 7 para 35
13.36	57(1), 75(1),(2)	27(1)(i), sch 3 para 11	sch 1 para 10(1)(i), sch 4 para 12, sch 6 para 12(1), sch 9 para 19(1)(c)	36(1)(i), 46(1), sch 5 para 12, sch 7 para 19(1)(c)
13.37	59	39(1)	sch 1 para 10(1), sch 11 para 2	36(1), 71
13.38	60	—	sch 11 paras 1(1), 3(1),(4),(6), 9(1), 10	70(1), 72(1),(4),(6), 78(1), 79
13.39	57(1), 59(6), 61	—	sch 11 paras 1(1), 9(1)(a)(ii),(b)(ii), 12, 13	70(1), 78(1)(a)(ii),(b)(ii), 81, 82
T13.9	60, 62	—	sch 6 para 17(6)-(9), sch 11 paras 1(1), 9	51(6)-(9), 70(1), 78
13.40	57(1)	—	sch 11 para 8	77
T13.10	61, 62	—	sch 6 para 17(6)-(9), sch 11 paras 1(1), 4	51(6)-(9), 70(1), 73
13.41	57(1)(g),(2)(b)	—	sch 11 paras 1(1), 11, 14(2)	70(1), 80, 83(2)
13.43	4(1), 57(1)(h),(2)(b)	—	2(1), sch 9 para 61, sch 10 para 52	2(1), sch 7 para 61, sch 9 para 52

	Working age SSI 2021 No. 249	Pension age SSI 2012 No. 319	Prescribed Requirements SI 2013 No.3029	Default Scheme SI 2013 No. 3035
13.44	57(1)	27(1)	sch 1 para 10(1), sch 6 para 12(1), sch 9 para 4	36(1), 46(1), sch 7 para 4
13.46	57(1)	31(12)	sch 1 para 11(13), sch 9 para 4	37(13), sch 7 para 4
13.47	—	sch 2 para 7, sch 3 paras 17, 18	sch 3 para 7, sch 4 paras 18, 19, sch 8 para 13, sch 9 paras 23, 24	sch 4 para 7, sch 5 paras 18, 19, sch 6 para 13, sch 7 paras 23, 24
13.48	57(1)(c), 70(2),(3), sch 3 paras 13, 14	27(1)(k), 31(7), sch 2 para 11, sch 3 paras 15, 16	sch 1 paras 10(1)(k), 11(8), sch 3 para 11, sch 4 paras 16, 17, sch 8 paras 15, 16, sch 9 paras 29, 39	36(1)(k), 37(8), sch 4 para 11, sch 5 paras 16, 17,sch 6 paras 15, 16, sch 7 paras 29, 39
13.49	—	sch 3 para 11(3)(b),(c),	sch 4 para 12(3)(b),(c), sch 9 para 40	sch 5 para 12(3)(b),(c), sch 7 para 40
T13.11(a)	57(1)	27(1)	sch 1 para 10(1), sch 9 para 5	36(1), sch 7 para 5
T13.11(b)	46(2), 49(3)(b), 50(3)(h), 57(1)	2(1), 32(2)(f)	2(1), sch 1 para 12(2)(f), sch 6 para 14(2)(d), sch 9 para 6	2(1), 38(2)(f), 48(2)(d), sch 7 para 6
T13.11(c)	50(3)(f), 53(1)(a)	27(1), 32(2)(b)	sch 1 paras 10(1), 12(2)(b), sch 6 para 14(2)(b), sch 8 para 7	36(1), 38(2)(b), 48(2)(b), sch 7 para 7
T13.11(d)	57(1)	27(1)	sch 1 para 10(1), sch 9 para 17	36(1), sch 7 para 17
T13.11 (e),(f)	57(1)	27(1)	sch 1 para 10(1), sch 9 para 46	36(1), sch 7 para 46
T13.11 (g),(h)	57(1)	27(1)	sch 1 para 10(1), sch 9 para 47	36(1), sch 7 para 47
T13.11(i)	57(1)	27(1)	sch 1 para 10(1), sch 9 para 48	36(1), sch 7 para 48
T13.11(j)	57(1)	27(1)	sch 1 para 10(1), sch 9 para 15	36(1), sch 7 para 15
T13.11(k)	49(2), 50(2)(a)	27(1)	sch 1 para 10(1), sch 6 para 14(2)(a), sch 9 para 28	36(1), 48(2)(a), sch 7 para 28
T13.11(l)	57(1)	27(1)	sch 1 para 10(1)	36(1)
T13.11(m)	57(1)	27(1)	sch 1 para 10(1), sch 9 para 44	36(1), sch 7 para 44
T13.11(n)	57(1)	27(1)	sch 1 para 10(1), sch 6 para 18(4), sch 9 para 18(1)(c)	36(1), 52(4), sch 7 para 18(1)(c)
13.53	55(1), 65(1)	21(1)	sch 1 para 5(1), sch 6 para 19(9),(10)	30(1), 53(9),(10)
13.54	55(1), 65(1)	41(1),(4)	sch 1 para 16(1),(4), sch 6 paras 19(2), 30(2)	42(1),(4), 53(2), 64(2)
13.55	65(3),(4)	38(1)-(7),(14)(a)	sch 1 para 16(1)-(8)	42(1)-(8)
13.56	55(6), 65(2)	—	sch 6 paras 19(2),(11), 30(2)	53(2),(11), 64(2)
13.57	55(5)	—	sch 6 paras 19(3)(c), 30(3)(c)	53(3)(c), 64(3)(c)
13.58	58, 65(3),(4)	39(1)	sch 1 para 17(1), sch 6 paras 19(3)(a),(b), 30(3)(a),(b), sch 9 para 28(2)	43(1), 53(3)(a),(b), 64(3)(a),(b), sch 7 para 28(2)
13.59	57(1)(g),(h),(2)(b), 55(6)	27(1), 39(2),(3)	sch 1 paras 10(1), 17(2),(3), sch 6 paras 19(4),(11), 30(4)	36(1), 43(2),(3), 53(4),(11), 64(4)
13.60	55(1), 65(1)	38(8)-(10),(13),(14)(b)	sch 1 para 16(9)-(12),(15),(16), sch 6 paras 19(1),(13)	42(9)-(12),(15),(16), 53(1),(13)
13.61	37	25(2)(f)	sch 1 para 8(2)(f), sch 6 para 8	31, 33(2)(f)

14.4	49(6), 50(3), 51,(2),(5),(9)	31(8)(a), 33(1), 36(1)	sch 1 paras 11(9)(a), 12(1), sch 6 para 14(1),(2), sch 6 para 24(1),(2)	37(9)(a), 39(1), 49(1),(2), 58(1),(2)
14.6	4(1)	2(1), 27(1)(a)	2(1), sch 1 para 10(1)(a)	2(1), 36(1)(a)
14.7	49(2),(4), 50(2),(3)	32	sch 1 para 12, sch 6 para 14	38, 48
T14.1(a)	49(2), 50(2)	32(1)	sch 1 para 12(1) sch 6 para 14(1)	38(1), 48(1)
T14.1(b)	49(2), 50(2)	31(4)	sch 1 para 11(5) sch 6 para 18(3)	37(5), 52(3)
T14.1(c)	49(2), 50(2)(k)	32(1)(m)	sch 1 para 12(1)(m), sch 6 para 14(1)(k)	38(1)(m), 48(1)(k)
T14.1(d)	49(2), 50(2)(j)	32(1)(h)-(l)	sch 1 para 12(1)(h)-(l), sch 6 para 14(1)(j)	38(1)(h)-(l), 48(1)(j)
T14.1(e)	49(2), 50(2)(d)	32(1)(d)	sch 1 para 12(1)(d), sch 6 para 14(1)(d)	38(1)(d), 48(1)(d)
T14.1(f)	49(2), 50(2)(e)	32(1)(e)	sch 1 para 12(1)(e), sch 6 para 14(1)(e)	38(1)(e), 48(1)(e)
T14.1(g)	49(2), 50(2)(a)	32(1)(a)	sch 1 para 12(1)(a), sch 6 para 14(1)(a)	38(1)(a), 48(1)(a)
T14.1(h)	50(2)	32(1)	sch 1 para 12(1), sch 6 para 14(1)	38(1), 48(1)
T14.1(i)	49(2), 50(2)(c)	32(1)(c)	sch 1 para 12(1)(c), sch 6 para 14(1)(c)	38(1)(c), 48(1)(c)
T14.1(j)	49(2), 50(2)(b)	32(1)(b)	sch 1 para 12(1)(b), sch 6 para 14(1)(b)	38(1)(b), 48(1)(b)
T14.1(k)	49(2), 50(2)(l)	32(1)(g)	sch 1 para 12(1)(g), sch 6 para 14(1)(l)	38(1)(g), 48(1)(l)
T14.1(l)	49(2), 50(2)	32(1)	sch 1 para 12(1), sch 6 para 14(1)	38(1), 48(1)
T14.1(m)	49(2), 50(2)	32(1)	sch 1 para 12(1), sch 6 para 14(1)	38(1), 48(1)
T14.1(n)	49(2), 50(2)(f),(3)(f)	32(1)(f),(2)(b)	sch 1 para 12(1)(f),(2)(b), sch 6 para 14(1)(f),(2)(b)	38(1)(f),(2)(b), 48(1)(f),(2)(b)
T14.1(o)	49(2), 50(2)(d)	32(2)(f)	sch 1 para 12(2)(f), sch 6 para 14(2)(d)	38(2)(f), 48(2)(d)
T14.1(p)	49(2), 50(2)(g)-(i)	32(2)(e)	sch 1 para 12(2)(e), sch 6 para 14(1)(g)-(i)	38(2)(e), 48(1)(g)-(i)
T14.1(q)	49(2), 50(2), 67(1)	32(1)(b), 41(1)	sch 1 para 12(1)(b), sch 6 para 14	38(1)(b), 48, 60(1)
T14.1(r)	50(3)(e)	32(2)(a),(3)	sch 1 para 12(2)(a),(3)	38(2)(a),(3)
T14.1(s)	49(2), 50(2)	—	sch 6 para 27(2)	61(2)
T14.1(t)	49(2), 50(2)	—	sch 6 para 27(6)	61(6)
T14.1(u)	49(2), 50(2)	—	sch 6 para 27(3)	61(3)
T14.1(v)	49(2), 50(2)(c)	32(2)(c)	sch 1 para 12(2)(c), sch 6 para 14(1)(c)	38(2)(c), 48(1)(c)
T14.1(w)	49(2), 50(2)	27(1)	sch 1 para 10(1), sch 6 para 14(1)	36(1), 48(1)
14.8	38(2), 39(1)-(3), 42(2)(a)	31(3), 28(1)(a)	sch 1 paras 11(2),(4), 18(1)(a), sch 6 paras 10(1)-(3), 20(1)(a)	37(2),(4), 44(1)-(3), 54(1)(a)
14.9	4(1), 39(1)-(3), 44	—	2(1), sch 6 paras 10(1)-(3)	2(1), 44(1)-(3)
14.10	—	2(1), 31(2),(3)	2(1), sch 1 paras 11(2)-(4)	2(1), 37(2)-(4)

	Working age SSI 2021 No. 249	Pension age SSI 2012 No. 319	Prescribed Requirements SI 2013 No.3029	Default Scheme SI 2013 No. 3035
14.12	39(2)	No equivalent	sch 1 paras 11(2),(4), 18(1)(a), sch 6 paras 10(1)-(3), 20(1)(a)	No equivalent
14.13	50(2)(d)	—	sch 6 paras 14(1)(d), 27(4)	48(1)(d), 61(4)
14.14	sch 3 paras 1(a),(c), 2	sch 2 para 9	sch 3 para 9, sch 8 paras 1(a),(b), 2(a),(b),(i), 19	sch 4 para 9, sch 6 paras 1(a),(b), 2(a),(b),(i), 19
14.15	50(2)(d)	—	sch 6 paras 14(1)(d), 27(4)	48(1)(d), 61(4)
14.16	sch 3 paras 1(d), 2	—	sch 8 paras 1(c), 2(a),(b),(ii), 19	sch 6 paras 1(c), 2(a),(b),(ii), 19
14.17	39(4), 40(2)	2(1), 26, 33	2(1), sch 1 paras 9, 13, sch 6 paras 10(4), 15	2(1), 35, 39, 44(4), 49
14.18	49, 50	32	sch 1 para 10, sch 6 para 14	38, 48
14.19	49(6)(b), 50(3)(a)	33(2)(a),(d)	sch 1 para 13(2)(a),(d), sch 6 paras 15(3)(a),(d)	39(2)(a),(d), 49(3)(a),(d)
14.20	50(5)(a),(b), 55(1)	2(1), 33(4)(a),(b)	2(1), sch 1 para 13(5)(a),(b), sch 6 paras 15(6)(a),(b), 19(10)(a),(b)	2(1), 39(5),(a),(b), 49(6),(a),(b), 53(10)(a),(b)
14.21	Not Scotland	Not Scotland	Not Wales	Not Wales
14.22	49(6)(a), 50(3)(c),(4),(5)(c)	33(2)(b),(c),(3),(4)(c)	sch 1 para 13(3)(b),(c),(4), (5),(6)(c), sch 6 paras 15(2)(b),(c), (3),(4),(5)(c), 19(10)(c)	39(3)(b),(c),(4),(5),(6)(c), 49(2)(b),(c),(3),(4),(5)(c), 53(10)(c)
14.23	39(4), 40(2), 55(1)	2(1), 26, 33	2(1), sch 1 paras 9, 13, sch 6 paras 10(4), 15	2(1), 35, 39, 44(4), 49
14.24	55(1),(3),(5)	—	sch 6 para 19(6),(10)	53(6),(10)
14.25	55(1),(3),(5),(6)	—	sch 6 para 19 (6),(7),(8),(11)	53(6),(7),(8),(11)
14.27	51(1)	2(1), 35(1)	2(1), sch 1 para 15(1), sch 6 para 16(1)	2(1), 41(1), 50(1)
14.28	51(1)	35(1)	sch 1 para 15(1), sch 6 para 16(1)	41(1), 50(1)
T14.2	51(6)	35(2)	sch 1 para 15(2), sch 6 para 16(2)	41(2), 50(2)
14.29	38(2)(a), 40(1), 42(2)(a)	28(1)(a), 34	sch 1 paras 14, 18(1)(a), sch 6 paras 11(1), 20(1)(a)	40, 45(1), 54(1)(a)
14.30	40(1)	2(1), 34	2(1), sch 1 para 14, sch 6 paras 11(1),	2(1), 40, 45(1)
14.34	sch 3 para 3	—	sch 8 para 3	sch 6 para 3
14.36	40(2), 51(2),(9)	2(1), 26, 36	2(1), sch 1 paras 9, 23, sch 6 paras 11(2), 24	2(1), 35, 45(2), 58
14.37	51(2),(6)	35(1)	sch 1 para 15(1), sch 6 para 16(1)	41(1), 50(1)
14.38	51(2),(9)	36(2)(a),(3),(6)	sch 1 para 23(2)(a),(3),(6), sch 6 para 24(3)(a),(4),(7)	58(3)(a),(4),(7)
T14.3 (a)-(e)	51(2),(9)	36(5),(7)(b)	sch 1 para 23(5),(7)(b), sch 6 para 24(6),(8)(b)	58(6),(8)(b)
T14.3(f)	51(2),(9)	36(2)(a),(3),(6)	sch 1 para 23(2)(a),(3),(6), sch 6 para 24(3)(a),(4),(7)	58(3)(a),(4),(7)
T14.3	51(2),(9)	36(4),(7)(a)	sch 1 para 23(4),(7)(a), sch 6 para 24(5),(8)(a)	58(5),(8)(a)
14.40	51(2),(9)	36(2)(a),(3)	sch 1 para 23(2)(a),(3), sch 6 para 24(3)(a),(4)	58(3)(a),(4)

14.45	51(2),(9)	36(6)	sch 1 para 23(6), sch 6 para 24(7)	58(7)
14.46	51(2),(9)	36(2)(a)	sch 1 para 23(2)(a), sch 6 para 24(3)(a)	58(3)(a)
14.47	51(2),(9)	36(1)(b)	sch 1 para 23(1)(b), sch 6 para 24(1)(b)	58(1)(b)
14.50	51(5),(9),(10)	36(9)	sch 1 para 23(9), sch 6 para 24(10)	58(10)
14.52	—	37(3)(b)	sch 1 para 24(4)(b), sch 6 para 25(4)(b)	59(4)(b)
14.53	51(5),(9),(10)	36(1)(b)(i),(8)(a), 37	sch 1 paras 23(1)(b)(i), (2)(b),(8)(a), 24, sch 6 paras 24(1)(b)(i),(3)(b),(9)(a), 25	58(1)(b)(i),(2)(b),(9)(a), 59
14.54	51(5),(9),(10)	2(1), 37(1),(2)	2(1), sch 1 paras 22, 24(1)-(3), sch 6 paras 23, 25(1)-(3)	2(1), 57, 59(1)-(3)
14.55	Not Scotland	Not Scotland	Not Wales	Not Wales
T14.4	—	2(1), 37	2(1), sch 1 para 24, sch 6 para 25	2(1), 59
14.56	51(5),(9),(10)	2(1), 36(1)(b)(ii), (2)(c),(8)(b),(10),(11)	2(1), sch 1 para 23 (1)(b)(ii),(2)(c), (8)(b),(10),(11); sch 6 para 24(1) (b)(ii),(3)(c),(9)(b),(11),(12)	2(1),58(1)(b)(ii),(3)(c), (9)(b),(11),(12)
14.57	51(9),(10)	2(1), 26, 36	2(1), sch 1 paras 9, 23, sch 6 paras 11(2), 24	2(1), 35, 45(2), 58
14.58	51(7)	27(1)(q),(r), 31(5),(8)(b),(9)	sch 1 paras 39(1)(q),(r), 11(6), (9)(b),(10), sch 6 para 16(3)	36(1)(q),(r), 37(6),(9)(b),(10), 50(3)
14.59	51(8)	31(4)	sch 1 para 11(5), sch 6 para 16(4)	37(5), 50(4)
14.61	4(1), 49(6)(d), 50(3)(i), sch 3 paras 4-12, 15	2(1), 28(1)(c),(2), 31(8), sch 4 paras 1-6, 8, 10(1),(3), sch 5 para 21	2(1), sch 1 paras 11(9), 18(1)(c),(2), sch 6 paras 15(2), 20(1)(c),(2), 24(2), sch 3 paras 1-6, 8, 10(1),(3), sch 4 para 21, sch 8 paras 4-12, sch 9 para 58	2(1), 37(9), 49(2), 54(1)(c),(2), 58(2), sch 4 paras 1-6, 8, 10(1),(3), sch 5 para 21, sch 6 paras 4-12, sch 7 para 58
14.62	sch 3 paras 4-12	sch 2 paras 1-6, 8	sch 3 paras 1-6, 8, sch 8 paras 4-12	sch 4 paras 1-6, 8, sch 6 paras 4-12
T14.5(a)	sch 3 para 12	sch 2 para 6	sch 3 para 6, sch 8 para 12	sch 4 para 6, sch 6 para 12
T14.5(b)	sch 3 para 5	sch 2 paras 1(a), 2	sch 3 paras 1(a), 2, sch 8 para 5	sch 4 paras 1(a), 2, sch 6 para 5
T14.5(c)	sch 3 para 4	—	sch 8 para 4	sch 6 para 4
T14.5(d)	—	sch 2 para 5	sch 3 para 5	sch 4 para 5
T14.5(e)	sch 3 paras 6, 7	sch 2 paras 1(b), 4	sch 3 paras 1(b), 4, sch 8 paras 6, 7	sch 4 paras 1(b), 4, sch 6 paras 6, 7
T14.5(f)	sch 3 paras 9, 10	sch 2 paras 1(b), 4	sch 3 paras 1(b), 4, sch 8 paras 9, 10	sch 4 paras 1(b), 4, sch 6 paras 9, 10
T14.5(g)	sch 3 para 8	sch 2 para 8(b)	sch 3 para 8(b), sch 8 para 8	sch 4 para 8(b), sch 6 para 8
T14.5(h)	sch 3 para 11	sch 2 para 8(a)	sch 3 para 8(a), sch 8 para 11	sch 4 para 8(a), sch 6 para 11
14.63	77(2)	29(1)	sch 1 para 19(1), sch 6 para 21(1)	55(1)
14.64	57(1)(l),(m), 67(3),(4)	28(3)	sch 1 para 18(3), sch 6 para 20(3)	54(3)
14.65	77(6),(11)	29(5),(10)	sch 1 para 19(5),(10), sch 6 para 21(5),(10)	55(5),(10)
T14.6	77(6),(8),(10)	29(5),(7)-(9)	sch 1 para 19(5),(7)-(9), sch 6 para 21(5),(7)-(9)	55(5),(7)-(9)
14.66	77(7),(10),(15)	29(6),(9),(14)	sch 1 para 19(6),(9),(14), sch 6 para 21(6),(9),(14)	55(6),(9),(14)

	Working age SSI 2021 No. 249	Pension age SSI 2012 No. 319	Prescribed Requirements SI 2013 No.3029	Default Scheme SI 2013 No. 3035
14.67	77(2)(c),(12)	29(1)(c),(11)	sch 1 para 19(1)(c),(11), sch 6 para 21(1)(c),(11)	55(1)(c),(11)
14.67(a)	7(12)(b)-(e)	29(11)(b)-(e)	sch 1 para 19(11)(b),(c), sch 6 para 21(11) (11)(a)-(c)	55(11)(b)-(e)
14.67 (b),(c)	77(12)(f),(h)	29(11)(h),(i),(m)	sch 1 para 19(11)(f)-(j), sch 6 para 21(11) (11)(f)-(j)	55(11)(h)-(l)
14.67(d)	77(12)(e),(g),(13),(14)	29(11)(f),(g),(12),(13)	sch 1 para 19(11)(d),(e),(12),(13), sch 6 para 21(11) (11)(f),(g),(12),(13)	55(11)(f),(g),(12),(13)
14.67(e)	77(12)(i)	29(11)(n)	sch 1 para 19(11)(l), sch 6 para 21(11)(l)	55(11)(n)
14.67(f)	—	29(11)(a)	sch 1 para 19(11)(a)	55(11)(a)
14.67 (g),(h)	77(2)(c)	29(1)(c)	sch 1 para 19(1)(c), sch 6 para 21(1)(c)	55(1)(c)
14.68	sch 3 para 15	sch 2 para 10	sch 3 para 10, sch 8 para 18	sch 4 para 10, sch 6 para 18
14.69	4(1), 10(1)	2(1), 6(1)	2(1), 10(1)	2(1), 10(1)
14.70	10(2)-(4)	6(2)-(4)	10(2)-(4)	10(2)-(4)
T14.7	sch 3 para 15(2)	sch 2 para 10(2)	sch 3 para 10(2), sch 8 para 18(2)	sch 4 para 10(2), sch 6 para 18(2)
14.71-72	4(1), 10(1),(5)-(8), 77(3)-(5),(15)-(18)	2(1), 6(1),(5)-(8), 29(2)-(4),(15)-(17)	2(1), 10(1),(5)-(8), sch 6 para 19(2)-(4),(15)-(17), sch 6 para 21(2)-(4),(15)-(17)	2(1), 10(1),(5)-(8), 55(2)-(4),(15)-(17)
14.73	sch 3 para 15(4)	sch 2 para 10(4)	sch 3 para 10(4), sch 8 para 18(4)	sch 4 para 10(4), sch 6 para 18(4)
15.1	67(1)	41(1)	sch 1 para 25(1), sch 6 para 26(1)	60(1)
15.2	36	21	sch 1 para 5, sch 6 paras 7, 26(3)	30(4), 60(4)
15.3	13(6)(a),(11)(a)	24	sch 1 para 7, sch 6 paras 8, 9	32, sch 8 paras 8, 9
15.4	38(2)(b),63,66, 67(1), sch 4	27(2), 28(1)(b), 40, 41(2), sch 4	27, 30, sch 1 paras 18(1)(b), 25(2), 31, sch 5, sch 6 paras 20(1)(b), 26(2), 33, sch 10	21, 35, 54(1)(b), 60(2), 68, 69, sch 8, sch 9
15.5	38(2)(b), 63	27(2), 28(1)(b)	sch 1 paras 18(1)(b), 31, sch 6 paras 20(1)(b), 33	54(1)(b), 68, 69
15.11	38(2),70(1)	28(1), 31(1), (6),(11), 41(1)	sch 1 paras 11(1),(7),(12), 18(1), 25(1), sch 6 paras 12(1),(2), , 20(1) 26(1)	37(1),(7),(12), 46(1),(2), 54(1), 60(1)
15.12	67(1)	41(1)	sch 1 para 25(1), sch 6 para 26(1)	60(1)
15.14	70(1)	42	sch 1 para 26, sch 6 para 28	62
15.15	70(1)	42	sch 1 para 26, sch 6 para 28	62
15.16	70(1)(a)	42(a)	sch 1 para 26(a), sch 6 para 28(a)	62(a)
15.17	70(1)(b)	42(b)	sch 1 para 26(b), sch 6 para 28(b)	62(b)
15.18	68	46	sch 1 para 30, sch 6 para 32	67
15.19	70(2)	43	sch 1 para 27, sch 6 para 29	63
15.20	70(3)	sch 4 para 23	sch 5 para 23, sch 10 para 28	sch 8 para 23, sch 9 para 28
15.22	67(1)	41(1)	sch 1 para 25(1), sch 6 para 26(1)	60(1)
15.23	67(1)	41(1)	sch 1 para 25(1), sch 6 para 26(1)	60(1)

15.24	67(1), 70(1)(a)	41(1), 42(a)	sch 1 paras 25(1), 26(a), sch 6 paras 26(1), 28(a)	60(1), 62(a)
15.25	67(3), sch 4 paras 10, 11	2(1), sch 4 paras 11, 12, 24, 33	2(1), sch 5 paras 11, 12, 24, 31, 33, sch 10 paras 16, 21, 35, 36, 63	2(1), sch 8 paras 11, 12, 24, 31, 33, sch 9 paras 16, 21, 35, 36, 63
15.26	63(3)	27(1)(i), 36(4), sch 3 para 22	sch 1 para 10(1)(i), sch 4 paras 22, 23, sch 6 para 27(5), sch 9 para 36	36(1)(i), 61(5), sch 5 paras 22, 23, sch 7 para 36
15.27	sch 4 para 7	sch 4 paras 5, 32	sch 9 paras 5, 30, sch 10 paras 10, 37	sch 8 paras 5, 30, sch 9 paras 10, 37
T15.1	67(1), 69(1), sch 4	41(1),(2), sch 4	sch 1 para 25(1),(2), sch 6 para 26(1),(2), sch 5, sch 10	60(1),(2), sch 8, sch 9
T15.1(a)	sch 4 para 1	sch 4 para 26	sch 5 para 26, sch 10 para 4	sch 8 para 26, sch 9 para 4
T15.1(b)	sch 4 para 2	sch 4 para 4(a)	sch 5 para 4(a), sch 10 para 7(a)	sch 8 para 4(a), sch 9 para 7(a)
T15.1(c)	sch 4 para 3	sch 4 para 4(b)	sch 5 para 4(b), sch 10 para 7(b)	sch 9 para 7(b)
T15.1(d)	sch 4 para 4	sch 4 paras 1-3	sch 5 paras 1-3, sch 10 paras 5, 32, 33	sch 8 paras 1-3, sch 9 paras 5, 32, 33
T15.1(e)	sch 4 para 5	sch 4 para 6	sch 5 para 6, sch 10 para 30	sch 8 para 6, sch 9 para 30
T15.1(f)	sch 4 para 6	sch 4 para 7	sch 5 para 7, sch 10 para 31	sch 8 para 7, sch 9 para 31
T15.1(g)	sch 4 para 7	sch 8 para 5	sch 5 para 5, sch 10 para 10	sch 8 para 5, sch 9 para 10
T15.1(h)	4(1), sch 4 para 16(a),(b)	—	2(1), sch 10 paras 6, 14(b)	2(1), sch 9 paras 6, 14(b)
T15.1(i)	sch 4 para 16(c)	—	sch 10 para 41	sch 9 para 41
T15.1(j)	sch 4 para 17	—	sch 10 para 13(a)	sch 9 para 13(a)
T15.1(k)	sch 4 para 18	—	sch 10 para 13(b)	sch 9 para 13(b)
T15.1(l)	4(1), sch 4 para 15	—	2(1), sch 10 para 14(a)	2(1), sch 9 para 14(a)
T15.1(m)	sch 4 para 27	—	sch 10 para 26	sch 9 para 26
T15.1(n)	—	sch 4 paras 18, 20(a)	sch 5 paras 18, 20(a)	sch 8 paras 18, 20(a)
T15.1(o)	—	sch 4 paras 18, 19	sch 5 paras 18, 19	sch 8 paras 18, 19
T15.1(p)	—	sch 4 paras 18, 20(a)	sch 5 paras 18, 20(a)	sch 8 paras 18, 20(a)
15.29	67(1), 69(1), sch 4	41(1),(2), sch 4	sch 1 para 25(1),(2), sch 6 para 26(1),(2), sch 5, sch 10	60(1),(2), sch 8, sch 9
15.30	sch 4	sch 4	sch 5, sch 10	sch 8, sch 9
15.31	67(1)	41(1)	sch 1 para 25(1), sch 6 para 26(1)	60(1)
15.32	67(2)	sch 4 para 8	sch 5 para 8, sch 10 para 15	sch 8 para 8, sch 9 para 15
15.33	sch 4 paras 8, 9	sch 4 paras 9, 10	sch 5 paras 9, 10, sch 10 para 11	sch 8 paras 9, 10, sch 9 para 11
15.34-35	76(1),(2)	44(3),(4)	sch 1 para 28(3),(4), sch 6 para 30(5),(6)	64(7),(8)
15.38	67(1)	41(1)	sch 1 para 25(1), sch 6 para 26(1)	60(1)
15.39	74(4), sch 4 para 7	sch 4 para 34	sch 5 para 32, sch 10 paras 10, 17	sch 8 para 32, sch 9 paras 10, 17
15.40	67(1)	41(1),(2)	sch 1 para 25(1),(2), sch 6 para 26(1),(2)	60(1),(2)
15.42	75	2(1), 27(1), sch 4 paras 14, 16	2(1), sch 1 para 10(1), sch 5 paras 14, 16, sch 9 para 41, sch 10 paras 29, 38, 57	2(1), 36(1), sch 7 para 41, sch 8 paras 14, 16, sch 9 paras 29, 38, 57
15.43	74(3)-(6)	sch 4 para 17	sch 5 para 17, sch 10 para 48	sch 8 para 17, sch 9 para 48
15.44	74(2)	sch 3 paras 13, 14	sch 4 paras 14, 15, sch 9 para 19(1)(c)-(e)	sch 5 paras 14, 15, sch 7 para 19(1)(c)-(e)
15.45	—	—	sch 10 paras 48, 49	sch 9 paras 48, 49

	Working age SSI 2021 No. 249	Pension age SSI 2012 No. 319	Prescribed Requirements SI 2013 No.3029	Default Scheme SI 2013 No. 3035
15.46	75(1)(a)	sch 4 paras 13, 15	sch 5 paras 13, 15, sch 10 paras 56, 58	sch 8 paras 13, 15, sch 9 paras 56, 58
15.48	sch 4 para 22	27(1), sch 4 para 15	sch 1 para 10(1), sch 9 para 15, sch 10 para 50	36(1), sch 8 para 15, sch 9 para 50
T15.2	sch 4 paras 21, 28	41(3), sch 4 paras 18, 21(a)-(d),(2), 22, 25	sch 1 para 25(3), sch 5 paras 18, 21(a)-(d),(2), 22, 25, sch 6 para 27(10), sch 10 paras 12, 40, 42	60(3), 61(10), sch 8 paras 18, 21(a)-(d),(2), 22, 25, sch 9 paras 12, 40, 42
15.51	67, 75(1)(b), sch 4 paras 23-25	27(1)(j)(xva), 41(1), sch 4 paras 30B, 30D, 30E, 30G	sch 1 paras 10(1)(j)(xiii), 25(1); sch 5 para 28C, sch 6 para 26(1), sch 10 para 65	36(1)(j)(xiii), 60(1), sch 8 para 28C, sch 9 para 65
15.52(a)	sch 4 para 32	—	sch 10 paras 46, 47	sch 9 paras 46, 47
15.52(b)	sch 4 paras 9(b), 33, 39	—	sch 6 para 27(8),(9), sch 10 paras 2, 3, 11(3),(4), 39, 51, 54	61(8),(9), sch 9 paras 2, 3, 11(3),(4), 39, 51, 54
15.53(a)	sch 4 paras 20, 35, 36	—	sch 10 paras 23, 24, 61, 62	sch 9 paras 23, 24, 61, 62
15.53 (b),(c)	sch 4 para 20	sch 4 para 29	sch 5 para 28, sch 10 para 60	sch 8 para 28, sch 9 para 60
15.53(d)	sch 4 para 20	41(1)	sch 5 paras 18, 21(1)(e), sch 10 para 59	sch 8 paras 18, 21(1)(e), sch 9 para 59
15.53(e)	sch 4 para 26	41(1)	sch 5 paras 18, 21(1)(f), sch 10 para 25(b)	sch 8 paras 18, 21(1)(f), sch 9 para 25(b)
15.54	67(1), (3)	41(1)	sch 1 para 25(1), sch 6 paras 26(1), 27(7), sch 10 para 38	60(1), 61(7), sch 9 para 38
15.56	67(1)	41(1)	sch 1 para 25(1), sch 6 para 26(1)	60(1)
15.60	71(1),(2)	44(5)	sch 1 para 28(5), sch 6 para 30(7)	64(9)
15.61	71(1)	44(1)	sch 1 para 28(1), sch 6 para 30(1)	64(1)
15.63	73(3)	44(2)	sch 1 para 28(2)	64(2)
15.64	67(1)	41(1),(2)	sch 1 paras 25(1),(2), 28(1),(2), sch 6 paras 26(1),(2), 30(1), sch 10 para 15	60(1),(2), 64(1),(2), sch 9 para 15
15.66	71(1)	44(1)	sch 1 paras 28(1), 29, sch 6 paras 30(1), 31	64(1), 65, 66
15.67	72(1)-(4),(8), 73	45(1)-(4),(8)	sch 1 para 29(1)-(5),(10), sch 6 para 31(1)-(5),(10)	65(1)-(5),(10), 66(1)-(5),(10)
15.68	72(1)(a),(2),(3),(8), 73	45(1)(a),(2),(3),(8)	sch 1 para 29(1)(a),(2),(3),(10), sch 6 para 31(1)(a),(2),(3),(10)	65(1)(a),(2),(3),(10), 66(1)(a),(2),(3),(10
15.70	72(1)(b),(4),(8), 73	45(1)(b),(4),(8)	sch 1 para 29(1)(b),(4),(5),(10), sch 6 para 31(1)(b),(4),(5),(10)	65(1)(b),(4),(5),(10), 66(1)(b),(4),(5),(10)
15.71	72(1)(b),(5)-(8), 73	45(1)(b),(5)-(8)	sch 1 para 29(1)(b),(7)-(10), sch 6 para 31(1)(b),(7)-(10)	65(1)(b),(7)-(10), 66(1)(b),(7)-(10)

Index

References in the index are to paragraph numbers (not page numbers), except that 'A' refers to appendices, 'T' refers to tables in the text and 'Ch' refers to a chapter.

A

Absence from home, T3.1, 3.5-12, 3.15-16, 4.23-25
Academic year, 2.49, T13.10
Access fund, 13.41, 13.49
Access to work, T13.1(p), T14.2
Accidental error, 20.41
Acts of Parliament, 1.18
Administrative penalty, 19.75-78
Adopted child, T4.2
Adoption allowance, T13.5
Adult disability payment, *see* personal independence payment
Advance claim, 3.19, 3.31-36, 16.35, 22.43
AFIP, T6.2, 12.22-23, 12.25, 12.39, T13.4
Agency arrangement, 1.13
Agent, landlord's, 7.9, 18.22 onwards, T18.1, 19.24, 19.30-32, 19.37, 19.40-50
Allowable expenses, 14.38-39, T14.3
Almshouse, T5.1
Annuity, 13.32

Appeal
  About HB, 10.29-30, 10.42-43, 20.26-41, 20.41-53, 20.56, 20.62 (NI only)
  Appeal tribunal, see First-tier tribunal
  Decision following, 20.26-27, 20.42-46
  Exempt accommodation, 10.42
  First-tier tribunal, 20.42 onwards
  How to, 20.29, 20.45
  Limit on arrears following, 17.11-12, T17.2, 20.38
  Local housing allowance, 10.29-30
  Matters which can/cannot be appealed, 20.43, T20.4
  Oral hearing, 20.52
  Payment of HB, 18.1 18.49, 20.43, T20.4
  Rent decision (NI only), 18.58
  Rent officer determination, 10.43, 18.51-57
  Time limits for, 20.28, T20.3, 20.38
  Upper tribunal, appeal to, 20.53
  Who may appeal, 18.47-48, 19.60, 20.2-3, 20.26, 20.42

Applicable amount
  Components, 12.42-44
  Children, 12.9-18
  ESA/ESA credits, 12.45-47
  Generally, 12.2
  Hospital in-patients, 12.51, T12.2

Personal Allowances, 12.4-18, T12.1
Polygamous marriages, 12.5, 12.20, 12.27, 12.35
Premiums, (*see also* Premium) 12.22-33, 12.37-41
Appointee, 16.5-7, 18.18, 20.2
Armed forces, T6.2, 11.15, *see also* AFIP
Assessed Income Figure, 13.15, T13.3
Assessment period, 14.9-10, 14.30-31
Assessment phase, ESA, 12.47
Asylum seeker, T2.5

Attendance allowance
  Benefit cap, T6.5
  Carer Premium, 12.29, 12.32, T12.2
  Hospital in-patient and premiums, 12.51, T12.2
  Non-dependants and, 6.15, T6.2
  Rates, A2
  Severe disability premium, 12.25-27
  Treatment of arrears as income, 15.50, T15.2
  Treatment as income, T13.1
Authority, 1.13

B

Backdating
  Good cause (working age claims), 16.39-46, T16.2
  Limit on arrears, 16.37-38, 16.40, 16.42, 17.11-15, T17.2, 20.34, T20.3, 20.38
  Pension age claims, 16.37-38
  Underpayment due to error or change of circumstances (revisions and supersessions), 17.11-15, T17.2, 20.34, T20.3, 20.38-41
  Working age claims, 16.39-46, T16.2
Bail hostel, 3.26, T5.2
Balance of probability, 20.20
Bankruptcy, effect on overpayment, 19.51
Bedroom, 11.42-44, T11.2
Bedroom tax, *see* Size criteria
Benefit award, termination of, 16.50, T17.2(d), 17.19, 17.24, 17.34-35
Benefit cap, 6.21-33, T6.4, T6.5
Benefit week, 16.49
Bereavement allowance, T6.4, T13.2
Bereavement payment, T13.2, 15.51
Bereavement support payment, T13.1(h), 15.51

Blind
  Definition, 12.54

Disability premium, 12.39
Disabled child premium, 12.22
Non-dependant charges where tenant is blind, T6.2
Severe disability premium, 12.25(b), 12.27

Boarder
Definition/who is, 10.39
Eligible rent T5.1, 10.40, T10.4
Ineligible charges (food), T8.1, 8.22, 8.28, T8.3, 8.39, T10.4
Living in claimant's home, 4.36-41
Local housing allowance, 10.39
Rent officer determinations and, 10.39, 10.40, T10.4
Treatment of income received from, T13.7
Bonuses, T14.1
Business assets and premises, 8.19, 15.33

C

Calculation of HB, Ch 6, 6.2, 6.5-6

Capital
Aggregation of, 15.2
Annuities, 15.25
Arrears of income/benefits, 15.11, 15.50, T15.2
Business assets, 15.33
Capital limit, 15.4
Charitable and voluntary, 15.54
Claimants on IS/JSA and pension credit, 13.15, T13.3, 15.3
Compensation for victims of war and terrorism, 15.42, 15.46-48
Deprivation, 15.61-65, T15.3
Distinguishing from income, 15.6, 15.10, 15.13
Held outside the UK, 15.19
Generally, 15.3-5, 15.56
Instalments of, 15.12
Jointly held, 15.18
Life interest, 15.31
Loans, 15.55
National Savings, 15.23
Notional, 15.35, 15.57-71
Personal injury, 15.43-44
Property and possessions, 15.28-35, T15.1
Savings and investments, 15.21-27
Trusts, 15.36-42
Valuation of, 15.14-20, 15.29
Caravan, T5.1, T7.1, 7.29-30, 10.32, T9.1, T10.4, 18.3
Care home, 3.18-22, 3.36, T5.2, 5.16
Care leaver aged 16-17, 2.40-42, 4.16
Carer premium, T12.1, 12.29-33
Carer, T3.1(f),(g), 4.33-35, 4.50, 8.18, T11.1, 11.19, 11.25-33
Carer's allowance, T6.5, 12.25, 12.29, 12.31, 12.32-33, T12.2, A2
Carer's allowance supplement, T13.1(g)

Case law, 1.20, 20.22
Change of circumstances
Changes requiring notice, T17.1
Continuing payments (66+s), 17.30
Date occurred, 17.11-12, T17.2, T17.3, T17.4
Date award altered, 17.11-36, T17.2, T17.3, T17.4
Decision notice following, 17.9, 19.59
Duty to notify, 17.2-3, T17.1
Extended payments, 1.29, T6.5, 17.32-33
Internet notification, 17.4
Late, 17.13
More than one change, 17.39
Moving home, 17.18, T17.3
On time, 17.11-15, T17.2
Pension credit, 17.25-26, 17.28, T17.4
Regulations, 17.37
Relevant benefit, 17.25, T17.4
Relevant change of, T10.3, 17.2
Rent referral, T10.3
Restoring, 17.42
Starting work, 17.31-33
Stopping work, 17.31
Suspending, 17.41
Tax credits, 17.26, T17.4
Telephone notification, 17.4, 17.6
Terminating, 17.44
Universal credit, 17.19-23, 17.21-24
Up-ratings, 17.37
Written notification, 17.9
Chargeable income, 14.46-52
Charitable payment, 15.54
Child
Applicable amount, 12.9-18, T12.1
Cannot share bedroom, 11.34-41
Definition, 4.15
Foster, T4.2, 11.19, 11.21-24, T13.5
Who is treated as a, 4.8, 4.23-30
Responsibility for, membership of family, 4.17-22, T4.2
Temporary absence, 4.23-25
Two child limit, 12.10-18
Child benefit, 4.16, 4.19, T4.1, T6.4, T13.1, A2
Childcare disregards, 14.63-67, T14.6
Child support, 13.28-29, T13.6
Child tax credit, T13.1(i), T13.2(d), 13.12, 13.21, 14.61, T15.2(a), T17.4
Child minder, 14.52
Children leaving care, 2.40-42
Circulars, 1.19
Civil penalties, 19.79-80
CJD (Creutzfeldt-Jacob disease trust payment), 15.42
Claim
Advance, 16.35, 22.43

Amending, 16.21

Appointee (claim by), 16.5-7

Backdating, 16.36-44, T16.2

Complete, 16.14-17

Couples, T2.2, 2.8-14, 16.4

Date of, T16.1

Defective, 16.14-17

DWP, made via, 16.8-13, T16.1

End of/termination, 16.50, T17.2, T17.3, 17.34-35,
17.44

Forms, 16.10

Hostel, 3.4, 16.27, 16.34

Incomplete and remedying, 16.16-17

Information and evidence, 16.15, 16.19, 16.22-24

Internet and electronic, 16.10

IS/JSA(IB)/ESA(IR)/guarantee credit claimants who
claim HB, 16.11, T16.1(c)

Life of a claim, 1.26-29, 2.2, 3.7, 16.50, T17.2, T 17.3,
17.34-35, 17.44

Local authority, made direct to, 16.10

Lost forms/claims, 16.46

National Insurance number, requirement for,
16.26-27

Nil income claim, 16.30

Not received, 16.46

Restoring (after suspension), 17.42

Suspension, 17.40-41

Telephone, 16.10, 16.11, T16.1(b)

UC claimants who claim HB, 16.11, T16.1(d), 16.41-42

Validly made/properly completed, 16.16-17

Verification, 16.24

Where to claim, 1.13, 16.8-10

Withdrawing, 16.21

Written claim, 16.10

Claimant, T1.1

Claim-related rent determination, T10.4

Cleaning, T8.1, 8.33, 8.37, 8.47

Closed period supersession, 20.33

Close relative, 5.27-28

Coal (and cash in-lieu of), T13.11, 13.59

Commercial v. non-commercial lettings, 5.22, T5.5

Commission payment, T14.1

Commissioner decisions, see Upper tribunal decisions

Commissioners, see Upper tribunal judge

Communal area, 8.3, T8.1, 8.15, 8.33, 8.34, 8.37-38,
8.47, 8.49-51

Company director, 5.36, 14.6, T14.2(I), 15.34-35

Company let, 5.36

Compensation payment, T14.1(p), 14.14, T15.1,
15.43-47

Components, ESA/Applicable amount, 12.42-44

Concessionary payment replacing a state benefit,
12.55, T13.1(q), 15.50

Conditional sale agreement, T5.2

Constant attendance allowance, see Attendance
allowance

Continuing payments, 17.30

Contribution-based ESA

Benefit cap, T6.4, T6.5

Claim, 16.11

Components, 12.42-44, 12.48-49

Contribution credits, 12.45

Disability premium, 12.37

Earned income disregards, T14.5, T14.7

Enhanced disability premium, 12.40

Income, T13.2

Linking rules, 12.47

Phases, 12.47-49

Contribution-based jobseeker's allowance, T6.4, T13.2,
16.11

Contrived liability for rent, 5.23, T5.6

Controlled and restricted tenancies in Northern
Ireland, 7.40-41, 9.4

Conversion to weekly figure, 6.34-38, 13.8, 14.23, 14.36

Co-operative tenants, T5.1

Co-ownership scheme, T5.2, T22.3

Correctly paid HB, 21.3

Cost of living payments, T13.5, T13.11, 15.53

Council tax, T8.1, 8.14, 8.24

Council tax rebates, 1.32-35, A3

Council tenant, T7.1, 7.11, 7.24, 7.45, 9.2, 9.4-16, T9.1,
21.39

Counselling and support, T8.1, 8.27, 8.30, 8.41-46

County council, 2.18, 7.19, 16.9

Couple(s)

Definition, T1.1, 4.4-7, 4.13

Income and capital of, 13.2

Living together as, 4.8-12

Meaning of, 4.9

Member treated as rent-payer, 5.13

Mixed age, 2.8-14, T9.1, 22.6, 22.8

National insurance number, 16.26-27

Students, 2.43, T2.6

Court procedure for recovering overpayments, 19.52-58

Credit sale agreement, T5.2

Croft land, T5.1

Crown tenant, T5.2, T22.3

D

Date of claim, 16.31, T16.1

Death, 7.52-54, 9.11, 10.15, T10.3, 12.53, T16.1(d),
17.36, 18.21, 18.29, 19.27

Debt relief order (DRO), 19.51

Decision

Changing (reconsideration), 17.10-12, 20.26-41

Definition (Decision v Determination), 20.9

Duty to make, 16.19, 20.8, 20.48-49
Making, generally, 9.36, 20.19-25
Notice, generally, 20.5-7, T20.1
Notice, overpayment, 19.59-62, T19.8
Notice, revision and appeal, 20.7, 20.31
Statement of reasons, 20.10
Time limit for making and remedies for delays,
     20.2-3, 20.11-15
Defective claim, 16.16-17
Deprivation of capital/income, 13.60, 15.61-65
Designated office, 16.9
Determination, T10.3, 10.39, 10.43, T10.4, 20.9, 20.55-60
DHP, 6.24, T13.5(k), 23.1-19
Diminishing capital rule, 19.13-15
Diminishing notional capital rule, 15.66-71
Direct earnings attachment (DEA), 19.47-49
Disability adaptations, 3.31-33, T15.1(d),(i),(k),(p)
Disability living allowance
     Benefit cap, T6.5
     Disability premium, 12.37-39
     Disabled child premium, 12.22
     Enhanced disability premium, 12.23, 12.40
     Hospital in-patient and premiums, T12.2
     Non-dependants and, T6.2, 6.15, 12.25(b)
     Rates, A2
     Severe disability premium, 12.25, 12.32
     Treatment of arrears as income, T15.2
     Treatment as income, T13.1
Disability premium, T12.1, 12.37-39
Disabled child payment, see disability living allowance
Disabled child premium, T12.1, 12.22
Disappeared, compensation for families of, 15.47
Discretion, 20.24
Discretionary assistance fund, see local welfare
assistance
Discretionary housing payment, 6.24, T13.5, T15.2,
23.1-19
Discretionary support, see local welfare assistance
Disputes process, 20.16-17, 20.26-30, T20.2, 20.42-43
Disregards, earned income, see Earnings
Domestic violence, T2.3, 2.21, 2.31, T2.5, 3.8, T3.1, 3.14-
17, 3.37, 3.40, T9.1, 12.15
Domiciliary care worker, T14.6
Drawings from business, 14.51
Dwelling, 3.3

E

Early years assistance (Scotland), T13.1(n)
Earnings
     Absences from work, 14.15-16
     Assessment of, 14.5 onwards
     Deductions/net earnings, 14.19-23
     Disregards, additional (30 hr), 14.61, 14.68, T14.7

Disregards, childcare, 14.61, 14.63-67, T14.6
Disregards, permitted work, T13.3, T14.5
Disregards, standard, 14.61-62, T14.5
Ending work, T14.1, 14.13-14, 17.31
Expenses, T14.1, 14.38-45, T14.3, 14.52
Self-employment, 14.26-59, T14.3, T14.4
Starting work, 14.12, 17.31
Types of earnings (bonuses, royalties etc), T14.1,
     14.58-59
Education maintenance allowance, 13.39
EEA nationals, T2.5(b)
Effective claim, 16.14-15
Eileen Trust, 6.15, 15.42, 16.25
Eligibility for HB, 2.1, T2.1
Eligible housing costs, T5.1, T5.2
Eligible rent, 5.5, T5.1, T5.2, 8.3-4, T8.1, 8.10, 8.25
Eligible rent restrictions (see also 'Maximum rent' and
'Protected Groups'), 7.44-45, 9.11, T9.2, 9.23, 10.40
Emergency alarm system, 8.41
Emergency services, T14.1(s), T14.5(f)
Employed earners, 14.4, 14.60
Employee living in claimant's home, 4.50
Employment and support allowance
     Assessment period, 12.20
     Benefit cap, T6.4, T6.5
     Change in, 17.25, T17.4
     Childcare disregard, 14.63, 14.67
     Components, 12.42-44, 12.49
     Contribution-based, 12.37, 12.45-46
     Income-based, see Income support
     Main phase, 12.47, 12.49, T14.5, 14.71
     New-style, 1.37, 1.38, 12.46, 13.11, 13.22, A2
     Passport benefit, 1.7
     Rates, A2
     Remunerative work, 14.71-72
     Support component, T6.5, 12.42-43, 12.49, T14.5,
        T14.7
     Work-related activity component, 12.44, T14.5,
        T14.7
End of claim/award, 2.2, 16.50, T17.2, T17.3, 17.19,
17.34-35, 17.44
Enhanced Disability Premium, 12.23, 12.40
Enterprise Allowance (New), T14.2
Equity sharer, T5.1
ESA, see Employment and support allowance
European nationals, T2.5(b)
Evidence, 16.22-25
Errors, correction of, 20.26-27, 20.32-34, T20.3, 20.38-41
Exceptionally high rent determination, T10.4
Excess income, 6.6
Excluded from HB, 2.38-44, T5.2, 5.20-38, T5.4
Exempt accommodation
     Benefit cap, 6.27, T6.4

Definition, T2.3, 2.17, T2.4, 9.18-19
Eligible rent, 9.21, T9.2, 9.23-35
Social landlord, 2.18, T7.1, 9.2, 9.18-19
Subsidy, 21.29-33
Expenses, T14.1, 14.38-45, T14.3, 14.52
Extended payment, 17.31-33
Extension of time, 16.17, T16.1(b), 17.15, 20.37, 20.47

F

Fact, finding of, 20.19-21
Family premium, T12.1, 12.24
Family, T1.1, 4.1-4, 4.17
Fear of violence, 3.14-17
First day and last day of HB, 2.2, 16.50, 17.11-12, T17.2, T17.3, 17.34-35, 17.44
First-tier tribunal (including appeal to)
Appealable decisions, 20.43, T20.4
How to appeal to, 20.45
Late appeals to, 20.47
Revisions prompted by, 20.49-50
Statement of reasons, 20.10, 20.53
Time limits for, T20.2, 20.46-47
Upper tribunal, appeal to, 20.53
Fit and proper person, landlord, 18.42-44
Foreign national, 2.39, T2.5
Foster child, T4.2, 11.13, 11.21-24
Fostering payment, T13.5
Foster parent, T11.1, 11.19, 11.21-24, T13.5, T14.6
Fraud, 19.69-77
Fraud, overpayment maximum deduction, T19.6
Fuel charge, T8.1, 8.22, 8.28, 8.34-37, T8.2, 10.6, 10.26, T10.4
Fund, the, 15.42
Funeral plan contracts, 15.25
Furniture and household equipment, T5.2, T8.1, 8.48
Further education, T2.6(c)

G

Garages and land, 8.15
Gardening, charges for, 8.51
George Cross, 15.48, T13.11
Good cause
Late claim, 16.36, 16.39, 16.42, 16.44-46, T16.2
Failure to provide evidence, 18.12-13
Grace period, T6.5, 6.29-30
Grant income, 13.39, T13.10
Guarantee credit, 1.7, 13.3, 17.25-26, 17.24, T17.4 (see also Income support), 22.5, 22.7, 22.10-18
Guardian's allowance, T6.5, T13.1, A2
Guidance Manual, 1.19
Gypsies and travellers, T5.1, 7.29-30, 10.32 (see also Caravan)

H

Habitual residence T2.5
Health benefits, T13.11
Higher education, T2.6
Hire purchase, T5.2
Holiday pay, 14.15
Home – capital valuation of, 15.14-18, 15.29, T15.1
Home income plan, 13.33
Homeless, 7.33, 21.34-38, T21.2
Homeless hostel, 3.4, T5.2, 10.20
Hospital patient, 3.6, 3.9-10, T3.1, 3.36, 12.51, T12.2, 13.21, 14.67
Hostel
Definition, T7.1, 7.26-27
Eligible for HB, T2.3, 3.4, T5.1, T5.2
Eligible rent, T5.1, T5.2, 7.28, 10.32, 10.37, T10.3, T10.4
National insurance number, 16.27
Payment to landlord, 18.28, 23.41, 23.47, 23.49
Time limit for claim, T16.1
Houseboat, T5.1, T7.1, 7.29, T9.1, 10.32, T10.4, 18.3
Household, 4.5, 4.20-22, 4.45-56
Household, absence from, 4.23-25
Household benefit cap, see Benefit cap
Housing association, 2.18, 7.12-18, 9.2, 9.4, 10.33, T10.4, 21.30
Housing costs, see Eligible housing costs
Housing Executive tenant, T7.1, 7.11, 7.45, 9.2, 9.4-16

I

Immigration control, persons subject to, T2.5
Improvement grant, T15.1
Incapacity benefit, T13.2, 13.21, T14.5
Incapacity for work, see Limited capability for work
Income
Aggregation of, 13.2, 13.20, 13.49
Arrears of, 13.7, 14.8, 15.50, T15.2
Benefits, 13.9-22, T13.1, T13.2, T13.3, T13.4
Bonds, 15.24
Charitable and voluntary payments, 13.30, 15.54
Concessionary coal and cash in lieu, T13.11, 13.59
Cost of living payments, T13.5, T13.11, 15.53
Council tax rebates, T13.5, A3
Disregards on unearned income, T13.1, T13.2(n), T13.4, T13.5, 13.28-29, T13.6-9, 13.49
Distinguishing from capital, 15.10-13
Earnings disregards, 14.61-62, T14.5, 14.63-64, 14.68, T14.7
Earnings, 14.4, 14.17, 14.36, 14.53, T14.4, 14.60-73
Generally, 13.1-8, 13.44, 13.49, 14.1-4, 14.17, 14.36
Government training schemes, T13.1(p) and welfare to work

Home income plans and equity release, 13.33-34

Income support, JSA(IB), ESA(IR) and guarantee credit, 6.3, T6.1, 13.3-5, T13.1, 15.50, T15.2

Loans, 13.34, T13.11(n), 13.38, T13.9, 15.55

Local authority care, T4.2

Local authority payments, 13.23-25, T13.5

Non dependants, 6.15-17, T6.2, T6.3, 13.61

Notional, 13.54

Outside the UK, 13.48

Pension credit, 6.3, 13.3-5, T13.1, 13.14-15, T13.3, 15.50, T15.2

Pensions, T13.2(e), 13.13, 13.27, 13.55

Rent, 13.31, T13.7, T13.8

Retirement pension, T13.2(e), 13.13, 13.55

Royalties, 14.58-59

Social security benefits, 13.3-5, 13.9-15, T13.1-3, 13.21-22, 17.25-26, T17.4

Students, 13.37-39, T13.9-10, 13.49

Tariff, 15.5

Tax credits (CTC and WTC), 13.12, 13.21, 14.61, T15.2, 17.26, T17.4

Treatment of, 13.3-8

Trusts and special trusts and compensation for injury, 13.36, 15.36-48

War pension and war widows' pensions, 13.16-19, T13.4, 13.49, T15.2

Income based jobseeker's allowance, *see* Income support

Income support (including income based JSA, income-related ESA and guarantee credit)

Amount of benefit and treatment as income, 6.3, T6.1, T13.1, 15.50, T15.2

Benefit cap, T6.4

Change of circumstance (IS etc ends), 17.19, 17.25-26, T17.4

Decision notice, T20.1

Direct payments of for rent arrears etc, and payment of HB, T18.1, 18.28, 23.38-56

Duty to notify change in, 17.2-3, T17.1

Income and arrears of, treatment, 13.3, T13.1, 15.50, T15.2

Making a claim via, 16.11, T16.1

Non-dependant deductions and, T6.2

Income tax, 13.46, 14.19-21, 14.53-55, T14.4

Independent hospital, see Care home

Independent Living Funds, 6.15, 13.36, 15.42

Industrial injuries disablement benefit, T6.5, T13.2, T15.2, A2

Information and evidence for assessing HB etc, 16.22-27, 17.8

Insurance, 15.25, T15.1(j),(o)

Interest from capital, 15.26

Interim payment, *see* Payment on account

Interpreting the law, 1.20, 20.22

Invalid vehicle, 12.39(c), 14.67

Investments, 15.24

J

Jobseeker's allowance

Benefit cap, T6.4

Contribution based, T13.2, 13.11, 16.11

Income based, see Income support

Joint liability for rent, 9.7-8, 9.13, 10.7-8, 10.17, T10.4

Joint tenant/occupier, 4.42-47, 6.19, 9.7, 9.16, 10.7-8, 10.17, 10.19, T10.4, 11.10

Judgment, 20.23

Juror's allowance, T13.11

L

Land, T5.1, T5.2, 8.15

Landlord

Agent, 7.9, 18.20, 18.22 onwards

Appeal, right to, 18.49, 19.30-32, 19.63-66, ,20.2-3, 20.6, 20.44

Claimant as a landlord, treatment of income etc, 13.31, T13.7, T13.8

Payment of HB to, 18.22-54, T18.1

Fit and proper person to receive direct payments, 18.42-44

Information when payment made to, 18.47-48

Notice of decision to be sent to and contents of, 18.47-48, 19.59-62, T19.8, 20.6-7

Overpayment, liable to recovery, 19.30-32

Overpayment, recovery of HB paid to, 19.30-32, 19.37, 19.40-50

Related to claimant etc, T5.4, T5.5, T5.6, 5.24-29, 5.36-38

Late notified advantageous change, T17.2(b)

Laundry facilities, 8.37. 8.51

Laundry, claimant's, 8.52

Leaseholder, T5.2

Letting agent, *see* Landlord

Liable to pay rent, Ch 5, 16.32, T16.1, 16.33

Liable relative, *see* Maintenance

Licence payment, T5.1, 5.9

Licensee, T5.1, 5.9

Life interest/life rent, 15.31

Living together as husband and wife or civil partners, 4.5, 4.8-12

Loan, 13.33-35, 13.38, T13.9, T14.1(t), T14.2(c), T14.3(b)-(d),(h), 15.55

Loan protection policy, 13.35

Local housing allowance

Amount, 10.5-6, 10.11, T10.1, 10.23-25

Appeals, 10.29-30, T20.4(b)

Broad rental market areas, 10.27-28

Categories and sizes of dwellings, 10.16-20, T10.2, T11.1

Claims made before 7/4/2008, T7.1, 7.36-39, 10.32

Claims that cannot be LHA cases, T7.1, 7.36-39, 10.4, 10.32

Eligible rent, 10.4-9

Four-bedroom limit, 10.16, T11.1, 11.20

Joint tenants, 10.7-8

Life of award, 10.9, 10.15

Maximum dwelling size, 10.16, T11.1, 11.20

Payment to landlord or agent, 7.9, 18.22-44, T18.1

Payment to tenant, 18.34, 18.66

Protected groups, 7.46-54, 10.5, 10.15

Service charges, 10.6, 10.26

Setting the LHA figures, 10.21-28

Size of dwelling, 11.4, T11.1, 11.20

When the LHA starts to apply, 10.12

When case is reviewed/amended, 10.9, 10.15, 10.29

Which cases it applies to, T7.1, 7.12, 7.25, 10.4, 10.32

Local reference rent determination, T10.4

Local scheme, war pensions, 13.18-19, T13.3, T13.4, 21.4

Local welfare assistance, 3.34-35, T13.5(j), 15.53, 23.35-37

Lodger

Eligible for HB / liability for rent, T5.1

Eligible rent, T5.1, 7.10, 7.22, 10.39

Income from, T13.7

Living in claimant's home, 4.36-41, 10.17

Meals provided, 10.39, *see also* Boarder

London bombings charitable relief fund, 6.15, 13.36, 15.42, 16.25

Lone parent, T1.1, T12.1, 12.15, T14.5, 14.63

Long leaseholder, T5.2, 22.26-39, T22.3

Lost claim form, 16.46

LSVT tenant, 7.14

M

Macfarlane Trusts, 6.15, 13.36, 15.42, 16.25

Main phase ESA, 12.47, 12.49, T14.5, 14.67, T17.4

Maintenance, 13.28-29, T13.6

Maternity benefits and pay, T6.4, 6.30, T13.2(h),(t), T14.1, 14.16, 14.71, 15.51, T15.2, A2

Maximum benefit, 6.2

Maximum rent, 9.5, 9.11, T9.2, 10.5, 10.40

Meal charge, T8.1, 8.22, 8.28, T8.3, 8.39-40, 10.38, 10.39, T10.4

Mesne profits, T5.1

Migration to UC, 1.26-30, 16.50, 17.19-23

Minimum benefit, 6.7

Mistake or error in fact or law, T19.1, 19.5-7, 20.26-27, 20.31-34, 20.38-41, 20.56, 20.59, 20.62

Mixed age couple, 2.8-14, T9.1, 22.6, 22.8

Mobile home, T5.1, T7.1, 7.29, T9.1, 10.32, T10.4, 18.3

Mobility supplement, 12.39, T13.4

Month, definition, 16.47-48

Mortgage protection policy, 13.35

Mortgage rescue schemes, 5.32-33

Moving home, 3.15-17, 3.29-38, 16.32, 17.18, T17.3

(*see also* Advance claims; Two homes)

N

National Insurance contributions, 14.17, 14.19-21, 14.53-55, T14.4

National Insurance number, 16.26-27

National Savings Certificates, 15.23

Nazi persecution victims, pension, 13.16

Neighbourhood, T10.4

New-style ESA/JSA, 1.37, 1.38, 12.46, 13.11, A2, *see also* Employment and Support Allowance

Night shelter, 3.4, T5.2

NIHE, 1.13, 9.2, 9.4-16, 10.35

Nominee, to receive payment on behalf of claimant, 18.19-20

Non-dependant

Amount of deduction, T6.3

Deduction for, 6.2, 6.9-20, T6.2, T6.3

Definition and generally, 4.26-32, T4.3, 4.40-41, 4.47, 6.10, T13.7(a)

Excluded from HB, 5.30

No deduction, T6.2

Severe disability premium, 12.25(b)

Tenancy with, 5.31, T13.7(a), 13.61

Northern Ireland

Administration, 1.13

Controlled and protected tenancies, 7.41, 9.2

NIHE tenants, 9.2, 9.4-16

Northern Ireland Housing Executive, *see* NIHE

Rent referrals/restrictions/decisions, 9.21, 9.23-35, 10.40, T10.4, 20.62

Notice of decision

Contents of, 17.9, 20.6-7, T20.1

Decision by authority, 18.39, 18.47

Overpayment, 19.59-62, T19.8

Payment to landlord, 18.47-48

Person affected, 20.2-3

Notional capital and income, 13.50-61, 15.57-71, T15.3

Notional income tax and national insurance, T14.4

Nursing home, *see* Care home

O

Occupier

Joint and eligible rent, 9.7, 9.13, 9.16, 10.7-8, 10.17, 10.19, T10.4, 11.10, 11.16

Living in claimant's home, Ch 4

Occupying accommodation as a home, 2.45, 3.1-8, 3.15-16

Official error, T19.1, 19.5-7, T19.2, 20.38-41
Old cases, eligible rent, 7.36-37, 9.17, 9.21, T9.2, 9.23-35
Old scheme, 7.37, 9.17, 9.21, 11.6
Overlapping social security benefits, 12.29(b), 12.33
Overnight carer, see Carer

Overpayment
  Amount/calculation, 19.12-22
  Cause of, T19.1
  Civil penalties, 19.79
  Deductions from HB, 19.40-43, T19.6, 19.66
  Definition of, 19.1-2
  Direct earnings attachment (DEA), 19.47-50
  Method of recovery, 19.34-58
  Notice of, 19.59-62, T19.8
  Persons liable to recovery, 19.23-33
  Rate of recovery, 19.43, T19.6
  Recoverable/non-recoverable, 20.44, T20.4
  19.3-7, T19.2, T19.3
  Recovered and rent arrears, 19.39, T19.4, T19.5
  Recovery from landlords, 19.30-33, 19.37-38, 19.42,
    19.45
  Subsidy, 21.10-26, T21.1,
  Time limit on recovery, 19.57-58
Owner occupier, T5.2, 22.26-39, T22.3

P

Parental contribution to student, 13.47
Partially sighted, see Severely sight impaired

Partner (see also Couple)
  Definition, 4.4-13, T1.1
  Liable for rent, treat as/as not, 5.13, 5.24, 5.25
  Temporary absence, 4.23-25

Payment
  Appeals about, 18.49
  Frequency of HB, 18.8-10
  Guidance, 18.31
  HB generally, 18.2, 18.4-10
  Landlord, fit and proper person, 18.42-44
  Landlord or agent, 7.9, 18.22-41, T18.1
  On account/interim payment, 18.11-16, T20.4
  Rent arrears, T18.1, 18.25-28, 18.33, 20.13
  Time limit following a decision, 18.5, 18.8
  Vulnerable, 18.34-36, 18.39
  Wrong person, made to, 18.50-52
Penalty, Administrative, 19.75-78
Penalty, Civil, 19.79-80
Pension, state and private, T13.2(e), 13.13, 13.27,
13.54-56, 15.25, A2
Pension age, 1.3, T2.2, 2.4, 2.8-14, 6.22, T9.1, 16.36-38
Pension contribution, 14.22, 14.56

Pension credit
  Backdating/past payments, T16.1(d), 16.38

Changes in, 17.25-26, 17.28, T17.4
Claim and, 16.11, 17.28, 22.42-43
Guarantee credit, 13.3-5, 16.38, 17.25-26, 17,28,
  T17.4, 22.10-18, see also Income support
Housing cost, 22.26-39, T22.3
Legacy benefits (end of), 17.30
Qualifying age, 2.4, T2.2, 2.13-14, 22.6, 22.8
Savings credit, T13.2, 13.14-15, T13.3, T15.2, 22.8,
  22.19-21, T22.2
Universal credit (end of), 17.29
Pension Protection Fund (PPF), 13.27, 13.59
Period of study, 2.49, T13.10
Permitted work, T13.3, T14.1

Personal independence payment
  Arrears of, T15.2
  Benefit cap, T6.5
  Earnings disregards, T14.5(d), 14.67
  Hospital, 12.51, T12.2
  Income, treatment, T13.1
  Non dependant, T6.2, 6.15, T6.2, 12.40
  Premiums, 12.22, 12.23, 12.25, 12.39, 12.40, T12.2
  Rates, A2
Person affected, 19.64, 20.2-3, 20.26, 20.42, 20.44
Person from abroad, 2.39, T2.5
Personal allowance, 12.4-9, 12.10-18, T12.1
Personal injury compensation, 15.43-45
Polygamous marriage, T1.1, 4.4, 12.5, 12.7, 12.20, 12.27
Possessions, 15.32, T15.3(g)
PPF, 13.27, 13.59

Premium
  Carer, 12.29-33
  Disability, 12.37-39
  Disabled child, 12.22
  Enhanced disability, 12.23, 12.40
  Family, 12.24
  Hospital, effect on, 12.51, T12.2
  Rates of, T12.1
  Severe disability, 12.25-28, 12.32-33
  Transitional protection, disability premium, 12.50
Pre-tenancy determination, 10.36
Prison visits payment, T13.11(i)
Prisoners, absence from home, 3.26-28
Private tenant, eligible rent, T5.1, T7.1, 7.21, 10.4-5,
10.32, 10.40
Probation hostel, see Bail hostel
Proof, 16.22-24, 19.4, T19.3, 20.20-21
Property, 15.28-35, T15.1

Protected groups and rent restrictions
  Bereavement, 7.52-54
  Exempt accommodation cases, 7.47
  9.18-19, T9.2, 9.22-35
  LHA cases, 7.17, 10.4-5, 10.15
  Old cases (pre-1996), 7.49-54, 10.1-2, 10.5-6, 10.21-25

Previously afford the rent, 7.49-51

Rent referral cases, 7.49-54, 10.15, 10.40, T10.4

Social renter cases, 7.49-54, 9.2, T9.1

Protected tenancies, T7.1, 7.38-41

R

Rate rebates, 1.36

Re-determination by rent officer, 20.56-59

Redundancy payment, T14.1

Referral to rent officer, 7.12, 10.31 onwards, 11.5, T11.1, 21.27-33

Referred rent, 10.36-37, T10.4

Refugee, T2.5(c)

Registered charity, 7.19-20, 9.18

Registered housing association, 2.18, 7.12-18, 9.2, 9.4, T9.1, 10.33, T10.4, 21.30

Registered provider, *see* Registered housing association

Registered rent cases, 7.38-39

Registered social landlord, *see* Registered housing association

Regulations, 1.18, T1.3, A1

Relative, 5.28, 7.56

Relevant benefit rule, 17.25-26, T17.4

Religious communities, orders, 5.35

Remunerative work, 6.14

Rent

Apportionment, 9.7-8

Business premises, 8.19

Carer, space for, 8.19

Council/NIHE tenants, 9.2, 9.4-16

Definition of, 5.4-5, T5.1

Discount (prompt payment etc.), 8.20

Eligible rent generally, 5.5, T5.1, 7.3, T7.1

Garages, 8.15

Housing association and stock transfer tenants, 7.12-18, 9.2, 9.4, T9.1, 10.33

Housing costs ineligible for HB (and exceptions), Ch 5, T5.2

Housing costs treated as rent, T5.1

Liability to pay, 5.6-19, T5.3, T16.1

Rent referral cases (maximum rent), 10.28-39, T10.2

Management costs, 8.16, 8.29, 8.47, 8.51, 8.52

Overheads, T8.1, 8.11-14

Private tenants, 10.5-6, 10.40, T10.4

Protected groups, 7.36-41, 7.46-54, 9.2, 9.4, T9.2, 10.34

Registered rents (fair rents), 7.38-39, 9.4, 10.34

Rent free periods, 6.35-36

Rent restrictions, 7.44-45, 7.46-54, 8.29-30, 9.5, 9.11, 9.22-35, 10.40

Service charges, T5.1, Ch 8, T8.1, 8.10, 8.25, 9.5, T9.2, 10.6, 10.26, 10.38, T10.4(g)

Rent allowance, T1.1, 18.6-10

Rent arrears

Charges to cover, 8.20

Direct payment of IS/JSA/ESA/PC to cover, 18.28, 23.38-56

Direct payments of HB to landlord, T18.1, 18.22-44

Recovered overpayments, 19.39, T19.4, T19.5

Rent decisions in Northern Ireland, 9.21-31, 10.35, 20.62, *see also* Rent officer

Rent charges, T22.3

Rent discounts, (prompt payment) 8.20

Rent officer

Accidental error, 10.30, 20.59

Appeals, 10.29-30, 20.55-59, 20.62 (NI only)

Claim related rent determinations, T10.4

Determinations, 10.35, T10.4

Exceptionally high rent, T10.4

Life of determination, 10.36-37, T10.3, 10.41

Local reference rent, T10.4

Pre-tenancy determinations, 10.36-37

Re-determination, 20.56-59, 20.62 (NI only)

Referral to, 9.21, 9.36-38, 10.32-34

Significantly high rent, T10.4

Single room rent, T10.4

Size related rent, T10.4, T11.1

Substitute determination, 20.59, 20.62 (NI only)

Rent rebate, T1.1, 18.2-5

Rent received, 13.31, T13.7, T13.8

Rent restrictions, 7.44-45, 9.5, 9.11, 9.21-35, T9.2, 10.40, T10.4

Rental purchase agreement, T5.1

Repair grant, T15.1(i),(k),(p)

Repairs, moving out while done, 3.13

Residential home, *see* Care home

Residing with (someone), 4.29-33, 5.29

Respite care payment, 13.25

Retainer, T14.1

Retirement pension, T13.2, 13.13, A2

Retirement age, *see* Pension age

Reversionary interest, 15.27, T15.1(g)

Revision of HB, 17.9-12, T17.2, 17.16 onwards, 19.4, 20.26-41, T20.3

Right to reside, T2.5

Rounding, 6.38

Royalties, 14.58-59

S

Safeguarding guidance, 18.32, 18.34-36

Sanctuary scheme, T9.1

Savings credit, T13.2, 13.14-15, T13.3, T15.2, 17.25-26, T17.4, 22.8, 22.19-21, T22.2

Savings, *see* Capital

Scottish welfare fund, *see* local welfare assistance

Second World War compensation, 15.46

Self-employed
Allowable expenses, 14.38-39, T14.3
Assessment of earnings, 14.36
Business assets, 15.33
Calculation of income from, 14.36, 14.46, 14.57
Earner, definition of, 14.27
Earnings disregards, 14.60, 14.62, T14.5, 14.63, 14.68
EEA national, T2.5(b)
Net profit, 14.57
Partnerships, 14.36, 14.47-48
Pension contributions, 14.56
Period of assessment, 14.30-31
Pre-tax profit/chargeable income, 14.46-52
Tax and national insurance, 14.53-55, T14.4

Service charges
Carer, space for, 8.18
Cleaning, T8.1, 8.33, 8.37, 8.47, 8.52
Communal areas, 8.3, T8.1, 8.12, 8.15, 8.33-35, 8.37
Council tax, T8.1, 8.14, 8.24
Decision making process, 8.22-31
Definition of, 8.22-24
Disability adaptations, 8.17
Eligible, T8.1, 8.25, 8.28, 8.33, 8.34, 8.47, 8.48, 8.49-51
Excessive, 8.4, 8.25, 8.28, 8.29-30
Fixtures, 8.17
Fuel, T8.1, 8.22, 8.24, 8.28, 8.34-36, 8.37, T8.2, 8.52
Furniture and household equipment, T8.1, 8.48
Garages and land, 8.20
Gardening/maintaining communal areas, 8.15, 8.51
Generally, T8.1, 8.22-31, T10.4
Ineligible, T8.1, 8.25, 8.33, 8.35, T8.2, T8.3, 8.39-41, 8.46, 8.52
Intensive housing management, 8.46
Laundry and laundry facilities, 8.37, 8.51, 8.52
Leaseholder, T22.3, 22.27-34
Leisure items, 8.52
LHA and, 10.6, 10.26
Management costs, T8.1, 8.11, 8.16, 8.29, 8.46, 8.47, 8.52
Meals, T8.1, 8.22, T8.3, 8.39-40
Owner occupier, T22.3, 22.27-34
Pension credit and, T22.3, 22.27-34
Rent referral cases, 8.53, T10.4
Sheltered housing, 8.37-38
Stair lift, 8.17
Support charges, 8.3, T8.1, 8.22, 8.27, 8.30, 8.41-46
TV and TV relay, 8.51, 8.52
Unreasonable, (see Excessive)
Valuing, 8.28, 8.53, T10.4
Who deals with, 8.28, 8.53, T10.4
Water, T8.1, 8.12-13, 8.24

Window cleaning, T8.1, 8.33, 8.37
Service user groups, T13.11(b), T14.1(o)
Severe disability premium, 10.20, T12.1, 12.25-28, 12.33, T12.2
Severe disablement allowance, T6.5, 14.67, A2
Severely sight impaired, T6.2, 12.22, 12.25, 12.27, 12.39, 12.54
Shared ownership, T5.1, 7.24, T9.1, 10.34
Shares, 15.24

Sheltered accommodation
Benefit cap, 2.35, 6.27, T6.4
Generally, 2.30
Eligible for HB/UC, T2.3, 2.15-17, T2.4, 2.26-29, 3.16, T17.3
Eligible rent, 2.32-34, 7.31-32, 8.37-38, 9.17-21
Sick pay, T13.2(t), T14.1, 14.15, 14.71
Significantly high rent determination, T10.4
Single claimant, T1.1
Single room rent determination, T10.4
Size-related rent determination, T10.4, T11.1

Size criteria
Additional bedroom allowed, 11.19-41
Bedroom, definition, 11.42-44, T11.2
Carer, 11.19-29
Disabled cannot share 11.34-41
Discretionary help, 11.7
Discrimination (unlawful), 11.8-19
Exempt accommodation, T9.1, 9.23-27, 9.30
Exemptions, 7.33, 7.47, 7.52-54, 9.10, T9.1, 23.9
Foster parent/child, 11.13, T11.1, 11.21-24
How many bedrooms T11.1, 11.17-20
LHA cases, 11.4
Occupiers, 10.16-18, 10.38, T10.3, 11.10-16
Old scheme cases, 11.6
Overnight carer, 11.25-33
Private renter (LHA), 10.16-20, T10.2, T10.3, T11.1
Protected groups, 7.47, 7.52-54, T9.2, 9.30
Rent referral cases, T10.3, T10.4, 11.5
Sanctuary scheme, T9.1
Scotland, 23.9
Social renter, 9.9-16, T9.1, 11.3, 23.9
Social fund, T13.1, 15.51
Social sector size criteria, 9.9-16, T9.1, 11.3, T11.1, see also Size criteria

Social security benefits
Arrears of, 15.50-51, T15.2
Benefit rates, A2
Change in award, 17.25-26, T17.4
Income, 13.9-15, T13.1-3
Social security commissioners, see Upper tribunal
Sports awards, T14.2, 14.72
Stair lift, 8.17
Starting work, 17.31

Statement of reasons, 18.49, 20.10, 20.53

State pension, *see* Pension

Statistics HB, T1.2

Statutory Instruments, 1.18, T1.3, A1

Statutory maternity pay/sick pay, T13.2(t), T14.1, 14.16, 14.71, A2

Stock transfer tenant, 7.14, 9.4-16

Stopping work, 17.31

Strike pay, T14.1

Student
  Accommodation, 2.44-45
  Definition, 2.46-49
  Eligibility, 2.43, T2.6
  Full-time vs. part-time, 2.48
  Grant income, 13.39, T13.10
  Loan income, T13.11(d), 13.38, T13.9, 13.40, 13.49, 15.55
  Other income, 13.39-43
  Period of study and summer vacation, 2.47-49, T6.2, T13.10(d)

Subsidy, 9.36-38, Ch 21

Substitute determination by rent officer, 20.59

Sub-tenant, 4.36-41, T5.3(h), T13.7(c)

Summer vacation, 2.47, 2.49, T6.2, T13.10

Supersession, closed period, 20.33

Supersession, superseding an HB decision, 17.10, 17.11-12, T17.2, 19.4, 20.32-33

Support charge, 8.3, T8.1, 8.22, 8.27, 8.30, 8.41-46

Support component, T12.1, 12.42-44, 12.49, T14.5, 14.67, T14.7(d)

Supporting People, T13.5(i), 15.53

Supported accommodation
  Benefit cap, 6.27, T6.4
  Eligible for HB/UC, T2.3, 2.15-18, T2.4, 2.32-34, 3.16, T17.3
  Eligible rent, 2.32-34, T5.1, T7.1, 7.31-32, 8.37-38, 8.41-46, 9.17-21

Suspending HB, 17.40-44

T

Taper, 6.6

Tariff income, 15.5

Tax contributions, 14-19-21, 14.53, T14.4

Tax refund, T14.1, T15.1(m)

Temporary absence of claimant, 3.5-8, T3.1, 3.15-16

Temporary absence of partner, child or young person, 4.23-25, 7.52

Temporary accommodation, 6.27, 7.33, T9.1, 21.34-38

Tenant
  Definition, T1.1, 4.48, 5.8
  Council, eligible rent, 7.11, 9.2, 9.4-16
  Housing association, eligible rent, 2.18, 7.12-18, 9.2, 9.4-16, 10.33

  Income received from, T13.7, T13.8
  Living in claimant's home, 4.36-41
  NIHE, eligible rent, 7.11, 9.2, 9.4-16
  Private sector, eligible rent, 10.5-6, 10.40, T10.4
  Stock transfer, eligible rent, 7.14, 9.2, 9.4-16

Tent, T5.2, T22.3

Termination of HB, 1.26-28, 2.2, 3.7, 16.50, T17.2, T17.3, 17.19-20, 17.34-35, 17.44

Tied accommodation, 5.34

Time limits for appeal/reviews etc T20.2, 20.35-38, 20.46-47

Time limits for dealing with claims, 20.8, 20.11-12

Time limit on overpayment recovery, 19.57-58

Tips, T14.1

Trainee, 2.50

Training allowance, 12.29, T13.1(p), 13.59

Transitional protection, 1.30, 7.36-37, 9.17, 9.21, 10.32, 10.34, 12.50

Transitional HB (UC migration), 17.20-23

Travellers, 10.32, 18.3 (*see also* Caravan)

Tribunal, *see* First-tier tribunal and Upper tribunal

Trust and trust fund, 5.37-38, 13.36, 13.49, 13.56, 13.59, 15.36-44

TV and TV relay, 8.51, 8.52

Two child limit, 12.10-18

Two homes, HB on, 2.45, 3.15-16, 3.25, 3.38-39, 3.40-43

Two-week run-on, 1.29, 17.20-23

U

Underlying entitlement, 19.16-19

Under-occupying, *see* Size criteria

Underpayment, T17.2, 20.34, T20.3, 20.38-40, *see also* Revision, Supersession and Backdating

Unit trust, 15.24

Universal credit
  Amount of HB award, 6.3
  Benefit cap, 6.27, T6.5
  Changing from HB to UC and vice versa, 1.22-30, 2.6-7, 2.16, T17.3, 17.19-23
  Claim for HB and, 2.6-7, 2.16, 16.11, T16.1(c), 16.41-42
  Entitled to HB, 2.6-7, T2.3, 2.16
  Excluded from HB, 1.26, 2.7
  Income, 13.3, 13.5, T13.1, T15.2
  Migration to UC 1.26-28, 2.6-10, 17.19-23
  Non-dependant deductions, T6.2
  Replacement of HB/JSA(IB) etc, 1.22, 1.37, 2.7
  Transitional HB & legacy benefits, 1.29, 17.19-20
  Transitional protection, 1.30
  Severe disability premium etc. 1.30
  Two homes (HB and UC), 3.16

Unreasonable rent (size, rent increase), 7.43-45, 8.3, 8.29-40, 9.11, 9.23, 10.33

Upper Tribunal, 20.53

Up-rating, 1.16, 17.37
Use and occupation payment, T5.1

V

Valuation Office Agency, 15.15
Variant Creutzfeldt-Jacob disease trust payment, 15.42
Vicinity, T10.4
Victoria Cross, 15.48
Violence, fleeing the family home, 3.14-17
Violent profits, T5.1
Voluntary organisation, 2.18-19, T7.1, 7.19-20, 7.27, 9.18
Voluntary payment, 13.30, 15.54
Voucher, T13.11(h),(k), T14.1(k),(r)
Vulnerable, 7.47, 9.32-35, 18.32, 18.34-36, 18.39

W

Wages, *see* Earnings
Waived liability for rent, 5.18
War pension, War widow's pension, T6.5, T13.3, 13.16-19, T13.4, 13.49, T15.2(d)
Water charge, T8.1, 8.12-13, 8.24, 8.28
Week, 16.49
Weekly amounts, conversion to, 6.34-37
Welfare benefits, *see* Social security benefits
Welfare supplementary payments, 23.20-34

Widow's pension, T6.4, T13.2
Widowed mother's/parent's allowance, T6.4, T13.2(n), 13.49
Window cleaning, T8.1, 8.33, 8.37
Working age, 1.4, T2.2, 2.6-7, 2.16, 9.11, 13.8, 15.4, 16.36-43
Working tax credit
    Arrears, T15.2(a)
    Benefit cap, T6.5
    Disability premium, 12.39
    Earnings disregards, 14.61, T14.6, T14.7(d)
    Income, T13.2, 13.12, 13.21
Work-related activity component, 12.44, 12.49, T14.5(c), 14.67, T14.7(d)
Work, starting and stopping, 17.31

Y

Young individual, T10.2, T10.4
Young person
    Care leaver, 2.40-42
    Definition, 4.16, T4.1
    Responsibility for/ membership of family 4.17-22, T4.2
    Shared accommodation rate/Single room rent (young individual), T10.2, 10.20, T10.4
    Temporary absence, 4.23-25